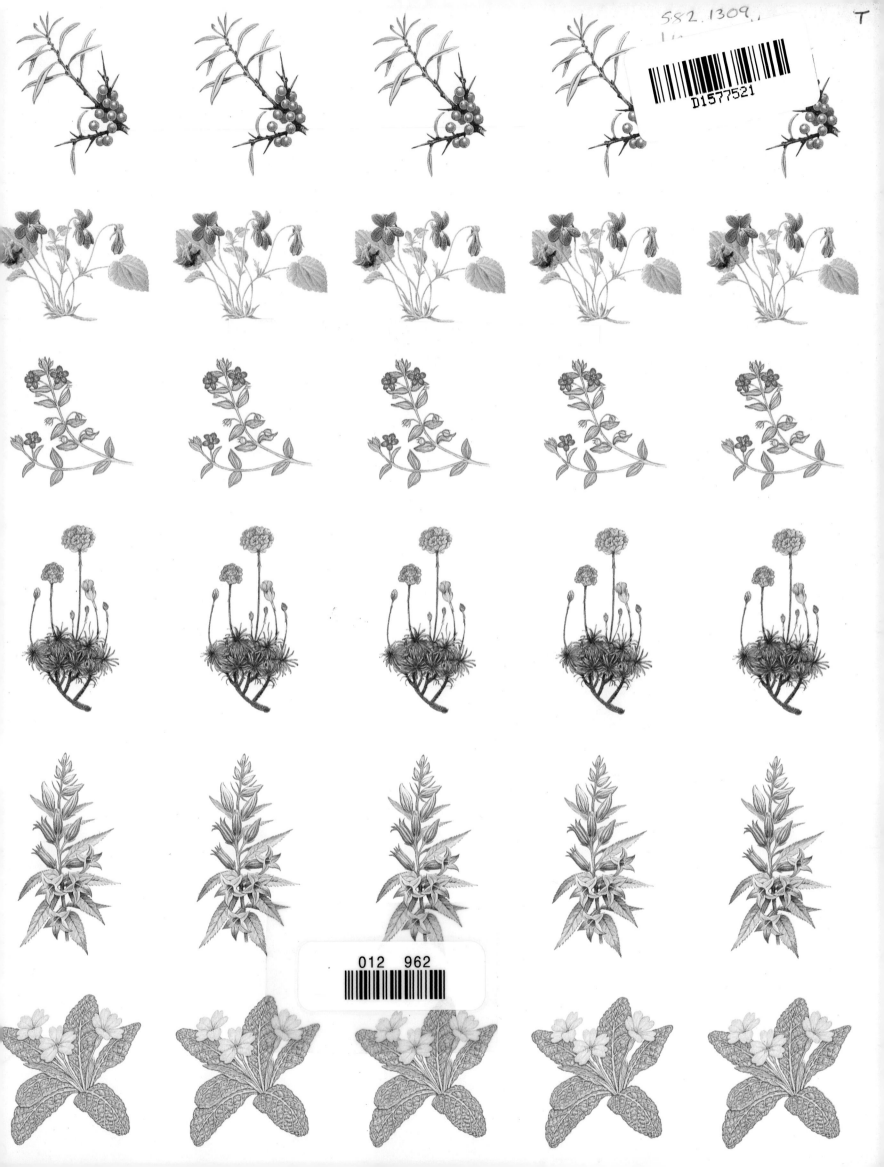

WILD FLOWERS

OF THE
BRITISH ISLES
AND
NORTHERN
EUROPE

Pond in late summer with White Water-lily floating in the water. In the foreground (from left to right) are Common Reed, Meadowsweet, Purple Loosestrife, Hemp Agrimony and Bulrushes.

WILD FLOWERS
OF THE
BRITISH ISLES
AND
NORTHERN EUROPE
Pamela Forey

DRAGON'S WORLD

Dragon's World Ltd
Limpsfield
Surrey RH8 0DY
Great Britain

First published by Dragon's World 1991

Editorial: Trish Burgess, Diana Steedman
Editorial Director: Pippa Rubinstein
Design: Mary Budd, Ann Doolan

British Library Cataloguing in Publication Data
Forey, Pamela
Wild flowers of Britain and Northern Europe.
1. Northern Europe. Flowering plants
I. Title
582. 130948

ISBN 1 85028 084 3

Typeset by Tradespools Ltd of Frome, Somerset

Printed in Singapore

CONTENTS

Introduction 7
Key to the Flower Families 10

Hemp family 14
Nettle family 14
Mistletoe family 14
Sandalwood family 16
Amaranth family 16
Pokeweed family 16
Purslane family 16
Dock family 18
Goosefoot family 22
Pink family 24
Buttercup family 32
Water-lily family 38
Sundew family 38
Pitcher-plant family 40
Birthwort family 40
St John's-wort family 40
Fumitory family 42
Poppy family 44
Mustard family 46
Mignonette family 56
Stonecrop family 58
Saxifrage family 60
Rose family 62
Pea family 70

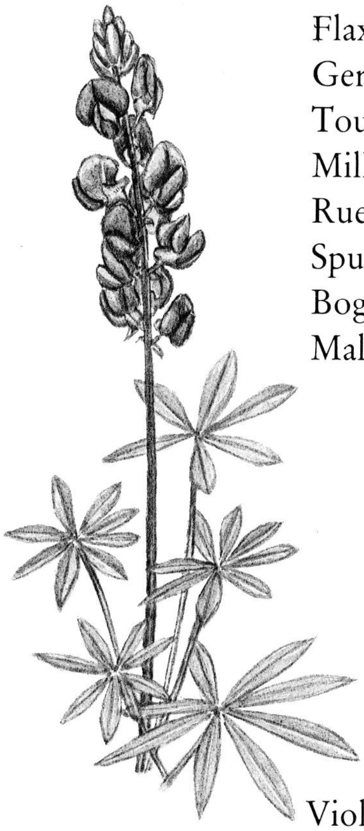

Wood Sorrel family 80
Flax family 82
Geranium family 82
Touch-me-not family 86
Milkwort family 86
Rue family 86
Spurge family 88
Bog Myrtle family 90
Mallow family 90

Violet family 92
Daphne family 94
Oleaster family 94
Rockrose family 94
Sea Heath family 96
Gourd family 96
Loosestrife family 96
Ivy family 98
Dogwood family 98
Willowherb family 98
Mare's-tail family 100

Water-milfoil family 100
Starwort family 102
Carrot family 102
Heath family 114
Crowberry family 116
Diapensia family 116
Wintergreen family 118
Bird's-nest family 118
Primrose family 118

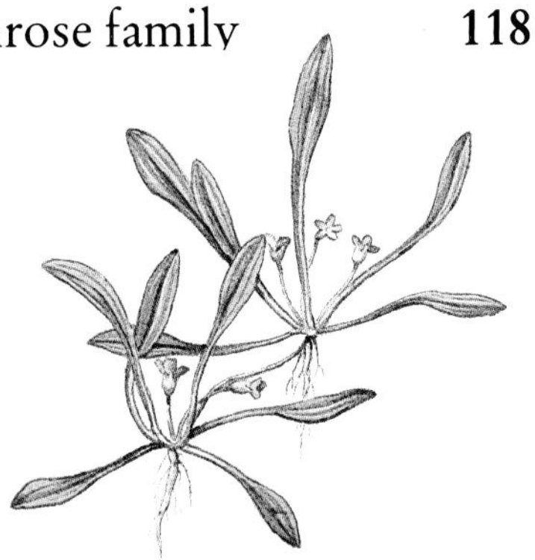

Sea Lavender family 122
Dogbane family 124
Milkweed family 124
Bogbean family 124
Gentian family 124
Bedstraw family 128
Phlox family 130
Bindweed family 130
Forget-me-not family 132
Vervain family 136
Mint family 138

Nightshade family 148
Figwort family 150
Broomrape family 160
Acanthus family 160
Butterwort family 162
Moschatel family 162
Plantain family 162
Honeysuckle family 164

Valerian family 166
Bellflower family 168
Teasel family 170
Daisy family 173
Water-plantain family 202
Flowering Rush family 202
Frogbit family 204
Pondweed family 204
Arrow-grass family 206
Lily family 206
Daffodil family 214
Iris family 216
Yam family 218
Rush family 218
Orchid family 220
Arum family 230
Duckweed family 230
Bulrush family 230
Bur-reed family 232
Sedge family 232
Grass family 236

Glossary 246
Index 250
Bibliography 256

INTRODUCTION

A world without plants would be a world without life, for it is plants that trap the sun's energy and make it available to animals. There are about 15,000 flowering plants in Britain and Europe, of which only some 2,500 are widespread, others being confined to one area of the Continent and only a few countries (many to the Mediterranean area), still others rare and even more limited in their distributions. They come in a wide variety of shapes, their forms linked to the places in which they live: oaks and other deciduous trees grow in the lowlands and valleys, leafy spring-flowering plants carpet the woodland floors, heathers grow in the acid soils of moors and heaths, low-growing, calcium-loving plants form mats and cushions on chalk downs and in the mountains, salt-resistant, water-storing plants survive the tough life on the coasts, while filmy water plants grow in ponds and streams. Other plants grow in the towns and cities, along roads and railways, adapted to survival in these latter-day, man-made habitats.

Plants adapt to their habitats from one main form. They have roots which enable them to absorb water from the soil and which anchor them in the ground. The stem forms the body of the plant, linking roots and leaves, and carrying water and nutrients to all parts. The leaves trap the sunlight in the process of photosynthesis and provide the plants with energy and food to grow. Flowering plants bear flowers, which produce the female ovules and the male pollen. Pollination results in the formation of seeds, which develop within the fruits and are then dispersed, spreading the plants to new areas.

Each species tends to be adapted to, and is often confined to, a particular kind of habitat, growing in that habitat and nowhere else. It is easy to see that water plants cannot survive on land, but the land also imposes distinctions, although in a more subtle form. Often many of the different plants found in a particular habitat develop similar adaptations, a response to the environment in which they grow.

Desert plants may have long and spreading roots to tap water sources deep in the ground, stems which store water, and spines or hairs and small thick leaves to reduce water loss. Coastal plants must withstand constant drying winds and must be able to grow in salt-laden soil; water is difficult to extract from such soil and coastal plants, like desert plants, frequently face water shortages; often they too have succulent stems and thick leaves. Alpine plants usually hug the ground to withstand the drying winds of summer and to gain protection from snow cover in winter. Water plants often lack roots and hairs, and many have dissected leaves; they absorb water directly through their stems and leaves, and hairs would hinder this process.

Plants which grow in meadows or woods do not need such extreme adaptations to survive in their much less harsh environments. However, these plants too have adapted. For instance, many plants of deciduous woods have their main growing and flowering season in spring, thus gaining maximum benefit from the higher light intensity in the woods before the leaves of the trees emerge. Once the trees are clothed in their full summer foliage the light intensity drops to too low a level to allow much growth on the woodland floor, and the ground cover plants often die back before midsummer, surviving underground until the following spring with food-stuffed rhizomes or bulbs formed by their leaves while the light levels were still high. Plants adapted to this regime cannot survive easily outside their woodland homes for several reasons. Their often soft or flimsy leaves appear in late winter and early spring, sheltered in the woods from the frosts, strong winds and battering rain or snow characteristic of that time of year; in the open they would be severely damaged by such weather and would survive only for a few years. Woodland plants are also generally unable to tolerate bright summer sunlight or the heat that comes with it in open places.

Deciduous woods are the natural climax vegetation of many parts of lowland Europe and last for centuries unless destroyed by disturbance or fire. By contrast the short grassland of the chalk downs and limestone uplands is an unstable habitat that, left to itself, tends to be invaded by scrub—shrubby plants like hawthorn and sloe—eventually, after several centuries, becoming deciduous woodland with beech or oak and ash trees. Grazing by rabbits or sheep is the key to the maintenance of short grassland as short grassland; in feeding, the grazing animals cut off and eat the tree seedlings before they

East coast salt marsh at mid tide in late summer. In the foreground are (from left to right) Sea Lavender, Scurvy-grass, and Sea Aster with Sea Purslane edging the hummocks.

can become established. The plants that survive in grazed grassland tend to form low-growing mats or cushions, where at least some of their tender shoots remain untouched by the animals. These open ground plants thrive on bright sunshine and tend to die out rapidly if the trees establish themselves enough to produce shade.

Plants also tend to be particular in their soil requirements; for instance, a species that grows well in a light, acid sand will not be found at all in a heavy, calcareous clay. Consequently, although chalk downland and moorland may appear to be similar in that they are both open, upland habitats, they are very different in that the first has a calcareous, alkaline soil and the second has a non-calcareous, acid soil. Plants that grow in the one will not grow in the other. In fact, far fewer plants grow in acid than in alkaline soils, and they tend to be confined to certain families; the Heath family particularly is one that is most often associated with acid soils.

The flowering plants have not arrived at their diversity overnight. Their history goes back more than 110 million years to a time when they began to replace Gymnosperms as the dominant plants on Earth. Since then they have evolved into many different families. Some families have been highly successful, with thousands of species in many different parts of the world and in many different habitats; others have remained small and confined to specific areas. Present-day families share similar features or may show patterns that reflect their evolutionary history. For instance, some families have a high proportion of members that are poisonous, often because they all contain the same kinds of poisonous alkaloids or other chemicals. Presumably the presence of the poisons prevented animals from eating the plants, so this became a survival characteristic—a feature that was positively useful in the competition for survival that goes on all the time among the plants and animals of our planet. Other families have a high proportion of edible members, some families have mainly white or yellow flowers, others blue ones. Some families are found primarily in deserts or water, others form bulbs or have bristly hairs. Some patterns may be of interest to people, others may not, so that some families are economically important, while others are not. Some families have bright, showy flowers while others have dull ones. This often reflects a difference in pollination mechanisms, bright, showy flowers designed to attract insects while dull ones rely on wind to spread the pollen.

It is this variety of patterns and differences that makes plants fascinating. What may seem interesting about one plant may seem dull in another; but this second one may have some other aspect of its biology that catches the attention. This book is intended as a celebration of the flowering plants of Britain and Europe. They are arranged in their families so that the patterns can be perceived clearly, and related families have also been kept together. Trees and shrubs have on the whole been omitted for reasons of space. The area covered ranges from Spain and northern Italy in the south to Scandinavia in the north, from Portugal and Ireland in the west to Germany in the east.

Some plants are common, others are rare or becoming scarcer. The habitats of many native plants and animals are being changed to suit the people who live there, not maintained to meet the needs of the plants and animals. Even the man-made habitats, like cornfields and hay meadows, are now poor instead of rich in wild flowers—a result of modern farming techniques. It is becoming clear that the process of habitat destruction cannot continue indefinitely if we wish to maintain the ancient diversity of our planet on which its health seems to depend. Preservation of habitats and of individual species is becoming an urgent priority, one to which all who value our heritage and who would wish to preserve our future need to give their support.

The continent of Europe has a wide variety of habitats in a relatively small area, a consequence of its complicated geological structure and varied terrain and soils, its position in the world and change in climate from north to south, and its long coastline and the consequent influence of the sea and the Gulf Stream on the western areas. Some of its habitats, like the lowland heaths and wetlands, are unique and found nowhere else in the world; for that reason, if for no other, they must be preserved. They cannot be replaced once they have disappeared under housing estates or once the peat that forms their foundation has been removed. In spite of its wide diversity of habitats, Europe does not have a wide variety of plants (in comparison with North America, for instance) because it has never recovered from the impoverishment of its flora which occurred during the Ice Ages. At that time many species became extinct, caught between the advancing glaciers and the Alps, unable to migrate southwards to survive because of the mountains in their path. The peaks also presented a barrier to recolonization of fresh species after the ice had retreated. Now Europe's species are under threat again, this time from the activities of man, but this time they can be saved.

This section will help you to identify unknown plants. A key provides you with a series of alternatives, the object being to lead you to one of the flower families in the book. The number at the end of each paragraph refers you to the next paragraph you should read in your search. It is a bit like following a maze with many endings. Once you

reach a family name, turn to the relevant page(s) and check there to find your plant.

A floral key can look daunting, but finding a wild flower and tracking it down through a key is a very satisfying experience. Unfamiliar terms are explained in the glossary at the back of the book.

1 □ Plants without chlorophyll. **2**
   □ Green plants. **4**

2 □ Flowers regular. **Bird's-nest fam.** p. 118, **Bindweed fam.** p. 130.
   □ Flowers bilaterally symmetrical. **3**

3 □ Petals fused into a corolla-tube. **Figwort fam.** (*Lathraea*) p. 150, **Broomrape fam.** p. 160.
   □ Petals free. **Orchid fam.** p. 220.

4 □ Parasitic plants forming clumps on the branches of trees. **Mistletoe fam.** p. 14.
   □ Plants not as above. **5**

5 □ Insectivorous plants with leaves modified into pitchers. **Pitcher-plant fam.** p. 40.
   □ Plants not as above. **6**

6 □ Plants aquatic and free-floating. **7**
   □ Land plants or rooted aquatic plants. **8**

7 □ Leaves finely divided, with bladders for catching water animals. **Butterwort fam.** p. 162.
   □ Leaves not finely divided and lacking bladders. **Frogbit fam.** p. 204, **Duckweed fam.** p. 230.

8 □ Perianth of two whorls (sepals and petals), differing from each other in colour, shape, function. **9**
   □ Perianth of two or more whorls, not markedly differing from each other, often all petal-like. **59**
   □ Perianth of one whorl, or perianth absent. **64**

9 □ Petals free. **10**
   □ Petals fused into a tube, at least at the base. **34**

10 □ Ovary superior. **11**
   □ Ovary inferior. **30**

11 □ Insectivorous plants, with sticky hairs on the leaves. **Sundew fam.** p. 38.
   □ Plants not as above. **12**

12 □ Flowers markedly bilaterally symmetrical. **13**
   □ Flowers more or less regular. **15**

13 □ Fruit a pod, flowers pea-like, with a five-lobed calyx and a corolla formed of a large standard petal at the back, two wing petals and two lower petals joined to form a keel. **Pea fam.** p. 70.
   □ Fruit a cluster of follicles, sepals petal-like, petals forming nectaries within the sepals. **Buttercup fam.** p. 32.
   □ Fruit a capsule or nutlet, flowers not as above. **14**

14 □ Stamens five, alternating with petals; sepals three, the lowest large and spurred, the lateral ones small; petals five, the upper one large, the two on each side joined together. **Touch-me-not fam.** p. 86.
   □ Stamens five, alternating with petals and the two lowest spurred; sepals five and free; petals five, free, the lowest spurred. **Violet fam.** p. 92.
   □ Stamens 12–25, crowded at front of flower; petals 4–7, divided and those at back of flower larger with deeper divisions. **Mignonette fam.** p. 56.
   □ Stamens two, each one divided into three; sepals two, small and soon falling; petals four, in two whorls, the inner ones often joined. **Fumitory fam.** p. 42.

15 □ Fruit consists of five sections, each with a long beak and a single seed in a swelling at the base. **Geranium fam.** p. 82.
   □ Fruit not as above. **16**

16 □ Fruit a capsule. **17**
   □ Fruit fleshy, or an achene or pod, not a capsule. **24**

17 □ Stamens 10 or less, or 12 and twice as many as petals. **18**
   □ Stamens numerous. **23**

18 □ Sepals two, free. **Purslane fam.** p. 16.
   □ Sepals 4–5, free or united into a calyx. **19**

19 □ Style one. **20**
   □ Styles 2–5. **21**

20 □ Leaves pinnate and pungently scented, stamens

8–10 (twice as many as petals). **Rue fam.** p. 86.
☐Leaves simple and linear, opposite; stamens six, petals five. **Sea Heath fam.** p. 96.
☐Leaves simple, rounded to elliptical with long stalks, opposite, spirally arranged or in basal rosette; stamens 10 and petals five. **Wintergreen fam.** p. 118.

21 ☐Stamens five, alternating with petals, but also with five sterile stamens. **Flax fam.** p. 82.
☐Stamens 8–10, twice as many as petals. **22**

22 ☐Leaves borne in opposite pairs, simple and usually narrow. **Pink fam.** p. 24.
☐Leaves alternate, pinnately divided with simple leaflets jointed to stalk. **Wood Sorrel fam.** p. 80.
☐Leaves alternate or borne in dense rosettes, simple and often thick. **Saxifrage fam.** p. 60.

23 ☐Sepals two. **Purslane fam.** p. 16, **Poppy fam.** p. 44.
☐Sepals three or five. **Rockrose fam.** p. 94.

24 ☐Fruits single-seeded nutlets arranged in a ring cupped in the calyx (and sometimes in epicalyx too). **Mallow fam.** p. 90.
☐Fruits a cluster (not a ring) of single-seeded achenes, or in pods, or fleshy. **25**

25 ☐Petals three. **Crowberry fam.** p. 116, **Water-plantain fam.** p. 202.
☐Petals four, five or more numerous. **26**

26 ☐Stipules present. **Rose fam.** p. 62.
☐Stipules absent. **27**

27 ☐Petals four, in the form of a cross; fruits siliquas, with two valves opening from below. **Mustard fam.** p. 46.
☐Petals five or more, or if four then not in the form of a cross. **28**

28 ☐Evergreen woody climber; fruit a berry. **Ivy fam.** p. 98.
☐Herbaceous plants; fruit a cluster of follicles or achenes. **29**

29 ☐Succulent plants, with thick, fleshy, entire leaves. Stamens as many as or twice as many as petals. **Stonecrop fam.** p. 58.
☐Plants not succulent and leaves usually lobed or divided. Stamens numerous. **Buttercup fam.** p. 32.

30 ☐Flowers bilaterally symmetrical. **Orchid fam.** p. 220.
☐Flowers more or less regular. **31**

31 ☐Flowers very small with tiny calyx and five petals, borne in umbels; fruits consist of two sections joined together across the top of a central axis. **Carrot fam.** p. 102.
☐Flowers not in umbels, or if they are, fruits not as above. **32**

32 ☐Stipules present; stamens numerous. **Rose fam.** p. 62.
☐Stipules absent or soon falling; stamens 10 or less. **33**

33 ☐Styles two. **Saxifrage fam.** p. 60.
☐Style one. **Dogwood fam.** p. 98, **Willowherb fam.** p. 98.

34 ☐Ovary superior. **35**
☐Ovary inferior. **49**

35 ☐Flowers regular. **36**
☐Flowers bilaterally symmetrical. **44**

36 ☐Flowers tiny, green and inconspicuous, in spikes. Stamens conspicuous with long filaments and large anthers. **Plantain fam.** p. 162.
☐Flowers not as above. **37**

37 ☐Flowers with five-lobed corolla and a five-part corona (formed of scales or appendages) between the petals and the stamens. Stamens five, either with anthers fused together around stigma, or anthers fused to stigma. Fruit is two pods. **Milkweed fam.** p. 124.
☐Flowers not as above. **38**

38 ☐Stamens twice as many as petals or petal-lobes. **Stonecrop fam.** (*Umbilicus*) p. 58, **Heath fam.** p. 114.
☐Stamens as many as petals or petal-lobes. **39**

39 ☐Stamens opposite petal-lobes. **40**
☐Stamens alternating with petal-lobes. **41**

40 ☐Sepals two, overlapping, free or united. **Purslane fam.** p. 16.
☐Sepals joined into a tubular calyx which has 5–10 ribs, expanding and becoming membranous at the top; styles five. **Sea Lavender fam.** p. 122.
☐Sepals joined into a tubular, toothed or lobed, often leafy, not membranous calyx (usually with five, sometimes up to nine lobes or teeth); style single. **Primrose fam.** p. 118.

41 ☐Fruit two or four nutlets. **Forget-me-not fam.** p. 132.
☐Fruit a follicle. **Dogbane fam.** p. 124.
☐Fruit a capsule. **42**

42 ☐Sepals free. **Bindweed fam.** p. 130.
☐Sepals joined into a five-lobed calyx. **43**

43 □Ovary one-celled. **Bogbean fam.** p. 124, **Gentian fam.** p. 124.
□Ovary two-celled. **Nightshade fam.** p. 148.
□Ovary three-celled. **Diapensia fam.** p. 116, **Phlox fam.** p. 130.

44 □Flower with four petals, outer two spurred, joined at tips, inner two often joined; stamens two, each one divided into three. Brittle plants with watery juice. **Fumitory fam.** p. 42.
□Flower not as above. **45**

45 □Flowers pea-like, with a five-lobed calyx and a corolla formed of a large standard petal at the back, two wing petals and two lower petals joined to form a keel. Fruit a pod. **Pea fam.** p. 70.
□Flowers not as above. **46**

46 □Flowers with five free sepals, three outer ones small, two large inner ones modified into coloured wings; and three petals joined together. **Milkwort fam.** p. 86.
□Flowers not as above. **47**

47 □Stems square in cross-section, at least near the top; fruit of four nutlets. **Vervain fam.** p. 136, **Mint fam.** p. 138.
□Stem round in cross-section; fruit a capsule. **48**

48 □Insectivorous plants with rosettes of soft, fleshy leaves; stamens two. **Butterwort fam.** p. 162.
□Plants not insectivorous; stamens four or five. **Figwort fam.** p. 150, **Acanthus fam.** p. 160.

49 □Flowers more or less regular. **50**
□Flowers markedly bilaterally symmetrical. **57**

50 □Flowers in four-sided heads, one flower on each side and one on top. **Moschatel fam.** p. 162.
□Flowers not as above. **51**

51 □Flowers in heads with involucre of bracts beneath; fruits dry, one-seeded achenes. **52**
□Flowers not in heads as above, or if flowers in heads, then fruit a capsule. **53**

52 □Stamens two or four, free. **Teasel fam.** p. 170.
□Stamens five, anthers united around the style. **Daisy fam.** p. 173.

53 □Climbing plants with male and female flowers on separate plants. Stamens five, with two pairs joined by their filaments and one free. **Gourd fam.** p. 96.
□Flowers hermaphrodite, or if flowers unisexual, then plant not climbing. **54**

54 □Stamens twice as many as petals or petal-lobes. **Heath fam.** p. 114.

55 □Stamens as many as or fewer than petal-lobes. **55**

55 □Leaves alternate. **Bellflower fam.** p. 168.
□Leaves opposite or in whorls. **56**

56 □Stamens 1–3, inserted at base of five-lobed corolla. **Valerian fam.** p. 166.
□Stamens four, alternating with four petal-lobes. **Bedstraw fam.** p. 128.
□Stamens five, alternating with five petal-lobes. **Honeysuckle fam.** p. 164.

57 □Sepals three, petals three, one of them forming a lip. **Orchid fam.** p. 220.
□Flowers not as above. Sepals united to form a toothed calyx, or calyx forming a ridge; corolla two-lipped, with five lobes. **58**

58 □Fruit a capsule. **Bellflower fam.** (*Lobelia*) p. 168.
□Fruit a berry. **Honeysuckle fam.** (*Lonicera*) p. 164.
□Fruit a one-seeded nut. **Valerian fam.** p. 166.

59 □Perianth petal-like, of many similar whorls, petals gradually becoming smaller towards the centre of the flower. **Water-lily fam.** p. 38.
□Perianth petal-like, formed of two similar whorls not markedly different from each other. **60**

60 □Stamens numerous. **Buttercup fam.** p. 32.
□Stamens nine or less. **61**

61 □Ovary superior. **62**
□Ovary inferior. **63**

62 □Stamens nine; fruit formed of partly fused follicles. **Flowering Rush fam.** p. 202.
□Stamens six; fruit a capsule or berry. **Lily fam.** p. 206.

63 □Stamens one or two, borne with three stigmas on a special structure, the column; one petal forming a hanging lip. **Orchid fam.** p. 220.
□Stamens three. **Iris fam.** p. 216.
□Stamens six. **Daffodil fam.** p. 214.

64 □Aquatic plants with strap-shaped or ribbon-like leaves; male and female flowers borne in separate globular heads, males above and females below. **Bur-reed fam.** p. 232.
□Plants not as above. **65**

65 □Tall, marginal aquatic plants with thick, sword-shaped leaves and flowers in dense, green or brown, cylindrical spikes, males above and females below. **Bulrush fam.** p. 230.
□Plants not as above. **66**

66 □Plants with linear, grass-like leaves, often with

sheathing bases, flat or channelled in cross-section; flowers green or brown, individually small and inconspicuous, although often borne in conspicuous inflorescences. **67**
□ Plants not as above; if leaves linear and grass-like, then flowers white or coloured and individually conspicuous. **68**

67 □ Flowers in spikelets. **Sedge fam.** p. 232, **Grass fam.** p. 236.
□ Flowers not in spikelets, but with sepal-like perianth segments and borne in spikes. **Arrow-grass fam.** p. 206.
□ Flowers not in spikelets, but with membranous perianth segments and borne in heads or clusters. **Rush fam.** p. 218.

68 □ Fully aquatic plants with submerged or floating leaves, flower spikes emerging from the water. **69**
□ Land plants, or marginal aquatic plants with both leaves and flowers emerging from the water. **71**

69 □ Leaves pinnately divided into fine, linear sections, usually borne in whorls of 4–6 (rarely 3–6). **Water-milfoil fam.** p. 100.
□ Leaves simple and linear, borne in close whorls of 6–12. **Mare's-tail fam.** p. 100.
□ Leaves simple, alternate or opposite, rarely in whorls of three. **70**

70 □ Flowers unisexual, solitary or one male and one female borne together in a leaf axil. Leaves opposite; stipules absent. **Starwort fam.** p. 102.
□ Flowers hermaphrodite in dense clusters or spikes on long stalks terminating the stems or growing from leaf axils. Leaves alternate with membranous sheathing stipules, or (rarely) leaves opposite and stipules absent. **Pondweed fam.** p. 204.

71 □ Flowers in dense cylindrical spikes, either hermaphrodite and growing at an angle at the side of the stem; or unisexual with males at the top, females below and the spike sheathed in a spathe. **Arum fam.** p. 230.
□ Flowers not as above. **72**

72 □ Flowers minute; male and female flowers separate but on same plant, and consisting of one stamen and one carpel. **Spurge fam.** p. 88.
□ Flowers not as above. **73**

73 □ Woody shrubs. **74**
□ Herbaceous or climbing plants. **76**

74 □ Thorny shrubs with silvery-brown, scale-like hairs. **Oleaster fam.** p. 94.
□ Shrubs not thorny, nor with silvery-brown hairs. **75**

75 □ Male and female flowers on separate plants, borne in catkins; they have no sepals or petals. **Bog Myrtle fam.** p. 90.
□ Hermaphrodite flowers with a brightly coloured calyx-tube which looks like a corolla. Petals absent. **Daphne fam.** p. 94.

76 □ Climbing plants. **77**
□ Herbaceous plants. **79**

77 □ Flowers unisexual. **Hemp fam.** p. 14, **Yam fam.** p. 218.
□ Flowers hermaphrodite. **78**

78 □ Flowers bilaterally symmetrical, each with a rounded, swollen base, a long tube and an expanded tip. **Birthwort fam.** (*Aristolochia*) p. 40.
□ Flowers regular, stipules sheathing. **Dock fam.** p. 18.
□ Flowers regular, stipules absent. **Buttercup fam.** p. 32.

79 □ Leaves with distinctive sheathing stipules (ochreae) at base of leaf stalk. **Dock fam.** p. 18.
□ Stipules absent or not as above. **80**

80 □ Flowers green and tiny, borne in spikes or in leaf axils, often dangling; male and female flowers often separate. **81**
□ Flowers not green and tiny. **82**

81 □ Stipules present. **Nettle fam.** p. 14, **Spurge fam.** (*Mercurialis*) p. 88.
□ Stipules absent. **Amaranth fam.** p. 16, **Goosefoot fam.** p. 22.

82 □ Petals free. **83**
□ Petals fused into a lobed corolla. **84**

83 □ Stamens numerous. **Buttercup fam.** p. 32.
□ Stamens six, ovary superior. **Lily fam.** p. 206.
□ Stamens six, ovary inferior. **Daffodil fam.** p. 214.

84 □ Fruits are purple berries borne in hanging racemes. **Pokeweed fam.** p. 16.
□ Fruits are small, green nuts crowned by remains of perianth segments. **Sandalwood fam.** p. 16.
□ Fruits are capsules. **Birthwort fam.** (*Asarum*) p. 40.

NOTE: Page references within the main text following relate to those plants whose illustrations do *not* fall on the page facing their accompanying text.

Hemp family
Cannabaceae

A very small family, with only 2 genera and 4 species, but economically significant despite its small size. Hemp, *Cannabis sativa*, comes in several varieties, all yielding different products: fibres from one variety are made into rope and sailcloth; seeds from a second yield an oil used to make paints and soaps; resin extracted from the flowers and fruits of a third can be refined to produce hashish (known also as cannabis and marijuana) but this process is illegal. Hemp is widely cultivated in Europe and also grows wild as a casual weed.

Family features The flowers are unisexual and borne on separate plants in clusters in the leaf axils. Male flowers grow on stalks; each has a five-part perianth with overlapping sections, and five stamens. Female flowers are stalkless and borne in conspicuous, persistent bracts; each has an entire perianth enfolding a one-celled ovary. The fruits are achenes. The leaves are alternate or opposite, simple or palmately lobed, and they have stipules.

Hop, *Humulus lupulus*, is best known in its cultivated form, grown on leaning ropes in hop fields. The female flowers (the hops) are gathered in summer, dried and used in the manufacture of beer. In the Middle Ages beer was brewed without hops (when it was called ale) and its bitter flavour came from such plants as Ground Ivy (called Alehoof), Sage, or Yarrow. True beer (as opposed to ale) is made with hops, which were introduced into Britain from northern Europe; they give a bitter flavour to the beer and also help it keep longer. Hop flowers are also used in herb medicine, as a sedative and to improve digestion. Young hop shoots can be cooked and eaten as a vegetable—they taste like asparagus. Hop is a perennial climbing plant with bristly stems that twist in a clockwise direction. Its leaves are large and deeply lobed. Female flowers, like small yellow cones, grow in clusters in the leaf axils; they enlarge in fruit to form cones up to 1.5cm ($^1/_2$in) long, with papery bracts. Hops grow wild in hedges and thickets throughout Europe and Britain (especially in England and Wales), probably as escapes from cultivation in many areas.

Nettle family
Urticaceae

A family of herbs and small shrubs, with about 45 genera and 550 species, found throughout the world, but more common and with all the shrubs in the tropics. Many have stinging hairs. Some are noxious weeds. Others have fibres in their stems which are used for making fishing nets and cord, while some, like several *Pilea* species, are grown as house plants.

Family features The flowers are unisexual, very small and usually borne in clusters. They lack petals but have four or five calyx lobes, with the same number of stamens opposite the calyx lobes in male flowers and a superior ovary in female flowers. The fruits are achenes or drupes. The leaves are simple, opposite or alternate. Stipules are usually present.

Stinging Nettle, *Urtica dioica*, is the most familiar nettle, found in waste places, often near buildings and among rubble, on roadsides, in hedgerows and woods throughout the British Isles and Europe. It is a perennial plant which can spread to form extensive colonies. Its four-angled stems grow 100–120cm (3–4ft) tall, and bear opposite, toothed leaves. Stems and leaves are all covered with stinging hairs which leave a burning red rash on the skin if the plant is handled incautiously. In summer tiny, greenish flowers grow in branched clusters in the leaf axils, males and females on separate plants. Surprisingly, nettles are edible, although gloves must be worn for gathering them. The leaves can be cooked as a green vegetable, like spinach, and are rich in vitamins and minerals.

The **Small Nettle**, *Urtica urens*, is a similar but smaller annual plant, growing only to 60cm (2ft) tall, with a single simple or branched stem. It has both male and female flowers on the same plant. This is a much more local species, growing in cultivated ground, arable land and waste places throughout Europe, mainly in the east in the British Isles.

Pellitory-of-the-wall, *Parietaria judaica*, is a branched perennial plant with soft, not stinging, hairs. It has sprawling, often reddish stems up to 40cm (15in) tall, and alternate, lance-shaped or ovate leaves. Dense clusters of flowers grow in the leaf axils, female flowers terminating the clusters and male flowers at the sides. This plant grows in old walls, in cracks between rocks and in hedge banks, locally throughout much of the British Isles (except in northern Scotland) and in western and southern Europe.

Mind-your-own-business or Mother-of-thousands, is usually known by its old Latin name of *Helxine soleirolii*. It may be grown as a house plant but is more often planted in patios, usually to the regret of the owner when it invades the flower beds, and comes up in every crack in the paths.

Mistletoe family
Loranthaceae

A family of shrubs which are semi-parasitic on trees. It contains about 30 genera and 400 species, found in tropical and temperate areas of the world.

Mistletoe, *Viscum album*, is one of only three species in this family found in Europe, and the only one in Britain. It is most familiar as the yellow-green plant with white berries used as decoration with holly at Christmas, but it has a long history in

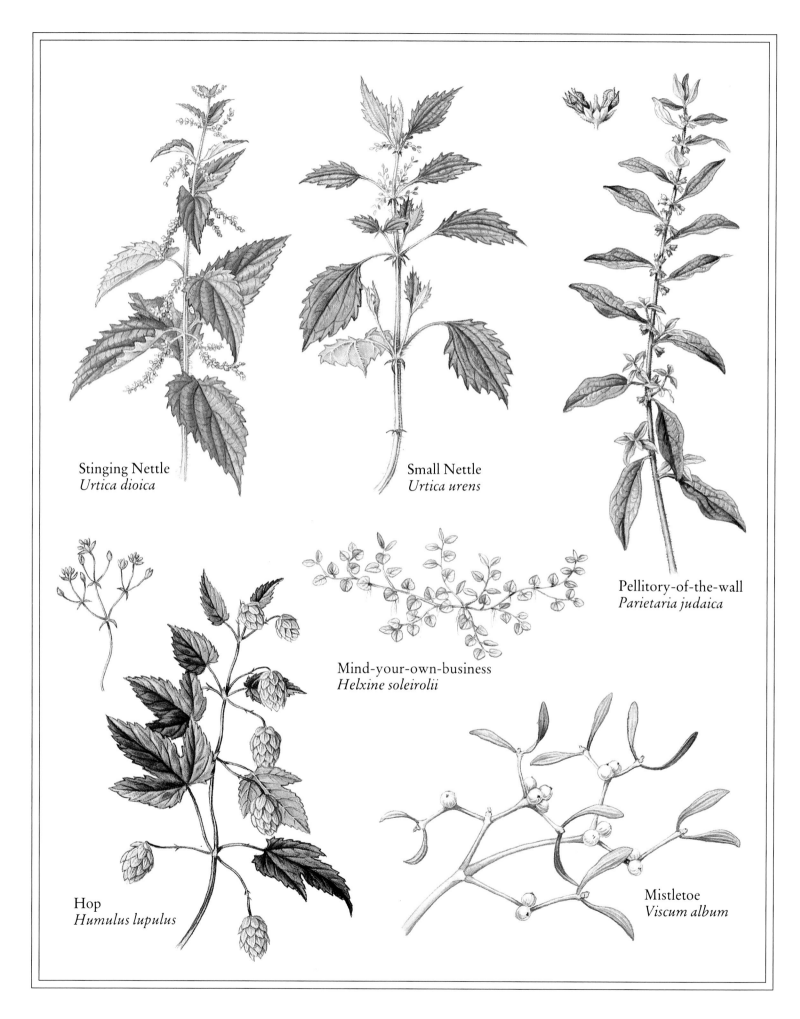

Stinging Nettle
Urtica dioica

Small Nettle
Urtica urens

Pellitory-of-the-wall
Parietaria judaica

Mind-your-own-business
Helxine soleirolii

Hop
Humulus lupulus

Mistletoe
Viscum album

folklore. It was used in the ceremonies of the Druids, cut from oak trees (on which it grows rarely) with golden sickles and not allowed to touch the ground, for then it lost its potency; it was believed to ward off evil and to make barren women fertile. Some hint of its magic properties survive in the tradition of kissing under the mistletoe. It was also a herbal plant, with a reputation for curing epilepsy and other nervous disorders. Its berries were used for making birdlime.

Mistletoe is an evergreen plant which grows on a variety of deciduous trees, most often on apples. It forms a clump of branched green stems with thick, leathery leaves in pairs. In spring tiny flowers appear in terminal clusters, males and females on separate plants. They have four green petals and the female flowers produce poisonous, white, sticky berries, ripening in winter. Mistletoe is found in England and Wales, and throughout Europe, except in the extreme north.

Sandalwood family
Santalaceae

A mostly tropical family of trees, shrubs and herbs, with about 30 genera and 400 species found in tropical and temperate regions of the world. Perhaps the most well known are the Sandalwood trees from the Pacific Islands and Australasia. Their sweet-scented wood is used for making boxes and gift items, and in the perfume industry.

A few species—members of the genus *Thesium*—occur in Europe. **Bastard Toadflax**, *T. humifusum*, grows locally in much of western Europe, and in Britain is found in the south in chalk and limestone grassland. It is becoming rarer as the chalk grasslands disappear. Bastard Toadflax is a slender perennial, with branched, spreading or prostrate stems and alternate, linear leaves. Although it looks like a normal green plant, it is parasitic on the roots of other plants. In summer it bears racemes of yellowish flowers terminating the stems, each flower growing in the axil of a linear bract and two smaller bracteoles. The flowers are regular and hermaphrodite, with only one perianth whorl and an inferior ovary. Their yellow colour comes from the bell-shaped, five-lobed perianth.

Amaranth family
Amaranthaceae

There are about 65 genera and 850 species in this family, mostly herbs, mainly from the tropical and warm temperate regions of the world. Many are weeds; others, like Cockscomb and Love-lies-bleeding, are grown as ornamental plants.

None of the members of this family are native to Britain or Europe, although more than 20 species grow as casuals, introduced from Asia and America. One of the most common in Europe, naturalized in cultivated and waste places in many countries but only a rare casual in Britain, is **Common Amaranth**, *Amaranthus retroflexus*. It is an annual from tropical America, with a branched stem up to 2m (6ft) tall and many long-stalked, triangular-ovate leaves. In the axils of the upper leaves and in a terminal spike are dense, ovoid clusters of green, petal-less flowers, males and females separate.

Pokeweed family
Phytolaccaceae

A family of herbs, shrubs and trees with about 12 genera and 100 species, mainly from South America and southern Africa.

Only one species is found in Europe and this one has been introduced from North America. It is **Pokeweed**, *Phytolacca americana*, grown as an ornamental and occasionally naturalized in waste places and around rubbish tips. It can be a weed in gardens, and its leaves and berries are poisonous. It is a perennial plant up to 3m (10ft) tall, with branched, reddish stems and alternate, tapering, ovate leaves up to 30cm (1ft) long. It has a strong, disagreeable scent. Its flowers are borne in vertical, long-stalked racemes opposite the leaves; each has five greenish-white sepals and a central ovary formed of a ring of about ten sections. The flowers lack petals.

Purslane family
Portulacaceae

A family of herbs, with about 17 genera and 200 species, mainly from North and South America. The plants are usually smooth and hairless, and many are succulent, with fleshy leaves, a feature which enables them to grow in hot, dry places. Some are grown as ornamentals, like the calandrinias and the garden hybrid forms of *Lewisia*.

Family features The flowers are regular and hermaphrodite, with two free or united sepals and 4–6 petals, free or united at the base and soon falling. The stamens either number the same as the petals and are opposite them, or are numerous. The ovary is usually superior. The fruits are capsules. The flowers are solitary or are borne in clusters, usually opposite the leaves. The leaves are entire, alternate or opposite, with bristly or papery stipules.

Most of the 40-odd *Montia* species come from North America, including the plant known in Europe as **Spring Beauty**, *Montia perfoliata*. In its native haunts in Alaska and western Canada it is known as Miner's Lettuce, for it was eaten by gold

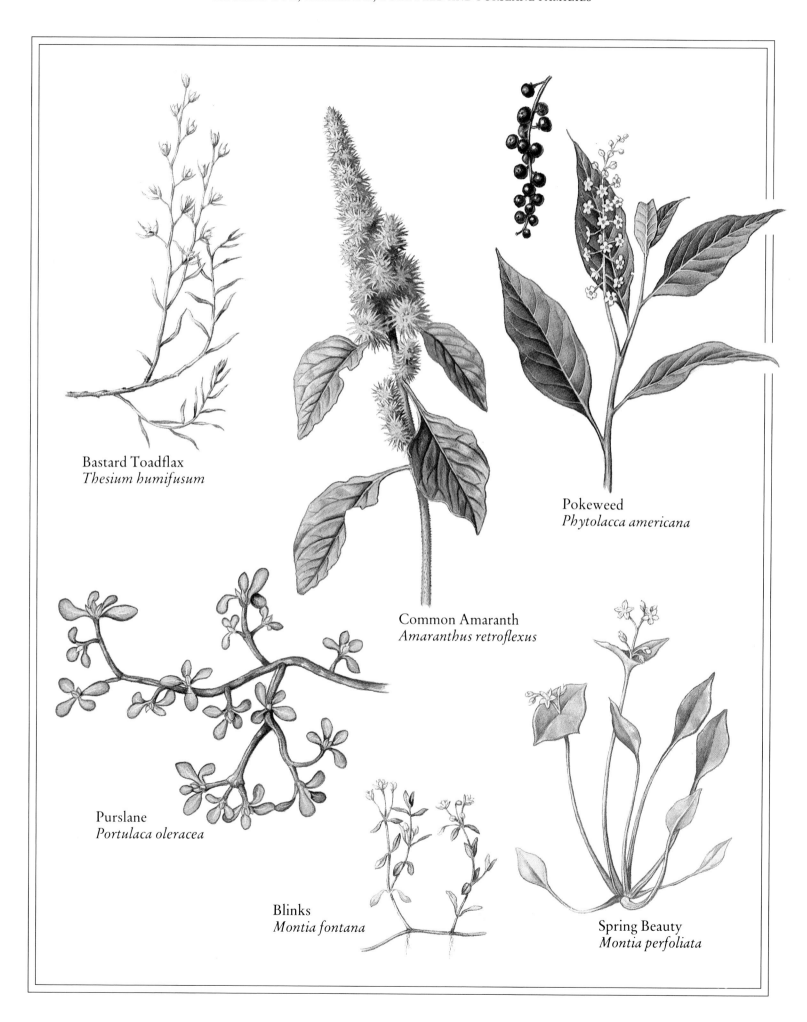

Bastard Toadflax
Thesium humifusum

Common Amaranth
Amaranthus retroflexus

Pokeweed
Phytolacca americana

Purslane
Portulaca oleracea

Blinks
Montia fontana

Spring Beauty
Montia perfoliata

miners as a salad and source of Vitamin C. It is a distinctive plant, growing up to 30cm (1ft) tall and forming small, annual clumps of fleshy, spoon-shaped leaves, together with several flowering stems which appear to terminate in broad, bowl-like disks. In the centre of each disk is a long-stalked cluster of small, pinkish flowers. In fact the disk is formed from a pair of leaves which have fused around the flowering stem. The plant flowers in late spring and early summer, and the flowers are followed by small capsules with shiny black seeds. In Europe and Great Britain the species is locally abundant, growing on cultivated and waste land, especially on sandy soils.

Blinks, *Montia fontana* (p. 17), is a species native to Europe—a low-growing, straggling, variable plant with several subspecies. It has much-branched stems, opposite, spoon-shaped leaves and terminal cymes of tiny, inconspicuous, white flowers, often blooming throughout the summer and into autumn. It may grow in water, beside streams, in wet flushes and meadows, or among wet rocks or in gravel, usually on acid soils, throughout the British Isles and Europe.

Purslane, *Portulaca oleracea* (p. 17), probably came originally from western Asia but now grows in warm, temperate regions throughout much of the world. It grows in cultivated land and on waste ground in Britain, in similar habitats and in vineyards in Europe. It is a prostrate, mat-forming, annual plant, with reddish stems which bear more or less opposite leaves and a final leaf rosette beneath the terminal flowers. The leaves are fleshy and shiny, ovate and blunt or spoon-shaped. The flowers are pale yellow, solitary or borne in small terminal clusters, and open only on sunny mornings. Young, leafy tips of this plant can be eaten as a vegetable or in salads.

Dock family
Polygonaceae

Most plants in this family are herbs or shrubs; there are about 40 genera and 800 species throughout the world, mainly found in temperate regions. Several of the *Polygonum* species are garden plants grown in flower borders and rock gardens; some species, like Russian-vine, are vigorous climbers; and there are several invasive weeds in the family. A few of the species are economically significant food plants, including Buckwheat, *Fagopyrum esculentum*, and Rhubarb, *Rheum rhaponticum*.

Family features The flowers are small and regular, and often borne in conspicuous inflorescences. Each has 3–6 perianth segments which may resemble petals or sepals, 4–9 stamens and a superior ovary. The perianth segments often persist to enclose the fruits, which are hard, dry, two-sided or three-sided achenes. The leaves are usually alternate and simple, with a distinctive stipule (or ochrea) sheathing the stem at the base of the leaf stalk.

The plants known as **Water-peppers** and **Bistorts** belong to the large genus *Polygonum*, with about 250 species found throughout the world, particularly in temperate regions. Some are grown in gardens, others are weeds. Several are associated with wet places like marshes and swamps, some, like certain forms of Amphibious Bistort, *P. amphibium*, growing in the shallow water of canals and slow-moving rivers.

Some of the *Polygonum* species are acrid (hence water-peppers), but **Redshank** or Persicaria, *Polygonum persicaria*, is edible; its young leaves can be used in salads or cooked as a vegetable. This is a smooth, hairless, annual plant, 25–75cm (12–30in) tall, with many branched, reddish stems, characteristically swollen above each node. It has small, lance-shaped leaves, often with a single black blotch on each leaf. The sheathing ochrea at the base of each leaf is fringed. Many pink flowers grow in dense, cylindrical spikes terminating the leafless flowering stems. This plant grows in moist places and beside ponds, and as a weed in damp waste and cultivated ground, beside tracks and on roadsides throughout Europe.

Pale Persicaria, *Polygonum lapathifolium*, is a similar but larger species, with green stems rather than red ones and nodding spikes of greenish-white, rarely pink flowers. Its ochreae are unfringed. This annual plant forms branched stems up to 1.5m (5ft) tall and grows in moist places throughout much of the temperate northern hemisphere.

Water-pepper, *Polygonum hydropiper*, is another annual, with lance-shaped leaves, short ochreae and spikes of greenish flowers. This is a very acrid plant, 25–75cm (12–30in) tall, that grows in acid soils, in wet places or in shallow ponds and ditches throughout the British Isles and Europe, except the extreme northern areas and northern Scotland.

Common Bistort or Snake-root, *Polygonum bistorta*, is a clump-forming, perennial species with contorted, creeping rhizomes and broadly heart-shaped basal leaves. In early summer it produces erect flowering stems about 60cm (2ft) tall, with triangular leaves and dense, terminal spikes of pink flowers. This is an attractive species, grown in gardens as well as being a wild plant. It is found throughout much of the British Isles and Europe, growing on grassy roadsides and in meadows, but is rare in Ireland and southeastern England, absent from Denmark and Scandinavia. In the English Lake District it is called Easter Ledges and made into a dish called Easter-ledge Pudding, eaten with bacon and eggs.

Knotgrass, *Polygonum aviculare*, is a ubiquitous weed found throughout much of the world, growing in lawns, streets and waste ground, as well as on seashores. It is a hairless, annual plant, often forming more or less prostrate mats, with branched stems up to 2m (6ft) long. It has small, linear or lance-shaped leaves with silvery, jagged ochreae and clusters of small pinkish flowers in the leaf axils. The brown, three-sided fruits can remain viable for years, so that the Knotgrasses spring up as if by magic on newly disturbed ground.

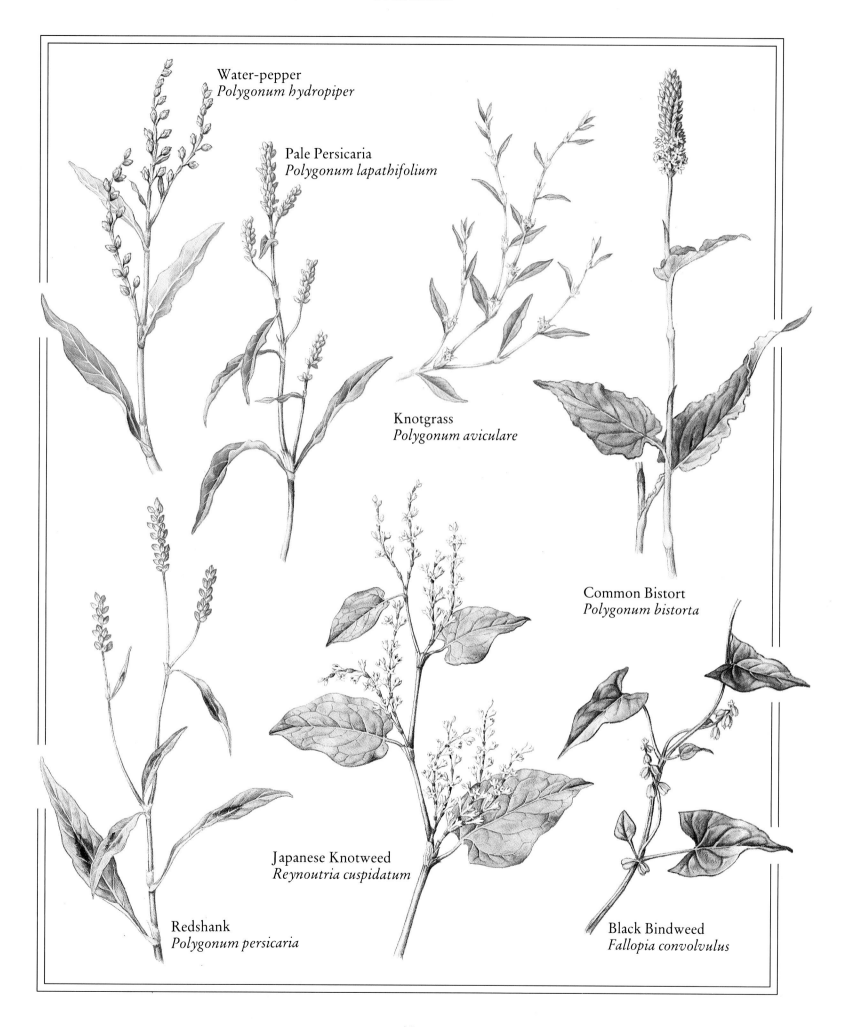

Water-pepper
Polygonum hydropiper

Pale Persicaria
Polygonum lapathifolium

Knotgrass
Polygonum aviculare

Common Bistort
Polygonum bistorta

Japanese Knotweed
Reynoutria cuspidatum

Redshank
Polygonum persicaria

Black Bindweed
Fallopia convolvulus

Japanese Knotweed, *Reynoutria cuspidatum* or *Polygonum cuspidatum* (p. 19), was introduced as a garden plant, but has become naturalized in wet places throughout much of the British Isles and northern Europe. It grows up to 3m (10ft) tall and has jointed stems like a bamboo (hence its other name of Japanese Bamboo) and invasive roots. It is extremely difficult to eradicate once established and poses a considerable menace to our native plants when it escapes into the wild.

Black Bindweed, *Fallopia convolvulus* or *Polygonum convolvulus* (p. 19), is a climbing annual plant which has thin, scrambling stems that reach 2m (6ft) in length. It has triangular leaves with small clusters of 3–6 greenish-pink flowers in the leaf axils. It grows in waste places and arable land, in hedges and gardens throughout Europe and the British Isles. Russianvine, *Fallopia baldschuanica*, is an extremely vigorous relative grown in gardens to cover garages and walls, covering itself with white flowers in late summer.

Buckwheat, *Fagopyrum esculentum*, is another cultivated member of this family, this species grown for its seeds which are ground into buckwheat flour or used in brewing. It is an erect annual plant, with little-branched, hollow, reddish stems up to 60cm (2ft) tall and arrow-shaped leaves. In the axils of the upper leaves grow the greenish-white or pink flowers in dense, branched inflorescences on long stalks. The fruits which follow are dull, dark brown, smooth and three-angled. This plant is grown in many parts of Europe and often seeds itself to grow wild in cultivated ground and waste places. In Britain it is most likely to be found in the Fens.

Mountain Sorrel, *Oxyria digyna*, is one of a number of alpine species in this family. It is a perennial plant which forms a clump of long-stalked leaves with kidney-shaped, rather fleshy blades. In late summer its leafless flowering stems bear terminal clusters of greenish or reddish flowers. The colour comes from the perianth segments which turn bright red and persist around the small winged fruits, so that the fruits are more conspicuous than the flowers. The leaves are sour and rich in Vitamin C, edible in salads or as a potherb. The plant grows in rocky places and mountains throughout much of Europe, in mountain areas in the British Isles.

There are many **Docks** and **Sorrels**, *Rumex* species, in Europe; this is a large genus with about 200 species found in temperate regions of the world. Some of the most familiar are weeds of waste places, roadsides, fields and gardens; others grow in grassland, in woods and beside streams, many of them preferring damp places.

Sheep Sorrel, *Rumex acetosella*, grows in acid soils, in grassland and heaths, and in cultivated land throughout the British Isles and Europe, and in many other temperate areas of the world. It is a perennial plant with a clump of bright green leaves in spring, many of the leaves like spearheads with spreading lobes on the bases. They have long stalks and each has a silvery, sheath-like ochrea where the stalk joins the stem.

The leaves are sour and can be eaten in salads, cooked as a potherb, or made into a refreshing drink. In summer the plants form leafy flowering stems up to 30cm (1ft) tall, with the flowers in whorls. Male and female flowers grow on separate plants. The fruits which follow are three-sided, golden brown nutlets, individually small, but conspicuous in masses.

Common Sorrel, *Rumex acetosa*, is a larger plant, with flowering stems up to 1m (3ft) tall. The spear-shaped leaves are broader than those of Sheep Sorrel, with fringed, silvery ochreae, and the leaves turn red in autumn. Like many members of the family, when the plants are in fruit the perianth segments of the female flowers enlarge to become heart-shaped and winged, red-brown in colour with conspicuous veins. This plant grows in grassland and on grassy roadside verges, less often in open places in woods and beside rivers, usually on neutral soils, throughout the British Isles and Europe. Its sour leaves can be used in salads or in sauces for fish.

Curled Dock, *Rumex crispus*, is one of the weedy species, the commonest dock in Britain, found throughout the British Isles and Europe. It grows in waste and grassy places, on shingle beaches and on cultivated land, where it can become a serious weed since its thick tap roots penetrate over 1m (3ft) deep into the ground and it produces thousands of seeds. Its leaves are a traditional remedy for nettle stings and were at one time also used to dress burns and scalds. They grow up to 30cm (1ft) long and have curly, 'crisped' edges. The flowering stems grow up to 1m (3ft) tall, with whorls of greenish flowers followed by three-angled, green fruits. Each is strongly veined and has three red tubercles, one larger than the others.

Broad-leaved Dock, *Rumex obtusifolius*, is another common, potentially serious weed, growing in waste and disturbed places, in poor pastures, around field edges and in hedgerows throughout the British Isles and much of Europe. It is similar to Curled Dock, but the edges of its broad leaves are wavy, not curly, and there is only one large red tubercle on each three-angled fruit. Fiddle Dock, *R. pulcher*, is another weed, this one found in dry, sandy places and on chalk and limestone in England south of the Humber, in Wales, southern Ireland and western Europe. Its name comes from its fiddle-shaped leaves.

Sharp Dock, *Rumex conglomeratus*, prefers damper grassy places, growing in marshy meadows, beside streams and ponds, less often in woods, throughout England, Wales and Ireland, rarely in Scotland. In Europe it is found north as far as southern Scandinavia. It is a more slender plant than many docks, a perennial with an erect stem up to 2m (6ft) tall, and large, oblong leaves. The small red flowers grow in widely separated whorls in the axils of the leaves (giving the plant its other name of Clustered Dock), and soon produce fruits, each one with three reddish tubercles.

Golden Dock, *Rumex maritimus*, is a rare plant becoming rarer as its specialized habitats disappear; it grows on bare muddy ground beside ponds and reservoirs, in dried-up ponds

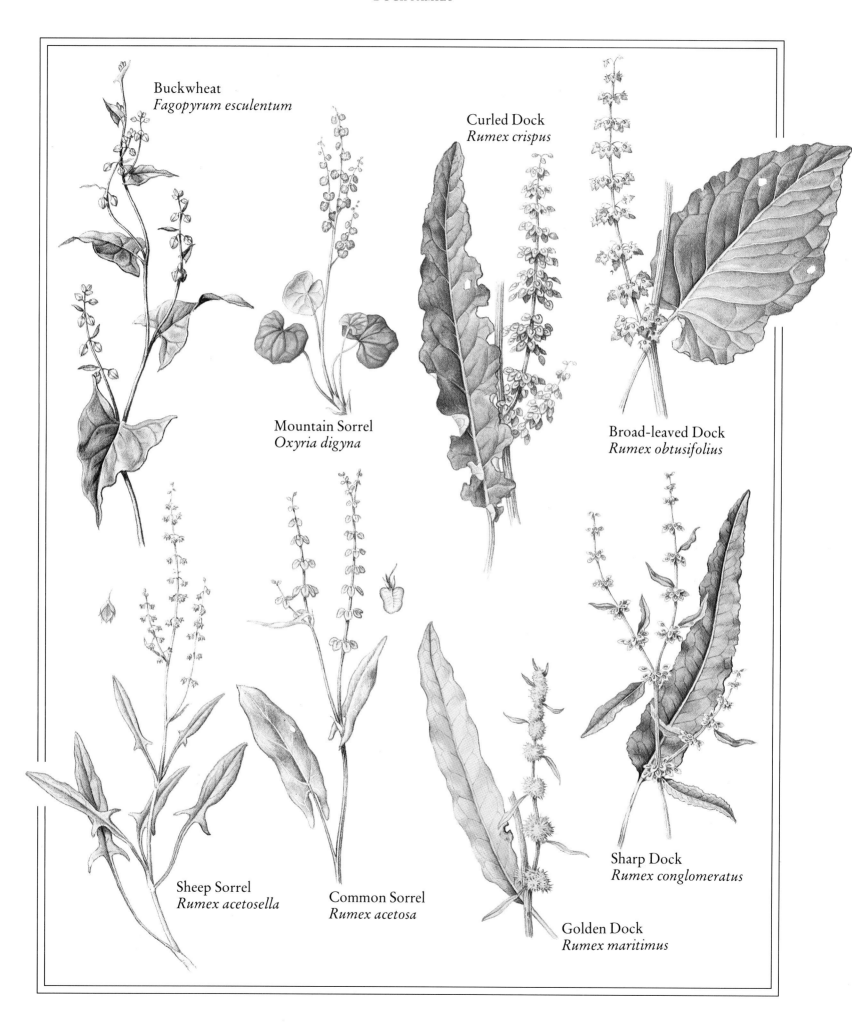

Buckwheat
Fagopyrum esculentum

Mountain Sorrel
Oxyria digyna

Curled Dock
Rumex crispus

Broad-leaved Dock
Rumex obtusifolius

Sheep Sorrel
Rumex acetosella

Common Sorrel
Rumex acetosa

Sharp Dock
Rumex conglomeratus

Golden Dock
Rumex maritimus

and ditches and on seashores throughout most of Europe, in England and into southern Scotland, particularly near the coast. It is an annual or biennial, often bushy plant, growing up to 1m (3ft) tall, with lance-shaped leaves. The flowers grow in leafy spikes formed of many crowded whorls. The feature of this plant that makes it special is the golden yellow colour that it turns when its fruits form.

Goosefoot family
Chenopodiaceae

A family of herbs and shrubs with about 100 genera and over 1400 species found throughout the world. Many are succulent and grow in arid or salt-rich habitats, many are weeds, like Fat Hen and Orache, but others, such as beetroot and spinach, are important vegetables.

Family features The flowers are small or minute and often green, with 3–5 fused sepals, and usually with the same number of stamens inserted opposite the sepals. The flowers lack petals. The ovary is usually superior. The flowers are borne in leaf axils or with bracts in spikes. They may be hermaphrodite, or male and female flowers may be separate on the same plant. The fruits are tiny nuts. The leaves are simple, alternate and lack stipules.

The **Goosefoots**, *Chenopodium* species, number both weeds and vegetables among their members. They are annual or perennial plants, many with large lobed leaves and spikes of reddish or greenish, hermaphrodite flowers, the spikes made up of many dense flower clusters.

Fat Hen, *Chenopodium album*, is an annual weed that grows in many parts of the world, including Europe and the British Isles, where it is the most common species in the genus, growing in rich soils, often as a weed on arable land or in waste places. It has branched, often reddish stems up to 1m (3ft) tall and diamond-shaped leaves. The leaves are dark green, variably covered with white bladder-like hairs, especially on the underside, and the larger ones are often toothed. In late summer the plant produces many dense spikes of tiny greenish flowers in the axils of the narrow upper leaves. Young leaves make a good vegetable, rich in vitamins and minerals and resembling spinach.

The young leaves and shoots of **Good King Henry**, *Chenopodium bonus-henricus*, are also edible and rich in minerals; the leaves can be eaten in salads and the shoots like asparagus. This plant grows in nitrogen-rich soils in farmyards, pastures and on roadsides throughout most of Europe; it has been introduced in the British Isles and is only common from England and Wales to southern Scotland, rare elsewhere and in Ireland. It is an erect, perennial plant up to 60cm (2ft tall), with broadly triangular leaves powdered with meal on the under-

sides when young. The small, greenish flowers are borne in many leafless spikes growing from the leaf axils in summer.

Oraches, *Atriplex* species, are often difficult to distinguish from goosefoots; however, they have separate male and female flowers on the same plant. **Common Orache**, *Atriplex patula*, is a common annual weed found in waste places and cultivated ground, particularly near the sea, in many parts of the northern hemisphere, including the British Isles and Europe. It is rather like Good King Henry, with triangular or arrow-shaped leaves more or less covered with white hairs. However, its female flowers are enclosed in two diamond-shaped bracts which persist to enclose the fruits; in contrast, the fruits of Good King Henry are exposed. Its leaves make a good vegetable—one that has gone out of fashion despite its flavour and high Vitamin C content. Hastate Orache, *A. hastata*, is a related species found in similar places, but its leaves lack white hairs or are hairy on the undersides only.

Many members of this family grow on the sea-shore or in salt marshes on the coast. **Sea Beet** is a subspecies of the same plant, which has given rise to Spinach, Beetroot and Sugar Beet, *Beta vulgaris*; it is *B. vulgaris* subsp. *maritima*. It grows wild around the coasts of the British Isles and on the European coast north to southern Sweden on shingle beaches and the edges of salt marshes, in grassy places and on sea walls. It is a variable plant, usually biennial, with sprawling, reddish stems and red-tinged leaves, rhombic in shape and leathery in texture. Its green flowers are borne in whorls of three in slender, branched spikes. They are followed by spikes of fruits enclosed by persistent brown petals. Unlike those of the cultivated Beetroot, the roots of Sea Beet are not swollen.

Sea Purslane, *Halimione portulacoides*, is a plant that often forms extensive colonies near the high tide mark, around the edges of estuaries and on the margins of channels and pools in salt marshes on the coasts of England, eastern Ireland and continental Europe north to Denmark. It is a small, creeping shrub, only 80cm (2–3ft) tall, with sprawling, rooting, leafy stems and a silvery appearance created by the tiny silver scales on the elliptical leaves. The leaves are thick and fleshy, able to retain water and withstand the drying winds that blow more or less constantly from the sea. In late summer the plants flower, producing dense yellow flower spikes terminating the stems and in the axils of the upper leaves, male and female flowers separate. The fruits that follow are enclosed in knobbly, yellow, three-lobed bracts.

Glasswort or Marsh Samphire, *Salicornia europaea*, grows on the sandy mud of salt marshes on the coasts of the British Isles and Europe. It is an annual, with erect, much-branched, jointed stems, its succulent and somewhat translucent aspect coming from its leaves. These are opposite, joined along their margins and form the 'segments'. The plants begin their life green but become flushed with yellow, then pink or red as the season progresses. They are edible, can be eaten raw in unpol-

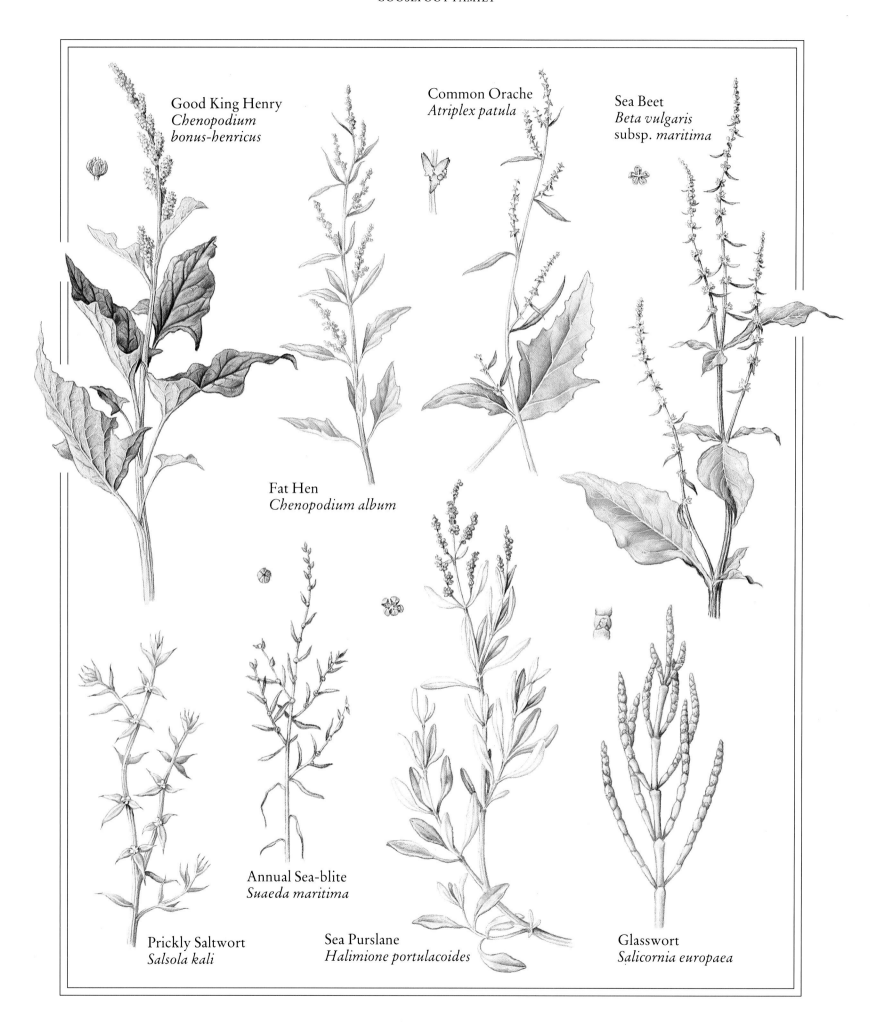

Good King Henry
*Chenopodium
bonus-henricus*

Common Orache
Atriplex patula

Sea Beet
Beta vulgaris
subsp. *maritima*

Fat Hen
Chenopodium album

Annual Sea-blite
Suaeda maritima

Prickly Saltwort
Salsola kali

Sea Purslane
Halimione portulacoides

Glasswort
Salicornia europaea

23

luted areas, added to salads or cooked in soups. Several similar species also grow in muddy places in salt marshes.

Annual Sea-blite, *Suaeda maritima* (p. 23), grows in salt marshes around the coasts of the British Isles and Europe. It is a small, sprawling annual, often blue-green plant, with fleshy leaves and small, button-like flowers in clusters in the axils of the upper leaves. It is edible and can be added to soups and casseroles. Shrubby Seablite, *S. vera*, is a small, shrubby plant, with branched stems and evergreen, greyish, linear leaves. It grows on shingle banks and in sandy places on the coast, often forming a line above the high tide mark.

Prickly Saltwort, *Salsola kali* (p. 23), is an annual plant, with much-branched stems and linear, fleshy, spine-tipped leaves. The flowers are solitary in the leaf axils and each one has two leaf-like, prickly-pointed bracts. When the fruits form, the bracts become hard and the calyx of each flower becomes reddish with conspicuous veins and membranous wings. This plant grows on the coasts of the British Isles and Europe, north to southern Scandinavia, often on developing sand-dunes and along the drift lines of sandy beaches.

Pink family
Caryophyllaceae

There are about 70 genera and 1750 species of herbs in this family. It is a group with many showy garden species and hybrids. Pinks may be simple rock garden or border plants, or they and their close relatives, the carnations, may be highly bred plants with double flowers, plants grown in greenhouses and used as cut flowers or buttonholes. Many of the old pinks were scented, the most famous being the Old Clove Pinks, also known as gillyflowers, with a fragrance like cloves. Modern pinks and carnations have largely lost this scent, bred out in the quest for yet more double or colourful flowers; some would say the loss is greater than the gain. Other well-known garden and cut flowers belonging to this family include Gypsophila and the *Lychnis* species.

Family features The flowers are regular, usually hermaphrodite. Each has four or five sepals, either free or united into a tube, often with papery margins. There are the same number of petals as sepals, or petals may be absent. Stamens number up to ten, often twice as many as the petals. The ovary is superior with one cell. The fruits are dry capsules, usually opening by valves or by teeth at the top. The flowers are solitary or borne in cymes. The leaves are entire, opposite and often connected by a transverse line; stipules are frequently absent but when present are usually papery.

Pinks and **Carnations** are members of the genus *Dianthus*, with 300 species, the majority of which grow in dry, sunny places. Most are perennial herbaceous plants, with clumps of basal, blue-green, linear leaves and attractive flowers.

Many pinks are small, mat-forming plants grown on rock gardens. In the wild they grow in mountain areas in Europe. **Cheddar Pink**, *Dianthus gratianopolitanus*, is a rare plant in Britain, growing only on the top of the cliffs at Cheddar Gorge in Somerset, where it is protected, but found also in mountains of western and central Europe. In early summer it forms dense tufts of linear leaves, long, non-flowering shoots and sprawling flowering shoots only 10–20cm (4–8in) tall, bearing a few rose-pink 'pink-type' flowers with fringed petals.

Maiden Pink, *Dianthus deltoides*, has a similar form but is a larger, looser plant. It has short, leafy, non-flowering shoots and sprawling flowering shoots that lie on the ground then turn upwards to grow 45cm (18in) tall with small, rose-coloured, spotted flowers terminating the stems. This plant grows on dry, grassy banks, in old quarries and beside tracks, in dry pastures and near the sea, usually on shallow soil over chalk or limestone. It is decreasing in numbers, but is still found locally throughout Great Britain and in most of Europe.

Deptford Pink, *Dianthus armeria*, forms a clump of stiff, dark green, linear leaves and bears erect, rigid but slender, flowering stems in summer. The bright reddish-pink flowers grow in flat terminal clusters on these stems. This is an annual plant, becoming increasingly rare, but likely to be found in dry, well-drained soils, in grassy places, in hedgerows and on banks, beside roads or railways and in other disturbed habitats in scattered places in England, Wales and southern Scotland, also in Europe north to southern Scandinavia.

Large Pink, *Dianthus superbus*, is found in dry woods and shady meadows in many parts of Europe, but is absent from the British Isles and the Iberian peninsula. It has large, sweetly scented, pink or lilac flowers with ragged petals cut into more than half their width to form deeply fringed lobes.

There are several garden species of pinks that have become naturalized in Britain and northern Europe, especially on old walls. The Common Pink, *Dianthus plumarius*, is one of these, a rock garden plant with tufts of leaves and fragrant, pale pink flowers, the petals turned up at the edges and fringed. **Sweet Williams** are garden plants belonging to the species *D. barbatus*; they are grown as biennials, flowering in early summer, then seeding freely if left alone, so that they too have become naturalized in many parts of Europe, growing in shady or grassy places. They form clumps of erect stems with linear leaves, the stems ending in dense, flat-topped clusters of white-spotted, red or purple flowers.

Soapwort or Bouncing Bett, *Saponaria officinalis*, spreads into wide patches, taking over large areas with its deep, invasive roots. Its erect stems, 30–90cm (1–3ft) tall, bear dark green, opposite leaves and terminal clusters of delicately scented, pink flowers. An attractive garden form has double blooms. This plant now grows in many grassy places and hedgerows near villages in England and Wales, northwards to

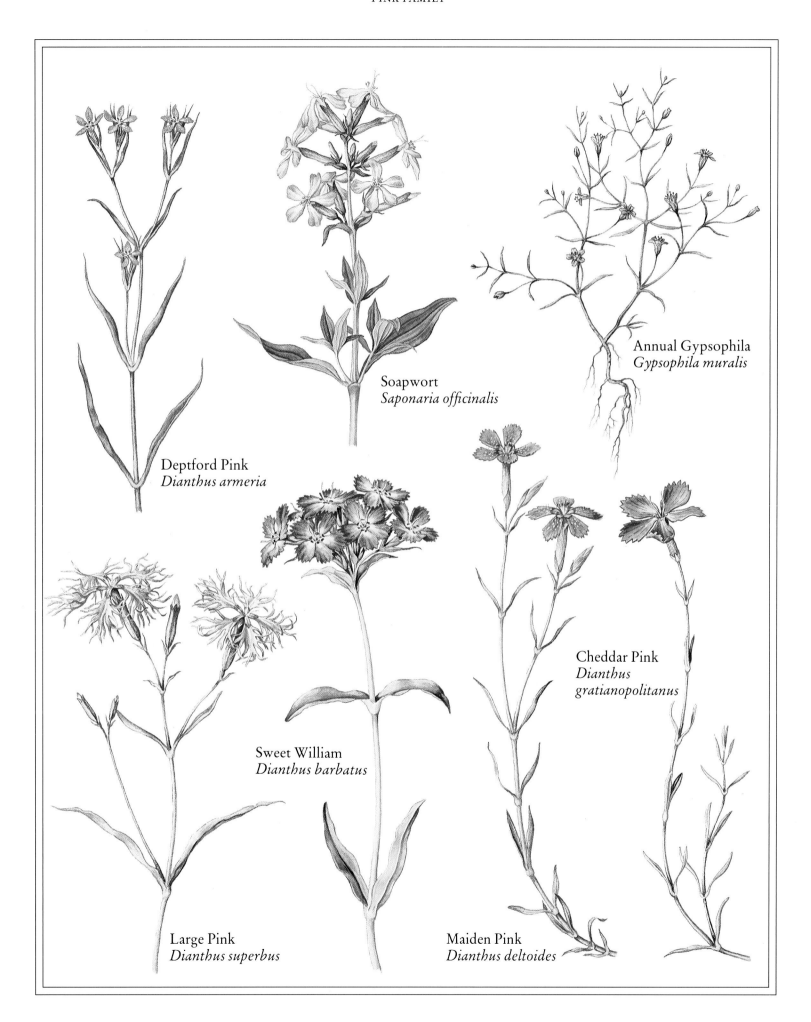

Deptford Pink
Dianthus armeria

Soapwort
Saponaria officinalis

Annual Gypsophila
Gypsophila muralis

Sweet William
Dianthus barbatus

Cheddar Pink
Dianthus gratianopolitanus

Large Pink
Dianthus superbus

Maiden Pink
Dianthus deltoides

Aberdeen and into Scandinavia in Europe. It was probably introduced to many of these areas and is native only to the southwestern parts of Britain. It may have been introduced as a garden plant or for the soapy liquid which can be obtained from boiling its stems, for before the advent of modern soaps it was widely used for washing wool and woollen cloth.

There are about ten species of *Gypsophila*, all native to southeastern Europe and Asia and none to the British Isles. **Annual Gypsophila**, *G. muralis* (p. 25), grows in damp woods and meadows in many parts of Europe, except the British Isles and Portugal. It is a very slender, much-branched, annual plant, with many linear leaves and tiny pink, red-veined flowers growing in loose clusters from all the leaf axils. The Cultivated Gypsophila, with its myriad tiny white flowers, which is sold for flower arrangements, is *G. paniculata*; it grows wild in stony places in eastern Europe and Asia, and is widely cultivated in western Europe.

Many **Stitchworts**, *Stellaria* species, are attractive plants with satiny white flowers, often found in damp and shady places. **Greater Stitchwort** or Satin Flower, *S. holostea*, is one of the showiest. Its flowers seem disproportionately large for the weak stems on which they grow—bright, satiny white with petals cleft for half their length. They appear in late spring and early summer. Like many stitchworts and chickweeds, this plant has short non-flowering shoots and taller flowering shoots, in this species reaching 60cm (2ft) tall. They are brittle, weak and straggling, often supported by other vegetation in the rough, shady places of woods and hedgerows where the plant most often grows. This stitchwort is found throughout the British Isles and much of Europe, north to southern Scandinavia but is rare in the south.

Lesser Stitchwort, *Stellaria graminea*, grows in grassy places, in hedgerows and woods through most of the British Isles and Europe. It is a perennial plant with slender, creeping rhizomes and numerous, slender, non-flowering shoots; these are brittle, sprawling and much-branched, with linear, grass-like leaves. In summer the plant produces flowering shoots which bear many small white flowers with deeply cleft petals. Wood Stitchwort, *S. nemorum*, is a similar but local species found in scattered, damp woods throughout much of Europe and Great Britain. It has weak stems, ovate leaves and large white flowers with deeply cleft petals.

Several stitchworts, such as the Marsh Stitchwort, *Stellaria palustris*, and the Bog Stitchwort, *S. alsine*, grow in wet places. The first is a relatively large species, with sprawling stems up to 60cm (2ft) tall and large white flowers; the second is a much smaller plant, only 40cm (15in) tall, with small flowers in which the white petals are shorter than the sepals.

Common Chickweed, *Stellaria media*, is a ubiquitous weed of gardens, woods, waste ground and cultivated land; it is an annual plant, germinating in autumn and growing through the winter in a mild year, and flowering from early spring to late autumn. It forms a sprawling clump of weak, leafy stems no more than 40cm (15in) high, with many tiny white flowers in terminal leafy cymes. Common Chickweed is edible; it is often recommended for salads, but has a fibrous texture and bitter taste and is better boiled briefly and eaten as a vegetable. The plant can be identified by the single line of hairs that runs down the stem from node to node.

Water Stitchwort or Water Chickweed, *Myosoton aquaticum*, grows in ditches and marshes, beside streams and ponds, in damp woods and other wet places throughout Europe, mainly in central and southern England in the British Isles. It is a perennial plant with fragile, straggling non-flowering and flowering shoots, stickily hairy towards the tops and with pointed ovate, often heart-shaped leaves. The white flowers appear in loose clusters in late summer; their petals are twice as long as the sepals and cleft to the base.

The **Mouse-ear Chickweeds**, *Cerastium* species, can be distinguished from *Stellaria* species because Mouse-ear flowers have three styles whereas Chickweed and Stitchworts have five. The Mouse-ear Chickweeds are so called because the short, downy hairs on the leaves of some of them resemble the fur on the ears of mice. Several are common weeds of short grassland, lawns and bare ground. Like the *Stellaria* species, they produce both non-flowering and flowering shoots.

Common Mouse-ear Chickweed, *Cerastium fontanum*, is a cosmopolitan weed found in grassy places, roadsides and waste places, sand-dunes and cultivated ground, a perennial creeping plant rooting at the nodes of its sprawling stems. Its non-flowering shoots remain less than 15cm (6in) tall but the flowering shoots turn upwards to reach 45cm (18in) in height. The stems are sticky-glandular and hairy, with opposite, grey-green, hairy leaves. The flowers grow in terminal, equally branched clusters; each has five hairy sepals and five cleft white petals, the latter just a little longer than the sepals.

Field Mouse-ear Chickweed, *Cerastium arvense*, is a similar plant and another common weed of dry grassland, found throughout Europe and the British Isles, but more common in the east in Britain. It can be distinguished from Common Mouse-ear Chickweed by its flowers—the petals are twice as long as the sepals. Many plants are also often much less hairy, although the species is very variable. **Sticky Mouse-ear Chickweed**, *C. glomeratum*, is a common weed of dry, waste places and cultivated land, a small, pale yellow-green plant with long white hairs on the leaves and a sticky texture. The petals are about as long as the sepals in its flowers.

A much more flamboyant and aggressive plant, very different to these small Mouse-ears, is **Snow-in-summer**, another *Cerastium* species, *C. tomentosum*, grown on rock gardens. It forms a wide-spreading mat with rooting stems, grey-white leaves and a froth of white flowers in early summer. This is a handsome plant, but one which takes over not only the garden but the roadside as well if left to its own devices. It often

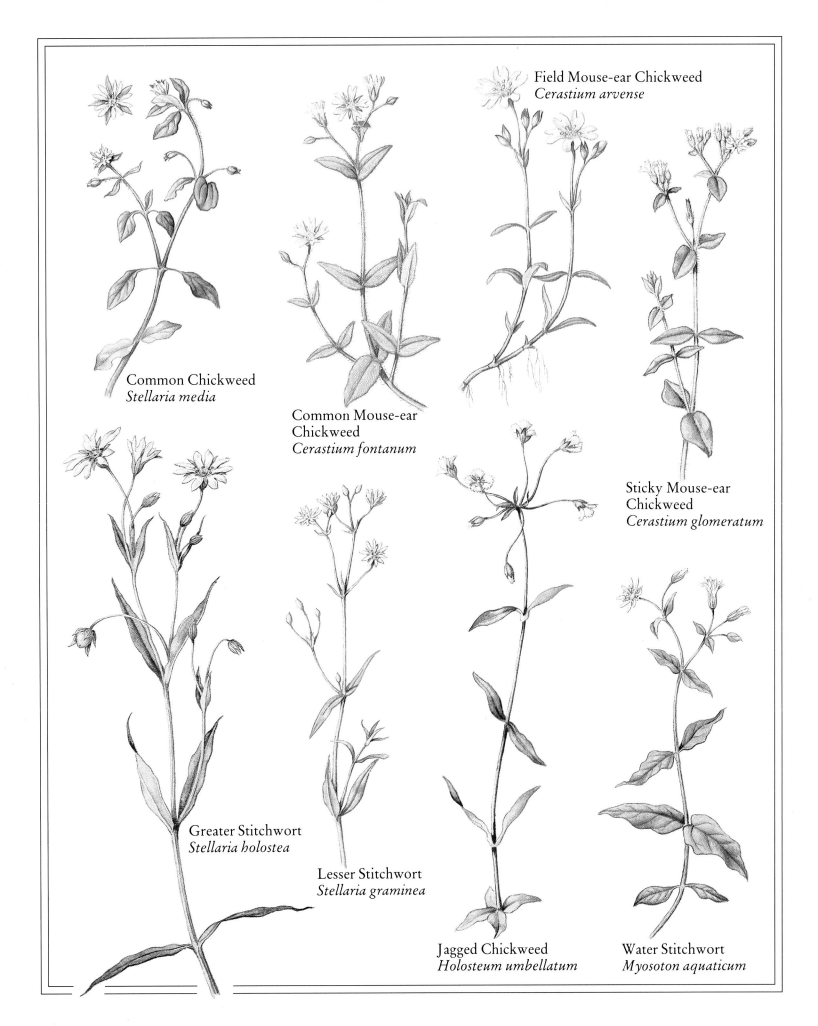

Common Chickweed
Stellaria media

Common Mouse-ear
Chickweed
Cerastium fontanum

Field Mouse-ear Chickweed
Cerastium arvense

Sticky Mouse-ear
Chickweed
Cerastium glomeratum

Greater Stitchwort
Stellaria holostea

Lesser Stitchwort
Stellaria graminea

Jagged Chickweed
Holosteum umbellatum

Water Stitchwort
Myosoton aquaticum

escapes to grow on walls and banks around towns and villages.

Jagged Chickweed, *Holosteum umbellatum* (p. 27), is more like the smaller mouse-ears. It is an annual plant, with a small clump of non-flowering shoots covered with greyish leaves, sticky on their upper surfaces. Flowering shoots grow up to 20cm (8in) tall and bear umbels of white flowers. This little plant grows in much of Europe in sandy or stony places, but is probably extinct in Britain. At one time it could be found on a few roofs or walls in East Anglia and Surrey.

Mouse-ears may be small plants but many members of this family are smaller, insignificant little plants with tiny, often inconspicuous flowers. **Pearlworts**, *Sagina* species, carry this tendency to an extreme. They are tiny mat-forming plants, with green tangled stems and linear leaves, the whole plant no more than a few centimetres across and 10cm (4in) tall.

Procumbent Pearlwort, *Sagina procumbens*, is a perennial weed that grows in damp places, often in lawns and paths in gardens, in damp arable land and beside streams. Although small, it seeds profusely, spreading slowly but surely and can soon cover large areas if left to its own devices. It produces tiny, greenish flowers on long stalks in the leaf axils, each flower with four sepals and often lacking petals. The plant grows throughout much of Europe and the British Isles. Knotted Pearlwort, *S. nodosa*, is similar in form and also grows in damp places, but it has larger, white flowers. Its name comes from the short side shoots which grow in the axils of the leaves, giving the stems a 'knotted' appearance.

There are several **Sandworts** in the genus *Minuartia*, which resemble the pearlworts in appearance. They are mat-forming plants with opposite, linear leaves and white flowers. However, they tend to be rare or local plants confined to specific habitats, like the Spring Sandwort, *M. verna*, which grows among base-rich rocks and on screes in suitable places throughout Europe. In Britain it is mostly confined to North Wales, the Lake District, the Peak District and the Pennines. Mossy Cyphel, *M. sedoides*, forms mossy, yellow-green cushions formed of densely leafy shoots. It grows on rocks and screes in the Highlands of Scotland, in the mountains of the Scottish islands and in the Alps, Pyrenees and Carpathians.

Thyme-leaved Sandwort, *Arenaria serpyllifolia*, is somewhat similar in appearance to Common Chickweed. It is an annual plant, untidy and sprawling, sometimes prostrate, with many stems and tiny, opposite, pointed-ovate leaves. However, it is wiry and rough to the touch, not succulent and not edible. Its white flowers have five uncleft petals. This plant is often found on bare ground, on roadsides and in waste places, in gardens and arable land, on walls, heaths and downs throughout the British Isles and Europe.

Sea Sandwort, *Honkenya peploides*, is a much larger species, a coastal plant found on beaches and sand-dunes all around the coasts of the British Isles and Europe; few plants grow in such conditions, and those that can are invaluable for stabilizing the sand. Sea Sandwort forms dense colonies with thick stems which run in and along the sand, frequently buried and then exposed by the shifting grains. Its stems have many fleshy leaves arranged in four overlapping ranks, and it bears small, whitish flowers in the axils of the leaves. Male and female flowers grow on separate plants, female flowers with minute petals. The succulence of the leaves is a common phenomenon in coastal plants, as in desert plants, for salt-laden soils are as difficult to extract water from as arid ones, and the leaves provide a means of storing water.

Corn Spurrey, *Spergula arvensis*, is an annual weed of arable and cultivated land on acid soils throughout the British Isles and Europe. It is also found on open ground in waste places and on roadsides. This plant is easy to spot, for it is distinctive, with slender green stems and fleshy, linear leaves which are opposite, but so divided that they look as if they are in whorls. It grows up to 40cm (15in) tall and in summer bears many terminal clusters of white flowers on thin stems.

Sand Spurrey, *Spergularia rubra*, has much-branched, often prostrate, stems and linear leaves. It is a small, usually annual plant, but individuals may survive for more than one year. It bears a few small pink flowers in clusters at the ends of the stems, the five petals of each flower alternating with the sepals and shorter than them. Sand Spurrey grows in lime-free, sandy or gravelly soils, on tracks and fields throughout Europe and Great Britain, and very locally in Ireland.

Lesser Sea-spurrey, *Spergularia marina*, is one of several succulent species growing in coastal areas. This one is found in salt marshes, along with Greater Sea-spurrey, *S. marginata*; both species may also be found on the sides of major roads treated with salt in winter. Lesser Sea-spurrey is a small, annual or biennial plant which forms prostrate mats of 20-cm (8-in) long fleshy stems with whorls of linear leaves, and terminal clusters of small pink, white-centred flowers. Greater Sea-spurrey is similar but a little larger, and a perennial plant, with pale pink or whitish flowers.

Rupturewort, *Herniaria glabra*, is another small plant, this one a mat-forming, annual species with numerous prostrate, branched stems growing about 15cm (6in) long and many tiny, elliptical leaves. It produces clusters of minute, pale pink flowers in the axils of the leaves on the side shoots. This is a rare and decreasing plant found in dry, sandy places in Europe north to southern Scandinavia, only in East Anglia and Lincolnshire in Great Britain.

Annual Knawel, *Scleranthus annuus*, is also a small annual, this one with sprawling, branched stems growing up to 25cm (10in) tall, and a spiky appearance coming from the narrow, pointed leaves. It flowers around midsummer, producing clusters of tiny, greenish, petal-less flowers hidden by bracts in the leaf axils. Annual Knawel grows in dry, sandy places, in waste places and cultivated land throughout Europe and Great Britain, locally in Ireland.

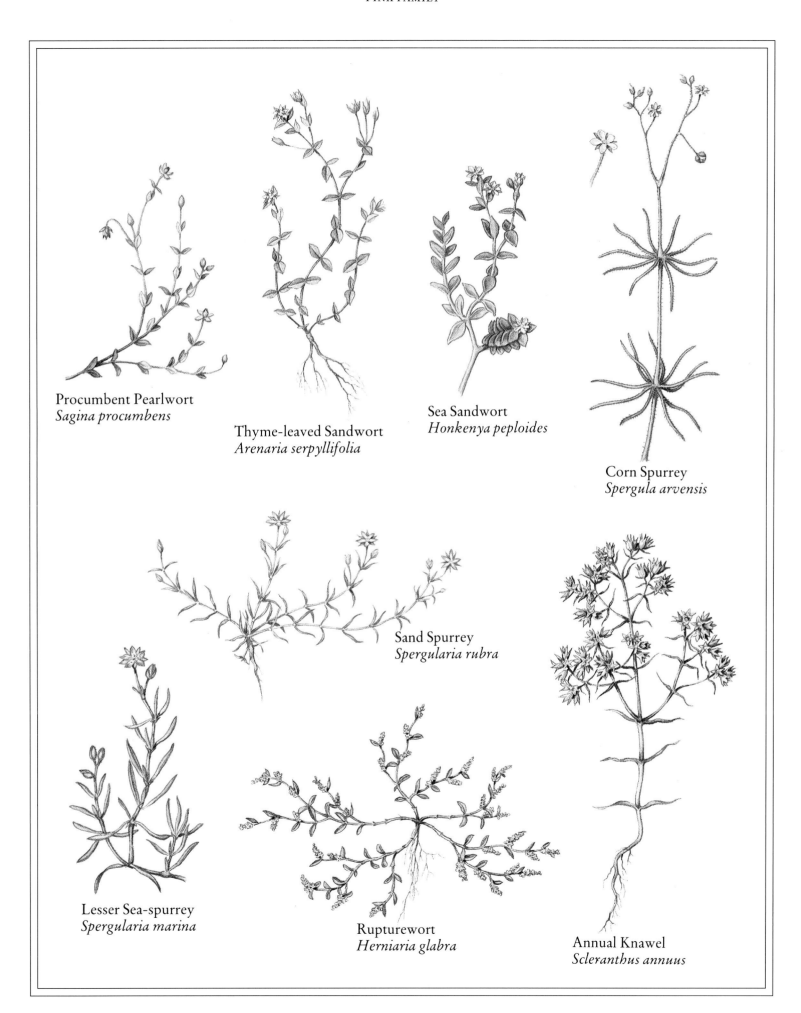

Procumbent Pearlwort
Sagina procumbens

Thyme-leaved Sandwort
Arenaria serpyllifolia

Sea Sandwort
Honkenya peploides

Corn Spurrey
Spergula arvensis

Sand Spurrey
Spergularia rubra

Lesser Sea-spurrey
Spergularia marina

Rupturewort
Herniaria glabra

Annual Knawel
Scleranthus annuus

Many of the **Campions** and **Catchflies**, members of the genera *Silene* and *Lychnis*, are similar to the Stitchworts but some of them are very much showier plants. There are about 300 *Silene* and 15 *Lychnis* species, the majority found in temperate areas of the world. Some are grown in gardens, but most are found only in the wild.

Red Campion, *Silene dioica*, must be one of the most attractive of these plants. It forms a short-lived perennial clump, with numerous non-flowering shoots about 20cm (8in) tall and many flowering shoots up to 90cm (3ft) tall in early summer. The shoots bear opposite pairs of soft, hairy leaves and many rose-red flowers with cleft petals protruding from sticky-hairy calyx tubes. Male and female flowers are separate. The flowers brighten a variety of habitats, mainly woods and hedgerows, but also limestone screes and coastal cliffs, usually in nutrient-rich places, throughout much of Europe and the British Isles, less commonly in Ireland.

The **White Campion**, *Silene alba*, is a similar but sticky-hairy plant, with pointed leaves and white flowers, slightly scented in the evening. It is found in hedgerows and grassy places, cultivated and waste land, most commonly in lowland areas and is probably not native to the British Isles, having been introduced from Europe in the Stone Age. It grows throughout Europe. White Campions and Red Campions hybridize freely, producing offspring with flowers in a variety of shades of pink. All the plants are fertile and it is often difficult to decide to which species they belong.

The **Bladder Campion**, *Silene vulgaris*, is a perennial plant, growing up to 1m (3ft) tall and found in a variety of disturbed habitats, in waste places and beside railway tracks, on roadsides and in cultivated land, in rough grassland and hedgerows throughout the British Isles and Europe. It forms a clump of erect, branched stems and opposite, pointed, lance-shaped leaves. Terminating the stems in early summer are many branched clusters of distinctive, nodding flowers. They have swollen, veined, bladder-like calyces enclosing the lower half of each flower, and the deeply cleft petals seem to emerge from the 'bladder' at all sorts of odd angles, so that the flowers often look vaguely dishevelled. The capsules that follow are globular, each with six teeth at the top; they are enclosed by the persistent calyces. The Sea Campion is a sprawling or cushion-forming subspecies of this plant with prostrate stems, *S. vulgaris* subsp. *maritima*. It rarely grows more than 20cm (8in) tall and may be found on cliffs, in sandy places and on shingle banks on the coasts of western Europe and the British Isles. It is often grown in rock gardens.

Nightflowering Catchfly, *Silene noctiflora*, is an annual plant found in sandy or chalky soils in arable land in southern and eastern England, much more rarely in western England and Scotland, very rarely in Ireland. It is also found through much of Europe. It has soft, downy hairs on its sticky-glandular stems and scattered hairs on the pointed, lance-shaped leaves. It bears few flowers and these have deeply cleft, white or pinkish petals which remain rolled inwards during the day, opening and spreading outwards at night, when their scent attracts moths. The calyx of each flower is somewhat swollen and egg-shaped, sticky and woolly in texture; it swells and remains around the egg-shaped capsule, which often bursts through as it enlarges in seed.

Small-flowered Catchfly, *Silene gallica*, is another sticky, annual species with small white or pink flowers in the axils of the leaves. It grows on sandy, arable land and in waste places, but is decreasing in numbers and is now confined to England and Wales in Britain, although plants are still found in much of continental Europe. The similar Sand Catchfly, *S. conica*, was never common and is becoming rare, found in sand-dunes and sandy or chalky fields in East Anglia. It has distinctive, very swollen calyces around the capsules.

Moss Campion, *Silene acaulis*, is a different sort of plant—a perennial, tufted, alpine species found on ledges, screes and mountain tops in Scotland, North Wales and the Lake District in Britain, and in the mountains of western Europe. It forms dense cushions of short stems with linear leaves, studded with deep rose-pink flowers in late summer. It is sometimes grown in troughs or rock gardens.

Another rock garden plant, one much more widely grown, is **Red German Catchfly**, *Lychnis viscaria*. In the wild in Europe it grows in sandy places and dry meadows, but in Britain it is rare and found in only a few places in Wales and Scotland, growing on igneous rocks. It forms perennial tufts of sticky, lance-shaped leaves from which grow erect flowering stems in early summer, reaching about 30–60cm (1–2ft) in height. They bear clusters of bright rose-pink flowers in the axils of the upper, linear leaves.

The related **Ragged Robin**, *Lychnis flos-cuculi*, is very different in appearance and in range. It is a perennial plant, with sprawling, leafy non-flowering shoots and erect flowering shoots growing to about 75cm (30in) tall and bearing their distinctive 'ragged', rose-red flowers around midsummer. Their appearance comes from the way that the petals are dissected into many linear segments. This attractive plant grows in damp meadows and marshes, wet woods and fens throughout the British Isles and Europe.

Corncockle, *Agrostemma githago*, was a common cornfield weed at one time but is now considered rare because of the improved techniques of seed screening and the use of herbicides. When the seeds of this plant were mixed with wheat, the resulting contaminated flour was poisoned by toxic glycosides present in the Corncockle seeds. The plant is an attractive one—an annual with erect stems 1m (3ft) tall, opposite, linear leaves and large, reddish-purple flowers in early summer. It is still found throughout Europe, while in Britain it is now most often found in waste places and on roadsides in lowland areas of England and Wales.

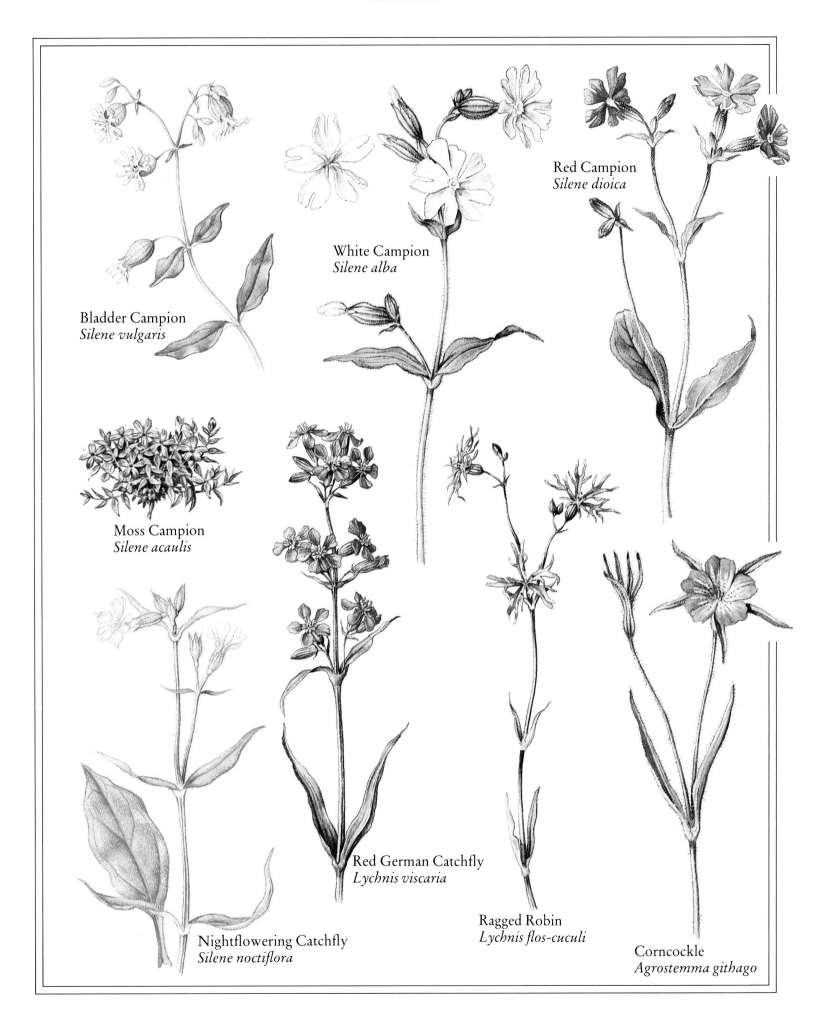

Bladder Campion
Silene vulgaris

White Campion
Silene alba

Red Campion
Silene dioica

Moss Campion
Silene acaulis

Red German Catchfly
Lychnis viscaria

Ragged Robin
Lychnis flos-cuculi

Nightflowering Catchfly
Silene noctiflora

Corncockle
Agrostemma githago

Buttercup family
Ranunculaceae

A family of herbs, shrubs and climbers, with about 50 genera and 1900 species found mostly in temperate and Arctic areas of the northern hemisphere. Some species have given rise to spectacular garden plants like delphiniums and clematis, or to interesting ones like anemones, hellebores and columbines.

All members of the buttercup family are poisonous. Buttercups, anemones and others are acrid and poisonous when fresh, causing ulceration and inflammation at the least and may cause diarrhoea, kidney damage and convulsions; poisoning is most common in livestock. When dried in hay the plants lose their toxicity since the alkaloids break down during drying. Other plants, like monkshoods, are much more poisonous and can cause death by heart failure.

Family features The flowers may be solitary or in terminal inflorescences. They are hermaphrodite and regular with all the parts free. There are 5–8 sepals in each flower, often overlapping, often falling, sometimes petaloid. Frequently there are five petals but they may be absent or numerous; usually they are overlapping and often each has a nectary at the base. The stamens are numerous and may be petaloid. The superior ovary is made up of one to many carpels and the fruits are usually either pod-like or achenes. The leaves are usually alternately arranged or may grow in a basal clump and they are often compound or divided. Stipules are usually absent.

There are about 14 **Monkshoods**, *Aconitum* species, in Europe. They are distinctive perennial plants with underground tubers, clumps of large, palmately-cleft leaves and flowering stems up to 1m (3ft) tall, bearing showy blue or yellow flowers, usually in late summer. The flowers have five petal-like sepals, the uppermost forming a helmet-shaped hood and concealing two nectaries, remnants of the petals. The flowers are followed by groups of 2–5 pods with many seeds.

The rhizomes of the plant usually known simply as **Monkshood**, *Aconitum napellus*, have been used for many years in commercial medicine and homoeopathy. They contain an alkaloid which is a painkiller and which reduces fever; monkshood is thus useful for treating rheumatism, inflammations and feverish colds. However, the plant is so poisonous that it can only be used under strict medical supervision. It has erect stems, palmately lobed leaves divided into linear segments and blue-mauve flowers in early summer followed by clusters of pods. In this species the hood in the flowers is broader than long and the nectary spurs are straight. Monkshood grows in damp mountain meadows and woods throughout much of Europe, except in the north, but is not common in Britain, found only in southwestern England and Wales.

Wolfsbane, *Aconitum vulparia*, is also found in much of Europe growing in damp mountain woods and meadows, but is absent from the British Isles. It forms clumps of palmately three-lobed leaves with erect flowering stems in summer; the flowers are yellow, with elongated, conical-cylindrical hoods and spirally twisted nectary spurs. It may be grown in gardens.

Larkspurs, members of the genus *Consolida*, are annual plants with much-divided leaves and racemes of distinctive flowers. Each flower is bilaterally symmetrical, with five outer petal-like sepals, the uppermost prolonged into a spur, and two inner petals joined together and forming a nectar-producing spur which is concealed within the sepal spur. The flowers are followed by many-seeded pods. There are about 12 species in Europe, found mostly in the Mediterranean area. None grow wild in the British Isles.

Forking Larkspur, *Consolida regalis*, grows in arable land and waste places across most of continental Europe. Its erect stems grow 1m (3ft) tall and end in showy racemes of light or dark blue flowers above leaves divided into linear lobes. Larkspur, *C. ambigua*, is the species most often grown in gardens. It usually has deep blue flowers, although cultivated varieties come in white, blue and pink forms. Wild plants originally come from the Mediterranean region.

Stinking Hellebore or Bear's-foot, *Helleborus foetidus*, is one of several hellebores that grow wild in Europe. It is sometimes grown in gardens along with its cousins, the Christmas Rose, *H. niger*, and Lenten Roses (garden hybrids of a variety of *Helleborus* species). Stinking Hellebore is a foetid perennial plant, with several leafy stems which persist over the winter, dying back when the new young stems appear above ground in late spring. The leaves are dark green and palmately lobed with narrowly lance-shaped, toothed segments. In early spring the pale green, bell-shaped flowers appear above the leaves and contrast vividly with the leaves. They grow in drooping, one-sided clusters and each one has a purple rim. The clusters of wrinkled green pods that follow remain on the plant for months. It grows wild in woods and rocky places in western and southern Europe, in southern and western England, and Wales, but may also be found in other parts of Britain and Europe where it has become naturalized.

Winter Aconite, *Eranthis hyemalis*, is another winter-flowering plant, but a much smaller one. It has tuberous underground rhizomes from which grow erect stems no more than 15cm (6in) tall, each with a ruff of three leaves beneath a single yellow, buttercup-like flower. The basal leaves appear after the flowers, each one rounded in outline and palmately lobed, dying down by early summer at the same time as the pods split open to release the seeds. This plant is native to the Mediterranean but is grown beneath trees in parks and gardens all over Europe and Britain, and has escaped in many areas to grow semi-wild in open, shady places.

Marsh Marigold or Kingcup, *Caltha palustris*, is a hairless, perennial plant only 60cm (2ft) tall. It forms a clump of long-stalked, dark green leaves with large, heart-shaped blades.

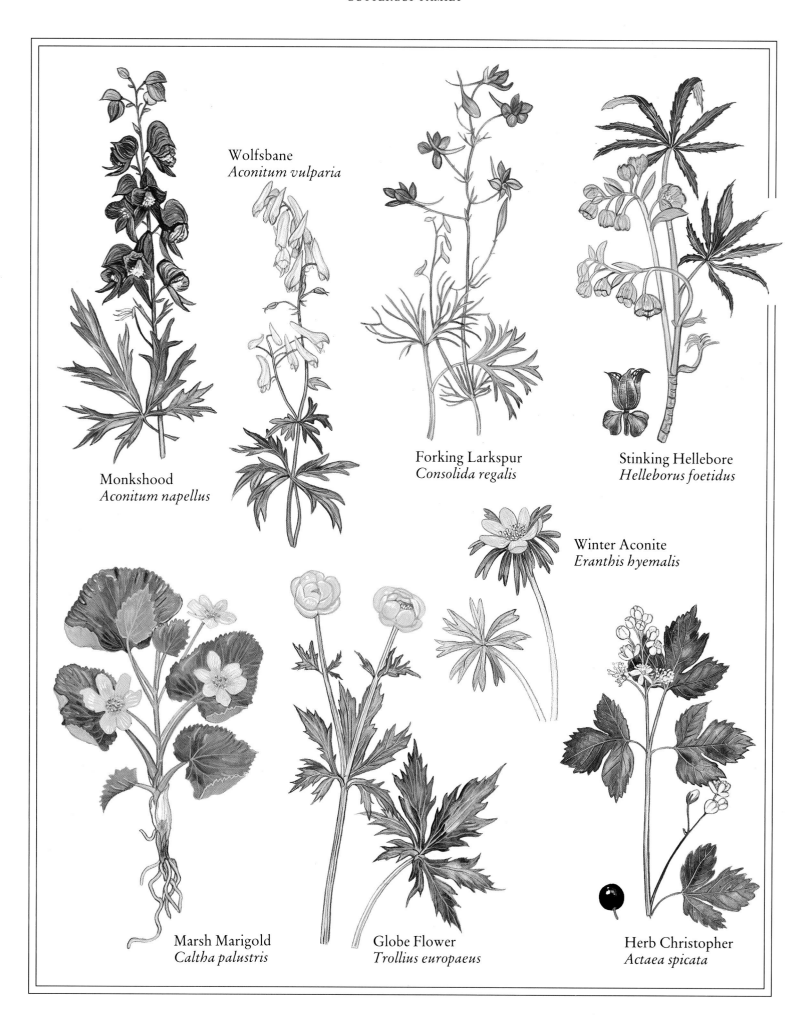

Wolfsbane
Aconitum vulparia

Monkshood
Aconitum napellus

Forking Larkspur
Consolida regalis

Stinking Hellebore
Helleborus foetidus

Winter Aconite
Eranthis hyemalis

Marsh Marigold
Caltha palustris

Globe Flower
Trollius europaeus

Herb Christopher
Actaea spicata

33

Many showy, bright yellow flowers, like large buttercups, grow on the branched, hollow stems in spring; each flower may have up to eight petals, 100 stamens and 5–12 carpels, which enlarge into pod-like fruits with many seeds. This attractive plant grows in marshy meadows and wet woods, in fens, along the edges of streams and ditches throughout Europe and the British Isles.

Globe Flower, *Trollius europaeus* (p. 33), resembles a buttercup but has much more gorgeous flowers—bowl-shaped and golden, each with about ten petal-like sepals. Inside the bowl are the hidden, nectar-producing petals, strap-shaped and clawed, somewhat resembling the stamens. The flowers grow at the tops of the 60-cm (2-ft) tall stems, hovering over the clump of long-stalked, palmately lobed basal leaves in early summer. They are followed by clusters of pods with many seeds. Globe Flowers grow in wet meadows and woods, in fens and marshes, usually in the mountains, across much of Europe. In Britain they grow in mountain areas of Wales, Scotland, northern England and northern Ireland, but they are also grown in gardens in many other areas.

Herb Christopher or Baneberry, *Actaea spicata* (p. 33), is a perennial, foetid plant, in appearance not unlike the Japanese Anemones grown in gardens. It has a black rhizome from which grows a clump of long-stalked, much-divided basal leaves with large, serrated leaflets. In early summer the flowering stems develop, having similar leaves and a terminal raceme of flowers. These have white sepals and petals which soon fall off, leaving the many white stamens still conspicuous. Unusually in this family, the fruits are berries, green at first, then ripening to glossy black. The berries, like the rest of the plant, are poisonous.

There are about 120 species of **Anemones**, genus *Anemone*, worldwide, mostly found in the northern hemisphere. Many species and cultivars are grown in gardens, especially the hybrid Japanese Anemones, which grow in shade and flower in late summer, the De Caen and St Brigid Anemones, cultivars of *A. coronaria*, the small, spring-flowering *A. blanda*, and rock garden plants, like *A. pulsatilla*, the Pasque Flower.

Anemones are usually small perennial plants, with a clump of palmately divided basal leaves, and flowers borne on separate stems. Each stem has a whorl of three or more leaves and from this whorl grow one or more flower stalks with one or a few flowers terminating the stalks. The flowers lack petals, although this is not immediately evident as the sepals have taken over the coloured role of the petals; they may be white, greenish, blue or red. The flowers have numerous stamens and carpels, the latter enlarging in fruit to form many achenes.

Wood Anemone or Windflower, *Anemone nemorosa*, is one of the most beautiful woodland spring flowers, especially when growing with bluebells. It is found in deciduous woods throughout Great Britain and Ireland, also throughout Europe. It has thin, creeping, brown rhizomes that colonize large areas; in spring they send up erect stems, each with a whorl of three leaves and a single white flower. Once the flowers are over, the basal leaves appear, long-stalked and palmately lobed, dying down by midsummer.

Yellow Wood Anemone, *Anemone ranunculoides*, is a similar species but it has fewer or no basal leaves, only leaves on the flowering stems and the flowers are yellow, like buttercups. It grows in woods and copses throughout much of Europe, but is not native to Britain. However, it is grown in woods and gardens and has become naturalized in a few localities.

Pasque Flower, *Pulsatilla vulgaris*, is a small plant, never growing more than 40cm (15in) tall, and a densely hairy one. It produces several solitary purple flowers cupped in finely divided, hairy leaves and growing on long stalks from the crown in spring; it then forms a clump of twice-pinnate, feathery-hairy leaves. As the flowers die and the fruits ripen, the achenes develop long, feathery tips, so that the plant is as noticeable in fruit as it is beautiful in flower. It grows in dry grassland, usually on chalk or limestone, and is now much less common than it was since many of these grassland areas have been ploughed. It is found in many parts of Europe, locally and decreasing in central and eastern England.

Hepatica, *Hepatica nobilis*, grows in mountain woods and copses across much of continental Europe but it is absent from Britain, except as a relatively uncommon garden plant. It is a low-growing, hairy perennial, only 15cm (6in) tall, with a clump of lobed, evergreen leaves and several solitary blue-violet flowers on long stalks in spring. The flowers lack petals and have 6–10 petal-like sepals.

Clematises, *Clematis* species, are unusual among members of the Buttercup family in that many are woody or herbaceous climbers. They include some popular garden plants and many hybrids have been developed, often with huge, brilliantly coloured flowers. **Traveller's Joy** or Old Man's Beard, *C. vitalba*, is a climbing plant up to 30m (100ft) tall, common on woodland edges, in hedgerows and thickets, on calcareous soils throughout much of Europe from Holland southwards, and in England and Wales, north to the Humber estuary. It has also been introduced further north. This is a very invasive plant, obvious especially in winter when the dead stems can be seen draped over hedges. It has twining stems and compound leaves with twining stalks; each leaf has three or five pointed-ovate, toothed leaflets and in the axils of many of the leaves grow clusters of fragrant flowers in summer. Each flower has four greenish-white, petal-like sepals, numerous white stamens and many carpels. These enlarge in fruit to form globular heads of achenes, each with a long, plume-like tail. The plants are often covered with these fruits, which persist from late summer long into the winter.

Pheasant's Eye, *Adonis annua*, is a small annual plant, with an erect stem only 40cm (15in) tall and dissected, feathery leaves. It is smooth and hairless in texture and bears bright

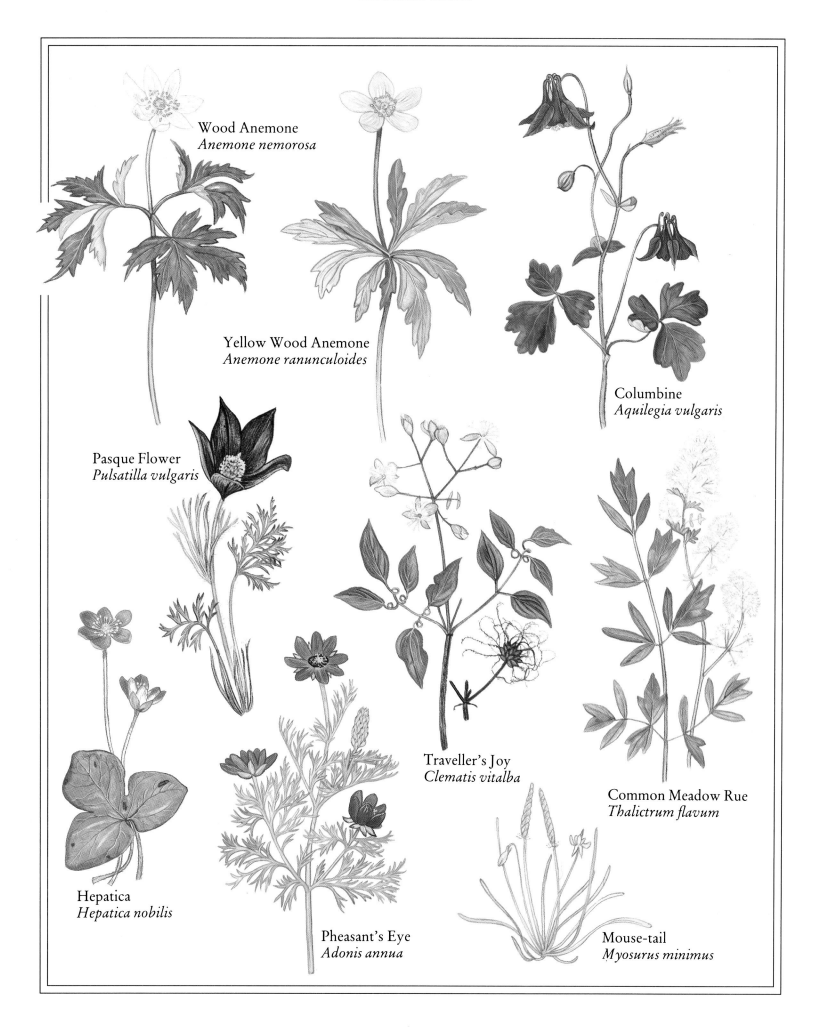

Wood Anemone
Anemone nemorosa

Yellow Wood Anemone
Anemone ranunculoides

Columbine
Aquilegia vulgaris

Pasque Flower
Pulsatilla vulgaris

Traveller's Joy
Clematis vitalba

Common Meadow Rue
Thalictrum flavum

Hepatica
Hepatica nobilis

Pheasant's Eye
Adonis annua

Mouse-tail
Myosurus minimus

scarlet flowers in the summer; each petal has a dark spot at the base. This plant grows as a weed in arable land and waste places, often in cornfields, on calcareous soils in western and southern Europe, but is only found as a very rare casual in Britain; it is no longer found in Ireland.

Columbine, *Aquilegia vulgaris* (p. 35), is a perennial plant, forming a clump of delicate, compound leaves and erect flowering stems, usually 60–100cm (2–3ft) tall, in early summer. The dumpy blue flowers are immediately recognizable; the five petal-like sepals have short claws and the five similar petals have elongated, hollow claws containing nectar. The flowers are followed by clusters of 5–10 pods. This attractive plant is one of those grown in gardens. In the wild it grows in woods and mountain meadows in much of Europe; in Britain it is found in wet woods and other wet places, scattered locally through England, Wales and southern Scotland, introduced and naturalized further north and in Ireland.

Common Meadow Rue, *Thalictrum flavum* (p. 35), is one of several *Thalictrum* species in Europe, inconspicuous but beautiful plants most often found in damp places. This is a perennial, with a clump of delicate, compound leaves divided into many lobed leaflets, dark green above, paler below. The flowers grow in branched inflorescences on stems 1m (3ft) tall; they have petal-like sepals enclosing the flowers in bud, but these fall as the flowers open and there are no petals, so that the impression is of many fluffy, yellow stamens. This plant grows in meadows and beside streams throughout Europe and Great Britain, north to Inverness. It is often grown in gardens, like the larger European species Great Meadow Rue, *T. aquilegifolium*, which has purplish sepals and stamens.

Mouse-tail, *Myosurus minimus* (p. 35), is a small annual plant with a basal rosette of somewhat fleshy, linear leaves and several leafless flowering stems, each one ending in a greenish-yellow flower. Its common name comes from the fruits, for the many achenes are borne in an elongated spike protruding from the centre of the flower. This is a rare plant, found only in southern and central England; it grows in damp, arable land and meadows where water stands in winter and its decline has coincided with improved drainage techniques.

There are about 130 species of **Buttercups**, **Crowfoots** and **Spearworts** in Europe, all belonging to the genus *Ranunculus*. They grow in many habitats, from mountain ridges to lowland woods and meadows, but many favour wet places and some grow in the water of streams and ponds. They have open, yellow or white flowers, usually with five petals, and there is a nectar-secreting pit or depression near the base of each petal. The flowers have numerous stamens and carpels in the centre and the carpels enlarge in fruit to form many single-seeded achenes. All buttercups are acrid and poisonous.

The **Meadow Buttercup**, *Ranunculus acris*, is a hairy, perennial plant with an erect, branched stem up to 1m (3ft) tall, compound, palmately cut leaves and many bright yellow,

glossy flowers around midsummer. It grows in damp hay meadows and pastures, near damp roadsides and ditches, in gullies and damp ledges in mountain areas throughout the British Isles and northern Europe, south to southern France and northern Italy. Cattle avoid it and it is not uncommon to see tall buttercups standing untouched in a meadow where other plants are grazed to the ground.

Bulbous Buttercup, *Ranunculus bulbosus*, is found in similar but drier places—on well-drained soils in meadows and pastures, on roadsides, banks and dunes; it is found throughout the British Isles and in much of Europe, north to southern Scandinavia. This plant is very like the Common Buttercup but it comes into flower earlier—in late spring and early summer—and is distinguished by its swollen stem base and by the way the sepals are reflexed beneath the flowers.

Creeping Buttercup, *Ranunculus repens*, grows in grassy places, often in damp meadows and pastures, but also in woods, marshes and dune slacks, and as a weed in gardens, arable land and roadsides. It is found throughout Europe and the British Isles. It has rosettes of long-stalked, three-lobed leaves with runners which form new plants, eventually making extensive mats. Its flowers are borne on long stalks in summer.

Goldilocks, *Ranunculus auricomus*, is a woodland and hedgerow plant, mostly found on moist, especially calcareous, soils. It grows in suitable habitats throughout much of Europe and in Great Britain and Ireland, most commonly in England. It is a perennial plant, with more or less erect stems up to 40cm (15in) tall and a few deeply divided leaves with linear segments. The flowers are typical buttercups but may have petals missing or absent. Most of the leaves form a basal clump; these are long-stalked, rounded in outline and deeply 3–5 lobed, the lobes with wavy edges.

Lesser Spearwort, *Ranunculus flammula*, is another very acrid and poisonous species found in wet places. It grows beside ponds and streams, in wet meadows and marshes, in wet woods and fens, usually on calcareous soils, throughout Europe and the British Isles. Its prostrate stems root at the nodes and turn up at the ends to bear linear or lance-shaped leaves and small, terminal clusters of glossy yellow flowers. Great Spearwort, *R. lingua*, is a larger plant with erect, hollow stems growing from creeping rhizomes. It is found in reed swamps, around the edges of fens and ponds, decreasing in numbers with improved drainage techniques. It is scattered through Europe and England, rare in Wales and Scotland.

Celery-leaved Crowfoot, *Ranunculus sceleratus*, is the most acrid of all the buttercups, causing blisters if handled and dangerous to livestock. It grows on the margins of muddy ditches, streams and ponds, or in wet meadows and marshes where the water is rich in nutrients, throughout Europe and in Great Britain and Ireland. It is only common in England, not in northern Scotland or western Wales. It is an annual plant, with hollow, hairless, branched stems up to 60cm (2ft) tall and

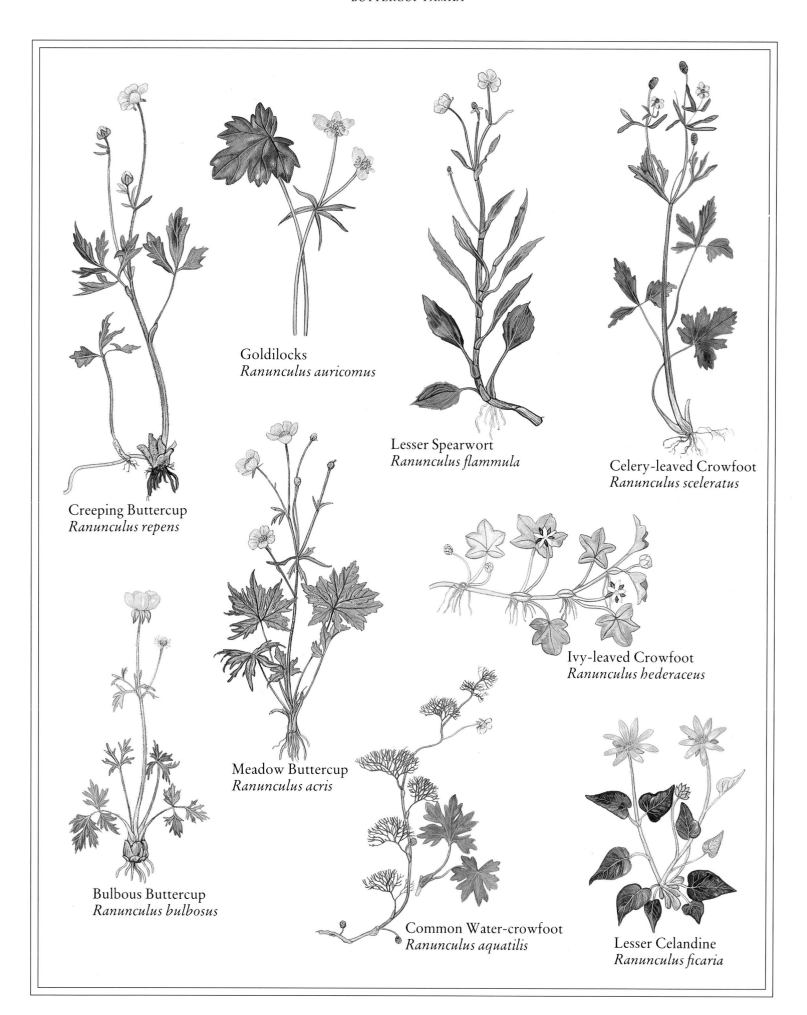

Goldilocks
Ranunculus auricomus

Lesser Spearwort
Ranunculus flammula

Celery-leaved Crowfoot
Ranunculus sceleratus

Creeping Buttercup
Ranunculus repens

Ivy-leaved Crowfoot
Ranunculus hederaceus

Meadow Buttercup
Ranunculus acris

Bulbous Buttercup
Ranunculus bulbosus

Common Water-crowfoot
Ranunculus aquatilis

Lesser Celandine
Ranunculus ficaria

deeply cut, palmate leaves, the upper ones with quite narrow segments. The plant bears many small, pale yellow flowers in summer, followed by cylindrical heads of achenes.

Many *Ranunculus* species are aquatic plants with white flowers. They have two kinds of leaves—floating leaves with normal blades and submerged leaves with finely dissected leaves—either or both on the same plant. This arrangement is related to the way they absorb oxygen and carbon dioxide, the submerged leaves having an enormous surface area in direct contact with the water, so the dissolved gases can diffuse in and out. The floating leaves are in contact with the air and have the air-holes of normal leaves on their upper surface.

Common Water-crowfoot, *Ranunculus aquatilis* (p. 37), is one of the most common of these species, growing in slow streams, ponds and ditches throughout Europe and lowland areas of the British Isles, but absent from northwestern Scotland. It has finely dissected, submerged leaves on very long, submerged stems, rounded, palmately lobed, floating leaves and small white flowers projecting above the surface of the water in early summer. Rounded heads of achenes follow the flowers and bend downwards, back into the water.

Ivy-leaved Crowfoot, *Ranunculus hederaceus* (p. 37), is an annual plant which may overwinter as a young plant or appear in spring. It grows in ponds and ditches, small streams or temporary pools, scattered throughout western Europe and the British Isles. It has only one kind of leaves and these are rounded, three- or five-lobed and they float on the water surface; the small white crowfoot flowers grow on long stalks in the leaf axils, their petals barely longer than the sepals.

Lesser Celandine or Pilewort, *Ranunculus ficaria* (p. 37), is a small, perennial plant which forms spreading mats of leaf rosettes. The leaves appear in late winter, the flowers in spring and the whole plant dies down by midsummer. It remains dormant for the rest of the year, surviving and spreading by means of its many root tubers. The basal leaves are glossy and hairless, long-stalked with heart-shaped blades. The flowering stems bear similar leaves and solitary, bright yellow flowers which fade to white as they age. This plant may be seen in spring in old deciduous woods and hedgerows, in damp pastures, beside streams, on damp roadsides and in disturbed places. It grows throughout Europe and the British Isles.

Water-lily family
Nymphaeaceae

A very small family of aquatic plants with about 6 genera and 70 species found throughout much of the world, with the notable exception of New Zealand. By far the largest genus is *Nymphaea*, from which most garden varieties of water-lilies come; they are famous for their beautiful floating flowers.

Family features These aquatic plants have floating, round or heart-shaped leaves with long stalks attaching them to the roots or rhizomes in the mud at the bottom of the water. Some species also have thin, translucent, submerged leaves. The flowers float on the water or project into the air on long stalks growing from the rhizome. Each flower is solitary, often showy, regular and hermaphrodite with 4–6 free sepals and numerous petals. In some species the petals become gradually more stamen-like near the flower centre. The flowers have numerous stamens and eight carpels. The fruits are capsules.

The **White Water-lily**, *Nymphaea alba*, is found in the still waters of ponds and lakes, and in slow-moving rivers and canals throughout many lowland areas of the British Isles and Europe, northwards to southern Scandinavia. It has a stout rhizome in the mud at the bottom of the water and long-stalked leaves with round blades floating on the surface. The flowers are floating, fragrant, white or pink-tinged, opening in the morning and closing again in late afternoon. As the flowers finish, their long stalks coil and pull them below the surface so that the fleshy capsules ripen under water. When they burst, the seeds rise to the surface and float away.

The **Yellow Water-lily** or Brandy-bottle, *Nuphar lutea*, also grows in ponds and slow-moving streams throughout lowland areas of Europe and the British Isles, but it is rare in Scotland. It has a branched rhizome, long-stalked leathery, heart-shaped floating leaves and thin, delicate submerged leaves, also heart-shaped or rounded. The flowers project above the water on stout stalks; they are bowl-shaped, with 5–6 thick, yellow sepals forming the edges of the bowl. In the flower centre are many similar petals and stamens surrounding the broad, disk-like stigma. The name of Brandy-bottle may come from the scent of alcohol given off by the flowers, or from the fruits which look like bottles. They ripen above water, eventually floating away as their stalks rot.

Sundew family
Droseraceae

This is a family of insectivorous plants, with rosettes of sticky, glandular leaves that function as insect traps. There are 4 genera and about 105 species found throughout the world in acid soils, in sandy and boggy places. Their insectivorous lifestyle enables them to live in these nitrogen-poor soils, since they obtain extra nitrogen from the insects they trap and absorb. The flowers are regular, usually with five separate sepals and petals, five stamens and a single ovary.

The **Round-leaved Sundew**, *Drosera rotundifolia*, is a typical member of the family. It grows in bogs and in wet, peaty places on moors and heaths, often in *Sphagnum* moss, throughout the temperate regions of the northern hemisphere,

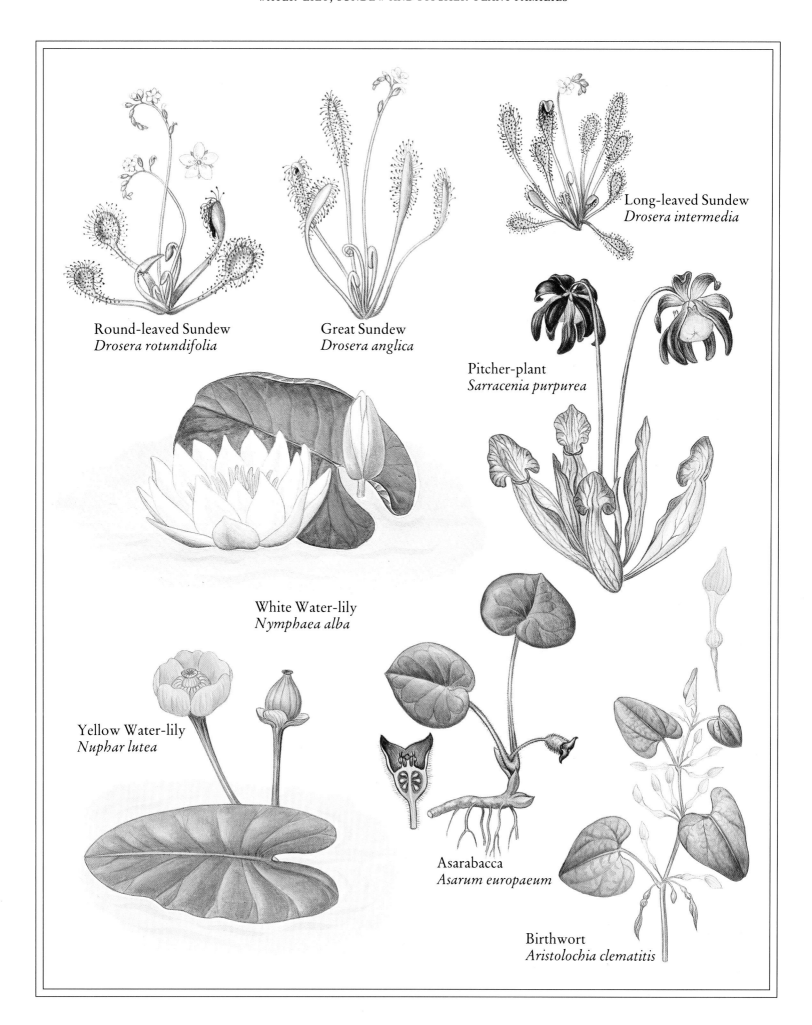

Round-leaved Sundew
Drosera rotundifolia

Great Sundew
Drosera anglica

Long-leaved Sundew
Drosera intermedia

Pitcher-plant
Sarracenia purpurea

White Water-lily
Nymphaea alba

Yellow Water-lily
Nuphar lutea

Asarabacca
Asarum europaeum

Birthwort
Aristolochia clematitis

including Europe and the British Isles. This is a small plant, which forms a flat rosette of long-stalked leaves with circular blades, conspicuous for the red-tipped glands that cover them and which secrete a sticky fluid. Insects—often small flies—get caught on the sticky leaves and die; they are then digested by enzymes in the fluid, and absorbed. In summer the plants produce erect, leafless flowering stems about 20cm (8in) tall, with one-sided clusters of small white or pink flowers.

Great Sundew, *Drosera anglica* (p. 39), is a circumboreal species, a plant which likes the wettest parts of bogs, growing among *Sphagnum* mosses. In the British Isles it is most common in northwest Scotland and other wetter areas, and is also found in northern Europe. It holds its leaves more or less erect and has long stalks and elongated blades.

Long-leaved Sundew, *Drosera intermedia* (p. 39), grows in damp, peaty places on heaths and moors, often many plants together and usually in drier places than the other sundews in northwestern Europe and mostly in western areas of the British Isles. It forms a rosette of more or less erect leaves, with short stems and ovate blades.

Pitcher-plant family
Sarraceniaceae

A small family of insectivorous plants, with 3 genera and about 17 species found in eastern North America, in California and in Guyana, South America. A few are grown in special greenhouses by collectors and some are very rare plants listed as endangered species. Like sundews, pitcher-plants grow in boggy, nitrogen-poor places and they obtain additional nitrogen from the insects that they digest and absorb.

Only one member of this family grows in Europe. It has been introduced from the US and become naturalized in bogs in central Ireland, where it was planted in 1906. This is the **Pitcher-plant**, *Sarracenia purpurea* (p. 39). Like other members of the family, it is a distinctive plant, with a rosette of tubular leaves forming pitchers in which it traps insects. The pitchers contain an acid digestive liquid at the bottom, are hooded and have a flaring lip covered with bristly, downward-pointing hairs. Insects are attracted to the pitchers by their colours and they crawl under the hood to try to reach the nectar secreted there. They are trapped by the downwardly directed hairs so that they cannot climb out again, and eventually slip down the smooth sides into the liquid below.

The conspicuous, solitary flowers are borne separately on long stalks in summer. They are regular and hermaphrodite, with five free sepals and five touching petals, both reddish-purple, but the petals are smaller than the sepals and pale green inside. The flowers have numerous stamens and a five-lobed, umbrella-like style.

Birthwort family
Aristolochiaceae

There are about 7 genera and 400 species of twining vines and herbs in this family, found in the tropics and temperate areas of the world.

Family features The flowers grow in clusters or singly in the leaf axils. They are usually bilaterally symmetrical and hermaphrodite. Each flower has a three-lobed, often tubular calyx that is frequently coloured like a corolla; petals are minute or absent. The flowers have 6 or 12 stamens and usually the ovary is inferior with 4–6 cells. The fruits are capsules. The leaves are alternate and simple without stipules.

Birthwort, *Aristolochia clematitis* (p. 39), is a foetid, hairless, perennial plant with a creeping rhizome from which grow many erect stems up to 80cm (30in) tall, with alternate, broadly heart-shaped leaves on long stalks. In the leaf axils grow characteristic flowers—they are dull yellow and tubular, with a curved tube, a flared, brownish opening and a swollen base. The flowers are followed by large, oval capsules. This plant has been used since ancient times to induce birth or abortion; however, it is poisonous and causes kidney damage. It is native to southern and eastern Europe but is naturalized in other parts of the continent in hedgerows and cultivated land. In Britain it is rare, but found mainly in the east.

Asarabacca, *Asarum europaeum* (p. 39), also has a thick, creeping rhizome but its stems grow only 5cm (2in) tall at most. There are two brown scales at the base of each stem and two glossy, dark green, kidney-shaped leaves growing on long stalks at the top. In the axils of the leaves droop the brown, bell-shaped flowers, appearing in summer and followed by small, rounded capsules. This little creeping plant is sometimes grown as ground cover in shady gardens. In the wild it grows in open woods throughout much of Europe; in Britain it is rare, found in a few English and Scottish woods. Like Birthwort, this plant has been used in herb medicine as a stimulant, but its use has been discontinued because of its harmful side effects. It is still powdered and used as an ingredient of snuff.

St John's-wort family
Hypericaceae

There are about 8 genera and 400 species of herbs, shrubs and trees in this family, found mainly in temperate regions and in mountainous areas in the tropics. Several shrubby species are used as ornamental plants in gardens.

Family features These plants have distinctive, showy, yellow or white flowers. Each is regular and hermaphrodite, with five sepals and petals and numerous stamens, often united

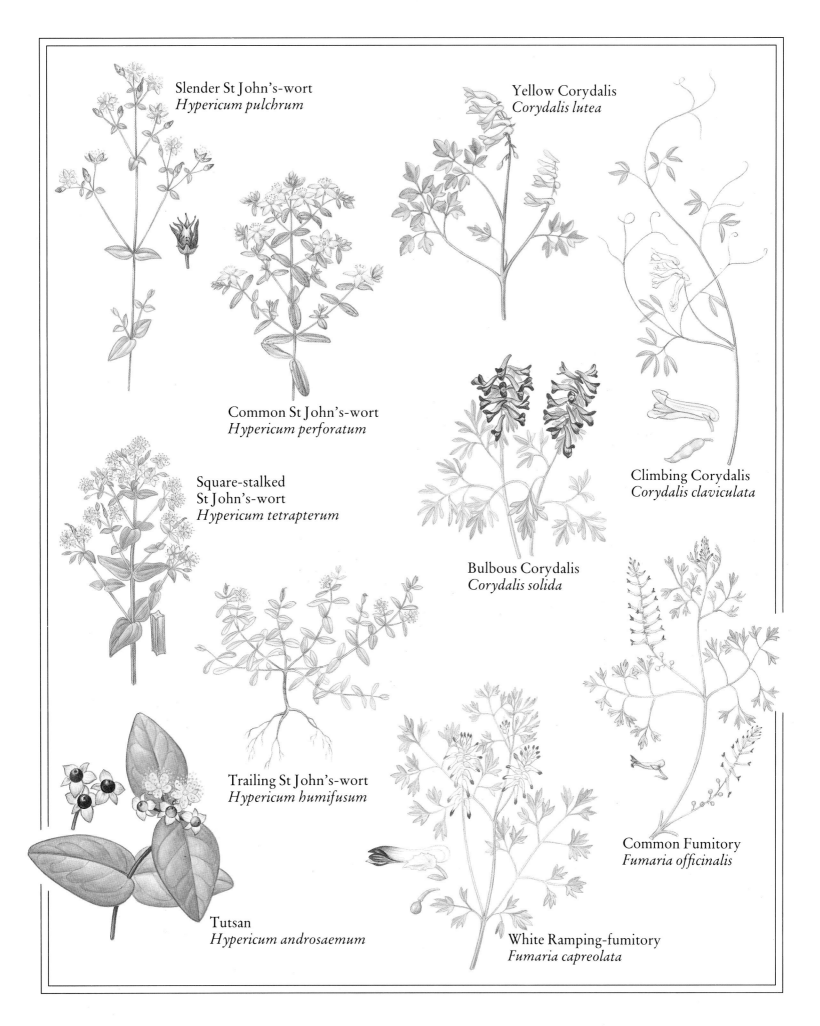

Slender St John's-wort
Hypericum pulchrum

Yellow Corydalis
Corydalis lutea

Common St John's-wort
Hypericum perforatum

Square-stalked
St John's-wort
Hypericum tetrapterum

Climbing Corydalis
Corydalis claviculata

Bulbous Corydalis
Corydalis solida

Trailing St John's-wort
Hypericum humifusum

Common Fumitory
Fumaria officinalis

Tutsan
Hypericum androsaemum

White Ramping-fumitory
Fumaria capreolata

into bundles, and appearing to fill the centre of the flower in *Hypericum*, by far the largest genus. The ovary is superior, with one, three or five carpels, usually forming a capsule in fruit. The leaves are opposite or in whorls, simple and often dotted with glands; they lack stipules.

Many St John's-worts, *Hypericum* species, grow in Europe. **Common St John's-wort**, *H. perforatum* (p. 41), is one of the most common herbaceous species, growing in open woods and hedgebanks, in rough grassland and on roadsides, especially on calcareous soils. It is found throughout Europe and much of the British Isles, but is absent from northern Scotland and parts of Ireland. This perennial plant has creeping rhizomes and many branched, leafy stems, each about 60cm (2ft) tall. The leaves are opposite, linear and stalkless, covered by translucent dots (glands), visible when they are held up to the light. The flowers are borne in a large inflorescence formed of many clusters growing from the upper leaf axils. They are typical of the genus, with five yellow petals and many stamens. In this species the petals have black dots around their margins.

Square-stalked St John's-wort, *Hypericum tetrapterum* (p. 41), is a similar plant about 1m (3ft) tall and with square instead of round stems. It grows in damp, grassy places, beside ponds and in marshes throughout much of Europe and the British Isles, but is absent from the north of Scotland.

Slender St John's-wort, *Hypericum pulchrum* (p. 41), is another perennial but has rather weakly erect, often reddish stems and red-tinged yellow flowers. It grows in dry heaths and woods, on acid soils throughout much of northwestern Europe and the British Isles but is only common locally.

Trailing St John's-wort, *Hypericum humifusum* (p. 41), has very slender, much-branched, trailing stems, many leaves and pale yellow flowers in summer. It grows in short grassland on heaths and moors, and in dry woods and scrub on acid soils throughout the British Isles and much of Europe.

Tutsan, *Hypericum androsaemum* (p. 41), is a shrubby species, growing about 1m (3ft) tall with spreading stems and semi-evergreen, stalkless, ovate leaves. It has a slight aromatic scent and many flowers. The sepals on the flowers are unequal in size, the largest as big as the petals; they persist and become deflexed in fruit, forming a base for the berries. These are red at first, ripening black. Tutsan grows in damp woods and hedgerows throughout western Europe and much of the British Isles, but is only common locally, becoming rarer in the north and east. It is often grown in gardens.

Fumitory family
Fumariaceae

This family has about 16 genera and 450 species, all herbs, in the northern temperate regions and north Africa. Several are outstanding garden plants, like Bleeding Heart and Dutchman's Breeches (both *Dicentra* species). These plants are allied to poppies—so closely that some botanists consider that they should be included in the Poppy family. They differ in having watery rather than coloured sap, in having characteristically shaped flowers and in the arrangement of their stamens.

Family features The flowers are bilaterally symmetrical and hermaphrodite, with two small sepals that soon fall and four petals. There are two inner petals, often joined together over the stigma, and two outer, spurred or pouched petals, separate at the base but joined at their tips. Each flower has six stamens, in two groups of three with joined filaments, opposite the outer petals. The ovary has a single cell which swells in fruit to form a capsule or nutlet. These are smooth, brittle plants with watery juice and alternate divided leaves.

Common Fumitory, *Fumaria officinalis* (p. 41), gets its name from the Latin for smoke, from the way its whitish, blue-green leaves spread over the ground and from the acrid gas given off by the roots when they are pulled up. This is a small, straggling plant with much-divided leaves and curious flowers growing in loose spikes. They are tubular, pink with red-tipped spurs and appear to be balanced on their stalks. It grows in light soils in cultivated ground throughout Europe and the British Isles, more commonly in the east than in the west.

White Ramping-fumitory, *Fumaria capreolata* (p. 41), is a robust perennial plant with much-branched stems that scramble through hedgerows, or trail over cultivated or waste land in many parts of Europe and the British Isles. It is a local plant, more often found in western Britain than in the east. Its branched stems grow up to 1m (3ft) tall, have typical fumitory-type leaves and dense racemes of flowers in the leaf axils. These are creamy white with red-black tips. Common Ramping-fumitory, *F. muralis*, is more common in both the British Isles and Europe; it is a slender, branched, erect or climbing plant with flowers similar to those of Common Fumitory.

In a garden **Yellow Corydalis**, *Corydalis lutea* (p. 41), is one of those plants designed to promote despair. Beautiful growing in an old wall, its seedlings try to take over the whole garden so that they have to be treated like weeds; then, once they are all pulled out, the parent plant dies! In the wild this plant is native to the foothills of the Alps, but it has become naturalized in old walls over much of Europe and the British Isles. It forms a clump of branched, rather brittle stems only 30cm (1ft) tall at most, with ferny leaves and an inexhaustible supply of yellow flowers. These have the form found in all **Corydalis** species, in which only the upper petal is spurred.

Bulbous Corydalis, *Corydalis solida* (p. 41), is a spring flower found in woods and hedgerows, on roadside verges and vineyards over much of Europe, but not in the British Isles. This little plant forms several erect stems, only 10–20cm (4–8in) tall, each with dissected leaves and a dense terminal cluster of purple flowers. It flowers in spring and dies down by

Yellow Horned-poppy
Glaucium flavum

Field Poppy
Papaver rhoeas

Long-headed Poppy
Papaver dubium

Welsh Poppy
Meconopsis cambrica

Celandine
Chelidonium majus

Prickly Long-headed Poppy
Papaver argemone

Opium Poppy
Papaver somniferum

early summer, remaining dormant for much of the year as a cluster of root tubers beneath the ground.

Climbing Corydalis, *Corydalis claviculata* (p. 41), is a different kind of plant—an annual with branched, slender climbing stems and pinnate leaves with elliptical segments ending in branched tendrils. In summer it bears racemes of creamy white flowers on long stalks opposite the leaves. It grows in woods and shady, rocky places on acid soils, locally in western Europe and the British Isles, except northern Scotland.

Poppy family
Papaveraceae

There are about 26 genera and 200 species in this family, mostly herbs with a very few shrubs and trees, found mainly in the subtropical and temperate regions of the northern hemisphere. Some members of the family are spectacular garden plants with showy flowers, including species and cultivars of *Papaver*, the true poppies, *Eschscholtzia californica*, the California Poppy, and *Sanguinaria canadensis*, the Bloodroot.

Family features The flowers are usually solitary, regular and hermaphrodite. Each has 2–3 sepals, which soon fall, and 4–6 or 8–12 often crumpled, separate petals. There are many stamens and a superior ovary of two or more united carpels. The fruits are capsules, opening by pores or valves and containing many tiny seeds. The leaves are alternate and often much divided; they lack stipules.

One of the most familiar of the *Papaver* species is the **Field Poppy** or Common Poppy, *Papaver rhoeas* (p. 43), the poppy that grew on Flanders fields after the First World War and which has become the symbol of Remembrance Day. At one time it was a common cornfield weed, but nowadays is more likely to be found on roadsides and in waste places, usually on light, calcareous soils. It grows throughout Europe and in much of the British Isles, mostly near the coast in Wales and in southern rather than northern Ireland, rarely in northwest Scotland. It is a stiffly hairy, annual plant with an erect stem up to 60cm (2ft) tall and divided leaves. At the tops of the stems are the red, four-petalled, bowl-shaped flowers, opening from nodding buds. At the centre of each flower is a ring of black anthers encircling a round stigma. The seed capsules are one of the wonders of the plant world, each resembling a pepperpot, with a ring of holes around the rim beneath the persistent lid of the stigma. The capsule contains many tiny seeds and as the wind blows the 'pot' to and fro, the seeds shoot out of the holes and are scattered over the surrounding area. The mechanism is simple, elegant and highly effective.

The **Long-headed Poppy**, *Papaver dubium* (p. 43), is a similar plant but its flowers are paler red and lack the black blotches. Whereas the capsules of the Field Poppy are more or less globular, those of the Long-headed Poppy are elongated, more than twice as long as wide. This plant grows in arable land and waste places, often with the Field Poppy, throughout most of Europe and the British Isles, but is more common in the north and west than the other species.

Prickly Long-headed Poppy, *Papaver argemone* (p. 43), gets its name from the bristles which cover stems and sepals, which tip its leaf segments and which cover its seed capsules. Like other poppies, it grows in arable land, in waste places and on roadsides, this species often on light, sandy soils in much of Europe, and in England, Wales and southern Scotland.

Probably the most famous member of the whole family is the **Opium Poppy**, *Papaver somniferum* (p. 43), whose seed heads are the source of the sap which is crude opium. From this can be derived the medicinally essential painkillers codeine and morphine, or the deadly addictive heroin. Poppy seeds are rich in oil, which is used in soaps, paints, salad oils and cattle cake. Opium Poppies are probably native to the Mediterranean and have been cultivated in many parts of Europe for centuries for their medicinal properties. Nowadays they still grow as casual weeds on cultivated land and in waste places in Britain and Europe. This is a tall, annual, more or less hairless plant, growing up to 1.5m (5ft) tall, with pinnately lobed or toothed leaves and large, pale purple flowers, often with black blotches.

Welsh Poppy, *Meconopsis cambrica* (p. 43), is a tufted perennial with a clump of pinnately lobed basal leaves. In early summer it produces erect, leafy flowering stems 30–60cm (1–2ft) tall, bearing solitary yellow flowers on long stalks in the axils of upper leaves. This attractive little plant grows in damp, shady places, beside walls and among rocks in Wales and southwest England, in the Massif Central in France and in northern Spain. It is also widely introduced and naturalized elsewhere in Europe and Britain, an escape from gardens.

Yellow Horned-poppy, *Glaucium flavum* (p. 43), is a maritime species, a member of a select community of plants found on shingle banks. It also grows on sand-dunes, cliffs and on coastal waste land. It can be found on the west and south coasts of Britain, also on the west coast of Europe. This is a grey-blue, somewhat fleshy perennial plant, with an erect, branched stem 30–90cm (1–3ft) tall and pinnately lobed leaves. In summer it produces a succession of yellow flowers followed by elongated, sickle-shaped capsules.

Greater Celandine, *Chelidonium majus* (p. 43), is a former herbal plant with a caustic orange sap which was used to treat warts. It may be found in hedgerows or beneath walls, usually near dwellings, throughout most of Europe and in lowland areas of Great Britain and Ireland, less commonly in Scotland. It is a perennial, with almost hairless, slightly blue-green, divided leaves on erect, brittle stems and grows up to 1m (3ft) tall. The small, pale yellow flowers grow in terminal clusters; they are followed by slender capsules which contain characteristic seeds—black with a fleshy white appendage.

Roadside flowers in July with arable land in the background, the wheat just beginning to ripen. In the foreground (from left to right) are Field Poppies, Scentless Mayweed, Fumitory, Charlock and Chicory.

Mustard family
Cruciferae

Also known as **Brassicaceae**. There are about 375 genera and 3200 species of herbs in this family, found throughout the world, but mainly in the north temperate regions. This is an important family with many crop plants, including cabbage and broccoli, kale, turnip and swede, watercress and mustard. Rape is now grown on a wide scale for the oil extracted from its seeds. Other members of the family, like alyssum, aubrieta and wallflowers, are ornamental plants for the garden, which transform the flower beds in spring. Some, like Shepherd's Purse, are familiar weeds of gardens, waste and arable land.

Family features The regular, hermaphrodite flowers are distinctive, with four separate petals in the shape of a cross alternating with four separate sepals. Each flower has six stamens and a superior ovary. The flowers grow in racemes. Fruits are specialized capsules called siliquas (known familiarly as pods), with two valves opening from below, exposing a central septum to which seeds are attached. The leaves are alternate and lack stipules.

The genus *Brassica* is one that has produced many of the most important crop members of the family. *Brassica oleracea* has produced cabbages, cauliflowers, broccoli, Brussels sprouts and kale; *B. rapa* is the turnip; *B. napus* has produced rape and swede; *B. nigra* has produced black mustard. At one time White Mustard and the wild Charlock were also included in this genus, as *B. hirta* and *B. kaber* respectively, but modern botanists usually place them in a separate genus, *Sinapis*.

Wild Cabbage, *Brassica oleracea*, is a maritime plant in its truly wild state, growing on cliffs on the coasts of France, Spain and Italy, southern England and Wales. Elsewhere plants are likely to be naturalized forms of cultivated cabbages. This is a biennial or perennial plant, with a strong tap root and a thick sprawling stem which becomes woody and scarred with the leaf bases of old leaves. The leaves are thick, hairless and pinnately lobed or with wavy margins, grey and cabbage-like in appearance. The flowers are borne in an erect, lengthening inflorescence, opening over a long period in summer and followed by cylindrical, beaked fruits.

Black Mustard, *Brassica nigra*, has long been cultivated for its seeds. These are used to make the kitchen condiment and also in herb medicine to make mustard plasters and as an emetic. Mustard flour, made from the ground seeds, is an excellent deodorizer and antiseptic. The plant grows wild in waste places and on roadsides, beside streams and ditches, and on coastal cliffs throughout Europe. In Britain it is most common beside streams in England and Wales, and it also grows in southern Scotland and southern Ireland. This is an annual plant, with a much-branched stem growing up to 1m (3ft) tall. It has large, bristly, lobed lower leaves and smaller, toothed upper leaves, all with stalks. The flowers are bright yellow and are followed by upright, quadrangular pods pressed closely against the stems. Each pod has strongly keeled valves, a short beak and constrictions between the dark red-brown seeds.

Field Mustard, *Brassica rapa*, is a wild plant belonging to the same species as the turnip, but wild plants usually lack the swollen roots of the cultivated varieties. They grow in waste places and on cultivated land, beside streams and ditches throughout Europe and the British Isles. This is an annual plant with an erect stem, lobed lower leaves and toothed upper ones. The flowers are bright yellow and the inflorescence is unusual in this family since it does not lengthen. The result is that open flowers on their long stalks overtop the still-closed buds in the centre of the inflorescence. The pods are held more or less erect and have long slender beaks.

Charlock or Wild Mustard, *Sinapis arvensis*, was at one time a serious weed of vegetable and grain crops, for it produced an abundance of seed which germinated so profusely that the weeds smothered large areas of the true crop. Sometimes wheat was not worth harvesting, for so much of the field had been taken over. In addition to competing with the crops for space, light and water, Charlock also acts as a host for insect and fungal pests which attack other cruciferous crop plants. With the advent of modern weedkillers, this species has become less of a menace; however, it may still be found in arable land, around the edges of fields and in waste places, especially in areas where the soil is heavy or calcareous. It grows throughout Europe, Great Britain and Ireland.

Charlock is an annual plant, with a stiffly hairy, erect stem and roughly hairy leaves. The lower leaves are coarsely toothed but upper ones become progressively simpler. The bright yellow flowers produce long, beaked pods held upright and away from the stem, each with 6–12 dark red-brown seeds. The seeds can be substituted for those of Black Mustard.

White Mustard, *Sinapis alba*, is grown for fodder, as a green manure and for its seeds which are made into mustard. The active ingredient of mustard is mustard oil, a substance that is highly irritant and poisonous in its pure form or in large quantities; condiment mustard is too strongly flavoured to be palatable in anything but small amounts. At one time mustard poultices were used as a remedy for rheumatism and chilblains, since they draw blood into an affected area, warming it and improving circulation. White Mustard grows as a weed of arable and waste land throughout Great Britain, Ireland and Europe, except in the extreme north. It is an annual plant, with an erect stem up to 80cm (30in) tall, stiffly hairy, pinnately lobed leaves and a lengthening inflorescence of bright yellow flowers followed by stiffly hairy, beaked capsules. These contain 1–4 yellowish or pale brown seeds.

Wild Radish or White Charlock, *Raphanus raphanistrum*, is a pernicious weed much disliked by vegetable farmers. It grows throughout Europe, in Great Britain and Ireland,

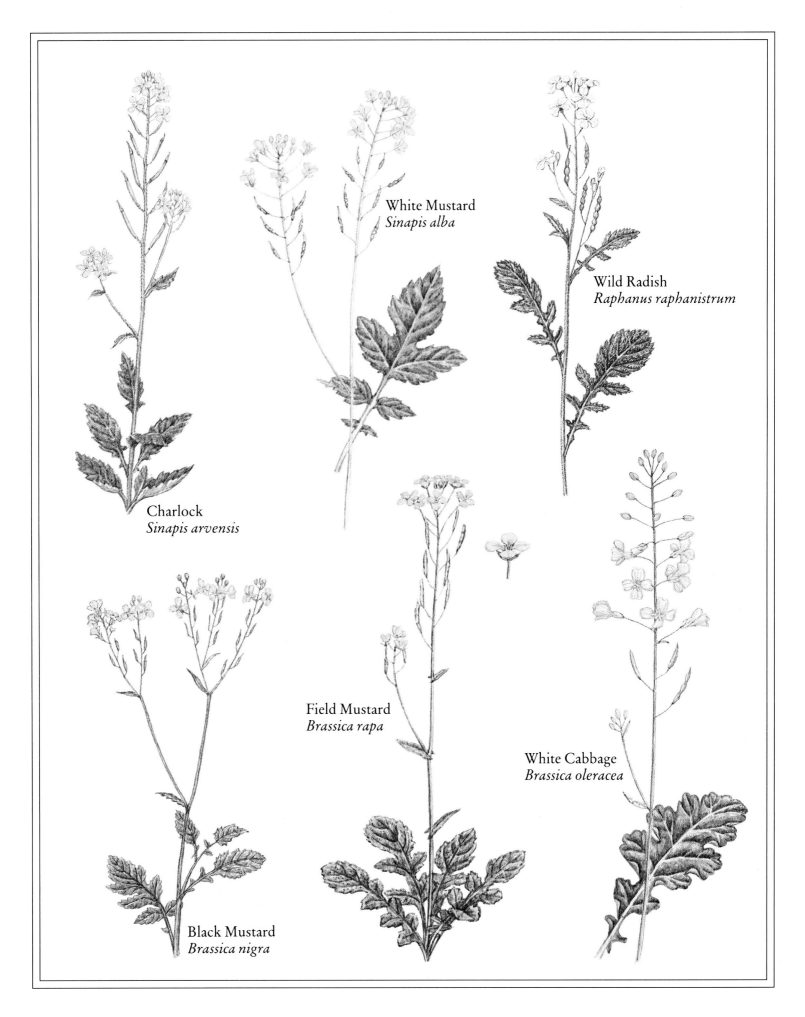

White Mustard
Sinapis alba

Wild Radish
Raphanus raphanistrum

Charlock
Sinapis arvensis

Field Mustard
Brassica rapa

White Cabbage
Brassica oleracea

Black Mustard
Brassica nigra

especially on calcareous soils. This is an annual plant, with rough, hairy stems, lobed leaves and yellowish flowers, becoming whiter with age. The petals have heavy mauve veins. Its fruits are distinctive—long cylindrical pods on ascending stalks, becoming ribbed and constricted between each seed as they dry out; eventually the pods break up and each seed is dispersed inside its section of pod. Wild Radish is related to garden radishes, the relationship becoming evident if garden plants go to seed, when they produce the same kind of pods.

Several members of this family are associated with the sea. **Seakale**, *Crambe maritima*, grows on shingle banks and sandy beaches, often on the drift line, or on cliffs and among rocks. It is not common, being restricted to suitable habitats, but is found all along the Baltic and Atlantic coasts of Europe, including those of Britain and Ireland. In Britain it is most common in the south. This plant is edible, the best parts being the young shoots which can be blanched and eaten like asparagus. It is a perennial, with a fleshy crown from which grow large clumps of leaves able to withstand burial in the shifting stones of the shingle. The leaves are blue-green, fleshy and pinnately lobed with a wavy outline. In summer the plant sends up erect stems ending in broad clusters of white flowers, followed by rounded fruits shaped like balloons.

Sea Rocket, *Cakile maritima*, is another maritime species, found on drift lines on shingle banks and sandy beaches around the coasts of Europe and the British Isles. It is an annual, with prostrate or sprawling, branched stems radiating outwards from a central tap root. The stems are leafy, with succulent, greyish leaves, varying in shape from pinnately lobed to entire. Purple flowers appear around midsummer in dense, terminal inflorescences; they are followed by stubby fruits.

Hare's-ear Cabbage, *Conringia orientalis*, grows as a casual weed of arable land and waste places in much of Europe, introduced from the southeast. It grows mostly near the coast in Britain. This annual plant has an erect stem up to 50cm (20in) tall, with characteristic leaves—elliptical with bases clasping the stem—and yellow-white flowers. The pods are elongated, curved and four-angled.

Wall Rocket, *Diplotaxis muralis*, is also known as Stinkweed, since it smells of rotten eggs if bruised. Coming originally from southeastern Europe, it now grows in limestone and chalk, on rocks and cliffs, old quarries and old walls throughout much of Europe, especially in southern England and Ireland in the British Isles. It is an annual or biennial, with a rosette of elliptical, often lobed leaves and one or more erect flowering stems in summer. The flowers are sulphur yellow, borne in an elongating inflorescence and followed by more or less erect fruits, each containing two rows of seeds. This feature serves to distinguish *Diplotaxis* species from many other cruciferous plants.

Perennial Wall Rocket, *Diplotaxis tenuifolia*, is a perennial plant; it lacks a rosette of leaves but has leafy stalks with deeply lobed leaves and yellow flowers in summer. It grows in old walls and waste places across much of Europe, except the north, and has been introduced in southern England.

The **Pepperworts** are members of the genus *Lepidium*, a variable group of annual to perennial plants, all with dense racemes of white flowers. There are 21 species in Europe. **Field Pepperwort**, *L. campestre*, is an annual, grey-green plant, with a branched, erect stem up to 60cm (2ft) tall. Its basal leaves are lyre-shaped but wither before flowering; the stem leaves are triangular with long basal lobes and they clasp the stem. The flowers are white and tiny, followed by rounded, notched fruits covered with white scales when mature. This plant grows in dry, grassy places, on roadsides and banks, in arable land and on walls throughout Europe and Great Britain; it is rare in Scotland and Ireland. The young shoots are edible, chopped up in salads like watercress, or added, with capers and gherkins, to mayonnaise for serving with fish.

Smith's Cress, *Lepidium heterophyllum*, is a greyish-hairy, perennial species, a smaller plant growing 45cm (18in) tall at most. It has a basal rosette of long-stalked, elliptical leaves that wither before flowering, and erect flowering stems with narrow, triangular leaves that have long basal lobes clasping the stem. The small, white flowers are followed by broadly winged, rounded, notched fruits that lack scales. This plant grows in dry, open places, in arable and waste land, and beside roads and railways throughout western Europe, Great Britain and in all but the northwest area of Ireland.

Swine-cress or Wart-cress, *Coronopus squamatus*, is a small, annual or biennial plant, with branched, prostrate stems and pinnately lobed leaves. The small white flowers grow in dense clusters in the leaf axils in summer and are followed by large, kidney-shaped, warty fruits, usually the first thing to catch the eye. This little plant grows in waste places, often on bare ground, throughout southern England, becoming rarer in the north, also in Ireland and throughout Europe. Lesser Swine-cress, *C. didymus*, is an introduced species from South America, a weed of cultivated land; it emits a sulphurous smell, has feathery leaves and pitted, rather than warty, fruits.

Hoary Cress, *Cardaria draba*, is another invader, this one from southeastern Europe, and a much more serious weed. It is a perennial plant which forms a spreading colony, smothering any other plants in its path. Its roots may penetrate to a depth of 3m (10ft) once it is well established, so that it becomes very difficult to eradicate. It is found in many parts of Europe, including much of Great Britain (most commonly in the south), and is scattered through Ireland. It grows in cultivated land, on roadsides, railway embankments and other disturbed places. Each shoot grows to about 90cm (3ft) tall, has hairy, deeply toothed leaves—those on the stem with clasping bases—and dense, umbel-like clusters of white flowers borne on long stalks in the upper leaf axils in early summer. The fruits are kidney-shaped and split into single-seeded sections.

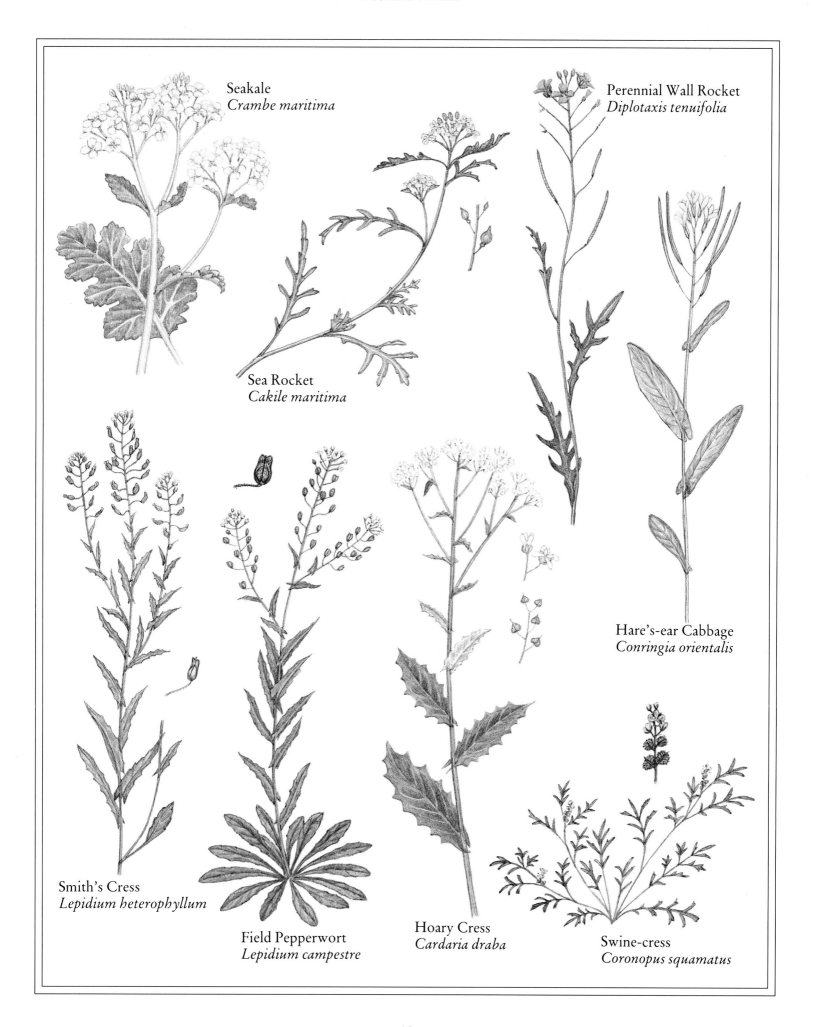

Seakale
Crambe maritima

Perennial Wall Rocket
Diplotaxis tenuifolia

Sea Rocket
Cakile maritima

Hare's-ear Cabbage
Conringia orientalis

Smith's Cress
Lepidium heterophyllum

Field Pepperwort
Lepidium campestre

Hoary Cress
Cardaria draba

Swine-cress
Coronopus squamatus

Field Pennycress, *Thlaspi arvense*, is a small, annual plant with a foetid scent. It has an erect stem 60cm (2ft) tall, with clasping, lance-shaped leaves and a cluster of white flowers which gradually give way to broadly winged, flattened fruits, each one notched at the top. The name Pennycress comes from these fruits, which resemble old pennies. The plant grows in waste places and cultivated land throughout Europe and the British Isles; it can be a serious weed.

Rock Hutchinsia, *Hornungia petraea*, is a rare species in Britain, found only in rocky places in a few counties in England and Wales, and on sand-dunes in Wales. It also grows throughout much of Europe. It is a small annual, with branched, erect stems only 15cm (6in) tall at most. They have a few pinnately lobed leaves near the base and elongating inflorescences of tiny, greenish-white flowers at the tips. The fruits are flattened, ovate pods on spreading stalks.

Shepherd's Cress, *Teesdalia nudicaulis*, grows in sandy and gravelly places throughout much of Great Britain, although it is rare in Scotland and Ireland; it is also found throughout much of Europe. This is another small annual, with a rosette of pinnately divided leaves and elongating racemes of white flowers followed by ovate, narrowly winged fruits.

Shepherd's Purse, *Capsella bursa-pastoris*, is one of the most familiar plants in the family, a garden weed found throughout the world. It is a small annual or biennial plant, with a basal rosette of simple, more or less lobed leaves and an erect flowering stem up to 40cm (15in) tall. The flowers are white and very small, borne in an elongating inflorescence, and are followed by heart-shaped capsules shaped like little purses.

Common Scurvy-grass, *Cochlearia officinalis*, is one of several Scurvy-grasses that grow on coasts all around Europe and the British Isles. This one grows mostly in salt marshes but also on grassy banks, cliffs and shingle. At one time plants were collected for the Vitamin C found in their leaves and eaten or made into a tonic to prevent scurvy. They were often taken by sailors bound on long sea voyages. Both plant and tonic taste very bitter and were replaced by orange juice when oranges became more freely available. Common Scurvy-grass is a biennial or perennial plant, growing up to 60cm (2ft) tall, with a rosette of fleshy, long-stalked, heart-shaped leaves and sprawling, leafy flowering stems with stalkless leaves, often with clasping bases. The many white flowers are borne in early summer, in elongating inflorescences on branched stems. They are followed by globular fruits.

Woad, *Isatis tinctoria*, was at one time cultivated in many areas of Britain and Europe for the blue dye which can be extracted from it. However, it has now largely been superseded by indigo and has become very rare in Britain, even though it is still found in waste places and fields in other parts of Europe. It usually grows as a blue-grey biennial, with several rosettes of softly hairy, lance-shaped basal leaves and erect, leafy flowering stems growing up to 120cm (4ft) tall. The stem leaves are arrow-shaped with clasping bases, becoming small and bract-like in the inflorescence. The stems branch near the top to form many dense racemes of yellow flowers, followed by purple-brown, drooping, flattened fruits.

Yellow Ball Mustard, *Neslia paniculata*, is found throughout most of Europe in waste and arable land, but is a very rare casual in Britain. It has an erect stem up to 60cm (2ft) tall, arrow-shaped leaves which clasp the stem and an elongating raceme of small yellow flowers. These are followed by globular, ball-like, wrinkled fruits.

Honesty, *Lunaria annua*, is a biennial plant grown in gardens throughout many parts of Europe and the British Isles. Its purple flowers are a familiar sight in late spring and its paper-like fruits are often used in dried flower arrangements. It rarely grows wild in Europe, unlike the related **Perennial Honesty**, *L. rediviva*, which can be found in woods throughout much of Europe, although it is absent from the British Isles. This plant spreads into colonies by underground stems and has erect, leafy stems up to 150cm (5ft) tall. It has long-stalked, finely toothed, pointed-oval leaves and a terminal cluster of very fragrant, purple flowers. The fruits which follow are not as attractive as those of Honesty, forming narrow ellipses rather than 'pennies'.

Some of the **Alisons**, *Alyssum* species, are popular garden plants, including the White Alyssum used with blue lobelias in summer bedding, and the Golden Alyssum grown in rock gardens. **Mountain Alison**, *A. montanum* (p. 53), is also grown in rock gardens, but in addition is a native European plant found in lowland and mountain areas, in sandy and stony places throughout many parts of Europe, but not in the north or the British Isles. It is a small perennial only 20cm (8in) tall, with rosettes of spoon-shaped leaves growing from sprawling stems. The stems turn upwards to bear bright yellow flowers in elongating racemes in summer, followed by round fruits.

The genus *Draba* has about 42 species in Europe, many known as **Whitlow Grasses**. They are mostly small, low-growing plants with tufts of simple, often lance-shaped leaves and little, erect flowering stems. Some are tiny cushion plants from the high mountains like the Alps and the Caucasus, and are often grown in rock gardens.

Common Whitlow Grass, *Erophila verna* (p. 53), is closely related to the *Draba* species and at one time was placed in the same genus. It is an annual plant with a small clump of hairy, spoon-shaped leaves and a flowering stem only 20cm (8in) tall at most. In adverse conditions this plant can be really tiny, with leaves less than 1cm ($\frac{1}{2}$in) long and an inflorescence only 5cm (2in) tall. Its minute flowers are white with deeply notched petals and they are followed by little elliptical pods. Common Whitlow Grass grows on walls and among rocks, in grassy places and dry banks, on arable land and roadsides, usually on calcareous or neutral soils, throughout the British Isles and Europe, north to central Norway.

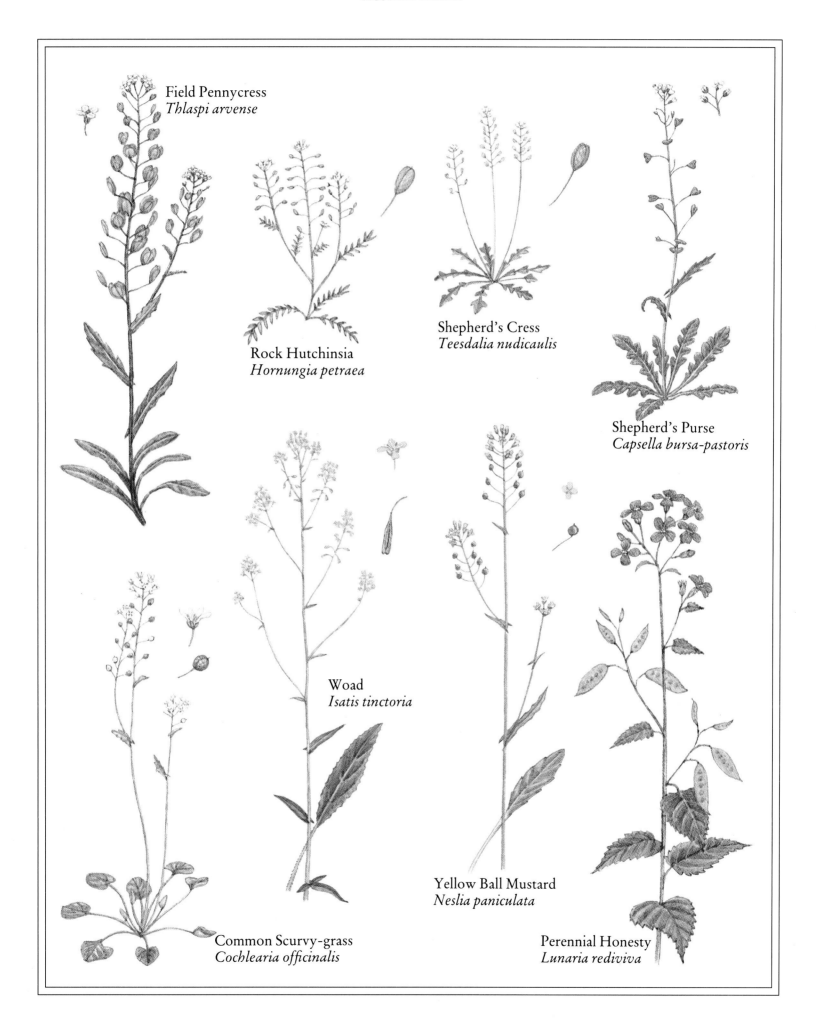

Field Pennycress
Thlaspi arvense

Rock Hutchinsia
Hornungia petraea

Shepherd's Cress
Teesdalia nudicaulis

Shepherd's Purse
Capsella bursa-pastoris

Woad
Isatis tinctoria

Yellow Ball Mustard
Neslia paniculata

Common Scurvy-grass
Cochlearia officinalis

Perennial Honesty
Lunaria rediviva

Horse Radish, *Armoracia rusticana*, probably came originally from southeastern Europe but has been cultivated for centuries; its roots are used to make horseradish sauce. It is now found in many parts of Europe, including England and Wales, rarely in Scotland and Ireland. It grows wild in fields and waste places, on roadsides and beside streams, especially near dwellings, and in lowland areas. In gardens it soon forms a wide colony with its creeping stems, each leaf rosette forming at the top of a long, fleshy tap root. The leaves are large and oblong, toothed and long-stalked. In early summer plants may produce erect flowering stems up to 120cm (4ft) tall, with spreading inflorescences and many white flowers, followed by globular fruits. However, northern plants often do not flower, and if they do, the seeds may not ripen.

Wintercress or Yellow Rocket, *Barbarea vulgaris*, is another edible crucifer. Its rosettes of leaves, appearing in late winter, are an excellent addition to salads, rich in Vitamin C and with a taste like watercress. The leaves may also be eaten as a green vegetable like spinach, and the early flower buds are like broccoli. The rosettes grow from perennial tap roots and have leaves with rounded lobes. From each rosette grow several erect, branched leafy stems, 30–90cm (1–3ft) tall, with elongating, terminal inflorescences of bright yellow flowers which open continuously through much of the summer. They are followed by long, straight fruits held erect. This plant grows on damp roadsides and beside ditches, in hedgerows and on stream banks throughout Great Britain and Ireland, and in Europe north to southern Finland. Several similar species grow more locally in Europe; in Britain two of them grow in damp places and a third grows as a weed of cultivated land.

The **Bittercresses**, belonging to the genus *Cardamine*, consist of a group of about 120 species found throughout the world, with over 35 in Europe. Some of them are beautiful and delicate wild flowers in a family not particularly renowned for the beauty of its members. **Cuckoo-flower** or Lady's Smock, *Cardamine pratensis*, may be seen adorning wet meadows and marshes, on the margins of ponds and streams, in open areas in woods and other damp, grassy places throughout the British Isles and Europe. It forms rosettes of pinnate leaves with ovate leaflets, and in late spring (when the cuckoo starts to call) produces delicate, lilac-pink flowers on an erect stem about 60cm (2ft) tall. The petals are notched and the fruits which follow are elongated and flattened.

Hairy Bittercress, *Cardamine hirsuta*, is an annual plant, also with rosettes of pinnate leaves, but the leaf segments in this plant are lobed or angled and sparsely hairy. It forms erect stems up to 30cm (1ft) tall, with similar leaves (but these have simpler and narrower leaflets) and terminal, elongating racemes of small, white flowers followed by long, thin fruits which overtop the unopened flower buds. This little plant grows as a weed on cultivated and bare ground—where it may be only 5cm (2in) tall—on walls and rocks throughout Europe

and the British Isles. It is familiar to gardeners as the plant that must be pulled out before it goes to seed, since the fruits open explosively and catapult seeds everywhere at the slightest touch. Just one missed plant in a flower border ensures hours of work for the following spring! These explosive seed pods are characteristic of all *Cardamine* species.

Coral-root, *Cardamine bulbifera*, is a rather different plant, sometimes placed in the genus *Dentaria*. It is a perennial with creeping rhizomes and erect, leafy flowering stems 30–70cm (1–2ft) tall in spring. The lowest stem leaves are pinnate with narrow, toothed leaflets, while the upper ones are simple, and often have brownish bulbils in their axils. In addition there may be a single pinnate basal leaf growing from the rhizome at the base of the flowering stem. The flowers are lilac with darker veins, borne in elongating racemes and followed by straight, spreading fruits. Coralroot grows in shady woods throughout much of Europe but is rare in Britain, confined to woods growing on chalk or limestone in England, in the Chilterns, the Peak District and similar areas.

Tall Rock-cress, *Cardaminopsis arenosa*, varies in its life plan from annual to biennial or perennial, and may have white, lilac or purple flowers. It is a robust, roughly hairy plant with a rosette of pinnately lobed leaves and an erect flowering stem 60–120cm (2–4ft) tall, with similar or toothed stem leaves and a branched inflorescence of many flowers. These are followed by long, straight fruits bulging with seeds. It grows in sandy places, on walls or among rocks throughout much of Europe, but is absent from the British Isles. Northern Rock-cress, *C. petraea*, is a perennial plant with white or purplish flowers. It is an arctic-alpine species found on mountains in Europe and in mountain areas of Wales, Scotland and Ireland.

The **Rock-cresses**, belonging to the genus *Arabis*, are a large group of some 120 species found throughout the temperate regions of the northern hemisphere, with about 35 in Europe. Some are well-known rock garden plants, like White Arabis, *A. albida*, an attractive plant with rosettes of grey-green leaves and white flowers, which is usually grown with aubrietas. Both flower in spring, carpeting the ground in red, purple and white, most often on walls and banks. **Hairy Rock-cress**, *Arabis hirsuta* (p. 55), is a variable member of the genus, a short-lived perennial or biennial plant with a rosette of simple basal leaves and an erect flowering stem. In this species the leaves are hairy and cover the flowering stalk as well as forming the basal rosette; the flowers are white. The pods are cylindrical and held erect, close to the stem. Hairy Rock-cress grows on walls and limestone rocks, on dry banks and dunes throughout the British Isles and most of Europe.

Tower Mustard, *Arabis glabra* (p. 55), is an overwintering annual or biennial plant, forming a rosette of linear, toothed leaves that wither before the flowers appear. The inflorescence is borne on an erect stem up to 120cm (6ft) tall, with clasping, arrow-like leaves. The flowers are pale yellow and the pods are

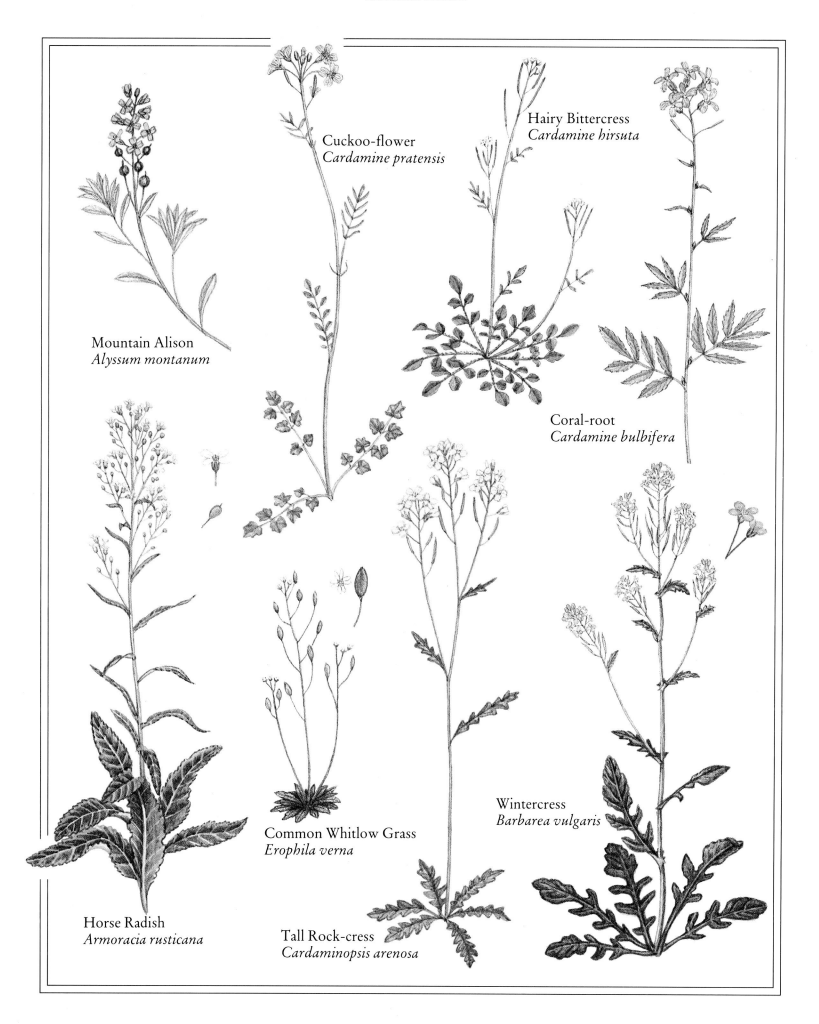

Mountain Alison
Alyssum montanum

Cuckoo-flower
Cardamine pratensis

Hairy Bittercress
Cardamine hirsuta

Coral-root
Cardamine bulbifera

Horse Radish
Armoracia rusticana

Common Whitlow Grass
Erophila verna

Tall Rock-cress
Cardaminopsis arenosa

Wintercress
Barbarea vulgaris

long and slender, held stiffly erect. This plant grows on dry banks and cliffs, on roadsides and in waste places, in open woods and heathland throughout much of Europe; it is absent from Ireland and Wales, rare in Scotland, local and declining in numbers in England.

Watercress, *Nasturtium officinale*, one of the most familiar members of the family, is a plant with a distinctive bitter taste, eaten in salads and rich in Vitamins A and C. The cultivated form is essentially the same as the wild form, which grows in the quiet waters of streams and springs throughout lowland areas of the British Isles and Europe, northwards to southern Scandinavia. It will not grow in stagnant ponds or in heavy shade. This is a dark green plant with hollow stems that root in the mud and then grow up towards the light to float on the surface. It has compound leaves with 5–9 leaflets. The racemes of white flowers appear in summer and are followed by erect, curving, cylindrical pods in which the outlines of the seeds can be seen quite clearly.

The **Yellowcresses**, belonging to the genus *Rorippa*, are a large group of species related to Watercress; at one time they were placed in the same genus, but the Yellowcresses have yellow flowers and are inedible. Many grow in wet places or beside streams and ditches. **Marsh Yellowcress**, *R. palustris*, is an annual or biennial plant, with a rosette of sinuately lobed basal leaves and an erect, leafy flowering stem in summer. The flowers are pale yellow and followed by egg-shaped fruits. This plant grows most often on bare ground where water stands in winter; it is found in much of Europe and in lowland areas of the British Isles.

Hoary Stock or Gilliflower, *Matthiola incana*, is the species from which most garden stocks are derived. Nowadays they come in a variety of forms, including Summer Stocks (also known as Ten-week Stocks) and Winter Stocks (including the Brompton and Perpetual Stocks). In the wild this species may be annual or perennial; it forms a stout tap root and an erect, woody shoot, unbranched at the base and branched above, with narrowly lance-shaped, downy-white leaves and terminal inflorescences of white, red or purple flowers. It grows on the coast of the Mediterranean Sea and western Europe, north to southern England. However, it is not common in Britain, found mainly on cliffs of the Channel Islands, the Isle of Wight and the Sussex coast.

Dame's Violet, *Hesperis matronalis*, is an attractive plant often grown in gardens for its white or lilac flowers and its sweet scent, most noticeable in the evenings. It is native to many areas of continental Europe and introduced elsewhere; in the British Isles it grows as a garden escape in damp hedgerows and on roadsides. It is a biennial or perennial plant, with branched, leafy stems up 90cm (3ft) tall; its leaves are lance-shaped and toothed, becoming smaller higher up the stem, and the flowers are borne in a branched inflorescence terminating the stem.

Wallflowers, garden forms of the species *Cheiranthus cheiri*, are grown in gardens all over Europe and in lowland areas of Great Britain and Ireland. The species is probably native to the eastern Mediterranean region, but has become naturalized throughout Europe, escaping from gardens to grow wild, mostly on walls, but also on cliffs and in stony places. Plants may be grown as annuals in gardens, but in the wild they act as perennials, the bases of their stems becoming woody and twisted, and progressively more straggly with the passing years. They produce new shoots every year, with lance-shaped leaves and fragrant, yellow or orange-brown flowers borne in early summer.

Treacle Mustard, *Erysimum cheiranthoides*, is a weed. It grows in waste places, on roadsides and in cultivated land in most of Europe, mainly in southern England in the British Isles, where it is never more than locally common. It is rare in the north, in Scotland, Wales and Ireland. It is a hairy, annual plant, with a rosette of irregularly toothed leaves withering before flowering, and branched, leafy stems up to 90cm (3ft) tall in summer. These stems end in flat-topped clusters of buds and bright yellow flowers above a gradually lengthening array of long, curved fruits. This is an old herbal plant often known as Wormseed, since its seeds were an effective, albeit extremely bitter and rather too potent, remedy for worms; too large a dose could be dangerous.

Garlic Mustard or Jack-by-the-hedge, *Alliaria petiolata* (p. 57), is most often found in hedgerows or on roadsides, frequently forming a row at the base of a wall or fence in woods, gardens, farmyards and waste places, growing best where the soil is rich in mineral nutrients. It can be recognized by the scent of garlic emitted by its bruised leaves; the leaves can be used in sauces as a substitute for garlic, or eaten in salads. Garlic Mustard is a biennial plant, with a rosette of long-stalked, dark green, kidney-shaped, toothed leaves in the first year and a leafy flowering stem in the second, growing about 1m (3ft) tall. This ends in a lengthening inflorescence of white flowers borne in late spring and early summer. The pods are long, cylindrical and curved.

There are many *Sisymbrium* species in Europe and Asia, a large number of them weeds of waste places, roadsides and cultivated land. They may be annual, biennial or perennial plants, but characteristically have yellow flowers and long, beakless fruits which contain one row of small seeds. **Hedge Mustard**, *S. officinale* (p. 57), is immediately recognizable for the way the flowering stems jut out from the main branches almost at right angles; when in fruit these stems become very elongated, with the long pods overlapping each other and pressed closely against the stems. This is an annual, much-branched, roughly bristly plant, growing about 60cm (2ft) tall, with deeply cut basal leaves and narrow, toothed stem leaves. The flowers are pale yellow, appearing over a long period during the summer, soon forming a small cluster over the elongating array of pods.

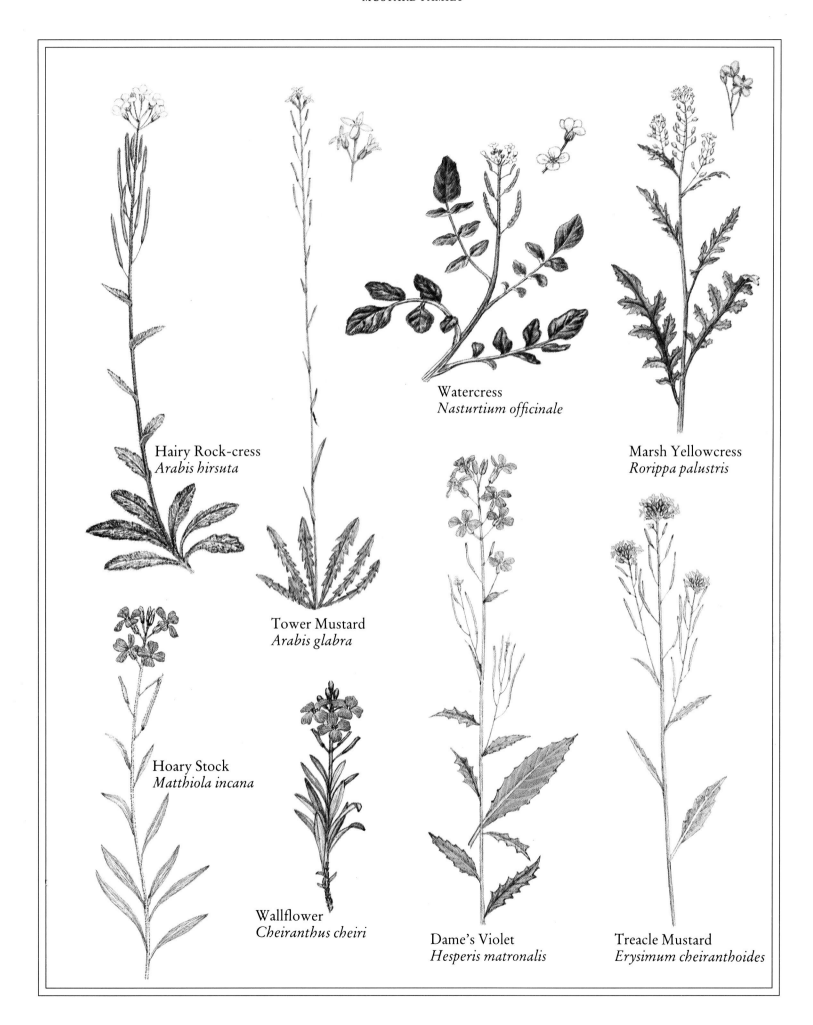

Hairy Rock-cress
Arabis hirsuta

Tower Mustard
Arabis glabra

Watercress
Nasturtium officinale

Marsh Yellowcress
Rorippa palustris

Hoary Stock
Matthiola incana

Wallflower
Cheiranthus cheiri

Dame's Violet
Hesperis matronalis

Treacle Mustard
Erysimum cheiranthoides

tivated land throughout Europe and the British Isles, but much less commonly in northern Scotland.

Tall Rocket, *Sisymbrium altissimum*, is another annual plant, with a rosette of deeply lobed leaves that wither before the plant flowers. It forms many branched stems, growing up to 1m (3ft) tall, bristly near the base, white-bloomed near the tops and with leaves so deeply divided that their segments are linear. It has pale yellow flowers in summer followed by pods carried at an oblique angle to the stems. This plant is native to southern and eastern Europe, but is naturalized in many other areas of the continent, as well as in parts of the British Isles. It grows in waste places, mainly in England and Wales, rarely in Scotland and Ireland.

London Rocket, *Sisymbrium irio*, became very common in London after the Great Fire of 1666, but is now found only occasionally in England, although it grows in waste places and on roadsides throughout much of Europe. Eastern Rocket, *S. orientale*, is another waste ground plant, this one found in England and Wales as well as Europe; it is like Tall Rocket.

Thale Cress, *Arabidopsis thaliana*, is another weedy species, but a native rather than an introduced one. It grows on walls and banks, in hedgerows and waste places, especially in sandy soils, throughout the British Isles and Europe. It is an annual plant, with a rosette of greyish-green, spoon-shaped or elliptical, often toothed leaves and erect stems up to 50cm (20in) tall. The stems have similar, usually untoothed, leaves and lengthening inflorescences of small white flowers, which are followed by long, linear fruits.

Gold-of-pleasure, *Camelina sativa*, gets its poetic name from its golden-yellow flowers. This is now only a casual plant in Britain where once it was a common weed of cultivated land, often growing with flax; its numbers have declined with the introduction of modern farming techniques. It is found scattered throughout much of Europe, introduced from the east. At one time it was extensively cultivated both for the fibres in its stems and for the oil which was extracted from its seeds. It is an annual plant, with erect stems up to 1m (3ft) tall, and arrow-shaped leaves with bases clasping the stems. The flowers grow in an elongating inflorescence and are followed by woody, pear-shaped fruits. Each contains two rows of seeds.

Flixweed, *Descurainia sophia*, was once a common weed of waste places and waysides in Britain, but is nowhere common now; it is found scattered through England and Wales, most frequently in East Anglia, but is rarer in Scotland and very rare in Ireland. It does grow throughout Europe. This is a bushy, annual plant with much-branched stems up to 80cm (40in) tall, greyish-green in colour, with star-shaped hairs on stem and leaves. The leaves are grey-green and ferny in appearance, very much divided with linear segments and the flowers are pale yellow. The fruits are long and slender, curving upwards and held more or less erect on long stalks.

Resedaceae

A small family of herbaceous plants, with only 6 genera and 700 species, found mainly in the Mediterranean region. Mignonette is grown in gardens for its fragrant flowers.

Family features The flowers are borne in spike-like racemes; they are irregular in form and hermaphrodite, with 4–7 sepals fused into a tube and 4–7 petals, those at the back of the flower larger and more deeply divided than those at the front. There are numerous, more or less free stamens crowded to the front of the flower and inserted on a nectar-secreting disk, and a superior ovary with 2–6 cells joined at the base. The fruits are one-celled capsules. The leaves are alternately arranged, simple or pinnately divided, with small, gland-like stipules. The plants contain watery juice.

Dyer's Rocket or Weld, *Reseda luteola*, has been known for centuries as the source of a brilliant yellow dye; it was used on a commercial scale to dye wool and other fabrics until finally replaced by modern synthetic dyes during the course of the present century. At one time it was grown on a large scale throughout much of Europe (including England), but now grows only as a wild plant. It is locally common in Europe north to southern Scandinavia; in Britain it grows north to southern Scotland and it is found in Ireland. It grows in waste places, old quarries and gravel pits, beside roads and on old walls, on fixed sand-dunes and dry banks, mostly on calcareous soils. Dyer's Rocket is a hairless, biennial plant, with a rosette of narrow, lance-shaped leaves in the first year, and an erect, leafy flowering stem in the second. The stem grows up to 1.5m (5ft) tall and may be branched or not; it has many stalkless, narrow leaves and a slender, terminal spike of yellow-green flowers. Each flower has four sepals and four petals, those at the back and sides divided into several lobes, while the front petal is linear in shape.

Wild Mignonette, *Reseda lutea*, is a smaller plant, only 60cm (2ft) tall, and often perennial in its growth pattern. It has a woody base and many much-branched stems, with pinnately divided leaves. These are quite distinctive in shape for their lobes are blunt and diverge widely from the narrow, central portion of the leaf, which is constricted above each lobe. The flowers are borne in conical racemes; each one has six petals, the back and side petals divided and the front two linear in shape. Wild Mignonette grows on calcareous soils, on dry banks and roadsides, in quarries and on cultivated ground and chalk downland throughout England and Wales, locally in Scotland and Ireland. It is also found in western Europe and the Mediterranean region. The similar White Mignonette, *R. alba*, has white flowers. Originally from the Mediterranean, it also grows in dry waste places, especially near ports, in western Europe and southwestern England.

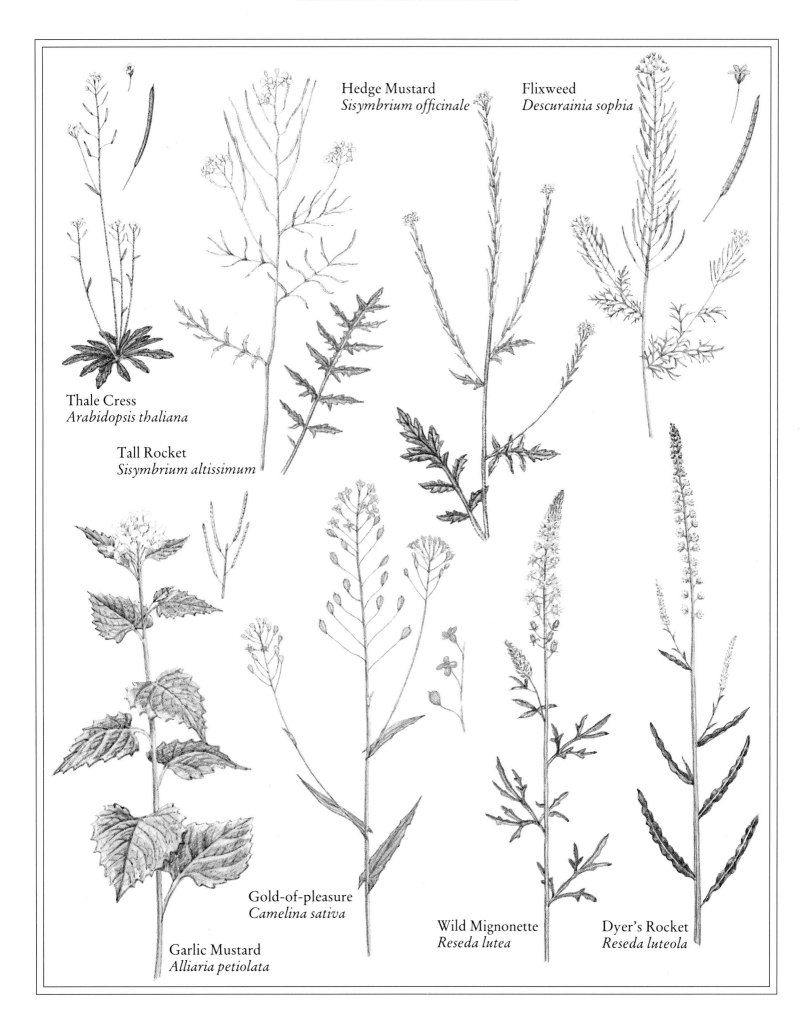

Hedge Mustard
Sisymbrium officinale

Flixweed
Descurainia sophia

Thale Cress
Arabidopsis thaliana

Tall Rocket
Sisymbrium altissimum

Gold-of-pleasure
Camelina sativa

Garlic Mustard
Alliaria petiolata

Wild Mignonette
Reseda lutea

Dyer's Rocket
Reseda luteola

Stonecrop family
Crassulaceae

There are about 35 genera and 1500 species of herbs and small shrubs in this family, mostly found in dry, warm, temperate regions of the world, many in South America. Some stonecrops and houseleeks are grown in rock gardens; *Crassula* and *Kalanchoe* species are grown as houseplants.

Family features Members of this family are almost all adapted to life in dry conditions and many are succulent. They often form dense leaf rosettes with fleshy stems, all with a waxy covering to cut down water loss. The leaves are opposite or alternate and lack stipules. The flowers are often star-like and borne in cymes, usually densely packed together. They are regular and hermaphrodite, with four or five sepals and petals, either free or united. They may have as many stamens as petals and alternating with the petals, or twice as many stamens as petals. The flowers have a superior ovary with as many carpels as petals; the carpels may be free or united at the base and there is a nectar-producing scale at the base of each carpel. The fruits are membranous or leathery pods.

The **Stonecrops** are a large group of about 600 species in the genus *Sedum*, with only one or two exceptions, in the northern hemisphere. Nearly 60 of them grow wild in Europe and more are grown in gardens, larger ones in flower borders, smaller, creeping ones in walls and rock gardens. They are all succulent plants with fleshy leaves.

Many stonecrops are small, mat-like plants with prostrate stems and leaves in rosettes, the leaves held close together or overlapping to reduce water loss. The plants often grow in the poorest of soils, on dry, stony ground or clinging to rocks; during a drought their fleshy leaves become puckered as they lose water, but they recover almost miraculously after rain. **Biting Stonecrop** or Wall-pepper, *Sedum acre*, is one of these species. It is an attractive little plant, with mats of bright green, often red-tinged leaves transformed by bright yellow flowers in summer. The leaves are borne on prostrate, rooting stems and the flowers on little, erect stems only 10cm (4in) tall at most, also leafy and with flowers in clusters at the top. Plants grow on walls and rocky banks, in dry grassland, on dunes and shingle, often in calcareous soils, throughout the British Isles and Europe. It is often grown in gardens, especially in a form which has bright yellow young leaves.

English Stonecrop, *Sedum anglicum*, is another creeping plant, only 5cm (2in) tall, with blue-green leaves on prostrate stems, and many upturned stems, some of which bear clusters of white flowers at the top. Their petals are tinged pink on the back. English Stonecrop grows among rocks on acid soils, less often on dunes and shingle, in western Europe and in the British Isles. In Britain it is most commonly found down the western side and in southern and western Ireland.

less neat in appearance and more straggly. Its creeping stems bear bright green leaves, sometimes red-tinged when the plant is growing in sun, and it also has many similar, upturned stems which may fall over if they cannot find support. The white flowers are borne in clusters at the tops of leafy stems 15cm (6in) tall. This plant grows wild across much of Europe and the British Isles, although it is probably naturalized rather than native in many places, having escaped from gardens. It grows in walls and rocks.

Reflexed Stonecrop, *Sedum reflexum*, grows wild on walls and rocks across much of Europe, but is introduced in Britain, where it is grown in gardens. It has the typical form of a creeping stonecrop, with prostrate stems and fleshy leaves, linear in shape in this species. It also has many upturned leafy stems and other flower-bearing stems. In these the lower leaves often wither and fall off; the yellow flowers are borne in terminal, umbel-like inflorescences.

Other stonecrops are larger plants, with clumps of more or less erect, leafy stems. **Orpine**, *Sedum telephium*, is grown in gardens and also grows wild in woods and hedgebanks, often on sandy soils, throughout much of Europe and the British Isles, becoming rare in northern Scotland and introduced into Ireland. It is a grey-green perennial plant, often tinged with red, forming clumps of erect stems 20–60cm (8in–2ft) tall, with alternate, toothed leaves. In late summer the stems bear dense clusters of red-purple flowers growing on long stalks from the axils of the upper leaves.

Roseroot, *Sedum rosea*, is another desirable garden species, but is also an alpine plant which grows in mountain crevices and on sea cliffs in northern Europe. In Britain it is found in northern England, Wales, Scotland and Ireland. Unlike most *Sedum* species, it bears male and female flowers on separate plants and is sometimes placed in another genus, *Rhodiola*. It is a perennial plant, with a thick, scaly rhizome and several fleshy stems up to 30cm (1ft) tall, with many stalkless, flat and broadly lance-shaped leaves, often crowded along the stems. The flowers are greenish-yellow and star-like; they appear in early summer, forming a terminal cluster to crown the stems.

The **Houseleek**, *Sempervivum tectorum*, is one of about 25 *Sempervivum* species found wild in the mountains of Europe; they are often grown in rock gardens and troughs, and a large number of varieties have been developed. Houseleek is the most common, grown for centuries on roofs in many parts of Europe to protect the house from fire and lightning according to folklore. It forms rosettes of pointed, red-tipped, blue-green leaves, each rosette growing up to 8cm (3in) across. The plant spreads by forming new rosettes on short, prostrate stems growing from the mother plant. Every year some rosettes in the patch will flower and then die; they produce erect, leafy stems 30–60cm (1–2ft) tall tipped with a flat cluster of spiky-looking, pink flowers.

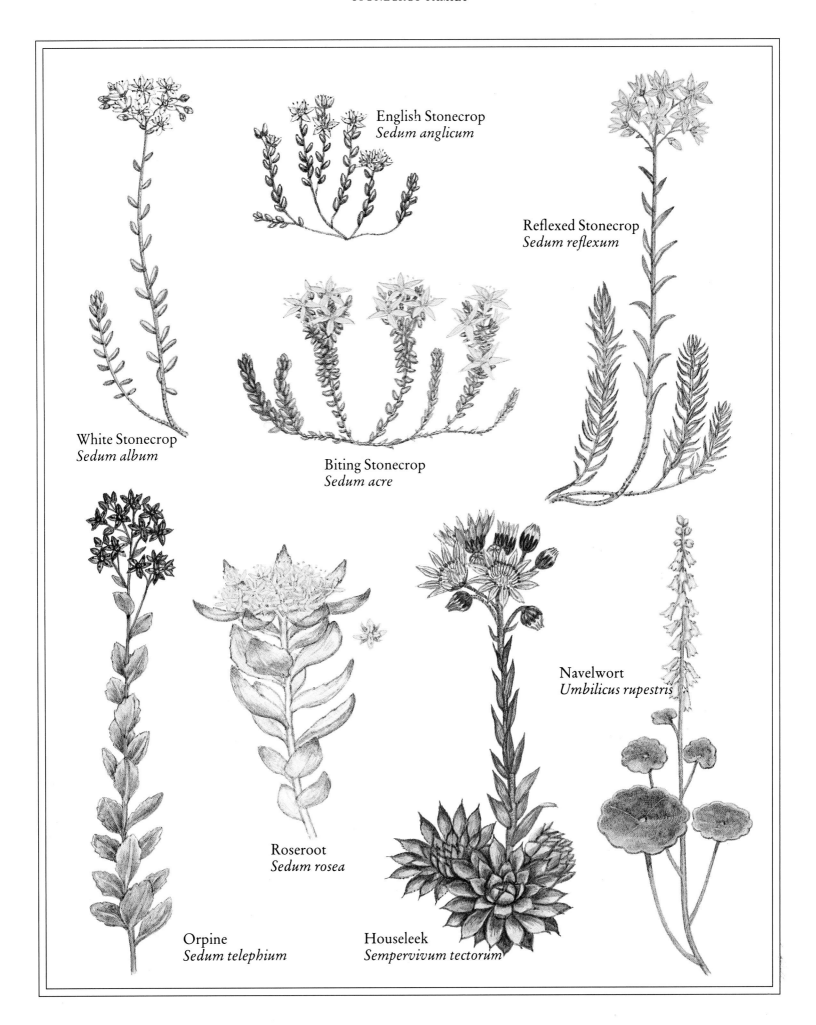

English Stonecrop
Sedum anglicum

Reflexed Stonecrop
Sedum reflexum

White Stonecrop
Sedum album

Biting Stonecrop
Sedum acre

Navelwort
Umbilicus rupestris

Orpine
Sedum telephium

Roseroot
Sedum rosea

Houseleek
Sempervivum tectorum

Navelwort or Wall Pennywort, *Umbilicus rupestris* (p. 59), forms characteristic clumps of thick, rounded leaves, each with a dimple in the centre where the stalk joins at the back. In the latter half of summer the plant produces erect flowering stems with long racemes of bell-shaped, greenish-white flowers. It grows in the sides of walls and banks, especially on acid soils, in Mediterranean Europe, Portugal, France, Ireland and western areas of Britain, north to southern Scotland.

Saxifrage family
Saxifragaceae

This family has about 30 genera and 580 species of herbs, mainly from temperate regions of the northern hemisphere. Many family members are beautiful and ornamental plants, including the saxifrages grown in rock gardens and astilbes, coral bells and Elephant's Ears grown in flower borders.

Family features The flowers are usually regular and hermaphrodite with five sepals and five petals alternating with the sepals; in some species petals are absent. There are 5–10 stamens and two carpels in the ovary, often joined together at the base but with free styles and stigmas. The flowers have a flat ring around the ovary on which the stamens, petals and sepals are inserted. The whole of this ring may glisten with nectar secreted by the ovary. The fruits are capsules. The leaves are alternate and lack stipules.

The **Saxifrages**, belonging to the genus *Saxifraga*, are much the largest group in the family, with over 300 species. Most people associate them with mountain crevices and many do grow in mountains, like the Alps or the Caucasus, but others grow at lower altitudes in woods and meadows.

Purple Saxifrage, *Saxifraga oppositifolia*, is a mountain species which forms loose mats or tufts of stems; these have opposite, fleshy leaves, so close together at the stem tips that they look like rosettes. This is a very small plant, growing 8–10cm (3–4in) high at most, and often just creeping over the surface of the ground; its solitary purple flowers look large in comparison, since they measure over a centimetre across. They are borne at the tips of the stems in late summer. Purple Saxifrage grows in limestone soils, among rock debris and on slopes in the high mountains of Europe. In Britain it is often quite common in the mountains of northern England, Wales, Scotland and Northern Ireland.

Starry Saxifrage, *Saxifraga stellaris*, is another mountain species, this one growing beside springs and streams, or on wet ledges and in flushes in many of the European mountain ranges. In Britain it is found in the mountains of Wales, northern England, Scotland and Ireland. It forms dense rosettes of slightly hairy, toothed and oblong leaves, the total effect being of a tufted plant. In summer erect, leafless stems bear terminal clusters of white flowers with pink anthers and yellow-spotted petals. London Pride, *S. x urbium*, is a related, old-fashioned plant grown in town gardens.

Meadow Saxifrage, *Saxifraga granulata*, is a much more widespread plant, since it is not confined to mountain areas. It grows in grassland, usually on well-drained neutral or alkaline soils, throughout most of Europe. In Britain it is more common in the east, absent from southwestern England and northern Scotland, rare in Ireland. It forms a clump of hairy basal leaves; they are kidney-shaped and lobed with long stalks, appearing in spring and dying down soon after the white flowers appear in early summer. The plant then remains dormant, surviving by bulbils produced in its leaf axils beneath the ground. A double form is sometimes grown in gardens.

Rue-leaved Saxifrage, *Saxifraga tridactylites*, is another lowland species. This one is found in dry, open places, among rocks and on walls, in dry grassland and on bare ground, usually on alkaline soils, throughout Europe and much of Britain and Ireland; it is not found in western Scotland. It is an annual (rare in saxifrages), a sticky-hairy, often reddish plant, which forms a small clump of long-stalked leaves, the lowermost spoon-shaped and withered by flowering time, the higher ones palmately lobed with 3–5 lobes. White flowers appear in early summer, borne on erect stalks.

Dovedale Moss or Mossy Saxifrage, *Saxifraga hypnoides*, is like a wild form of the mossy saxifrages grown in rock gardens and flower borders. It grows on rock ledges and screes, in damp, grassy places and beside streams, in the hills and mountains of northwestern Europe and those of Great Britain and Ireland. It is a mat-forming plant, with many prostrate, leafy shoots and flowering rosettes. The flowers are white, borne in clusters on erect stalks in early summer.

Golden Saxifrages are a group of about 55 species in the genus *Chrysosplenium*, found mainly in eastern Asia but with five species in Europe. **Opposite-leaved Golden Saxifrage**, *C. oppositifolium*, grows in shady, wet places, beside springs and streams in western and central Europe, and throughout much of the British Isles, more commonly in the west than the east. It often spreads into large patches with its creeping, leafy stems. The leaves are opposite, rounded or kidney-shaped with wavy edges and long stalks. In summer the stems turn upwards to flower, producing tiny, yellow-green flowers surrounded by bright yellow-green bracts. The flowers have no petals.

Alternate-leaved Golden Saxifrage, *Chrysosplenium alternifolium*, grows in similar places across much of Europe and in Great Britain, but is absent from the extreme west of Britain and Ireland. Its creeping stems are leafless and its long-stalked, rounded leaves grow in rosettes. The leaves are thick with rounded teeth on their margins and they grow alternately on the flowering stalks, as well as in the rosettes. The small yellow flowers lack petals and are surrounded by yellow-green bracts, larger than those of the former species.

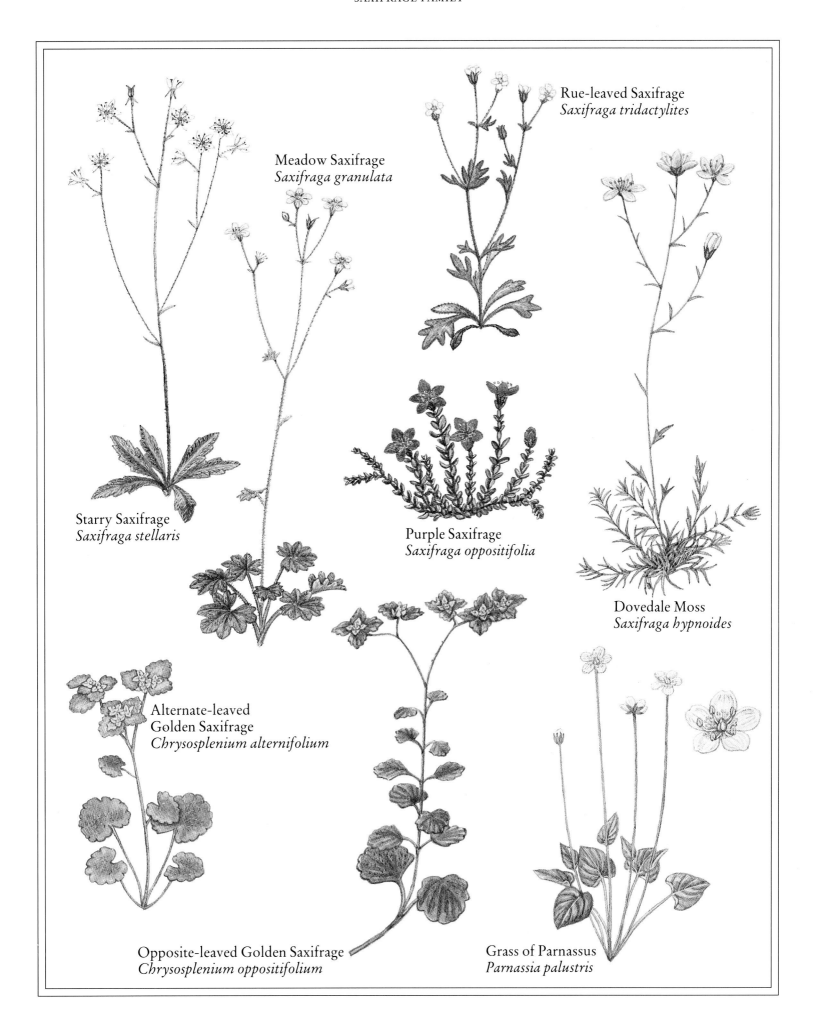

Meadow Saxifrage
Saxifraga granulata

Rue-leaved Saxifrage
Saxifraga tridactylites

Starry Saxifrage
Saxifraga stellaris

Purple Saxifrage
Saxifraga oppositifolia

Dovedale Moss
Saxifraga hypnoides

Alternate-leaved
Golden Saxifrage
Chrysosplenium alternifolium

Opposite-leaved Golden Saxifrage
Chrysosplenium oppositifolium

Grass of Parnassus
Parnassia palustris

Grass of Parnassus, *Parnassia palustris* (p. 61), grows in wet meadows, beside streams and lakes, in bogs and marshes across most of Europe and locally in Great Britain and Ireland. It is declining in numbers, however, and is probably extinct in parts of the south and Midlands. This perennial plant has a rosette of long-stalked, heart-shaped leaves and solitary white flowers on erect flowering stalks. Grass of Parnassus can be identified by the pattern of the stamens in each flower—five fertile stamens between the petals and five fringed sterile ones opposite the petals. There are many *Parnassia* species in the northern hemisphere; the stamens make them sufficiently distinctive to be placed by some botanists in a separate family of their own, the Parnassiaceae.

Rose family
Rosaceae

A large and important family, with about 100 genera and over 2000 species, found throughout the world, especially in the temperate regions. The family includes many fruit trees, such as apple, pear, cherry, peach and plum. Almond trees provide nuts. Other trees, like mountain ash and whitebeam, crab apple, hawthorn and ornamental cherry, are planted in city parks and streets, as well as in gardens. The family is also rich in shrubs, including the roses themselves, spiraeas, potentillas and cotoneasters. Herbaceous garden plants include geums, lady's mantles and strawberries.

Family features The flowers are hermaphrodite and regular, with five separate, often overlapping sepals and petals. The flowers have numerous stamens. The ovary is usually superior, with the floral parts in rings around its base, or it is inferior, with the floral parts in rings above it. The ovary has one to many carpels, variously free or united; the styles usually remain free. The fruits are achenes, drupes or pomes. The leaves are simple or compound, usually alternate, often with a pair of stipules attached to the leaf stalk.

Meadowsweet, *Filipendula ulmaria*, grows throughout Europe and the British Isles, often in abundance in wet meadows, fens and marshes, in wet woods and on the banks of rivers. It is a perennial plant, forming clumps of dark green, pinnate leaves and erect, leafy flowering stems 60–120cm (2–4ft) tall in summer. Each leaf has up to five pairs of large leaflets, with smaller leaflets between the larger ones. The flowers are small with creamy-white petals, sweetly scented and borne in clusters, with a fluffy appearance that comes from the long stamens. The fruits consist of several carpels which become twisted around each other, so that they look like spirals.

Dropwort, *Filipendula vulgaris*, grows in quite a different environment—in calcareous grassland, often on downs and limestone uplands, throughout much of Europe north to southern Norway. In the British Isles it is widespread only in England. This perennial plant forms clumps of pinnate leaves with many toothed leaflets, larger leaflets alternating with smaller ones. In summer it bears almost leafless flowering stems up to 80cm (2–3ft) tall, tipped with a spreading, flat-topped cluster of creamy white flowers opening from pink buds. The fruits are hairy and the carpels do not form a spiral.

Goatsbeard, *Aruncus dioicus*, is an impressive perennial plant, with several erect, leafy stems up to 2m (6ft) tall, topped in early to mid summer with plumes of white, fluffy flowers. It has large compound leaves up to 50cm (20in) long, with long stalks and pointed-oblong, serrated leaflets. The branched flower plumes have separate male and female flowers, the males with many stamens and the females with three carpels each. The plant grows in damp, shady places and woods in western and central Europe. It is grown in gardens in Britain.

Lady's Mantles belong to the large genus *Alchemilla*, with probably over 100 species in Europe. However, species are very difficult to distinguish in this genus, for Lady's Mantles produce seed without pollination (like hawkweeds), so there is no exchange of genes between individuals. In consequence the seeds from one individual form a closed population and could be said to be a species. These perennial plants have palmate or palmately lobed leaves and numerous flowers in branched cymes. The flowers are green or yellow-green, the colour coming from the calyx and epicalyx, for they lack petals.

Common Lady's Mantle, *Alchemilla vulgaris*, grows in damp grassland and woods, on stream banks and rocky ledges, especially on basic soils, throughout most of Europe and the British Isles. It is rare in southeastern England. It forms large clumps of attractive, palmately lobed leaves that hold drops of water after rain or heavy dew. The yellow-green flowers are less attractive, borne in large, branched clusters on leafy stalks in summer and followed by many seeds.

Alpine Lady's Mantle, *Alchemilla alpina*, is a mountain species, growing in grassland and in rock crevices, often on acid substrates, in the mountains throughout much of Europe, in Scotland and northern England, rarely in Ireland. It forms small clumps of palmately divided leaves with lance-shaped leaflets, dark green above and silvery-hairy beneath, growing on long stalks from a woody crown. The flowers are borne in small clusters on long stalks, often hidden between the leaves. This plant is sometimes grown in rock gardens.

Parsley Piert, *Aphanes arvensis*, grows on bare ground in arable land, gardens, waste places and roadsides, also in grassland and heaths throughout much of Europe and the British Isles. This is a very small, pale green, annual plant, often only 2cm (1in) tall. It has branched, sprawling stems covered with fringed, cup-like stipules and fan-shaped, lobed leaves, each lobe further divided into three sections. The flowers are tiny and petal-less, borne in dense clusters opposite the leaves, each cluster half cupped in one of the leafy stipules.

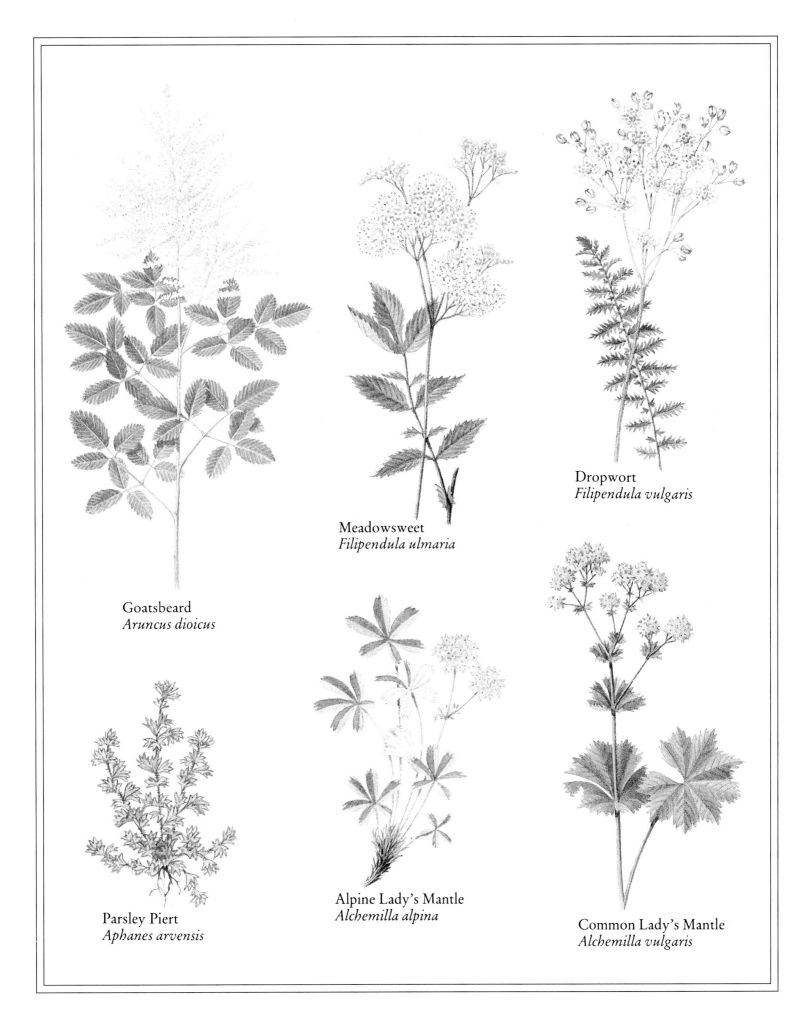

Goatsbeard
Aruncus dioicus

Meadowsweet
Filipendula ulmaria

Dropwort
Filipendula vulgaris

Parsley Piert
Aphanes arvensis

Alpine Lady's Mantle
Alchemilla alpina

Common Lady's Mantle
Alchemilla vulgaris

There are about 13 different **Avens**, *Geum* species, in Europe. **Water Avens**, *G. rivale*, is a wetland plant growing in wet meadows and marshes, in wet woods and beside streams, usually in shady places on base-rich soils. It forms a clump of compound pinnate leaves, each one with a very broad terminal leaflet. The flowers are borne on leafy flowering stems in loose terminal clusters; they are nodding, with purplish sepals and orange-pink petals. The centre of each flower, like those of all avens, contains many ovaries which enlarge into numerous achenes. In Water Avens the long styles are hooked in fruit, so that the fruit forms a burr which catches in fur or clothing.

Wood Avens or Herb Bennet, *Geum urbanum*, is a perennial plant forming a clump of hairy compound leaves; each leaf has 2–3 pairs of lateral leaflets and one large, lobed terminal leaflet. In early summer the small, yellow flowers appear in loose clusters on separate, leafy stalks 20–60cm (8in–2ft) tall. The fruits form hooked burrs, the hooks jointed and often pointing downwards. This plant grows in shady, damp places in woods and hedgerows throughout Europe and the British Isles, except the extreme north.

White Mountain Avens, *Dryas octopetala*, grows on sea cliffs and rocky grassland in the extreme north of Scotland and Europe, in mountain rock crevices and on ledges further south in its range. It is found in the mountains of Europe, Scotland, Ireland and northern England, rarely in Wales. It has prostrate, semi-woody stems and many dark green leaves, like miniature oak leaves but with pale undersides. White flowers grow on erect stalks in early summer and are followed by plumed achenes with white feathery styles. The plant is always attractive, in flower and in fruit, and even in winter for it is evergreen. It is sometimes grown in rock gardens.

Agrimony, *Agrimonia eupatoria*, grows in open woods and woodland edges, in hedgebanks, on roadsides and on the edges of fields throughout Europe and the British Isles, but rarely in northern Scotland. It forms an erect, leafy stem 30–60cm (1–2ft) tall, with dark green, compound leaves in which large leaflets are interspersed with small ones; the leaflets have toothed margins. In late summer a spike of small yellow flowers forms at the top of the stem. The fruits which follow are distinctive; each is top-shaped, with several rows of hooked bristles on its top surface—an aid to dispersal since they get tangled in the hair of passing animals.

Great Burnet, *Sanguisorba officinalis*, is an old herbal plant, highly astringent, used to stop internal bleeding and to check diarrhoea and dysentery. It has become much less common since its damp, grassland habitats have disappeared with modern farming methods. It is found throughout much of Europe, most commonly in England and Wales in Britain. It is a hairless perennial with a rosette of pinnate leaves. Each leaf has 3–7 pairs of long-stalked, toothed leaflets that become larger towards the tip. In summer the flowering stems appear, 30–100cm (1–3ft) tall, with a few similar leaves and dense,

oblong heads of reddish flowers terminating the stems. The colour comes from the sepals for the flowers lack petals.

Salad Burnet, *Sanguisorba minor*, is a smaller plant found in calcareous grassland, usually on chalk and limestone uplands, across much of Europe. In Britain it is most common in England and Wales, occurring much more locally in Scotland and Ireland. It forms small, perennial clumps of pinnate leaves, each with 4–12 pairs of toothed leaflets. In summer the flowering stems grow about 60cm (2ft) tall, with pinnate leaves near the base and rounded flower heads at the top. Unlike the heads of Great Burnet, which has hermaphrodite flowers, those of Salad Burnet vary—female flowers with reddish styles at the top of each head, hermaphrodite ones in the centre and hermaphrodite or male flowers at the base. This plant smells of cucumber when bruised and the leaves can be added to punch.

Sibbaldia, *Sibbaldia procumbens*, is a very small, tufted, perennial plant, often only 3cm (1in) tall, with a rosette of long-stalked, three-lobed leaves. The leaves are hairy and the leaflets three-toothed at their tips. The tiny flowers are borne on separate stalks in dense, terminal clusters; their petals are narrow and yellowish, sometimes absent, smaller than the purplish calyces and epicalyces. This is a mountain plant found in high rock crevices and alpine pastures, in the mountains of northern and central Europe, also in the Highlands of Scotland and Cumbria. It is related to the Cinquefoils.

The **Cinquefoils**, members of the genus *Potentilla*, are a large group of mostly perennial plants, with over 75 species in Europe. Their flowers have five petals cupped not only in a calyx of green sepals, but also in an epicalyx—this looks like a second set of sepals beneath the true sepals. Most have yellow flowers, although a few have white or dark red petals. Their fruits are clusters of dry achenes, often partly enclosed by the persistent calyx. Cinquefoils are often confused with buttercups and do resemble those plants, with their yellow flowers and their dark green leaves. But buttercups have simple or divided leaves rather than compound ones with separate leaflets; buttercups lack stipules, whereas members of the rose family have conspicuous stipules; buttercups do not have an epicalyx; and buttercups have a superior ovary while cinquefoils have an inferior one. These last two factors give the flowers of buttercups and cinquefoils quite a different appearance.

Creeping Cinquefoil, *Potentilla reptans* (p. 67), has leaves typical of Five-finger Cinquefoils; there are several species of these, all with leaves that are long-stalked and palmately compound, with several toothed leaflets (often five, hence cinquefoil and five-finger). This one has prostrate stems rooting at the nodes and rosettes of long-stalked leaves. In summer it produces solitary flowers on long stalks, bright yellow with notched petals. This plant is a common sight on roadside verges, in waste places and hedgebanks, less often in grassland, mostly on basic and neutral soils, throughout the British Isles and Europe, except the extreme north.

Water Avens
Geum rivale

White Mountain Avens
Dryas octopetala

Wood Avens
Geum urbanum

Agrimony
Agrimonia eupatoria

Sibbaldia
Sibbaldia procumbens

Salad Burnet
Sanguisorba minor

Great Burnet
Sanguisorba officinalis

Hoary Cinquefoil, *Potentilla argentea*, is another five-finger cinquefoil, this one with deeply toothed leaflets. The leaves are dark green above, white-hairy beneath, borne in a basal rosette. Yellow flowers appear in branched clusters on sprawling, leafy stems in summer. This plant is found in dry grassland, on sandy soils throughout most of Europe. It is scattered through England and southern Scotland, but absent from much of the west, from most of Wales and from Ireland.

Tormentil, *Potentilla erecta*, is associated with acid grasslands, growing on heaths and moors, in lawns and grassy tracks, in marshes and fens, and open woods throughout Europe and the British Isles. It is a little, perennial plant with leafy, trailing flowering stems often only 10cm (4in) long; the leaves are palmately lobed, usually with three toothed leaflets (they may appear to be five-lobed, for they lack stalks and the two stipules look like extra leaflets). Its flowers distinguish it from other cinquefoils, for they have only four petals.

Silverweed, *Potentilla anserina*, is a lover of damp and grassy places, growing in moist meadows, on damp roadsides, in open woods, in waste places and on sand-dunes. It is found across much of Europe, except the south, and throughout the British Isles. It can be distinguished from other cinquefoils by its leaves; they are pinnately compound, with pairs of small toothed leaflets alternating with larger ones, dark green above and silver-hairy beneath. This is a creeping plant with stems that hug the ground and root at the nodes. The flowers are the usual cinquefoil ones, with yellow petals. Silverweed has many folk tales associated with it, including the story that it was grown as a root crop in ancient Britain. This may be true but the roots, although reminiscent of parsnips in flavour, are very small and often not worth the effort of gathering. Silverweed has also been used as a medicinal plant to treat mouth ulcers and other sores, and as a cosmetic to remove freckles and spots.

Barren Strawberry, *Potentilla sterilis*, looks like a Wild Strawberry in leaf form and flowers, and produces runners, but these are prostrate instead of arching. However, its fruits are small, dry clusters of achenes rather than juicy strawberries. The plant forms small rosettes of long-stalked, three-lobed, blue-green leaves, the leaflets broad and toothed towards their tips, silky beneath. The flowering stems are slender and sprawling, with small clusters of white flowers in the leaf axils; the flowers have widely separated petals. This little plant grows in hedgebanks, woodland edges and open woods, grassy places and roadside verges, usually on dry soils. It is found in western and central Europe, and throughout the British Isles, more rarely in northern Scotland.

Marsh Cinquefoil, *Potentilla palustris*, is a wetland plant, growing in wet meadows, marshes and fens, wet heaths and moors throughout much of Europe and the British Isles, most commonly in northern Britain and in Ireland. It has long, creeping rhizomes from which grow erect, leafy stems 15–45cm (6–18in) tall, with palmately lobed leaves and loose clusters of flowers in the early part of summer. The flowers are unusual for potentillas—reddish-purple in colour, with large purplish sepals and smaller, darker petals.

Shrubby Cinquefoil, *Potentilla fruticosa*, has typical cinquefoil flowers, but is a deciduous shrub about 1m (3ft) tall. It has branched, woody stems and small, compound leaves, each with 5–7 narrow leaflets, the three terminal ones often joined together. This is not a common wild plant in Europe; it grows in damp, rocky places in the mountains of southern Europe, also in a few places in the Lake District, in Upper Teesdale and in Ireland. Many varieties are grown in gardens, however, including ones with red and orange flowers.

Wild Strawberries, the fruits of *Fragaria vesca*, are smaller but sweeter than cultivated ones. Wild Strawberry is a small, perennial plant found in woods and scrub, grassy places and hedgebanks, usually on base-rich soils, throughout Europe and the British Isles. It forms rosettes of compound leaves, each leaf with three toothed leaflets. The plants produce arching runners—long thin stems which grow out all around the mother plant to root at the nodes and then grow on so that spreading mats of plants develop. The white flowers, and then the fruits, grow in small clusters on leafless stalks. In the centre of each flower the many carpels are borne on a conical receptacle; this enlarges to produce the 'fruit'—a false fruit since it forms from the receptacle rather than from the ovary. The real fruits are the 'seeds' on the strawberries.

Roses are prickly shrubs belonging to the genus *Rosa*; they have erect or arching stems and pinnate leaves with obvious stipules. Garden Roses are familiar to everyone; there are many forms, from the modern Floribunda and Hybrid Teas to climbing roses and Old Shrub Roses, tens of thousands of varieties from about 250 cultivated species. Their flowers may resemble those of wild roses, with five sepals and petals, or may be double; they may be scented or unscented, and mostly come in shades of pink, red, yellow or white. Rose petals are used in pot-pourris, both for their colour and fragrance. Rose-water is made from the petals of the French Rose, *R. gallica*, and used in beauty preparations. Attar of Roses is an oil extracted from the petals of French Roses and Damask Roses, *R. damascena*, and used in perfumery and in medicines.

The fruits of roses are hips; they are formed from the inferior ovary (in roses the ovary is below the flower), which swells up and becomes fleshy and brightly coloured. Hips are rich in Vitamin C and minerals, and the flesh can be made into syrups or wine once the seeds and hairs in the centre have been removed. These hairs are used by children as itching powder.

The **French Rose**, *Rosa gallica*, is a small spreading shrub only 40–80cm (15–30in) tall, forming large patches of prickly stems with rather leathery leaves. The stems bear not only straight prickles but also gland-tipped bristles; the leaves have 3–7 dull blue-green, hairy leaflets with double-toothed margins. This plant has very beautiful solitary flowers, 6–9cm

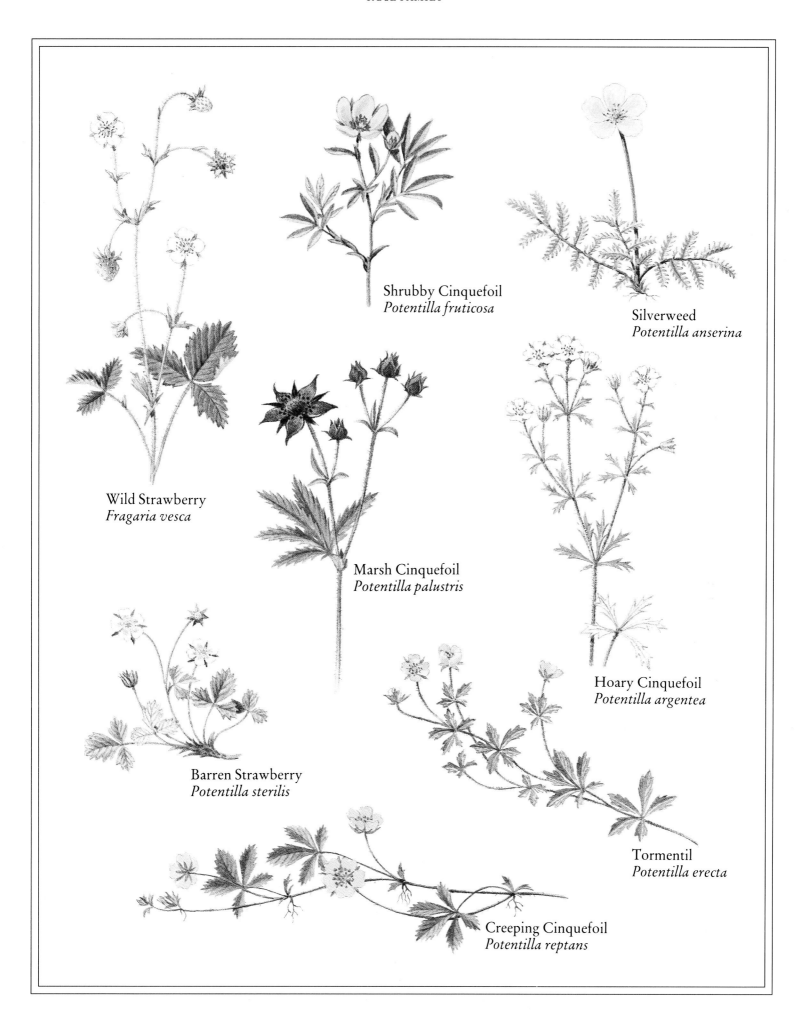

Shrubby Cinquefoil
Potentilla fruticosa

Silverweed
Potentilla anserina

Wild Strawberry
Fragaria vesca

Marsh Cinquefoil
Potentilla palustris

Hoary Cinquefoil
Potentilla argentea

Barren Strawberry
Potentilla sterilis

Tormentil
Potentilla erecta

Creeping Cinquefoil
Potentilla reptans

(2–4in) across, deep rose pink in colour and very fragrant, with the old-fashioned rose perfume. They are followed by bright red hips covered by many glandular hairs. This plant grows in woods and hedgerows in much of Europe, but is absent from the north and the British Isles. It is also grown as an ornamental and for its rose petals, especially in Provence.

About 45 species of Wild Roses grow in Europe. The most familiar one in Britain is the **Dog Rose**, *Rosa canina*, its arching branches forming conspicuous flower-studded patches in hedgerows and woodland margins. It is found throughout Europe northwards to southern Scandinavia, and throughout the British Isles, although relatively rarely in Scotland. It has stout stems that grow up to 3m (10ft) tall, pinnate leaves with 2–3 pairs of hairless, oval, toothed leaflets, stout, curved prickles and small clusters of pink or white flowers in summer. These are followed by elliptical, hairless hips.

The **Field Rose**, *Rosa arvensis*, is often mistaken for a Dog Rose, but has weaker, trailing, often purplish stems and characteristic white flowers that distinguish it from most other roses. The flowers have fused styles forming a column as long as the stamens (in most roses the styles are free or fused into a short column). Field Roses may form low bushes or trail over other shrubs in woods and hedgerows; they are found in western and southern Europe, in Ireland, southern England and Wales, much less commonly in northern England, and have been introduced into Scotland. The White Rose of York may have been a double form of this species.

Sweetbriar or Eglantine, *Rosa rubiginosa*, is usually found on calcareous soils, often on chalk downs or limestone uplands, also on the coast in rough grassland and scrub. It is found throughout most of Europe; in the British Isles it is common in suitable habitats throughout England and Wales, locally in Ireland and more rarely in Scotland. It is a dense shrub with stout, arching stems 2–3m (6–9ft) tall armed with unequal, flattened, broad-based thorns. The leaves are sticky with red-brown, stalked glands, particularly on the undersides; they smell of green apples when crushed. The fragrant, bright pink flowers appear in early summer and are followed by elongated red hips with persistent sepals.

Burnet Rose, *Rosa pimpinellifolia*, is a coastal plant, forming dense thickets of erect, extremely prickly stems with many suckers. The stems grow up to 60cm (2ft) tall and are covered, not only with numerous straight prickles, but also with many stiff bristles. They bear small, hairless leaves, each with 7–11 rounded, serrated leaflets, and solitary, creamy white flowers in early summer. The flowers are followed by small, rounded hips, turning purplish-black when ripe. Burnet Rose grows in dry, open places and on limestone pavements, and particularly in dune slacks and on stabilized sand-dunes along the coasts of Scotland, more especially in the west, and more locally on the Irish Coast. It is also found in similar places on the European coast, except in parts of the north.

There seems to be an inexhaustible supply of *Rubus* species, a group found mainly in the temperate regions of the northern hemisphere. At present the count is over 250 species, but new ones are described every year and the naming problem is complicated by hybridization and apomixis (the production of seeds without pollination). The group includes blackberries and loganberries, raspberries, dewberries and cloudberries.

Many *Rubus* species follow a distinctive growth pattern. They are shrubby, perennial plants that nevertheless have a biennial pattern of growth. Each year new shoots grow from the base of the plant; these first-year shoots are unbranched, have compound leaves and do not flower. In the second year the shoots produce side shoots with smaller, simpler leaves, then flowers and fruits. The whole shoot dies after fruiting.

Blackberries, *Rubus fruticosus*, follow this growth pattern, their stems often growing to 1m (3ft) tall and then arching over and rooting at the tips, or lying prostrate along the ground. This is a prickly plant, bearing a variety of hooked prickles, bristles and glands on the stems and leaf stalks. The white or pink flowers appear around midsummer and are followed by the popular fruits—the blackberries—sweet and juicy, glossy black fruits made up of many single-seeded sections. Blackberry bushes are found in heathland, in hedgerows and woods throughout the British Isles and Europe.

Dewberry, *Rubus caesius*, forms weak, sprawling stems with scattered, weak prickles and leaves with three leaflets. The flowers are numerous, borne in large clusters in late summer, and white or pink in colour; they are followed by bluish, blackberry-type fruits. The fruits are waxy and covered by a whitish bloom, as are the stems. Dewberries usually grow on basic soils, in rough grassland and scrub, also in fen carr, throughout much of Europe. They also grow throughout the British Isles, most commonly in central and eastern England.

Raspberry, *Rubus idaeus*, is found throughout the British Isles and most of Europe (in mountains in the south). It grows most commonly in hills and woods, on heaths, moors and commons, and in waste places. Its first-year shoots grow up to 2m (6ft) tall and are densely armed with slender prickles and stiff bristles. Around midsummer the second-year shoots produce side shoots with clusters of white flowers, followed by the fruits—raspberries. This is the same species as grown in gardens and the raspberries are just as edible.

Cloudberry, *Rubus chamaemorus*, is a rather different plant, a creeping herbaceous species that grows in *Sphagnum* bogs and on wet mountain moors in northern Europe. In Britain it is found in North Wales and northern England, north to Sutherland in Scotland. Cloudberry has erect stems with long-stalked, shallowly lobed leaves and no prickles. Its solitary white flowers appear around midsummer, the male and female flowers on separate plants. They are followed by orange fruits; these are considered a delicacy in northern Europe, especially as their season is short and they are difficult to gather.

Dog Rose
Rosa canina

Dewberry
Rubus caesius

Blackberry
Rubus fruticosus

Field Rose
Rosa arvensis

French Rose
Rosa gallica

Raspberry
Rubus idaeus

Burnet Rose
Rosa pimpinellifolia

Sweetbriar
Rosa rubiginosa

Cloudberry
Rubus chamaemorus

Pea family
Leguminosae

This is the third largest family of flowering plants in the world, with about 600 genera and 12,000 species. It has a bewildering variety of plants, including herbs, shrubs, trees and climbers. Important crop plants in the family include peas and beans, peanuts, soybeans, lentils, liquorice and alfalfa. Timber comes from tropical trees like the Acacias. Gum arabic comes from *Acacia senegal*, senna comes from the *Cassia* species, the insecticide derris comes from species of *Derris*, and other plants yield dyes, bark for tanning leather, fibres and resins. Among the many decorative garden plants are laburnums and mimosas, sweet peas and wisterias, brooms and lupins.

There are three subfamilies in the Leguminosae: the Mimosoideae (the Mimosa subfamily), the Caesalpinioideae (the Senna subfamily) and the Papilionoideae (the Pea subfamily). Sometimes these subfamilies are given separate family status. Most members of the Caesalpinioideae and the Mimosoideae are found in the tropics and few are herbaceous plants.

The **Pea subfamily**, the Papilionoideae, is much the biggest of the three in temperate regions of the world. Members of this group have the typical pea-type flowers with five unequal petals; each flower has one standard petal at the back, one wing petal each side of the standard and two lower petals often joined together to form the keel which encloses the stamens and ovary. The five sepals are fused into a five-toothed tube. There are 10 stamens, which may all be joined together, or nine may be fused and one left free. The ovary is superior and enlarges to form the characteristic fruit of the family—the legume, a pod which splits open along one or both seams to release the large seeds. The leaves may be simple or compound, the latter often having leaflets modified as tendrils. Stipules may be large and leaf-like, small, or modified to form spines.

Most plants need a supply of nitrogen, which they use in the synthesis of proteins; since they cannot obtain nitrogen from the air, they absorb it as soluble nitrates from the soil and are dependent on soil bacteria to fix nitrogen from the air into nitrates. Artificial fertilizers are a substitute for this process. However, members of the Papilionoideae have special nodules on their roots which contain nitrogen-fixing bacteria, and the nitrates are thus directly available to the plants. Leguminous plants are often planted in poor soils and then dug in as a natural way to enrich the soil. In the same way, wild plants enrich the soil where they are growing.

Broom, *Cytisus scoparius*, is a shrub, growing up to 2m (6ft) tall, with branched, green, flexible, five-angled stems and small, three-leaflet leaves. In early summer its green stems are transformed by the many yellow flowers that open in the leaf axils. They are followed by black pods which open explosively with sudden cracking sounds on hot days in late summer. This plant grows on acid sandy soils, in heathland and woods, in waste places and on roadsides throughout the British Isles and much of Europe, north to southern Scandinavia.

Dyer's Greenweed, *Genista tinctoria*, is a much-branched plant 1–2m (3–6ft) tall, with sprawling, smooth green stems and stalkless, lance-shaped or pointed-oblong leaves. In late summer the solitary yellow flowers appear in the axils of the uppermost leaves. The pods are smooth and flattened, opening explosively to scatter the seeds. This plant gets its name from the yellow dye extracted from it for centuries, mostly used for dying wool. It was also combined with woad to produce a green dye known as Kendal Green. It grows in pastures and meadows throughout much of Europe, except Portugal; in Britain it is found in England, Wales and southern Scotland, but not in Ireland. Hairy Greenweed, *G. pilosa*, is a similar but more or less prostrate plant found on heaths, stony hills and cliffs in western and central Europe. It is rare in Britain, found in a few places along the coasts of southern England and Wales.

Petty Whin or Needle Furze, *Genista anglica*, is like a spiny, woody version of Dyer's Greenweed, with similar leaves and flowers on brown, spiny stems. The spines are curved, held in the axils of the leaves. The plant grows on dry moors and heaths, scattered throughout western Europe and much of Great Britain, but is not found in Ireland. **Spanish Gorse**, *G. hispanica*, is another spiny shrub, with the majority of spines on old branches. It has head-like clusters of 5–12 bright yellow flowers terminating its stems in summer. This plant is found in mountain meadows in Spain and France.

Spanish Broom, *Spartium junceum*, is a wild plant from the dry hills of the Mediterranean region and southwestern Europe; it is grown in gardens in other parts of Europe, including the south of England, and has escaped in some areas. This spindly shrub grows up to 3m (9ft) tall and has flexible, green, cylindrical stems with few leaves (and these soon fall off). The flowers appear around midsummer; they are bright yellow and fragrant, borne all along the stems and followed by silky-hairy, flattened pods, each with several poisonous seeds.

Gorse or Whin, *Ulex europaeus*, is another spiny plant, with numerous branched spines replacing the leaves on older stems. It is a much-branched shrub growing up to 2m (6ft) tall, with many green stems and flowering from December to June. It grows in heaths and grassy places, usually on acid soils, throughout western Europe and the British Isles. The similar but smaller Western Gorse, *U. galli*, grows only in acid soils, often on heaths, also throughout western Europe and the British Isles, but more commonly in the west. It comes into bloom just as the flowering season of Whin comes to a close, blooming from July to September, with bright golden-yellow flowers often tinged with red. Both species produce hairy pods, those of gorse bursting in the hot sun of summer and those of Western Gorse in spring. Gorse flowers can be made into wine if the collector is willing to battle with the spines.

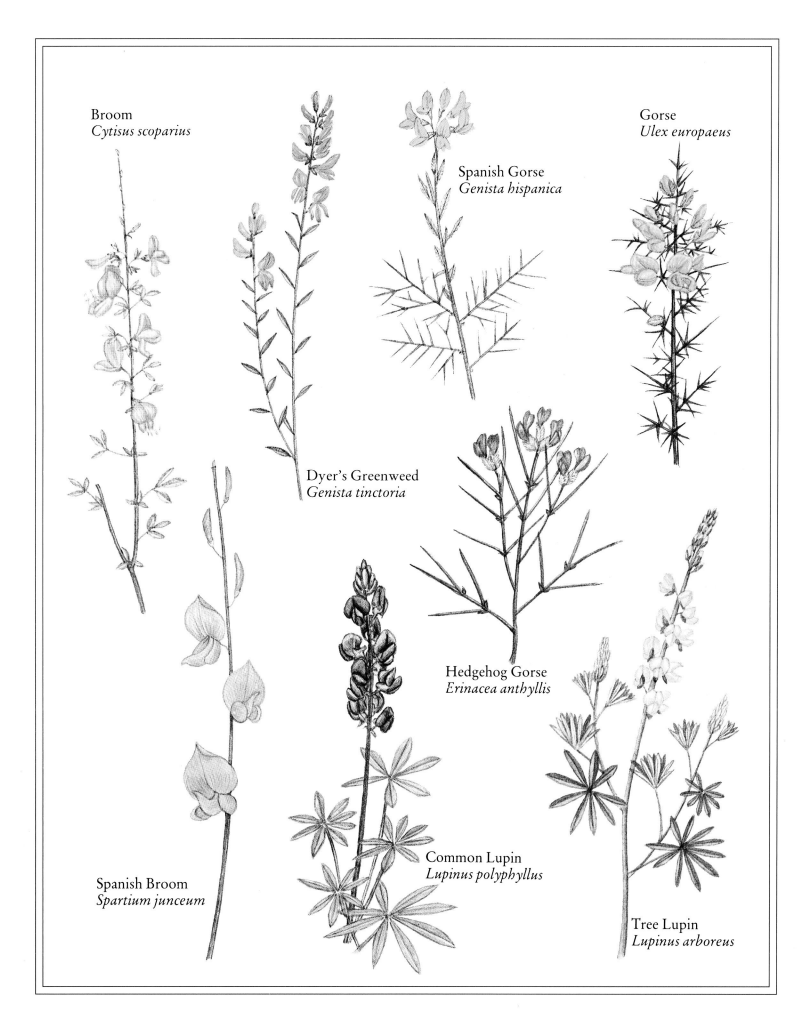

Broom
Cytisus scoparius

Spanish Gorse
Genista hispanica

Gorse
Ulex europaeus

Dyer's Greenweed
Genista tinctoria

Hedgehog Gorse
Erinacea anthyllis

Spanish Broom
Spartium junceum

Common Lupin
Lupinus polyphyllus

Tree Lupin
Lupinus arboreus

Hedgehog Gorse, *Erinacea anthyllis* (p. 71), grows in Spain and France in dry places in the mountains, and is planted in rock gardens elsewhere in Europe, including Britain. It is a low-growing, intricately branched plant only 30cm (1ft) tall, forming cushions of stiff, spiny, grey-green stems with few leaves but many blue-violet, pea-like flowers in early summer.

Lupins, *Lupinus* species, are herbaceous plants with alternate, palmately compound leaves and racemes of showy flowers terminating the erect stems. The flowers are typically pea-like in form, the standard with its sides bent backwards. Most lupins are native to North America and the Mediterranean but some, like **Common Lupin**, *L. polyphyllus* (p. 71), are grown for ornament and fodder in other areas across much of Europe and Britain. It has stout, erect stems up to 1.5m (5ft) tall, palmate leaves with 9–13 broadly lance-shaped leaflets, and long, dense terminal racemes of blue flowers. This has been one of the most important species in the development of garden varieties. Both it and its hybrid offspring may grow wild in grassy waste places, roadsides and railway embankments.

Tree Lupin, *Lupinus arboreus* (p. 71), is a semi-shrubby plant, with erect branched stems up to 2m (6ft) tall and more or less silky palmate leaves. Each one has 5–12 leaflets. The flowers grow in loose racemes and are usually yellow or white. This plant is a native of California, now naturalized around the coasts of Great Britain, southern Ireland and southern Europe. It grows on sand-dunes and in waste places, stabilizing the sand and enriching the poor 'soil' with its root nodules. White Lupin, *L. albus*, is native to southeastern Europe but is grown for fodder in other areas. It has a few white, blue-tipped flowers growing in loose racemes.

Goat's-rue or French Lilac, *Galega officinalis*, grows wild in Europe, beside streams and in ditches, or in damp meadows and fields; in Britain it is most often found as a garden plant, but may grow wild in waste places. It is a perennial, producing a clump of erect, leafy stems 60–150cm (2–5ft) tall; the leaves are pinnate with 9–17 pointed-oblong leaflets and the flowers grow in erect racemes on long stalks in the leaf axils in early summer. They are pale lilac or white in colour and followed by long, red-brown pods.

Liquorice, *Glycyrrhiza glabra*, comes originally from southeastern Europe; it is also cultivated in many other parts of Europe (but not in Britain), grown for its rhizomes from which liquorice is extracted, and sometimes escapes to grow wild. Liquorice is used in cough medicines and laxatives, and as a flavouring for medicines and sweets. It is also used in brewing and in the tobacco industry. The plant is a perennial, with deep-growing, sweet-tasting rhizomes and erect, hairless stems up to 1.5m (5ft) tall, with many pinnate leaves. Each has 9–17 elliptical leaflets, sticky on the underside. The bluish or violet flowers are borne in summer in dense spike-like racemes on long stalks growing from the leaf axils. They are followed by flattened, hairless pods.

The **Milk-vetches** are a very large group of about 2000 species in the genus *Astragalus*, found throughout most of the world, with over 130 in Europe. These are herbaceous plants with pinnate leaves and typical pea flowers growing in racemes in the leaf axils. They have characteristic ovoid or oblong, often two-celled pods which may be smooth or very hairy.

Wild Liquorice or Milk-vetch, *Astragalus glycyphyllos*, is a straggling, hairless, perennial plant with branched stems 30–100cm (1–3ft) tall and many pinnate leaves. Each leaf has 4–6 pairs of rounded leaflets. The creamy-white or greenish-cream flowers appear in the latter half of summer in dense racemes terminating long stalks in the leaf axils; they are followed by narrow, slightly curved pods. This plant grows in rough grassy places and scrub, locally throughout Great Britain to central Scotland; it is absent from Ireland. It is found across much of Europe, except the extreme north.

Purple Milk-vetch, *Astragalus danica*, is a much more slender plant which grows only 40cm (15in) tall. It has pinnate leaves with 6–13 pairs of leaflets and dense, head-like racemes of purple flowers terminating long stalks growing from the leaf axils. In Great Britain it grows in short grassland, on chalk and limestone, sometimes in sand-dunes, mainly in the east; it is also found across much of Europe, north to southern Sweden and in mountains in the south of its range.

The Wild Peas or Vetchlings, *Lathyrus* species, and the Vetches and Tares, *Vicia* species, are both groups of climbing or scrambling plants, clinging to anything within reach with modified leaflets which have become tendrils.

Many of the *Lathyrus* species, such as the Sweet Peas and the Everlasting Pea of gardens, have winged stems. There are over 50 wild species in this genus in Europe. **Yellow Vetchling**, *L. aphaca*, is a scrambling annual plant, its thin, winged stems growing up to 1m (3ft) tall. Its leaves lack leaflets, for they have been replaced by simple coiled tendrils which grow from the axils of large, broadly arrow-shaped stipules. The flowers are yellow, borne singly on erect stalks in the axils of the stipules. This plant grows in dry, grassy places, often in sandy soils or chalk, across much of Europe, except the north. It has become naturalized in southern England, but is not common.

Meadow Vetchling, *Lathyrus pratensis*, is a scrambling perennial plant, its thin, angled stems climbing by means of the tendrils on its leaves. The leaves are pinnate, each with one pair of leaflets and a branched tendril, and they grow from the axils of arrow-shaped, leaf-like stipules. Its flowers are yellow, borne in erect racemes on long stalks in the leaf axils, and followed by compressed black pods. This plant grows in rough, grassy places and meadows, on roadsides, in hedgerows and woodland margins throughout Europe and the British Isles.

Tuberous Pea, *Lathyrus tuberosus*, is yet another clambering species, this one a perennial up to 120cm (4ft) tall. It has angled stems, one pair of rounded leaflets and a branched tendril on each leaf, and relatively small arrow-shaped stipules. Its

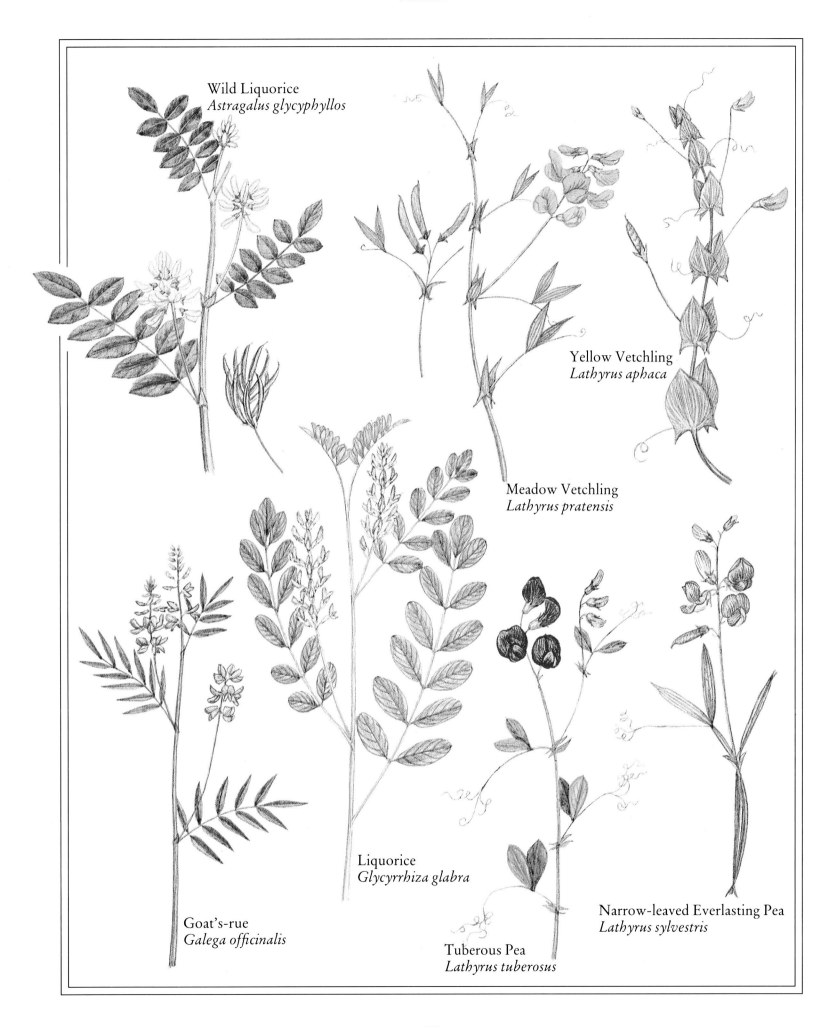

Wild Liquorice
Astragalus glycyphyllos

Yellow Vetchling
Lathyrus aphaca

Meadow Vetchling
Lathyrus pratensis

Liquorice
Glycyrrhiza glabra

Goat's-rue
Galega officinalis

Tuberous Pea
Lathyrus tuberosus

Narrow-leaved Everlasting Pea
Lathyrus sylvestris

racemes of crimson flowers are borne on erect stalks. Its roots bear fleshy, edible tubers. This plant is found in fields and vineyards across much of Europe, except the north and Portugal. It has been introduced into England and southern Scotland, where it is a rare inhabitant of cornfields and hedges; it is sometimes grown in gardens.

Narrow-leaved Everlasting Pea, *Lathyrus sylvestris* (p. 73), has broadly winged stems and a pair of narrow leaflets on each tendrilled leaf. Stems and leaflets look similar. The flowers are rose pink, often tinged with green or purple; they grow in racemes on erect stems and are followed by compressed, brown pods. This plant grows in woods, hedgerows and thickets, scattered across most of Europe and Great Britain. It is most common in southern England and absent from Ireland.

The **Sea Pea**, *Lathyrus japonicus*, is a very local plant, growing on dunes and shingle beaches on the coast of western and northern Europe; in Britain it is found from East Anglia to Cornwall. It has prostrate, angled stems, 3–6 pairs of soft, slightly fleshy, often bluish, elliptical leaflets on each tendrilled leaf, and broadly triangular stipules. In the axils of the leaves grow racemes of flowers on long stalks; they are purple at first, becoming blue as they age.

In **Bitter Vetch**, *Lathyrus montanus*, the tendrils are reduced to fine points at the tips of the leaves. This is an erect, not a scrambling plant, with winged stems up to 50cm (20in) tall, and leaves with 2–4 pairs of linear to elliptical leaflets. It produces loose racemes of crimson flowers on long stalks, the flowers turning blue or green as they age, and followed by hairless, red-brown pods. This perennial plant has swollen, tuberous roots and creeping rhizomes. It grows in hills and mountains, in rough grassland, woods and hedgerows across much of Europe; it is scattered throughout the British Isles, except in East Anglia, more commonly in the west.

There are about 55 *Vicia* species in Europe. Some are crop plants, like *Vicia faba*, the Broad Bean. One subspecies of **Common Vetch**, *V. sativa* subsp. *sativa*, is cultivated for fodder and as a green manure. However, the subspecies *nigra* is a native wild plant, growing in grassy places, fields and hedges throughout Europe and the British Isles. It is an annual, with slender stems and pairs of violet or purple flowers in the axils of the pinnate leaves. Its stipules are often toothed and dark-blotched and its tendrils are branched.

Bush Vetch, *Vicia sepium*, is an almost hairless perennial species, a trailing plant which may take over a large patch of ground with its branched stems, pinnate leaves and hungry tendrils. The stems grow to 1m (3ft) tall and are slender, the leaves have 5–9 pairs of ovate leaflets and a branched tendril at the tip, and the stipules are half arrow-shaped and usually untoothed. The flowers appear in summer in clusters of 2–6 in the leaf axils; they are pale bluish-purple and followed by black, beaked pods. Plants may be found in grassy places, in hedgerows and thickets across Europe and the British Isles.

Yellow Vetch, *Vicia lutea*, is a tufted perennial plant, with branched, often prostrate stems and pinnate leaves. It varies in texture from smooth to hairy, has 3–10 pairs of lance-shaped leaflets on each leaf, together with a branched tendril, and has small, triangular stipules. The flowers appear in summer and are pale yellow, borne on short stalks singly or in small clusters in the leaf axils. Yellow Vetch is a relatively uncommon plant found on cliffs and shingle beaches on the coasts of southern and western Europe, rarely in Great Britain (and then mostly in England). It is also introduced inland in some places.

Tufted Vetch, *Vicia cracca*, also called Cats-peas and Tinegrass, is probably one of the most familiar vetches, growing in meadows and fields, along roadsides and in woods throughout Europe and the British Isles. It is a scrambling plant up to 1m (3ft) tall, with pinnate leaves ending in branched tendrils that twine around anything they contact. In summer it produces showy, one-sided racemes of bright bluish-purple flowers growing on long stalks in the axils of the leaves. They are followed by squarish pods which crack open in hot summer sun to release the seeds.

Wood Vetch, *Vicia sylvatica*, grows in hills and mountains, in rocky woods and bushy places, or by the sea on shingle banks and cliffs. It is scattered throughout most of Europe and Great Britain. This is a hairless perennial plant, scrambling up to 2m (6ft) in height (but often only half this size), with pinnate leaves, branched tendrils and semi-circular, toothed stipules. The flowers appear in summer in loose, one-sided racemes in the leaf axils; they are white with purple veins.

Some of the *Vicia* species are weeds—the tares of the Bible. **Hairy Tare**, *V. hirsuta*, was once a troublesome weed of grain fields, contaminating the harvest so that the flour was unpalatable. It grows throughout Europe and the British Isles in fields and grassy places. This little annual plant is often only 30cm (1ft) tall, with branched, slender stems and very narrow leaflets on its pinnate leaves, scrambling through other plants with branched tendrils. In summer it bears small racemes of purplish or whitish flowers. Smooth Tare, *V. tetrasperma*, is a similar plant found in grassy places. It has only 3–6 pairs of leaflets on each leaf (compared to 4–10 pairs in Hairy Tare) and pale purple flowers borne singly or in pairs.

The **Restharrows**, *Ononis* species, are small shrubs or herbaceous plants. They have simple or clover-like leaves in which the veins end in teeth at the edges of the leaflets, and conspicuous stipules fused to the leaf stalks. There are nearly 50 species in Europe. **Common Restharrow**, *O. repens* (p. 77), is a subshrubby plant, with woody, branched stems, often prostrate and rooting near the base, turning upwards near the tips and growing about 60cm (2ft) tall. Both stems and clover-like leaves are hairy. The plants flower in summer, producing loose, leafy racemes of pinkish-purple flowers in the axils of the leaves. This restharrow grows in rough grassy places, on

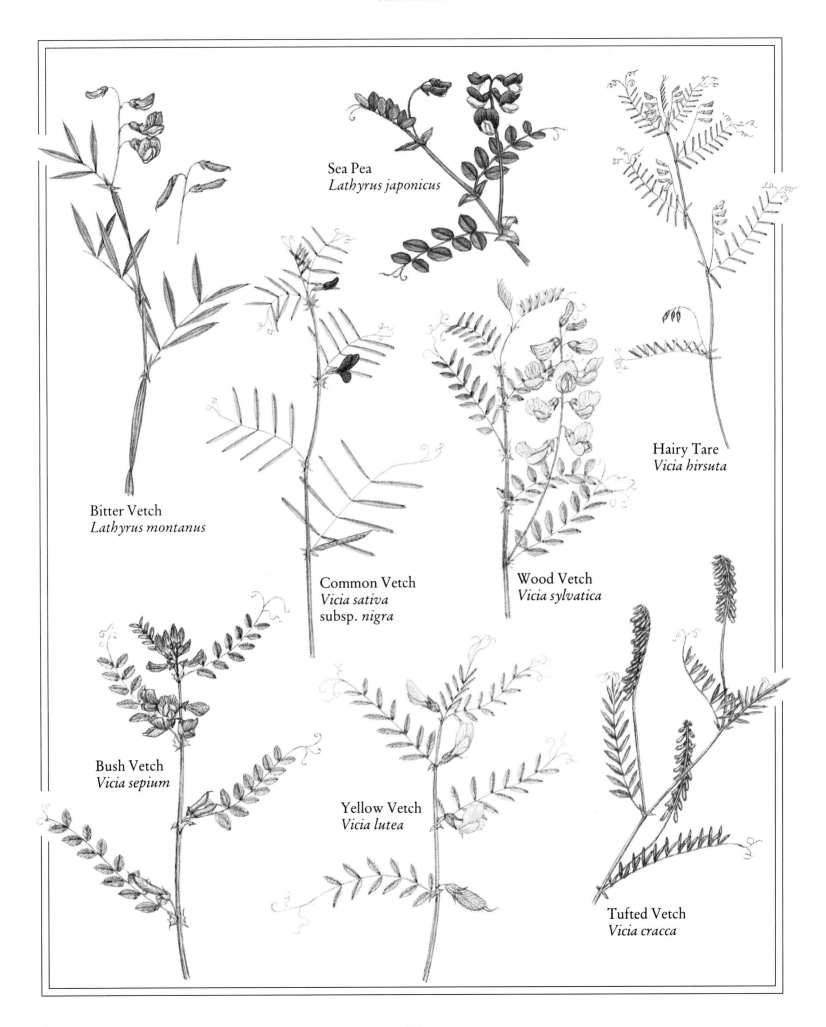

Sea Pea
Lathyrus japonicus

Hairy Tare
Vicia hirsuta

Bitter Vetch
Lathyrus montanus

Common Vetch
Vicia sativa
subsp. *nigra*

Wood Vetch
Vicia sylvatica

Bush Vetch
Vicia sepium

Yellow Vetch
Vicia lutea

Tufted Vetch
Vicia cracca

banks, roadsides and in pastures, on dry calcareous or basic soils across much of Europe, and is scattered throughout the British Isles, becoming rare in western Scotland and Ireland.

Spiny Restharrow, *Ononis spinosa*, is a similar, slightly taller plant, but its stems do not root at the base; instead, they have two lines of hairs rather than hairs all over, and their side shoots end in stiff spines. The leaves have narrow leaflets and the flowers are pink or reddish-purple. This species grows in rough grassy places, on banks, roadsides and pastures on dry calcareous soils throughout Europe. It is scattered across England, becoming rare in Wales and the southwest.

Ribbed Melilot, *Melilotus officinalis*, is a tall biennial plant up to 1.5m (5ft) in height, with many slender racemes of yellow flowers in late summer. It has clover-like leaves with toothed, elliptical leaflets and a scent of coumarin (new-mown hay), especially when drying. It grows beside roadsides, in waste places and fields throughout continental Europe and has been introduced to the British Isles, where it is common in England and eastern Ireland, rare in Wales and Scotland. **Tall Melilot**, *M. altissima*, is often perennial in its growth. It has a similar distribution to Ribbed Melilot. **White Melilot**, *M. alba*, with white flowers, also grows in similar places across Europe and has become naturalized in England.

Several small annual plants in the genus *Medicago*, are found in Europe and the British Isles. **Black Medick**, *M. lupulina*, is a much-branched, trailing, often prostrate plant, sometimes growing 30cm (1ft) tall or more, especially if supported by surrounding vegetation. It has small, clover-like leaves with rounded, often toothed and notched leaflets, and heads of tiny, bright yellow flowers on long stalks in the leaf axils. The plant is easy to distinguish in fruit because its ripe pods resemble tiny, black, coiled, kidney-shaped shells. Black Medick grows in grassy places throughout Europe and the British Isles, becoming more local in Scotland.

Spotted Medick, *Medicago arabica*, is another annual, a sprawling plant with stems growing up to 50cm (20in) tall. Its clover-like leaves have dark blotches in the centre of each leaflet and its larger, yellow flowers are borne in small clusters on long stalks in the leaf axils. The pods form round, spiny spirals. This plant grows in grassy and waste places, especially on sandy soils across most of Europe; in Britain it is confined mostly to southern and eastern England.

Alfalfa or Lucerne, *Medicago sativa*, is a hairy perennial with erect or sprawling stems growing up to 90cm (3ft) tall. It has clover-like leaves and racemes of blue-violet flowers in the leaf axils and terminating the stems. The pods that follow are twisted into a spiral with a hole through the centre. This plant comes originally from Asia, is cultivated as a forage plant in many parts of Europe and has become naturalized in grassy, waste and cultivated places in many countries. In the British Isles it is most likely to be found in England, more locally in Scotland, Wales and Ireland.

Classical Fenugreek, *Trigonella foenum-graecum*, has been used in herb medicine since the times of the ancient Egyptians (and probably before that). Today it is grown as cattle fodder in central and southern Europe and used in veterinary medicine; its seeds are still used in herbal medicine, especially made into a poultice to relieve abscesses and boils, or as a tonic; the seeds are also used in curry. Fenugreek is an erect, annual plant, growing about 50cm (20in) tall. It has many clover-like leaves and solitary or paired, creamy-white flowers in the axils of the uppermost leaves. The pods are narrow and sickle-like. This plant comes from Asia; it has been introduced to much of Europe but is absent from the north and from the British Isles. Several other *Trigonella* species grow wild in Europe, including Star-fruited Fenugreek, *T. monspeliaca*. It is a small annual with clover-like leaves and yellow flowers found in waste places across much of Europe, except the north.

Bird's-foot Fenugreek, *Trifolium ornithopodioides* (p. 79), was at one time placed in the genus *Trigonella* with Classical Fenugreek, but modern botanists think it more closely related to the clovers. It is a branched, little annual plant growing 20cm (8in) tall at most, with slender stems and clover-like leaves, each with three oval, serrated leaflets. In summer it produces small clusters of 2–4 pinkish-white flowers on long stalks in the leaf axils, followed by curved pods. This plant grows in dry, sandy and gravelly places, often near the coast in short grassland, in scattered localities around western and southern Europe, England, Wales and eastern Ireland.

Clovers are more familiar members of the genus *Trifolium*. White Clover, with its creeping stems, white-banded leaflets and heads of white flowers is known to everyone who has played in grass as a child; or to anyone who has searched for the proverbial lucky leaf with four leaflets instead of three. Red Clover is almost as familiar, with its much bigger clumps of leafy stems and large red flower heads, on roadsides and rough grassland. There are nearly 300 *Trifolium* species, mostly found in north temperate regions, with about 100 in Europe. Several are grown as fodder or forage crops.

Clovers are, in general, distinguishable from other leguminous plants by their leaves with three leaflets, their stipules joined to the leaf stalks, and particularly by their heads or dense head-like spikes of flowers. Their flowers are rich in nectar and much sought out by bees, both hive bees and bumble bees. Honey made from clover nectar is one of the best kinds. The petals, and often the sepals, persist on the flower heads when the pods are formed, so that the whole thing looks like a brown, withered parody of its former self.

White Clover, *Trifolium repens* (p. 79), is the one found most often in lawns. Often unwanted, it is actually useful, since the presence of its roots, with their nodules, improves the soil; it is often grown as a forage plant. In the wild it grows in all kinds of grassy places, usually on heavy soils, throughout Europe and the British Isles. This is a creeping species with

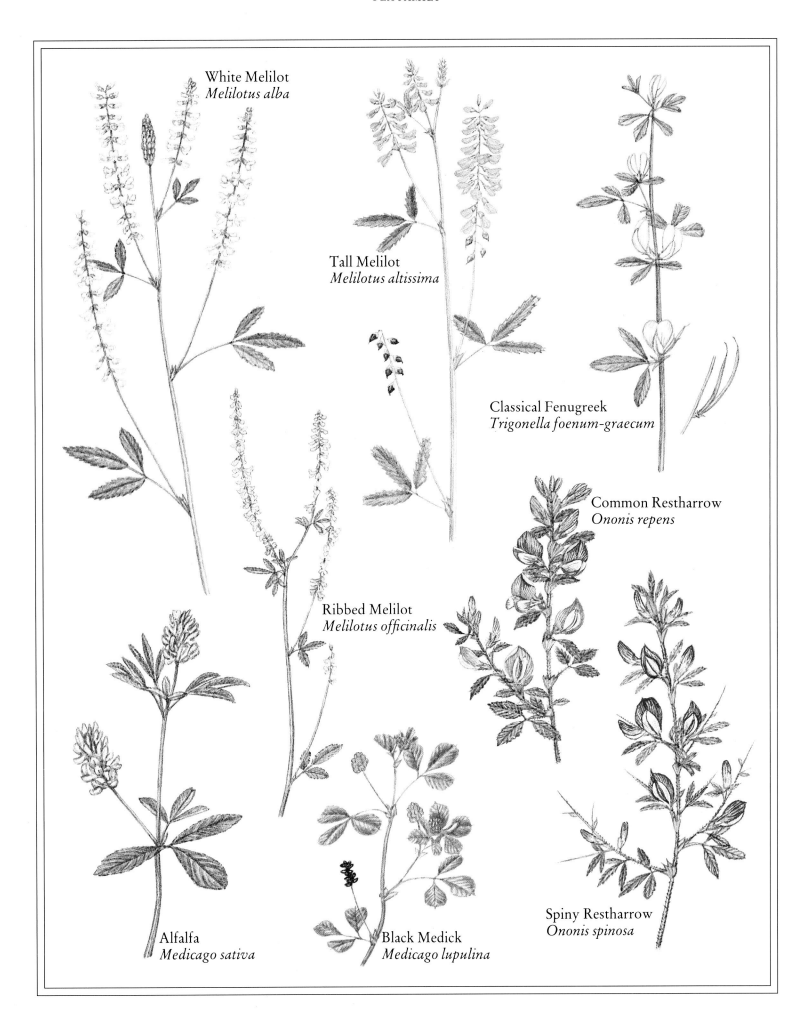

White Melilot
Melilotus alba

Tall Melilot
Melilotus altissima

Classical Fenugreek
Trigonella foenum-graecum

Common Restharrow
Ononis repens

Ribbed Melilot
Melilotus officinalis

Alfalfa
Medicago sativa

Black Medick
Medicago lupulina

Spiny Restharrow
Ononis spinosa

stems that root at the nodes and leaves with three rounded leaflets; there is a white, angled band partly encircling the base of each leaflet. The globular heads of white or pinkish flowers grow on long stalks from the leaf axils in summer; each head has numerous flowers and, as in many clovers, the petals are more or less united into a tube with the standard folded around the wings. As the flowers wither, the whole head assumes a drooping appearance. -

Alsike Clover, *Trifolium hybridum*, is also grown for fodder and as a forage crop. It is similar to White Clover, but its stems are more erect and do not root at the nodes, its leaflets lack white markings and its flowers are purple at first, becoming pink or white as they age. This plant grows on roadsides and fields throughout Europe and the British Isles (where it is most common in the south and east).

Strawberry Clover, *Trifolium fragiferum*, is another creeping species, with prostrate stems rooting at the nodes and long-stalked leaves with oval, unmarked leaflets. It is often mistaken for White Clover, but its flower heads are pink and its fruiting heads are quite distinctive. The upper lip of each calyx becomes inflated so that, when all the flowers have formed pods, the head comes to resemble a hairy strawberry. This plant grows in grassy places throughout much of Europe; in Great Britain it is most common in pastures on heavy soils south and east of a line from the Humber to the Severn, although it is found throughout, and it grows locally in Ireland.

Many varieties of **Red Clover**, *Trifolium pratense*, are grown as forage crops, each one depending on a different bee for pollination. This is because they flower at different times of the summer, when different species of bees are flying, and because the bees can only pollinate the flowers if their tongues are long enough to reach the bottom of the flower tube. In the wild Red Clovers are found in all kinds of grassy places throughout Europe and the British Isles. This is a variable perennial plant, forming a straggling clump up to 60cm (2ft) tall, with thin stems and many leaves. The leaves have narrow, pointed leaflets, often with a whitish, crescent-shaped mark towards the base. The pink-purple, ovoid heads of flowers are terminal, borne in summer between two leaves.

Zigzag Clover, *Trifolium medium*, gets its name from the way its stems appear to zigzag from node to node. It is rather like Red Clover, a straggling perennial plant with reddish-purple flowers, but its narrow leaflets lack markings. It is sometimes grown for forage; in the wild it grows in grassy places, fields and open woods, found locally across Europe and the British Isles.

Sulphur Clover, *Trifolium ochroleucon*, has yellow-white flowers in globular heads. It is a hairy perennial plant, with more or less erect stems and lance-shaped or elliptical, unmarked leaflets. It grows in grassy places across much of Europe, but is more or less confined to East Anglia in Britain, growing in damp, shady places on heavy clay soils.

Crimson Clover, *Trifolium incarnatum*, is a distinctive clover, cultivated throughout much of Europe as a fodder crop and often escaping to grow wild in grassy places. In Britain it is grown mostly in southern England. It is an annual, usually with a single unbranched stem, papery stipules, leaves with rounded leaflets and a terminal, cylindrical head of crimson flowers. The head look hairy because the calyces are covered in dense hairs. Occasionally the flowers may be pink or white.

Hare's-foot Clover, *Trifolium arvense*, has many striking heads of flowers, silky-hairy from their downy calyces which are longer than the petals. The flowers are tiny, pink or white in colour. This is an annual or biennial species, often only 10–20cm (4–8in) tall, with branched stems and leaves with narrow leaflets, the uppermost stalkless. It grows in dry, sandy fields and grassy heaths, in waste places and roadsides, often on acid soils, sometimes on sand-dunes, throughout Europe and scattered across the British Isles.

Hop-trefoil, *Trifolium campestre*, is one of several small *Trifolium* species. These trefoils are annual or biennial, straggling, branched plants, with clover-like leaves and tiny heads of yellow flowers in summer. Hop-trefoil grows 20–30cm (8–12in) tall at most; even so it is more robust than Lesser Yellow Trefoil, *T. dubium*, which has more slender stems and smaller flower heads (only 8–9mm [$^1/_4$in] in diameter as opposed to 10–15mm [$^1/_3$–$^2/_3$in]). They both have one-seeded pods folded in dried petals; the whole head is supposed to resemble a hop flower, hence the name hop-trefoil. Both species grow in dry, grassy places, on roadsides and banks, commons and waste places throughout Europe and the British Isles, rarely in the far north.

Bird's-foot Trefoil is one of over 70 common names given to the species *Lotus corniculatus* (p. 81). Others include Eggs-and-bacon, Cat's Claw, Devil's Fingers, Shoes-and-stockings and Fingers-and-thumbs, together with variations on these themes. The question of why this plant has merited such attention seems to have no answer. For this is a small, more or less prostrate, trailing plant with no economic significance, nor any medicinal folklore. It is found throughout Europe and the British Isles, in grassy places, pastures and heaths. It is a perennial, with a clump of slender, leafy stems and many compound leaves, each with three leaflets. In summer the plant bears heads of yellow, often red-tinged flowers growing on long stalks from the leaf axils and followed by elongated pods, which twist and split open when ripe and dry. Greater Bird's-foot Trefoil, *L. uliginosus*, is a less common but larger plant, with hairier, more erect stems. It is found in damp, grassy places across much of Europe and the British Isles.

Dragon's Teeth, *Tetragonolobus maritimus* (p. 81), resembles the *Lotus* species; it is a downy perennial with sprawling stems and clover-like leaves with oval leaflets. The pale yellow flowers appear in summer, borne singly in the leaf axils and followed by oblong pods; these are square in cross-section

Hop-trefoil
Trifolium campestre

Sulphur Clover
Trifolium ochroleucon

Crimson Clover
Trifolium incarnatum

White Clover
Trifolium repens

Bird's-foot Fenugreek
Trifolium ornithopodioides

Zigzag Clover
Trifolium medium

Alsike Clover
Trifolium hybridum

Hare's-foot Clover
Trifolium arvense

Strawberry Clover
Trifolium fragiferum

Red Clover
Trifolium pratense

and winged on the angles. This plant grows in marshes and damp grassland in western and central Europe, north to southern Sweden. It has become naturalized in rough grassland on calcareous soils in a few parts of southern England.

Bird's-foot, *Ornithopus perpusillus*, is a spreading, prostrate plant, a finely hairy annual with slender stems and pinnate leaves. Each leaf has 7–13 pairs of elliptical leaflets, the lowest pair right at the base of the leaf stalk and looking a bit like stipules; the real stipules are minute. The flowers appear in summer in small clusters subtended by pinnate bracts at the ends of long stalks in the leaf axils; each one is white with red veins. The clusters of pods that follow look like birds' feet; each pod is beaked and segmented and splits into segments rather than splitting open. This little plant grows in dry, sandy and gravelly places, in short grassland and pastures, waste and cultivated ground. It is scattered across much of Europe north to southern Sweden, also across England and Wales, but rarely in Scotland and Ireland.

Kidney Vetch or Ladies' Fingers, *Anthyllis vulneraria*, is a traditional medicinal plant used to treat wounds and slow-healing cuts (hence *vulneraria*). It is a perennial, with sprawling, leafy stems up to 60cm (2ft) tall and pinnate leaves, each leaf with 5–15 pointed-elliptical leaflets, the terminal leaflet much larger than the others. The flowers are almost showy, borne in heads cupped by leaf-like bracts at the ends of erect stems in summer. They are normally yellow but may be red, and turn brown as they fade; and their attraction comes not only from their bright colours but also from their white-woolly calyces. Plants grow in dry grassland, often on calcareous soils and near the sea, in mountains and on screes, scattered throughout Europe and the British Isles.

Crown Vetch, *Coronilla varia*, is another medicinal plant, containing a glycoside that stimulates heart action; because of this it is quite poisonous. It is a straggling, hairless, perennial growing up to 1m (3ft) tall, with spreading stems and pinnate leaves. These have 7–12 pairs of elliptical leaflets. The flowers are multicoloured, with a pink standard, whitish wings and a pink, purple-tipped keel; they are borne in heads on long stalks growing from leaf axils in summer. The pods are narrow and four-angled, and they break into segments. This plant grows in grassy places and waste ground across much of Europe; it is naturalized in a number of places in Britain.

Horseshoe Vetch, *Hippocrepis comosa*, is a variable perennial plant, woody at the base, with spreading, branched stems, often prostrate and bearing pinnate leaves on long stalks. The leaves have 7–17 linear to ovate leaflets; in their axils are long stalks with loose, umbel-like clusters of yellow flowers followed by distinctive pods. These are compressed from side to side and twisted into many horseshoe-shaped sections. Horseshoe Vetch grows in dry grassland on chalk and limestone, and on sea cliffs across much of Europe, except the north. It is also found in England, rarely in Wales.

Sainfoin, *Onobrychis viciifolia*, is probably native to central Europe but has been cultivated in other areas of the Continent and in England as a fodder plant; nowadays it can still be found wild as a relict of this pattern in areas where it is no longer grown, usually in grassy and waste places on calcareous soils. It is an erect perennial plant up to 60cm (2ft) tall, with pinnate leaves; each leaf has 6–14 pairs of pointed-oblong leaflets. The bright pink, purple-veined flowers grow in dense racemes on long stalks in the leaf axils, so that they overtop the leaves. The pods are distinctive, small, reticulate and single-seeded, spiny on the lower margins.

Wood Sorrel family
Oxalidaceae

There are 3 genera and nearly 900 species in this family, mainly tropical in their distribution but also found in temperate regions. They are mostly herbs, several being grown in gardens and rock gardens. Others are weeds of the kind that cause gardeners to despair because although they are small and fragile-looking plants, they are often difficult to eradicate.

Family features The flowers are hermaphrodite and regular, with five sepals and petals, ten stamens and a superior ovary with five carpels. They are either solitary or borne in cymes. The fruits are usually capsules. The leaves are compound and clover-like, with three rounded leaflets notched at the tips and jointed to the leaf stalk; they often exhibit sleep movements by folding downwards at night.

Most plants in this family belong to the genus *Oxalis*, with about 800 species. **Wood Sorrel**, *O. acetosella* (p. 83), forms attractive carpets of bright green leaves on shady banks, growing among rocks and wherever there is plenty of humus, sometimes on rotting trees, in woods and hedgebanks (especially beneath beech and oak) throughout Europe and the British Isles. Its leaves grow directly from many thin rhizomes, on long stalks only 15cm (6in) tall at most; each has three leaflets which fold down at night. The flowers appear in spring, growing singly on long stalks directly from the rhizomes; they are white with lilac veins. These flowers produce few seeds; most of the seeds come from the summer flowers which do not open, forming capsules without pollination.

Upright Yellow Sorrel, *Oxalis europaea* (p. 83), is a cosmopolitan garden weed, probably native to North America originally but now found in many parts of Europe and scattered throughout the British Isles. This is a perennial, spreading by slender underground stems and with solitary, more or less upright, leafy stems. The leaves are clover-like and fold down at night, and the yellow flowers grow in small clusters on long stalks from the leaf axils. They are followed by seedpods borne on erect stalks, a feature that serves to distinguish this species

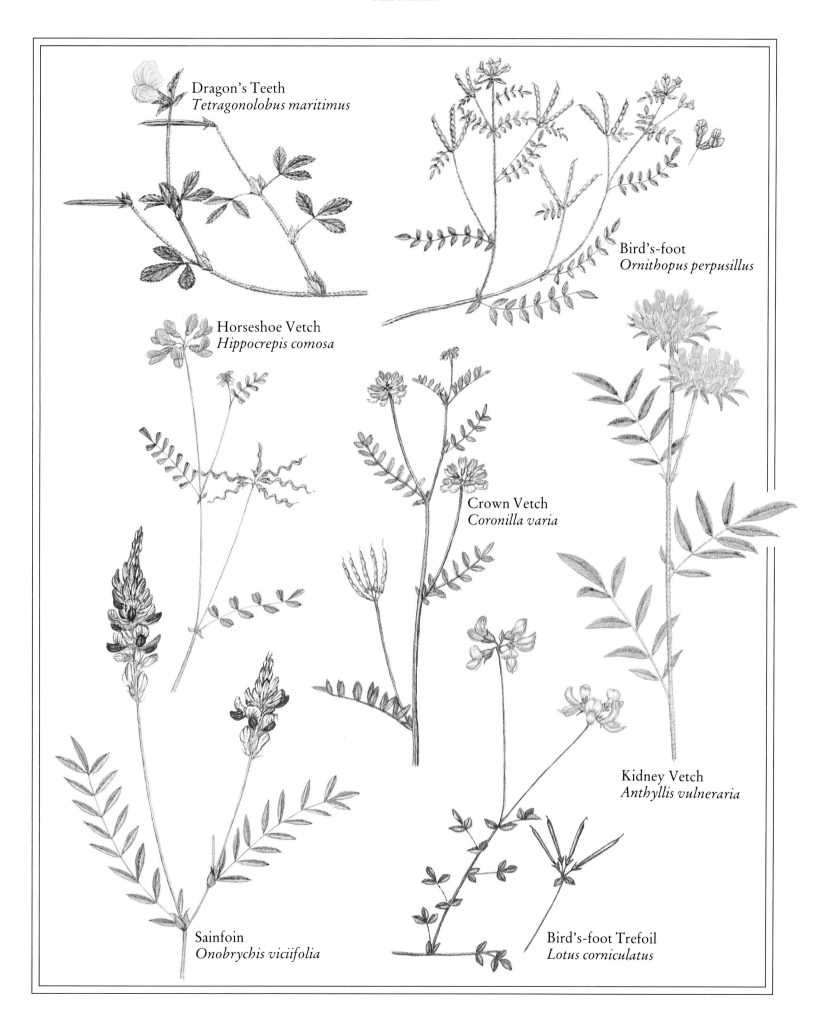

Dragon's Teeth
Tetragonolobus maritimus

Bird's-foot
Ornithopus perpusillus

Horseshoe Vetch
Hippocrepis comosa

Crown Vetch
Coronilla varia

Kidney Vetch
Anthyllis vulneraria

Sainfoin
Onobrychis viciifolia

Bird's-foot Trefoil
Lotus corniculatus

from **Procumbent Yellow Sorrel**, *O. corniculata*, which bears its seedpods on deflexed stalks. This latter species lacks underground stems, but roots at the nodes of its rather sprawling stems instead. It is another garden weed, often present as a variety with purple leaves, introduced to Europe and the British Isles from the tropics. In Britain it is most often found in southwestern England, becoming less common further north and in Ireland.

Flax family
Linaceae

There are about 12 genera and nearly 300 species in this family of herbs and shrubs, found in tropical and temperate regions of the world. Many have flowers similar to those of the Oxalidaceae, but flaxes have simple entire leaves, a feature that immediately distinguishes them from the wood sorrels.

Family features The flowers are hermaphrodite and regular, with five overlapping sepals and five contorted, often fleeting petals. There are five stamens, often joined into a ring at the base of the filaments, sometimes alternating with five sterile stamens. The ovary is superior, with 2–6 carpels. The flowers are frequently borne in cymes or racemes. The fruits are usually capsules. The leaves are simple and usually alternately arranged, with or without stipules.

There are several garden plants in the family, including **Perennial Flax**, *Linum perenne*, with flowers of sky blue. This smooth, blue-green plant is a perennial, with several erect, rigid stems, 30–90cm (1–3ft) tall, and numerous erect, linear leaves (each with a single vein). It bears loosely branched, leafy clusters of flowers around midsummer. In the wild it grows very locally in calcareous grassland in eastern England, and in mountain meadows in central and western Europe.

Pale Flax, *Linum bienne*, is similar, but may be biennial or perennial in its growth pattern, has branched stems and smaller, pale blue flowers with petals that fall soon after the flowers open. Its linear leaves mostly have three veins. This plant grows in dry grassland, often on calcareous soils and near the sea, mostly in southern England, south Wales and southeastern Ireland in the British Isles, also in France, Portugal and the Mediterranean region.

Common Flax, *Linum usitatissimum*, is a more robust, annual plant, with stems up to 60cm (2ft) tall, and lance-shaped leaves. It has pale blue flowers. Cultivated since ancient Egyptian times, it may escape to grow wild on roadsides and in waste places; however, it does not seem to be able to establish itself in the wild. Linen is produced from the fibres in the stems; the fibres are made into thread and then woven into cloth, or used to make canvas. Shorter fibres are used to make fine papers. The heated seeds are crushed to produce linseed oil, used in the manufacture of paints and varnishes, inks and soaps. Residues from these seeds are used for cattle feed.

Fairy Flax, *Linum catharticum*, is a tiny annual plant, only 5–20cm (2–8in) tall, with several wiry stems, a few lance-shaped, opposite leaves and numerous, minute white flowers in summer. It grows in grassland, often on calcareous soils, but also on heaths and moors, dunes and cliffs throughout Europe and the British Isles.

Allseed, *Radiola linoides*, is an even smaller annual, a scrap of a plant only 8cm (3in) tall at most. Usually its thread-like stems are repeatedly branched so that it looks like a tiny bush with many elliptical leaves and a multitude of white flowers; indeed, it resembles a chickweed rather than a flax. It grows on damp, bare patches, in sandy or peaty soils, on heaths and grassland locally throughout the British Isles and across much of Europe, except the north.

Geranium family
Geraniaceae

There are 5 genera and about 750 species, mostly herbs, in this small but familiar family. Almost everyone has grown potted geraniums at some time or another and the bright red or pink flowers of the most common varieties are seen in millions of window boxes. Their leaves have a peculiar scent which clings to the hands. Many geraniums have scented leaves, the scent varying with species, from lemon to apple, mint or eucalyptus.

Family features The flowers are more or less regular and hermaphrodite, with parts in fives: five free overlapping sepals, five free overlapping petals, 10–15 stamens, often joined at the base, and 3–5 carpels in the ovary. The fruits are lobed capsules in which the stigmas elongate to form long beaks, one to each lobe and with one seed in each lobe. The leaves are alternate, simple or compound, often palmately lobed, and they have stipules.

The houseplants known as 'geraniums' do, in fact, belong to the mostly tropical genus *Pelargonium*, whereas the true 'geraniums' are the wild crane's-bills which belong to the genus *Geranium*. The latter genus contains about 300 species of mainly temperate region plants, many of which are fine garden plants not as widely known or grown as they deserve to be.

Wild Crane's-bills, the *Geranium* species, are annual or perennial herbs, about 40 of which grow wild in Europe. **Meadow Crane's-bill**, *G. pratense* (p. 85), grows in meadows and on roadsides throughout much of Great Britain and across most of Europe (except Portugal). Several of its varieties and cultivars are also grown in gardens. It is typical of many members of the genus, a perennial plant with thick rhizomes and clumps of palmately compound leaves, sprinkled with blue-violet flowers in summer. The basal leaves of the clump are all

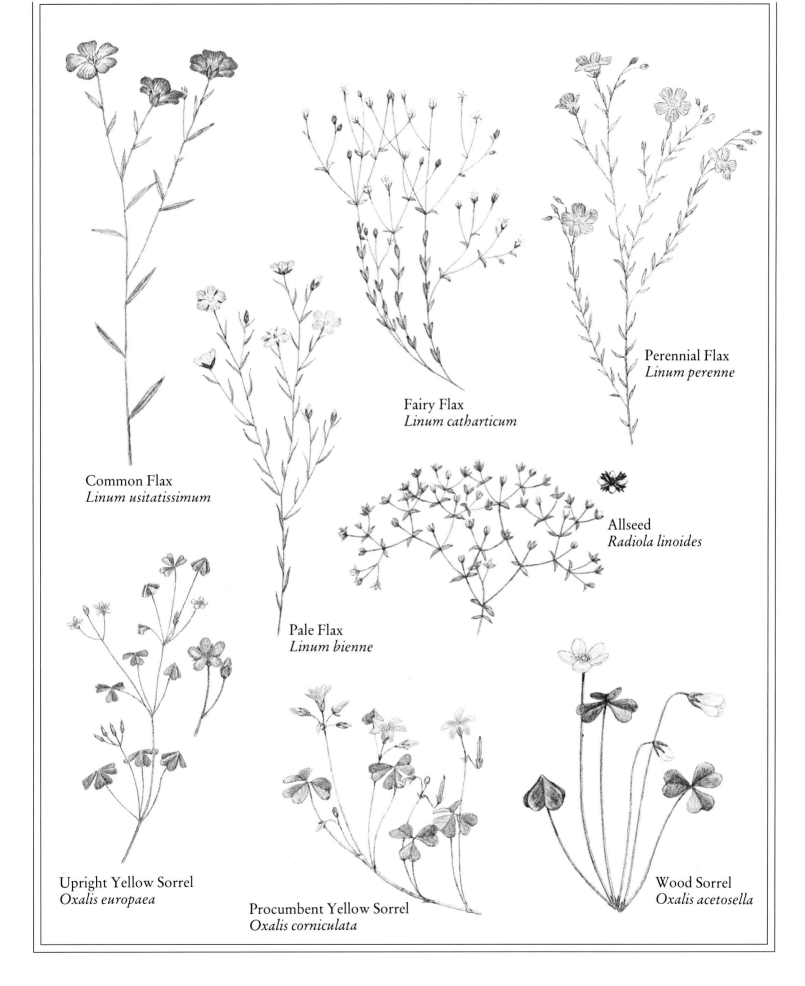

Common Flax
Linum usitatissimum

Fairy Flax
Linum catharticum

Perennial Flax
Linum perenne

Pale Flax
Linum bienne

Allseed
Radiola linoides

Upright Yellow Sorrel
Oxalis europaea

Procumbent Yellow Sorrel
Oxalis corniculata

Wood Sorrel
Oxalis acetosella

which measure up to 15cm (6in) across. The flowers are borne on separate flowering stalks, in loose terminal clusters on long stalks growing from the axil of a pair of leaves, which are formed about halfway up each flowering stalk. Within each flower cluster the flowers grow in pairs. This arrangement of leaves and flowers is characteristic of many crane's-bills.

The flowers of Meadow Crane's-bill are large and bowl-shaped, over 35mm (1$\frac{1}{2}$in) across, and followed by distinctive fruits that are characteristic of many crane's-bills. Each fruit consists of five spoon-shaped sections, with the bowls of the spoons at the bottom and containing the seeds, and all the handles of the spoons forming a 'beak'. When the seeds are ripe, the handle of each spoon contracts and pulls the bowl of the spoon upwards, flinging out the seed. Afterwards the spoons are left curled about the central axis of the fruit.

Wood Crane's-bill, *Geranium sylvaticum*, is similar to Meadow Crane's-bill, but its leaves are less deeply cut and its flowers are smaller (30mm across at most), varying in colour from blue-violet to reddish-purple. It grows in damp woods and hedgebanks, in meadows and often in mountains in Scotland and northern England; it also grows across much of Europe, in mountains in the south. It is also grown in gardens.

Bloody Crane's-bill, *Geranium sanguineum*, has flowers not so much red as bright reddish-purple. It forms bushy clumps of leafy stems, often sprawling and branched from the base, only 40cm (15in) tall at most. There are no basal leaves. The stem leaves are rounded or polygonal in outline, deeply 5–7 lobed, each lobe narrow and cut into three segments. The flowers are borne singly on long stalks. This plant grows in grassland and woods, among rocks and sometimes on fixed dunes, scattered across much of Europe. In Britain it grows locally, mainly in Scotland, northern England and north Wales, often as a rather more prostrate coastal plant, var. *prostratum*. It is also found in western Ireland and several varieties are grown in gardens.

Dusky Crane's-bill, *Geranium phaeum*, is characteristic of several species with dark purple flowers and reflexed petals; the projecting stamens and style are more noticeable in these flowers. This is a perennial, clump-forming plant that grows in woods, hedges and meadows across much of Europe, except the north; it has been introduced to Great Britain as a garden plant, escaping to grow wild in many places.

Hedgerow Crane's-bill, *Geranium pyrenaicum*, is another perennial plant, with clumps of lobed basal leaves and taller flowering stems up to 60cm (2ft) tall. The leaves have 5–9 rounded lobes, each lobe divided at the tip into three blunt teeth. The flowers are borne in pairs, about 20mm ($\frac{3}{4}$in) across and purple in colour. This plant grows in hedges, on the edges of fields and in waste places scattered across the British Isles, much more commonly in southern England than anywhere else, also across most of Europe, north to southern Sweden.

weeds, thriving in disturbed places and prolific in seed. **Cut-leaved Crane's-bill**, *Geranium dissectum*, is one such plant. It has branched, straggling stems 60cm (2ft) tall at most, leaves divided almost to the base and many small, reddish-pink flowers in summer. It is found throughout the British Isles and in Europe, except the north, in waste places, cultivated ground, grassland, roadsides and hedgerows.

Dove's-foot Crane's-bill, *Geranium molle*, is another weedy annual species, this one grey-green with long silky hairs, round-lobed leaves and sprawling stems. Its flowers are tiny, only 6–10mm ($\frac{1}{2}$–$\frac{3}{4}$in) across, and pinkish-purple in colour. It grows in waste and cultivated places, dry grassland and dunes throughout Europe and the British Isles. **Small-flowered Crane's-bill**, *G. pusillum*, is similar but its leaves are more deeply lobed with shorter hairs, and its reddish-purple flowers are smaller (only 4–6mm ($\frac{1}{4}$–$\frac{1}{2}$in) across). It grows in waste and cultivated ground, in dry grassland and other open places across much of Europe, except the north, mainly in England in the British Isles.

Herb Robert, *Geranium robertianum*, has some of the most deeply dissected leaves of all the crane's-bills, almost ferny in appearance but still palmately lobed. They have a disagreeable scent when handled but are attractive in appearance, especially when they turn red in the sun or late in the season. This is an annual, often hairy plant, quite small with many branched, straggling stems growing up to about 30cm (1ft) tall. It produces bright pink flowers throughout the summer. The fruits of this plant are rather different to those of most crane's-bills in the way the seeds are flung out. In Herb Robert the whole spoon-shaped section of the fruit comes away with the seed, leaving the central axis of the fruit naked. Seed and 'spoon' separate in the process. The plant is found in hedges and woods, especially among rocks or on crumbling walls, on shingle near the coasts throughout Europe and the British Isles.

The **Stork's-bills**, from the genus *Erodium*, also belong to this family. They mostly come from the Mediterranean, but **Common Stork's-bill**, *E. cicutarium*, grows throughout Europe and much of Great Britain, near the coast in Ireland. It is found in dry grassland, waste places and arable land, usually in sandy soils, often in dunes near the sea. It is an annual, forming rosettes of pinnate, ferny leaves at first, then prostrate, branched stems with similar leaves and terminal umbels of pink flowers. The fruits do resemble the long beaks of storks; they are similar to crane's-bill fruits, but with much longer 'handles' to the 'spoons'. When ripe, the fruits split into single-seeded sections, the beaks remaining attached to the seeds and becoming spirally coiled like a corkscrew. On the ground this corkscrew unwinds or winds closer with changes in humidity, and the movements screw the seed into the ground; it is prevented from re-emerging by backward-pointing hairs. The seeds are thus 'planted' at exactly the right depth!

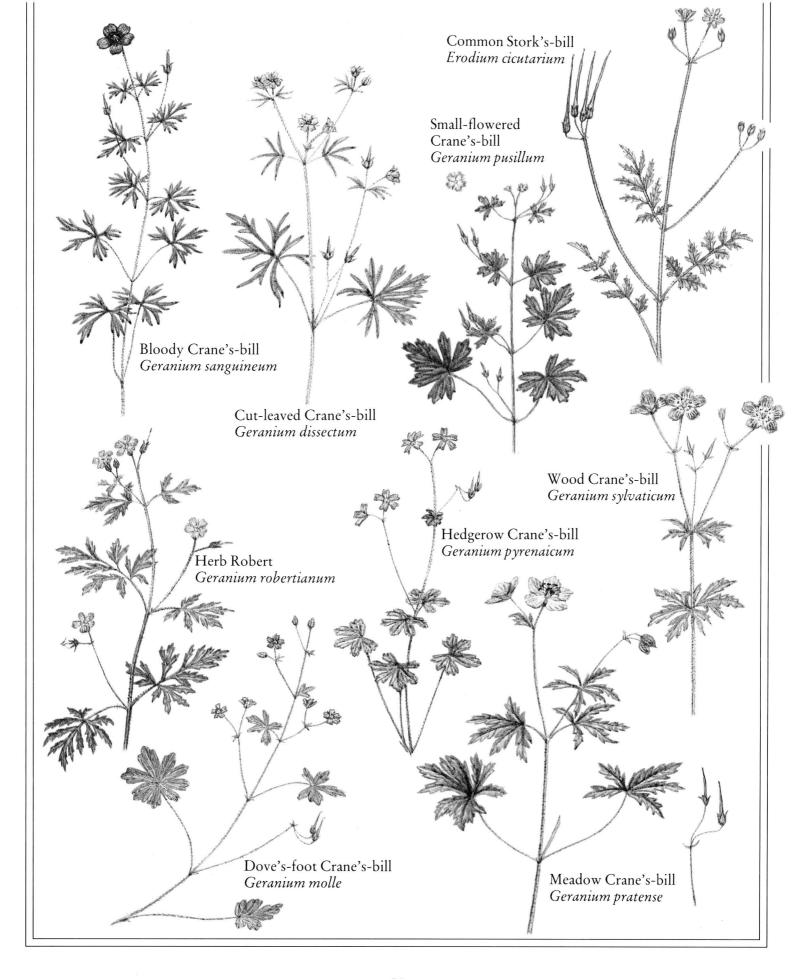

Common Stork's-bill
Erodium cicutarium

Small-flowered
Crane's-bill
Geranium pusillum

Bloody Crane's-bill
Geranium sanguineum

Cut-leaved Crane's-bill
Geranium dissectum

Wood Crane's-bill
Geranium sylvaticum

Herb Robert
Geranium robertianum

Hedgerow Crane's-bill
Geranium pyrenaicum

Dove's-foot Crane's-bill
Geranium molle

Meadow Crane's-bill
Geranium pratense

This family has 4 genera and 600 species, over 500 in the genus *Impatiens*. They are mostly rather succulent herbs with watery, translucent stems, found in tropical Asia and Africa. Many have large, showy flowers, and Busy-Lizzies, varieties of *Impatiens wallerana*, are popular house and garden plants.

Family features The flowers are bilaterally symmetrical and hermaphrodite. Each has 3–5 sepals, one larger than the others and forming a spur at the back of the flower; the sepals are often petal-like in appearance. Each flower has five petals, the uppermost the largest, and two on each side usually fused together, so that the flower may appear to have only three petals. Five stamens alternate with the petals. The ovary is superior with five cells. The flowers are often drooping, solitary or borne in racemes in the leaf axils. The fruits are capsules, with sides formed of several elastic sections, so that when they are ripe a light touch or even a rain drop will trigger them into sudden explosive opening, flinging the seeds in all directions. It is this feature which has given the family its name of Touch-me-not. The leaves are simple, alternate, opposite or in whorls.

Policeman's Helmet, *Impatiens glandulifera*, is an introduced plant brought to Europe from the Himalayas, now naturalized and still spreading along river banks in many countries of Europe. In Britain it is most common in England and Wales. It is an unmistakable plant, a hairless annual that grows 1–2m (3–6ft) tall, with stout, translucent stems and a rather sickly scent. The leaves are opposite or in whorls, elliptical to lance-shaped with serrated edges. The flowers are large and distinctively shaped, like pinkish-purple helmets, borne in clusters on long, drooping stalks in the axils of the uppermost leaves. They are followed by pear-shaped fruits that explode under the slightest pressure when ripe, leaving the coiled valves behind and flinging the seeds out.

Small Balsam, *Impatiens parviflora*, is another introduced plant from Asia, now naturalized across much of Europe, including England and Wales, growing in shady waste places and woods. It is an annual, growing 30–90cm (1–3ft) tall, with alternate, pointed-ovate leaves, serrated at the edges and tapering to winged leafstalks. The flowers are small, pale yellow and unspotted, borne in clusters in the leaf axils and followed by explosive, club-shaped capsules.

The similar **Touch-me-not**, *Impatiens noli-tangere*, is a native plant, with broader, ovate leaves and larger, bright yellow flowers spotted with brown, growing in small clusters in the leaf axils. It grows in wet places in woods, beside streams and ditches, and in shady ravines across most of Europe, except Portugal and the far north. It is limited to the Lake District in Great Britain and absent from Ireland.

There are about 12 genera and 800 species of herbs, shrubs and climbers in this family, found in temperate and tropical regions throughout the world, except New Zealand and Polynesia.

Family features The flowers are often borne on jointed stalks. They are hermaphrodite and bilaterally symmetrical, each one with five free, overlapping sepals, the two inner sepals often coloured like petals and resembling wings, and 3–5 petals, the outer two free or united with the lowermost (this is often boat-shaped and known as the keel), the two upper free or absent. The flowers usually have eight stamens, their filaments often joined together into a sheath which is split above and joined to the petals. The ovary is superior, usually with two cells. The fruit may be a capsule or fleshy. The leaves are simple and usually alternate; they lack stipules.

There are 500–600 **Milkworts**, *Polygala* species, found throughout much of the world, with about 30 in Europe. Most are herbaceous plants. **Common Milkwort**, *P. vulgaris*, is a small perennial, only 30cm (1ft) tall at most, with a woody base, spreading, sprawling, much-branched stems and many alternate, narrowly ovate leaves. The flowers are borne in racemes at the tops of the stems in early summer. They may be blue, pink or white, with greenish outer sepals and inner sepals the same colour as the petals. This plant grows in grassland on chalk and limestone, on heaths and dunes; it is found across Europe and throughout the British Isles. **Heath Milkwort**, *P. serpyllifolia*, is very similar to Common Milkwort, but is a more slender plant in which at least the lower leaves are opposite. It usually has blue flowers. This little plant grows in acid soils, on heaths and in other grassy places in western and central Europe, and throughout the British Isles.

Tufted Milkwort, *Polygala comosa*, is not found in Britain, but grows in dry, grassy places and woods across most of Europe. It has erect stems growing up to 20cm (8in) tall, ovate, alternate leaves tapering towards the stalk and pink flowers borne in a dense spike at the top of each stem.

Rue family
Rutaceae

A large family with about 150 genera and 900 species, mostly of shrubs and trees, mostly from tropical and temperate regions of the world. It includes all citrus fruits—oranges, lemons and their relatives. None grow wild in Britain.

Family features The flowers are usually hermaphrodite and regular, with 4–5 overlapping sepals, free or joined at the base, and 4–5 overlapping petals. There are as many stamens as

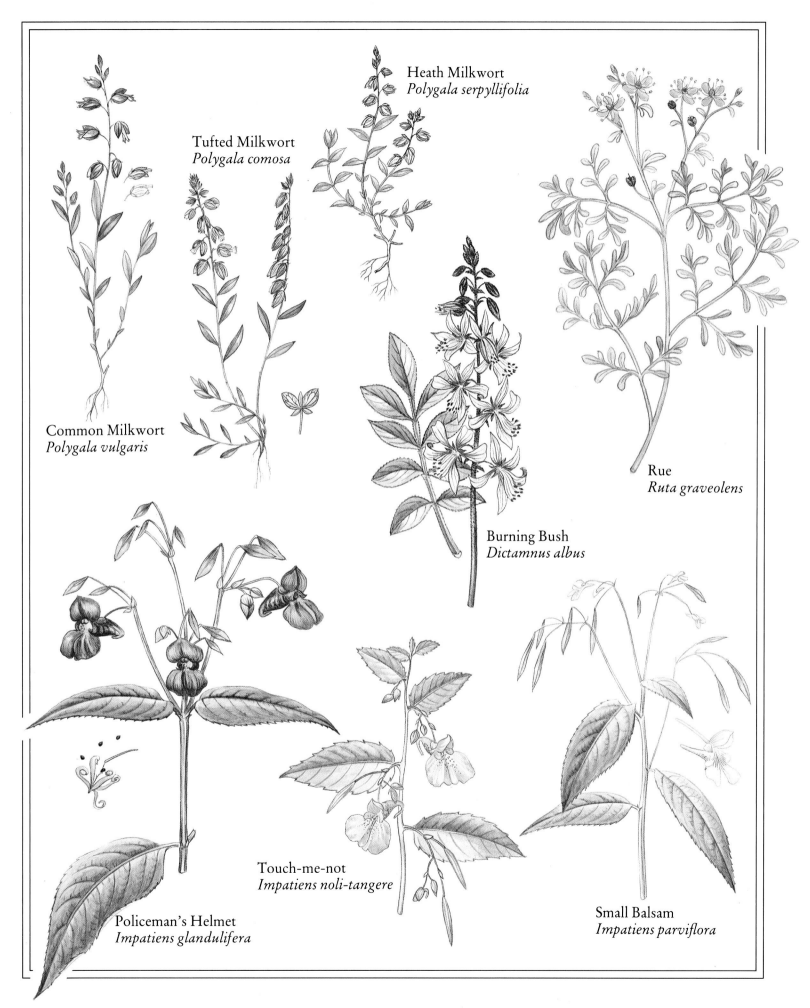

Tufted Milkwort
Polygala comosa

Heath Milkwort
Polygala serpyllifolia

Common Milkwort
Polygala vulgaris

Burning Bush
Dictamnus albus

Rue
Ruta graveolens

Policeman's Helmet
Impatiens glandulifera

Touch-me-not
Impatiens noli-tangere

Small Balsam
Impatiens parviflora

petals, or twice as many stamens as petals, and the ovary is superior with 4–5 cells. The fruit is often a fleshy berry, but may be a capsule. The leaves are often evergreen, simple or compound and dotted with glands that release volatile oils. Stipules are absent.

Rue, *Ruta graveolens* (p. 87), is native to the Mediterranean but is grown in other parts of Europe, including the British Isles, as a garden plant and for its use in medicine. This is a shrubby plant, with a woody base and many branched stems about 90cm (3ft) tall. Both stems and deeply divided leaves are hairless, rather fleshy and blue-green in colour, with a not altogether pleasant scent. In late summer the plant bears terminal clusters of glandular yellow flowers.

Burning Bush, *Dictamnus albus* (p. 87), gets its name from the inflammable gas that it releases on hot summer days. It comes from the Mediterranean region but is grown in gardens in other countries, including Britain. This is one of the few herbaceous plants in this family—a glandular, pungent perennial about 1m (3ft) tall, with erect stems and alternate, pinnate leaves. In early summer it bears dense, showy racemes of purple-veined, white or pink flowers with long purple stamens.

Spurge family
Euphorbiaceae

A very large and varied family of trees, shrubs and herbs found throughout the tropics and temperate regions of the world, with the majority in the tropics. It contains 300 genera and 5000 species, including economically important ones like rubber trees, cassava and tapioca. Castor Oil, which comes from *Ricinus communis*, is used in paints, textile finishes, dyes and inks, as well as medicinally. The family also supplies garden and greenhouse plants, including poinsettias and crotons.

Family features The flowers are regular. Male and female flowers are separate, generally on the same plant. Sepals are usually present, petals usually absent, but both may be missing. The flowers contain one to many stamens and a superior ovary with three cells. The fruits are capsules or drupes. The leaves are usually simple, alternate, usually with stipules.

Most European representatives of this family are herbs. **Dog's Mercury**, *Mercurialis perennis*, is a poisonous, hairy, perennial plant with creeping rhizomes; in spring its erect, leafy stems carpet the floor of deciduous woods, especially beech woods on chalk, or grow in shady hedgerows and among mountain rocks. It is found throughout Europe and much of Great Britain, rarely in northern Scotland and Ireland. Each stem grows 15–40cm (6–15in) tall and has opposite, lance-shaped leaves with serrated edges, crowded near the top. They have the scent of decaying fish if bruised. Greenish male and female flowers grow on separate plants, females singly or in small clusters on long stalks, males in erect spikes. Annual Mercury, *M. annua*, has a branched, erect stem and lance-shaped serrated leaves; it grows as a weed across most of Europe, mainly in southern England in the British Isles.

The **Spurges**, *Euphorbia* species, are a vast group of 2000 herbs, shrubs and trees spread throughout the tropics and warmer temperate regions of the world. Their flowers are very reduced, the males consisting of a single stamen, the females of a single pistil. Several male flowers are arranged around a female one and together they form the centre of a cup-like bract, the whole arrangement looking like a single flower. These are grouped together in clusters with special leaves beneath. Spurges have white, milky sap, often caustic and sometimes very poisonous. Many are grown in gardens.

Over 100 *Euphorbia* species grow in Europe. Some are weeds, like the **Sun Spurge**, *E. helioscopia*, found in cultivated ground, gardens and waste places throughout Europe and the British Isles. It is a hairless annual plant, with a single leafy stem 20–50cm (8–20in) tall ending in umbels of spurge flowers cupped in broad, leafy bracts, those nearest the flowers often bright yellow. Leaves and bracts are all finely toothed on the ends, a feature characteristic of this plant.

Petty Spurge, *Euphorbia peplus*, is another weedy annual also found in cultivated ground and waste places throughout Europe and the British Isles. It is a leafy plant, no more than 30cm (1ft) tall, with a simple or branched stem, often branched towards the top to form loose, leafy umbels of flowers. Like many other spurges, this plant was at one time used in herb medicine, a practice largely discontinued because of the acrid nature of its sap, which makes it dangerous.

Cypress Spurge, *Euphorbia cyparissias*, is a perennial, hairless plant with creeping rhizomes and many erect, branched stems, only 30cm (1ft) tall, with dense, linear leaves. Flowers grow at the tops of many of the stems, the yellow-green leaves of the umbels round rather than linear and turning red in the sun. This plant grows in cultivated land, beside roads, in scrub, grassy and rocky places in Europe. In Britain it is most likely to be seen in gardens or as a casual weed in waste places in England or Scotland. Its white juice may irritate the skin. **Leafy Spurge**, *E. esula*, is a similar species with wider, lance-shaped or ovate, less crowded leaves. It grows wild in Europe on cultivated ground and roadsides, in sandy and stony soils. It has become naturalized in grassy places and woods in Britain, mainly in England but also in Scotland.

Wood Spurge, *Euphorbia amygdaloides*, is a clump-forming perennial spurge, its stems sterile in the first year, growing taller and flowering in the second—a pattern seen in many garden spurges. The dark green leaves are present at the tops of the first-year stems. The flowers are borne in umbels, the yellowish bracts beneath each umbel joined into pairs. This plant grows in damp woods across Europe, except in the north, mainly in southern England and Wales in Great Britain.

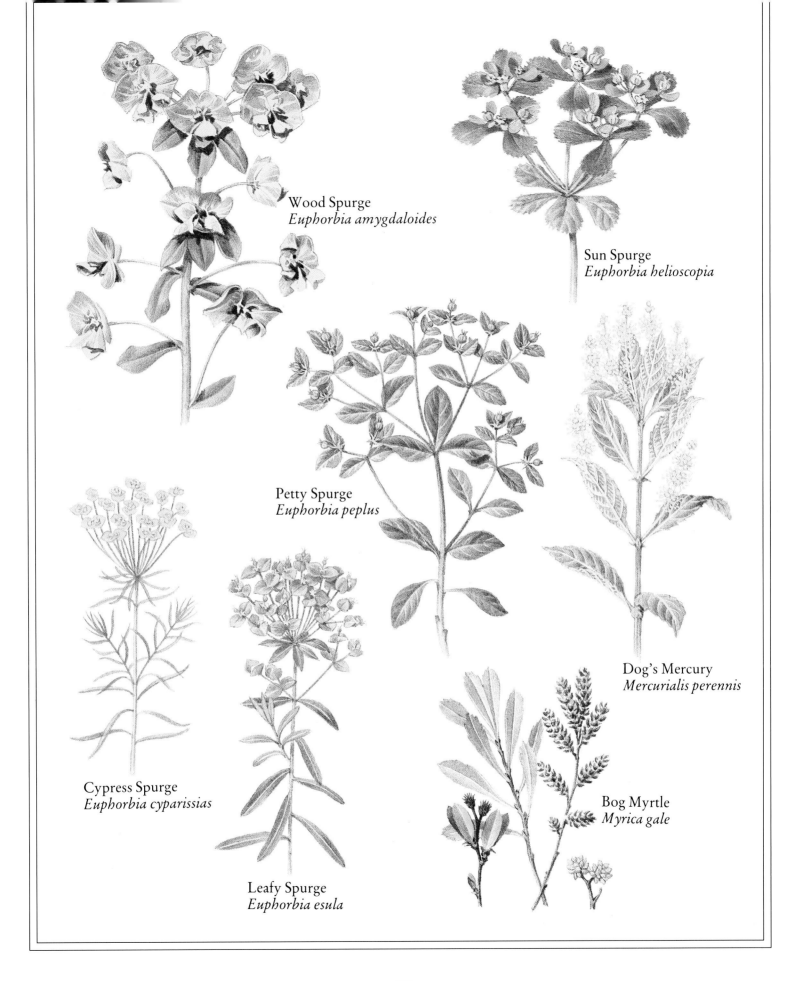

Wood Spurge
Euphorbia amygdaloides

Sun Spurge
Euphorbia helioscopia

Petty Spurge
Euphorbia peplus

Dog's Mercury
Mercurialis perennis

Cypress Spurge
Euphorbia cyparissias

Leafy Spurge
Euphorbia esula

Bog Myrtle
Myrica gale

89

Bog Myrtle family
Myriaceae

A very small family of shrubs and trees, with only 4 genera and about 40 species, found throughout the world.

Only three species grow in Europe. **Bog Myrtle** or Sweet Gale, *Myrica gale* (p. 89), is a deciduous shrub, growing 60–200cm (2–6ft) tall and spreading by suckers into thickets, with red-brown twigs and buds. Its grey-green, oval leaves have many short hairs on the undersides. Both twigs and leaves have an aromatic scent and may be added to pot pourris for their fragrance or carried to repel midges. The flowers appear before the leaves in spring, forming erect catkins on last year's shoots, males and females on separate plants, the males larger than the females. They lack petals or sepals, but grow in the axils of bracts, and the female flowers each have two smaller bracts as well. Fruiting catkins are formed of many two-winged fruits covered with a waxy bloom; they may be boiled in water to extract their wax, which is good for making candles. Bog Myrtle grows in wet heaths, bogs and fens in western and northern Europe and locally throughout Scotland, parts of northern England, north Wales and Ireland, more rarely elsewhere. It is absent from central England.

Mallow family
Malvaceae

This family has about 75 genera and 1000 species of herbs, shrubs and trees in tropical and temperate regions of the world. Many family members are grown in gardens—shrubs like *Hibiscus* and *Lavatera* species, herbaceous plants like mallows and hollyhocks. Cotton plants come from this family, providing not only cotton, but also oil extracted from their seeds and used in soap and cosmetics; the residue from the seeds is used in paper and cellulose manufacture.

Family features The flowers may be borne singly in the leaf axils or in branched racemes; they are hermaphrodite and regular, with five sepals and petals, the sepals often united and the petals more or less separate. Often there is also an epicalyx outside the sepals. The numerous stamens are joined at the base to form a tube, and the ovary is superior with two to many carpels. The fruit may be a capsule or schizocarpic, i.e. splitting into many one-seeded sections. The leaves are alternate, entire or palmately lobed, with stipules. The plants are often velvety with star-shaped hairs.

The **Mallows** are a group of about 30 Old World species in the genus *Malva*, with about 13 in Europe. Mallows have fruits like round cheeses cut into segments. The base of the fruit is formed from the receptacle cupped in the calyx and the seg-

mon Mallow, *M. sylvestris*, forms a clump of sprawling, hairy stems up to 90cm (3ft) tall, with long-stalked, heart-shaped or kidney-shaped leaves, their edges indented into 3–7 lobes. Clusters of flowers appear in the leaf axils in summer; they are pink-purple, veined with darker purple, and followed by the fruits formed of wrinkled, brownish-green nutlets. Common Mallow is a conspicuous perennial plant of dry roadsides and waste places, grassland and hedgerows, found throughout Europe and the British Isles, more rarely in the north.

Musk Mallow, *Malva moschata*, grows on more fertile soils, on the edges of fields and meadows, in hedgerows and on roadsides throughout Europe and Great Britain. This perennial plant has a clump of kidney-shaped basal leaves and branched, hairy stems up to 90cm (3ft) tall. The stem leaves are more deeply divided higher up on the stems until the topmost have linear segments. Both stems and leaves smell of musk if handled. The rose pink or purple flowers are mostly borne in dense terminal clusters; they have triangular, notched petals. The dark fruits are rounded and densely hairy.

Dwarf Mallow, *Malva neglecta*, is one of the smaller mallows, an annual with prostrate or sprawling, branched stems growing up to 60cm (2ft) tall. It has many downy hairs on the stems and long-stalked, rounded, palmately lobed leaves. The flowers are whitish, veined or tinged with lilac, with notched petals, and they grow in clusters in the leaf axils in summer. The nutlets that follow are greenish-brown and finely hairy.

Marsh Mallow, *Althaea officinalis*, is an erect, branched, grey-velvety, perennial plant, up to 120cm (4ft) tall, with triangular toothed leaves, the lowermost slightly lobed and the upper ones folded like a fan. In late summer it bears clusters of pink flowers in the axils of the upper leaves. The roots of this plant are rich in mucilage and were used to make the original marshmallows. They are still used in herb medicine to soothe intestinal disorders and to make poultices.

Hollyhock, *Alcea rosea*, has been introduced from China as a garden plant to Europe and the British Isles, escaping in many areas to grow wild, especially on walls and in waste places. This is a statuesque plant, with an erect stem up to 3m (9ft) tall and many shallowly lobed leaves on long stalks. The flowers are large, 6–8cm (2–3in) across, usually pink or white, borne in a long leafy spike.

Tree Mallow, *Lavatera arborea*, is a biennial plant, in spite of its name and its large size. In its second, flowering year, it reaches 3m (9ft) in height and has many branched stems, woody at the base and softly woolly at the tips. Its leaves are large—up to 20cm (8in) across—and rounded with 5–7 shallow lobes and long stalks. The showy flowers grow in small clusters terminating the branches; they are purple with much darker purple veins. The flowers are followed by rings of yellowish, wrinkled nutlets. This plant grows in rocky places and waste ground near the sea on the Mediterranean and Atlan-

Hollyhock
Alcea rosea

Marsh Mallow
Althaea officinalis

Small Tree Mallow
Lavatera cretica

Tree Mallow
Lavatera arborea

Musk Mallow
Malva moschata

Common Mallow
Malva sylvestris

Dwarf Mallow
Malva neglecta

Flower-of-an-hour
Hibiscus trionum

England and Wales, and on the south coast of Ireland. If found elsewhere it is likely to have been introduced.

Small Tree Mallow, *Lavatera cretica* (p. 91), is a smaller annual or biennial plant with herbaceous stems, lobed leaves and lilac flowers with widely separated petals. It grows in waste places near the sea on the Mediterranean and west coasts of Europe, north to Cornwall, the Scilly Isles and Jersey.

Hibiscus is a large genus, with about 200 species of shrubs and herbs from the warmer regions of the world. **Flower-of-an-hour**, *H. trionum* (p. 91), comes from southeastern Europe but is grown in France, Spain and Portugal. It is an annual, with an erect, branched stem up to 60cm (2ft) tall and three-lobed, wavy-margined leaves. Solitary flowers grow in the leaf axils in summer; they are quite large, pale yellow with purple centres and last for only a few hours. The fruits are hairy capsules divided into five sections, each enclosed in the bristly, five-angled calyx which becomes inflated and papery.

Violet family
Violaceae

For many people this family is synonymous with the pansies and violets, *Viola* species, although there are actually 22 genera and 900 species in the family, and only 500 of them are in the genus *Viola*. They are found in temperate and tropical regions, and are mostly herbaceous plants.

Family features The flowers are solitary or borne in racemes; they are regular or bilaterally symmetrical. Each has five persistent, overlapping sepals and five petals; these are usually unequal and the lowermost is spurred. There are five stamens, the lower two often spurred at the base and with the anthers of all five joined around the ovary. The ovary is superior with one cell. The fruits are capsules or berries. The leaves are simple and alternate with leafy stipules.

There are over 90 *Viola* species in Europe. Many appear to flower only in spring, but actually bloom through spring and summer, producing two kinds of flowers. The familiar ones, with bright petals, are spring flowers; summer flowers remain hidden beneath the foliage, do not open and are self-pollinated. It is these that form most of the seed. Violet flowers are quite distinctive, with five petals forming a bilaterally symmetrical and spurred flower. They come in variations on three colours (blue-violet, yellow and white), are often veined and the two lateral petals are often bearded near the base. Plants may form rosettes of leaves with flowers on separate stalks or may have long, leafy stems with flowers in the leaf axils.

Sweet Violet, *Viola odorata*, is a small perennial plant only 20cm (8in) tall, with rosettes of long-stalked, broadly heart-shaped leaves and long, leafless runners which root and pro-duce new plants. In spring sweet-scented, deep purple or white flowers grow from the crown of the plant; closed flowers are produced throughout the summer, never appearing above the leaves. Sweet Violets grow in hedgerows, coppiced woodland, thickets and plantations, usually on calcareous soils, throughout Europe, in England, Wales and central Ireland. They are also grown in gardens, valued for their perfume and used in herb medicine, in remedies for coughs and colds and in headache treatments. **Hairy Violet**, *V. hirta*, is similar but lacks runners, has narrower leaves and scentless, paler blue-violet flowers. It grows in calcareous grassland and scrub throughout most of Europe, mostly in England in the British Isles.

Common Dog-violet, *Viola riviniana*, is probably the most familiar violet for many people, abundant throughout Europe and the British Isles, found in open woods and hedgerows, heaths and pastures. It is a little perennial plant, often only 15cm (6in) tall, with a central clump of long-stalked, heart-shaped leaves. The spring flowers grow on separate stems, each one in the axil of a long-stalked leaf; they are blue-violet with a paler, often whitish spur. Closed flowers appear in summer.

Heath Dog-violet, *Viola canina*, has no central leaf rosette; instead the leaves all grow on sprawling stems and the plant may reach 30cm (1ft) tall. The leaves are ovate to somewhat triangular in shape, borne on long stalks, and the spring flowers are blue with a yellowish spur. This is a very variable species found scattered throughout Europe and the British Isles, in dry grassland and heaths, sand-dunes and open woods, also in fens, often on acid soils.

Marsh Violet, *Viola palustris*, has long, slender rhizomes with leaves growing from the nodes; these have broad, almost kidney-shaped blades and long stalks. The spring flowers are borne singly on long stalks; they are lilac with darker veins. This little plant grows in marshes and wet heaths, fens and bogs, in acid soils across much of Europe and the British Isles (but is absent from much of the Midlands and East Anglia).

Yellow Wood Violet, *Viola biflora*, grows in the mountains of western Europe, in damp, shady woods or among rocks; it is not found in the British Isles. It is a delicate plant, with slender, leafy stems bearing kidney-shaped leaves on long stalks and pairs of golden-yellow flowers veined with brown.

Pansies do not produce closed flowers in summer; instead they go on producing showy flowers for a much longer period than violets. **Wild Pansy** or Heartsease, *Viola tricolor*, is one of the plants from which Garden Pansies are derived, with much smaller flowers than its offspring, but the same sprawling, leafy stems. It has two subspecies. Subsp. *tricolor* is found in cultivated ground and waste places across most of Europe and the British Isles; it is an annual with blue-violet flowers. Subsp. *curtisii* grows on dunes and in grassy places near the sea around much of the British and Irish coastline, and on the coasts of the North and Baltic Seas. It is a perennial plant and may have blue-violet, yellow, or multicoloured flowers.

Sweet Violet
Viola odorata

Field Pansy
Viola arvensis

Mountain Pansy
Viola lutea

Marsh Violet
Viola palustris

Wild Pansy
Viola tricolor

Yellow Wood Violet
Viola biflora

Heath Dog-violet
Viola canina

Common Dog-violet
Viola riviniana

Mountain Pansy, *Viola lutea* (p. 93), is the other ancestor of Garden Pansies, the cross between the two species resulting in the large hybrid varieties. Mountain Pansy is a perennial, with creeping rhizomes and sprawling stems. The lowermost leaves are ovate, but upper ones are much divided and so are their stipules. The flowers are coloured in combinations of blue-violet, red and yellow, but the lowest petal is always yellow at the base. This plant grows in hills, in short grassland and among rocks, often on base-rich soils; it grows throughout much of western and central Europe, in north Wales, northern England and Scotland, and a few places in Ireland.

Field Pansy, *Viola arvensis* (p. 93), has sprawling, branched, leafy stems, and small, creamy-white flowers, often with blue-tinged upper petals. It grows in waste places and may become a weed in cultivated land, usually in neutral or basic soils, throughout Europe and the British Isles.

Daphne family
Thymelaeaceae

A family of about 50 genera and 500 species of trees and shrubs (rarely herbs), found throughout most of the world.

There are about 70 *Daphne* species in the temperate regions of the world, several grown in gardens for their fragrant flowers. About 17 are found in Europe. **Mezereon**, *D. mezereum*, is a deciduous shrub about 1m (3ft) tall, with a few erect branches and smooth, light green, lance-shaped leaves. The flowers are pinkish-purple, sweetly scented and appear before the leaves in early spring. They are characteristic of *Daphne* flowers in having a corolla-like calyx-tube enclosing the cylindrical receptacle and no petals. Very poisonous 'berries' follow the flowers, ripening bright red in autumn; they may be mistaken for redcurrants with fatal results. The fruits are technically drupes since they have one seed rather than many. This plant grows in woods and scrub on calcareous soils, but is becoming less common all the time due to overcollecting and changes in land management. It is, or was, found across most of Europe, and can still be found in some places in England.

Spurge-laurel, *Daphne laureola*, is an evergreen shrub, also with a few erect branches, growing about 1m (3ft) tall. The leaves are leathery and glossy dark green, ovate to lance-shaped and crowded towards the tops of the branches on the young green shoots. The flowers appear in spring, little clusters of scented, green bells in the axils of the leaves; they are followed by deadly poisonous black berries in the autumn. In fact, the whole plant is poisonous, like many *Daphne* species. Spurge-laurel grows in woods, usually on calcareous soils, locally throughout much of Europe, except the north and Portugal. It is local but widespread in England and Wales, not found in Ireland or Scotland, unless introduced.

Annual Thymelaea, *Thymelaea passerina*, is unusual among members of this family, in being an annual herbaceous plant. It grows 20–50cm (8–20in) tall, has erect, rigid stems with pointed, narrow leaves and tiny greenish flowers in the leaf axils. It grows in dry waste places across much of continental Europe, except the north. It is absent from the British Isles.

Oleaster family
Elaeagnaceae

A family of trees and shrubs, with only 3 genera and about 50 species, found in northern temperate and subtropical areas of the world. Several species of *Elaeagnus* are grown in gardens.

Sea-buckthorn, *Hippophaë rhamnoides*, is a branched, spiny shrub, its old stems brown, its young twigs and narrow grey leaves covered with silvery scales. The leaves are crowded on to lateral shoots, expanding after the flowers appear in spring. Male and female flowers grow in small clusters on separate plants; they are petal-less, tiny and greenish, and the female flowers are followed in autumn by bright orange, poisonous berries. Sea-buckthorn forms thickets up to 3m (9ft) tall, with many suckers, on fixed dunes, sometimes on cliffs, on the Atlantic and Baltic coasts of Europe, and around the coast of Great Britain. It has been introduced to Ireland and also grows on shingle banks in the rivers of central Europe.

Rockrose family
Cistaceae

There are about 8 genera and 200 species in this small family of herbs and shrubs, the majority found in the Mediterranean region. Some, like the *Cistus* species, are grown in gardens.

Family features The flowers are hermaphrodite and regular, with three or five contorted free sepals, five often contorted, overlapping petals which soon fall, many free stamens and a superior ovary with one, three or five cells. The fruits are capsules. The leaves are usually opposite and simple and the plants often have star-shaped hairs.

Common Rockrose, *Helianthemum nummularium*, is a small shrub with sprawling, often rooting stems 30cm (1ft) tall at most and often prostrate. The stems bear opposite pairs of leaves, green above with dense white hairs beneath, and produce a succession of bright yellow flowers in summer. This plant grows in dry, basic grassland, often among rocks or on banks, throughout Europe and most of Great Britain; it is absent from Cornwall and northwest Scotland, very rare in Ireland. Many varieties are grown in rock gardens. **White Rockrose**, *H. apenninum*, is a similar plant but has white

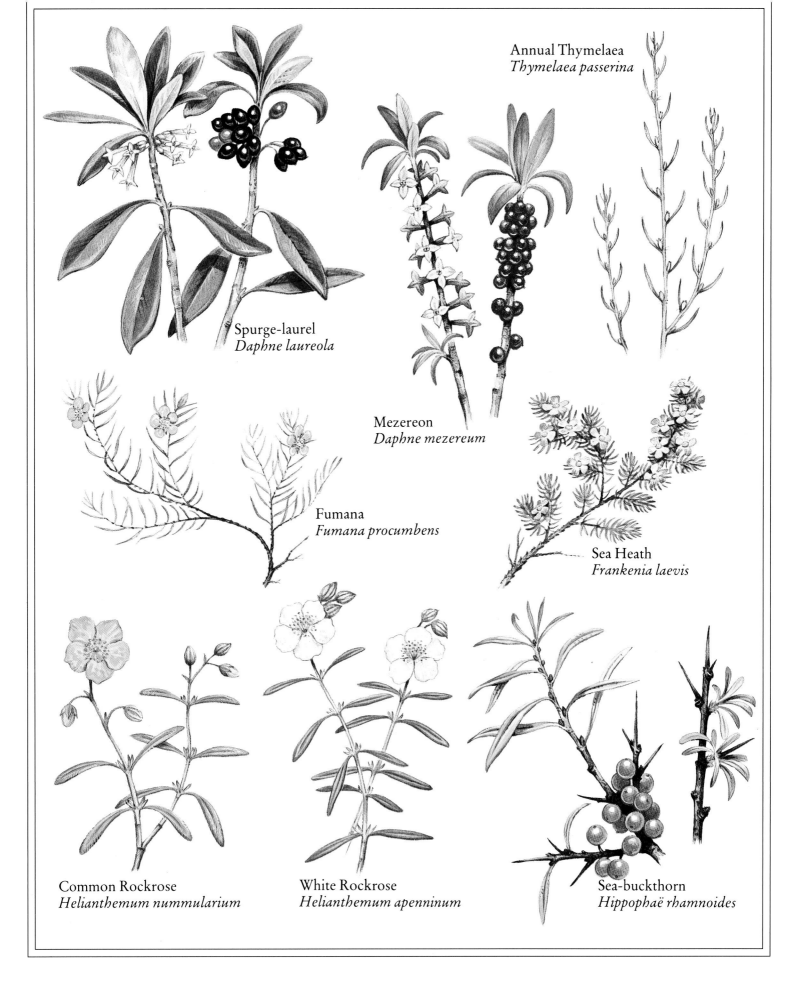

Annual Thymelaea
Thymelaea passerina

Spurge-laurel
Daphne laureola

Mezereon
Daphne mezereum

Fumana
Fumana procumbens

Sea Heath
Frankenia laevis

Common Rockrose
Helianthemum nummularium

White Rockrose
Helianthemum apenninum

Sea-buckthorn
Hippophaë rhamnoides

flowers. It grows among rocks, in grassland and open woods in western and southern Europe, and in southwestern England.

Fumana, *Fumana procumbens* (p. 95), is a small, much-branched subshrubby plant about 40cm (15in) tall, with many linear leaves and yellow flowers in early summer. The flowers may be solitary or borne in small lateral clusters. This plant grows across much of Europe, except the north, and the British Isles, in dry, rocky places and bare, sandy ground.

Sea Heath family
Frankeniaceae

A small family, with 4 genera and about 90 species, mostly found in salt marshes and saline deserts in temperate and subtropical regions of the world.

Sea Heath, *Frankenia laevis* (p. 95), is one of about 80 species in this genus, only six of which are found in Europe. It is a prostrate plant, with branched stems forming a dense mat. It has numerous opposite, linear leaves rolled in at the margins and mostly borne on short, lateral shoots. The flowers appear in late summer, singly or in small clusters, usually in the forks of the branches; each has five sepals and five pink petals. Sea Heath grows at the edges of salt marshes in western Europe, from Norfolk and the south coast of England to Italy.

Gourd family
Cucurbitaceae

Also called the **Cucumber family**. A family of about 100 genera and 900 species, mostly trailing herbs or vines from the tropical regions of the world. There are many economically important food species in this family, including melons, marrows, pumpkins and cucumbers. Gourds and calabashes are used as containers in tropical countries.

Few species are found in Europe. **White Bryony** or Red Bryony, *Bryonia cretica*, is a climber, with long, angled stems branched and covered with bristly hairs. It has palmate leaves, usually with five lobes, and long, coiled tendrils opposite the leaves. Male and female flowers grow on separate plants in clusters in the leaf axils; both have spreading sepals and five greenish-white, net-veined petals, but the petals in male flowers are larger. Male flowers have three stamens, two joined together; females have three bilobed stigmas and an inferior ovary. The fruits are red berries. This plant scrambles over other plants in hedgerows and woodland margins, usually on calcareous soils. It is found across much of Europe, except Scandinavia, throughout England and eastern Wales, becoming rarer in the north and west, absent from much of Scotland.

Loosestrife family
Lythraceae

There are about 25 genera and 550 species of herbs and shrubs in this family, distributed all over the world, except in the cold regions. Some are grown as ornamentals in the garden. Some members of the family yield dyes, including the Middle Eastern species, *Lawsonia inermis*, from which comes henna.

Family features The flowers are hermaphrodite and regular. The calyx is tubular, usually with five teeth; there are usually 4–6 free petals, often crumpled in bud and inserted near the top of the calyx-tube. There are 2–12 stamens, often as many as or twice as many as the petals, inserted below the petals. The ovary is superior, with 2–4 cells and many seeds. The flowers are borne singly or in complex clusters. The fruits are usually capsules. The leaves are usually opposite or whorled and lack stipules, or the stipules are minute.

Lythrum is a genus of about 30 species of herbs and shrubs found throughout the world, with 13 in Europe. **Purple Loosestrife**, *L. salicaria*, is found throughout most of the northern hemisphere, growing beside streams and lakes and in marshes. This perennial plant has clumps of tall, unbranched flowering stems, conspicuous in late summer when they have reddish-purple flowers. The flower spikes are formed of many whorls of flowers, each with six crumpled petals.

There are three different flower forms in Purple Loosestrife, occurring on separate plants. In the first form the flower has short styles, with long and medium-length stamens; the second kind has medium-length styles, with short and long stamens; the third kind has long styles, with short and medium-length stamens. The three kinds of stamens produce different size pollen. This extraordinarily complex arrangement is designed to ensure cross-pollination, so that the ovules of one plant cannot be fertilized by pollen from the same plant. The mechanism maintains the vigour of the species.

Grass Poly, *Lythrum hyssopifolia*, is a hairless annual plant, only 25cm (10in) tall at most, with sprawling, branched stems and alternate, linear leaves held erect. In the axils of the upper leaves grow solitary, small, pale pink flowers, forming a flowering spike at the top of each stem in summer. This is a local, even rare, plant, very unpredictable in its appearances, growing in winter-flooded bare ground and damp fields. It is found in much of Europe, occasionally in Britain, mainly in East Anglia, southern England and the Midlands.

Water Purslane, *Lythrum portula*, is another annual plant of wet places, this one found creeping on the margins of muddy ponds, around puddles or on bare ground, never on calcareous soils. It is scattered throughout Europe and the British Isles, becoming rare in the north. It has many branched, prostrate stems, rooting at the nodes, opposite, rather fleshy leaves and solitary purple flowers in the leaf axils.

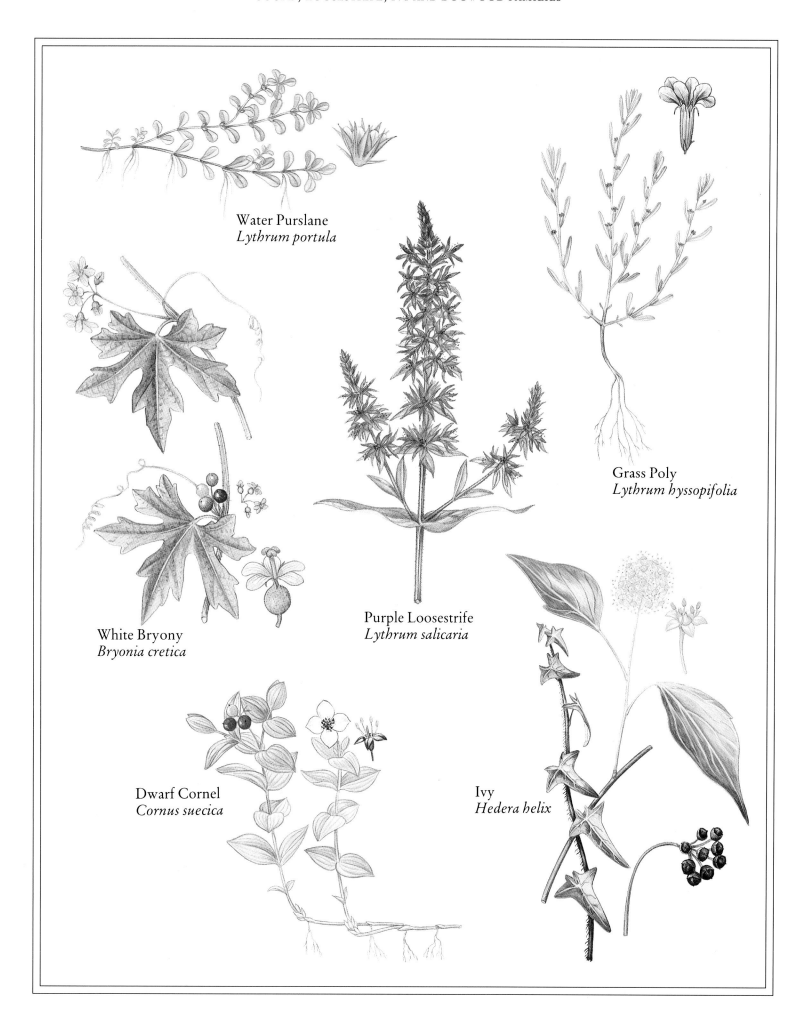

Water Purslane
Lythrum portula

Grass Poly
Lythrum hyssopifolia

White Bryony
Bryonia cretica

Purple Loosestrife
Lythrum salicaria

Dwarf Cornel
Cornus suecica

Ivy
Hedera helix

Ivy family
Araliaceae

A mostly tropical family of 55 genera and about 700 species, chiefly trees and shrubs. Some are grown in gardens, by far the most familiar being the ivies, *Hedera* species. One of the most famous members of the family is Ginseng, the Chinese plant whose roots were believed to be a cure for all ills.

Ivy, *Hedera helix* (p. 97), is the only member of the family found wild in Europe. It is an evergreen, woody climber, growing in woods and other shady places, climbing on trees, rocks and walls, hedgerows and old buildings, tolerant of dry soil and deep shade, clinging by means of rootlets on the woody stems or creeping over the ground into wide carpets. Its leaves are dark green and glossy, shade leaves with 3–5 lobes, those produced in sun (usually at the top of the plant where it emerges into sunlight) elliptical and lacking lobes or teeth. The flowers are produced only on sunlit plants; they are borne in terminal umbels and each one has a five-toothed calyx, a five-lobed, yellow-green corolla, five stamens and an inferior, five-celled ovary. This later swells to produce the rounded black berries. Ivy berries and leaves are poisonous.

Dogwood family
Cornaceae

A small family, mainly of trees and shrubs, with 12 genera and about 100 species, most from northern temperate regions.

Several *Cornus* species are found in Europe, most of them large shrubs. Some, like Cornelian Cherry and Dogwood, are grown in gardens. **Dwarf Cornel**, *C. suecica* (p. 97), is an unusual member of the family, a creeping herbaceous plant with underground rhizomes. Every year it sends up erect, often unbranched stems growing up to 20cm (8in) tall, with opposite pairs of stalkless, ovate leaves. At the top of each stem is what looks like a single flower, but is actually an umbel of tiny, dark purple flowers subtended by four large, oval white bracts; this arrangement is typical of many dogwoods. The fruits are red, egg-shaped drupes. This plant grows in acid soils on moors, heaths and mountains in northern Europe, locally in the Scottish Highlands and rarely in northern England.

Willowherb family
Onagraceae

There are about 20 genera and 650 species in this family of herbs and shrubs, found throughout the world, but most commonly in the temperate regions. There are some highly ornamental garden plants in the family, including the fuchsias.

Family features The flowers are hermaphrodite and more or less regular or bilaterally symmetrical. Each has a calyx-tube attached to the ovary, and two, four or five free sepals; there are the same number of often contorted or overlapping petals. There are as many stamens or twice as many stamens as sepals. The ovary is usually inferior, with 2–5 cells and few to many seeds. The fruits are usually capsules or berries, or they may be indehiscent. The leaves are simple, whorled, opposite or alternate, usually without stipules.

Rosebay Willowherb, *Chamaenerion angustifolium*, is one of the most easily recognizable willowherbs, forming great drifts of red-purple flowers in late summer, especially after fires or in disturbed areas. It spreads by means of creeping underground rhizomes, forming many erect, leafy stems up to 2m (6ft) tall. These are topped by long spikes of showy red-purple flowers in mid and late summer. The inferior ovaries develop into capsules 7cm (3in) long, which open to reveal silky-haired seeds. These are blown in huge numbers to invade new areas. This species has become widespread only in the last 50 years; before that it was a local plant, growing in rocky places and scree slopes in mountains. Now it is common across Europe and the British Isles, in waste places, open woods and riverbanks, on roadsides, in cities and open countryside.

Most of the **Willowherbs** belong to the genus *Epilobium*, a large group with over 100 species (about 25 in Europe), found throughout the world, except in the tropics. The European species are perennial plants with pink or purple flowers, many of them growing in wet places, beside rivers, in marshes and damp woods, others in disturbed habitats.

Great Hairy Willowherb or Codlins-and-cream, *Epilobium hirsutum*, are both splendid plant names, guaranteed to raise eyebrows. This is indeed a large, hairy willowherb; its second name comes from the creamy-white stigmas in the pale pinkish-purple flowers—like cream in cooked apples (or codlins). It grows along the edges of ponds and rivers, in marshes and fens throughout Europe and Great Britain, absent from parts of northern Scotland and Ireland. It forms patches of erect, leafy stems up to 1.5m (5ft) tall, with lance-shaped, toothed leaves all covered with soft hairs, and bears its large, attractive flowers at the tops of elongated ovaries in summer.

Small-flowered Hairy Willowherb, *Epilobium parviflorum*, is another wetland plant, growing in damp places and beside streams, in marshes and fens throughout Europe and the British Isles. It has erect stems about 60cm (2ft) tall, with lance-shaped, toothed leaves, hairy on both sides, the lower ones opposite and the upper ones alternate. Its purplish-pink flowers are small, perched at the tops of long ovaries in the leaf axils. The plant spreads, like several *Epilobium* species, by producing short creeping stems ending in leaf rosettes, so that a widening patch of rosettes develops after several years.

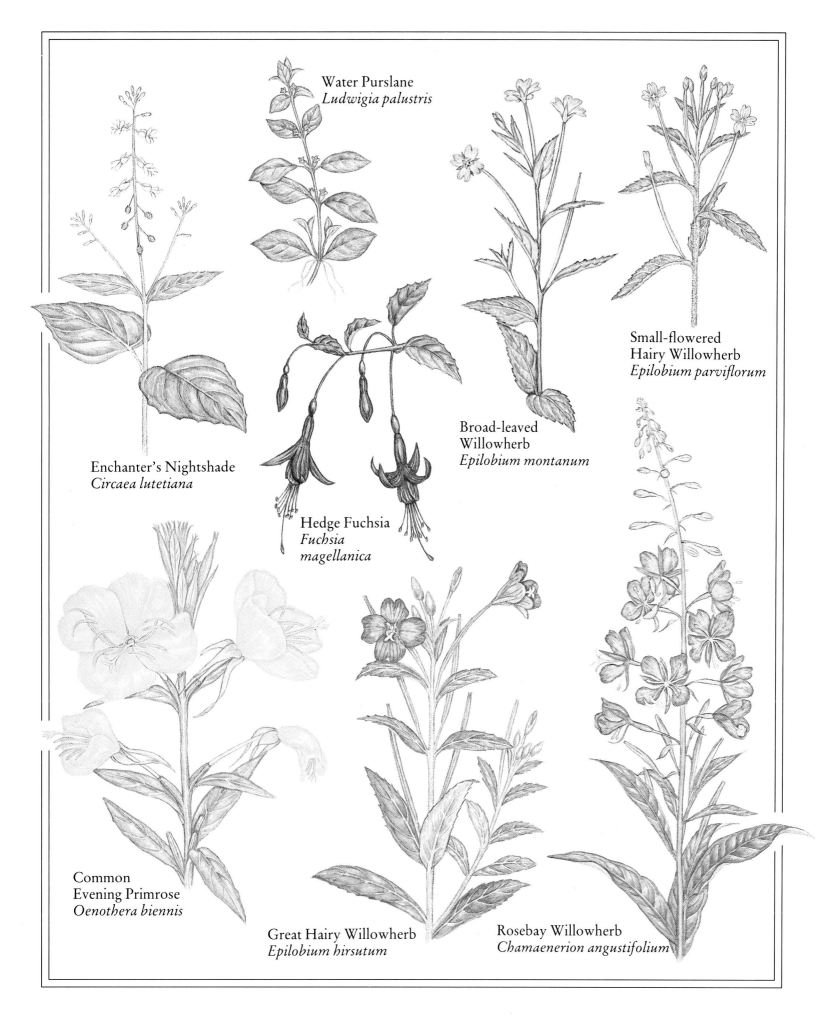

Water Purslane
Ludwigia palustris

Small-flowered
Hairy Willowherb
Epilobium parviflorum

Broad-leaved
Willowherb
Epilobium montanum

Enchanter's Nightshade
Circaea lutetiana

Hedge Fuchsia
Fuchsia magellanica

Common
Evening Primrose
Oenothera biennis

Great Hairy Willowherb
Epilobium hirsutum

Rosebay Willowherb
Chamaenerion angustifolium

Several willowherbs are weeds of gardens and cultivated land. **Broad-leaved Willowherb**, *Epilobium montanum* (p. 99), is one of these, found in gardens, hedgerows and woods, in waste places, among rocks and on walls throughout Europe and the British Isles. It is a perennial plant, with erect, leafy stems about 60cm (2ft) tall, developing a patch of leaf rosettes in time. The flowers are small, opening pale pink from drooping, reddish buds, and have deeply notched petals.

The **Evening Primroses**, members of the genus *Oenothera*, are a large group of about 200 New World species. Several have become established in the wild in Europe, in England in the British Isles. **Common Evening Primrose**, *O. biennis* (p. 99), is probably the best known. It is a biennial, with a rosette of lance-shaped, often wavy leaves in the first year and a leafy flowering spike up to 1.5m (5ft) tall in the second. The scented, showy yellow flowers open in the evening. Each flower has four reflexed sepals, four petals, prominent stamens and a cross-shaped stigma. The fruits are large, oblong capsules held more or less upright. This is the plant from which comes Evening Primrose Oil, now the focus of much research. It soothes eczema and coughs, and helps prevent heart disease.

Water Purslane, *Ludwigia palustris* (p. 99), grows in streams and fens in acid water across much of Europe, except the north. It is very rare in Britain, found only in the New Forest and Jersey. This is a creeping perennial plant, its prostrate stems either rooting in the mud at the water margins or floating in the shallows. The stems are reddish and leafy, with opposite, ovate leaves, smooth and shiny in appearance. In the latter half of summer tiny, petal-less flowers appear in the leaf axils; they have green calyces, often with red edges.

The **Fuchsias**, *Fuchsia* species, are best known as plants for hanging baskets and patio tubs, beautiful frost-sensitive plants with exotic flowers. However, some of them can resist a cold climate, and **Hedge Fuchsia**, *F. magellanica* (p. 99), introduced from South America and grown as a hedge plant in the British Isles, has escaped to grow wild in some places. It does best in the west, in Ireland, southwestern England, Wales and up into western Scotland. This shrub grows up to 3m (9ft) or so in warmer situations, but is cut to the ground each winter by frost and reaches only 90cm (3ft) in colder areas. It has arching stems, toothed, oval leaves and pendant flowers growing in the axils of the uppermost leaves in summer. The flowers are small and relatively dull by fuchsia standards, but even so have reddish stems, red calyx-tubes and red sepals, purple petals, long protruding stamens and an even longer style.

Enchanter's Nightshade, *Circaea lutetiana* (p. 99), forms wide colonies in woods, hedgerows and shady places throughout most of Europe and the British Isles, rarely in the northeast. Its erect stems grow up to 60cm (2ft) tall, have large, pointed-ovate leaves near the base and sparse, elongated racemes of tiny white flowers in late summer. Each flower points downwards on a long stalk, has two sepals, two deeply notched petals and two stamens. The fruits are bristly capsules, pointing downwards like the flowers. Alpine Enchanter's Nightshade, *C. alpina*, has weaker stems and pointed, heart-shaped leaves. It grows in upland woods in northern and central Europe, very locally in northern England, Wales and Arran in Britain. There is also a more widespread hybrid between these two, also found in upland woods.

Mare's-tail family
Hippuridaceae

There is one species in this family—the **Mare's-tail**, *Hippuris vulgaris*. It is found in lakes, ponds and quiet streams, especially in base-rich water, throughout the British Isles and Europe. This is a perennial plant, with creeping rhizomes at the bottom of the water and erect stems which project well above the surface. The stems are hairless and leafy, with many whorls of 6–12 linear leaves both above and beneath the water. In summer the plants bear tiny flowers in the axils of the upper leaves. They have no sepals or petals, and either have a single stamen with a one-celled ovary beneath, or a single stamen alone. The fruits are smooth green achenes.

Water-milfoil family
Haloragidaceae

A small family of herbaceous plants, with 7 genera and about 170 species found throughout the world. Most are aquatic or marsh plants. *Gunnera manicata*, a plant like a giant rhubarb, is sometimes planted in marshy areas in large gardens.

There are five species of **Water-milfoils** in Europe, belonging to the genus *Myriophyllum*. They are aquatic herbs with erect stems and dissected leaves, 3–6 in a whorl. The flowers are small and borne in terminal spikes, often with male flowers at the top, females below. Male flowers have a four-lobed calyx, four petals and usually eight stamens. Females lack sepals and petals, and have a four-celled ovary.

Spiked Water-milfoil, *M. spicatum*, grows in calcium-rich waters of lakes, ditches and streams scattered throughout the British Isles and Europe, north to southern Scandinavia. It has erect, branched stems with whorls of 3–4 leaves beneath the water and flowering stems emerging from the water. These are almost leafless, with whorls of tiny reddish flowers in the axils of small bracts. **Whorled Water-milfoil**, *M. verticillatum*, has leafy flowering spikes above the water, the leaves similar to, but smaller than, the dissected underwater leaves. It grows in base-rich waters of lakes and ponds in lowland areas of Europe, England, Wales and Scotland, but is not common.

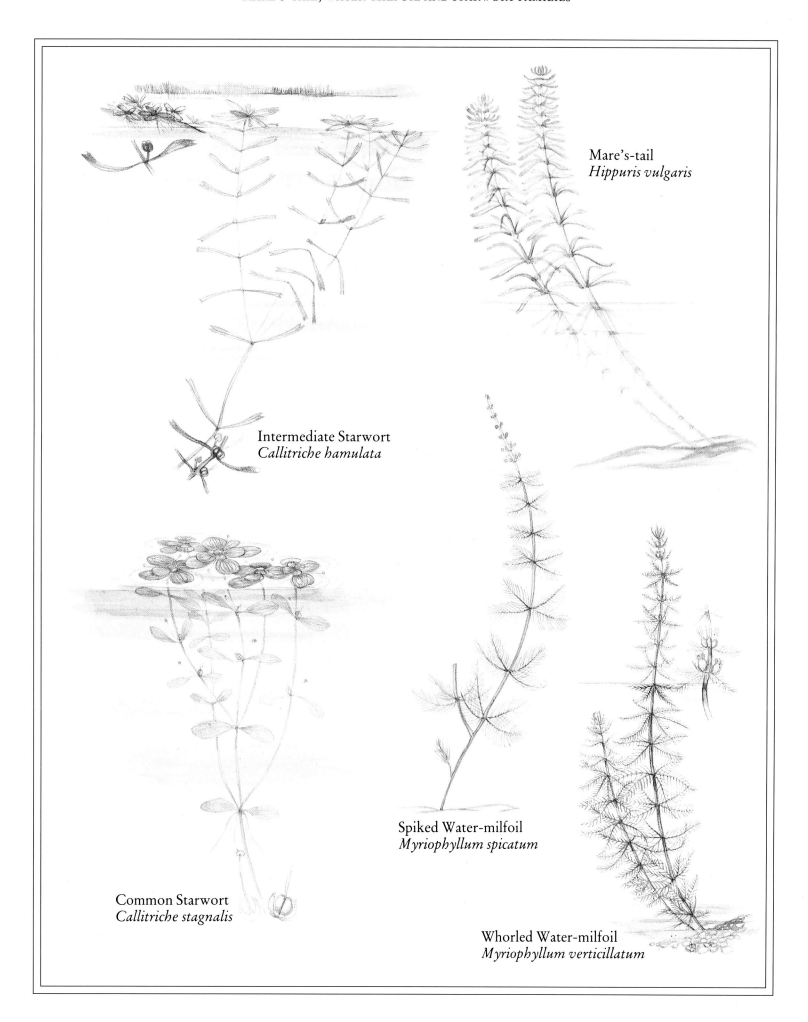

Mare's-tail
Hippuris vulgaris

Intermediate Starwort
Callitriche hamulata

Spiked Water-milfoil
Myriophyllum spicatum

Common Starwort
Callitriche stagnalis

Whorled Water-milfoil
Myriophyllum verticillatum

Starwort family
Callitrichaceae

There is only one genus in this small family. The **Starworts**, 17 *Callitriche* species, are aquatic or amphibious herbaceous plants found throughout the world. They may be annuals or perennials, have simple, opposite leaves and usually male and female flowers are on separate plants. Species are difficult to identify and ripe fruits are often necessary for accurate identification; the fruits are four-lobed with winged or keeled lobes, separating when ripe into two or four sections.

Common Starwort, *Callitriche stagnalis* (p. 101), is common in ponds, ditches and streams throughout the British Isles and Europe. From the surface it looks like a mat of flat leaf rosettes, each one formed of six or eight almost circular leaves. These rosettes terminate the submerged stems, which grow up to 60cm (2ft) long and have many opposite, elliptical leaves. The flowers grow in the axils of the rosette leaves and are followed by pale, subrounded fruits, each with four winged lobes separated by deep grooves. The plant may also be found on wet mud at the margins of ponds when it is much smaller; it may be annual or perennial.

Intermediate Starwort, *Callitriche hamulata* (p. 101), is a perennial with stems about 60cm (2ft) long. It has linear leaves in deep water, broader, parallel-sided leaves in shallow water and a loose, concave rosette of elliptical or ovate leaves on the surface. The leaves have a characteristic notch at the apex. Flowers and fruits are borne in the axils of both floating and submerged leaves; the fruits are subrounded, with parallel sides, sharp keels and narrow wings borne without stalks. This plant grows in ponds and reservoirs, ditches and slow-moving streams throughout the British Isles, central and northwestern Europe. It also grows as a smaller form on mud.

Carrot family
Umbelliferae

Also known as the **Parsley family** and the **Apiaceae**. A large family of herbaceous plants, with about 275 genera and 2850 species, mostly from northern temperate regions. This is a family of great economic importance, supplying vegetables like celery, carrots and parsnips, and culinary herbs such as parsley, caraway, fennel, coriander and dill. Some are grown in flower gardens, notably the *Eryngium* and *Astrantia* species. Others, such as Hemlock and Cowbane, are among the most poisonous plants known.

Family features The flowers are tiny, regular and hermaphrodite, usually borne in simple or compound umbels, sometimes in heads. Each flower has a five-lobed calyx fused to the ovary and five free petals, which soon fall. There are five stamens alternating with the petals and a two-celled inferior ovary. The fruit develops below the flower and is quite distinctive, consisting of two sections (known as mericarps), one each side of the central axis of the fruit, and often joined together and suspended across the top of this central axis. When the fruit is ripe it splits open from the bottom into two sections, often leaving the two mericarps swinging from the top. The fruits are often elongated, or rounded and flattened. Many umbellifers (as they are called) have furrowed stems, either with soft pith, or hollow in the centre. Their leaves are alternate, usually compound and often much divided, with sheathing bases and lacking stipules. Many species are aromatically scented.

Marsh Pennywort, *Hydrocotyle vulgaris*, is one of a small group of species in the genus *Hydrocotyle*, plants rather different to other umbellifers and sometimes put in a family of their own. They are small perennials associated with wet places or growing in water, with creeping or floating stems and rounded leaves like pennies. Marsh Pennywort has slender, creeping stems, rooting at the nodes, and long-stalked, shallowly lobed, round leaves with a dimple in the centre where the stalk joins at the back. The tiny, pinkish-green flowers are borne in whorl-like umbels on separate stalks, hidden beneath the leaves in summer. This little plant grows in marshes, fens and bogs, beside streams and in wet meadows, often on acid soils. It is found throughout the British Isles and much of Europe, north to southern Scandinavia.

Sanicle, *Sanicula europaea*, is a woodland plant, growing in large colonies in deciduous woods beneath beech, oak and ash, especially on calcareous or base-rich soils. It is found throughout the British Isles and Europe. This is a perennial with a clump of shiny, palmately lobed, bristle-toothed leaves and flowering stems growing up to 60cm (2ft) tall in summer. The latter bear small, dense umbels of pink or white flowers, male on the outside, hermaphrodite in the centre. The fruits are covered with numerous hooked bristles and catch in the fur of passing animals. At one time this plant was an important medicinal herb, now more or less out of fashion, and used only in ointments for treating wounds and in gargles.

Great Masterwort, *Astrantia major*, grows in the wild in continental Europe in mountain woods and meadows. It is more familiar as a garden plant in Britain, where it may seed so profusely that it becomes a weed, but it does not grow wild. It is a perennial, with clumps of palmately lobed, toothed leaves growing on long stalks and unbranched flowering stems up to 1m (3ft) tall. The flowers are unmistakable, borne in dense umbels like posies or pincushions (one old garden name for this plant is Hattie's Pincushion). Each umbel has a ruff of white, often pink-tinged, pointed bracts beneath the white or pink flowers. The fruits are like small ridged cylinders. Several smaller species also grow in Europe and are grown in gardens.

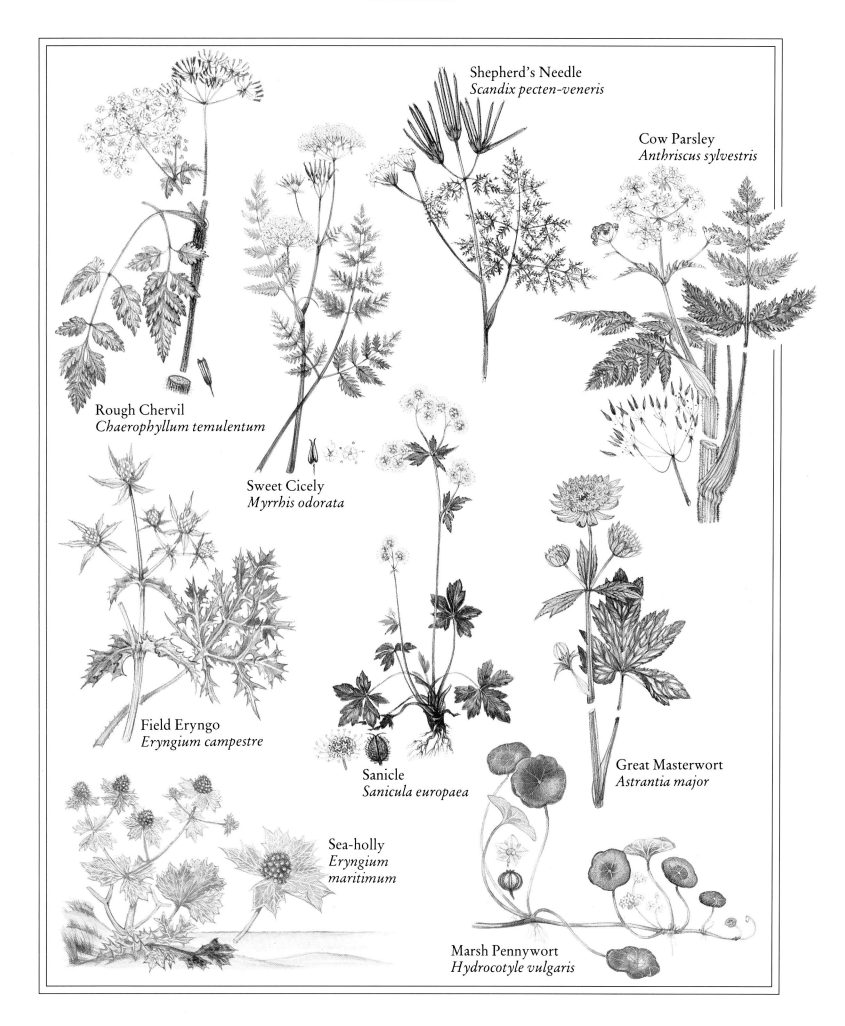

Shepherd's Needle
Scandix pecten-veneris

Cow Parsley
Anthriscus sylvestris

Rough Chervil
Chaerophyllum temulentum

Sweet Cicely
Myrrhis odorata

Field Eryngo
Eryngium campestre

Sanicle
Sanicula europaea

Great Masterwort
Astrantia major

Sea-holly
Eryngium maritimum

Marsh Pennywort
Hydrocotyle vulgaris

Sea-holly, *Eryngium maritimum* (p. 103), is not immediately recognizable as an umbellifer; its flowers are borne in heads rather than umbels and its leathery leaves are spiny, like those of thistles, with white veins and a thickened white margin. This stiff perennial plant is blue-grey in colour, with a clump of three-lobed, spine-edged basal leaves and branched flowering stems up to 60cm (2ft) tall in late summer; these have palmately lobed, also spiny leaves. The metallic blue flower heads are borne in clusters terminating the stems, cupped in spiny bracts. This plant is not very popular with holiday-makers; it grows on sandy beaches, sand-dunes and shingle banks around the coasts of the British Isles and western Europe, north to southern Scandinavia. It can be grown in gardens and the flower heads dried for flower arrangements.

Field Eryngo, *Eryngium campestre* (p. 103), is a less prickly species, a perennial with a clump of pinnate basal leaves on long stalks and erect flowering stems growing up to 60cm (2ft) tall. These are well endowed with spiny leaves, their bases clasping the stem, and with a terminal, branched inflorescence of many pale green, egg-shaped flower heads. Each head is cupped in several narrow, spine-edged bracts. This plant grows in dry, grassy places throughout much of Europe, except the north. In Britain it is not common, found only at a few scattered sites in southern England.

Rough Chervil, *Chaerophyllum temulentum* (p. 103), is a much more typical member of the Carrot family, as are the rest of the plants included here. It is a biennial, with a clump of twice- or three-times pinnate leaves in the first year and leafy flowering stems up to 1m (3ft) tall, with compound umbels of white flowers, in the second. The stems are solid, stiffly hairy and purple spotted; the leaves are also hairy and turn from dark green to purple as they age. The umbels are nodding when the flowers are in bud, each one has several narrow bracts beneath and 8–10 slender rays. This plant is found in most of Europe and much of the British Isles; it is absent from western Ireland and north and west Scotland. It is one of several umbellifers found in hedgebanks, flowering in sequence throughout the summer; this one is the second, coming into bloom just after Cow Parsley, from which it can be distinguished by its purple-spotted stems. It is poisonous, causing dizziness.

Cow Parsley, *Anthriscus sylvestris* (p. 103), is the first of the common hedgebank umbellifers to flower, blooming in early summer with a froth of lacy flowers (its other name is Queen Anne's Lace). It is another biennial plant, with twice- to three-times pinnate leaves in the first year and leafy, furrowed flowering stems in the second. They grow up to 1m (3ft) tall and bear many compound umbels of white flowers. Each umbel has 6–12 rays, 4–6 narrow bracts and an outer ring of flowers in which the outside petals are larger than the others. The fruits are black and bristly. This plant is often abundant in woodland margins and hedges, or in waste places throughout most of the British Isles and Europe.

Bur Chervil, *Anthriscus caucalis*, is a related annual plant, with hollow stems, twice- or three-times pinnate leaves and small umbels of white flowers in early summer. Its fruits are distinctive—covered in hooked bristles like small burs. It grows in hedgebanks and waste places scattered throughout much of the British Isles, especially near the sea but not in the north and west, throughout Europe, except the north.

Shepherd's Needle, *Scandix pecten-veneris* (p. 103), was a common weed at one time, found in arable land throughout Europe, including southeastern England. However, it is now rather rare as a result of the use of modern weed-killers, together with techniques for producing cleaner seed. It is a winter annual, a more or less hairless plant, with an erect branched stem up to 60cm (2ft tall) and two- to three-times pinnate, ferny leaves. The small white flowers are borne in simple umbels, usually growing in pairs in early summer. The plant becomes highly distinctive when the fruits form, for they are 15–80mm ($\frac{1}{2}$–3in) long with extremely long beaks. This plant has many names, as it has been familiar to farm workers for centuries; the names mostly describe the fruits, for they form at harvest time when the men were in the fields gathering the wheat. Folk names range from Venus' Comb and Ladies' Comb, to Darning Needles, Adam's Needles and even Devil's Needles.

Sweet Cicely, *Myrrhis odorata* (p. 103), is one of the edible members of this family; its leaves and fruits taste of aniseed and can be added to salads or used as a sweetener. The young roots can be eaten as a vegetable. This is a perennial plant, with hollow, rather grooved stems growing up to 2m (6ft) tall and twice- or three-times pinnate leaves with serrated segments. It blooms in early summer, with compound umbels of white flowers, some umbels with hermaphrodite flowers, others with male flowers only and these with shorter, more slender rays. The outer flowers of the umbels have unequal petals. The ripe fruits are shiny brown, oblong and deeply ridged with bristly hairs on the ridges. Plants grow in grassy places, hedges and woods, hills and mountains across Europe, in Wales, northern England, northern Ireland and Scotland.

Alexanders, *Smyrnium olusatrum*, is a mainly maritime plant found on coastal cliffs, but also in waste places, woods and hedgebanks, both near the sea and less often inland. It comes originally from the Mediterranean region, but has become naturalized northwards to France, Holland and the British Isles (rarely in Scotland). At one time it was cultivated and eaten as a vegetable, but has been replaced by celery. This is a stout biennial plant, its second-year stems growing up to 1.5m (5ft) tall; they are solid when young, becoming hollow with age and furrowed, branched near the top to produce dense, rounded umbels of yellow-green flowers in early summer. Each compound umbel has 7–15 rays. The leaves are dark green and shiny, basal ones up to 30cm (1ft) long and three-times divided into three leaflets; all the leaves have broadly sheathing bases.

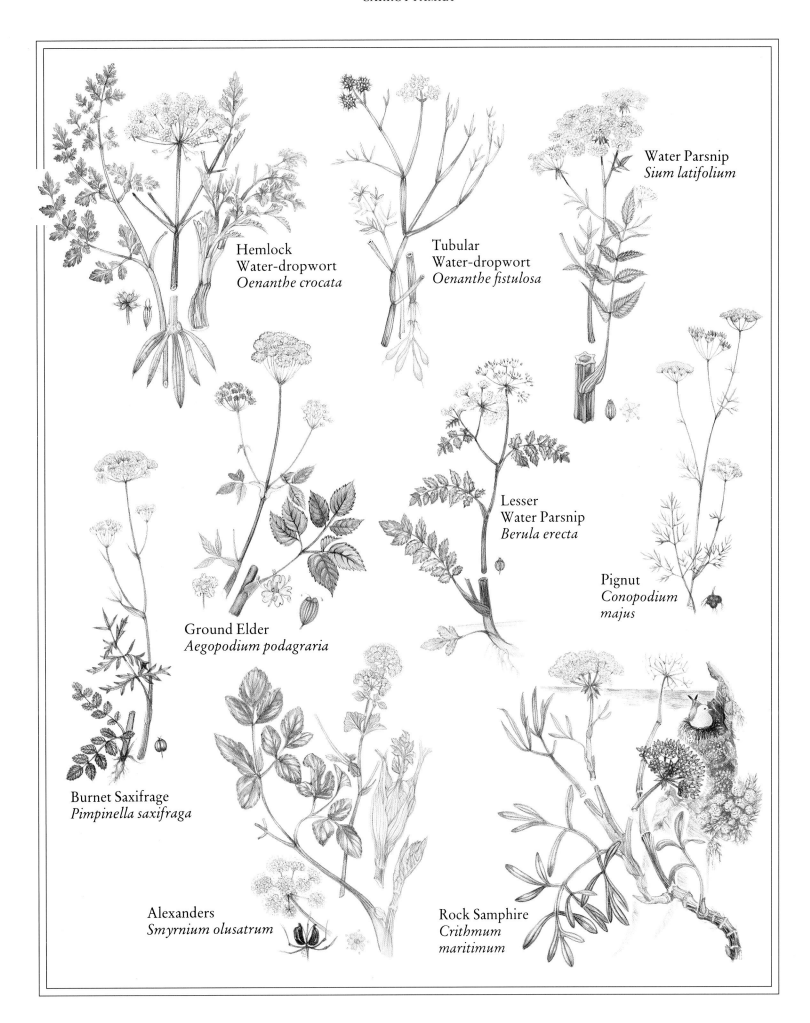

Hemlock
Water-dropwort
Oenanthe crocata

Tubular
Water-dropwort
Oenanthe fistulosa

Water Parsnip
Sium latifolium

Lesser
Water Parsnip
Berula erecta

Pignut
*Conopodium
majus*

Ground Elder
Aegopodium podagraria

Burnet Saxifrage
Pimpinella saxifraga

Alexanders
Smyrnium olusatrum

Rock Samphire
*Crithmum
maritimum*

Pignut or Earthnut, *Conopodium majus* (p. 105), is a slender plant, a perennial growing in woods and fields on acid soils throughout the British Isles and western Europe, north to Norway. It grows from a dark brown, irregular tuber (edible and with a nutty taste), producing broad, twice-pinnate basal leaves which soon wither, and sending up a slender stem about 50cm (20in) tall, its upper leaves finely divided with linear segments. It flowers in early summer, producing a few compound umbels with 6–12 rays; each is nodding in bud and opens into white flowers, unequal on the outside.

Burnet Saxifrage, *Pimpinella saxifraga* (p. 105), is another relatively slender perennial plant, this one found in dry, grassy places, often on calcareous soils, scattered throughout the British Isles and across most of Europe. It has an erect stem, rough in texture and solid, with pinnate leaves and serrated leaflets, the lower leaves twice-pinnate. It blooms in late summer, producing flat-topped, compound umbels with 10–22 rays and white flowers. At one time this plant was used in herb medicine, mainly to soothe coughs and bronchitis. Its less common relative, Greater Burnet Saxifrage, *P. major*, was used in the same way. It is a larger plant with hollow, angled stems, once-pinnate leaves and white or pinkish flowers. It grows in grassy places in hedges and woodland edges in England and Ireland, and across much of Europe.

Ground Elder, *Aegopodium podagraria* (p. 105), was used as a medicinal herb at one time to treat gout and rheumatism (hence its other name of Goutweed). It was also grown in gardens for its leaves, which were eaten like spinach; since it spreads into what are often ineradicable colonies with its creeping rhizomes, many owners of old gardens regret this practice. The plant sends up carpets of pinnate leaves in spring and flowering stems in summer. These bear dense, rounded umbels of white flowers, with 10–20 rays in each umbel. It is found throughout the British Isles and most of Europe.

Rock Samphire, *Crithmum maritimum* (p. 105), is a coastal plant, most often growing on cliffs and rocks around the Atlantic and Mediterranean coasts of Europe, around Ireland, on the west coast of Britain from northern England southwards, and on the south coast to East Anglia. It is a branched, perennial, blue-grey plant, with solid, narrowly ridged stems and fleshy, pinnate leaves with narrow leaflets. Yellow-green flowers appear after midsummer, borne in stout umbels with 8–36 rays. Young leaves and stems can be gathered in spring and pickled; young seed pods can be pickled later in the year.

Water Parsnip, *Sium latifolium* (p. 105), is one of several umbellifers found in wet places, growing in fens and marshes across Europe; in Britain it is found in England, mainly in the east, and in central Ireland but is declining in numbers with improved techniques of drainage in farming. This is a perennial plant, with a grooved, hollow stem up to 2m (6ft) tall, twice- or three-times pinnate submerged leaves with linear segments, and aerial pinnate leaves with 9–17 leaflets. The flowers are white, borne in dense, flat-topped umbels with 20–30 rays and large, leaf-like bracts. They appear in late summer.

Lesser Water Parsnip, *Berula erecta* (p. 105), is a similar plant, but it has sprawling stems which root where they touch the ground or the mud beneath the water. This is another semi-aquatic plant, growing in ditches and canals, marshes and ponds across much of Europe and lowland areas of the British Isles; it is rare in Wales and Scotland. It has hollow, narrowly ridged stems, pinnate leaves with serrated leaflets and umbels of white flowers opposite the leaves in late summer. The umbels are rather irregular, with 7–18 rays and leaf-like, often three-lobed bracts. The fruits are more or less globular.

The risk in eating wild umbellifers or using them in herb medicine is that some of the most poisonous of all flowering plants belong to this family and several resemble the useful species. Accurate identification of the family members is thus essential for anyone tempted to use them.

The **Water-dropworts** are a group of about 35 species in the genus *Oenanthe*, found in the north temperate regions of the world, with 13 in Europe. They are hairless perennials, all aquatic or marsh plants, and some are poisonous. **Hemlock Water-dropwort**, *O. crocata* (p. 105), is one of the most deadly umbellifers; its stems may be eaten in mistake for celery and the tuberous roots for parsnips. Death follows rapidly, but poisoning is more common in livestock than in humans. This plant grows in acid soils in wet, grassy places, on woodland edges, in ditches and beside water in western Europe, mostly in the south and west, and in Ireland. Its erect stems are hollow and grooved, up to 1.5m (5ft) tall and its leaves are large—30cm (1ft) long and ferny in appearance, three- to four-times pinnate, with serrated leaflets and sheathing bases to the leaf stalks. Plants flower around midsummer, bearing large, terminal umbels with 10–40 rays and white flowers.

Tubular Water-dropwort, *Oenanthe fistulosa* (p. 105), is also poisonous, although less so. It has erect, hollow stems, 30–90cm (1–3ft) tall, constricted at the nodes and rooting at the lower nodes. The stems grow from a clump of swollen, spindle-shaped roots. The leaves are pinnate with tubular leaf stalks and linear leaflets, and the white flowers are borne in late summer in dense umbels with 2–4 rays. The partial umbels become globular in fruit, with cylindrical fruits. This plant grows in marshes and shallow water across most of Europe; in the British Isles it is found mainly in the east, less commonly in Ireland, rarely in Scotland. Fine-leaved Water-dropwort, *O. aquatica*, is another poisonous species, found in slow-moving or still waters in England, eastern Wales and central Ireland, and across most of Europe. It has submerged leaves with thread-like segments, and three- to four-times pinnate, aerial leaves. Its white flowers grow in umbels opposite the leaves and terminating the stems; each has 4–16 rays.

Fool's Parsley, *Aethusa cynapium*, is another poisonous umbellifer, its chief danger that it may be mistaken for Parsley,

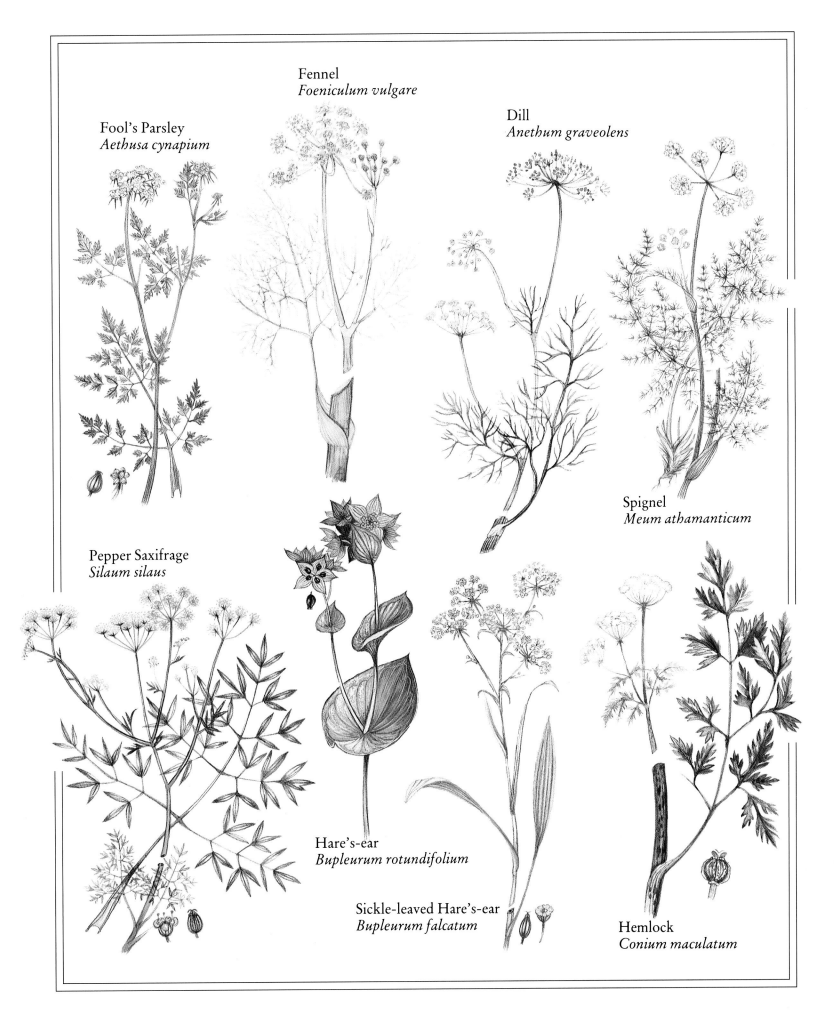

Fool's Parsley
Aethusa cynapium

Fennel
Foeniculum vulgare

Dill
Anethum graveolens

Spignel
Meum athamanticum

Pepper Saxifrage
Silaum silaus

Hare's-ear
Bupleurum rotundifolium

Sickle-leaved Hare's-ear
Bupleurum falcatum

Hemlock
Conium maculatum

as it can be lethal if eaten. Animals avoid it as it has a foetid scent when green; however, the poisons disappear with drying so it is harmless in hay. This plant grows as a weed of arable land, gardens and waste places throughout most of Europe and the British Isles, becoming rarer in Scotland and Ireland. It is a hairless annual plant, with branched, leafy stems, twice-pinnate leaves with leaflets in threes and umbels of white flowers in the latter half of summer. Each umbel has 10–20 rays and three or four linear bracts hang beneath one side of each partial umbel.

Young shoots of **Fennel**, *Foeniculum vulgare* (p. 107), have a distinctive anise-like scent and taste (like the whole plant), and are eaten in salads or as a vegetable. Stems and leaves are dried and chopped for flavouring sauces that are especially good with fish. The fruits are also used for flavouring. Fennel is native to the Mediterranean region, but is grown as a herb and naturalized over much of continental Europe, also in England and Ireland. It grows in waste places and roadsides inland, on cliffs near the sea. Both the normal grey-green and a bronze-leaved form are grown for decoration in gardens. This is a hairless, perennial plant, but individuals seldom live for more than a few years and they seed prolifically. Each plant has an erect, solid stem up to 2m (6ft) tall, with many extremely finely divided leaves with linear segments, quite characteristic of the plant. Growing opposite the upper leaves are long stalks bearing compound umbels of yellow flowers, each one with 10–40 rays and no bracts.

Dill, *Anethum graveolens* (p. 107), is one of several aromatic umbellifers cultivated for their seeds, which are used as fla-vouring in food and to aid digestion; they are used in herbal medicine to counteract indigestion and settle upset stomachs. Dill is one of the ingredients of gripe water, given to infants to relieve colic; other active constituents are Fennel and Anise, both also umbellifers. Dill is native to Asia, but is cultivated in the Mediterranean and other parts of Europe, escaping to grow wild in fields and waste places, only as a casual in Britain. It is an erect, branched, annual plant up to 1.5m (5ft) tall, hairless and blue-green in colour, with many compound leaves so finely divided that their segments appear threadlike. The flowers are greenish-yellow and borne in large compound umbels above the leaves, with 30–40 rays in each. The fruits are flattened and elliptical, strongly ridged.

Pepper Saxifrage, *Silaum silaus* (p. 107), is a branched perennial plant, hairless in texture, with erect, narrowly ridged, solid stems growing up to 1m (3ft) tall. It has twice- to four-times pinnate lower leaves and a few upper leaves often reduced to sheaths. Umbels of yellow flowers appear in the latter half of summer. The umbels are borne on long stalks, have 4–15 rays and are irregular in appearance. This plant grows in meadows, on grassy roadsides and other grassy places across much of Europe, but is absent from the north and Portugal; in Britain it is found in England and Wales, mainly in the south and east.

Spignel or Baldmoney, *Meum athamanticum* (p. 107), is a very aromatic, hairless plant, a perennial with branched, hollow stems growing up to 60cm (2ft) tall. It has twice-pinnate leaves, mostly growing in a basal clump and leaving the fibrous remains of their leaf bases from year to year. Terminating the stems are open, compound umbels of white flowers, each with 6–15 rays, and widely separated small, dense, partial umbels. These have 3–8 small, linear bracts hanging beneath. This plant grows in rough, grassy places in mountain areas in western and central Europe, in a few places in northern England and Wales, locally in Scotland where the roots were eaten at one time. The origin of its strange names is obscure.

Hemlock, *Conium maculatum* (p. 107), is one of the poiso-nous umbellifers; it can cause paralysis and death but is not necessarily lethal. It is, of course, most well known for its part in the death of Socrates in ancient Greece. It grows in damp places and often on heavy soils in woods and meadows, in fields and on roadsides, beside ditches and streams throughout Europe and the British Isles, less commonly in the north. It is a biennial, with a branched, furrowed flowering stem up to 3m (9ft) tall in the second year, distinctive for its smooth texture, its greyish colour and its purple spots. It has a characteristic foetid scent likened to that of mice, and soft, twice- to four-times pinnate leaves with coarsely serrated leaflets. The umbels of white flowers appear at the tops of the stems and in the leaf axils around midsummer. Its dark brown fruits are globular, with wavy, pale brown ridges.

The **Thorow-waxes**, *Bupleurum* species, are rather differ-ent umbellifers, with simple, entire leaves. There are about 150 species in the genus and 39 in Europe. **Hare's-ear** or Thorow-wax, *B. rotundifolium* (p. 107), is an annual plant, with an erect, hollow stem only 30cm (1ft) tall, often purple-tinged, and with round leaves. The lower ones have stalks but the upper ones encircle the stem. Yellow flowers are borne at the tops of the stems, in compound umbels with 4–8 rays; each partial umbel is cupped in conspicuous, broad, yellow-green bracts. This little plant grows as a weed in arable land and waste places in western and central Europe. At one time it was widely naturalized in southeastern England but is now probably extinct in Britain. False Thorow-Wax, *B. subovatum*, is simi-lar but has more pointed leaves. It has been introduced into Britain from Europe in bird seed to grow as a casual weed.

Sickle-leaved Hare's-ear, *Bupleurum falcatum* (p. 107), was at one time introduced into southeastern Britain but has now declined almost to extinction. It is found across much of Europe, except the north and Portugal, in grassy places and woods. This is a perennial plant, with a hollow stem up to 1m (3ft) tall and sickle-shaped leaves, the lower ones with stalks, upper ones linear and partly clasping the stems. Yellow flowers grow in sparse, compound umbels at the tops of the stem; each has 5–11 rays and 2–5 prominent linear bracts cupping the base of the rays. Slender Hare's-ear, *B. tenuissimum*, is an annual,

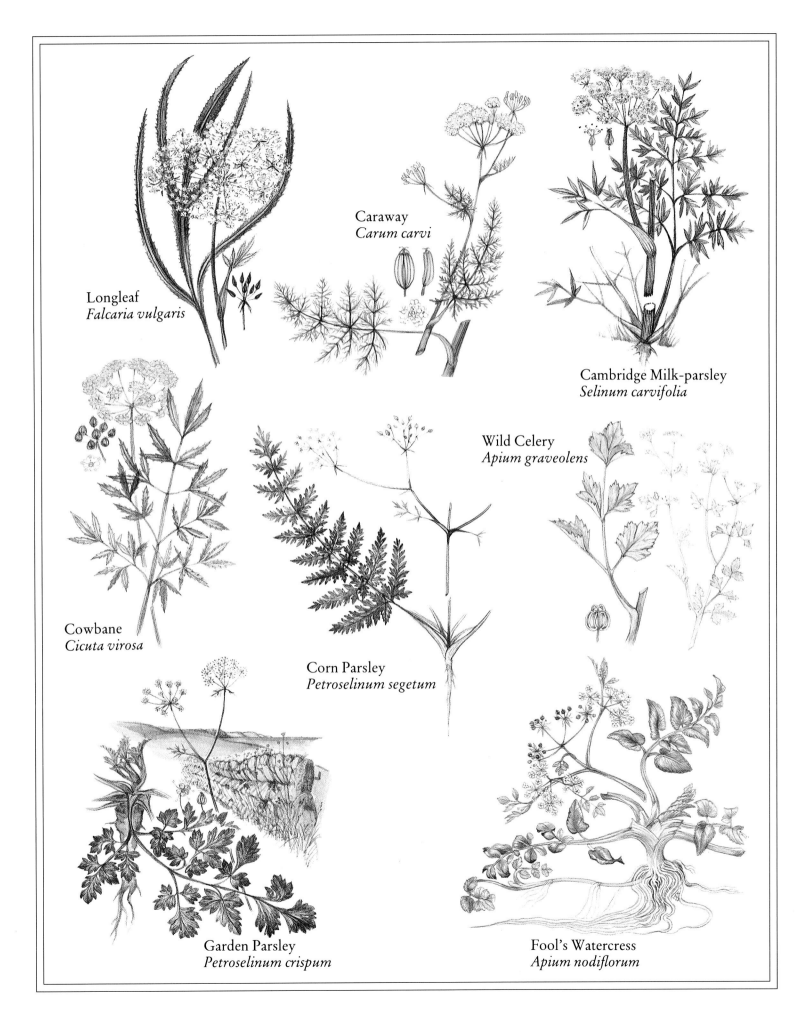

Longleaf
Falcaria vulgaris

Caraway
Carum carvi

Cambridge Milk-parsley
Selinum carvifolia

Cowbane
Cicuta virosa

Wild Celery
Apium graveolens

Corn Parsley
Petroselinum segetum

Garden Parsley
Petroselinum crispum

Fool's Watercress
Apium nodiflorum

with branched, wiry stems and small umbels of yellow flowers in the axils of the leaves. It is widespread in southern and central Europe, and also found in Britain in salt marshes around the coast of England, much more rarely in waste places inland.

Fool's Watercress, *Apium nodiflorum* (p. 109), is not poisonous, even though its name implies danger. It grows in shallow ponds and ditches often with Watercress, and the leaves of the two plants are similar; both are edible. It is a sprawling plant, with furrowed stems rooting at the lower nodes and shiny, bright green, pinnate leaves with ovate leaflets. The white flowers appear in late summer in small compound umbels opposite the leaves; each umbel has 3–15 rays, with 4–7 small bracts beneath each partial umbel. This plant is found in western and southern Europe and much of the British Isles, most commonly in the south and rare in Scotland.

Wild Celery, *Apium graveolens* (p. 109), is a branched biennial, with erect, grooved stems, pinnate leaves with lobed, toothed leaflets on the lower part of the stem, three-leaflet leaves on the upper. The plant has the characteristic yellow-green colour and scent of celery. Its flowers are greenish-white, borne in dense, compound umbels on short stalks subtended by small upper leaves. This plant grows locally in damp places, especially where the soil is brackish near the sea, in Europe north to Denmark and in the maritime counties of the British Isles. It is edible but stronger than cultivated celery, which is a milder variety of this species.

Garden Parsley, *Petroselinum crispum* (p. 109), is the familiar kitchen herb used for seasoning sauces and in salads; fresh leaves are rich in Vitamin C. Parsley is also used in herb medicine as a diuretic and to promote menstruation. It is not only cultivated but also grows wild throughout Europe and the British Isles, except in northern Scotland, on rocks and walls, in waste and grassy places. However, it is not wise to eat wild plants because of the danger of picking Fool's Parsley by mistake. It is a stout biennial plant, with stems up to 75cm (30in) tall, erect and branched, solid and finely ridged, with shiny, three-times pinnate leaves, often crisped at the edges of the leaflets and with the characteristic scent of parsley. The plant produces flat-topped umbels of yellowish flowers around midsummer; the umbels are compound, with 8–20 rays and the flowers are followed by ridged, egg-shaped fruits.

Corn Parsley, *Petroselinum segetum* (p. 109), is a related plant, whose stems and fruits have the parsley scent. It is a hairless biennial, with branched, slender, leafy stems growing up to 1m (3ft) tall in the second year. The stems are solid and finely ridged and the leaves are pinnate with toothed, ovate leaflets. The plant produces white flowers in late summer, borne in umbels with 2–5 very unequal rays; each umbel is made up of small partial umbels with very few (often only 3–5) flowers. Corn Parsley grows in grassy places and hedgerows in western and southern Europe, in southern and eastern England, and in a few places near the Welsh coast.

Cowbane, *Cicuta virosa* (p. 109), is an extremely poisonous plant, causing convulsions and death in both livestock and people. Its roots are deadly and may be mistaken for parsnips since they have a similar scent; they are most likely to be found on the banks of ditches after the ditch has been cleaned out. Fortunately, this is not a particularly common plant; it grows in ditches and marshes, locally in Great Britain and parts of northern Ireland, also scattered in northern and central Europe. It is a stout perennial, with erect, hollow stems up to 120cm (4ft) tall, large twice- or three-times pinnate leaves with linear or lance-shaped segments, and dense, flat-topped umbels of white flowers in late summer. Each umbel has 10–30 rays and many small linear bracts beneath each partial umbel.

Longleaf, *Falcaria vulgaris* (p. 109), is a Continental species found only in East Anglia and southeastern England in Britain, and there it is naturalized. In Europe it grows on roadsides, in waste places and fields. This is a tangled perennial plant, grey-green in colour, with solid stems up to 50cm (20in) tall and leaves divided into linear, three-lobed, serrated segments. It has white flowers in late summer, borne in loose umbels with 10–20 slender rays and many linear bracts.

Cambridge Milk-parsley, *Selinum carvifolia* (p. 109), is another rare plant in Britain but a native one, found in fens and damp meadows in Cambridgeshire, at one time also in Lincolnshire and Nottinghamshire; it grows across much of Europe. It is a hairless perennial plant, with erect, solid, angled stems up to 1m (3ft) tall, and twice- or three-times pinnate leaves with oval or linear segments. It bears umbels of white flowers in late summer and autumn; each umbel grows on a long stalk and has 15–30 rays. This is another plant that smells like parsley.

Caraway, *Carum carvi* (p. 109), is native to western Europe but was probably introduced to the British Isles for its seeds. These are used in baking and cheese-making, in sauerkraut and for flavouring liqueurs. It grows in meadows and woods in mountain regions of Europe and is naturalized in waste and grassy places in lowland areas scattered throughout the British Isles. This is a biennial plant, its leaves twice- or three-times pinnate so that they appear finely dissected with linear segments, all in a basal rosette in the first year. In the second year the flowering stems develop; they are ridged and hollow, with dissected leaves and compound umbels of white or pinkish flowers, each umbel with 5–16 rays. The fruits that follow—the caraway 'seeds'—are elliptical and ribbed, with a pleasant aromatic scent when crushed.

Scots Lovage, *Ligusticum scoticum*, is a northern plant, as its name implies, found on rocky coasts in Scotland, northern Ireland and the coasts of northwestern Europe. It is a glossy, bright green perennial plant, growing up to 90cm (3ft) tall, with erect, ribbed stems, often reddish towards the base. The leaves are twice-pinnate, with ovate, serrated, sometimes lobed, leaflets. Around midsummer the plant bears umbels of greenish-white flowers; the umbels have 8–14 rays.

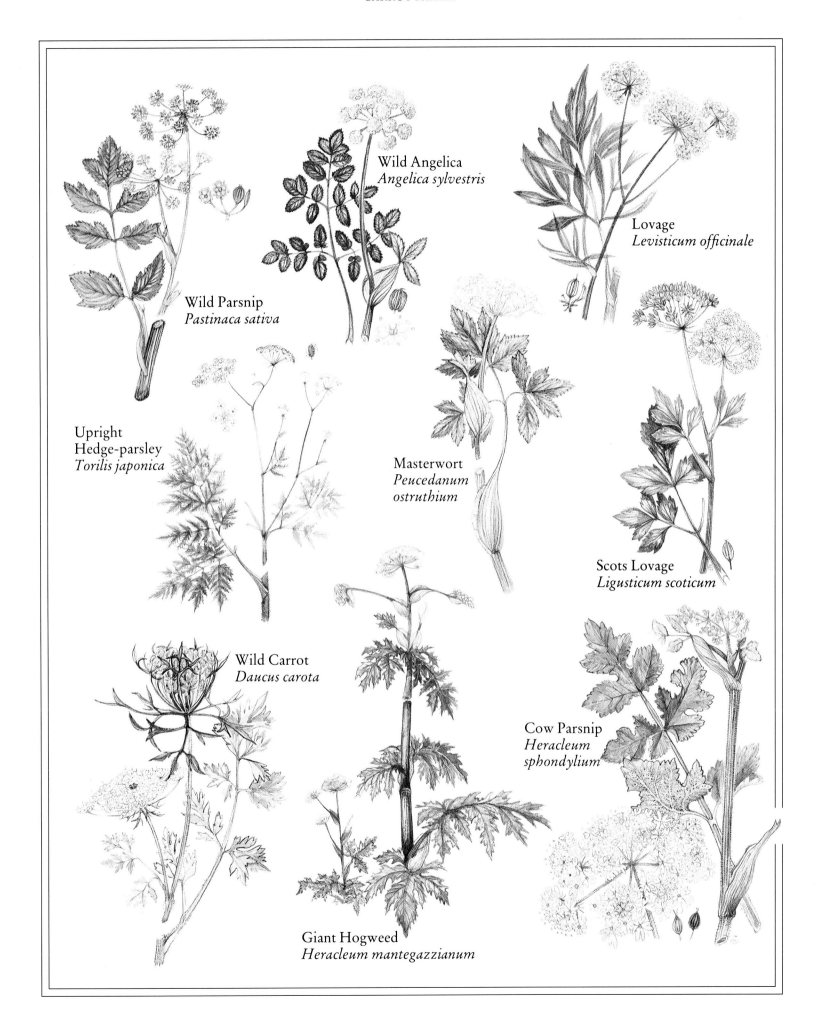

Wild Parsnip
Pastinaca sativa

Wild Angelica
Angelica sylvestris

Lovage
Levisticum officinale

Upright
Hedge-parsley
Torilis japonica

Masterwort
*Peucedanum
ostruthium*

Scots Lovage
Ligusticum scoticum

Wild Carrot
Daucus carota

Cow Parsnip
*Heracleum
sphondylium*

Giant Hogweed
Heracleum mantegazzianum

The original **Lovage** is a culinary and medicinal herb, *Levisticum officinale* (p. 111). It comes from Iran but is now naturalized throughout much of Europe, sometimes in the British Isles. This is an aromatically scented, large perennial plant, with hollow, branched stems growing up to 2.5m (8ft) tall. It has large, shiny green leaves, twice- or three-times pinnate, with irregularly toothed, wedge-shaped segments and umbels of yellowish flowers in late summer. The umbels measure up to 20cm (8in) across and have 12–20 rays. The fruits of this plant are characteristic, with narrow wings on all the ribs. Young leaves are used commercially for flavouring vegetable extracts and can be added to salads and sauces, or rubbed on meat.

Wild Angelica, *Angelica sylvestris* (p. 111), is a stout, almost hairless plant, with hollow, finely ribbed stems growing up to 2m (6ft) tall, often tinged with purple and with a whitish bloom. The lower leaves measure up to 60cm (2ft) long and are twice- or three-times pinnate, with long stalks and lance-shaped, serrated segments; upper leaves are reduced to inflated sheaths partly enclosing the developing umbels. The flowers may be white or pink, borne in large umbels with 15–40 rays. The fruits are oval with membranous wings. This plant grows in damp meadows, woods and fens throughout Europe and the British Isles. Garden Angelica, *A. archangelica*, is native to northern Europe and grown for its stems, which are candied and used in baking. It has greenish-white flowers.

Masterwort, *Peucedanum ostruthium* (p. 111), is one of about 30 species in this genus in Europe, with three in Britain, few of them common. Masterwort grows in mountain woods and meadows in central Europe and has been introduced into western Europe and Britain as a herbal plant. It is found mainly in northern England and Scotland. This is an erect perennial up to 1m (3ft) tall, with ridged, hollow stems; the once- or twice-ternate leaves have lobed, toothed leaflets and greatly inflated sheathing bases to the stalks. The plant has white or pinkish flowers, borne in late summer; the umbels have 30–60 rays.

Wild Parsnip, *Pastinaca sativa* (p. 111), is the wild form of the cultivated plant. It is a biennial, with a clump of once-pinnate leaves in the first year and erect flowering stems up to 1.5 (5ft) tall in the second. The taproots, formed by the first-year plants as a food store for the following year, are the edible vegetables. The whole plant smells strongly of parsnips. The flowering plant has hollow, furrowed stems and pinnate, bright green leaves with serrated leaflets. It also has dense, compound umbels of tiny yellow flowers in late summer. Each flower has five inrolled petals. Wild Parsnip is most likely to be found on chalk or limestone, growing in grassy waste places and along roadsides throughout much of Europe and in England.

Cow Parsnip or Hogweed, *Heracleum sphondylium* (p. 111), is a large, bristly-hairy perennial plant growing up to 2m (6ft) tall. It has an erect stem, hollow and ridged with conspicuous resin canals in the furrows, and large pinnate leaves with lobed, serrated leaflets, the lower ones with stalks and the upper ones with inflated, sheath-like bases. The flowers may be white, greenish-white or pinkish and are borne in large umbels up to 20cm (8in) across; each has 7–10 stout rays and there are reflexed, linear bracts beneath each partial umbel. Rim flowers have enlarged, notched petals pointing towards the outside and smaller inner petals. This large, conspicuous plant grows in rough, grassy places, in open woods, on roadsides and in hedgerows throughout the British Isles and Europe. Its young shoots and leaves can be eaten as a vegetable.

If Cow Parsnip is big, then its big brother is a giant. **Giant Hogweed**, *Heracleum mantegazzianum* (p. 111), grows up to 5m (15ft) tall in its second year (it is a biennial) and has hollow, purple-spotted stems 10cm (4in) across. Its huge leaves grow up to 2.5m (8ft) across and are divided into broad, irregularly lobed, coarsely toothed sections. The white flowers are borne in very large umbels up to 50cm (20in) across, with 50–150 stout, hairy rays. The outermost petals of the rim flowers are much larger than the others. This plant is native to the Caucasus but has been introduced into other parts of Europe (including Britain) as an ornamental garden plant; it has escaped in many areas to grow in waste places, often near rivers. However, it is not a welcome plant, since its sap reacts with sunlight and can cause blisters if it is handled in hot, sunny weather, and it seeds prolifically, soon becoming a weed.

Upright Hedge-parsley, *Torilis japonica* (p. 111), is one of the three common roadside umbellifers, flowering just after Rough Chervil. It is found in hedgerows and grassy places throughout the British Isles and Europe, except the far north. It is a hairy, annual plant, with stiff, erect, ridged stems up to 120cm (4ft) tall and once- to three-times pinnate leaves. The leaflets are lance-shaped and toothed. The flowers grow in compound umbels with 5–12 rays and several bracts at the base; the flowers may be white or pinkish and are followed by egg-shaped fruits covered with hooked spines. Spreading Hedge-parsley, *T. arvensis*, is a smaller plant, with only one or no bracts at the base of its umbels and straight-spined fruits. It grows in arable fields in many parts of Europe, except the north, and in southeastern England.

Wild Carrot, *Daucus carota* (p. 111), is the species that gave rise to cultivated carrots, but the wild variety has thin, tough, inedible roots. It does have the characteristic carroty smell, however. It grows in dry, grassy places and fields, often on calcareous soils, and near the sea throughout the British Isles and Europe. Wild Carrots are biennial plants, forming clumps of ferny leaves in the first year and overwintering by taproots. From these grow the flowering stems in the second year, reaching 1m (3ft) in height. They have divided, fern-like leaves up to three-times pinnate, and dense, flat-topped umbels of creamy-white flowers, usually with one central purplish or red flower in each umbel. The fruiting umbels are easily recognizable, for they close up and come to resemble birds' nests, containing many flattened, spiky fruits.

A Scottish heather moor in August with the heather in full bloom. In the foreground (from left to right) are Heather, Bilberry and Bell-heather.

Heath family
Ericaceae

This is a large family, with about 70 genera and 1500 species, found throughout much of the world. Many grow in acid soils, where other plants would find difficulty absorbing nutrients; heath family members can probably survive in these soils because they have roots associated with mycorrhizal fungi. The fungi help them absorb the nutrients they need. All members of the family are woody to a greater or lesser extent and some are large shrubs or trees. Others are small, creeping, sub-shrubby plants. There are many fine garden plants among them, including rhododendrons, azaleas and heathers.

Family features The flowers are often showy, usually regular and hermaphrodite, with four or five sepals united to form a tubular calyx and four or five petals united to form a tubular or bell-like corolla. There are usually twice as many stamens as petal-lobes in the corolla and the ovary may be inferior or superior with 4–5 cells. The fruits are capsules, berries or drupes. The flowers are borne singly or in clusters. The leaves are usually evergreen, mostly simple, usually arranged alternately; they lack stipules.

Trailing Azalea, *Loiseleuria procumbens*, is an attractive, far northern plant, growing across northern Europe, in the Alps and other mountains and in Scotland. It forms bushy mats in exposed rocky areas and moors, with many diffusely branched woody stems and opposite, evergreen leaves. These leaves are typical of those found on many plants growing where water may be scarce; they are leathery, with hairs on the undersides and they have inrolled margins, all ways of conserving water. The plant bears small, terminal clusters of pink, bell-shaped flowers in summer followed by ovoid capsules.

St Dabeoc's Heath, *Daboecia cantabrica*, is a straggling shrub about 60cm (2ft) tall, with evergreen, elliptical leaves; these are dark green above, downy white beneath. In late summer the flowers appear, borne in loose racemes at the tops of the stems; they are reddish-purple and bell-shaped, followed by dry capsules. This plant grows in heaths in Galway and County Mayo in western Ireland, in western France, Portugal and northwestern Spain. It is also grown in gardens.

Bog Rosemary, *Andromeda polifolia*, is an evergreen shrub about 30cm (1ft) tall, with spreading stems and narrow leaves, white on their undersides when young. In early summer bell-shaped, pink or white flowers grow in umbel-like clusters terminating the stems, followed by greyish capsules. This plant grows in acid bogs from Wales and northern England into southern Scotland, in central Ireland and across northern Europe, south in the mountains on the Continent.

Bearberry, *Arctostaphylos uva-ursi*, is found across Europe, in northern England, Scotland and Ireland. It grows on moors and in open woods, often in rocky places and on banks. It is a prostrate, shrubby plant with woody stems and leathery, spoon-shaped leaves; these are used in herb medicine and for tanning leather. In early summer the plant bears pink-tinged, white bell-like flowers; they are followed by bright red, mealy, edible berries which cover the stems in winter.

There are about 150 species of *Vaccinium* in the world, but only five in Europe. They include cranberries and blueberries from North America, bilberries in Europe. **Bilberry**, *V. myrtillus*, also known as Whortleberry and Blaeberry, has edible blue-black berries, a real treat eaten fresh with cream or in pies. This plant forms spreading patches of erect stems 30–60cm (1–2ft) tall, with green twigs and ovate, deciduous leaves; in late summer drooping, pink-tinged, urn-shaped flowers appear in the leaf axils. They are followed by the berries. This creeping plant grows in dry, acid soils, on moors and heaths, in open birch and pine woods throughout much of the British Isles, becoming less common in the south. It is also found throughout much of Europe, in mountains in the south.

Bog Bilberry, *Vaccinium uliginosum*, is another deciduous creeping shrub, this one growing up to 50cm (20in) tall, with more spreading branches and brownish twigs. It has ovate, blue-green leaves, pink-tinged white, globular flowers in late summer and edible, sweet, blue-black berries. This plant grows in damp, acid soils, on moors and heaths, and in open coniferous woods in northern England and Scotland and across northern Europe, often in association with Bilberry.

Cowberry, *Vaccinium vitis-idaea*, grows in acid soils on moors and heaths, and in coniferous woods in Ireland and Scotland, extending south into northern England and Wales, and across northern Europe. This creeping shrub grows only 30cm (1ft) tall and has arching branches with leathery, evergreen leaves. It bears drooping clusters of bell-shaped, pink-tinged white flowers terminating the stems in summer, then red, edible but rather tasteless berries in the autumn.

Cranberry, *Vaccinium oxycoccus*, is a trailing shrub with slender, rooting stems, evergreen, pointed-oblong leaves and clusters of nodding, pinkish-white flowers, each with four backwardly-pointing petals and a cone of fused stamens. The flowers are followed in late summer by rounded or pear-shaped, edible red berries. This plant grows among *Sphagnum* mosses in bogs, less often in wet heaths and woods, in many parts of Ireland and Great Britain, least commonly in southern England and the Midlands. It is found across much of Europe.

One of the most familiar plants in this family is **Heather** or Ling, *Calluna vulgaris* (p. 117), the dominant plant over great stretches of moors and heaths on acid soils throughout the British Isles and western Europe, becoming less common further east and south on the Continent. It also grows in open woods. This is an evergreen shrub growing up to 60cm (2ft) tall, its sprawling branches rooting at the nodes and bearing many leafy side shoots. The leaves are small and scale-like, borne in opposite pairs and pressed closely to the stems. In late

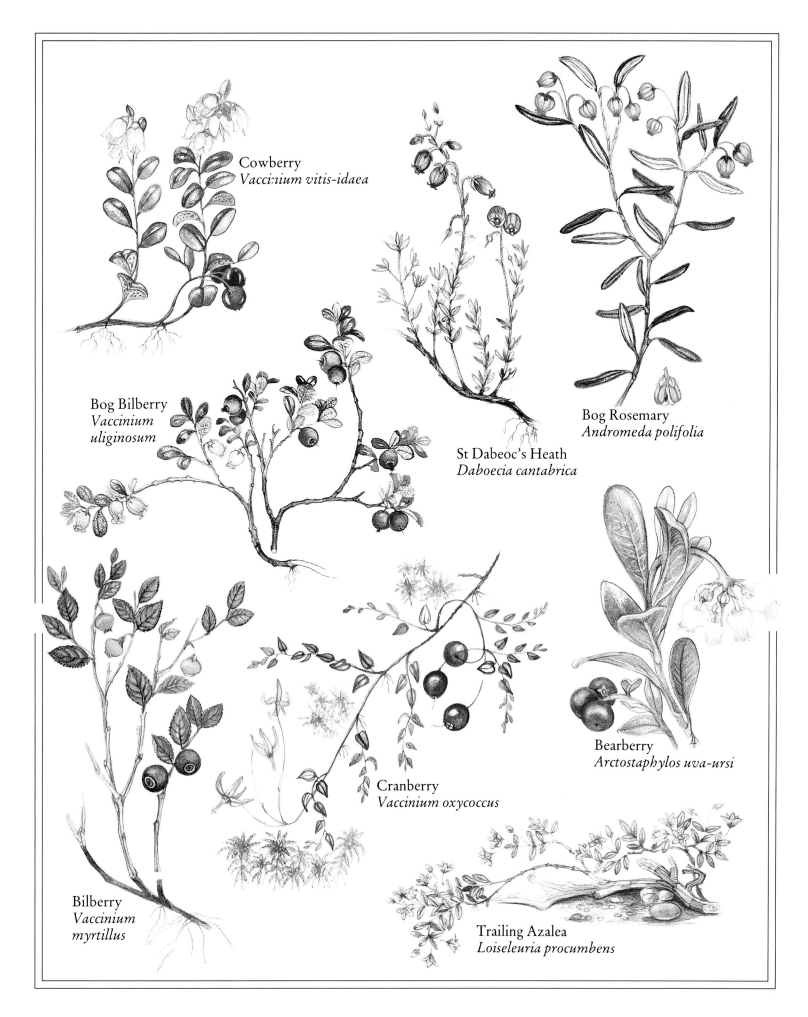

Cowberry
Vaccinium vitis-idaea

Bog Bilberry
Vaccinium uliginosum

St Dabeoc's Heath
Daboecia cantabrica

Bog Rosemary
Andromeda polifolia

Bearberry
Arctostaphylos uva-ursi

Cranberry
Vaccinium oxycoccus

Bilberry
Vaccinium myrtillus

Trailing Azalea
Loiseleuria procumbens

summer this rather dowdy shrub is transformed by the small, bell-like flowers borne along the tops of the stems and along the side shoots; the flowers are pale pinkish-purple, the colour coming from both calyx and corolla. At one time Heather was used for fuel and bedding, as animal fodder and for making brushes and baskets. Heather honey is one of the finest.

Many other heathers or heaths belong to the genus *Erica*, with about 17 species in Europe. This is, however, only a small percentage of the world total of 500, the majority of which are found in South Africa. All the *Erica* species are evergreen shrubs, with small, entire leaves in whorls and bell-shaped or urn-shaped flowers. Their fruits are dry capsules.

Bell-heather, *Erica cinerea*, is one of the most attractive and widespread species, found on dry heaths and moors throughout the British Isles and western Europe, north to Norway. It is a branched shrub about 60cm (2ft) tall, with many upward-growing stems and numerous leafy side shoots; the leaves are linear with inrolled margins, dark green and hairless, borne in whorls of three. In late summer the plants flower, transforming the moors (with Heather) into purple instead of dark green. The flowers are reddish-purple, urn-shaped and constricted at the mouth, borne along the tops of the stems.

Cross-leaved Heath, *Erica tetralix*, is also widespread, found in wetter heaths and moors, also in bogs and pinewoods throughout the British Isles but less commonly in parts of central and southern England than elsewhere. It is also found in western and northern Europe. It is another much-branched shrub about 60cm (2ft) tall, with more or less upright stems. These bear many linear leaves with margins inrolled almost to the midrib, hairy when young and arranged in cross-like whorls of four (hence Cross-leaved Heath). The flowers appear in late summer in little umbel-like clusters nodding at the tops of the stems; they are rose-pink in colour and urn-shaped with a constricted mouth.

Other European heathers are much more restricted in their distributions. **Dorset Heath**, *Erica ciliaris*, grows locally in heathland in Dorset, south Devon and Cornwall in England, also in Connemara in Ireland, and in France, Spain and Portugal. It is not unlike Bell-heather, a small shrub up to 60cm (2ft) tall, with more or less erect branches and leaves in whorls of three on side shoots. The leaves have inrolled margins and a white underside. The flowers are bright pink, urn-shaped and slightly curved above, slightly swollen beneath; they are borne in one-sided racemes at the tops of the stems in summer.

Cornish Heath, *Erica vagans*, is found only on heathland around the Lizard in Cornwall, in Fermanagh in Ireland and in parts of France and northern Spain. It grows up to 80cm (30in) tall, and has erect branches with no side shoots. The leaves are linear with inrolled margins, and borne four or five in a whorl. The flowers are small and bell-shaped, pale lilac with purple-brown anthers protruding from the mouth, borne in dense, leafy racemes at the tops of the stems in late summer.

Irish Heath, *Erica erigena*, grows in bogs and wet heaths in Galway and Mayo in Ireland, also from western France to Spain and Portugal. This is a larger shrub, up to 2m (6ft) tall, with many more or less upright branches without side shoots. It has dark green linear leaves with inrolled margins, borne four in a whorl. The flowers are tubular and dull pinkish-purple, with dark purple anthers half-protruding; they are borne in one-sided racemes at the tops of the stems.

Crowberry family
Empetraceae

A very small family, with 3 genera and 9 species, found in north temperate and Arctic regions, southern South America and the island of Tristan da Cunha. They are evergreen shrubs resembling the heathers.

Crowberry, *Empetrum nigrum* (p. 119), is the only widespread or common member of the family in Europe. It is a low-growing shrub with numerous erect and sprawling stems forming low mounds, the stems becoming prostrate and rooting at the edges of the mounds. The stems are densely covered with small, leathery, needle-like leaves alternately arranged. The leaves have strongly inrolled margins to reduce water loss. Tiny pink flowers grow in the axils of the leaves, male and female flowers on separate plants, and the female plants go on to produce juicy black berries. Crowberry grows in peaty soils on moors and the drier parts of bogs, in birch and pine woods in Ireland, Scotland, Wales and northern England, becoming rare in the Midlands and south. It is also found in suitable habitats across much of Europe. Mountain Crowberry is a subspecies of this plant, subsp. *hermaphroditum*, found at higher altitudes; its stems do not root at the edges of the mounds and its flowers are hermaphrodite.

Diapensia family
Diapensiaceae

A very small family, with 6 genera and about 20 species of evergreen herbs or dwarf shrubs, found in the north temperate and Arctic regions of the world. Some are beautiful plants grown in gardens. They are related to the heathers.

Diapensia, *Diapensia lapponica* (p. 119), is an evergreen cushion-like plant, with branched stems and crowded, overlapping leaves. In spring white, bell-shaped flowers (with their parts in fives) appear on short, erect branches all over the mat. This is a far northern plant, growing in rocky places in the Arctic mountains and tundra. It is found in two places in the Scottish mountains, on exposed ridges in Inverness.

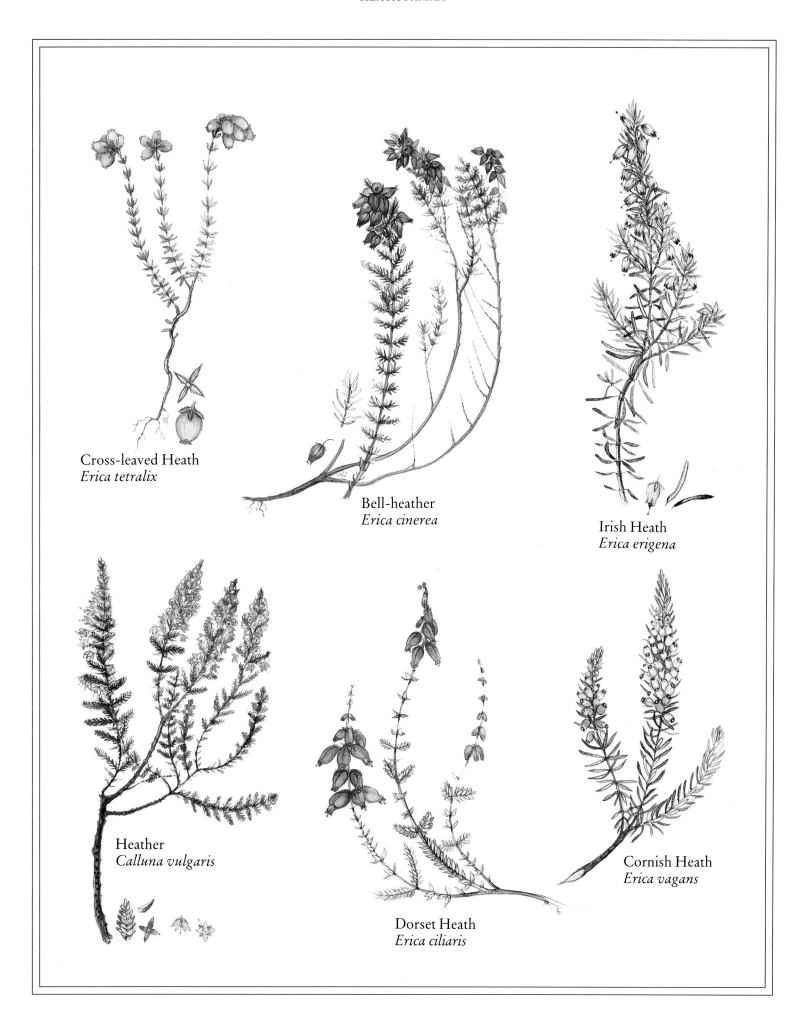

Cross-leaved Heath
Erica tetralix

Bell-heather
Erica cinerea

Irish Heath
Erica erigena

Heather
Calluna vulgaris

Dorset Heath
Erica ciliaris

Cornish Heath
Erica vagans

Wintergreen family
Pyrolaceae

A small family with 4 genera and about 40 species of evergreen herbs, mostly found in Arctic and northern temperate regions, sometimes included in the Ericaceae, the Heath family. All the species are partially saprophytic and associated with raw humus, often growing in pine woods.

Family features The flowers are solitary or borne in clusters, often nodding, white, pink or purple. They are regular and hermaphrodite, each one with four or five sepals fused to form a calyx, and five free petals. There are 10 stamens and the ovary is superior with five cells. The fruit is a globular capsule with many small seeds. The leaves are simple, in basal rosettes or, if on the stems, alternate or in whorls; they lack stipules.

The **Wintergreens**, *Pyrola* species, have creeping rhizomes from which grow rosettes of evergreen leaves and erect, leafless flowering stalks with terminal racemes of nodding flowers. There are about five in Europe. **Small Wintergreen**, *P. minor*, is typical, with broadly elliptical leaves and pinkish-white flowers. It grows in woods, on damp moors and on damp ledges, usually in mountain areas and on calcareous soils, scattered throughout Europe, northern England and Scotland; it is also found more rarely in southern England and Ireland.

Nodding Wintergreen, *Orthilia secunda*, is a similar plant with creeping rhizomes and tufts of light green, ovate leaves on long stalks. However, its nodding, greenish-white flowers grow in one-sided racemes on their erect stalks. This little plant grows in woods and on damp, rocky ledges in the mountains of Scotland and the Scottish islands, in a few places in northern England, Wales and Ireland. It is also found in mountain woods across much of Europe.

One-flowered Wintergreen, *Moneses uniflora*, is a small creeping plant forming rosettes of opposite, long-stalked leaves with ovate blades. In summer the flowers appear, borne singly at the tops of stems only 15cm (6in) tall at most. The flowers are white and sweetly scented, bowl-shaped with a broad base accommodating the 10 stamens and spreading petals. This plant grows in damp mountain woods, usually in coniferous woods on acid soils, in many parts of northern Europe but is quite uncommon; in Britain it is a rare plant found in Scotland.

Bird's-nest family
Monotropaceae

These are specialized plants, lacking chlorophyll and feeding as saprophytes, growing in soils rich in raw humus, often in coniferous woods. They are white, pink or brownish in colour, with a mass of roots covered in mycorrhizal fungi. The fungi presumably enable them to absorb their nutrients from the humus in the soil. These plants are often included in the Wintergreen family and have similar family features other than their totally saprophytic lifestyle. There are about 12 genera and 30 species in the north temperate regions.

Yellow Bird's-nest, *Monotropa hypopitys*, is a distinctive, waxy-looking plant, only 30cm (1ft) tall at most with a clump of fleshy stems covered with alternating, yellowish or ivory-white scale leaves, especially near the base. Each stem is bent over at the top when the flowers are in bud, gradually straightening as the flowers open and are pollinated, so that the capsules are held erect. The flowers are like tubular, yellowish bells, opening in the latter half of summer. This plant is widespread in Europe, occurring locally in England in the British Isles, rarely in Wales and Ireland. It grows in beech and pine woods, and on sand-dunes on the coast.

Primrose family
Primulaceae

There are about 20 genera and 1000 species of herbs in this family, mostly found in the northern hemisphere. They include some choice garden plants: primroses and polyanthus, cyclamens for the greenhouse, androsaces for the rock garden and dodecatheons for the bog garden.

Family features The flowers are hermaphrodite and regular, with a toothed calyx formed of five fused sepals, and a lobed corolla formed of five fused petals. Each flower has five stamens opposite the petal-lobes and a superior ovary with one cell and a single style. The fruits are capsules. The flowers may be solitary, or borne in branched clusters or umbels. The majority of plants have their leaves in basal rosettes. Others have leafy stems with simple or lobed leaves in a variety of arrangements. Stipules are absent.

The **Primulas**, genus *Primula*, are a large group of 500 species centred in Asia and beloved of gardeners throughout the temperate world. Primroses and polyanthus are favourites for spring gardens, drumstick and candelabra primulas for bog gardens, auriculas for the greenhouse and several Asiatic species are grown as pot plants. About 35 are found in Europe.

Primrose, *Primula vulgaris* (p. 120), is one of the most beloved of spring flowers, nestling into hedgerows and on shady banks in woods and meadows throughout much of Europe and the British Isles. Sadly, it is much less common than in former years as many plants have been destroyed by modern farming techniques or dug up and taken away. This is a perennial plant, with a short rhizome and a clump of wrinkled, lance-shaped leaves tapering to the base, bright green and hairless above, paler and hairy on the underside, growing up to

118

One-flowered Wintergreen
Moneses uniflora

Small Wintergreen
Pyrola minor

Nodding Wintergreen
Orthilia secunda

Crowberry
Empetrum nigrum

Diapensia
Diapensia lapponica

Yellow Bird's-nest
Monotropa hypopitys

25cm (10in) long. In spring the pale yellow, scented flowers appear, growing singly on hairy stalks. At one time this plant was used in herb medicine as a sedative and remedy for gout and rheumatism. Many garden varieties have been developed, including forms with double flowers and hose-in-hose flowers (where one flower grows out of another).

Primroses show a feature common to many members of this family, designed to ensure cross-pollination. The flowers of some plants have a long style and shorter stamens so that the stigma appears at the mouth of the corolla-tube; such plants are called 'pin-eyed'. The flowers of other plants have a short style and long stamens so that it is the anthers that appear at the corolla mouth; such plants are called 'thrum-eyed'. This system prevents self-pollination. Primroses are pollinated by insects: pollen grains from pin-eyed plants are fertile only when they catch on stigmas of thrum-eyed plants; conversely, pollen grains from the anthers of thrum-eyed plants are effective only on stigmas of pin-eyed plants. Clever!

Another much-loved plant is the **Cowslip**, *Primula veris*, blooming a little later than Primroses on grassy banks and roadsides, pastures and meadows, generally on calcareous and base-rich soils. It is found throughout Europe, England and Wales, but is mostly absent from Scotland and found mainly in the centre in Ireland. It has a clump of wrinkled leaves, much like those of the Primrose, but the drooping flowers grow in a one-sided umbel on a much stouter stalk. They are deeper yellow with orange spots in the centre, much more tubular in form with only small lobes around the mouth, sweetly scented. Cowslip wine, made with the flowers, is an excellent sedative. However, these plants are much reduced in numbers and should be left to bloom undisturbed. Hybrids between cowslips and primroses occur where they grow together, intermediate in form between the two species. Hybrids between primroses and oxlips also occur.

In Britain the **Oxlip**, *Primula elatior*, is found only in eastern England, mainly in East Anglia, growing in woods in chalky boulder clay. It is also found in damp woods and meadows in many other parts of Europe, north to southern Sweden. It has a rosette of wrinkled leaves and a stout flowering stalk bearing a one-sided umbel of pale yellow flowers. They are like small, unscented primroses with orange markings.

The **Bird's-eye Primrose**, *Primula farinosa*, is similar in form to the Oxlip but only about half the size of a Primrose. Its leaves are spoon-shaped and unwrinkled, with toothed edges and mealy-white beneath. The flowers are borne in umbels at the tops of erect, mealy stalks; they are pinkish-purple with yellow 'eyes'. This little plant grows in damp, grassy and peaty places on basic soils, mainly in northern England in Britain, across much of Europe but mostly in the mountains.

Scarlet Pimpernel, *Anagallis arvensis*, is a little annual plant found throughout much of the world, growing on cultivated land, in gardens, waste land and on roadsides, on dunes near the coast. It is common throughout Europe and the British Isles, mainly near the coast in Scotland. It has sprawling, often prostrate, stems with opposite, pointed-ovate leaves and many solitary red flowers on long stalks in the leaf axils. These flowers open only in the morning, closing at about 3 o'clock in the afternoon and remaining closed or closing early in dull weather. Because of this the plant has many folk names relating to time and weather, such as Poor Man's Weatherglass, Jack-go-to-bed-at-noon and Shepherd's Clock, together with innumerable variations and combinations of these.

Bog Pimpernel, *Anagallis tenella*, also has prostrate stems, which root at the nodes, and many opposite, rounded leaves. It has pink, funnel-shaped flowers borne singly on long stalks in the leaf axils in summer. This is a perennial plant, growing in damp, grassy places, in marshes and bogs, wet open woods and beside pools. It is found in western Europe and scattered throughout many parts of the British Isles, more commonly in the west and absent from much of Scotland.

Chaffweed, *Anagallis minima*, is a tiny annual, with slender, erect stems only 10cm (4in) tall at most and alternate oval leaves. It has minute, pale pink flowers in the leaf axils, their petals almost hidden by the larger sepals. Chaffweed grows in damp, open places, often in sandy soil, on heaths and commons, and in sand-dunes by the sea. It is scattered throughout much of Europe and the British Isles.

Sowbread, *Cyclamen hederifolium*, forms spreading mats of many plants, each forming a tuft of leaves growing from a corm below the surface of the ground. The leaves are attractive, appearing after the flowers and remaining green through the winter, dying down in spring; they are heart-shaped but with angled edges, with a white margin around a dark green centre, often purplish beneath. The solitary flowers appear in late summer and early autumn. Like all cyclamen flowers they are nodding, with reflexed petal-lobes, and quite distinctive. They are followed by globular capsules, pulled back to ground level by the coiled stalks, remaining on the ground until the following year, when they split open to release the seeds just before the new flowers appear. The seeds are attractive to ants, which carry them away. This plant grows wild in woods in southern Europe but is planted in gardens elsewhere, including the British Isles, sometimes escaping to grow wild. A number of other cyclamen species are also found in Europe.

Water Violet, *Hottonia palustris* (p. 123), is a very different plant, a perennial aquatic species found in ponds, marshes and ditches in many parts of Europe, including England and Wales (mainly in the east). It has floating, much-dissected leaves with linear segments, and erect flowering stems up to 40cm (15in) tall in early summer. These bear whorls of lilac, yellow-throated flowers.

The **Loosestrifes** are a large group of about 200 species in the genus *Lysimachia*, found in many parts of the world but with only nine in Europe. The most familiar of these is probably

Cowslip
Primula veris

Bird's-eye Primrose
Primula farinosa

Oxlip
Primula elatior

Primrose
Primula vulgaris

Chaffweed
Anagallis minima

Sowbread
Cyclamen hederifolium

Scarlet Pimpernel
Anagallis arvensis

Bog Pimpernel
Anagallis tenella

Creeping Jenny, *L. nummularia*. It has prostrate, creeping stems forming a leafy mat studded with yellow, saucer-shaped flowers around midsummer. The leaves are opposite, rounded and are supposed to resemble pennies. In the wild the plant grows in damp woods and shady hedgebanks, on the edges of streams and ditches; it is found throughout Europe, in England and Wales in the British Isles, rarely in Ireland and absent from much of Scotland. It is often grown in gardens, taking over the damp, shady spots if left undisturbed.

Yellow Pimpernel, *Lysimachia nemorum*, is a similar plant, but more tolerant of sunlight and more widespread, found throughout the British Isles and Europe. It is perennial and evergreen, with sprawling stems up to 40cm (15in) long, opposite, pointed-ovate leaves and yellow flowers on long, slender stalks throughout the summer. It may be found in damp and shady places.

Many of the *Lysimachia* species are erect plants, with leafy stems and yellow flowers in the axils of the upper leaves. The most familiar of these is probably **Yellow Loosestrife**, *L. vulgaris*, which grows beside rivers and lakes, in fens and marshes, scattered throughout Europe and the British Isles, except the north of Scotland. This is a softly hairy, perennial plant, with creeping rhizomes and erect, leafy stems up to 1.5m (5ft) tall. The leaves are broadly lance-shaped, borne in opposite pairs or in whorls of 3–4, with clusters of late summer flowers in the axils of the uppermost.

Tufted Loosestrife, *Lysimachia thyrsiflora*, is found across much of Europe in marshes and beside shallow water, but is rare in Britain, found in a few places in Yorkshire and southern Scotland. It has erect leafy stems up to 60cm (2ft) tall, with opposite, lance-shaped leaves and dense racemes of yellow flowers in the leaf axils about half way up the stems. The flowers are bell-shaped with long, protruding stamens.

Chickweed Wintergreen, *Trientalis europaea*, is a perennial plant with creeping rhizomes, from which grow erect stems in spring. Each stem has a whorl of five or six shiny, dark green leaves at the top, with one or more white, star-like flowers on long stalks growing from the centre of the whorl. This attractive plant grows in pine woods and heaths, among moss or in damp, grassy places across much of northern Europe and in Scotland, more rarely in northern England.

Brookweed, *Samolus valerandi*, is a perennial plant that grows in wet places, beside water and in damp meadows throughout Europe and the British Isles, except northeastern Scotland, usually near the sea. It forms tufts of pale green, spoon-shaped leaves and in early summer produces branched, leafy stems up to 60cm (2ft) tall with loose racemes of tiny, white, bell-shaped flowers.

Sea Milkwort, *Glaux maritima*, is another coastal plant, this one growing in grassy salt marshes, on rocks, cliffs and in estuaries, also in alkaline places inland. It is found all around the coasts of Europe and the British Isles. This is a small peren-nial plant only 30cm (1ft) tall at most, hairless and succulent in appearance, with prostrate stems rooting at the nodes and bearing many pairs of pointed-ovate, blue-green leaves. The solitary flowers grow in the leaf axils in summer; they have no petals but the bell-shaped calyx is white or pink and looks like a corolla. The fruits are globular capsules which split into five valves to release the few seeds.

Sea Lavender family
Plumbaginaceae

This is a family of herbs and shrubs closely related to the primroses. There are 19 genera and 780 species, many associated with the coast and some with mountains. They are especially numerous in the Mediterranean region of Europe and in Asia.

Family features The flowers are hermaphrodite and regular, with five sepals fused to form a ribbed, often papery calyx, and five petals which may be free or joined together and which often persist around the fruits. There are five stamens opposite the petals and the ovary is superior with one cell and five styles. The fruits are dry and often split open by lids. The flowers are borne in one-sided inflorescences or in heads, with sheathing, often dry, papery bracts. The leaves are simple, often in a basal rosette; they lack stipules.

There are some good ornamental plants in this family, with the *Statice* and *Limonium* species being the best known. These are Everlasting Flowers, whose papery flowers feel dry even when fresh, and which are used in dried flower arrangements.

Sea Lavender, *Limonium vulgare* (p. 125), is one of about 50 *Limonium* species found in Europe (out of about 300 altogether, found all over the world, near the sea or in salt-laden soil inland). Sea Lavender grows in muddy salt marshes on the coasts of southern and western Europe, and around Great Britain north to southern Scotland. It is a perennial plant, often carpeting the ground with clumps of leathery, elliptical or lance-shaped, long-stalked leaves. The plants bloom in late summer or autumn, sending up angular stems about 30cm (1ft) tall, which branch near the top into striking inflorescences of blue-purple flowers. Each branch of the inflorescence is curved while the flowers are in bud, straightening as they open to reveal dense spikes of flowers in two rows along the upper side of the stems. Other Sea Lavenders resemble this plant but vary in details—the shape of the leaves, the density of the flowers, the degree of branching in the inflorescence and in where they grow; several grow on rocks and cliffs.

Thrift or Sea Pink, *Armeria maritima* (p. 125), is another mainly maritime plant, found on coastal rocks and cliffs and in salt marshes on the coasts of western and northern Europe and around the British Isles, but also in mountains inland. It is an attractive, cushion-forming plant, spreading into carpets as it

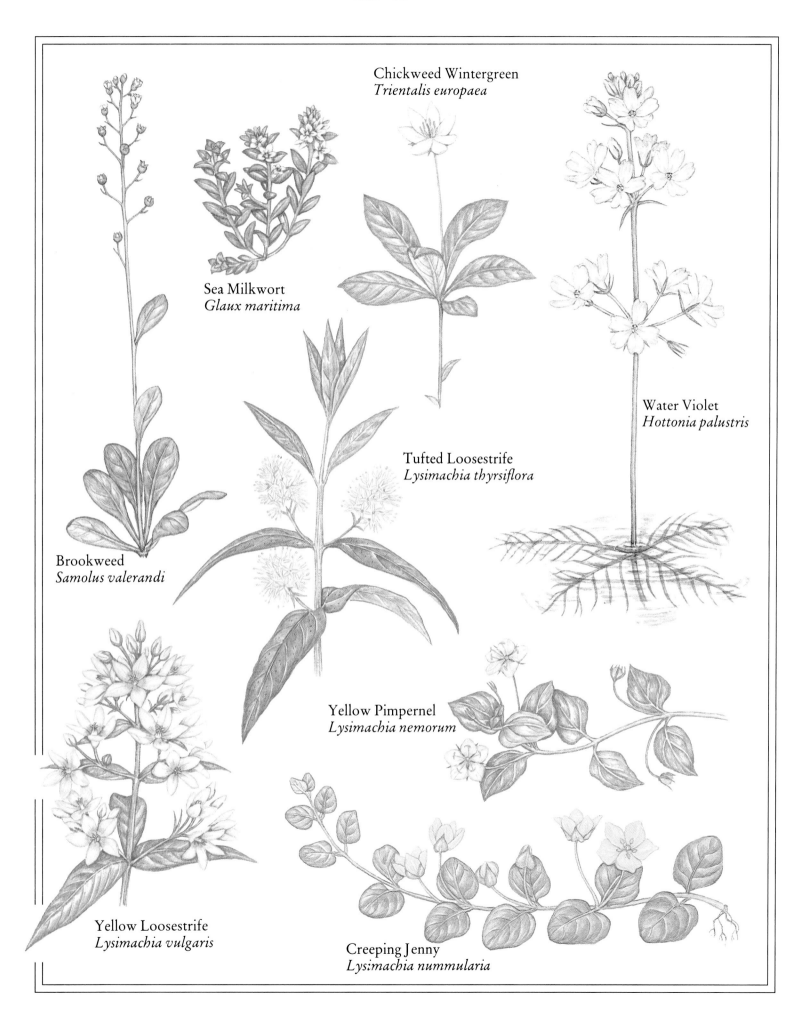

Chickweed Wintergreen
Trientalis europaea

Sea Milkwort
Glaux maritima

Water Violet
Hottonia palustris

Tufted Loosestrife
Lysimachia thyrsiflora

Brookweed
Samolus valerandi

Yellow Pimpernel
Lysimachia nemorum

Yellow Loosestrife
Lysimachia vulgaris

Creeping Jenny
Lysimachia nummularia

grows older and often becoming bare in the centre. The carpets are formed from tufts of narrow, rather fleshy leaves growing from the branches of a woody rootstock. In the summer the flowers appear—heads of fragrant, red-purple flowers with papery bracts, waving on long stalks. They are rich in nectar and visited by bees. Thrift has been grown in gardens for centuries, usually beside paths.

Dogbane family
Apocynaceae

This is a mostly tropical and subtropical family, with about 180 genera and over 1500 species of herbs, shrubs and climbing plants. Some members of the family, like the African Bushman's Poison Tree, have poisonous sap, which is used to tip arrows for hunting. Ornamental plants in the family include Oleander and Frangipani—both beautiful but poisonous.

Few species are represented in Europe. There are five **Periwinkles**, *Vinca* species, trailing or herbaceous plants with funnel-shaped flowers typical of the family as a whole. **Lesser Periwinkle**, *V. minor*, has prostrate stems which root at the nodes and upright, leafy stems little more than 30cm (1ft) tall. **Greater Periwinkle**, *V. major*, has more erect, trailing stems which grow up to 1m (3ft) tall, arching over to root at the tips. Both have opposite, evergreen leaves and blue flowers with a curious wheel-like appearance, an effect created by the petals, which all curve in one direction, and by a white ring at the 'hub'. The flowers appear in spring and are followed in southern Europe by pairs of follicles. These plants grow in woods and hedgerows, Lesser Periwinkle across much of Europe, including Great Britain. Greater Periwinkle is native to the Mediterranean region but has been introduced to other areas, including southern England. Both are grown in gardens, especially as varieties with variegated leaves.

Milkweed family
Asclepiadaceae

There are about 200 genera and 2000 species in this family of herbs, shrubs and climbing vines distributed most commonly in the warmer regions of the world. They are closely related to the Apocynaceae and, like the members of that family, contain milky juice that is poisonous in many species.

Few members of this family are found in Europe. **Swallowwort**, *Vincetoxicum hirundinaria*, is one of 10 European species in this genus. It is a perennial plant, with erect, unbranched stems up to 1m (3ft) tall and opposite, lance-shaped to heart-shaped leaves. In the axils of the leaves and terminating the stems grow the flowers in clusters of 6–8 on long stalks. They are dull greenish-white or yellowish in colour, tubular in shape with five spreading corolla-lobes and a corona formed of five rounded scales in the centre. The anthers are joined together above the stigma. The fruits that follow the flowers are pairs of follicles which split open along one side to release many seeds, each adorned with a tuft of hairs and carried away by the wind. This is a very poisonous plant.

Bogbean family
Menyanthaceae

This is a small family of aquatic herbs, with 5 genera and 33 species, found throughout many parts of the world. They are often included in the Gentian family.

Family features The flowers are hermaphrodite and regular, with five fused sepals forming a lobed calyx and a five-lobed corolla. Each flower has five stamens and a superior, one-celled ovary. The fruit is a capsule with many seeds. The leaves are alternate, simple or compound.

Bogbean or Buckbean, *Menyanthes trifoliata*, grows on the edges of lakes and ponds, and may be planted as an ornamental in such places in gardens. It is also found in marshes, fens and bogs, where it may spread into wide patches among other like-minded plants, spreading in the mud beneath the water by means of long, creeping rhizomes and producing many leaves which grow above the surface. Each leaf has three broad leaflets. In early summer the pink-tinged white flowers grow in terminal clusters on separate, leafless stalks, bringing an exotic feel to the marshes and pond margins. They have delicate, fringed margins to the petals. Bogbean is found throughout the British Isles and Europe, becoming rare in the Mediterranean.

Fringed Water-lily, *Nymphoides peltata*, looks much like a smaller version of the true Water Lilies, with floating, rounded, heart-shaped leaves on long stalks growing from rhizomes at the bottom of the water. The shiny leaves grow up to 10cm (4in) across and are spotted with purple on the upper surface, purplish below. However, the flowers are different—golden-yellow with five fringed petals, borne in clusters growing on long stalks from the leaf axils. They appear in late summer to float on the surface among the leaves.

Gentian family
Gentianaceae

A family of herbaceous plants, with about 80 genera and 900 species mostly from temperate regions. Many people think of it as a mountain family, but in fact its members occupy an array

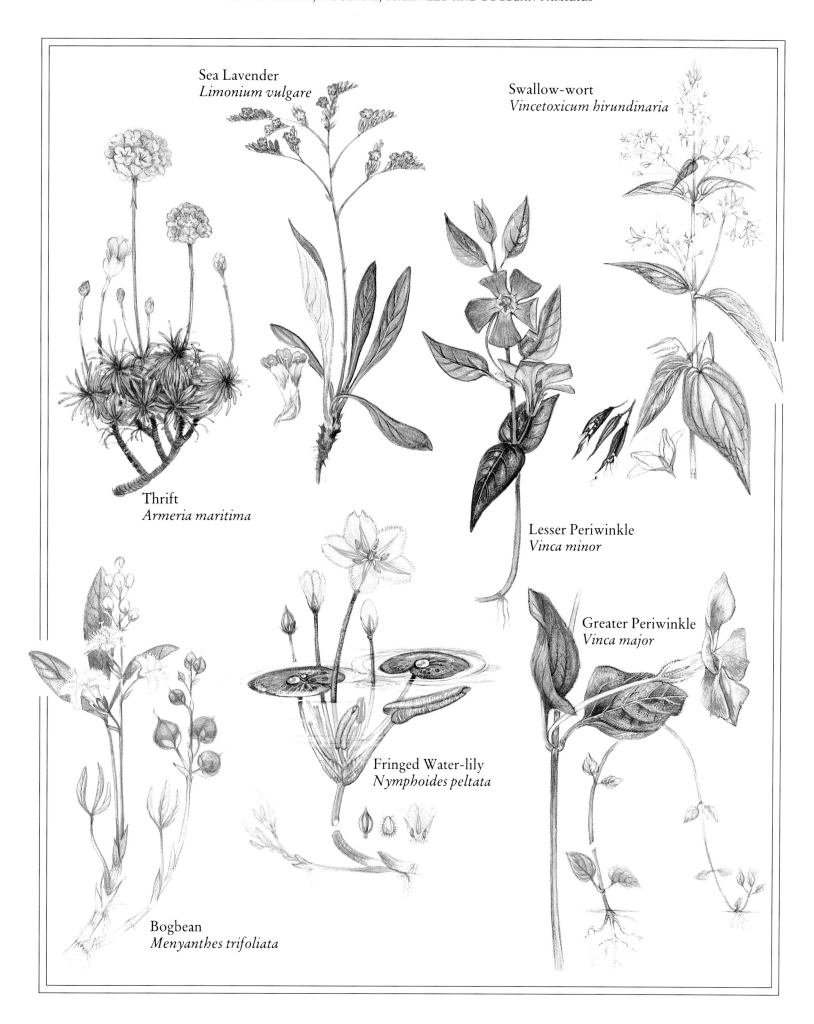

Sea Lavender
Limonium vulgare

Swallow-wort
Vincetoxicum hirundinaria

Thrift
Armeria maritima

Lesser Periwinkle
Vinca minor

Greater Periwinkle
Vinca major

Fringed Water-lily
Nymphoides peltata

Bogbean
Menyanthes trifoliata

of habitats, from brackish marshes to lowland woods and grassland, as well as mountain slopes and valleys. Some *Gentiana* species are coveted rock garden plants.

Family features The flowers are borne singly or in clusters; they are hermaphrodite and regular, usually showy, with 4–5 sepals usually fused to form a calyx-tube, and 4–5 brightly coloured petals fused to form a tubular or wheel-shaped corolla. The petal-lobes are twisted in bud. There are as many stamens as petal-lobes, inserted on the corolla-tube so that they alternate with the petal-lobes. The ovary is superior, usually with one cell. The fruit is a capsule with many small seeds. The leaves are opposite and entire, often connected to each other in pairs across the stem.

About 15 **Centauries**, *Centaurium* species, grow in Europe. They have erect stems topped with branched, often flat-topped clusters of pink, more or less funnel-shaped flowers. **Common Centaury**, *C. erythraea*, is typical of many. It is a biennial plant, with a rosette of elliptical to spoon-shaped leaves from which grows an erect flowering stem in the second year, up to 50cm (20in) tall. This has several pairs of opposite leaves and a branched inflorescence of pink flowers in summer. This plant grows in dry, grassy places, in woodland margins and dunes throughout Europe and much of the British Isles, becoming much less common in eastern Scotland.

Yellow-wort, *Blackstonia perfoliata*, is a greyish annual plant, with a rosette of leaves and an erect stem about 45cm (18in) tall at most; the stem looks as if it is growing through its opposite leaves, for they are fused around it. In summer the plant produces terminal cymes of yellow flowers, their petals widely spreading from a funnel-shaped base. Yellow-wort grows in calcareous soils, in short grassland and dunes, across most of Europe, except the north, in England, Wales and Ireland, becoming rarer in the north and absent from Scotland.

The **Gentians**, *Gentiana* species, are by far the biggest group in the family, with about 400 species mainly found in the mountains and cool regions of the northern hemisphere, about 30 in Europe. They all contain bitter substances and many are used in herb medicine, some to a much greater extent than others. The **Great Yellow Gentian**, *G. lutea*, is the most useful in this respect, and its rhizomes are the source of Gentian Bitter, used to flavour liqueurs and in herb medicine as a tonic for the digestive system. This is a large perennial plant, with erect stems up to 2m (6ft) tall and large, opposite, blue-green leaves. The lower leaves are stalked, while upper ones clasp the stem; all have prominent parallel veins. In summer dense whorls of flowers grow in the upper leaf axils; they are yellow, each with 5–9 linear petal-lobes forming a star-shaped, rather than a bell-shaped, corolla. Great Yellow Gentian grows in damp mountain woods and meadows across much of Europe, but is absent from the north and from the British Isles.

Most gentians are perennial plants, many with rosettes of basal leaves and erect stems with opposite leaves. They have bell-shaped or funnel-shaped, often showy, flowers, bright blue or purple, borne in the upper leaf axils. **Marsh Gentian**, *Gentiana pneumonanthe*, has slender, unbranched stems up to 40cm (15in) tall, linear leaves and blue flowers with green streaks on the outside. They are borne in a dense cluster at the top of each stem. This plant grows in acid soils, in wet heaths, marshes and bogs across most of Europe, but is declining in numbers. It has always been local in Britain, found mainly in southern England, absent from Ireland and Scotland.

Spring Gentian, *Gentiana verna*, is a mountain species, a typical alpine plant, with rosettes of leaves pressed close to the ground. The leaves are elliptical to lance-shaped, only 2cm (1in) long and smaller than the solitary flowers which seem absurdly large for this small plant. The flowers are glorious trumpets of brilliant deep blue borne in spring and early summer. In the wild this plant grows in stony, grassy places in the mountains of central and southern Europe; it is also found on limestone in a few places in northern England and western Ireland. It is one of the most popular rock garden gentians.

Unlike the gentians, the *Gentianella* species are usually annual or biennial plants and their flowers are often purple or whitish; there are usually long hairs in the throat of the flowers. **Felwort**, *G. amarella*, is a biennial, with a rosette of lance-shaped leaves in the first year and an erect, leafy, often branched stem in the second, growing about 30cm (1ft) tall. Its flowers grow in clusters in the upper leaf axils; they are tubular with a fringe of hairs in the throat and four or five spreading petal-lobes, varying in colour from reddish-purple to dull purple, to blue, pink or white. This little plant grows on basic soils in pastures and short grassland, on sand-dunes and cliffs; it is found throughout Europe and many parts of the British Isles, less widespread in the west.

Field Gentian, *Gentianella campestris*, is a similar plant, another biennial with more or less branched stems and opposite, ovate or lance-shaped leaves. Its flowers are borne in axillary clusters but are bluish-lilac or occasionally white and have only four petal-lobes. These flowers have four uneven calyx-lobes, the two outer ones wider, overlapping and hiding much of the two narrower, inner ones. This plant grows in acid or neutral soils in short grassland and pastures, also on dunes and heaths across northern and central Europe. In Britain it is common in Scotland and northern England, found more locally in Wales and Ireland, more rarely in the rest of England.

Marsh Felwort, *Swertia perennis*, is a perennial, branched plant with purplish stems up to 60cm (2ft) tall and opposite, yellow-green leaves, the uppermost clasping the stem. The flowers are borne in clusters in the upper leaf axils and terminating the stems; they are star-shaped, with petals separate almost to the base of the corolla, usually dark purple but sometimes yellow-green. This plant grows in bogs and wet mountain meadows from northern France to Germany and across much of central Europe; it is not found in the British Isles.

126

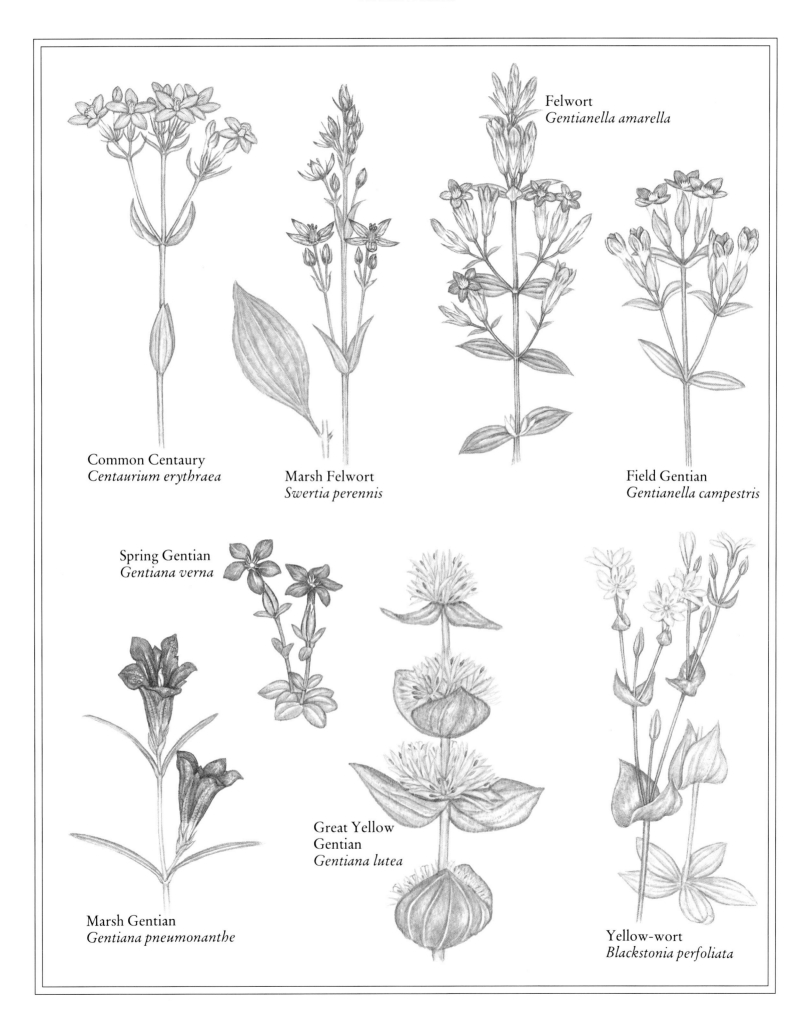

Common Centaury
Centaurium erythraea

Marsh Felwort
Swertia perennis

Felwort
Gentianella amarella

Field Gentian
Gentianella campestris

Spring Gentian
Gentiana verna

Marsh Gentian
Gentiana pneumonanthe

Great Yellow
Gentian
Gentiana lutea

Yellow-wort
Blackstonia perfoliata

Bedstraw family
Rubiaceae

Also known as the **Madder family**. This is one of the largest families of flowering plants, with about 500 genera and 6000 species of herbs and shrubs, mostly found in the tropical regions. Coffee, quinine and gardenias all come from this family.

Family features The flowers are small and arranged in cymes or heads. They are hermaphrodite and regular, with 4–5 free sepals and petals fused into a corolla with four or five lobes. There are as many stamens as petal-lobes, inserted in the tube of the corolla and alternating with the petal-lobes. The ovary is inferior, with two or more cells. The fruits are berries or capsules, or dry and schizocarpic. The leaves are simple and usually entire, sometimes toothed, opposite or borne in whorls. They have stipules which may resemble leaves.

There are not that many members of the family in temperate regions, about 170 in Europe, the majority small herbaceous plants belonging to the **Bedstraws**, *Galium* species, and their relatives. They are slender plants, with four-angled, squarish stems and leaves in whorls. The flowers are small and either borne in clusters on every branch of the stems, or in the leaf axils. Their fruits are dry, one-seeded nuts borne in pairs.

Lady's Bedstraw, *Galium verum*, gets its name from the legend that it was present in the straw in the stable where Christ was born; the legend was expanded to include the belief that childbirth was easier if this plant was in the mattress when women were in labour. The plant has the pleasant scent of new-mown hay for it contains coumarin. Lady's Bedstraw can be used in cheese-making, as its flowers curdle milk. It is used in herb medicine and it yields a red dye used at one time for dying wool. It is a low-growing, perennial plant, with wiry, much-branched, creeping stems and upright leafy stems forming dense patches in short grassland and fixed dunes, along roadsides and hedgebanks throughout Europe and the British Isles. It has whorls of 8–12 leaves on its squarish stems and dense clusters of yellow flowers in late summer.

Many bedstraws are similar in form to Lady's Bedstraw, but the majority have white flowers, like **Heath Bedstraw**, *Galium saxatile*. This is another low-growing plant, forming a mat of prostrate non-flowering stems with ovate leaves in whorls of 6–8. In summer the upright flowering shoots grow about 10–20cm (4–8in) tall, with narrower leaves and clusters of white flowers. The plant becomes black if it is dried. It grows in acid soils, on heaths and moors, grassland and scrub throughout most of Europe and the British Isles.

Hedge Bedstraw, *Galium mollugo*, is a taller, almost scrambling plant, often seen tangled in the grasses at the base of a hedgebank, but also found in woods and waste places, in rough grassland and scrub on calcareous soils throughout much of Europe and southern areas of the British Isles, diminishing in

Scotland, Wales and Ireland. It is a perennial with numerous, much-branched, weak stems with many whorls of 6–8 oblong to elliptical leaves and loose, branched clusters of flowers in the latter half of summer. It does not turn black on drying.

Marsh Bedstraw, *Galium palustre*, is a variable, straggling, much-branched plant, often with weak stems, rough on the angles and blackening when dried. It has whorls of 4–6 elliptical or oblong leaves and white flowers borne in loose clusters terminating the stems. This plant grows in wet meadows and fens throughout the British Isles and Europe. It has several forms sometimes considered to be separate species, varying in size from 30cm (1ft) to 120cm (4ft) tall or more.

Cleavers or Goosegrass, *Galium aparine*, is an annual plant, with weak, scrambling, angled stems growing up to 120cm (4ft) tall and clinging to vegetation (or clothing!) by hooked bristles on the angles. The narrow leaves grow in whorls of 6–8, and small clusters of tiny, greenish-white flowers grow in the leaf axils. The pairs of globular fruits that follow are covered in tiny hooks and catch on everything that brushes past them, a superb distribution mechanism and obviously successful, for the plant grows in damp, shady places all over Europe and the British Isles. It can be a nuisance as a weed, but its fruits can be roasted as a coffee substitute and its young shoots can be eaten as a green vegetable or in salads. It is also used in herb medicine for purifying the blood.

Sweet Woodruff, *Galium odoratum*, is rather different—a perennial with branched, creeping rhizomes and many erect, unbranched stems, 45cm (18in) tall at most. Each stem has several whorls of 6–8 firm, lance-shaped leaves and a branched cluster of white flowers at the top. This attractive plant grows in shady places and damp woods on base-rich soils, forming carpets of leaves and flowers in early summer; it is found throughout Europe and the British Isles. The whole plant has the scent of new-mown hay and retains its fragrance when dried; at one time it was kept in drawers and cupboards to keep clothes and linens sweet, and added to liqueurs and perfumes.

Squinancy-wort, *Asperula cynanchica*, is a small tufted, grey-green, perennial plant, with much-branched, prostrate non-flowering shoots and erect flowering shoots up to 50cm (20in) tall. All the stems are four-angled and bear whorls of four linear 'leaves', the two true leaves often longer than the others, which are really stipules. The vanilla-scented flowers are borne in clusters at the ends of the flowering shoots; they are funnel-shaped, warty and pale pink outside, white inside. Squinancy-wort grows in dry grassland and dunes on calcareous soils across much of Europe, except the north, in southern England and south Wales, and in southwestern Ireland.

Crosswort or Mugwort, *Cruciata laevipes*, is another creeping perennial, with slender rhizomes and many weak, four-angled stems branched from the base and growing up to 60cm (2ft) tall. They are softly hairy with whorls of four similarly hairy, yellow-green, elliptical leaves and clusters of pale

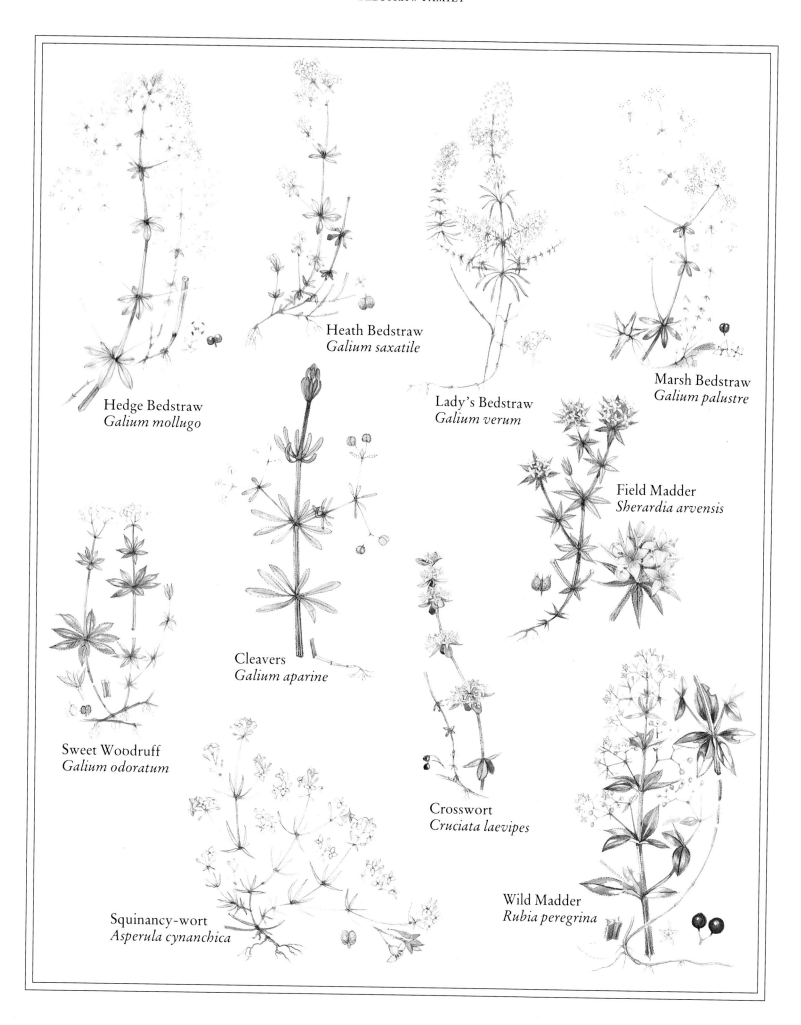

Hedge Bedstraw
Galium mollugo

Heath Bedstraw
Galium saxatile

Lady's Bedstraw
Galium verum

Marsh Bedstraw
Galium palustre

Field Madder
Sherardia arvensis

Cleavers
Galium aparine

Sweet Woodruff
Galium odoratum

Crosswort
Cruciata laevipes

Wild Madder
Rubia peregrina

Squinancy-wort
Asperula cynanchica

yellow, honey-scented flowers in the leaf axils in summer. This little plant grows on calcareous soils, on roadsides and walls, on the sides of chalk pits and in other dry places. It is widespread in Great Britain but absent from Ireland, also found across Europe, except in the north.

Field Madder, *Sherardia arvensis* (p. 129), is a small annual plant found as a weed in arable land and waste places, most commonly in dry soils on chalk or limestone. It forms a patch of branched, sprawling stems up to 1m (3ft) across, the stems four-angled with whorls of four leaves on the lower parts, 5–6 on the upper parts. Stem angles and leaves are both rough with tiny prickles. The pale lilac flowers are funnel-shaped, borne in terminal clusters and cupped in a ruff of 8–10 lance-shaped bracts like leaves. This plant grows across Europe and much of the British Isles, less commonly in Scotland.

Wild Madder, *Rubia peregrina* (p. 129), is a prickly, rough-textured, scrambling plant, a perennial found in hedgerows, woods and scrub near the coasts of western and southern Europe, and on British coasts from southern England to Wales and southern Ireland. It has trailing stems up to 120cm (4ft) tall, with prickles on the angles and whorls of 4–6 leaves; these are stiff, persistent and shiny dark green, elliptical in shape and prickly on margins and midribs. In summer loose clusters of pale yellow-green flowers appear, terminating the stems and in the leaf axils. The fruits are fleshy black berries. Madder, *R. tinctorum*, has been known since prehistoric times as a source of madder dye, used to dye fabrics various shades of red, until replaced by synthetics.

Phlox family
Polemoniaceae

A small family with about 15 genera and 300 species, most from western North America. The majority are herbs. Many species and varieties of phlox are grown in flower gardens.

This family has few representatives in Europe, the only native species being several in the genus *Polemonium*. **Jacob's Ladder**, *P. caeruleum*, is a perennial plant, with a clump of erect stems up to 90cm (3ft) tall and many alternate, pinnate leaves. The leaves are large, with 6–12 pairs of pointed-elliptical leaflets and one terminal leaflet, the lower leaves with winged stalks, the upper ones almost stalkless. The flowers are showy and blue, borne in dense clusters at the tops of the stems. Each has a funnel-shaped corolla with five wide-spreading petal-lobes sitting in a five-toothed calyx. This plant grows on grassy slopes and rock ledges on limestone hills in a few places in northern England; it is also found in northern and central Europe. Several *Polemonium* species are grown in gardens. Jacob's Ladder is a name given to many of them because of the ladder-like aspect of their leaves.

Bindweed family
Convolvulaceae

This is a mostly tropical family, with about 55 genera and 1650 species of herbs and shrubs; many of them are climbers with twining stems. Some, like morning glories (*Ipomoea* species), are ornamental garden plants with showy flowers, but some of the bindweeds (*Convolvulus* species) are pernicious weeds. Sweet potatoes are the edible tubers of *Ipomoea batatas*.

Family features The flowers are hermaphrodite and regular, usually with five free, often overlapping sepals and five fused petals forming a funnel-shaped corolla. Each has five stamens inserted at the base of the corolla alternating with the petal-lobes. The ovary is superior with 1–4 cells. The fruits are usually capsules. The leaves are simple and alternate; they lack stipules. The stems contain milky juice.

Field Bindweed, *Convolvulus arvensis*, is a weed that grows in waste places and on roadsides, in cultivated land, short grassland and near the sea throughout the temperate regions of the world. In the British Isles it is common in England and Wales, less so in Ireland, and becomes rare in Scotland. It is a perennial plant with stout, underground rhizomes which penetrate to a depth of 2m (6ft) or more, so deeply that they are very difficult to eradicate and even small fragments can grow into new plants. The plant spreads into tangles of climbing stems that festoon fences and twist around other plants, strangling them if left alone for long enough. The stems twist in a counterclockwise direction. They bear variably arrow-shaped leaves and many white or pink, funnel-shaped flowers on long stalks opposite the leaves. This is an attractive plant but so invasive that it is always unwelcome.

Field Bindweed is like a scaled-down version of the **Hedge Bindweed** or Bellbine, *Calystegia sepium*, for its leaves are 2–5cm (1–2in) long and its flowers are less than 3cm (1¼in) across, whereas the leaves of the latter plant are 5–15cm (2–5in) long and its funnel-shaped flowers are about 6cm (2½in) across. The flowers of Field Bindweed tend to be pink, while those of Hedge Bindweed tend to be white. Hedge Bindweed is just as difficult a weed as Field Bindweed, but its rhizomes do not penetrate as deeply, though they spread far and wide. This is another strangler, with twining stems twisting counterclockwise, but because it is bigger it can do more damage more quickly, swamping surrounding plants with its foliage. It is widely distributed in the temperate regions of the northern hemisphere and is found throughout Europe and the British Isles, becoming less common in Scotland. It grows in waste places, in hedges and woodland margins, in gardens and on roadsides and often near the sea.

Sea Bindweed, *Calystegia soldanella*, grows on seashores, sand-dunes and shingle along the Atlantic and Mediterranean coasts of Europe and all around the British Isles. It has pen-

Great Dodder
Cuscuta europaea

Common Dodder
Cuscuta epithymum

Hedge Bindweed
Calystegia sepium

Field Bindweed
Convolvulus arvensis

Jacob's Ladder
Polemonium caeruleum

Sea Bindweed
Calystegia soldanella

etrating rhizomes and spreading, sprawling stems with fleshy, kidney-shaped leaves on long stalks. In summer the flowers appear, growing singly in the leaf axils; they are large and funnel-shaped, pink or purple in colour.

The **Dodders**, members of the genus *Cuscuta*, are sometimes included in a separate family because they are parasitic plants, quite unlike any others. They lack roots but have yellow or brown twining stems, with leaves reduced to tiny scales, and clusters of small white or yellow flowers in late summer. The plants spread by seed. When dodder seeds germinate, the seedlings must find a host very quickly or die, since they have no roots. The stem of the seedling rotates and if it finds the stem of another plant, twines around it and develops special suckers which penetrate the conduction vessels of the host from which it can then absorb food and water.

There are about 15 Dodder species in Europe. **Common Dodder**, *Cuscuta epithymum* (p. 131), is found across most of Europe, mainly in southern England in the British Isles. It most often grows on gorse and heathers, sometimes covering many plants with its thread-like, reddish stems. It may also parasitize crop plants like clovers and alfalfa and can cause considerable damage. Dense, head-like clusters of scented, pink flowers appear on the stems in summer. **Great Dodder**, *C. europaea* (p. 131), is a similar but larger plant, usually found on nettles but also on hops. It grows throughout much of Europe but is rare and decreasing in southern England, the only part of the British Isles where it is found.

Forget-me-not family
Boraginaceae

Also called the **Borage family**. There are about 100 genera and 2000 species of herbaceous plants in this family found in tropical and temperate regions of the world, especially in the Mediterranean region and eastern Asia. There are many ornamental plants in the family, both annuals and perennials grown in flower borders, including forget-me-nots and pulmonarias. The roots of Dyer's Alkanet, *Alkanna tinctoria*, yield a red dye used to colour medicines and to stain wood; and several species, like Comfrey and Borage, are used in herb medicine.

Family features The flowers are borne in one-sided clusters which are curled tightly at first, uncoiling as the flowers open gradually from the bottom. Each flower is hermaphrodite and regular, with five fused sepals and five petals fused to form a lobed corolla-tube. There are five stamens inserted on the corolla, alternating with the petal-lobes. The ovary is superior with two or four cells, entire or four-lobed, with the style protruding from the middle of the lobes. The fruit consists of four nutlets. The leaves are simple, usually alternate, and stipules are absent. These plants are often coarsely hairy or bristly.

Houndstongue, *Cynoglossum officinale*, was a medicinal plant at one time, its large leaves recommended for wrapping around dog bites; since they resemble dog's tongues it was thought they could cure the bites! It was also used to treat bruises and wounds but is rarely used in modern herb medicine since it can cause dermatitis. It grows in dry, grassy places and in woodland margins on dry soils across much of Europe and in England and Wales (much less commonly in Scotland and Ireland), often on fixed dunes and in sandy places near the sea. This is a biennial plant, with a clump of large, broadly lance-shaped basal leaves and erect leafy stems growing up to 90cm (3ft) tall, all covered with soft grey hairs. Its stems branch near the top to end in curled clusters of dull red, funnel-shaped flowers, the clusters lengthening and straightening as the flowers open. The nutlets are covered with barbed spines which catch on clothes.

Bur Forget-me-not, *Lappula myosotis*, also has spiny nutlets, the spines on the fruits of this species in two rows on the margins. This is a continental plant, growing in vineyards and dry waste places across much of Europe, on sand-dunes on the coast; in Britain it is found only as a casual weed. It is a stiffly hairy, annual or biennial plant, with erect branched stems and lance-shaped leaves. The sky blue flowers resemble those of forget-me-nots and are borne in loose, leafy clusters at the tops of the stems in summer.

Madwort, *Asperugo procumbens*, is a rough-textured, spreading annual plant, its bristly, opposite, elliptical leaves much more obvious than the small flowers in their axils. The flowers may be solitary or paired and are funnel-shaped, violet to purple in colour. As they fade and the fruits develop, the calyx enlarges into two conspicuous kidney-shaped lobes completely surrounding the nutlets. This is a continental plant found only as a casual in the British Isles; it grows in fields, in waste places and on roadsides across much of Europe.

Common Comfrey, *Symphytum officinale*, is one of 12 *Symphytum* species found in Europe. It is a coarse perennial plant, forming clumps of large, bristly stems and leaves, the stems growing up to 120cm (4ft) tall and ending in coiled clusters of tubular, yellowish-white, pinkish or blue flowers in early summer. The bases of the leaves run down the stems, making them appear winged. This Comfrey grows in damp places, on the banks of rivers and canals, in ditches and wet meadows across much of Europe and Great Britain, becoming much less common in the north; it has been introduced into Ireland. It has a long history of use in herb medicine, especially for healing wounds, sprains and broken bones, and was called Knitbone or Boneset in many old herbals.

Tuberous Comfrey, *Symphytum tuberosum*, is a similar but smaller plant, just as bristly but only 50cm (20in) tall at most, with thick, creeping rhizomes, unbranched stems and large, elliptical leaves halfway up the stems (the smaller lower leaves soon wither). The flowers are yellowish-white. It grows in

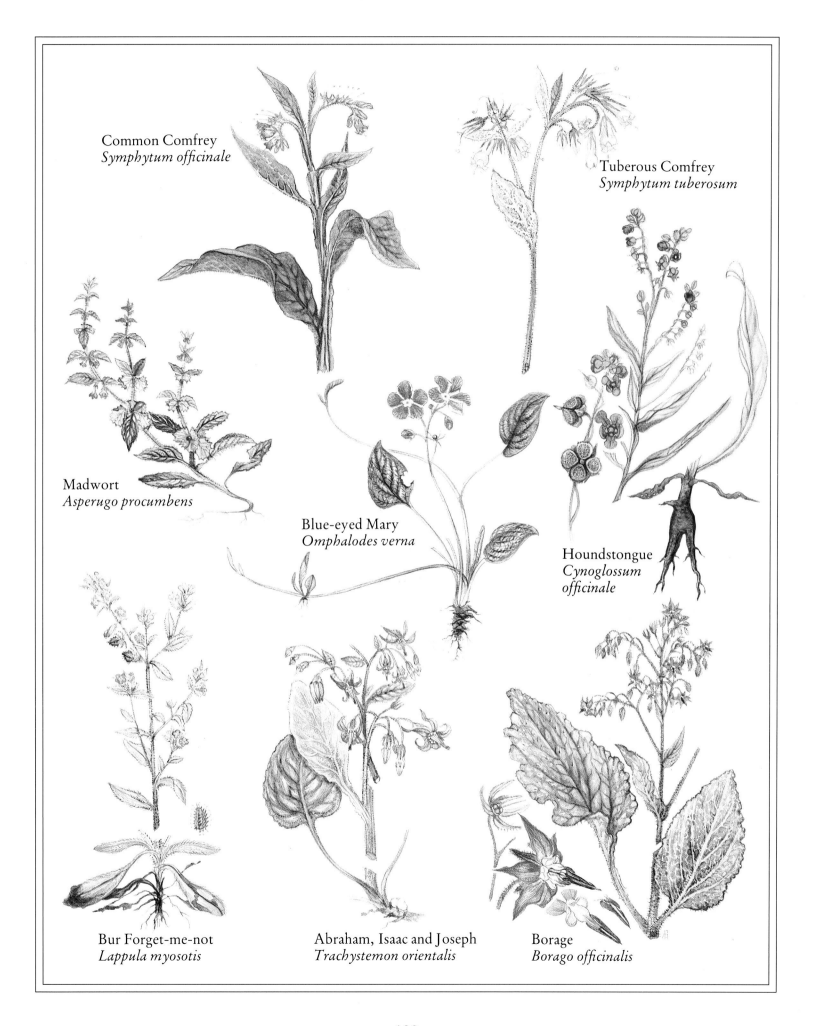

Common Comfrey
Symphytum officinale

Tuberous Comfrey
Symphytum tuberosum

Madwort
Asperugo procumbens

Blue-eyed Mary
Omphalodes verna

Houndstongue
Cynoglossum officinale

Bur Forget-me-not
Lappula myosotis

Abraham, Isaac and Joseph
Trachystemon orientalis

Borage
Borago officinalis

damp woods and hedges, in wet meadows and beside streams across most of Europe, except the north and Portugal; it is scattered in England and Wales, more common in Scotland.

Borage, *Borago officinalis* (p. 133), is an old medicinal and culinary herb known for its fresh scent and taste of cucumber, its young leaves and flowers an attractive addition to fruit punch or salads. In medicine it has anti-inflammatory properties that make it a good remedy for colds and rheumatism. This is a bristly annual plant from the Mediterranean region, now cultivated in many other parts of Europe, including the British Isles. It may escape to grow in waste places near gardens. It forms a rosette of ovate bristly leaves with wavy margins, then a stout branched stem up to 75cm (30in) tall, with ovate leaves, the upper ones clasping the stems. The flowers are unmistakable—bright blue and star-shaped, with spreading petal-lobes and a projecting cone of purple anthers.

Abraham, Isaac and Joseph, *Trachystemon orientalis* (p. 133), is sometimes known as Eastern Borage, and its flowers are similar to those of Borage, with the same kind of reflexed petals and a cone of anthers. However, it is a much larger plant, a perennial with spreading clumps of large, bristly, heart-shaped basal leaves growing from creeping rhizomes, and erect, leafy flowering stems about 60cm (2ft) tall in spring. These produce clusters of the small, bluish-violet, starry flowers. This plant grows in damp woods and shady places, wild in the Mediterranean, in gardens elsewhere in Europe and in Britain, escaping in some places.

Blue-eyed Mary, *Omphalodes verna* (p. 133), is a softer plant than many species in this family, with only slightly hairy leaves. It is a perennial, with long, prostrate stems and low carpets of ovate or heart-shaped leaves on long stalks. In spring sky blue flowers like large forget-me-nots peep out from between the leaves, growing in loose racemes on erect, leafy stalks. This little plant grows wild in woods of western and southern Europe, but has been widely introduced into gardens elsewhere, including parts of Britain.

Lungwort, *Pulmonaria officinalis*, is another plant grown in gardens for its clumps of white-spotted, heart-shaped or ovate leaves and spring flowers borne in clusters on short, erect stalks. The flowers open pink from pink buds and then turn blue. Lungwort grows wild across much of Europe in woods and hedgerows, and is found in scattered places in Great Britain, probably as a garden escape in many areas. At one time it was used as a medicinal plant; since the spotted leaves were mucilaginous and resembled lungs, they were used to treat coughs and bronchitis. Other *Pulmonaria* species are found in Europe, including Narrow-leaved Lungwort, *P. longifolia*, a species with long, lance-shaped, spotted or unspotted leaves; it grows wild in a few places in southern England.

Green Alkanet, *Pentaglottis sempervirens*, is a bristly perennial plant, with a basal clump of pointed-oval leaves on long stalks and several erect, leafy flowering stems ending in curled clusters of bright blue flowers in early summer. Each flower is tubular, with spreading petal-lobes and white scales in the centre closing the throat. This plant grows in woods and damp, shady places in western Europe; it was introduced into Britain many centuries ago, although why is not clear for it is not mentioned in the old herbals. It now grows wild in hedgerows and woodland margins all over Great Britain.

Alkanet, *Anchusa officinalis*, is a bristly perennial plant, with erect stems up to 90cm (3ft) tall, leafy with long, lance-shaped leaves and ending in coiled clusters of funnel-shaped flowers. These open red and turn blue as they age. It grows in meadows and arable land, in waste places and on roadsides throughout continental Europe, only as a casual in southern England in the British Isles. At one time it was used in herb medicine to treat ulcers, cuts and bruises.

Bugloss, *Anchusa arvensis*, is a more straggly annual or biennial plant, very bristly, with stems only 15–20cm (6–8in) tall and lance-shaped, wavy-margined leaves, the upper ones clasping the stems. The flowers are borne in a branched inflorescence at the top of the stem, the clusters elongating as more of the bright blue flowers open. Each one has five white, hairy scales at the centre. This little plant grows in arable land and heaths, especially on sandy or chalky soils, and near the sea; it is found throughout Europe and much of Great Britain, also on the east and north coast of Ireland.

The **Forget-me-nots**, *Myosotis* species, are probably the most familiar plants in this family; there are about 20 species in Europe. Cultivated varieties of the **Wood Forget-me-not**, *M. sylvatica*, are those grown in gardens, forming a blue froth among tulips and wallflowers. The wild plant is common throughout Europe, growing in woods and damp meadows, mainly found in England and southern Scotland in the British Isles, rare in the west. It is a biennial or perennial, with a rosette of hairy, ovate or spoon-shaped leaves, and erect stems in spring growing up to 45cm (18in) tall and branching a little to bear the flowers. As is common to all the forget-me-nots, the flower clusters are coiled at first, unfurling as the bright blue flowers gradually open.

The **Water Forget-me-not**, *Myosotis scorpioides*, grows in wet places and in water, beside streams and ponds, in marshes and wet meadows throughout Europe and the British Isles. This is a perennial plant, with leafy stems which creep a little and root into fresh soil, turning upwards to unfurl coiled clusters of sky blue, yellow-eyed flowers. It is a sprawling plant, only 60cm (2ft) tall at most and often smaller.

The **Field Forget-me-not**, *Myosotis arvensis*, has smaller flowers than either of the former species, the corolla only 3mm (1/8in) across. It is like a smaller Wood Forget-me-not, with a rosette of elliptical leaves and erect, leafy stems growing up to 30cm (1ft) tall and bearing coiled clusters of grey-blue flowers at the top. It grows in cultivated ground and on roadsides, also on dunes, throughout Europe and the British Isles.

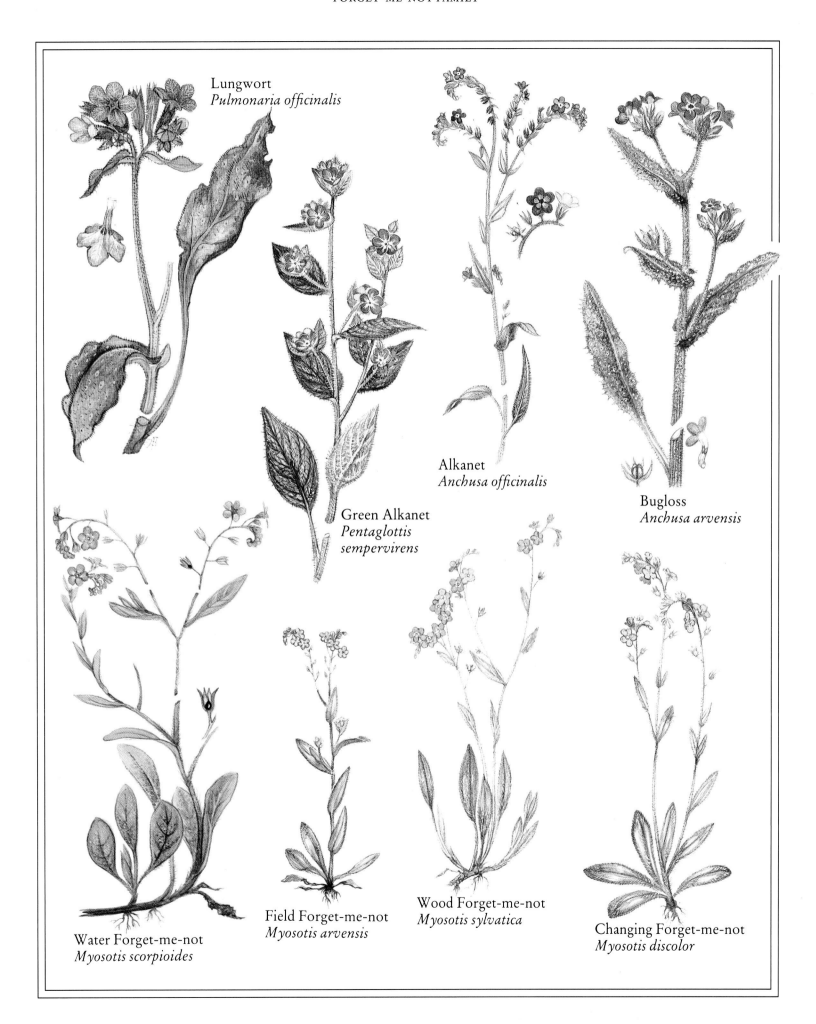

Lungwort
Pulmonaria officinalis

Alkanet
Anchusa officinalis

Bugloss
Anchusa arvensis

Green Alkanet
Pentaglottis sempervirens

Water Forget-me-not
Myosotis scorpioides

Field Forget-me-not
Myosotis arvensis

Wood Forget-me-not
Myosotis sylvatica

Changing Forget-me-not
Myosotis discolor

Changing Forget-me-not, *Myosotis discolor* (p. 135), gets its name from its flowers—they open creamy-white, then change colour to pink and blue. This is a small annual plant, with a rosette of hairy, lance-shaped leaves and slender, leafy stems up to 30cm (1ft) tall ending in coiled clusters of the very small, changing flowers. It grows in grassy places on light soils throughout Europe and the British Isles.

Golden Drop is a name given to about 20 *Onosma* species found in Europe, but not in the British Isles. They are biennial and perennial plants, with narrow leaves and tubular yellow flowers. Several are alpine plants. *Onosma echioides* is a perennial, a stiff, bristly plant, with several erect stems up to 40cm (15in) tall, yellow-green leaves covered with bristly yellow hairs, lower ones linear, upper ones lance-shaped. The flowers are borne in leafy cymes at the tops of the stems. This plant grows in dry, stony places and among rocks across much of Europe from France and Germany southwards. A red dye extracted from its roots is used as a food colouring.

Gromwell is a name given to several *Lithospermum* species, of which there are about 17 in Europe, out of a world total of 60-odd. **Common Gromwell**, *L. officinale*, is a perennial plant, rather bristly and up to 80cm (30in) tall, with much-branched, leafy stems; many coiled clusters of yellowish-white flowers grow in the leaf axils and at the tops of the branches. The clusters lengthen and straighten as they age. This plant grows in hedgerows and woodland margins throughout Europe, mainly in England in the British Isles.

Corn Gromwell, *Lithospermum arvense*, is a weed of arable land, a rather bristly annual plant, with a little-branched, erect stem usually about 50cm (20in) tall at most. It has many leaves, the lower ones bluntly oblong and the upper ones linear and stalkless. Leafy clusters of small white flowers terminate the stems in early summer. It is found throughout Europe, mainly in England in the British Isles.

Blue Gromwell, *Lithospermum purpurocaeruleum*, grows in woods and hedgerows across much of Europe, except the north, but is rare in Britain, found only in a few places in the southwest and Wales. This is a perennial plant, with creeping non-flowering shoots and erect flowering shoots in early summer. Both are leafy, with rough, narrowly lance-shaped leaves, darker above than beneath. The flowers grow in leafy clusters at the tops of the stems, opening reddish-purple but quickly turning intense, bright blue.

Oyster Plant, *Mertensia maritima*, in contrast to many members of this family, is hairless and rather fleshy, an adaptation to its life on the seashore. It grows on sand and shingle beaches on the Atlantic coast of Europe from Jutland northwards, and on the coasts of northern England, Scotland and northern Ireland, but is rare everywhere and decreasing. It forms a mat of sprawling stems with two rows of opposite, blue-grey, spoon-shaped leaves and clusters of flowers in summer; they are pink at first, soon turning blue and pink.

Viper's Bugloss, *Echium vulgare*, by contrast is almost prickly, with very large bristly hairs. This biennial plant has a rosette of large, lance-shaped leaves in the first year and a leafy flowering stem up to 90cm (3ft) tall in the second. The flowers grow in many coiled clusters in the axils of the upper leaves, pink in bud, opening bright blue and funnel-shaped; each one has four or five long stamens protruding from it. At one time this was a medicinal herb used to treat snakebites (particularly from vipers) and scorpion stings, but this use has now fallen into disrepute. An infusion of the leaves makes a good cordial. The plant grows in dry soils, in waste ground and grassy places, on cliffs near the sea and on sand-dunes throughout Europe and much of England and Wales; it is rare in Scotland, found only on the east coast in Ireland.

There are about 20 other *Echium* species in Europe. **Purple Viper's Bugloss**, *Echium plantagineum*, is similar in appearance to Viper's Bugloss but may be annual in its growth pattern and has much softer leaves, the upper ones heart-shaped. The flowers are reddish-purple at first, turning blue-purple, with only two of the stamens protruding from each flower; the clusters become very elongated as they age. This plant grows in dry, sandy places in the Mediterranean region and France, in a few places on the coast in Cornwall, Jersey and the Scilly Isles in Britain, where it is a rare plant.

Vervain family
Verbenaceae

This is a mainly tropical and subtropical family, with about 75 genera and 3000 species of herbs, shrubs and trees. Some species are ornamental garden plants, like verbenas, which are annuals and perennials for the flower border, and Lemon Verbena, a shrub grown in gardens and used in herb medicine. Teak comes from a member of this family—the Asian tree *Tectona grandis*; the wood is one of the hardest and most durable, and so heavy that it tends to sink in water.

Few members of the family are native to Europe and of the ones that are, most are shrubs. However, **Vervain**, *Verbena officinalis*, is a perennial plant, growing 30–75cm (12–30in) tall, with stiffly branched, four-angled stems resembling a candelabrum and rough, opposite, pinnately cut leaves, becoming less divided higher up the stem. Its pale lilac flowers are borne in long spikes terminating the stems; individually they are small and tubular with five petal-lobes, and they open a few at a time in late summer. Each flower is followed by four reddish-brown nutlets, separating when ripe. Vervain grows on roadsides and in waste places throughout much of Europe, except the north, mainly in England, Wales and southern Ireland in the British Isles. It is well known in herb medicine, as a cold and fever remedy.

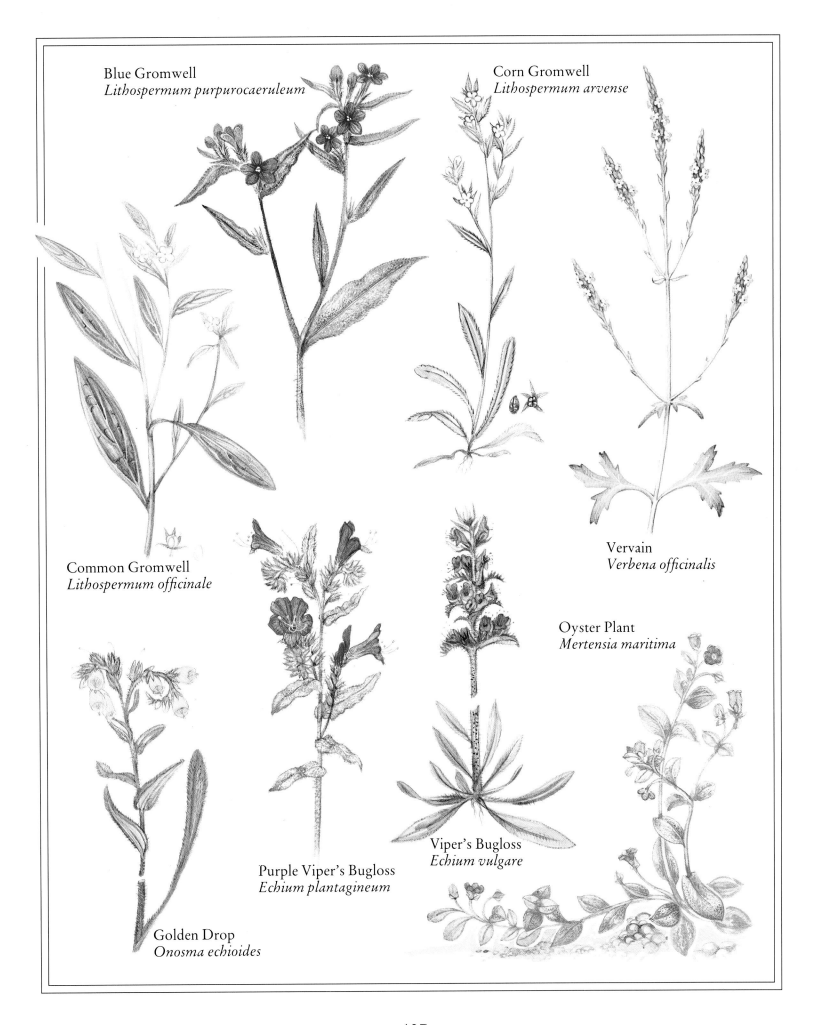

Blue Gromwell
Lithospermum purpurocaeruleum

Corn Gromwell
Lithospermum arvense

Common Gromwell
Lithospermum officinale

Vervain
Verbena officinalis

Oyster Plant
Mertensia maritima

Viper's Bugloss
Echium vulgare

Purple Viper's Bugloss
Echium plantagineum

Golden Drop
Onosma echioides

Mint family
Labiatae

Also known as the **Lamiaceae**. A relatively large family, with about 180 genera and 3500 species, mostly herbs and some shrubs, found in tropical and temperate regions of the world, with many in the Mediterranean area. Plants like mint, basil, sage, rosemary and thyme are used as kitchen herbs. Other species, such as betony, balm, peppermint and horehound, have been used for centuries in herb medicine. Lavender, clary and patchouli are important in the perfume industry. Bergamot is used to flavour Earl Grey tea, and rosemary, balm and peppermint are used to flavour liqueurs. Garden plants include annual and perennial salvias, lavender, catmint and monardas.

Family features The flowers are often borne in spikes made up of whorls of flowers in the axils of bracts; they are hermaphrodite and bilaterally symmetrical. The sepals are united into a tubular, often two-lipped calyx with five teeth and the petals are united to form a tubular, five-lobed, often two-lipped corolla. Each flower has two or four stamens inserted on the corolla-tube. The ovary is superior, with two deeply lobed cells, and the divided style arises from the cleft in the centre. The fruit consists of four nutlets, free or in pairs. The stems are usually square and the leaves opposite. Stipules are absent. Many species contain aromatic oils.

There are about 20 **Mints**, *Mentha* species, in Europe, all more or less scented plants, often difficult to identify as they hybridize freely and intermediates are common. They have small, tubular, weakly two-lipped flowers, each one with four petal-lobes. The flowers come in shades of lilac or white and are borne in dense whorls or spikes. Several mints are cultivated as culinary herbs and ornamental plants. There are garden species which smell of apple or pineapple, as well as the more ordinary spearmint or peppermint.

Peppermint, *Mentha x piperita*, is a hybrid between Water Mint and Spearmint. It is widely grown for the oil of peppermint extracted from it and used to flavour sweets, liqueurs, medicines and toothpaste. The active ingredient is menthol, one of the best remedies for indigestion. In the wild Peppermint has become naturalized in ditches and along damp roadsides throughout much of Europe and the British Isles. It is a greyish, often purple-tinged, hairy perennial plant, with creeping rhizomes (like all mints), erect, branched stems and opposite, toothed, lance-shaped leaves. The lilac-pink flowers are borne in dense, terminal spikes broken into whorls near the bottom of the spikes.

Spearmint, *Mentha spicata*, is mostly used as a culinary herb, grown in many gardens and made into mint sauce. It is another perennial plant, variably hairy, with branched stems 90cm (3ft) tall, serrated, lance-shaped leaves and the unmistakable scent of garden mint. In late summer each stem bears a terminal flower spike formed of whorls of pink or lilac flowers, the whorls often well separated. The origin of this plant is unknown, but it is widespread in the wild in Europe, found in damp places, often beside roads and in waste ground.

Horsemint, *Mentha longifolia*, is similar to Spearmint, with tall stems growing up to 1m (3ft) tall and lance-shaped, toothed leaves. However, it has downy white stems and hairy leaves, grey on the upper surface and whitish on the undersides. The flowers are lilac or white, borne in dense terminal spikes and in other spikes growing from the uppermost leaf axils. This mint grows in damp places and beside water throughout much of Europe but is relatively rare in Britain. It has been used in the past in medicines and for flavour.

Water Mint, *Mentha aquatica*, is a wild species common throughout Europe and the British Isles in marshes and fens, beside streams and ponds, and in wet woods. It is a perennial, with a strong scent of spearmint, erect, branched stems up to 90cm (3ft) tall and pointed-ovate, serrated leaves on long stalks. The lilac flowers appear in late summer, borne in dense, oblong heads often broken into several whorls, terminating the stems and in the axils of the upper leaves.

Corn Mint, *Mentha arvensis*, has a strong, rather sickly scent. This perennial plant has erect stems up to 60cm (2ft) tall and toothed, ovate or elliptical leaves. Its flowers grow in dense, widely spaced whorls in the axils of the upper leaves; they are usually lilac or white, sometimes pink. Plants grow in damp places, in grassy openings in woods, in meadows and arable fields throughout most of Europe and the British Isles. They sometimes get into fields of peppermint and will ruin the flavour of the mint if gathered with the crop.

Pennyroyal, *Mentha pulegium*, has a different form to these other mints—it is a smaller plant, with prostrate stems and opposite, ovate leaves; it flowers in late summer, producing erect flowering stems 30cm (1ft) tall at most, with dense whorls of lilac flowers in the upper leaf axils. The whole plant smells of peppermint. It grows in wet places, grassy spots, beside ponds and streams across much of Europe, except the north, mainly in England and Wales in Britain where it is not common. However, it is grown in gardens and at one time was popular for making mint tea and as a flea deterrent, also as a remedy for headaches. Corsican Mint, *M. requienii*, is even smaller, a tiny mat-forming plant with thread-like stems, tiny oval leaves and whorls of minute lilac flowers in late summer. Its strong scent of peppermint seems out of all proportion to its size. It is grown in gardens in many parts of Europe.

Gipsywort, *Lycopus europaeus*, is related to the mints but is without scent. It is a perennial plant, with creeping rhizomes from which grow erect, leafy stems up to 1m (3ft) tall, much-branched with opposite pairs of pinnately lobed, elliptical leaves. Its white flowers grow in dense whorls in axils of the upper leaves in summer; each one is tubular with four lobes. This plant grows in marshes and wet woods, beside rivers and

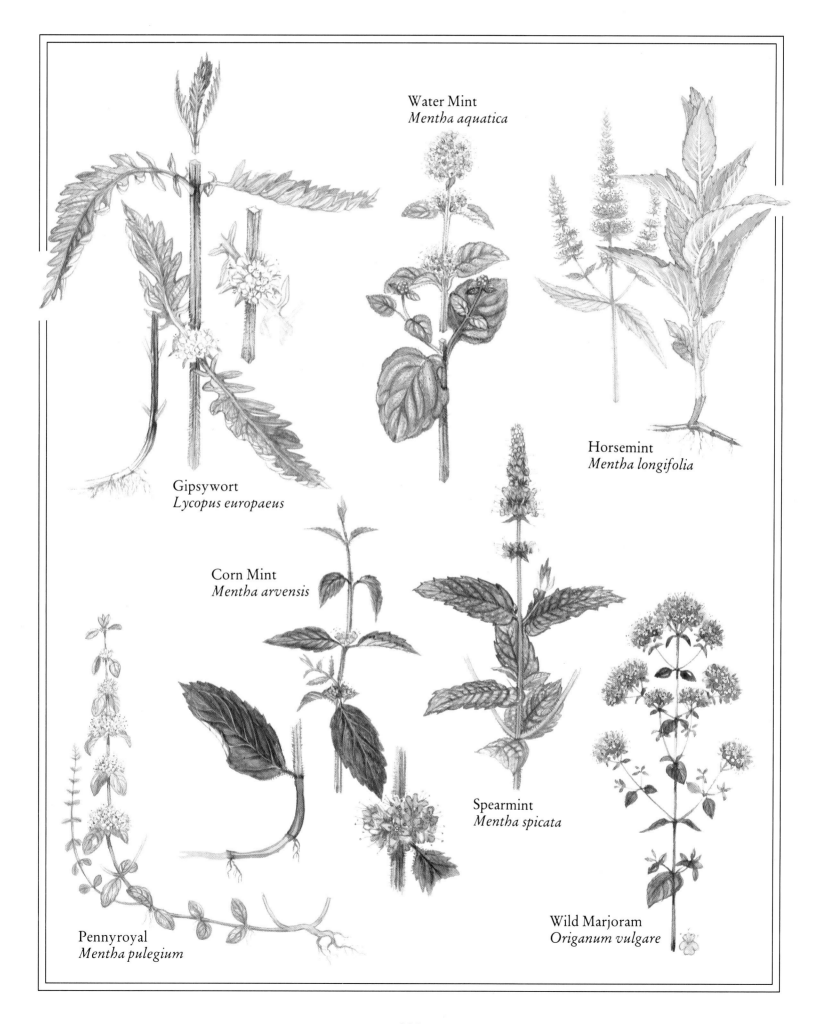

Water Mint
Mentha aquatica

Horsemint
Mentha longifolia

Gipsywort
Lycopus europaeus

Corn Mint
Mentha arvensis

Spearmint
Mentha spicata

Pennyroyal
Mentha pulegium

Wild Marjoram
Origanum vulgare

139

ditches throughout Europe and much of the British Isles, most commonly in England, Wales and western Scotland. It is rare in eastern Scotland, scattered in Ireland. The plant yields a black dye, which legend says was used by rogues in medieval Europe to darken their skin so that they could masquerade as Egyptian fortune-tellers—hence Gipsywort.

Of all the kitchen herbs provided by this family, two of the best known are Sweet Marjoram, *Origanum majorana*, (usually just called marjoram) and **Wild Marjoram** or Oregano, *O. vulgare* (p. 139). Sweet Marjoram grows only in the Mediterranean region, but Wild Marjoram grows wild all over Europe and over much of the British Isles, becoming rare in Scotland and in parts of Ireland. It favours calcareous soils and can usually be found in dry, grassy places, in hedgebanks and on roadsides, or in scrub. It forms patches of erect, purplish stems about 60cm (2ft) tall, with opposite, ovate leaves and the characteristic marjoram scent. In late summer its dense, rounded clusters of reddish-purple to pale pink, two-lipped flowers develop on long stalks in the leaf axils and at the tops of the stems. They are extremely attractive to butterflies and bees, and on a sunny day the whole patch seems to hum.

Wild Thyme, *Thymus praecox*, is a small, matted perennial plant, with branched, prostrate stems and small, elliptical leaves. The plants flower in summer, producing rows of side stems along the main shoots, each with a terminal head of small, purple, two-lipped flowers. This plant grows in dry, grassy places, on downs and heaths, on banks and screes, sometimes in fixed dunes, throughout Europe and much of the British Isles. It has a scent similar to, but weaker than, that of Garden Thyme. Large Thyme, *T. pulegioides*, has a stronger scent; it is a taller, tufted, subshrubby plant, with prostrate or sprawling stems and flower branches turning upwards to reach 25cm (10in) in height. It grows in dry, calcareous grassland in many parts of Europe, mainly in southern and eastern England in the British Isles. The kitchen herb is Garden Thyme, *T. vulgaris*, a small, bushy shrublet from southern Europe.

Common Calamint, *Calamintha sylvatica* subsp. *adscendens*, is a perennial plant, with a creeping rhizome and little-branched, erect, hairy stems about 30–60cm (1–2ft) tall. They bear ovate, serrated leaves in opposite pairs and with long stalks; in the axils of the upper ones the flowers appear in late summer, borne in racemes. They are two-lipped, lilac or pink, spotted or lined with purple on the lower lip. This plant grows locally on calcareous soils, on banks and dry, grassy places in England, Wales and southern England; it is also found in central and southern Europe. The very similar Wood Calamint, *C. sylvatica* subsp. *sylvatica*, is found throughout much of Europe, except the north, only in the Isle of Wight in Britain; it has larger flowers. Lesser Calamint, *C. nepeta*, grows on dry, calcareous banks in eastern England and across southern Europe; it is greyer than Calamint, with much-branched stems, similar leaves and lilac, little-spotted flowers.

Basil Thyme, *Acinos arvensis*, is an old medicinal plant used to treat bruises and toothache, little used today. It has an aromatic scent like Thyme but not so strong. This is a small, bushy, annual plant no more than 20cm (8in) tall, with branched stems and ovate or lance-shaped leaves. Whorls of flowers grow in the axils of the upper leaves; they are similar to those of Calamint—two-lipped and violet with white marks on the lower lip. Plants grow in dry, calcareous soils, in arable fields, grassy places or among rocks, locally in England, more rarely in Wales and Ireland, also across most of Europe.

Wild Basil, *Clinopodium vulgare*, is a somewhat straggling, softly hairy, perennial plant, with a faint aromatic scent. It has erect, little-branched stems up to 80cm (30in) tall and opposite pairs of short-stalked, ovate leaves with serrated margins. The flowers are two-lipped, pinkish-purple, borne in dense whorls in the axils of the upper leaves in late summer. They fall to leave hairy, purplish calyces containing the nutlets. This plant grows in dry, usually calcareous soils, in hedgebanks and scrub on rocky banks and slopes throughout Europe and much of Great Britain, becoming much less common in Scotland and rare in Ireland. This is not the same species as the kitchen herb, Basil. That is another labiate, *Ocimum basilicum*, a plant native to the Middle East and southern Asia.

Balm, *Melissa officinalis*, is another medicinal plant, its leaves made into tea and used as a remedy for indigestion and nervous tension. They are lemon-scented and make a fine addition to pot-pourris or herb pillows; they can also be used in the kitchen with other herbs, or in cold drinks and salads. Balm is a perennial plant which forms spreading clumps of erect, leafy stems about 30–60cm (1–2ft) tall, with ovate, serrated leaves growing on long stalks. In late summer the whorls of flowers appear in the upper leaf axils; the flowers are two-lipped, pale yellow or white, becoming pinkish as they age. As they fall they leave behind whorls of toothed, hairy calyces containing smooth nutlets. This plant grows wild in continental Europe, in woods and hedges, also in vineyards; it is found only in gardens in Britain, as a green form in the herb garden, as a variegated or yellow-leaved form in flower beds. It has become naturalized in a few places.

There are about 700 species of **Sage** in the warmer temperate and tropical regions of the world, which belong to the genus *Salvia*. Some are grown as ornamentals in shrub and flower gardens, a few are used in herb medicine and as kitchen herbs. They are a variable group of plants; many are small, leafy shrubs, others are small herbs, but they all have terminal spikes of flowers which grow in whorls in the axils of the upper leaves and they are usually aromatic. About 45 of them are found in Europe, the majority in the Mediterranean region.

The true **Sage**, *Salvia officinalis*, is famous for Christmas stuffing, for flavouring cheese and for making sage tea. It comes from the Mediterranean regions, but is grown commercially and in gardens all over Europe.

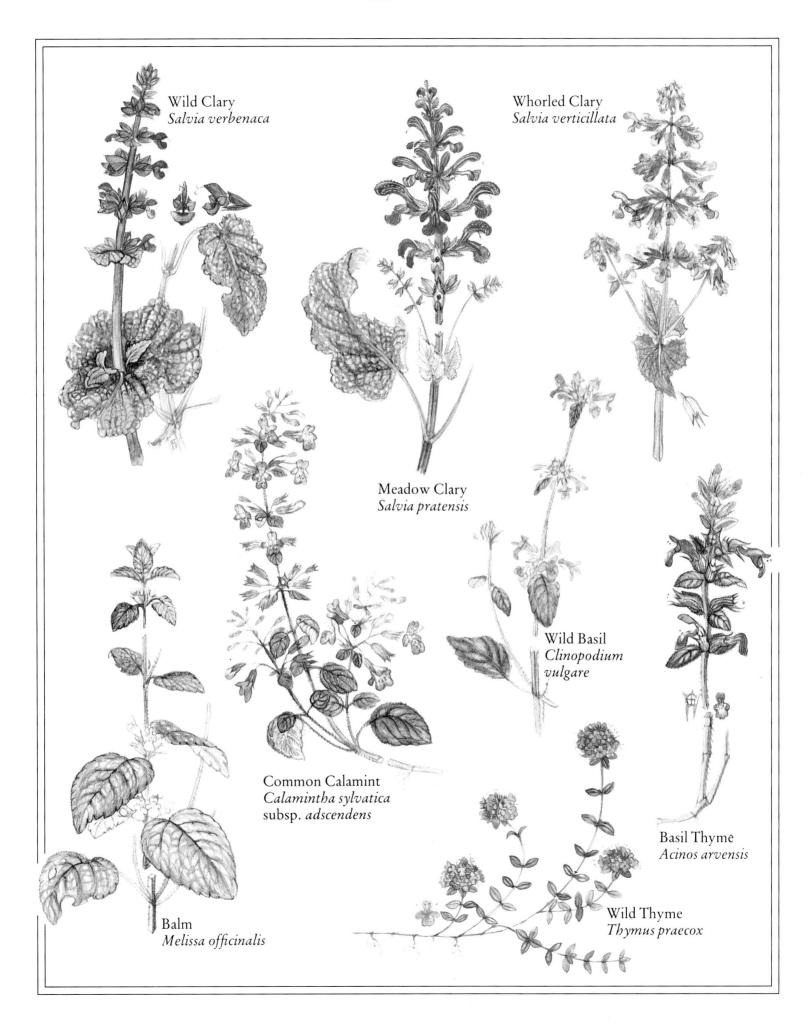

Wild Clary
Salvia verbenaca

Whorled Clary
Salvia verticillata

Meadow Clary
Salvia pratensis

Wild Basil
*Clinopodium
vulgare*

Common Calamint
Calamintha sylvatica
subsp. *adscendens*

Basil Thyme
Acinos arvensis

Balm
Melissa officinalis

Wild Thyme
Thymus praecox

Meadow Clary, *Salvia pratensis*, is one of the few found in the north, growing in meadows and other grassy places, usually on calcareous soils, throughout Europe, except Portugal and Ireland, locally in England. It is a tufted, perennial plant with a clump of oblong, heart-shaped leaves, long-stalked, rather wrinkled and with serrated margins. In summer the flowering stems grow up to 1m (3ft) tall, the lower leaves long-stalked, upper ones stalkless, flowers growing in whorls at the top from toothed, hairy calyces. The flowers are tubular and two-lipped, with a curved, hooded upper lip, and two stamens and/or the style protruding from beneath the hood (this kind of flower is typical of many sage species). The flowers are violet-blue and may be hermaphrodite or female, usually the two kinds on separate plants, and the female flowers much smaller than the hermaphrodite ones.

Wild Clary, *Salvia verbenaca* (p. 141), is a similar but smaller plant, only 80cm (30in) tall at most, often tinged with blue-purple at the tops of the stems and with deeply toothed, almost lobed leaves. Its flowers are smaller, blue or lilac with two white spots at the base of the lower lip, either female or hermaphrodite. Many of the flowers never open but are self-pollinated. This plant grows in dry grassland and along roadsides, occasionally in sand-dunes, throughout much of western and Mediterranean Europe; in Britain it is found mainly in southern and eastern England, in a few places on the coasts of Wales and southern Ireland.

Whorled Clary, *Salvia verticillata* (p. 141), in contrast to many members of this family, has a foetid scent rather than a pleasant one. It is another perennial plant with serrated leaves and whorls of violet flowers growing in the axils of brown bracts and forming long spikes at the tops of the stems. It grows on dry banks and roadsides, in bare, stony ground and waste places across much of Europe, and has been introduced into England, in a few places in Wales and Ireland.

Bastard Balm, *Melittis melissophyllum*, has a strong scent like sage but is not used as a culinary or medicinal herb. It is a hairy perennial with sprawling, unbranched stems up to 50cm (20in) tall and opposite, coarsely toothed, heart-shaped leaves on long stalks. The flowers are large and fragrant, pink or white spotted with pink, two-lipped, in whorls of 2–6 in the upper leaf axils. Bastard Balm grows in woods and hedges across much of Europe, except the north, very locally in south Wales, southwest and southern England.

Self-heal, *Prunella vulgaris*, sounds as if it ought to be a medicinal plant; in fact, it was once highly recommended for the treatment of wounds, but is little used today. It is found throughout Europe and the British Isles in waste and grassy places, gardens and roadsides, pastures and open woods. It is a small perennial, with erect stems up to 50cm (20in) tall and ovate or lance-shaped, sometimes toothed leaves. In summer its blue-violet, two-lipped flowers are borne in dense clusters amid hairy bracts at the tops of the stems.

Cut-leaved Self-heal, *Prunella laciniata*, has pinnately lobed leaves, the lowermost oblong to lance-shaped, the upper ones much narrower, but all deeply cut. The flowers are borne in dense terminal clusters, like those of Self-heal, but are creamy-white. This plant is native to Europe, growing in dry, grassy places, usually on calcareous soils, except in the north; it has been introduced into the British Isles and is now found mainly in southern and eastern England.

The **Woundworts** are a large group of about 300 species in the genus *Stachys*, found worldwide, with about 65 in Europe. They may be annuals or perennials, with leafy, erect stems and whorls of flowers in the upper leaf axils, forming spike-like inflorescences. The flowers are two-lipped, the lower lip three-lobed and the upper lip flat or hooded.

Betony, *Stachys officinalis*, is sometimes placed with several other species in a separate genus, *Betonica*, based on small differences in its flower structure. It is a perennial plant, with a clump of wrinkled, basal leaves—long-stalked with oblong blades and toothed margins. The erect flowering stalks, almost leafless, grow in summer to about 60cm (2ft) tall and bear many whorls of bright reddish-purple flowers with toothed calyces, the lower whorls often separated from each other. This plant grows in open woods and hedgerows, in grassland and heaths, usually in light soils, throughout most of Europe north to southern Sweden, in England and Wales, rarely in Scotland and Ireland. In the past the plant was an important medicinal herb, mainly used to cure headaches and made into poultices to treat cuts and bruises. The leaves were also dried for use as tea or tobacco.

Hedge Woundwort, *Stachys sylvatica*, has long green rhizomes and leafy stems growing up to 1m (3ft) tall. Rhizome and leaves both have an unpleasant scent if bruised. The stems are glandular-hairy, the leaves heart-shaped with serrated margins and long stalks. In late summer the flowers form spikes at the ends of the stems, growing in well-separated whorls in the axils of bracts; they are dull reddish-purple with white markings and have toothed calyces. This perennial plant grows in shady places, woods and hedgebanks throughout Europe and the British Isles. It has antiseptic properties and at one time its leaves were made into poultices to bind around wounds.

Marsh Woundwort, *Stachys palustris*, was used in the same ways. It is similar to Hedge Woundwort but is almost odourless, its rhizomes produce small tubers at the ends, and its leaves are lance-shaped. Its late summer flowers are dull purple with white markings. Marsh Woundwort grows in wet places, in marshes and fens, beside streams and ponds throughout Europe and the British Isles, except parts of the north.

Field Woundwort, *Stachys arvensis*, is a little annual plant, with a clump of slender, branched stems, only 25cm (10in) tall at most. The stems are leafy, with long-stalked, ovate or heart-shaped leaves, wavy-margined or toothed and hairy like the stalks. The flowers are pale purple, borne in whorls in the axils

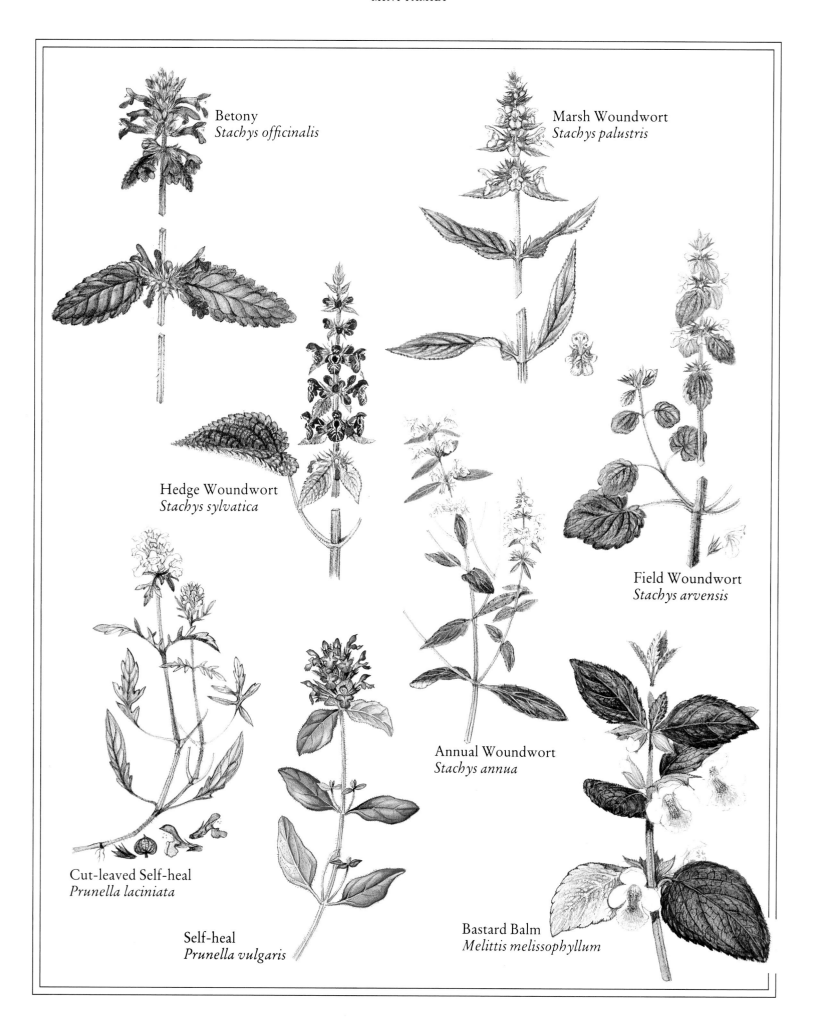

Betony
Stachys officinalis

Marsh Woundwort
Stachys palustris

Hedge Woundwort
Stachys sylvatica

Field Woundwort
Stachys arvensis

Annual Woundwort
Stachys annua

Cut-leaved Self-heal
Prunella laciniata

Self-heal
Prunella vulgaris

Bastard Balm
Melittis melissophyllum

of bracts, forming a very loose, interrupted spike at the tops of the stems; plants can be found in flower for much of the year. This little plant grows in acid soils in lowland areas, often in sandy, arable fields; it is found throughout Europe and much of Great Britain but is absent from many parts of northern England and Scotland, scattered in Ireland.

Annual Woundwort, *Stachys annua* (p. 143), is an annual of fields and waste places, found in southern and central Europe. At one time it was a common cornfield weed in southern England, but is now rarely found in Britain. It has branched stems up to 30cm (1ft) tall, oblong, toothed leaves, the lower ones with short stalks, upper ones almost stalkless, and whorls of pale yellow or white flowers.

The **Deadnettles** are a group of about 40 *Lamium* species found in Europe and Asia. They are annual or perennial plants, with leafy stems and dense whorls of flowers in the axils of leafy bracts high up on the stems; the flowers are two-lipped, with a hooded upper lip and a three-lobed lower lip in which the two lateral lobes are very small. **Spotted Deadnettle**, *L. maculatum*, a species with white-centred leaves and pinkish-purple flowers, is grown as a ground cover plant in British gardens. It grows wild in woods and waste places across much of Europe, except the north.

White Deadnettle, *Lamium album*, is found across most of Europe and much of the British Isles, commonly in England, rarely in northern Scotland, western and southern Ireland. It grows in grassy hedgebanks, along roadsides and in waste places. This small, hairy, perennial plant has a clump of erect stems up to 60cm (2ft) tall and opposite, coarsely toothed and heart-shaped leaves. The whorls of white flowers grow at the tops of the stems in the axils of purple-tinged, leaf-like bracts. Plants may be found in flower from spring to autumn, but when not in flower they are often mistaken for Stinging Nettle—all they lack is the sting, hence Deadnettle.

Red Deadnettle, *Lamium purpureum*, is a weedy annual plant with a pungent scent when bruised, growing in waste places and cultivated ground throughout the British Isles and Europe. It forms a small clump of branched stems with heart-shaped, long-stalked leaves, stems and leaves hairy and often purple-tinged. Plants may be found in flower from early spring to late autumn; the flowers are pinkish-purple, borne in dense whorls often crowded towards the top of each stem, with purple bracts. Both Red and White Deadnettle are old herbal plants used to treat diarrhoea and to stop bleeding.

Henbit, *Lamium amplexicaule*, is an annual plant, with branched, rather sprawling stems only 25cm (10in) tall at most, and scalloped, rounded leaves, the lower ones with long stalks, the upper ones clasping the stem. In summer a few whorls of pinkish-purple flowers grow in the axils of bracts at the tops of the stems. Henbit grows in light, cultivated soils, in arable land and waste places throughout Europe and most of the British Isles, less commonly in the west and in Ireland.

Yellow Archangel, *Lamiastrum galeobdolon*, resembles the deadnettles, but unlike them, it has creeping stems that produce new leaf rosettes, often formed after the parent plant has flowered. It forms large patches of erect, leafy stems up to 60cm (2ft) tall, with pointed-oval, coarsely toothed leaves and showy yellow flowers in early summer. The flowers grow in the axils of leaf-like bracts at the tops of the stems; each has a helmet-shaped upper lip and a three-lobed lower lip marked with red-brown streaks. Yellow Archangel grows in heavy soils in woods and other shady places throughout Europe; it is common in much of England and Wales, becoming rare in the north and in Scotland, also rare in Ireland.

There are about 10 **Hempnettles**, *Galeopsis* species, nine found in Europe. Like all of them, **Common Hempnettle**, *G. tetrahit*, is an annual plant, with two-lipped flowers borne in dense whorls in the axils of bracts at the tops of the stems. The flowers grow in spiny-toothed calyces. Common Hempnettle is a roughly hairy plant, with erect, branched stems up to 1m (3ft) tall and coarse, toothed leaves like those of nettles, but without the stinging hairs. The stems are especially hairy and swollen just below the nodes. The flowers are pink or purple with darker markings. This plant grows in moist places, often in arable land, also in marshes and fens across Europe and throughout the British Isles.

Large-flowered Hempnettle, *Galeopsis speciosa*, is like Common Hempnettle in form, but has much larger yellow flowers, often with a purple blotch on the lower lip. It grows in arable land, often in peaty soils, across much of Europe, scattered throughout most of the British Isles.

The stems of **Red Hempnettle**, *Galeopsis angustifolia*, are not hairy, only downy or even smooth in texture, and not swollen below the nodes. The stems grow up to 80cm (30in) tall and have opposite, hairy, lance-shaped leaves, with small side stems growing out of the axils of the lower ones and whorls of flowers in the axils of bracts at the top. The flowers are large, deep reddish-pink with hairy, toothed calyces. This plant grows in arable fields and bare, stony ground across central Europe, in England, Wales and southern Ireland, becoming less common from east to west in the British Isles.

Motherwort, *Leonurus cardiaca* (p. 147), is an old medicinal plant used to treat nervous and heart disorders. It grows in waste places, in hedgebanks and beside roads across much of central Europe, but is a rare introduction in the British Isles, found scattered only in England. This is a perennial plant, with branched stems 60–120cm (2–4ft) tall, and many long-stalked, palmately lobed leaves; they have a pungent scent if bruised. The lower leaves have 5–7 irregularly toothed lobes and the upper ones and the bracts have three pointed lobes. The flowers appear in late summer, borne in whorls in the axils of the three-lobed bracts at the tops of the stems; they are pink and two-lipped, with a white-bearded upper lip, and spine-tipped lobes on the calyces.

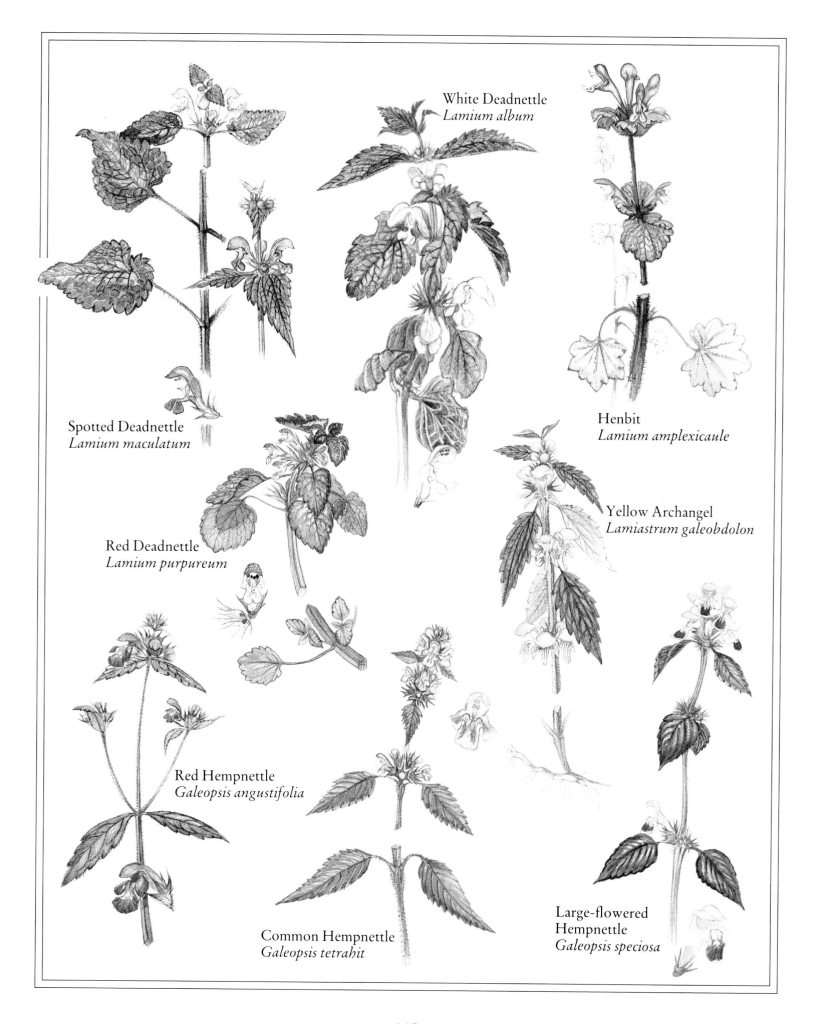

White Deadnettle
Lamium album

Spotted Deadnettle
Lamium maculatum

Henbit
Lamium amplexicaule

Red Deadnettle
Lamium purpureum

Yellow Archangel
Lamiastrum galeobdolon

Red Hempnettle
Galeopsis angustifolia

Common Hempnettle
Galeopsis tetrahit

Large-flowered
Hempnettle
Galeopsis speciosa

Black Horehound, *Ballota nigra*, has a disagreeable scent, dull dark green foliage and unattractive, dull purple flowers in summer. It is found on roadsides and in hedgebanks across most of Europe and much of England, found more locally in Wales, rarely in Scotland and Ireland. It is a hairy perennial, with branched stems, toothed, ovate leaves and whorls of two-lipped flowers at the tops of the stems. They grow in the axils of leaf-like bracts and in toothed calyces.

Catmint, *Nepeta cataria*, grows wild in hedgebanks and on roadsides throughout Europe, scattered in England, Wales and Ireland, only in the south in Scotland. It is grown in flower gardens and gets its name from the attraction it has for cats, who seem to love its scent and will rub themselves against it. However, many insects dislike it and its presence can protect other plants from their attacks. In herb medicine it is used to promote perspiration, so is useful for treating a fever. Catmint is a perennial plant, forming a patch of more or less erect stems up to 1m (3ft) tall, with toothed, ovate leaves whitened by soft, dense hairs. In late summer clusters of red-spotted white, two-lipped flowers grow in the axils of the upper leaves and terminating the stems.

Ground Ivy, *Glechoma hederacea*, was also called Alehoof at one time, since before the advent of hops it was used to give the bitter flavour to beer. It is also used in herb medicine as an astringent, a remedy for diarrhoea and colds. This is a low-growing perennial plant, with creeping, prostrate stems up to 60cm (2ft) long and rooting at the nodes, and rounded, heart-shaped leaves with wavy margins. In spring and early summer its stems turn upwards at the ends to bear blue-purple, two-lipped flowers in twos or fours in the axils of the leaves. Ground Ivy grows in damp places, often in heavy soils, in woods and hedgebanks, in grassland and waste places throughout Europe and the British Isles, rarely in northern Scotland.

White Horehound, *Marrubium vulgare*, is another medicinal plant, used in cough medicines and teas to treat coughs, bronchitis and other throat and chest problems. It is an aromatic perennial plant with much-branched, erect stems, 30–60cm (2–3ft) tall, and wrinkled, ovate leaves, all thickly covered with woolly white hairs; many of the stems are non-flowering. In summer dense whorls of white, two-lipped flowers appear in the axils of the upper leaves; each has a notched upper lip and a three-lobed lower lip. This plant is found in dry, open places, in waste ground, on grassy slopes and downs, and on roadsides throughout much of Europe, scattered in England and Wales, rare in Scotland and Ireland.

The **Skullcaps** are a group of about 300 species in the genus *Scutellaria*, found in many areas of the world, with about 12 in Europe. They are perennial herbaceous plants, with simple leaves and two-lipped, frequently S-shaped flowers, often borne in pairs in the leaf axils. **Skullcap**, *S. galericulata*, forms patches of erect, often branched stems up to 50cm (20in) tall, growing from creeping rhizomes. The stems have toothed, lance-shaped leaves and bright blue flowers in the axils of bracts at the tops of the stems; the flowers may be solitary or borne in pairs. This plant grows in wet meadows and fens, in marshes and beside rivers and ponds throughout Europe and the British Isles. Lesser Skullcap, *S. minor*, is a smaller species with pale pinkish-purple flowers. It grows in wet heathland and woods across western and central Europe, in southern England and Wales and up the west coast to the Scottish islands, also in southwestern and southeastern Ireland.

The **Germanders** are a large group of about 300 species in the genus *Teucrium*, found worldwide, with about 50 in Europe. Some are herbaceous plants, others dwarf shrubs. The flowers are distinctive, with a corolla that lacks an upper lip, but has a five-lobed lower lip, the central lobe the largest and often hanging. **Wood Sage**, *T. scorodonia*, grows in heaths and woods, usually in dry, non-calcareous soils, sometimes on dunes or shingle; it is found in western and central Europe and throughout much of Great Britain, around Ireland but not in the centre. It is immediately recognizable with its long spikes of yellow-green flowers growing above a clump of branched stems with wrinkled leaves. It is a perennial, with creeping rhizomes and stems up to 60cm (2ft) tall in late summer when it is in flower. The sage green leaves are rounded heart-shaped with a texture similar to Sage leaves; the flowers have hanging lips and because they have no upper lip the arching, brown stamens are exposed. At one time this plant was used in brewing in place of hops, but it gives a strong colour and bitter taste to the beer. Tea made from the dried leaves is used in folk medicine to treat rheumatism and cleanse sores.

Wall Germander, *Teucrium chamaedrys*, is a shrubby perennial plant, with sprawling stems only 30cm (1ft) tall, woody at the base and forming a dense, spreading patch with many opposite, dark green leaves like tiny oak leaves. In late summer whorls of small, pinkish-purple flowers appear in the axils of the upper leaves, each one with a toothed calyx, a lobed lower lip and protruding stamens. This plant grows in dry, open places and woods across most of Europe, except the north, but is not native to the British Isles. It is often grown in gardens and has escaped to grow wild on the Sussex downs.

Bugle, *Ajuga reptans* (p. 149), is a creeping perennial plant, with leafy, prostrate stems rooting at the nodes and forming rosettes of smooth, ovate leaves often tinged with bronze. In summer the flowering stems grow up to 30cm (1ft) tall, each with a terminal, leafy inflorescence formed of many whorls of blue flowers. Each flower has a short upper lip and a three-lobed lower lip; the stamens are exposed. This plant grows in damp woods and meadows throughout Europe and the British Isles. It is also grown in gardens. At one time Bugle was used as a medicinal plant for its astringent properties.

Pyramidal Bugle, *Ajuga pyramidalis* (p. 000), forms rosettes of hairy, ovate leaves and erect flowering stems in summer, bearing tapering, pyramidal, very leafy inflores-

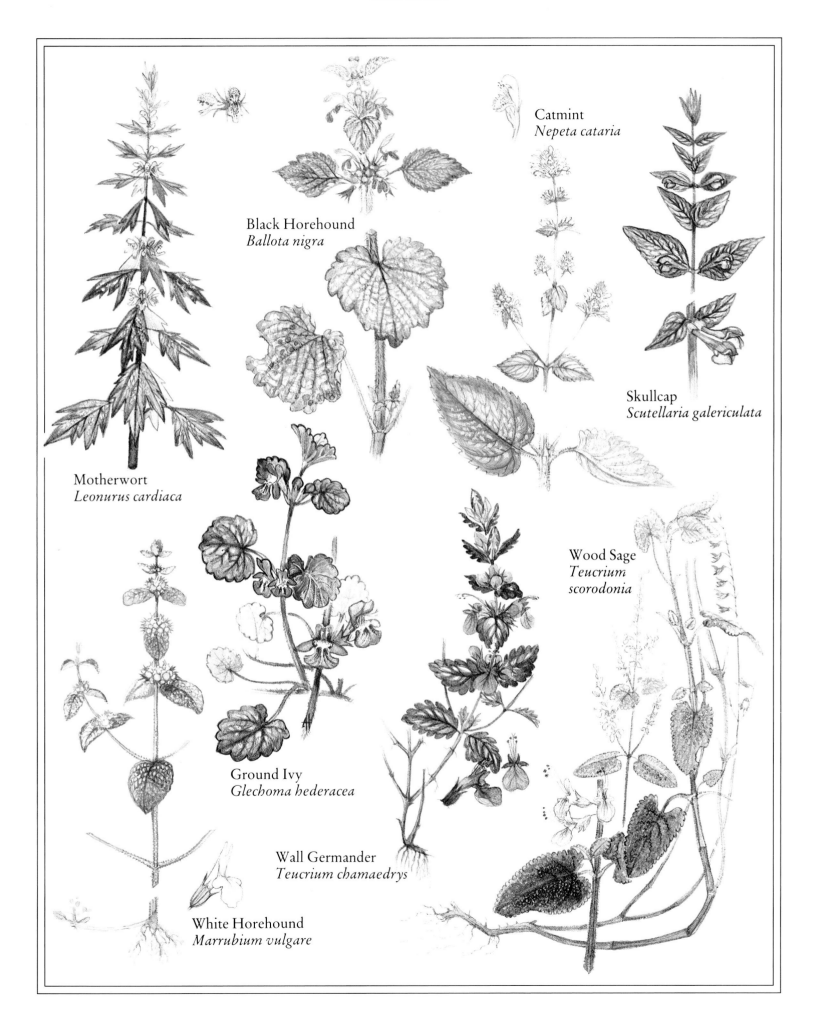

Black Horehound
Ballota nigra

Catmint
Nepeta cataria

Skullcap
Scutellaria galericulata

Motherwort
Leonurus cardiaca

Wood Sage
Teucrium scorodonia

Ground Ivy
Glechoma hederacea

Wall Germander
Teucrium chamaedrys

White Horehound
Marrubium vulgare

cences made up of many whorls of blue flowers like those of Bugle. It grows in mountain meadows in Europe, in the Scottish mountains and is also grown in gardens elsewhere.

Ground Pine, *Ajuga chamaepitys*, is a strange-looking annual plant, its stem almost hidden by the many leaves, each leaf divided into three linear lobes and smelling of pine when crushed. It has yellow flowers almost hidden among the leaves. It grows in fields and dry, stony places across much of Europe, except the north, very locally in southern England.

Nightshade family
Solanaceae

A large and important family, with about 90 genera and 2000 species, mostly herbs and twining plants, the majority found in the tropics and warm temperate regions, especially in Central and South America. There are several important food plants in this family, including potatoes, tomatoes, chillies, peppers and aubergines. Some members of the family are very poisonous, including Belladonna and Henbane; they contain powerful alkaloids used in medicine. Tobacco also belongs to the family and ornamental plants include petunias and Chinese lanterns.

Family features The flowers are solitary or borne in cymes. They are usually hermaphrodite and regular. The calyx has 3–6 (usually five) lobes and is persistent, and the corolla usually has five lobes. The stamens are inserted on the corolla and alternate with the corolla lobes. The ovary is superior with two cells. The fruit is a berry or capsule. The leaves are alternate and simple. Stipules are absent.

Belladonna, *Atropa belladonna*, is one of the most poisonous plants known and just a few of its berries can be lethal for a child. The poisons are the alkaloids atropine and hyoscyamine, which cause visual disturbance, hallucinations, coma and death from heart failure. Ironically these alkaloids are extracted from the plant and used to treat heart failure and ulcers; atropine is used in surgery to dilate the pupils of the eye. Belladonna is a glandular, perennial plant, with a clump of branched, leafy stems 1.5m (5ft) or more tall. The leaves are large, up to 20cm (8in) long, pointed-ovate and alternately arranged or in uneven pairs. Around midsummer and later the plant produces bell-shaped, violet-brown flowers drooping in the leaf axils and followed by berries, green at first, ripening black and glossy, and cupped in calyx-lobes. The plant grows in calcareous soils, in woods, thickets and hedgerows across most of Europe. It is relatively rare in the British Isles, found mainly in England and Wales.

By far the largest genus in the family is *Solanum*, the **Nightshades** themselves, with about 1500 mainly tropical species; few are found in Europe. The flowers of nightshades have characteristic stamens, with short filaments and large anthers;

these anthers protrude from the flat or reflexed petal-lobes and their tips are pressed, or even joined, together so that they form a cone around the style. The flowers are followed by black or brightly coloured berries. Nightshades contain the alkaloid solanine, less lethal than atropine or hyoscyamine, especially to adults, but the plants are still dangerous to children, particularly the berries.

Black Nightshade, *Solanum nigrum*, grows as a weed of gardens and waste places, cultivated land and vineyards in many parts of Europe, mainly in England and Wales in the British Isles. It is a leafy, annual plant with branched green stems up to 60cm (2ft) tall, and leaves that are ovoid or broadly triangular and irregularly toothed. Its flowers grow in drooping clusters opposite the leaves; each has five white, spreading petal-lobes and yellow anthers. They are followed by clusters of poisonous berries, green at first, ripening to dull black.

Woody Nightshade or Bittersweet, *Solanum dulcamara*, is a climbing plant, woody at the base, with branched stems scrambling over shrubs or fences, commonly reaching 2m (6ft) in height. It grows in waste places, woodland margins and hedgerows, often in shingle or on dunes near the coast, throughout Europe and the British Isles, but rarely in Scotland and Ireland. It has simple or lobed leaves and eye-catching racemes of blue-purple flowers with reflexed petal-lobes and yellow anthers. These are followed by clusters of berries, green at first and ripening red. This is an old medicinal herb used mainly to treat skin diseases, asthma and whooping cough.

Thorn-apple, *Datura stramonium*, is much more poisonous than the nightshades—a few seeds can be lethal to children and adolescents. The poisons are hyoscyamine and atropine, with the effects described in Belladonna. Thorn-apple is a coarse, hairless, annual plant, with an unpleasant scent, a branched, often purplish stem up to 2m (6ft) tall, and large, coarsely toothed leaves. Its solitary flowers have an elongated, winged calyx and a funnel-shaped, white corolla. The fruits are prickly capsules containing rough, black seeds. This plant grows in waste places and cultivated land, also in riverine sandbanks, across much of Europe; it has been introduced into Great Britain to become an uncommon casual of waste ground.

Henbane, *Hyoscyamus niger*, contains the same poisons and has the same effects as Thorn-apple. Hyoscyamine and atropine are both extracted from it for use in medicine. This is a coarse, annual or biennial plant with an unpleasant scent like Thorn-apple, but unlike that species it is stickily hairy. Its erect, branched stems grow about 80cm (30in) tall and are very leafy, with leaves so coarsely toothed they are almost lobed. In late summer it bears one-sided clusters of conspicuous flowers—funnel-shaped and greenish-yellow with purple veins. They are followed by capsules enclosed in calyces. This plant grows in disturbed places, often in sandy soils, around farms or near the sea throughout Europe and scattered through the British Isles, more rarely in the north and Ireland.

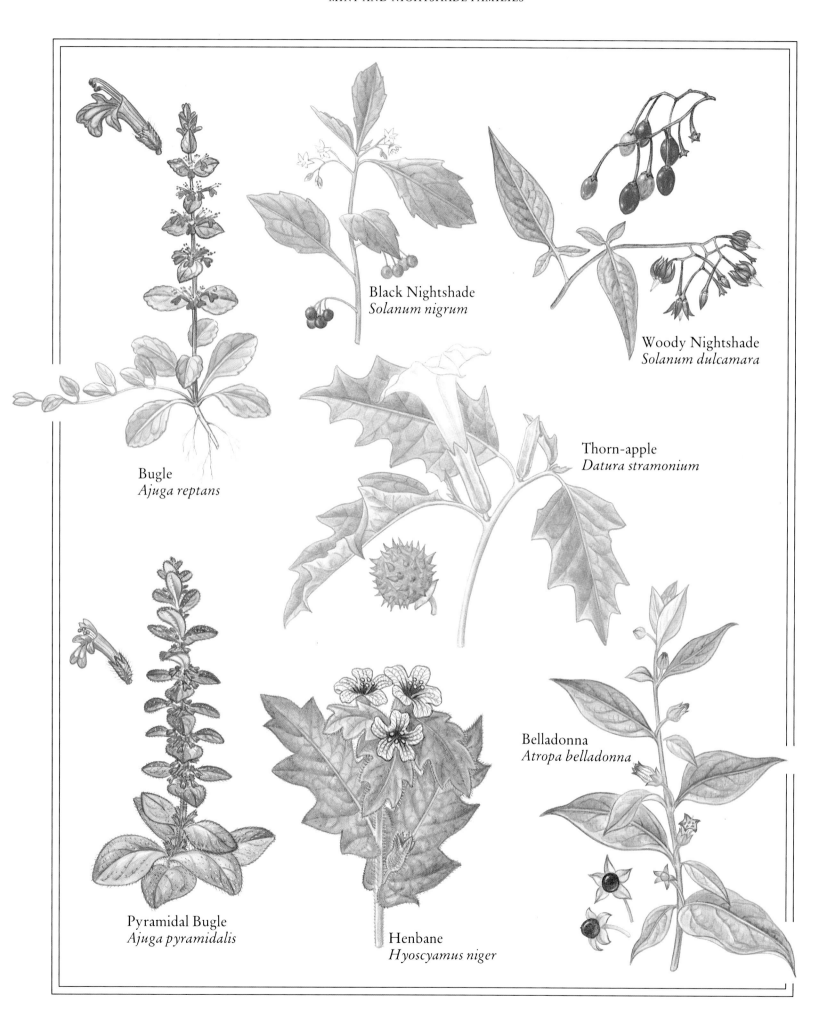

Black Nightshade
Solanum nigrum

Woody Nightshade
Solanum dulcamara

Bugle
Ajuga reptans

Thorn-apple
Datura stramonium

Belladonna
Atropa belladonna

Pyramidal Bugle
Ajuga pyramidalis

Henbane
Hyoscyamus niger

Figwort family
Scrophulariaceae

A large family of herbs and shrubs, with over 200 genera and nearly 3000 species, found almost throughout the world. Many have large, showy or brightly coloured flowers; some, like veronicas, penstemons, verbascums and antirrhinums, are grown in gardens.

Family features The flowers are hermaphrodite and usually bilaterally symmetrical. Each has a five-lobed calyx and a corolla formed of 4–5 fused petals; the corolla may be lobed or two-lipped. The flowers normally have two or four stamens inserted in pairs on the corolla. If a fifth stamen is present, it is usually different and sterile. The ovary is superior and two-celled. The fruits are capsules or, rarely, berries. The leaves are simple or pinnate, and stipules are absent.

The **Mulleins**, *Verbascum* species, are stately plants with tall stems and spikes of many flowers. They are usually biennials, forming a rosette of leaves in the first year and the tall flowering stem in the second. Several are grown in gardens. **Great Mullein** or Aaron's Rod, *V. thapsus*, grows on sunny banks and roadsides, in waste places and rough grassland, usually in dry soils, throughout Europe and the British Isles, becoming rarer in Scotland and Ireland. The stout flowering spike, 2m (6ft) tall, bears many yellow flowers that open over a long period of time. The grey-woolly leaves have had many uses in folklore: they were used as shoe-liners to keep feet warm in winter; they were soaked in saltpetre and used as wicks; women rubbed them on their cheeks to make them red; the leaves were dried and added to tobacco; they were used as poultices and still are used in herb medicine as a remedy for chest diseases. For the plant the leaves have different uses: they are arranged in such a way as to direct water running down the stem into the roots, and the wool cuts down water loss—both useful functions for a plant that grows in dry places.

White Mullein, *Verbascum lychnitis*, is another woolly species, this one with grey, woolly stems and dense, white hairs beneath the leaves; the upper leaf surfaces are green. It is a biennial, with lance-shaped leaves, long-stalked in the basal clump, becoming stalkless higher up the stem, and a flowering stem up to 1.5m (5ft) tall in the second year. This is often branched and usually has white flowers. White Mullein grows in dry, often calcareous soils in waste places, on banks and rocks across most of Europe; in Britain it is a very local plant found mainly in England and Wales.

Dark Mullein, *Verbascum nigrum*, is another biennial plant, this one with a basal clump of hairy, heart-shaped leaves, green on the upper surface, paler below. The whole plant is green, without the mealy, white hairs characteristic of some other mulleins. In summer its flowering spike grows up to 2m (6ft) tall and is usually straight but sometimes branched, with many yellow or white flowers, purple-spotted at the base of each petal-lobe. As in all mulleins, the five stamens are hairy; in this species they have purple hairs on their filaments. Dark Mullein grows on banks and in open places, often on roadsides, usually in dry, calcareous soils; it is found across most of Europe south to northern Spain and northern Italy. In Great Britain it is most common in southern England, becoming rarer in the north and absent from Ireland.

Moth Mullein, *Verbascum blattaria*, is a smaller plant, with stems only 1m (3ft) tall, and shiny, hairless leaves, the basal ones lobed and the higher stem leaves triangular. It has a looser, more graceful raceme of yellow flowers than Dark Mullein, although the flowers have similar purple-haired stamens. This plant grows on banks and roadsides, or in waste places across much of Europe, except the north. It has been introduced as a garden plant into the British Isles, growing occasionally in waste places in England and Wales.

Snapdragon, *Antirrhinum majus*, comes originally from southern Europe but is grown in gardens all over the Continent and the British Isles. It seeds prolifically and often escapes on to old walls and dry places in the wild. In gardens it is grown as an annual but in the wild it survives for several years, often becoming bushy and woody at the base. Each year it forms fresh shoots with almost hairless, lance-shaped leaves and racemes of red-purple, yellow or two-tone flowers. They are typical 'snapdragons'—strongly two-lipped, with a two-lobed upper lip and a three-lobed lower lip, pouched at the base and with a swelling at the throat (the palate), often in a contrasting colour to the rest of the flower. The fruits are characteristic capsules, opening by three pores.

There are about 150 **Toadflax** species in the genus *Linaria*, the majority found in the Mediterranean region, with about 90 in Europe altogether. They have snapdragon-type flowers like those of *Antirrhinum*. **Common Toadflax**, *L. vulgaris*, is found throughout Europe and the British Isles, although less commonly in Ireland and northern Scotland. It grows in grassy places and on roadside verges, in hedgebanks and waste places. It can be a persistent, spreading weed in the wrong place, for it is a perennial plant which forms colonies of erect stems. They grow 30–90cm (1–3ft) tall and have linear leaves and bright yellow and orange flowers. The flowers open in summer, forming long, dense spikes terminating the erect stems; each is two-lipped with a straight spur and an orange palate. The name 'toadflax' comes from the supposed resemblance of an open flower to a toad's mouth, and from the way the plants resemble flax before they flower. This species has a long history of use in herb medicine and was recommended for treating jaundice and dropsy. Steeped in milk it makes good fly poison.

Pale Toadflax, *Linaria repens*, is one of several species with mauve or purple flowers. It has creeping rhizomes and numerous erect stems, growing about 30–90cm (1–3ft) tall, with whorls of linear leaves and long terminal racemes of pale lilac

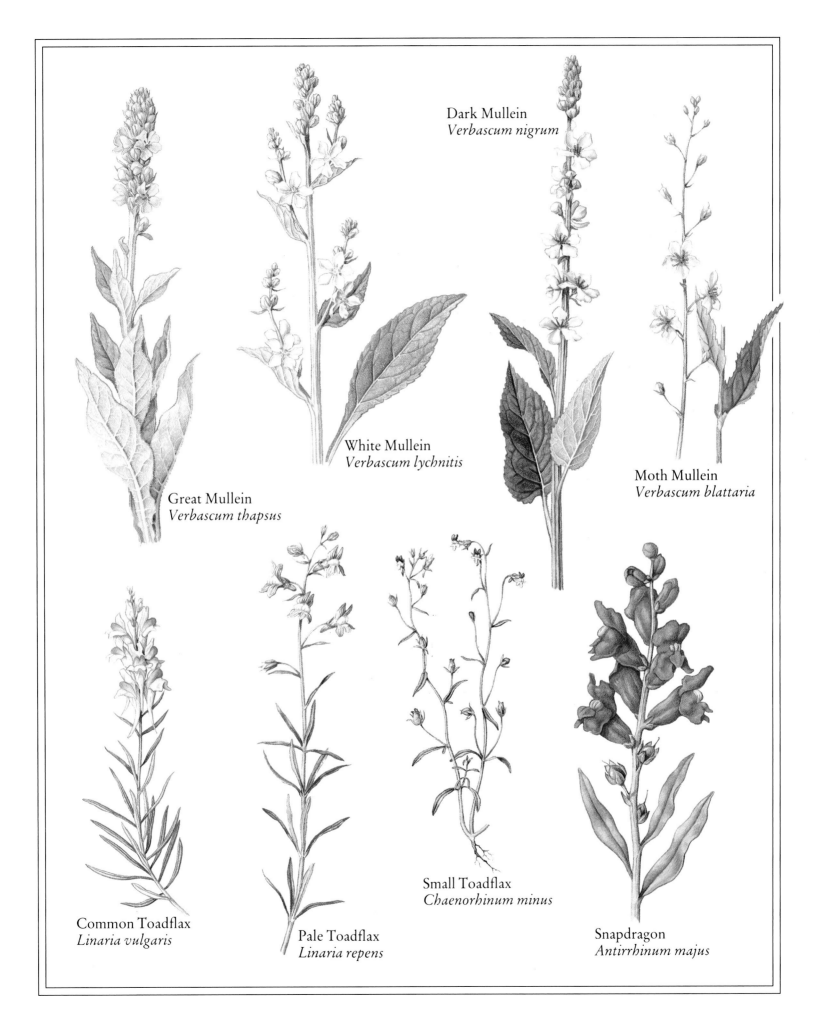

Dark Mullein
Verbascum nigrum

White Mullein
Verbascum lychnitis

Great Mullein
Verbascum thapsus

Moth Mullein
Verbascum blattaria

Common Toadflax
Linaria vulgaris

Pale Toadflax
Linaria repens

Small Toadflax
Chaenorhinum minus

Snapdragon
Antirrhinum majus

or white flowers veined with darker violet and with an orange spot on the palate. This toadflax grows in dry, cultivated and waste places, in stony fields in western and central Europe, mainly in England and Wales in the British Isles.

Small Toadflax, *Chaenorhinum minus* (p. 151), is a slender, annual plant with branched, erect stems up to 25cm (10in) tall, many linear leaves and small, solitary flowers in the leaf axils. The flowers are purple with a yellow palate, an open mouth and a short, curved spur. This little plant grows in grassy places, arable land and waste ground, especially near railway lines, across most of Europe and in much of the British Isles, except northern Scotland.

Round-leaved Fluellen, *Kicksia spuria*, is related to toadflaxes, its relationship clearly evident in its flowers. This is an annual plant, with sprawling, branched stems up to 50cm (20in) long and long-stalked, ovate or rounded leaves; both stems and leaves are glandular and hairy. The solitary flowers appear in late summer on long, hairy stalks in the leaf axils; they are yellow with a violet upper lip and a long spur. **Sharp-leaved Fluellen**, *K. elatine*, is similar and has yellow and purple flowers, but it has arrow-shaped leaves which are less hairy and not glandular, and its flowers grow on hairless stalks. Both species grow in arable fields, often among the stubble in cornfields, and are found across most of Europe; they are local plants in Britain, found mainly in England and parts of Wales.

Ivy-leaved Toadflax, *Cymbalaria muralis*, is another toadflax relative, originally from Mediterranean Europe, but now found wild further north and throughout most of the British Isles. It was introduced as a garden plant and now grows on old walls, sometimes on rocks. This is a small, hairless perennial with trailing, purplish stems rooting at the nodes, and long-stalked, palmate, rather thick leaves. The little flowers grow on long stems in the leaf axils for much of the summer; they are blue-mauve with yellow palates and long spurs.

The genus *Scrophularia* is a large one with about 300 species of **Figworts**, mostly Old World plants. About 40 are found in Europe. They are biennials or perennials with erect, often square stems and opposite leaves. The flowers grow in cymes in the axils of the upper leaves and are usually dull in colour. They have a distinctive shape, with a barrel-shaped tube and five small lobes (often forming an upper and a lower lip) around the opening, and they are attractive to wasps, which pollinate the flowers. Each flower has four fertile stamens and a single sterile, scale-like one just inside the upper lip.

Common Figwort, *Scrophularia nodosa*, grows in damp places, in woods and hedgerows, beside streams and in moist waste places throughout Europe and the British Isles. Its erect stem grows up to 80cm (30in) tall, ending in a branched inflorescence of many flowers at the top. This is a hairless, perennial plant, with pointed-ovate, sharply serrated leaves, the lower ones long-stalked. The flowers have a greenish tube and a brown upper lip, and an unpleasant scent obviously meant to attract wasps. At one time this was an important herbal plant, believed to be a remedy for scrofula (a form of tuberculosis that produced abscesses and skin sores).

Water Figwort, *Scrophularia auriculata*, was also used to treat scrofula, as well as other sores and wounds. It is taller than Common Figwort, up to 1m (3ft) in height; its square stems are winged on the angles and its leaves are oblong or elliptical, often with two small lobes at the base of the blade. This plant grows beside water, in wet woods and marshes in western Europe, commonly in England and eastern Wales, locally in western Wales and Ireland, rarely in Scotland.

Yellow Figwort, *Scrophularia vernalis*, grows in European woods and shady places, and is naturalized in a few parts of Great Britain. It has erect stems up to 80cm (30in) tall, with broadly heart-shaped, serrated leaves, the whole plant softly glandular-hairy. In early summer racemes of yellow flowers grow in the axils of the uppermost leaves. The flowers are globular with five even lobes at the constricted mouth.

Monkeyflower, *Mimulus guttatus*, and **Blood-spot-emlets**, *M. luteus*, are two of the *Mimulus* species introduced into British and European gardens from North America and now naturalized in wet places in many countries. Monkeyflower is a perennial, hairless plant, with leafy, creeping stems which root at the nodes and form overlapping mats. In summer the shoots turn upwards and develop into erect stems 20–50cm (8–20in) tall with opposite, rounded leaves and showy yellow flowers in the upper leaf axils. The flowers are two-lipped, with orange spots on the palate. Blood-spot-emlets has more sprawling flower stems and large red spots all over the flowers. Both plants grow on the banks of streams and ponds, and in marshes in the wild, although Monkeyflower is much more common. They hybridize when growing together.

Gratiole, *Gratiola officinalis*, is a leafy, perennial plant, with stems that creep and root at the base, then turn upwards to reach 60cm (2ft) tall; they have many linear or lance-shaped leaves which may or may not be toothed, and solitary, pinkish-white flowers in the leaf axils. The flowers are held upright and are tubular in shape, with five more or less even lobes around the mouth. Gratiole grows in marshes and wet meadows, on the banks of streams and ditches across most of Europe, except the north, but not in the British Isles.

Mudwort, *Limosella aquatica*, is another wetland plant, this one found in wet mud around ponds, or in places subjected to periodic flooding; the plant is erratic in its appearance, coming and going with the water. It is an annual, with creeping stems rooting at the nodes and forming rosettes of linear, elliptical or spoon-shaped leaves, the stalks of the leaves several times longer than the blades. The white or pink flowers grow singly on separate stems and are bell-shaped with five petal-lobes. Mudwort is found mainly in England and Wales in the British Isles and across Europe, except in the Mediterranean region; however, it is not common and often rare.

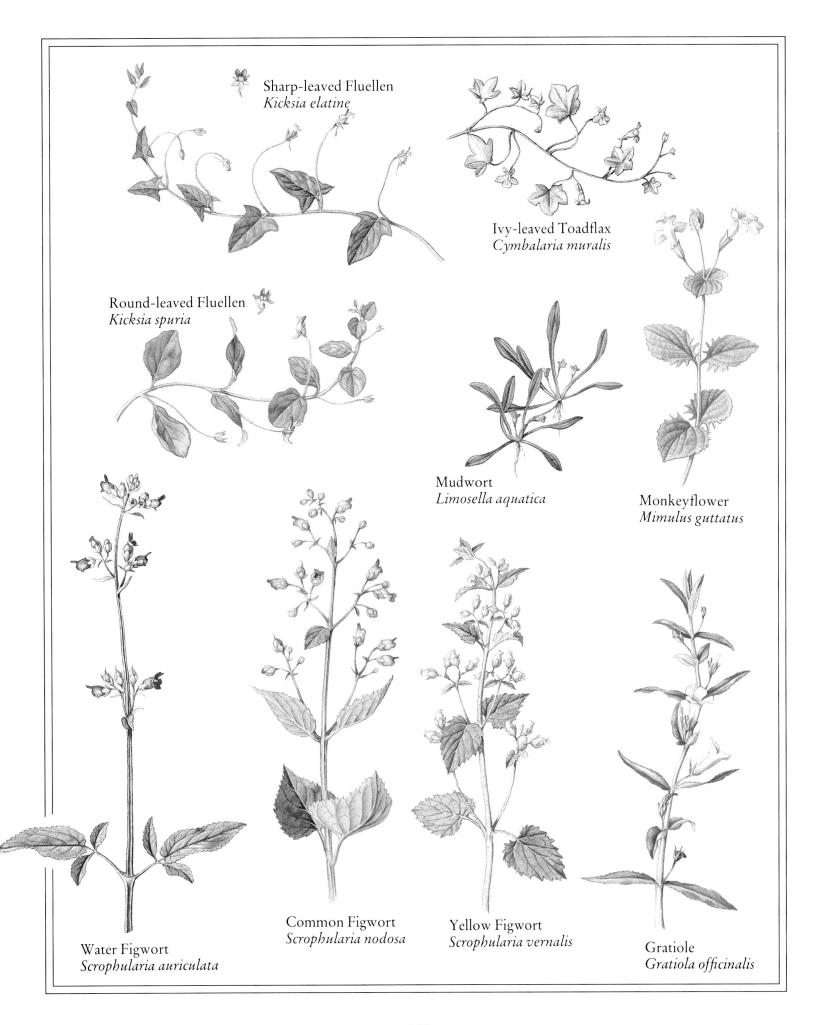

Sharp-leaved Fluellen
Kicksia elatine

Ivy-leaved Toadflax
Cymbalaria muralis

Round-leaved Fluellen
Kicksia spuria

Mudwort
Limosella aquatica

Monkeyflower
Mimulus guttatus

Water Figwort
Scrophularia auriculata

Common Figwort
Scrophularia nodosa

Yellow Figwort
Scrophularia vernalis

Gratiole
Gratiola officinalis

The **Speedwells**, *Veronica* species, are mostly small, spreading, often prostrate annual or perennial plants, with opposite leaves and blue or white flowers. Speedwell flowers are distinctive, with a very short tube and four lobes looking like four petals in the form of a broad, upright cross. The upper lobe is larger than any of the others. Two long stamens project beyond the petals towards the sides of the flower. Out of a total of 300 *Veronica* species found in temperate regions of the world, about 70 grow in Europe, many native and others naturalized from other parts of the world.

Brooklime, *Veronica beccabunga*, is larger than most *Veronica* species, growing up to 60cm (2ft) tall. It is found in ponds and streams, in marshes, wet meadows and springs throughout Europe and the British Isles. This is a fleshy, hairless, perennial plant with creeping, sprawling stems that root in the mud and then turn upwards. It has opposite, rather thick, ovate leaves with serrated margins and loose racemes of blue flowers in summer growing on long stalks in the upper leaf axils. Brooklime is edible and its young shoots can be eaten in salads like watercress, but they are bitter and need to be mixed with other salad plants.

Water Speedwell, *Veronica anagallis-aquatica*, is a similar but smaller plant, found also in wet meadows, ponds and streams throughout Europe. It also grows in much of the British Isles, but is absent from parts of the southwest, Wales and western Scotland. Its creeping, rooting stems grow 30cm (1ft) tall at most, its leaves are ovate on the lower stems, oblong with clasping bases higher up the stems, and its flowers are pale blue with darker veins. Pink Water Speedwell, *V. catenata*, is often found with Water Speedwell, but has purple-tinged stems, linear or lance-shaped leaves and pink flowers.

Heath Speedwell, *Veronica officinalis*, is a typical small speedwell, a perennial plant with rooting stems often forming wide mats, and other stems turning upwards to grow 40cm (15in) tall at most. It has softly hairy, oval or elliptical, toothed leaves and in summer dense, pyramidal racemes of lilac flowers appear, usually in one axil of a pair of leaves. This little plant grows in grassland, heaths and woods, usually in dry soils, throughout Europe and the British Isles. It is an old medicinal herb used to treat coughs and skin problems.

Germander Speedwell, *Veronica chamaedrys*, has some of the bluest flowers in the whole plant world—surprising on a plant that qualifies as a weed when growing in the wrong place, as it sometimes does. This is another creeping, perennial plant with upturned stems; it has hairy, serrated leaves with very short stalks, and flowers on long stalks in the upper leaf axils. The plant blooms in spring and early summer. It grows in woods and hedgerows, in grassland, waste places and gardens throughout Europe and the British Isles.

Thyme-leaved Speedwell, *Veronica serpyllifolia*, grows in similar places to Germander Speedwell: in grassy places, heaths, waste ground and gardens, often in somewhat moist spots, throughout Europe and the British Isles. It is a perennial plant, with creeping, rather hairy, somewhat sticky stems and ovate leaves, some of the stems turning upwards to bear leafy racemes of many small flowers. The flowers are white or lilac with dark violet veins. There is a subspecies of this plant with bright blue flowers, which is found in damp, grassy places in mountains across much of Europe, including the British Isles.

Wall Speedwell, *Veronica arvensis*, also has leafy spikes of flowers at the tops of the stems, but they are tiny in this species and bright blue. This is a little annual plant, with sprawling stems only 25cm (10in) tall at most, and often much smaller, with coarsely toothed, ovate leaves; plants can be found in flower from spring to late autumn. Wall Speedwell grows as an inconspicuous weed of cultivated land and gardens, also in heaths, dry grassland and other open places throughout Europe and the British Isles.

Ivy-leaved Speedwell, *Veronica hederifolia*, is another annual species, another weed of cultivated land found throughout Europe and much of the British Isles, becoming less common in western Scotland and Ireland. It has hairy, branched, sprawling stems up to 60cm (2ft) long and forming mats with many kidney-shaped, palmately-lobed leaves, light green and rather thick for a speedwell. The pale blue flowers grow singly on long stalks in the upper leaf axils.

Buxbaum's Speedwell, *Veronica persica*, is one of several introduced species found in Europe, this one from southwestern Asia. It grows as a weed, probably the most common speedwell in cultivated land throughout Europe and the British Isles. It is an annual, with branched, sprawling stems up to 40cm (15in) long and coarsely toothed, triangular-ovate leaves; the stems are hairy, as are the veins on the undersides of the leaves. The flowers grow singly on long stalks in the axils of the leaves; they are bright blue, the lowest petal-lobe often paler than the others or white.

Slender Speedwell, *Veronica filiformis*, is another introduced garden species, now a persistent weed in lawns and other grassy places, naturalized in much of Europe and the British Isles. It has numerous creeping stems that root at the nodes and the plant soon takes over wide areas, even displacing grasses in shady, damp places. The leaves are kidney-shaped with rounded teeth, and the flowers are solitary, growing on long, slender stalks in the leaf axils. They are pale lilac-blue, the lowest petal-lobe narrower than the others and paler.

Spiked Speedwell, *Veronica spicata*, resembles some of the showier garden species, with flowers borne in dense spikes at the tops of the stems. Several varieties of this species are grown in gardens, but the plant is also native to Europe and the British Isles. In the wild it is found in dry grassland and among rocks, in basic or calcareous soils across most of Europe; in Britain it is confined to a few localities in the west where it grows on limestone. It is a perennial plant, with a woody rhizome and numerous erect, leafy flowering stems, the leaves grey-green in

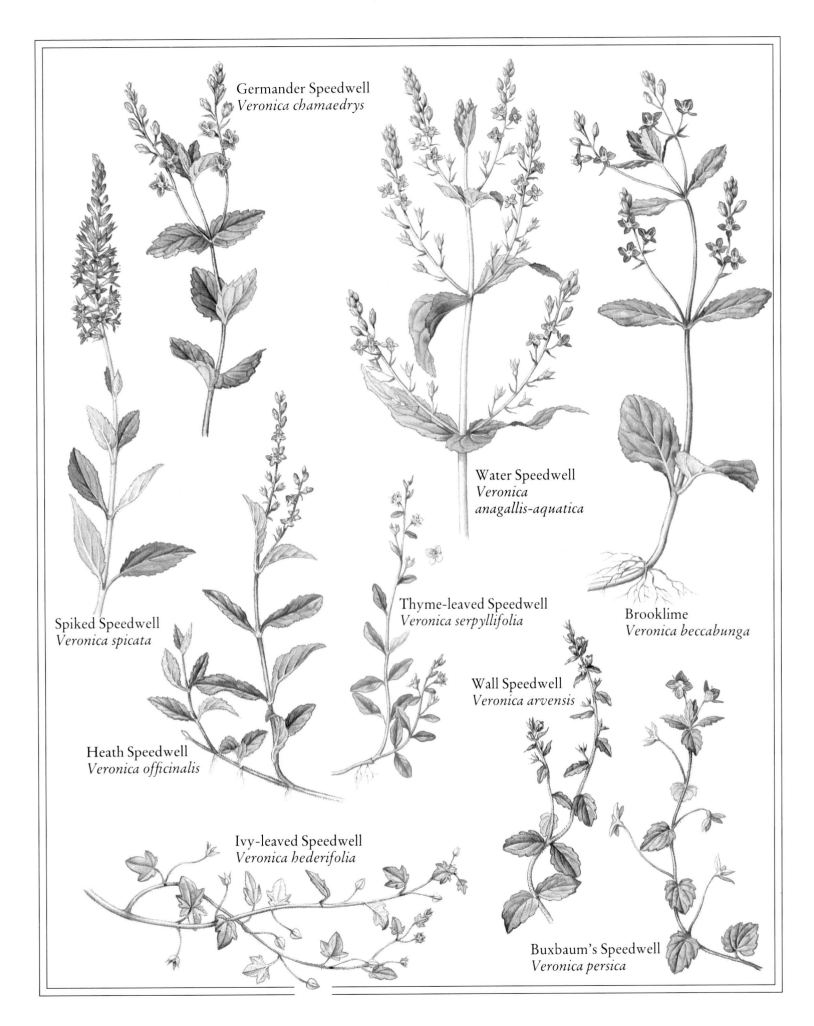

Germander Speedwell
Veronica chamaedrys

Water Speedwell
*Veronica
anagallis-aquatica*

Brooklime
Veronica beccabunga

Spiked Speedwell
Veronica spicata

Thyme-leaved Speedwell
Veronica serpyllifolia

Heath Speedwell
Veronica officinalis

Wall Speedwell
Veronica arvensis

Ivy-leaved Speedwell
Veronica hederifolia

Buxbaum's Speedwell
Veronica persica

155

colour from their glandular hairs, varying in shape from ovate with long stalks at the base of the stems to linear and stalkless higher up. The flowers are violet-blue, each with a long tube and four narrow petal-lobes.

Cornish Moneywort, *Sibthorpia europaea*, is a relatively rare plant, found only locally in a few places in southern England and Wales, in southern Ireland and the Channel Islands, and in the mountains of western Europe and Greece. It grows in damp, shady places. This is a small perennial, with creeping, thread-like stems rooting at the nodes and many pale green leaves on long stalks. The leaf blades are rounded, often kidney-shaped, bluntly lobed into 5–7 sections at the margins. The flowers appear in late summer, growing singly on long stalks in the leaf axils; each one has five petal-lobes, the two upper lobes cream-coloured, the three lower pinkish. Forms with variegated leaves are sometimes grown in rock gardens.

Fairy Foxglove, *Erinus alpinus*, is seen only in gardens in Britain, growing in rock gardens or in patio cracks, sometimes escaping on to walls or into woods. It is native to western and central Europe, found in mountain woods, among rocks or screes, on old walls in lowland areas. It is a very small plant, a hairy perennial, forming tufts of toothed, lance-shaped leaves and flowering in early summer. The flowering stems grow 15cm (6in) tall at most and bear terminal clusters of bright purple flowers; each flower is tubular with five more or less equal petal-lobes. This little plant is poisonous, containing the same poison as Foxglove.

Foxgloves, *Digitalis purpurea*, are familiar plants of woods, heaths and mountains, with their tall flowering spikes of hanging bells adorning the open areas in early summer. Plants grow in acid soils throughout the British Isles and in western and central Europe. Foxglove is a biennial plant, with a rosette of softly hairy, large, lance-shaped leaves in the first year and an erect, leafy flowering stem 1–2m (3–6ft) tall in the second. The large tubular flowers are mauve-pink in colour, lighter on the inside with dark pink spots. Foxgloves are poisonous, containing the glycoside digitoxin, which affects the heart. They are grown commercially for this drug which is used in medicine to regulate heart function.

Large Yellow Foxglove, *Digitalis grandiflora*, is a Continental species not found in the British Isles. It grows across much of Europe, except the north, in open mountain woods, among rocks and on screes. This is a perennial plant, with an erect stem up to 1m (3ft) tall, glandular-hairy in texture and with alternate, broadly lance-shaped leaves, hairless and shiny above, downy beneath. The stem ends in a long spike of hanging, pale yellow flowers, each one tubular in shape with a network of brown lines inside, hairy on the outside and with reflexed sepal-lobes. Small Yellow Foxglove, *D. lutea*, is similar, but its flowers are smaller, hairless on the outside and without the brown veins inside. It grows in woods and hills in central Europe. Both species are very poisonous.

Many members of this family are semi-parasites. They have well-developed green stems and leaves, but their root systems are poorly developed and they attach themselves to the roots of other plants, especially to grasses, and obtain water and mineral salts from their hosts. Some species cannot survive without a host, while others do grow and survive, but are stunted and do not do well. Sometimes the area of host plants affected can be seen, for a patch of short grass, which appears to have been trampled, will surround the parasite. All the following plants are semi-parasites.

Red Bartsia, *Odontites verna*, is a much-branched, downy, annual plant, with erect stems up to 50cm (20in) tall and opposite, lance-shaped leaves. The leaves have toothed margins and are often flushed with purple. The plants bloom in summer, producing long, one-sided, leafy spikes of purplish-pink flowers at the tops of the stems; each flower has a hooded upper lip, a three-lobed lower lip and anthers protruding from beneath the upper lip. This plant grows in waste places, in pastures, cultivated land and roadsides throughout Europe and the British Isles. Yellow Odontites, *O. lutea*, is a similar plant with yellow flowers; it grows in dry grassland and stony ground in central Europe.

Yellow Bartsia, *Parentucellia viscosa*, is another annual, but a sticky-hairy one with an unbranched stem growing up to 50cm (20in) tall. It has coarsely toothed, lance-shaped leaves growing in opposite pairs, and yellow flowers in a spike at the top of the stem. Each flower is tubular and two-lipped, with a hooded upper lip and a three-lobed lower lip. The plant grows in damp, grassy places in the Mediterranean region and in western Europe, in southwestern Ireland, southwestern and southern England, and in a few places elsewhere in the British Isles, but not in Scotland.

Alpine Bartsia, *Bartsia alpina*, is an arctic and alpine plant, found in meadows and on ledges in the mountains of Europe, in a few places in northern England and Scotland. It is a creeping perennial, glandular-hairy in texture, with erect, leafy stems up to 30cm (1ft) tall. The leaves are wrinkled and ovate with toothed margins. The flowers are borne singly, growing in the axils of purple-tinged bracts which resemble the leaves in shape; the flowers are dark purple, two-lipped with a hooded upper lip and a three-lobed lower lip.

Eyebrights, *Euphrasia* species, are a complex group difficult to identify, prone to hybridize with one another and mostly confined to very specific habitats and with limited distributions. Thus, although there are about 50 species in Europe, most are confined to a small area. They are all annual plants, usually with branched stems and often no more than 30cm (1ft) tall, leafy with many small toothed, often opposite leaves. The solitary flowers grow in the axils of leaf-like bracts (which resemble the leaves but often have more teeth), forming a spike-like inflorescence at the top of each stem. Each flower is two-lipped, the upper lip two-lobed and the lower lip with

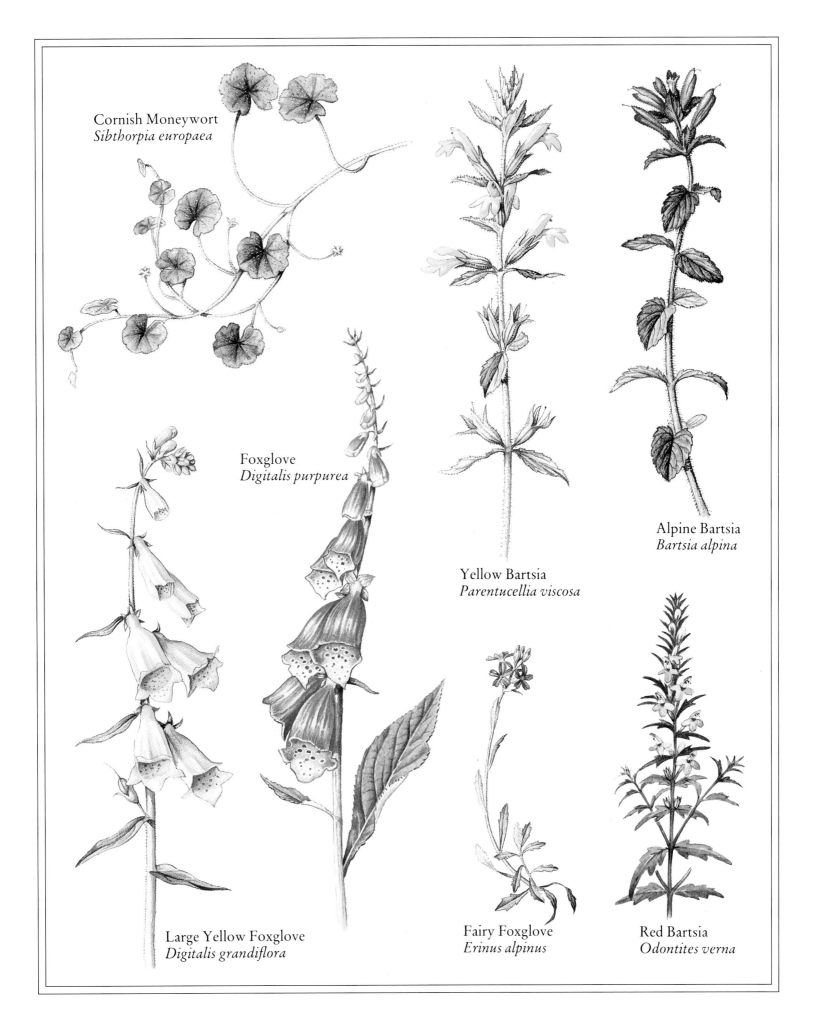

Cornish Moneywort
Sibthorpia europaea

Foxglove
Digitalis purpurea

Alpine Bartsia
Bartsia alpina

Yellow Bartsia
Parentucellia viscosa

Large Yellow Foxglove
Digitalis grandiflora

Fairy Foxglove
Erinus alpinus

Red Bartsia
Odontites verna

three spreading lobes. The flowers are usually white or purple, with a yellow blotch and purple veins on the lower lip. Eyebrights grow in a variety of habitats: in grassy meadows and pastures, in heaths and woods, marshes and wet moorland, on dunes and in the mountains, some near the sea, some in cultivated land. They are called Eyebright because they are used in herb medicine to treat sore and tired eyes.

Common Eyebright, *Euphrasia rostkoviana*, is taller than many, its branched stems growing up to 50cm (20in) in height. Its opposite leaves are ovate with 3–5 teeth on the margins and its flowers are white, the upper lip often veined with lilac and the lower lip yellow-blotched. This species is widespread compared to many eyebrights, found in moist meadows in much of Europe, except the north, and throughout the British Isles.

There are about 500 **Louseworts**, *Pedicularis* species, in the northern hemisphere, the majority in the mountains of Asia; about 50 grow in Europe, many of them in the mountains. They are often parasitic on grasses. They may be annual or perennial plants and have divided leaves, usually alternately arranged, and spike-like racemes of two-lipped flowers. Each flower has a hooded upper lip and a three-lobed lower lip. The name 'lousewort' is supposed to come from an old belief that cattle picked up lice from these plants; various explanations have been given at different times to account for this erroneous belief, none of which are convincing. The plants are poisonous and livestock usually avoid them.

Lousewort, *Pedicularis sylvatica*, grows in marshes and bogs, damp heathland and moors throughout much of Europe and the British Isles. It is a tufted, perennial plant, with many sprawling stems and deeply divided or pinnately lobed leaves, the leaflets toothed. The red or pink flowers appear in summer, borne with bracts similar to but smaller than the leaves, in dense spikes on erect stems. They have cylindrical calyces and are followed by compressed capsules with a few large seeds.

Marsh Lousewort, *Pedicularis palustris*, is an annual or biennial plant with a single erect but branched stem growing up to 60cm (2ft) tall, pinnately divided leaves with toothed segments, and terminal spikes of reddish-pink flowers. The flowers grow in the axils of bracts which look like small leaves. The flowers have reddish, two-lipped calyces which become inflated around the capsules; the seeds rattle in the dried, ripe capsules, providing the plant with its other name of Red Rattle. This plant grows in wet meadows and heaths throughout Europe and the British Isles.

Yellow Rattle, *Rhinanthus minor*, is an annual plant, with an erect, often branched, black-spotted stem up to 50cm (20in) tall and opposite, stalkless, toothed leaves. The tubular, two-lipped flowers are yellow, the upper lip of each flower hooded and the lower lip three-lobed. The flowers have characteristic calyces, inflated with reticulate veins and four teeth; the calyx becomes more inflated than ever in fruit, enclosing the flattened capsule with its winged seeds. Like Red Rattle, this plant

gets its name from its capsules because as they mature their tissues dry and shrink inside, freeing the seeds which then rattle every time the plant blows in the wind. Yellow Rattle grows in a variety of grassy places, dry pastures, wet meadows and fens, mountain meadows, often on basic or calcareous soils, throughout Europe and the British Isles.

Yellow Rattle is one of about 50 *Rhinanthus* species, all found in the temperate regions of the northern hemisphere, with about 20 species in Europe. They are difficult to identify and prone to hybridization, but all are annuals and basically similar. Greater Yellow Rattle, *R. angustifolius*, grows up to 60cm (2ft) tall and its stems lack black spots; it grows in cornfields and meadows throughout Europe, in a few scattered places in England and Scotland.

The **Cow-wheats**, *Melampyrum* species, are annual plants with simple, opposite leaves and tubular, two-lipped flowers; the upper lip is hooded and the lower lip three-lobed. They are poisonous and avoided by livestock, semi-parasitic on grasses, with about 15 species in Europe. **Common Cow-wheat**, *M. pratense*, grows in open woods and heaths throughout Europe and the British Isles, locally rather than commonly in many areas. It is a small plant, with branched, often sprawling, slender stems and ovate to linear leaves, flowering in summer. The yellow flowers grow singly in the axils of opposite, leaf-like bracts at the tops of the stems; both flowers in each pair are turned towards the same side of the stem. Small Cow-wheat, *M. sylvaticum*, is a similar but smaller plant found in mountain woods in Europe, northern England and Scotland.

Crested Cow-wheat, *Melampyrum cristatum*, has one or several erect or spreading stems growing up to 50cm (20in) tall, with opposite, linear or lance-shaped leaves. The flowers are borne in dense, four-sided spikes in the axils of highly characteristic bracts. The bracts are elongated heart-shaped with a long, pointed tip, folded along the midrib and reflexed at the tip, toothed at the base where they become rose-purple rather than green. The flowers are pale yellow tinged with purple and the mouth is closed. This plant grows in dry grassland, often in rocky places and in woodland margins, across most of Europe. In Britain it is found very locally in East Anglia and scattered into surrounding areas of England.

Field Cow-wheat, *Melampyrum arvense*, is similar to Crested Cow-wheat, but has spreading, branched stems up to 60cm (2ft) tall, and the flowering spikes are loose and cylindrical instead of dense and four-sided. The bracts are held erect and are not folded, their toothed bases reddish-purple at first. The flowers are purplish-pink with a yellow throat and a closed mouth. This plant grows in dry, grassy places and cultivated land across most of Europe, except Portugal, very locally in England, mainly in the south.

For a long time **Toothwort**, *Lathraea squamaria* (p. 161), was placed in the Broomrape family. However, many modern botanists believe its affinities lie with some members of the Fig-

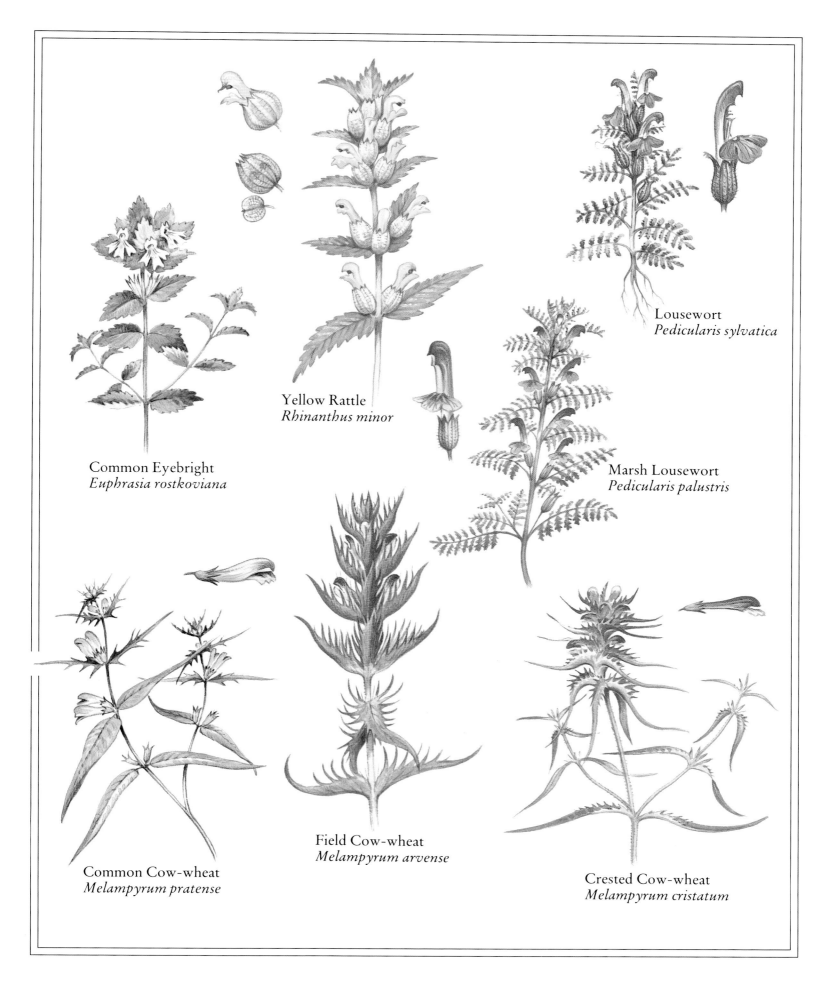

Lousewort
Pedicularis sylvatica

Yellow Rattle
Rhinanthus minor

Common Eyebright
Euphrasia rostkoviana

Marsh Lousewort
Pedicularis palustris

Field Cow-wheat
Melampyrum arvense

Common Cow-wheat
Melampyrum pratense

Crested Cow-wheat
Melampyrum cristatum

wort family rather than with the Broomrapes, so it has been included here. Toothwort is a total parasite, its branched, creeping rhizomes attaching themselves to the roots of certain trees, especially hazel and elms, but also beech and alders. It grows in woods and hedgerows, usually on fertile soils, across much of Europe, scattered throughout Great Britain north to Inverness, and in eastern Ireland. The plant appears in spring, forming several flowering shoots, white or pale pink in colour (the plant lacks chlorophyll), and covered with many fleshy, heart-shaped scale-leaves; the shoots are arched over at the top at first, straightening and becoming erect, up to 30cm (1ft) tall. The flowers are borne in a one-sided spike at the top of the stem, each one in the axil of a bract resembling the leaves; the flowers are white tinged with purple. Each one has a hairy calyx and a two-lipped corolla, with a strongly curved upper lip and a smaller, three-lobed lower lip.

Broomrape family
Orobanchaceae

A small family of strange, parasitic plants with about 10 genera and 170 species, mainly found in the warm, temperate regions of the Old World. They are mostly perennial herbs, lacking chlorophyll and parasitic on the roots of other flowering plants and trees. They are closely related to the Figwort family.

Family features The flowers are hermaphrodite and bilaterally symmetrical, with a toothed or lobed calyx and a five-lobed corolla which is often curved or two-lipped. There are four stamens (two long and two short) alternating with the corolla lobes. The ovary is superior with one cell. The fruit is a capsule with many tiny seeds. These plants have erect stems, with alternately arranged, often fleshy scale-leaves at the base and dense, terminal spikes of flowers.

The **Broomrapes**, members of the genus *Orobanche*, are by far the largest group in the family, with about 100 species worldwide, 90 of which occur in Europe. They are parasitic on a wide variety of plants, often on members of the pea and daisy families. Some attack crops like clovers or potatoes.

Common Broomrape, *Orobanche minor*, is one of the smaller species, with an erect stem up to 50cm (20in) tall, the stem yellowish and often tinged with purple, its scale leaves brownish and crowded mostly at the base, which is swollen. The flowers are borne in a loose spike, each one in the axil of a bract; they are yellowish with purple veins, tubular in shape and curved, two-lipped at the mouth with a notched upper lip and a three-lobed lower lip. This broomrape is often parasitic on members of the Pea family, sometimes on crop clovers, also on Cat's Ear and other members of the Daisy family. One variety, *maritima*, attacks Wild Carrot. Plants can be found in meadows and other grassy places, on roadsides and railway embankments, in fixed dunes and cultivated land throughout Europe, mainly in southern England and southern Ireland in the British Isles.

Greater Broomrape, *Orobanche rapum-genistae*, has a larger, stouter spike up to 80cm (30in) tall, glandular-hairy in texture and with many linear or lance-shaped bracts. The flowers are borne in the axils of bracts in a long, compact spike at the top of the stem; they are similar to those of Common Broomrape but the upper lip is not notched and both lips have wavy margins. This plant is almost always parasitic on Broom (hence Broomrape), sometimes on Gorse. At one time it was found throughout much of England and Wales, but it is now rare and found only in a few scattered localities within its former range. It is also found in central and western Europe.

Yarrow Broomrape, *Orobanche purpurea*, is parasitic on Yarrow and other members of the Daisy family; it is found across much of Europe but is very rare in Britain, and confined to southern England. It has bluish stems and blue-purple flowers. Ivy Broomrape, *O. hederae*, attacks Ivy; it is widespread in Europe, scattered in England, Wales and Ireland, most common near the sea. It has a purplish stem and creamy, purple-veined flowers. Hemp Broomrape, *O. ramosa*, attacks Hemp, tobacco, potatoes and tomatoes. It is a small species with pale blue flowers, found in Europe and probably introduced into southern England with cultivated Hemp.

Acanthus family
Acanthaceae

This is another family closely related to the Figworts. They are mainly tropical plants, with a few representatives in warmer temperate regions. There are about 250 genera and 2500 species of herbs and shrubs in the family; some, like gloxinias, are grown as house plants or in greenhouses.

Bear's Breeches, *Acanthus mollis*, is native to areas around the Mediterranean, but is grown in gardens and has become naturalized in many countries, including southwestern England. It is a robust, perennial plant, with a clump of large, dark green leaves often up to 60cm (2ft) long, pinnately divided with softly spine-toothed sections. In summer the stout flowering stems grow up to 1m (3ft) tall and bear many ovate, purple bracts with flowers in their axils. Often the bracts are more obvious than the flowers. These are tubular with a two-lipped calyx, the upper lip arching over the corolla and violet or green in colour; the corolla is white and veined with purple, without an upper lip but with a three-lobed lower lip. The plants are statuesque rather than beautiful; they are often grown in cities as they can withstand poor soil and polluted air. The leaves were used as the model for the decorative carvings on the Corinthian columns in ancient Greece.

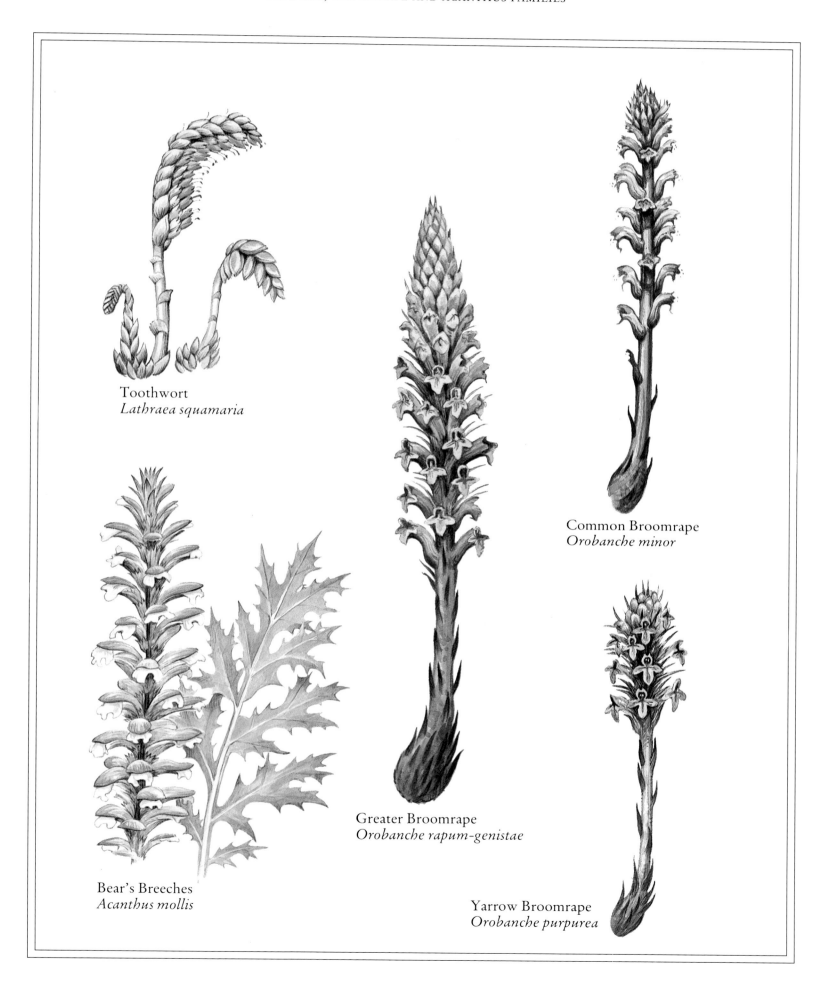

Toothwort
Lathraea squamaria

Bear's Breeches
Acanthus mollis

Greater Broomrape
Orobanche rapum-genistae

Common Broomrape
Orobanche minor

Yarrow Broomrape
Orobanche purpurea

Butterwort family
Lentibulariaceae

A family of insectivorous plants, some living in bogs or in water, others on land or as epiphytes. This is a small family with 4 genera and about 170 species found throughout the world. They are related to the Figwort family.

Family features The flowers are solitary or borne in racemes, hermaphrodite and bilaterally symmetrical. The calyx may be five-lobed or two-lipped, and the corolla is two-lipped, the upper lip two-lobed and the lower lip three-lobed, with a spur at the back. The flowers have two stamens inserted at the base of the corolla and a superior ovary with one cell. The fruits are capsules. The leaves form traps for insects.

The leaves of **Common Butterwort**, *Pinguicula vulgaris*, are borne in a small rosette; their oblong blades are yellowish and fleshy, with a soft, slimy texture and rolled-up edges. Insects land on the leaves and are held by the stickiness; their struggles trigger the leaves into rolling up, and the luckless creatures are then digested. The purple flowers are borne on erect, leafless stalks growing up to 15cm tall in early summer. This Butterwort grows in bogs and wet heaths, or among wet rocks, across much of Europe and the British Isles, rarely in England south of the Midlands and rarely in southern Ireland.

Pale Butterwort, *Pinguicula lusitanica*, is a similar plant, but its yellowish leaves are tinged purple and it has pale lilac, yellow-throated flowers. It grows in bogs and wet heaths in western Europe, in Ireland (mainly in the west), western Scotland, southwestern England and east to Hampshire. **Alpine Butterwort**, *P. alpina*, has yellow-spotted, white flowers; it grows in springs and wet mountain meadows in Arctic and mountain areas of Europe; at one time it was found in northeast Scotland but is now extinct there.

The **Bladderworts**, *Utricularia* species, are found in quiet waters where their tiny, elaborate traps catch water fleas and other aquatic creatures. **Greater Bladderwort**, *U. vulgaris*, grows in lakes and ponds, usually in deep water, throughout Europe and the British Isles. It forms a network of branching stems with finely dissected leaves floating beneath the surface. The stems bear traps—translucent bladders with a few hairs at one end which act as a trigger. If a water flea touches the hairs, a trap door opens on the bladder and water rushes in, carrying the crustacean with it. In late summer the bright yellow flowers grow on erect stalks above the water.

Lesser Bladderwort, *Utricularia minor*, is a smaller plant found in ponds and ditches, fens and marshes across much of Europe and in parts of the British Isles, most commonly in the north and west. Its branching stems are of two kinds, some with reduced leaves and many bladders often buried in the mud, others with larger leaves and few bladders. Its pale yellow flowers are smaller than those of Greater Bladderwort.

Moschatel family
Adoxaceae

Moschatel, *Adoxa moschatellina*, looks quite unlike any other plant and is the only species in its family. It is a small perennial, 30cm (1ft) tall at most, with creeping rhizomes and clumps of light green, more or less three-lobed leaves growing on long stems. In early summer it bears extraordinary flowers growing in terminal clusters on stems that have a single leaf about half-way up. The clusters are unique, each one with five flowers, four of them forming the sides of a square and the fifth on top facing the sky. The side flowers have three sepals and five petals, the top flower two sepals and four petals; all are yellow-green. If fruits are formed, they are drupes, produced in the same formation as the flowers and heavy enough to make the stems droop; however, the flowers often fail to set seed and the plant spreads mostly by its creeping rhizomes. The strange appearance of this plant has earned it the names of Townhall Clock and Five-faced Bishop, while the name of Moschatel comes from its musky scent. It grows locally in woods and hedgerows, but is widespread across most of Europe and the British Isles, absent from Portugal and Ireland.

Plantain family
Plantaginaceae

A small family found throughout the world but mainly in northern temperate regions of the world, with 3 genera and about 270 species of herbs.

The **Plantains** themselves, plants belonging to the genus *Plantago*, account for 260 of these. Some are weeds of gardens and roadsides, others grow in grassy places, some are associated with the coast. Plantains are annual or perennial plants with dense heads or spikes of small, inconspicuous flowers; each flower has four green sepals and four membranous petals. The stamens, however, are coloured and noticeable, often protruding from the flowers to display their anthers, and the flowers are pollinated by wind. The spikes remain long after flowering, with the withered petals around the fruiting capsules until they finally break up.

Many plantains have a rosette of basal leaves and leafless, unbranched flower stalks. Several are cosmopolitan weeds, like **Greater Plantain**, *Plantago major* (p. 165), a species that probably originated in Europe and Asia but is now found throughout most of the world. It grows in cultivated fields and lawns, on roadsides and in waste ground, especially on paths or in places where the ground is well trodden, throughout Europe and the British Isles. It is a perennial plant, forming rosettes of broadly ovate, almost hairless leaves, their blades

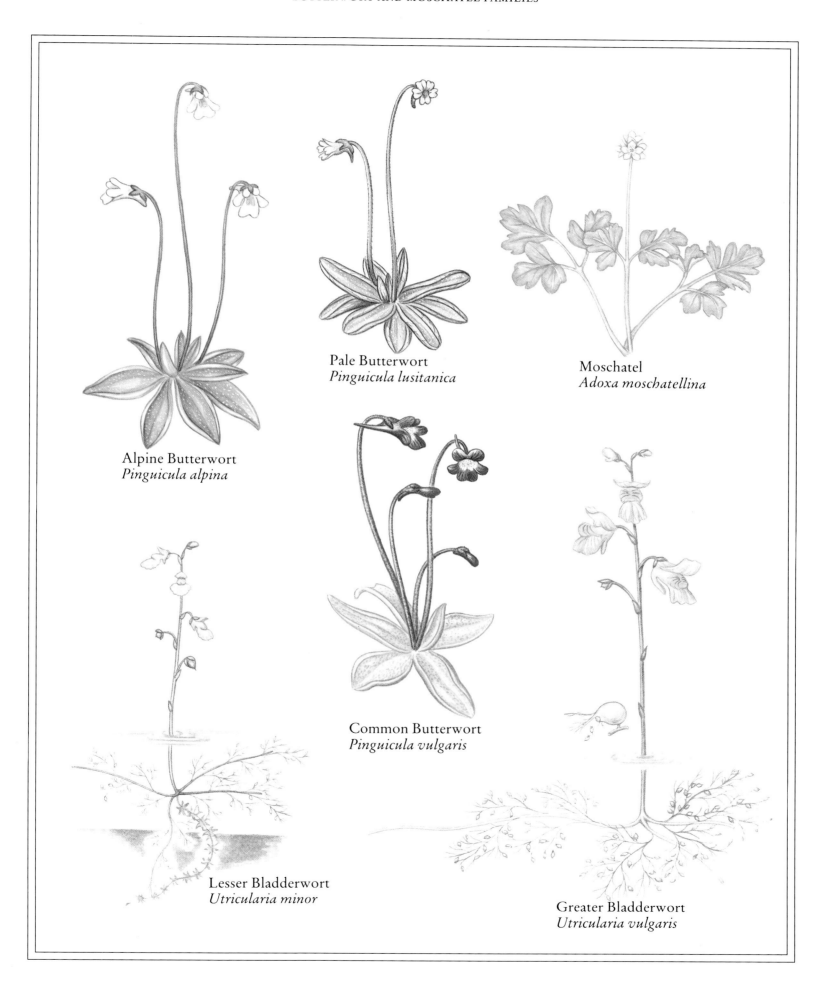

Alpine Butterwort
Pinguicula alpina

Pale Butterwort
Pinguicula lusitanica

Moschatel
Adoxa moschatellina

Common Butterwort
Pinguicula vulgaris

Lesser Bladderwort
Utricularia minor

Greater Bladderwort
Utricularia vulgaris

narrowing abruptly into stalks that are almost as long as the blades. The leaves have 5–9 parallel veins and are more or less hairless. In summer the plant bears long, narrow spikes of green flowers with purple anthers, the spikes reaching nearly 60cm (2ft) in height if conditions are right. If a plant is growing in a path where it is well trampled, it may have tiny flower spikes with only a few flowers.

Hoary Plantain, *Plantago media*, also has broad-bladed leaves, with elliptical or ovate blades about twice as long as the stalks. Each leaf has 5–9 parallel veins, is covered in fine hairs and greyish in colour. The leaves grow in basal rosettes. The plants bloom in summer, the flowers growing in dense, cylindrical spikes at the tops of stems about 30cm (1ft) tall, hovering over the leaves; the flowers are scented and the stamens have purple filaments and lilac anthers. This plant grows in grassy places, often on calcareous soils, across much of Europe, mainly in southern England and the Midlands in Great Britain; it has been introduced into Ireland.

Ribwort, *Plantago lanceolata*, has rosettes of lance-shaped leaves held more or less upright and gradually narrowing into very short stalks at the base; the leaves have a strongly ribbed appearance caused by the 3–7 prominent, parallel veins on each. The flowering stalks appear in summer, growing to about twice the height of the leaves, up to 45cm (18in) tall, each one with five furrows running along its length. They end in dense cylindrical spikes of green flowers with whitish stamens. The flower stems and leaves have long, silky hairs. This plant is a common weed of grassy places, roadsides and waste ground, growing in basic or neutral soils throughout Europe and the British Isles. Both Greater Plantain and Ribwort are used as medicinal plants, the mucilage they contain making them effective as cough remedies.

Sea Plantain, *Plantago maritima*, forms several leaf rosettes growing from a woody base, with many thick, rather fleshy, linear leaves, sometimes toothed at the margins, each with 3–5 faint veins. The brownish flowers are borne in long, narrow spikes and have yellow anthers. This perennial plant grows in short grass near the sea, in salt marshes and beside mountain streams inland; it is found in most of Europe, around the British coasts and inland in the Scottish Highlands, the Welsh mountains, the Pennines and western Ireland.

Buck's-horn Plantain, *Plantago coronopus*, may be biennial or perennial. It forms distinctive leaf rosettes, the leaves linear in shape and deeply toothed or pinnately lobed, their bases prostrate then turning upwards so that they may form a circle on the ground. The long flowering stalks are also prostrate at the base, then turn upwards to bear elongated spikes of yellow-brown flowers with pale yellow anthers. This plant grows in dry, sandy and gravelly places and among rocks, often near the sea. It is found around the coasts of southern and central Europe, and all around the British and Irish coasts, inland in some areas of southern England.

Branched Plantain, *Plantago arenaria*, is a very different plant to the previous plantains. It is a much-branched, hairy annual, with more or less erect, leafy stems growing up to 50cm (20in) tall, the leaves long and linear and in opposite pairs, the lower ones with leafy shoots in their axils. The brownish-white flowers grow with hairy bracts in dense, rounded heads borne on long stalks growing from the upper leaf axils. This plant is found in sandy soils, in dry fields and on roadsides across most of Europe, except the north; it is not native to the British Isles but may be found occasionally, growing as a casual in disturbed places or on sand-dunes.

Shore-weed, *Littorella uniflora*, is a hairless aquatic plant growing in shallow, acid waters on the sandy shores of lakes and ponds or beside the sea. It is found across most of Europe, most commonly in Scotland and the Scottish islands in the British Isles. It often forms extensive carpets of leaf rosettes submerged beneath the water surface and spreading over the mud with many creeping stems. These root at the nodes and form rosettes of linear, half-cylindrical leaves, usually about 10cm (4in) tall. The plants flower in the latter half of summer, but only if they are above the surface of the water; male and female flowers are separate, the male flowers borne singly on a stalk less than the height of the leaves, female flowers several together at the base of the stalk.

Honeysuckle family
Caprifoliaceae

A family of shrubs and herbs, with 13 genera and about 490 species, found mainly in north temperate regions and in mountains in the tropics. Several beautiful garden shrubs belong to this family, including weigelas and viburnums.

Family features The flowers are hermaphrodite, bilaterally symmetrical or regular, usually borne in cymes. The calyx is usually small with five teeth, often joined to the ovary; the corolla is tubular, sometimes two-lipped, formed of four or five fused petals. There are four or five stamens inserted on the corolla and alternating with the corolla lobes. The ovary is inferior, with 2–5 cells. The fruit is a fleshy berry, drupe or achene. The leaves are opposite, simple or divided and stipules are small or absent.

The *Sambucus* species are mostly large shrubs or trees, with few species in Europe, the best known being Elder, *S. nigra*, found in hedgerows, waste places and woods throughout Europe and the British Isles. This large shrub is famous for its flowers and berries which can be made into wine and preserves; its bark and leaves are used in herb medicine and its flowers were at one time used in cosmetic preparations.

It has a much less well-known herbaceous relative, **Danewort** or Dwarf Elder, *Sambucus ebulus* (p. 167), which grows

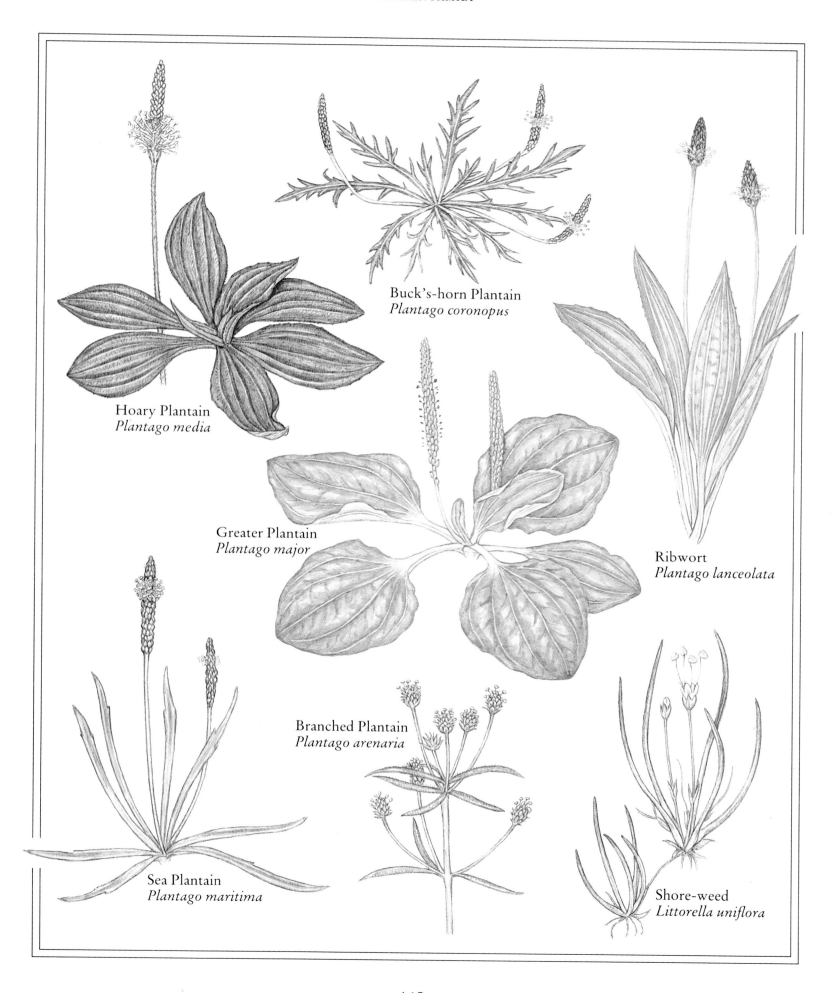

Buck's-horn Plantain
Plantago coronopus

Hoary Plantain
Plantago media

Greater Plantain
Plantago major

Ribwort
Plantago lanceolata

Branched Plantain
Plantago arenaria

Sea Plantain
Plantago maritima

Shore-weed
Littorella uniflora

in waste places, hedgerows and roadsides throughout Europe, scattered throughout the British Isles but much more rarely in Scotland. It has creeping rhizomes and numerous erect, grooved stems growing up to 120cm (4ft) tall, with pinnate leaves. The whole plant is hairless and has an unpleasant, foetid smell. The leaves are divided into 7–13 pointed-oblong leaflets with serrated margins. In the latter half of summer the plant bears flat-topped, umbel-like clusters of white flowers followed by many round black berries.

The **Honeysuckles**, *Lonicera* species, form the largest genus in the family, with about 200 species spread across the northern hemisphere in both temperate and tropical climes. The majority are shrubs, many with ornamental flowers, but some are climbers. Their flowers have long tubes and are rich in nectar, attracting insects but only those with the longest proboscis can reach the sweet riches. Many are scented, with a scent that is strongest in the evening, and these attract moths. The flowers are irregular at the mouth of the tube, with four petal-lobes forming the top and a single petal-lobe below.

Honeysuckle or Woodbine, *Lonicera periclymenum*, grows in woods and hedgerows in western and central Europe, and is the only one native and widespread in the British Isles, where it is found throughout. It has twining, woody stems growing through and over other plants, reaching 6m (20ft) tall in a tree but usually much less. It has dark green, pointed-ovate leaves, the lower ones with stalks and the upper stalkless. In summer its distinctive clusters of creamy-yellow and pink, evening-scented flowers grow in the axils of the uppermost pairs of leaves. The flowers are followed by clusters of red berries. Perfoliate Honeysuckle, *L. caprifolium*, is another climber, found in woods and hedgerows in Europe, grown in gardens in the British Isles. Its flowers grow in a leaflike cup formed by the two uppermost leaves fused together.

Twinflower, *Linnaea borealis*, is a complete contrast to these vigorous honeysuckles. It is a delicate, creeping shrublet found in coniferous woods among shady rocks, with trailing stems which run along the ground, sending up leafy shoots only (10cm) 4in tall. Each shoot has small, opposite, broadly ovate leaves and ends in a pair of nodding, bell-shaped, pink or white flowers. Twinflower is a rare plant, found in northern and central Europe and in northern Scotland.

Valerian family
Valerianaceae

This is a small family, with about 13 genera and 400 species of herbs, found throughout the world, except in Australia.

Family features The flowers are usually bilaterally symmetrical and may be hermaphrodite or unisexual; they are mostly small and borne in dense, head-like inflorescences. The calyx is usually small and toothed, often inrolled in the flowers and forming a feathery pappus in the fruits. The corolla is often funnel-shaped, usually with five lobes, often spurred or swollen at one side of the base. There are usually 1–3 stamens inserted at the base of the corolla tube. The ovary is inferior, with 1–3 cells, only one of which is fertile. The fruit is dry and indehiscent. The leaves are opposite or form a rosette. Stipules are absent. Plants often have strongly scented rhizomes.

Valerians, *Valeriana* species, are perennial plants with thick, often scented roots or rhizomes and several erect, leafy stems. Often the whole plant is scented, with a distinctive, peculiar smell very attractive to cats. Their leaves may be entire or pinnately divided and their pink or white flowers are borne in compound inflorescences, often resembling heads or umbels. There are about 25 species in Europe.

The roots of **Common Valerian**, *Valeriana officinalis*, have been used in herb medicine since the times of the ancient Greeks as a highly effective nerve tonic and sedative. This valerian is a stout, almost hairless, perennial plant, with erect stems up to 1.5m (5ft) tall and large, pinnate leaves up to 20cm (8in) long; the leaflets are large and lance-shaped, often irregularly toothed. The pink or white flowers are hermaphrodite, appearing around midsummer. This plant often grows in damp places, in rough grassland, meadows and woods throughout Europe and the British Isles.

Marsh Valerian, *Valeriana dioica*, is a much smaller plant with creeping, rooting stems, clumps of elliptical, long-stalked basal leaves and erect, leafy stems often only 30cm (1ft) tall. Its stem leaves are pinnately lobed. The pink flowers are unisexual, males and females borne on separate plants, males in loose heads and females in dense heads. Plants grow in marshes and wet meadows across most of Europe and Great Britain, north to southern Scotland.

Red Valerian, *Centranthus ruber*, is not native to the British Isles, but is grown in gardens and has become well naturalized in southern and western England, Wales and southern Ireland, growing on cliffs and rocks, often on old walls which its strong, penetrating roots gradually demolish. It comes originally from the Mediterranean region. This perennial plant has erect, leafy stems up to 80cm (30in) tall, with oval to lance-shaped, often toothed leaves, rather waxy and grey-green in appearance. It bears terminal, head-like clusters of showy red flowers around midsummer.

Lamb's Lettuce or Corn Salad, *Valerianella locusta*, is a little annual plant, one of over 20 similar species found in this genus in Europe. It is often cultivated as a salad plant, but also grows wild in dry soils, in arable and waste land, in dunes, on walls and hedgebanks throughout Europe and the British Isles, rarely in Scotland. It has brittle, much-branched stems and many leaves, the lowermost spoon-shaped and the upper ones oblong. In early summer head-like clusters of pale lilac flowers appear in the axils of the uppermost leaves.

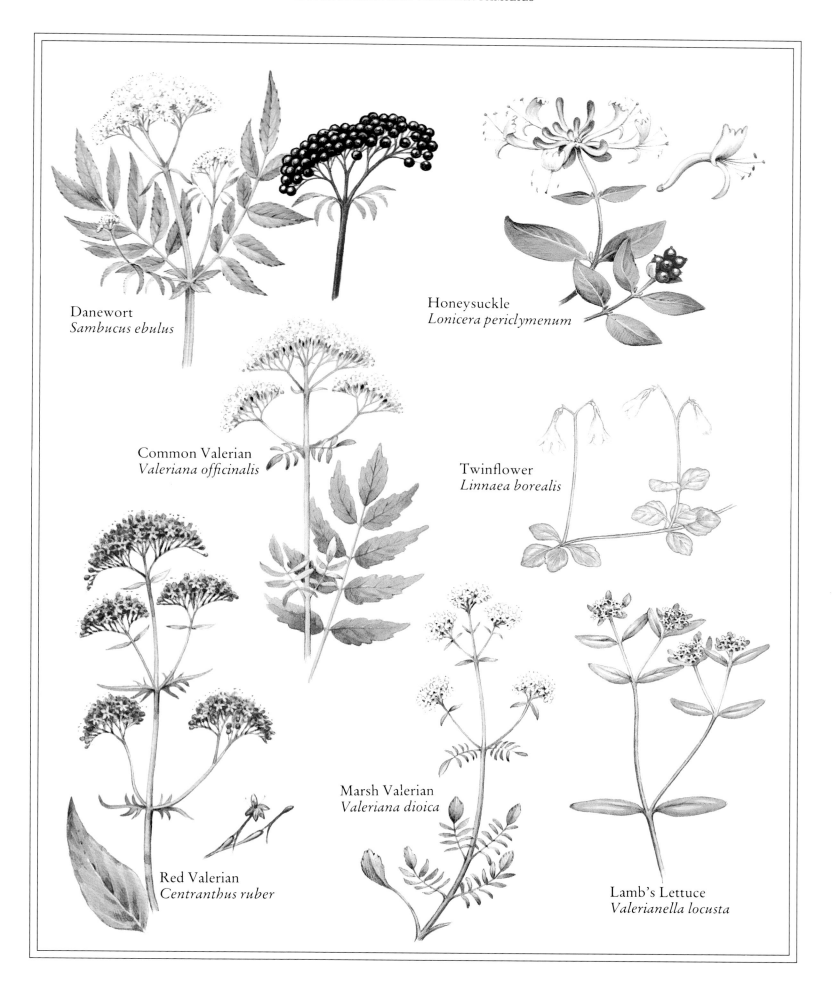

Danewort
Sambucus ebulus

Honeysuckle
Lonicera periclymenum

Common Valerian
Valeriana officinalis

Twinflower
Linnaea borealis

Red Valerian
Centranthus ruber

Marsh Valerian
Valeriana dioica

Lamb's Lettuce
Valerianella locusta

Bellflower family
Campanulaceae

There are about 60 genera and 2000 species in this family, mostly herbs, found throughout much of the world. It contains many garden plants, including Canterbury Bells and the blue lobelias used in summer bedding.

Family features The flowers are often showy, regular or bilaterally symmetrical, and hermaphrodite. The calyx is usually five-lobed and joined to the ovary. The corolla is tubular, bell-shaped or one or two-lipped, and there are as many stamens as corolla lobes, alternating with the lobes. The ovary is inferior, with two or more cells. The fruit is a capsule. The leaves are alternate and simple, and stipules are absent. Plants usually contain milky juice.

There are about 300 species of **Bellflowers**, *Campanula* species, the majority found in the Old World. Many are perennial plants, with erect, leafy stems and blue, bell-like flowers in the axils of the upper leaves. **Giant Bellflower**, *C. latifolia*, is one such species found in woods and hedgebanks, near streams and in mountain meadows across most of Europe, except in Portugal, and in much of Great Britain, becoming rarer in northern Scotland and southern England. It has clumps of pointed-ovate, basal leaves and stout, erect stems often 1m (3ft) or more tall, leafy and with showy, blue, bell-like flowers in the leaf axils, each bell pointing upwards. This species is often grown in gardens.

Bats-in-the-belfry, *Campanula trachelium*, is another garden plant but it also grows wild as a native species in woods and hedges, usually on clay soils, throughout Europe, mainly in eastern Wales and England in Britain, and absent from the southwest. It too has clumps of basal leaves—long-stalked and heart-shaped in this species—and erect flowering stems in summer. The bell-like flowers are blue-purple and point upwards in the axils of heart-shaped leaves; both leaves and stems are bristly-hairy in this species.

Peach-leaved Bellflower, *Campanula persicifolia*, is one of the most common garden species in Britain, grown in varieties with blue or white flowers. It is also found wild in woods and hedgerows across Europe, where it opens its broadly lobed bells in summer. It has basal rosettes of narrow leaves remaining green throughout the year. **Creeping Bellflower**, *C. rapunculoides*, can be a weed in gardens, its creeping stems and clumps of basal leaves taking over large areas. In summer it produces erect, leafy stems, with funnel-shaped, blue-purple bells hanging from each leaf axil. It grows wild across most of Europe, in open woods and fields, and has been introduced as a garden plant to Britain, escaping to invade cultivated land and disturbed, grassy places in many areas.

Clustered Bellflower, *Campanula glomerata*, is rather different in appearance to these other bellflowers since its flowers are clustered at the top of the stems. It is a perennial plant, its basal leaves long-stalked with ovate blades, its flowering stems often only 30cm (1ft) tall and leafy with stalkless leaves, bearing a terminal cluster of stalkless, blue-purple bells pointing upwards, and often with flowers in the axils of the uppermost leaves as well. It grows in grassy places, often on chalk, also on cliffs and in open woods, mainly in southern and eastern England, in Britain and across most of Europe.

Harebell, *Campanula rotundifolia*, is a much smaller perennial, its basal leaves long-stalked with rounded blades, its flowering stems slender, only 40cm (15in) tall at most, with narrow leaves and nodding blue, bell-like flowers. The flowers appear in the latter half of summer. Harebells grow in dry grassland, often on poor, shallow soils, on heaths and dunes throughout Europe and the British Isles. The plant is called the Bluebell in Scotland.

Ivy-leaved Bellflower, *Wahlenbergia hederacea*, is a little trailing plant, a hairless perennial with weak stems growing up to 30cm (1ft) long and long-stalked, palmately lobed leaves. The pale blue, nodding, bell-like flowers appear in late summer. This bellflower grows in acid, peaty soils on moors and heaths in western Europe, mainly in Wales and southwestern England in the British Isles.

Venus' Looking Glass, *Legousia hybrida*, is a bristly, annual plant, with an erect, often branched stem up to 30cm (1ft) tall and wavy, oblong leaves. The flowers resemble those of bellflowers, but are shallower, reddish-purple or lilac in colour, and have an enlarged, elongated ovary below; this later develops into a cylindrical capsule. Plants grow in arable fields and sandy places across western and into central Europe; in Britain the species is found mainly in England but its numbers are decreasing.

At first sight, **Sheep's-bit**, *Jasione montana* (p. 171), looks more like a Scabious than a bellflower, for its blue flowers are all gathered into terminal heads. This is a small biennial plant, with a rosette of narrow, hairy leaves in the first year and spreading flowering stems up to 50cm (20in) tall in the second. These are leafy near the base, with flower heads cupped in two rows of leafy bracts at the tops of long, bare stems in summer. Each flower has a globular calyx, five narrow petal-lobes and protruding purple anthers. Plants grow in grassland, in sandy, usually acid soils, often on banks and cliffs, throughout Europe, mainly in the west in Great Britain, and around Ireland but not in the centre.

The **Rampions**, *Phyteuma* species, also have flowers gathered into heads. There are about 15 species in Europe, most of them from the Mediterranean area, but **Spiked Rampion**, *P. spicatum* (p. 171), is more widespread, found in woods and mountain meadows across most of Europe, only in East Sussex in Britain. It is a robust, hairless, perennial plant, forming a clump of long-stalked, heart-shaped leaves with serrated margins. In summer the flowering stems develop, growing up to

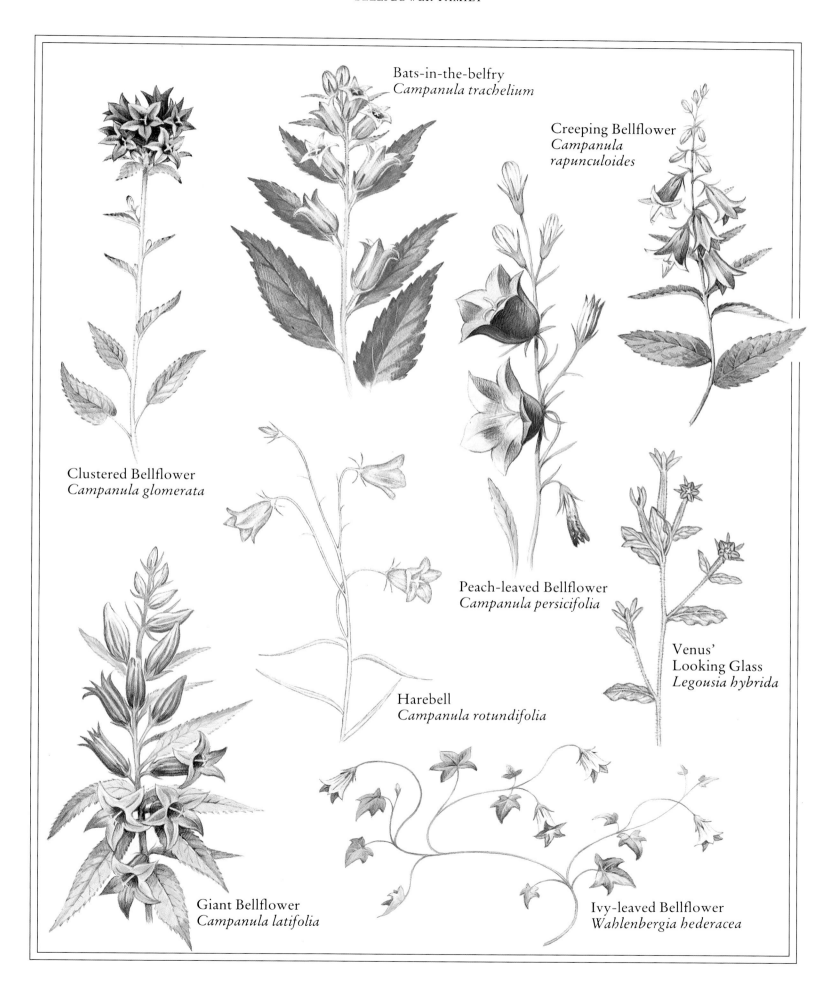

Bats-in-the-belfry
Campanula trachelium

Creeping Bellflower
Campanula rapunculoides

Clustered Bellflower
Campanula glomerata

Peach-leaved Bellflower
Campanula persicifolia

Venus'
Looking Glass
Legousia hybrida

Harebell
Campanula rotundifolia

Giant Bellflower
Campanula latifolia

Ivy-leaved Bellflower
Wahlenbergia hederacea

80cm (30in) tall, their lower leaves similar to the basal ones but becoming smaller and stalkless at the tops of the stems, and the yellowish-white flowers borne in terminal, cylindrical spikes. Each flower has five narrow petal-lobes closed together into a curved tube in bud, spreading as the flowers open.

Round-headed Rampion, *Phyteuma orbiculare*, is a similar but smaller plant, its erect, leafy stems growing only up to 50cm (20in) tall. However, its flowers are deep violet-blue and borne in rounded heads. This plant grows in dry meadows and woods in western and central Europe, on chalk grassland in southern England.

The **Lobelias** are a large group of about 250 species in the genus *Lobelia*, found in most of the warm and temperate regions of the world; few, however, are found in Europe. They are often placed in the Bellflower family, as in this book, but are sometimes put into another family, the Lobeliaceae, since they have bilaterally symmetrical, not bell-like flowers.

Water Lobelia, *Lobelia dortmanna*, is an aquatic plant, growing in acid lakes and tarns in western Europe, northern Scotland, the Lake District, north Wales, northern and western Ireland. It has creeping stems and tufts of linear leaves submerged below the water surface. In summer the flowering stems emerge above the surface, growing about 60cm (2ft) tall and bearing a few of the distinctive lobelia-type flowers, pale lilac in this species.

Heath Lobelia, *Lobelia urens*, is a perennial plant found in rough grassland and heaths on acid soils in western Europe and near the south coast of England. It has erect stems about 60cm (2ft) tall, irregularly serrated, oblong leaves and spikes of blue-purple, lobelia-type flowers in late summer.

Teasel family
Dipsacaceae

A small family of 9 genera and about 155 species, mostly herbs, the majority in the Mediterranean region and western Asia. The Scabiouses are often attractive plants and several are grown in flower gardens.

Family features The flowers are small, often borne in dense heads with an involucre; they may be hermaphrodite or unisexual and are bilaterally symmetrical. The calyx is small, cup-like, deeply divided into sections or into numerous hairs. The corolla has 4–5 lobes and is often two-lipped. There are two or four stamens alternating with the corolla lobes, their filaments free or joined in pairs. The ovary is inferior with one cell. The fruits are dry and indehiscent. The leaves are opposite or in whorls. Stipules are absent.

Wild Teasel, *Dipsacus fullonum*, grows in damp places, often in heavy soil, beside water, on roadsides, in woods and hedgerows, in field margins and by the sea throughout most of Europe, mainly in England in the British Isles, less commonly in Wales and southern Scotland, in a few places in Ireland. Many books make a distinction between Wild Teasel, which they call *D. sylvestris*, and Fuller's Teasel, *D. fullonum*, but they are both subspecies of the same plant. Fuller's Teasel has cylindrical rather than conical heads, with stouter, more recurved prickles—features which were useful when the heads were used by fullers. (A fuller was a man who finished cloth by brushing it with teasel heads to bring up the nap.) Teasel heads are still used to brush some fabrics, particularly the green baize of snooker tables, and can be used for brushing clothes and carding wool. Teasel is a biennial plant, with a tall, prickly flowering stem in the second year, often 1.5–2m (5–6ft) tall, with prickly leaves, the lower ones joined across the stem, making a cup in which water collects and insects drown. The pale purple flowers grow with prickly bracts in heads. They open in the latter half of summer, forming a band which gradually 'travels' from the bottom to the top of the head.

Several members of the family have the common name of Scabious, a name given to them because they were believed to be useful remedies for skin diseases, like scabies. One of these is **Field Scabious**, *Knautia arvensis*, a small perennial plant found in rough, dry, grassy places, roadsides, hedgebanks and woodland margins, especially on chalk or limestone, throughout Europe and the British Isles, but relatively rarely in western and northern Scotland. It has rosettes of lance-shaped, somewhat toothed leaves in spring and erect stems growing up to 1m (3ft) tall, with smaller but more divided leaves and terminal flower heads in late summer. The lilac-blue flowers are borne in flat heads where the outer flowers have very unequal petals, the largest petals forming a ring around the outside of the head. The larger heads contain hermaphrodite flowers, smaller ones female flowers.

Small Scabious, *Scabiosa columbaria*, is another plant found in dry, calcareous grassland, on banks and pastures throughout Europe, England and Wales, north into southern Scotland. It is a perennial species similar to Field Scabious, but only 60cm (2ft) tall, with stem leaves deeply divided into pinnate lobes, the sections becoming progressively narrower higher up the stem. Its lilac-blue flowers are borne in heads, each one with a ring of larger flowers around the circumference; all flowers are hermaphrodite. This is one of about 40 *Scabiosa* species found in Europe.

Devil's-bit Scabious, *Succisa pratensis*, grows in wet meadows, marshes and fens throughout Europe and the British Isles. It is a perennial plant, with a rosette of firm, elliptical, basal leaves and an erect stem up to 1m (3ft) tall in summer. This has a few narrow leaves and terminal heads of mauve or blue-purple flowers, all the flowers in the head the same size, even the marginal flowers. The heads may be small with female flowers only, or larger with hermaphrodite flowers and protruding red-purple anthers.

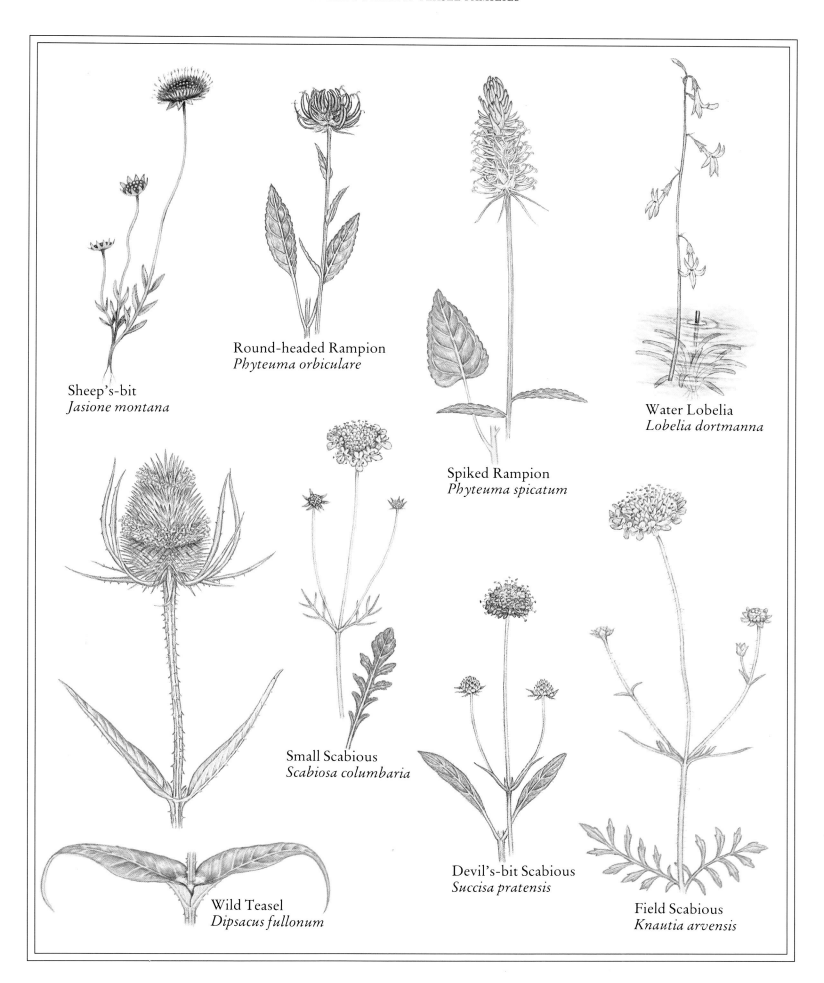

Sheep's-bit
Jasione montana

Round-headed Rampion
Phyteuma orbiculare

Spiked Rampion
Phyteuma spicatum

Water Lobelia
Lobelia dortmanna

Wild Teasel
Dipsacus fullonum

Small Scabious
Scabiosa columbaria

Devil's-bit Scabious
Succisa pratensis

Field Scabious
Knautia arvensis

Limestone grassland around midsummer. In the foreground are some of the flowers associated with this habitat: (from left to right) Rockrose, Bird's-foot Trefoil and Salad Burnet, with Wild Thyme and Stemless Thistles just beyond them. Many members of the Daisy family are also found in such areas.

Daisy family
Compositae

Also known as the **Sunflower family** and the **Asteraceae**. This is by far the largest family of flowering plants, with over 900 genera and 14,000 species found throughout the world. Most are herbaceous plants, some are shrubs and others are climbers. There are many decorative plants in the family, grown in flower borders, in greenhouses and as cut flowers. Chrysanthemums are probably the most popular of cut flowers, available throughout the year and easy to arrange. Dahlias are grown in many gardens, along with perennial plants like heleniums, gaillardias, rudbeckias, goldenrods, asters and a host of others. Annual plants used in summer bedding schemes include zinnias, ageratums and African marigolds. Greenhouse and house plants include cinerarias and mutisias.

Not all composites are as popular. Dandelions, daisies and groundsels are garden weeds, while other species, like chamomiles, thistles, ragworts, hawkweeds and mugwort, are common weeds of roadsides and waste ground. Ragweeds cause problems for thousands of hay fever sufferers every year in North America.

Some important vegetable and salad plants come from this family, including lettuce and chicory, artichokes, cardoons, salsify and endive. Sunflower seeds are an important source of polyunsaturated oils, along with other less well known members of the family. Several species are used in herb medicine; for instance, coltsfoot is a component of many cough medicines, elecampane is used to combat chest infections, and arnica is a traditional remedy for sprains. Several species provide dyes, including safflower, goldenrod and marigolds.

Family features The flower structure in this family is unique and is presumed to account for its success. Individual flowers are small but are gathered into flower heads surrounded by green bracts. The heads are often conspicuous and highly attractive to insects. Because of the design of the individual flowers within each head, a high proportion are pollinated and many seeds are produced. In addition, many species have very effective dispersal mechanisms for their seeds. Individual flowers are called florets and they have a corolla which may be tubular in form or strap-shaped. A flower head may be made up of all tubular florets or all strap-shaped florets, but a common arrangement in many species is to have tubular florets (or disk florets) forming the centre of each flower head (which is then called the disk), and strap-shaped florets (or ray florets) around the margins. Each floret has a calyx formed of hairs, bristles, teeth or a membranous ring. Flowers may be male, with five stamens, or female with an inferior ovary, or hermaphrodite. The fruits are achenes—hard, nut-like structures which contain a single seed and which are crowned by the pappus, the remains of the calyx.

Like other families, this one is split into tribes. Usually the tribes are of interest only to botanists, but because this is so large a family, they form a convenient way of breaking the family down into more manageable and recognizable portions.

Members of the **Sunflower tribe**, the Heliantheae, usually have opposite leaves. Their flower heads are often formed of tubular disk florets which may be hermaphrodite or male, and strap-shaped ray florets which may be female or neuter. Where the flowers are formed of tubular florets only, the florets are hermaphrodite. The achenes never have a hairy pappus, but they may be awned or have a pappus formed of scales. Many members of this tribe are familiar garden plants, including dahlias, coreopsis, zinnias, rudbeckias, heliopsis and cosmos.

Sunflowers, *Helianthus annuus* (p. 000), are among the most familiar of the composites, their huge late-summer flowers towering over most other plants in the garden, on stout stems often 3m (10ft) tall. They are not native to Europe, but are grown in gardens and cultivated on a wide scale for their oil-rich seeds and sometimes escape to grow wild for a season or two. The Sunflower is an annual plant, with an erect stem, little branched in cultivated forms, and alternate, large, toothed leaves up to 30cm (1ft) long, ovate or heart-shaped in outline and roughly hairy in texture. The often drooping flower heads may reach 30cm (1ft) across and have brownish disk florets with bright yellow ray florets; disk florets are followed by the characteristic black and white achenes. These may be eaten raw, roasted and made into coffee, crushed and boiled for their oil or fed to hamsters and gerbils. Jerusalem Artichoke, *H. tuberosus*, is grown for its tubers, which are eaten as vegetables. It is a smaller plant, only 2.5m (8ft) tall at most, with opposite, ovate, serrated leaves and all-yellow flower heads.

The **Coneflowers**, *Rudbeckia* species, come from North America but are often grown in gardens in Europe and sometimes escape to grow wild. **Green-headed Coneflower**, *R. laciniata* (p. 000), is a perennial plant, with a clump of erect stems growing up to 2.5m (8ft) tall, with leaves deeply cleft into three or five sections. The terminal flower heads are showy, with a domed, greenish disk and long, drooping, yellow ray florets. This species has escaped into the wild in many parts of Europe. Black-eyed Susan, *R. hirta*, also grown in gardens and sometimes escaping, has showy flowers, so it is not a plant that can be missed. It has yellow ray florets and a domed, purple-black disk.

The **Bur-marigolds**, *Bidens* species, are waterside plants found in ditches, beside streams and ponds and in marshes. Most of the 120-odd species are found in the New World, with only a few in Europe. They are annual or perennial, often more or less hairless plants, with erect stems and opposite, simple or dissected leaves. A feature that many of them share are the barbed spines found on the achenes; these stick to animal hair or clothing and so the plants are dispersed.

Nodding Bur-marigold, *Bidens cernua*, grows beside streams and ponds, especially in places that are wet in winter, dry in summer, throughout much of the British Isles and Europe, becoming rare in the north. It is an annual plant, with branched stems up to 60cm (2ft) tall, many lance-shaped, toothed leaves borne in opposite pairs, and many flower heads borne in late summer on long stalks, nodding as they age. The species has two varieties; in one the flower heads have large yellow disks and broad yellow ray florets, while in the other ray florets are absent. In both varieties there are leafy bracts behind the heads which are longer than the rays. Each spiky fruit has four barbed spines that catch on clothes.

Tripartite Bur-marigold, *Bidens tripartita*, also grows in ditches, beside streams and ponds, locally throughout Europe and the British Isles, north to the south of Scotland and southern Scandinavia. It is similar to Bur-marigold but has divided leaves, each one cleft into three or five lance-shaped sections. The dull yellow flower heads have disk florets but no rays, and are cupped in green, leafy bracts.

Gallant Soldier is a big name for a little annual plant, a corruption of its Latin name *Galinsoga parviflora*. It came originally from South America but is now a cosmopolitan weed, introduced into the British Isles via Kew Gardens and now spreading in waste places and arable land in many parts of southern England, especially in the southeast. It is repeating the pattern in Europe. Its success is due to its many tiny fruits, which are flattened and bristly with a parachute of silvery scales; they both cling to clothing and are also transported by wind for short distances. The plant grows 60cm (2ft) tall at most, has many branching stems, ovate, toothed leaves and many tiny white flowers, each only 5mm ($^1/_4$ in) across, usually with five white ray florets and a yellow disk.

Common Ragweed, *Ambrosia artemisiifolia*, and **Great Ragweed**, *A. trifida*, have arrived in the British Isles and Europe from North America, at present growing only as casuals in waste places. They are coarse plants, with male and female flowers in separate heads, the numerous yellow-green male heads in elongated inflorescences at the top of the plant and the green female heads in leaf axils lower down. Common Ragweed grows 1–1.5m (3–5ft) tall and has dissected, light green leaves; Great Ragweed is bigger, often over 2–2.5m (6–8ft) tall, with palmate, three-lobed leaves. Because they are wind-pollinated they produce huge amounts of pollen, and in North America are one of the worst causes of hay fever.

Common Cocklebur, *Xanthium strumarium*, is a strange plant, probably native to central and southern Europe, where it grows in waste places, beside rivers and roads; in the British Isles it is most likely to be found on rubbish tips in southeastern England. It is an annual plant with rough, branched stems and broad, rounded-triangular, often lobed leaves. Its male and female flowers are borne separately, in rounded heads in the leaf axils, the female heads below the males. The female heads are prickly and enlarge in fruit to form ovoid burs covered with slender spines; these catch on the fur of animals or on clothes. Plants are found throughout temperate and subtropical regions of the world, probably travelling from one country to another with the wool trade and in animal skins.

Spiny Cocklebur, *Xanthium spinosum*, is a related plant, an annual with branched stems like Common Cocklebur, but with tripartite yellow spines at the base of each leafstalk, and with much narrower, tapering leaves. The leaves have pointed lobes and are dark green on the upper surface, white-felted beneath. The flowers and burs are similar to those of Common Cocklebur, but are borne in small clusters or singly, and the burs are hairy and covered in hooked spines. This is another cosmopolitan weed, this one from tropical America, now found in rubbish tips, waste places and on railway sidings, usually near wool mills and factories or near coastal ports, in many parts of Europe, England and southern Scotland.

The **Sneezeweed tribe**, the Helenieae, is not represented in the wild in Europe, but many of its members are familiar garden plants. The yellows, browns and oranges of late summer gardens often come from the Sneezeweeds, *Helenium* species, and the Blanket Flowers or Gaillardias, *Gaillardia* species. French and African Marigolds of summer bedding schemes also belong here, members of the genus *Tagetes*.

Members of the **Aster tribe**, the Astereae, have alternate leaves. The involucre beneath each flower head is formed of numerous bracts in overlapping rows, the bracts becoming progressively shorter towards the outside; the heads may be formed entirely of tubular florets or they may have marginal florets which are strap-shaped or thread-like. This tribe also contributes to the garden flora, with goldenrods, Michaelmas daisies and erigerons.

Goldenrods, about 120 *Solidago* species, come mainly from North America; some are showy plants grown in gardens in Britain and Europe, blooming in late summer. The European **Goldenrod**, *S. virgaurea* (p. 177), is less impressive, however. This perennial plant has a clump of basal leaves, lance-shaped with toothed margins, and a leafy flowering stem up to 75cm (30in) tall, with a terminal inflorescence of yellow flower heads on straight, erect stems. Individual flower heads are small, with the involucre forming a cup for the yellow ray florets and central yellow disk. Plants may be found in dry woods and grassland, on rocks and cliffs, hedgebanks and sand-dunes throughout Europe and the British Isles.

The impact of the showier species comes from the way in which their small flower heads are borne in large, striking inflorescences, like that of Canadian Goldenrod, *Solidago canadensis*. This species has plume-like inflorescences with the flower heads borne all along the upper sides of the arching branches. It is a tall plant, with erect stems up to 1.5m (5ft) tall, grown in gardens throughout Britain and Europe and often escaping to grow wild.

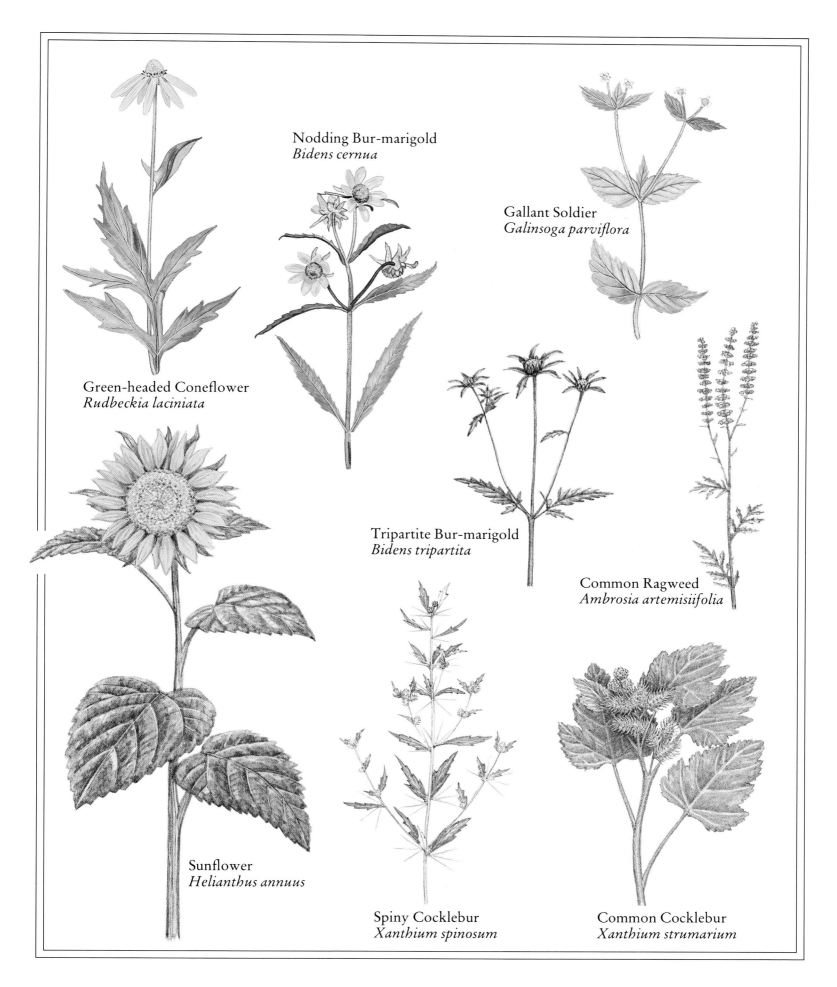

Nodding Bur-marigold
Bidens cernua

Gallant Soldier
Galinsoga parviflora

Green-headed Coneflower
Rudbeckia laciniata

Tripartite Bur-marigold
Bidens tripartita

Common Ragweed
Ambrosia artemisiifolia

Sunflower
Helianthus annuus

Spiny Cocklebur
Xanthium spinosum

Common Cocklebur
Xanthium strumarium

Michaelmas Daisies are familiar garden plants which flower in late summer or autumn, around Michaelmas. They are often associated with harvest festivals, their purple, blue or white flowers contrasting with the yellows and bronzes of golden-rods, heleniums and the other composites of the season. Their popularity has grown during the course of this century, mainly with the development of the Ballard hybrids; today they come with flowers in many shades, in single and double forms, from tall, back-of-the-border plants to tight mounds for the front. Some of the more vigorous garden species have escaped to grow wild, usually in waste places or on railway embankments, but also on the margins of streams and ditches.

Michaelmas Daisies belong to the genus *Aster*, a large group of about 500 species, many from North America and Asia, with about 15 in Europe. The **European Michaelmas Daisy**, *A. amellus*, has erect or straggly stems up to 60cm (2ft) tall, roughly hairy leaves and a loose cluster of flower heads at the top of the stem; each head has bluish-lilac rays and a yellow disk. This species grows wild in central and southeastern Europe, in open woods and meadows, and several varieties of it are grown in gardens elsewhere.

Sea Aster, *Aster tripolium*, is a maritime species, growing in salt marshes, on rocks and cliffs all around the British and European coastline. It is a short-lived perennial plant, hairless in texture with branched stems up to 1m (3ft) tall, and narrow, fleshy leaves. In late summer the flower heads grow in loose clusters at the tops of the stems; each has bluish-purple rays and a yellow disk.

Goldilocks, *Aster linosyris*, is a rather different plant and has been placed in several genera since it was first described. It has rayless, yellow flowers borne in dense, flat-topped clusters at the tops of the stems in late summer. It is a perennial, its erect stems growing up to 50cm (20in) tall and clothed with numerous linear leaves. It grows in rocky places, on cliffs and open grassland, usually on calcareous soils, across much of Europe, but its numbers are declining and it is rare in Britain, found only on limestone cliffs in a few places on the coasts of south-west England and Wales.

The **Fleabanes**, members of the genus *Erigeron*, are another large group with over 200 species, the majority from America. Many hybrids are grown in gardens, with flowers in shades of pink and purple. One of their most attractive features is the large number of narrow ray florets in each flower, 100–200 being not uncommon; the florets are usually arranged in two rows. Fleabanes are not unlike asters and may be mistaken for them, except that fleabanes generally flower in spring and summer, whereas asters flower in late summer and autumn.

Blue Fleabane, *Erigeron acer*, is a roughly hairy, annual or biennial plant, with a clump of oblong basal leaves and an erect, leafy stem up to 40cm (15in) tall, branched near the top to bear a cluster of small flower heads. The leaves are linear to lance-shaped with bases half-clasping the stem; the flower heads have erect, blue-purple ray florets not much longer than the yellow disk which they surround. This plant grows in dry grassland, on banks and walls, especially on calcareous soils, across Europe and in England and Wales, locally in Ireland.

Alpine Fleabane, *Erigeron borealis*, grows on limestone rocks in European mountains, but is a rare plant in the wild in Britain, found only in a few mountains in Scotland. It is, however, grown in rock gardens. It forms tufts of hairy, lance-shaped leaves with erect flowering stalks in the latter half of summer, each one bearing a single terminal flower head. These have purple rays and a yellow disk.

Canadian Fleabane, *Conyza canadensis*, came to Europe from North America late in the seventeenth century but did not become widespread until the building of the roads and railways, for this is one of those plants associated with disturbed ground. It cannot survive much competition and is not found in settled plant communities. It is used in herb medicine as a remedy for diarrhoea and to stop bleeding, and also has insecticidal properties. It is a coarse, bristly annual, with a rosette of basal leaves and a stem up to 1m (3ft) tall, very leafy with lance-shaped, more or less toothed leaves. From the upper leaf axils grow clusters of tiny flowers, each one with minute, white ray florets and a yellow disk. The flowers are followed by tiny achenes, each with a tuft of white hairs.

Daisies, *Bellis perennis*, must be one of the most well-known wild flowers, growing in lawns and other places where the grass is short, throughout the British Isles and Europe. Daisies form many small rosettes of spoon-shaped leaves and flower for much of the year, producing numerous, solitary flower heads on slender, leafless stalks. The ray florets may be white or tinged with pink.

Members of the **Mayweed tribe**, the Anthemideae, usually have alternate, often pinnately divided leaves. The bracts in the involucre often have membranous margins and the heads have both tubular disk and strap-shaped ray florets. The disk florets are hermaphrodite; ray florets may be female or neuter. The pappus on the fruits is almost entirely undeveloped or missing. Shasta Daisies, chrysanthemums, and achilleas belong here.

Mayweeds and **Chamomiles** are a confusing group, not least because they keep changing their Latin names. For instance, the old name for **Chamomile** (p. 179), the plant used in chamomile tea, is *Anthemis nobilis*, and it is still given this name in many herbal and garden books. But it has been known more accurately for many years as *Chamaemelum nobile*, the name used in botanical literature. Chamomile has many creeping, rooting stems and pleasantly scented, feathery leaves, which form a dense mat if left alone. It is sometimes planted in gardens as a Chamomile lawn (usually in the variety 'Treneague' which does not flower). Wild plants produce daisy-like flower heads, solitary on long stalks, around midsummer; the heads have white rays around a domed yellow disk, and the rays droop as they age. This species grows in western Europe

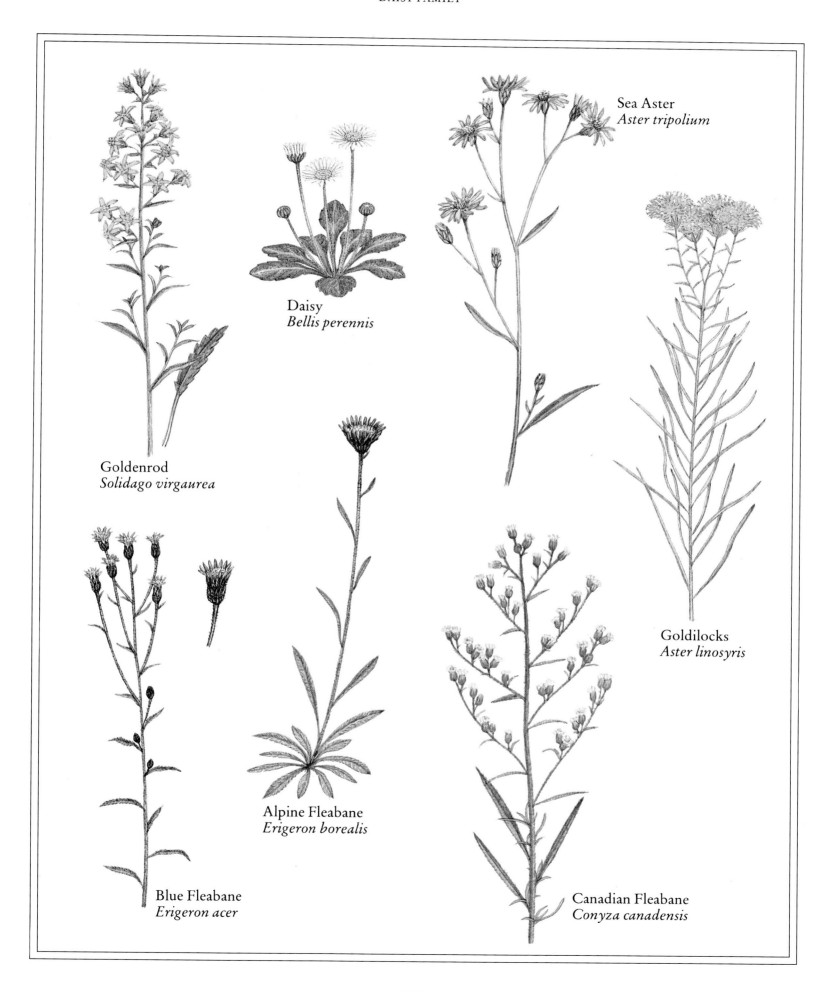

Goldenrod
Solidago virgaurea

Daisy
Bellis perennis

Sea Aster
Aster tripolium

Goldilocks
Aster linosyris

Blue Fleabane
Erigeron acer

Alpine Fleabane
Erigeron borealis

Canadian Fleabane
Conyza canadensis

south from Belgium, in southern England, Wales and Ireland, usually in sandy soils, in grassy places, on heaths and commons, banks and roadsides.

Stinking Chamomile, *Anthemis cotula*, grows in waste places and arable land, generally on heavy soils, throughout Europe, mainly in England and Wales in the British Isles. Its common name is appropriate, for the plant has an unpleasant odour that comes from glands on its leaves; the acrid secretion can cause blisters. This is an annual plant, with a branched, erect stem up to 60cm (2ft) tall and soft, finely dissected, quite smooth leaves. It bears daisy-like flowers in summer, with sterile, white ray florets and dome-shaped, yellow disks.

Corn Chamomile, *Anthemis arvensis*, often grows as an annual weed of arable land, especially on calcareous soils, but may also be found in waste places and on roadsides; it grows throughout Europe, locally in England and Wales, rarely in Ireland and Scotland. It resembles Stinking Chamomile but has hairy or even woolly leaves with a slight, pleasant scent.

Yellow Chamomile, *Anthemis tinctoria*, is a popular garden plant, introduced and escaping to grow widely as a casual in England and Scotland, native to much of Europe, where it may be found in rocky places and walls, on slopes and banks. It is a short-lived perennial plant, with woolly stems up to 60cm (2ft) tall and twice-pinnate leaves, white woolly beneath and with toothed margins on the leaflets. The yellow flower heads are borne singly at the tops of the stems.

Scentless Mayweed, *Tripleurospermum inodorum*, is one of those with several name changes in its past. It was thought to be an inland subspecies of Sea Mayweed and called at the time *Matricaria maritima* subsp. *inodora*. Both plants were later transferred into the genus *Tripleurospermum*, and Scentless Mayweed became *T. maritima* subsp. *inodorum*; it has recently been made into a full species as *T. inodorum*. These name changes may seem unimportant, and in a sense they are, for the plant does not change. But the problem that arises when a plant has a history like this is tracking it down, for it may be found under any of these names in different books, and then it may appear that the books are describing different plants, when in fact they are all describing the same one. Scentless Mayweed is an annual, almost scentless, hairless plant, with a branched, sprawling stem up to 60cm (2ft) tall and leaves so divided that their segments are linear. In the latter part of summer it bears many daisy-like flowers, with white ray florets which droop as the flowers age, and dome-shaped yellow disks. It is an abundant weed of cultivated land and waste places throughout the British Isles and is found across Europe.

Sea Mayweed, *Tripleurospermum maritimum*, is a similar and closely related plant, but it has sprawling stems and fleshy leaves. As its name suggests, this is a coastal plant, found on the drift line on shingle beaches, on cliffs and rocks on the shore, and on the sea edge of sand-dunes all around the British Isles and on the coasts of western and northern Europe.

Wild Chamomile or Scented Mayweed, *Matricaria recutita* (old name *M. chamomilla*), is a hairless, aromatic annual plant, with divided, fern-like leaves and many daisy-like flower heads around midsummer. The leaves have bristle-tipped segments and each flower head has a conical yellow disk and white rays which become reflexed soon after the flowers open. Wild Chamomile is a common weed of waste places and arable land, usually growing in sandy or loamy soils, across much of Europe and in England and Wales; it is rare in Scotland and Ireland. It has a long history of use as a medicinal plant; a tea made from its flowers is useful for treating digestive disorders.

Pineapple Weed or Rayless Mayweed, *Matricaria matricarioides*, is another weed but an introduced one this time, brought from Asia or North America and now found in waste places, on the sides of roads and tracks, especially where the ground is trampled, throughout the British Isles and Europe. It is a scented, hairless, annual plant, its crushed foliage smelling of pineapples and giving it its common name. It has a branched, often sprawling stem, only about 30cm (1ft) tall, and pinnate leaves divided into linear segments. It bears many distinctive flower heads, each with a highly domed, greenish-yellow disk and no ray florets. The disk is cupped by green bracts with papery edges.

Corn Marigold, *Chrysanthemum segetum*, is also a weed and at one time a troublesome one of cornfields in light acid or sandy soils, but its numbers have decreased with improved techniques of cleaning seed. Nowadays it is not often seen in cornfields but grows in waste places and on roadsides instead, locally throughout the British Isles and across Europe. It is an annual plant, hairless in texture and greyish in colour, with erect, branched stems up to 60cm (2ft) tall and irregularly toothed, oblong leaves, their bases clasping the stems. The flowers appear at the tops of the stems in summer; they have yellow ray florets and flat yellow disks.

The **Ox-eye Daisy**, *Leucanthemum vulgare* (p. 181), is a common native plant found in grassland throughout the British Isles and Europe. But it is also a perennial grown in flower borders in many gardens, usually in the large-flowered varieties known as Moon Daisies, Shasta Daisies and Marguerites. In the wild it forms spreading colonies of leaf rosettes, from which grow erect stems up to 1m (3ft) tall, with dark green, pinnately divided leaves, the upper ones clasping the stem. Each stem bears a solitary, large, daisy-like flower, with white ray florets and a flat yellow disk. It has an old Latin name still used in many books, *Chrysanthemum leucanthemum*.

Yarrow or Milfoil, *Achillea millefolium* (p. 181), is an aromatic plant used in herb medicine, yarrow tea being a remedy for colds. Traditionally it was used as a wound herb—the Greek hero Achilles is supposed to have recommended it for treating wounds made with iron weapons, especially if pounded with grease. It is very variable, growing tall in shady positions but flat to the ground in open, exposed sites, in a var-

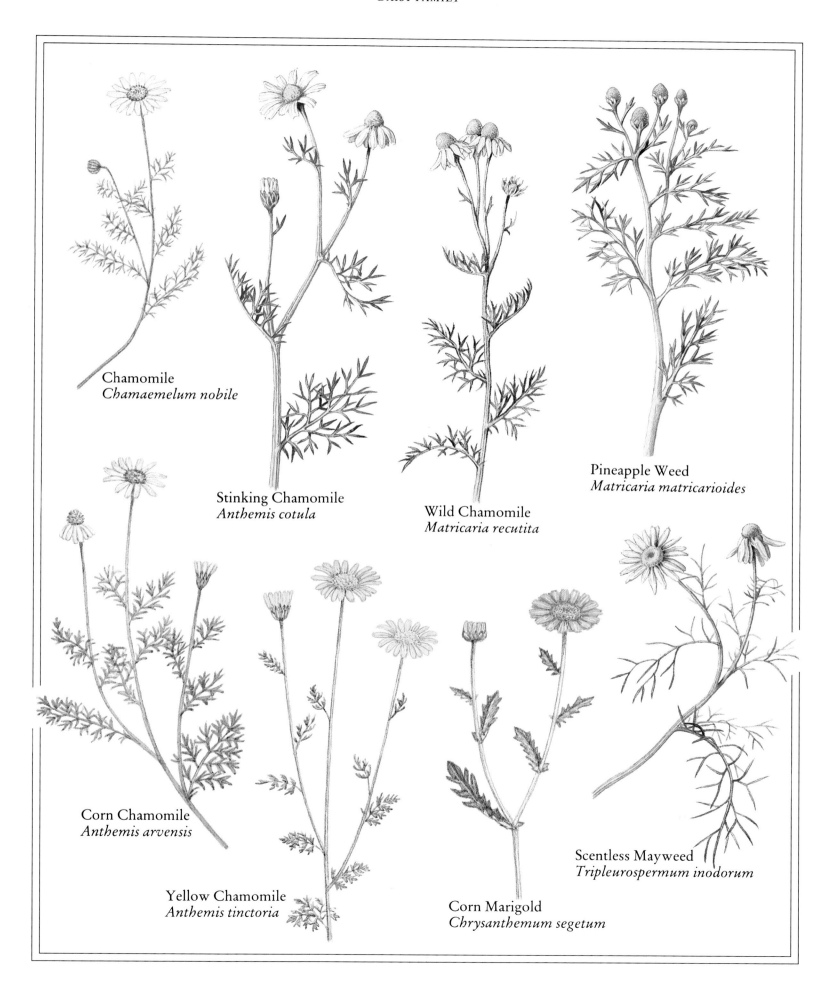

Chamomile
Chamaemelum nobile

Stinking Chamomile
Anthemis cotula

Wild Chamomile
Matricaria recutita

Pineapple Weed
Matricaria matricarioides

Corn Chamomile
Anthemis arvensis

Yellow Chamomile
Anthemis tinctoria

Corn Marigold
Chrysanthemum segetum

Scentless Mayweed
Tripleurospermum inodorum

iety of habitats but most often in meadows, grassy banks, roadsides and hedgerows, throughout Europe and the British Isles. It has many underground stems and creeps into large colonies if left alone, with soft, ferny, much dissected, dark green leaves. The erect stems bear more or less flattened, terminal clusters of white flower heads. Each head is small, with roughly five broad ray florets and 10–20 disk florets.

Sneezewort, *Achillea ptarmica*, is closely related to Yarrow, but is a taller plant, with erect stems up to 60cm (2ft) tall, lance-shaped leaves with serrated margins, and loosely branched, terminal clusters of larger white flower heads. It grows in marshes and damp meadows, and beside streams throughout the British Isles and across much of Europe. Its dried and powdered leaves were at one time used in herb medicine to promote sneezing.

Tansy, *Tanacetum vulgare*, is another old medicinal plant. Its name comes from the Greek word for 'immortal' and it was strewn over corpses to keep worms and flies away from them. Certainly it does keep insects away; they seem not to like its bitter scent. It is little used in modern herb medicine because an overdose can be fatal, but it is sometimes recommended as a wash for sprains and bruises. It is a perennial, with creeping underground stems and erect, robust stems with soft, ferny, pinnately divided leaves. In the latter half of summer, when the stems are about 1m (3ft) tall, they bear terminal, branched clusters of yellowish flower heads; the heads contain only disk florets, many of them packed densely together.

Feverfew, *Tanacetum parthenium*, was once *Chrysanthemum parthenium* and before that was *Matricaria parthenium*. It is a medicinal herb, traditionally used to reduce fevers as its name suggests. It can also be used as an insecticide, like pyrethrum. This is a perennial plant, with a much-branched, erect stem about 60cm (2ft) tall and pinnately divided leaves. In the latter part of summer it bears many small flower heads, each with white rays and a yellow disk. Feverfew is native to south-eastern Europe, but has been widely introduced further north and in Great Britain, found most often on walls, on roadsides and in waste places, but also grown in gardens.

The **Wormwoods**, about 400 members of the genus *Artemisia*, are generally aromatic, herbaceous or shrubby plants, found mostly in the grasslands of Eurasia and North America, with about 50 species in Europe. Several are medicinal and kitchen herbs, including Wormwood itself, Tarragon and Mugwort; others, like Southernwood and Dusty Miller, are grown in gardens for their silver or grey foliage.

Wormwood, *Artemisia absinthium*, has been called the bitterest of all the herbs, apart from rue; it is best known as the active ingredient of absinthe and gives this drink its bitter taste. It is also used in herb medicine as a nerve tonic to stimulate digestion and promote appetite. Wormwood is a perennial plant, silky-hairy in texture, with rosettes of thrice-pinnate leaves and erect flowering stems in summer, growing up to 1m (3ft) tall and often woody at the base. The stems are grooved and angled, with leaves becoming progressively simpler higher up, and they branch to form large, complex inflorescences of many small flower heads. The heads are rounded and drooping, yellowish in colour and containing only disk florets. Wormwood grows in rocky and uncultivated places across Europe, in waste places and on roadsides in England and Wales, much more rarely in Scotland and Ireland.

Sea Wormwood, *Artemisia maritima*, grows on salt marshes and sea walls locally around the coasts of Europe, mostly on the coasts of England and south Wales in the British Isles. It is an aromatic perennial plant, with rosettes of twice or thrice-pinnate leaves, grey-woolly on both surfaces and with linear segments. In late summer the sprawling flowering stems reach 50cm (20in) in height and produce numerous egg-shaped flowering heads on side shoots growing from the leaf axils; the heads may be drooping or erect, yellow or orange in colour.

Field Southernwood, *Artemisia campestris*, has similarly shaped leaves and flowers, but its leaves are silky-hairy only when young, becoming hairless as they age, and the plant is almost scentless. The flower heads may be greenish or reddish. This species grows in bare, sandy ground, waste places and roadsides across Europe, but is confined to the Brecklands of East Anglia in Britain.

Mugwort, *Artemisia vulgaris*, is a creeping perennial plant, a weed of roadsides and waste places, found throughout Europe and the British Isles. It has strong, erect stems up to 120cm (4ft) tall, with many clasping, deeply cleft leaves. These leaves are smooth and very dark green above, white with cottony hairs below. The plant produces numerous flower heads growing on long, branched, leafy stems from every leaf axil, each head small, reddish-brown and inconspicuous. The plant is very dull in appearance, but also very obvious with its dark and light leaves. It has a strong, aromatic odour and is used in herb medicine to treat digestive disorders; in Europe it is added to stuffings and sauces for eating with geese.

Members of the **Ragwort tribe**, the Senecioneae, usually have alternate leaves. The involucre beneath the flower heads is usually formed of a single row of bracts which do not have membranous margins. The heads always have hermaphrodite, tubular disk florets in the centre, often with female florets around the margin; these marginal florets may be tubular or strap-shaped. The fruits have a pappus consisting of many simple hairs. Cinerarias and doronicums belong to this tribe.

Coltsfoot, *Tussilago farfara* (p. 183), is a plant to be noticed, both in early spring when it flowers and in summer when its large, basal leaves cover the ground. The flower heads are yellow, formed of ray florets and borne singly on reddish, scaly stems only 15cm (6in) tall; they often appear in large clumps, for this plant spreads into wide colonies by means of underground stems. The flowers are followed by clock-like fruits and finally the leaves emerge, white-felted all over at

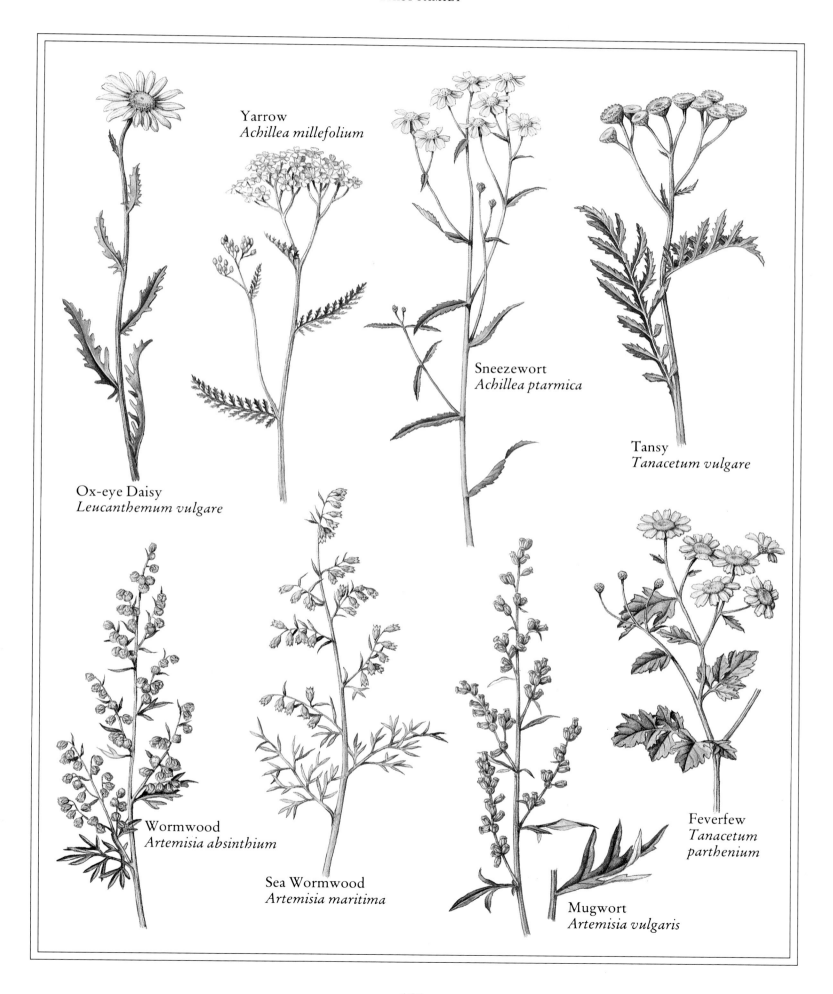

Yarrow
Achillea millefolium

Sneezewort
Achillea ptarmica

Tansy
Tanacetum vulgare

Ox-eye Daisy
Leucanthemum vulgare

Wormwood
Artemisia absinthium

Sea Wormwood
Artemisia maritima

Mugwort
Artemisia vulgaris

Feverfew
Tanacetum parthenium

first, remaining white-felted beneath as they unfurl. They are large and rounded, shallowly lobed and deep green above once mature. This plant grows in arable land, on banks and in waste places, on cliffs and landslides, shingle banks and dunes, riversides and woodland margins, often in damp places. It is rich in mucilage and an effective cough remedy used both in herb medicine and in commercially produced cough mixtures.

Like Coltsfoot, **Butterbur**, *Petasites hybridus*, produces its flowers before the leaves emerge. It grows from stout, creeping rhizomes which may reach 1.5m (5ft) in length, so that the plant gradually forms broad patches; in spring the rhizomes send up thick, purplish flowering shoots covered with lance-shaped, greenish scales and bearing terminal clusters of pale red-violet flower heads. Plants bear either male or female flowers, the male heads mostly formed of tubular florets, the female flowers of strap-shaped florets. In female plants the flowering stems grow about twice as tall after flowering is over and develop many hairy fruits. The leaves emerge in summer and are very large—up to 90cm (3ft) across—grey-downy at first but losing their hairs on the upper surface as they mature; they are rounded heart-shaped with toothed margins and hollow, channelled stalks. Butterbur grows in wet places, beside streams, in wet meadows, marshes and woods across Europe and the British Isles. Most British plants are male.

White Butterbur, *Petasites albus*, is like a smaller version of Butterbur with scented, white flowers. Its leaves grow only 30cm (1ft) across and are white-woolly beneath, even when mature; the scales on the flowering stems are pale green and the inflorescence is almost as broad as it is long. This plant grows beside streams and springs in the hills and mountains of Europe; it has been introduced into Great Britain, where it is found mainly in northeastern Scotland and northern England in waste places, on roadsides and in woods.

Winter Heliotrope, *Petasites fragrans*, flowers in winter and early spring, its flowering stems appearing at the same time as the leaves. It has pale lilac, vanilla-scented flowers and kidney-shaped leaves up to 20cm (8in) across; these are quite shiny on the upper surface and almost hairless beneath. This plant grows in damp, shady places, in hedgerows and on roadsides, in waste places and beside streams across central and southeastern Europe; introduced as a garden plant into the British Isles, it has become widely naturalized.

Alpine Coltsfoot, *Homogyne alpina*, grows in the damp meadows and woods of the mountains in central and southeastern Europe, but it has also been introduced to two places in the British Isles—Scotland and the Outer Hebrides. This is a miniature coltsfoot, with rosettes of long-stalked, rounded heart-shaped leaves growing from creeping stems. The leaves are dark green above, often purplish beneath and have toothed margins; their blades grow only 4cm (1½in) across. Flowers and leaves appear together in summer, the purple-red flowers in a terminal head on an erect stalk about 30cm (1ft) tall.

Arnica, *Arnica montana*, is a famous herbal plant, used as a remedy for bruises and strains, and at one time recommended for reducing fever and to treat some heart conditions. Since some people can react very badly to it, however, its internal use is now largely discontinued. Arnica is a perennial plant, with a clump of oval to elliptical basal leaves, glandular-hairy in texture and with an aromatic scent. The flower heads are borne singly, terminating erect stems up to 60cm (2ft) tall, with only one or two pairs of small, opposite leaves. The heads are bright yellow and like those of daisies, with a circle of strap-like ray florets around a central disk. Arnica grows in mountain pastures and woods in many of the mountains of Europe; it is not found in the British Isles.

About 12 **Leopard's-banes** are found in Europe, all members of the genus *Doronicum*. They are attractive plants and several are grown in gardens. **Great Leopard's-bane**, *D. pardalianches*, is a perennial, with clumps of broadly heart-shaped leaves, pale green in colour, thin and hairy in texture. In early summer the leafy flowering stems grow up to 90cm (3ft) tall, branching near the tops to bear bright yellow flower heads, each one with a circle of ray florets and a central disk cupped in a saucer-shaped involucre of bracts. This plant grows in woods and plantations in the hills of central and southeastern Europe; it has been introduced into Great Britain and now grows wild in many scattered areas.

At first glance, **Groundsels** and **Ragworts** appear very different, but they belong to the same genus, *Senecio*, united by botanical details of the flowers. In fact, if the bright ray florets of ragworts were removed they would resemble groundsels. *Senecio* is a very large genus, with about 1000 species worldwide, including not only herbaceous plants, but also shrubs and climbers. Some 65 species are found in Europe.

Common Ragwort, *Senecio jacobaea* (p. 185), is a biennial or perennial plant, with a rosette of sinuately toothed basal leaves and erect, leafy flowering stems growing up to 1.5m (5ft) tall. The stems are furrowed, often cottony, with many crisped, sinuate leaves, dark green on the upper surface and paler, sometimes with cottony hairs beneath; the upper ones have clasping bases. The stems branch above the middle to bear dense, flat-topped inflorescences of many flower heads; both ray florets and disk florets are bright golden yellow and the heads are cupped in green, black-tipped bracts. They are followed by fruits with hairy parachutes. This is an attractive but unwelcome plant; with its windborne fruits it spreads rapidly and may take over large areas of farmland if left alone. Grazing animals sensibly avoid it, as it is poisonous and causes liver damage (like all ragworts and groundsels), but it seeds undisturbed in the grazed pastures and retains its poisons when dried in hay or in silage, causing many deaths every year. It is found in abundance in overgrazed pastures, in waste places and roadsides, on sand-dunes and open woods throughout Europe and the British Isles.

Butterbur
Petasites hybridus

Winter Heliotrope
Petasites fragrans

White Butterbur
Petasites albus

Coltsfoot
Tussilago farfara

Alpine Coltsfoot
Homogyne alpina

Arnica
Arnica montana

Great Leopard's-bane
Doronicum pardalianches

Marsh Ragwort, *Senecio aquaticus*, is a similar plant but is a biennial, with a rosette of unlobed basal leaves in the first year and erect, reddish flowering stems up to 80cm (30in) tall in the second. These are leafy with half-clasping, irregularly lobed leaves, and they branch to bear large, loose clusters of golden yellow flowers, larger than those of Common Ragwort. Marsh Ragwort grows in marshes and wet meadows, in ditches and on the banks of streams and rivers throughout the British Isles and much of Europe.

Oxford Ragwort, *Senecio squalidus*, is a smaller annual plant, with sprawling stems only 30cm (1ft) tall. It has dark green, pinnately lobed leaves and an irregular inflorescence of bright golden yellow flower heads, each head borne in a bell-shaped cup of black-tipped bracts. This plant comes from the mountains of central and southern Europe, but was brought to the Oxford Botanical Gardens in the eighteenth century, escaping to grow wild around Oxford in the nineteenth century, finally expanding explosively with the building of the railways. Today it grows in waste places and on roadsides, on railway embankments, in arable land and on walls throughout lowland areas of England, locally in southern Scotland and southern Ireland; it is also naturalized in western Europe.

Hoary Ragwort, *Senecio erucifolius*, is a creeping, greyish, perennial plant, with many rosettes of basal leaves, more or less pinnately lobed in shape. In summer the furrowed flowering stems grow up to 120cm (4ft) tall; they have firm, pinnately lobed leaves and a branching inflorescence of bright yellow flower heads. Both stem and leaves are cottony, the stems sparsely covered with the white hairs and the leaves with theirs mostly beneath; the leaves have narrow segments and slightly inrolled margins. This plant grows in rough grassland, around fields and on roadsides, often on heavy calcareous soils, also on shingle banks throughout much of Europe, except in the north, in England and Wales, rarely in southern Scotland and eastern Ireland.

Groundsel, *Senecio vulgaris*, is a cosmopolitan weed, familiar to anyone who has a vegetable patch, and growing also in waste places and on roadsides, in disturbed environments everywhere. It is a small annual plant, no more than 30cm (1ft) tall, with a branched stem and crisp, irregularly toothed leaves. It bears many small flower heads, each one with a cup of green, black-tipped bracts and many yellow disk florets, so that the head resembles a shaving brush. The flowers do not have ray florets. After flowering, each head becomes a dome of white-haired fruits, which are blown away on the wind. This plant has several generations a year and is so successful at colonizing that it may take over whole areas of waste ground or whole vegetable gardens, if left to its own devices.

Sticky Groundsel, *Senecio viscosus*, is an annual similar in appearance to Groundsel but is a taller plant growing up to 60cm (2ft) in height; it has a foetid scent, very sticky, glandular-hairy stems and leaves, and the bracts of the flower heads are not black-tipped. This groundsel grows in waste places and on tracks, on roadsides and railway embankments, sand-dunes and shingle beaches across much of Europe and in lowland areas of Great Britain.

Members of the **Hemp Agrimony tribe**, the Eupatorieae, often have opposite leaves and their flower heads contain only tubular, hermaphrodite florets. The ageratums of summer bedding schemes belong to this tribe.

Hemp Agrimony, *Eupatorium cannabinum*, is the only species of this large genus found in Europe; most of the 1200 members are American. Like several of the American species, it is a medicinal herb, little used today but useful in treating colds and flu. It is a handsome plant, a large perennial with a clump of erect, often reddish, leafy stems up to 120cm (4ft) tall, with opposite, palmately-lobed leaves. The leaves have lance-shaped, serrated leaflets. The stems branch at the top to form dense, flat-topped inflorescences of fluffy, reddish-mauve flowers; the flowers are all tubular, their fluffy appearance coming from the protruding white styles. This plant grows in damp and wet places, in marshes and fens, on the banks of rivers and in wet woods throughout Europe and most of the British Isles, but less commonly in Scotland.

Members of the **Cudweed tribe**, the Inuleae, usually have simple, alternate leaves, often with white-woolly hairs. The flower heads usually have hermaphrodite, tubular florets in the centre, while the marginal florets are female, either strap-shaped or tubular and thread-like. The pappus on the fruits is often formed of simple or feathery hairs. Garden flowers in the tribe include helichrysums, antennarias and inulas.

Elecampane, *Inula helenium* (p. 187), is an ancient herbal plant, known to the Greeks and Romans, used to treat asthma, bronchitis and other chest complaints, in which use it is very effective. In the Middle Ages its roots were candied and eaten, and it is still used in the preparation of absinthe. Elecampane grows in waste places and hedgerows, in woods and rough pastures, scattered across Europe, Great Britain and Ireland, probably naturalized in most of this area and native only to southeastern Europe. It is a stout perennial, with a basal rosette of pointed-ovate leaves, each up to 60cm (2ft) in length, and thick stems up to 1.5m (5ft) tall, bearing similar but smaller leaves, their bases clasping the stem. The stems and the undersides of the leaves are softly hairy. The stems branch near the top to bear clusters of bright yellow flower heads with hemispherical involucres and numerous long, narrow ray florets around the yellow disk.

Irish Fleabane, *Inula salicina* (p. 187), is a much more slender perennial, with stiff, leafy stems growing up to 50cm (20in) tall, the lower leaves lance-shaped and upper ones pointed heart-shaped with their bases clasping the stems, all the leaves firm and hairless with rough margins. The flower heads terminate the stems and smaller ones may grow on side shoots from the upper leaf axils; each head has a hemispherical

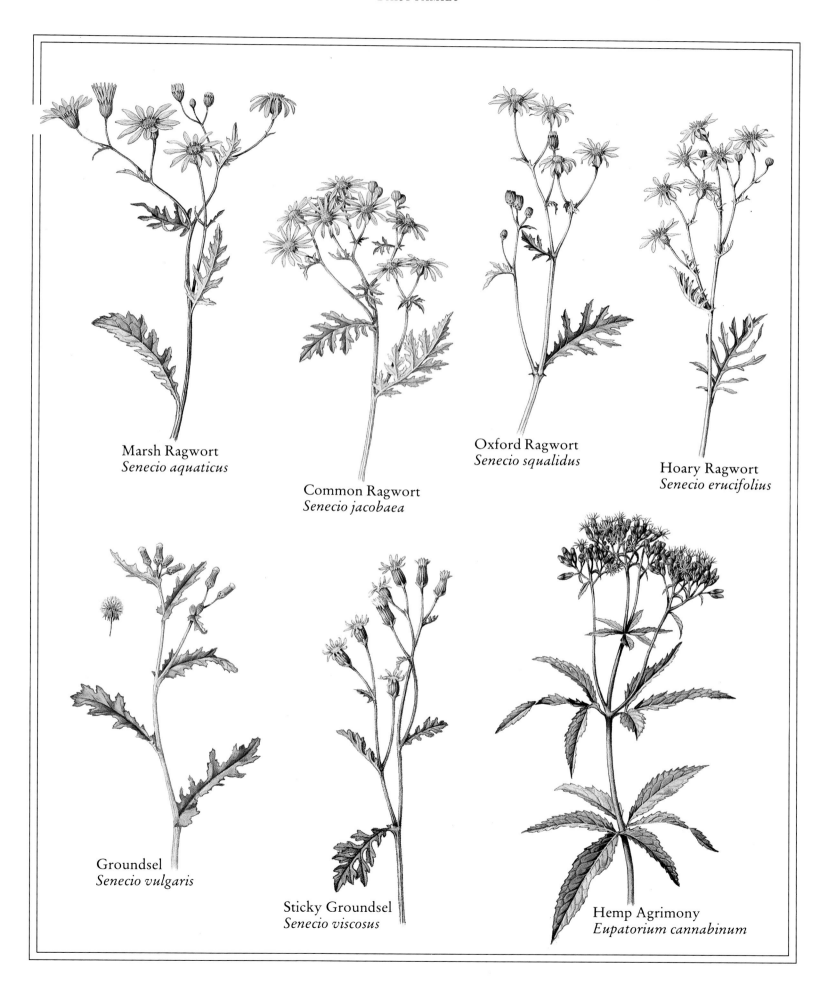

Marsh Ragwort
Senecio aquaticus

Common Ragwort
Senecio jacobaea

Oxford Ragwort
Senecio squalidus

Hoary Ragwort
Senecio erucifolius

Groundsel
Senecio vulgaris

Sticky Groundsel
Senecio viscosus

Hemp Agrimony
Eupatorium cannabinum

involucre of bracts, numerous yellow ray florets and a central yellow disk. This plant grows in rocky and wooded slopes, in wet, calcareous grassland and marshes throughout Europe, but in the British Isles is confined to the limestone shores of Lough Derg in Ireland.

Ploughman's Spikenard, *Inula conyza*, is a biennial or perennial plant, with a rosette of basal leaves which may be mistaken for those of a Foxglove; they are softly hairy and ovate in shape. From this rosette grow erect, purplish stems up to 120cm (4ft) tall, with downy, pointed-elliptical leaves and a branched, terminal cluster of flower heads in late summer. Each head is cupped in an involucre, the outer bracts green and the inner ones purplish; the florets are yellowish, the inner ones tubular and the outer ones often with small rays. This plant grows in dry, calcareous soils, in open woods and scrub, on rocky slopes and cliffs, and in grassy places throughout much of Europe, except the north, in England and Wales, north to Cumbria.

Golden Samphire, *Inula crithmoides*, is a maritime plant growing on cliffs and rocks, on shingle banks and salt marshes, locally on the coasts of western Europe south to the Mediterranean, around the coasts of England, Wales and southern Ireland. This perennial, rather shrubby species has branched, fleshy stems about 60cm (2ft) tall and many linear or lance-shaped leaves which often have three teeth at their tips. The plants flower in the latter half of summer, with a branched inflorescence terminating the stems; the many flower heads have golden yellow ray florets and orange-yellow disks.

Fleabane, *Pulicaria dysenterica*, gets its name from its old use as a flea deterrent—when it was burned the smoke was said to drive fleas away. It is a perennial plant with creeping stems, forming patches of erect, leafy stems up to 60cm (2ft) tall, hoary from the white hairs which cover stems and leaves. The leaves are oblong to lance-shaped with wavy margins, those higher up with heart-shaped, clasping bases. The stems branch near the top to form a cluster of yellow flower heads; each head has a yellow disk and numerous linear ray florets. The flowers are followed by hairy fruits. Fleabane grows in wet meadows and marshes, in ditches and on the banks of streams throughout much of Europe, except the north, in England and into southern Scotland, in Wales and Ireland.

Small Fleabane, *Pulicaria vulgaris*, is similar but is an annual plant with smaller flower heads, and is much less obviously hairy. Its stems grow to about 45cm (18in) tall and branch near the top to produce yellow flower heads with very short, more or less erect rays. This plant grows in moist, sandy soils where water stands in winter, across much of Europe, except in the north; at one time it was widespread in central and southeastern England, but is now very rare and found only in a few places in the extreme south.

Some members of this tribe have flowers with a curious texture like paper. They are often known as **Everlasting Flowers**,

for their naturally dry blooms last long beyond the normal time-span of most flowers. Some, like **Pearly Everlasting**, *Anaphalis margaritacea*, a North American plant, are used in dried flower arrangements, but also grown in gardens in Britain and Europe and widely naturalized. Its flower heads are surrounded by white, papery bracts which look like part of the flower, as if they could be ray florets. It is these which give the flowers their special texture and which last so long.

The most famous Everlasting Flowers are the *Helichrysum* species, of which about 20 are found in Europe. **Sand Everlasting**, *H. arenarium*, is one of the most attractive, with some varieties grown in gardens. In the wild it is a relatively rare plant, found in dry, sandy places, in open grassland and pine woods, on dunes and tracks, scattered across central and western Europe. It is a greyish perennial, all covered with woolly hairs; it has a rosette of spoon-shaped leaves and leafy flowering stems up to 30cm (1ft) tall ending in dense clusters of golden yellow flower heads. Their shiny appearance comes from the bright orange-yellow bracts which surround the yellow disk florets (it is these coloured bracts which give the characteristic texture to *Helichrysum* flowers).

Mountain Everlasting or Cat's-foot, *Antennaria dioica* (p. 189), also has flowers which answer to the description of 'everlasting'. This small perennial plant has short, creeping stems and spreading mats of leaf rosettes, the spoon-shaped leaves green on the upper surface, white woolly beneath. Its erect flower-bearing stems grow only 20cm (8in) tall and bear dense, terminal clusters of small flower heads in summer, males and females on separate plants. The smaller male heads have white bracts like ray florets encircling the tubular florets; female heads have pink bracts held erect. The variety 'Rosea' is grown in rock gardens and troughs. In the wild plants grow in dry mountain meadows and heaths, on slopes and banks, usually on calcareous or base-rich soils, in northern and central Europe, mainly in Scotland and the Scottish islands, in northern England and Ireland in the British Isles.

Edelweiss, *Leontopodium alpinum* (p. 189), is a famous alpine plant often used to symbolize the mountains of Europe, where it grows in dry meadows on calcareous or base-rich soils. It is a tufted perennial, with rosettes of densely woolly, grey-green, spoon-shaped leaves. In the latter half of summer the flowering stems appear, leafy and with terminal clusters of globular flower heads cupped in star-shaped ruffs of large, white-woolly leaves. Each head has a white involucre surrounding yellow disk florets.

The **Cudweeds**, a large group of about 200 species in the genus *Gnaphalium*, are found in temperate regions of the world, but with only seven or so in Europe. They are woolly-haired plants, with alternate entire leaves and clusters of small, often whitish or yellowish flower heads all formed of disk florets. The bracts which surround the flower heads may be completely papery or may have only papery tips. **Heath Cudweed**,

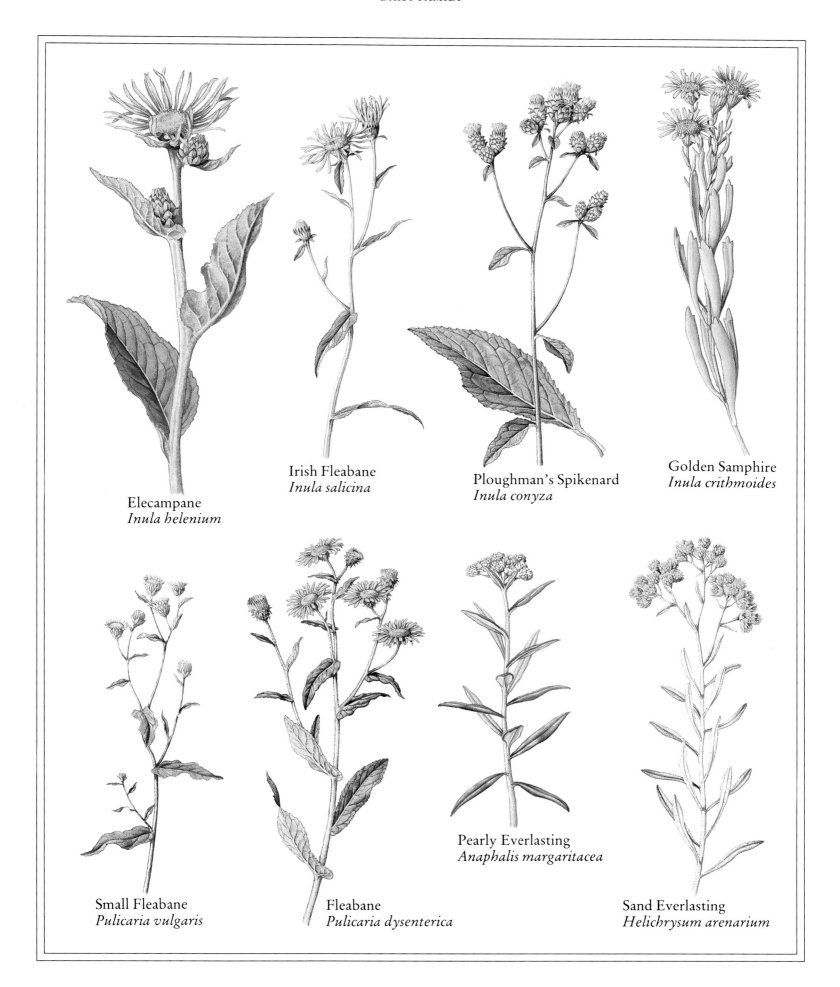

Elecampane
Inula helenium

Irish Fleabane
Inula salicina

Ploughman's Spikenard
Inula conyza

Golden Samphire
Inula crithmoides

Small Fleabane
Pulicaria vulgaris

Fleabane
Pulicaria dysenterica

Pearly Everlasting
Anaphalis margaritacea

Sand Everlasting
Helichrysum arenarium

G. sylvaticum, grows in dry heaths and open woods, in grassland and commons, on acid soils throughout Europe and the British Isles, less commonly in the north. It is a perennial plant, with sprawling, leafy non-flowering shoots and erect flowering shoots growing up to 60cm (2ft) tall. These bear dense clusters of flower heads in the leaf axils, so that the inflorescence looks like an interrupted leafy spike; the heads are pale brown, the outer bracts brown with clear, membranous tips, the inner bracts with a green stripe in the centre and pink or white tips and margins.

Dwarf Cudweed, *Gnaphalium supinum*, is an alpine species, a low, tufted, perennial plant, with many leafy, non-flowering shoots and erect flowering shoots in summer. The pale brown flower heads grow in clusters, forming a dense, terminal spike at the tops of the shoots; each head is cupped in 3–4 rows of green-striped bracts, which have papery brown margins. This little plant grows on cliffs, among rocks and in pastures in the European and Scottish mountains.

Marsh Cudweed, *Gnaphalium uliginosum*, is found in damp places, on the banks of streams and ditches, in woodland rides and tracks, in damp, arable fields and gardens, generally on acid soils, throughout Europe and the British Isles. This is an inconspicuous plant, no more than 20cm (8in) tall, an annual with grey-woolly stems and leaves. The stem is branched, with many overlapping linear leaves and small clusters of curious little brownish-white flower heads appearing in the axils of the leaves and terminating the stems in late summer.

Members of the genus *Filago* are also called Cudweeds, a group of about 25 species, with about 12 in Europe. They are small annual plants, many of them greyish-white in colour from the dense hairs which cover their stems and leaves. **Common Cudweed**, *F. vulgaris*, has erect stems, often branched at the base, about 30cm (1ft) tall, and densely covered with white-woolly, linear, often wavy leaves. Dense clusters of tiny flower heads terminate both stems and the wide-spreading side branches which often grow taller than the main stems. The heads contain only tubular florets, the inner ones hermaphrodite and the outer ones female; they are yellow, cupped in densely woolly outer bracts, membranous, yellowish inner ones, all half sunk into a mass of white woolly hairs. This little plant grows in acid, sandy soils, in dry grassland and heaths, fields and roadsides throughout Europe and Great Britain, north into southern Scotland, occasionally in Ireland.

Small Cudweed, *Filago minima*, has forked stems and linear leaves held close against the stems, all grey with silky hairs. It usually reaches only 15cm (6in) in height and bears small clusters of flower heads in the forks; these are yellowish with pale bracts. Small Cudweed grows in sandy or gravelly soils, in grassland and heaths, in waste land and fields, on walls and in old quarries throughout much of Europe north to southern Scandinavia, mainly in the east in Great Britain and rarely in eastern Ireland.

Members of the **Thistle tribe**, the Cynareae, have alternate, often spiny leaves. There are many rows of bracts forming the involucre beneath each flower head; and the heads contain only tubular florets, either all hermaphrodite or the outer ones female or neuter. The pappus on the fruits is formed of many hairs or scales. Garden flowers include the echinops species and the centaureas, but many more members of this tribe are weeds than are ornamental plants.

On sunny days when its flowers are open, the **Carline Thistle**, *Carlina vulgaris* (p. 191), is a striking plant. The flower heads are surrounded by pointed, shiny-yellow bracts which spread out in dry weather and close up when wet—in the past the dried flowers have been used as primitive hygrometers. This biennial plant has a rosette of cottony, thistle-like leaves in the first year and an erect flowering stem growing up to 60cm (2ft) tall in the second; the rosette leaves wither before flowering. The stem leaves are numerous, wavy with weak spines on the lobed margins and with bases half-clasping the stems. In late summer the flower heads appear in clusters at the tops of the stems; they consist of hermaphrodite, golden yellow disk florets encircled by an outer ring of spiny, greenish bracts and an inner ring of the conspicuous yellow ones. Carline Thistles grow in dry, usually calcareous grassland throughout Europe, in England, Wales and central Ireland, on the east coast of Scotland and in the Inner Hebrides.

Stemless Carline Thistle, *Carlina acaulis* (p. 191), is like a compressed version of a Carline Thistle, with virtually no stem and the flower heads nestled into the rosette of spiny leaves. The rosette may develop for several years before the plant flowers and then it dies; the flower heads have whitish disk florets and shiny, silvery white inner bracts rather than yellow ones, but they are just as weather wise, only spreading out when dry. This plant grows in poor pastures and on rocky slopes in many of the European mountains; it is not found in the British Isles.

Lesser Burdock, *Arctium minus* (p. 191), and **Greater Burdock**, *A. lappa* (p. 191), were thought to be one species until around the turn of the century, when botanists realized that they were at least two separate species. The original composite species was known as *Arctium lappa*, and still sometimes it is unclear, in books on herbal medicine in particular, which species is under discussion. The problem is compounded by the fact that the two grow in the same places and hybrids are often found. Lesser Burdock is the widespread, common species, Greater Burdock the less common one; yet in many herbal books, Burdock is still named as *A. lappa* and also described as common and widespread. It seems that the books are perpetuating the original name, when in fact the plant under discussion may be Lesser Burdock, *A. minus*, or encompass both species. Burdock is used in herbal medicine to purify the blood, and in poultices to relieve inflammation. It is also high in Vitamin C and young leaves and roots are edible.

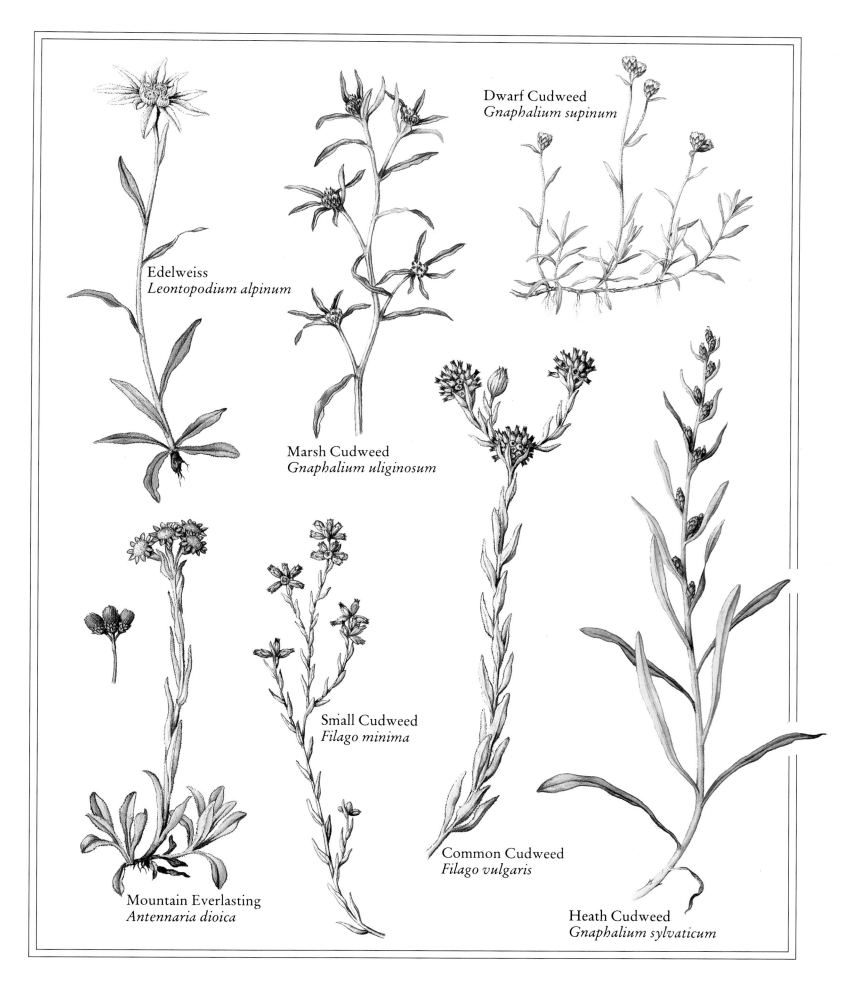

Edelweiss
Leontopodium alpinum

Dwarf Cudweed
Gnaphalium supinum

Marsh Cudweed
Gnaphalium uliginosum

Small Cudweed
Filago minima

Common Cudweed
Filago vulgaris

Mountain Everlasting
Antennaria dioica

Heath Cudweed
Gnaphalium sylvaticum

Both Burdocks are weeds of waste places and roadsides, in fields and open woods. Lesser Burdock is common throughout Europe and the British Isles. Greater Burdock is scattered across Europe north to southern Scandinavia, and also in lowland areas of England and Wales. It is absent from Scotland and much of northern England, rare in Ireland. Lesser Burdock grows to about 1.2m (4ft) tall, whereas Greater Burdock reaches 1.5m (5ft). Both form branched, bushy plants with furrowed, reddish, often cottony stems, and large, long-stalked, pointed-ovate and rather heart-shaped lower leaves, the leaves becoming smaller and less heart-shaped higher up the plant, those of Lesser Burdock rather narrower. Their flower heads have red-purple, tubular florets and hooked bracts making up the involucre. In Lesser Burdock the flower heads are generally less than 2.5cm (1in) across and borne in tight clusters on short stalks in the leaf axils; in Greater Burdock the heads are generally 3–4cm (1¼–1½in) across and borne in loose clusters on long stalks. The fruits are the hooked 'burs', which cling to animal fur and to clothing; those of Greater Burdock are straw-coloured and wide open, while those of Lesser Burdock are darker and closed at the top. Their purpose is to ensure the dispersal of the plants.

Woolly Burdock, *Arctium tomentosum*, is quite similar to Greater Burdock, but its numerous flower heads have distinctive involucres covered with cobwebby hairs. It grows in hedgerows and woodland margins, on roadsides and riverbanks across much of Europe but is generally absent from the British Isles, found there only as an occasional casual.

Many of the most common **Thistles** belong to two genera, *Carduus* and *Cirsium*. There are about 120 *Carduus* species altogether, with about 45 in Europe; and about 150 *Cirsium* species, with 65 or so in Europe. Several are considered to be troublesome weeds. They are more or less spiny plants, with alternate toothed or divided leaves, usually with prickles on their margins. Their flower heads are formed only of disk florets cupped in an involucre formed of overlapping, spiny bracts. Most species have red or purple flowers, others have white or yellow ones. One of the easiest ways to distinguish between the two genera is to look at the achenes. In *Carduus* species the hairs on the achenes are simple and unbranched, while in *Cirsium* species, the hairs on the achenes are feathery. A hand lens may be required to see this clearly.

Musk Thistle, *Carduus nutans*, is a biennial, like many of the thistles, with a rosette of wavy, spiny leaves in the first year and an erect, cottony flowering stem in the second. This grows up to 1m (3ft) tall and is winged, with interrupted, narrow, spiny wings ending some distance below the flower heads. The stem leaves are deeply lobed, with wavy, spiny margins and woolly veins beneath. The flower heads are large and drooping, solitary or borne in small clusters at the tops of the stems, formed of purple disk florets and surrounded by large, reflexed, spine-tipped bracts. They are followed by clusters of achenes with long, whitish hairs. Musk Thistles grow in waste and grassy places, in fields and pastures (where it is considered a weed), and on roadsides throughout Europe north to southern Scandinavia, and in England, Wales and southern Scotland. The name of Musk Thistle is a very old one and refers to the scent of the plant when warmed by the sun.

Welted Thistle, *Carduus acanthoides*, is another biennial, with a rosette of wavy-lobed, spiny leaves in the first year and a tall, branched flowering stem in the second, reaching 120cm (4ft) in height. The stems have uninterrupted, narrow, spiny wings running along their length, ending just beneath the flower heads. The stem leaves are wavy and lobed, with weak spines on their margins and their bases running into the wings. The reddish-purple flower heads are borne in dense clusters at the tops of the stems; they are smaller than those of the Musk Thistle, held erect over involucres formed of many linear, spine-tipped bracts. Welted Thistle grows in damp, grassy places, beside rivers, on roadsides and in hedgerows in lowland areas of England, Wales and southern Scotland, scattered in Ireland and in Europe north to southern Scandinavia. In many places it is treated as a weed.

Slender Thistle, *Carduus tenuiflorus*, may be annual or biennial, has a branched stem which grows up to 120cm (4ft) tall with continuous spiny wings along the whole length, and wavy-lobed, spiny-margined leaves, their bases running into the wings. Its flowers are much smaller than those of Welted Thistle, with pale purple-red florets over cylindrical involucres; they are borne in dense terminal clusters. This plant grows in dry, grassy and waste places, and on roadsides, especially near the sea, in western Europe, England and Wales north to southern Scotland, and in Ireland.

Creeping Thistle, *Cirsium arvense* (p. 193), is an aggressive weed, forming spreading colonies in arable land and pastures, in open woods, waste places, paths and roadsides, creeping by means of its far-ranging lateral roots throughout Europe and the British Isles. It can be difficult to eradicate since every piece of root left in the ground can form a new plant. The colonies are formed of many erect, branched, unwinged stems growing up to 1.5m (5ft) tall, with wavy, lobed, spiny-edged leaves. The pale purple flower heads are solitary or borne in small clusters in the axils of the upper leaves, male and female heads usually on separate plants. Many of the colonies are sterile, even though they appear to produce an abundance of the fluffy, brown-haired fruits; very few of these contain viable seed. Only when female plants are growing near male plants are fertile seeds produced.

Spear Thistle, *Cirsium vulgare* (p. 193), is another weed found in gardens, waste places, and on roadsides, especially on calcareous or base-rich soils, throughout the British Isles and Europe. This one spreads by seed rather than by creeping roots for it is a biennial plant; it forms a large rosette of deeply divided, wavy, spine-tipped leaves in the first year and a flowering

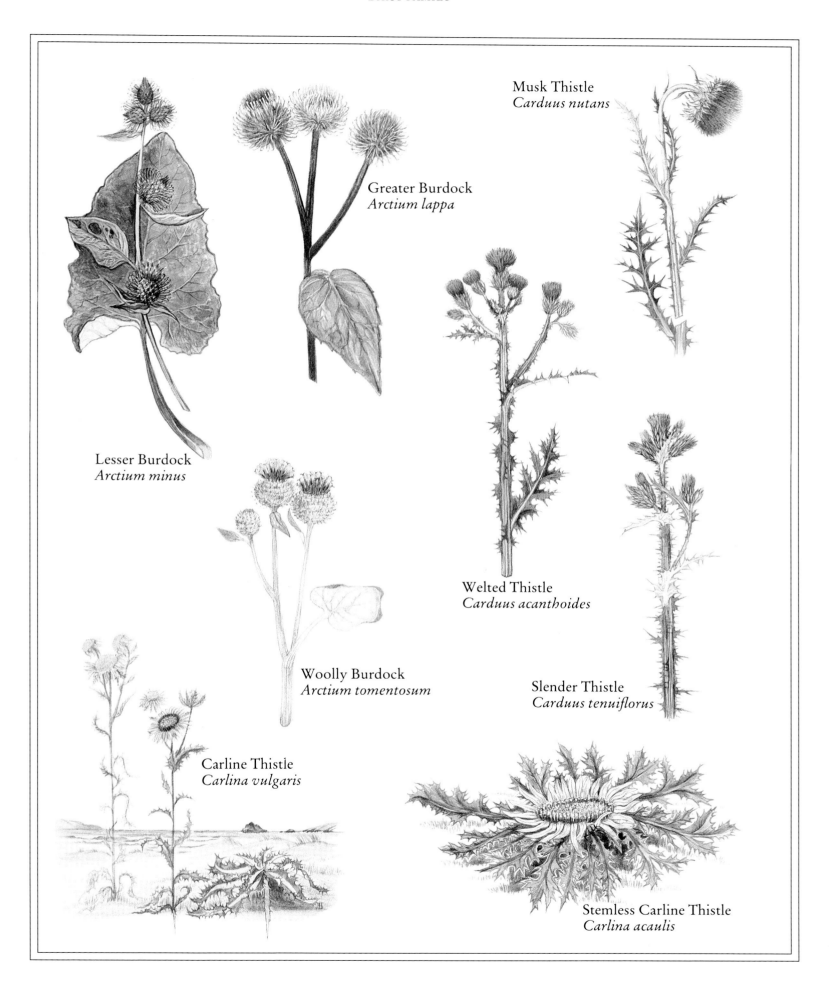

Greater Burdock
Arctium lappa

Musk Thistle
Carduus nutans

Lesser Burdock
Arctium minus

Welted Thistle
Carduus acanthoides

Woolly Burdock
Arctium tomentosum

Slender Thistle
Carduus tenuiflorus

Carline Thistle
Carlina vulgaris

Stemless Carline Thistle
Carlina acaulis

stem in the second, growing up 1.5m (5ft) in height. The stem is furrowed and cottony, with interrupted, spiny wings running along its length. Its many leaves are large, deeply lobed and spine-tipped, with shorter spines on the upper surface. The flower heads are solitary or borne in small clusters on long stalks in the upper leaf axils; they are large and showy, with spiny involucres and red-purple florets. The flowers are followed by achenes with white hairs, borne away by the wind to colonize new areas.

Marsh Thistle, *Cirsium palustre*, resembles the Creeping Thistle to some extent, but it is a biennial and lacks creeping roots, its stems are interruptedly spiny-winged, its many flower heads are dark red-purple and its fruits have dirty white hairs. Marsh Thistles grow in damp places, in wet meadows and marshes, in woods and hedgerows throughout Europe and the British Isles.

Stemless Thistle, *Cirsium acaule*, is the one sprinkled in the short grassland of downs and limestone uplands of southern England, so that it is sometimes difficult to find a place to sit down. It forms flat rosettes of spiny, lobed leaves concealed among the grasses. In late summer the flowers appear, a single bright red-purple flowering head sitting in the centre of each rosette. This plant is no longer as common as it was at one time, since so many of the downs which once were grassy and sheep-grazed now grow wheat; it is found across much of Europe, mainly in southern and eastern England in Great Britain, not at all in Ireland.

Melancholy Thistle, *Cirsium helenioides*, is rather different in appearance to many other thistles. It is another colonial plant, with creeping underground stems and a patch of erect, cottony, very leafy stems up to 120cm (4ft) tall. But the leaves are broadly lance-shaped, thin and flaccid, white-felted beneath with softly prickly margins, the upper ones with bases that clasp the stem. There is a solitary flower head at the top of each stem, the florets red-purple, the involucre broadly egg-shaped with purple-tipped bracts. This plant grows in hills and mountains, beside streams, in damp meadows and in open woods across much of Europe, in northern England and Scotland, less commonly in north Wales.

Cabbage Thistle, *Cirsium oleraceum*, is another less typical thistle, a perennial plant, with erect stems up to 120cm (4ft) tall, the stems ribbed but unwinged and often unbranched. The leaves are thin and greenish-yellow with weakly spiny margins, the lower ones pinnately lobed, the upper ones pointed-ovate with bases clasping the stems. The uppermost leaves form cups concealing the clusters of yellowish-white flower heads produced in the latter half of summer. Cabbage Thistle grows in marshes and wet flushes, wet meadows and woods, and beside streams across most of central Europe, except Spain and Portugal, and it is not native to the British Isles. However, it has been introduced into a few scattered localities in Great Britain and Ireland.

Scotch Thistle or Cotton Thistle, *Onopordon acanthium*, is similar to some of the *Cirsium* species, a large biennial plant with erect, broadly spine-winged, white-cottony stems up to 1.5m (5ft) tall. It has large, prickly-margined leaves near the base of the stem and solitary flower heads terminating the many branches at the top of the stem. The heads are purple and cupped in rounded involucres of spiny bracts. This plant grows in waste places and fields, on roadsides and in hedge-banks throughout Europe, and has been introduced into Great Britain, where it is scattered in England and Wales but rare in Scotland. It was given the name of Cotton Thistle because of the 'cotton' which was collected from its stems and used to stuff mattresses and pillows. However, its name of Scotch Thistle is curious, since it does not grow in Scotland!

Milk Thistle, *Silybum marianum*, is native to the Mediterranean region and southeastern Europe, but is also naturalized in waste places, in cultivated land and on roadsides throughout central Europe, and in lowland areas of Great Britain as far north as central Scotland. It is rare in Ireland. Milk Thistle is an annual or biennial plant, with a rosette of pale green, shiny, white-mottled leaves, lobed in shape and with spiny margins. The erect stem grows up to 120cm (4ft) tall, has smaller clasping leaves, and in early summer it produces large, solitary, nodding flower heads, with red-purple florets. The plant is used in herb medicine for the treatment of liver complaints and at one time it was thought to increase the flow of milk in nursing mothers, hence Milk Thistle.

Blessed Thistle, *Cnicus benedictus* (p. 000), is a distinctive plant, its flower heads quite unlike those of other thistles. It forms a branched, brown stem up to 50cm (20in) tall, with many lobed, spiny-margined, white-veined leaves. A single yellow flower head is produced at the top of each stem branch; the head is cupped in several rows of bracts, green and white-veined with spreading spines at their tips—it is the bracts that make the flower heads look so strange. This is a Mediterranean plant, introduced into central Europe, growing in dry, sandy places and found occasionally as a casual in Great Britain. It was probably introduced as a medicinal plant, as people in the Middle Ages thought it a cure for all ills. It is still used to treat liver and digestive disorders.

Alpine Saw-wort, *Saussurea alpina* (p. 195), is an alpine plant found in rock crevices, on cliffs and ridges in the mountains of Scandinavia and central Europe, also in the islands and mountains of Scotland, northern England, north Wales and northern Ireland, and in the Carpathians. It is a perennial, with short, creeping stems and many rosettes of ovate to lance-shaped, non-spiny leaves, white-cottony beneath like the stem leaves. The plants flower in late summer, producing flower heads in dense clusters at the tops of leafy stems, 45cm (18in) tall at most. Each flower head is white at the base, purple at the tip; the heads are borne in ovoid involucres formed of woolly, purplish bracts.

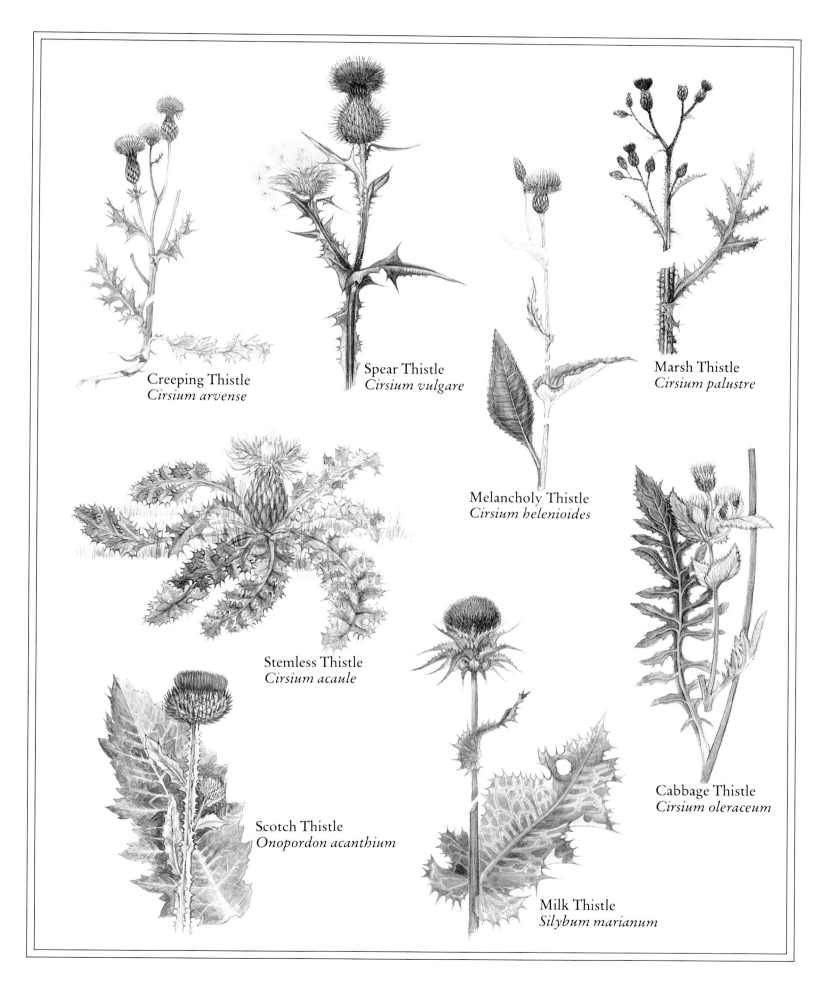

Creeping Thistle
Cirsium arvense

Spear Thistle
Cirsium vulgare

Melancholy Thistle
Cirsium helenioides

Marsh Thistle
Cirsium palustre

Stemless Thistle
Cirsium acaule

Scotch Thistle
Onopordon acanthium

Milk Thistle
Silybum marianum

Cabbage Thistle
Cirsium oleraceum

Saw-wort, *Serratula tinctoria*, is a related plant found in damp grassland, in meadows and marshes, in woodland rides and margins, often growing in calcareous soils. It is scattered throughout Europe, England and Wales, found in a few places in southern Scotland and in one place in Ireland. This is a perennial, with a wiry, erect stem, branched near the top to bear several flower heads. Its leaves, both basal and those on the stems, are highly variable in their shape, from undivided to pinnately lobed, the lower ones with stalks, upper ones stalkless; however, all have fine, bristle-tipped teeth on their margins. The reddish-purple flower heads appear in late summer in involucres formed of chaffy scales. The fruits are hairy, each with many rows of rough, bristly hairs.

The genus *Centaurea* is a very large one, with about 600 species altogether, 200 of which are found in Europe, many in the Mediterranean region. They are often known as **Knapweeds** or Star-thistles, the name 'knapweed' coming from the appearance and hardness of the involucre, for it has the shape and hardness of a head ('knap' in Old English). Knapweeds may be annual or perennial plants, and are frequently rather tough, with alternate or basal leaves; often they have relatively few flower heads terminating the erect stems. Their flower heads are distinctive, with several series of dark bracts forming the involucre; the bracts may have papery edges or may be spine-tipped. The heads are formed entirely of conspicuous, tubular florets, pink or purple in many species. Some of the most attractive are grown in gardens; in the showiest of these the outermost florets are enlarged and may be dissected into linear segments.

Greater Knapweed, *Centaurea scabiosa*, is one of the most striking species, a perennial that grows in dry grassland, on rough banks and in hedgebanks, among rocks and on cliffs, usually on calcareous soils, throughout Europe and lowland areas of England and Wales, mainly in the centre in Ireland, rarely in Scotland. It is a perennial, with erect, grooved stems branching above the middle and growing up to 90cm (3ft) tall. Its dark green leaves are pinnately divided with oblong or linear segments, firm in texture and sparsely hairy beneath; its flower heads are reddish-purple, with the outer florets enlarged and much divided; and the bracts of the involucre are fringed with what look like brown or black horseshoe-shaped combs. The flowers appear in the latter half of summer. At one time this plant was used in herb medicine to treat wounds and bruises. Brown Knapweed, *C. jacea*, is mainly a Continental plant found occasionally in southern England. It is similar to Greater Knapweed, but its involucral bracts have pale brown tips with white comb-like margins.

Lesser Knapweed or Hardheads, *Centaurea nigra*, grows in similar places to Greater Knapweed—in dry grassland, on cliffs and among rocks, but on a wider variety of soils and in more disturbed places like roadsides and railway embankments; it is found throughout western Europe and the British Isles. It is another summer-flowering perennial, with tough, erect stems up to 60cm (2ft) tall, sinuate basal leaves and entire stem leaves, and red-purple flower heads, usually with the marginal florets the same as all the others, so that the flower heads are less showy than those of Greater Knapweed. The bracts of the involucre have triangular, brown or black fringed tips concealing the adjoining bracts.

Cornflower or Bluebottle, *Centaurea cyanus*, is a rather different member of the genus, a plant with a long history as an agricultural weed. It is often associated with Red Poppies and Corncockles and, like them, is now far less common in the wild than it was before the advent of modern farming methods. However, since it is also a favourite garden plant, it is unlikely to become extinct. In may still be found on roadsides and waste places, less often in cornfields, throughout Europe and Great Britain, but is rare. Cornflower is an annual plant, with an erect, wiry, grooved stem up to 90cm (3ft) tall, many slender branches and a cottony texture, especially when young. It has linear leaves and numerous flower heads with tubular florets, mostly blue but also sometimes in shades of pink and white, especially in garden varieties. The marginal florets are much enlarged and conspicuous. The involucre of each flower head is bell-shaped and the bracts have fringed, membranous edges.

The **Star-thistle**, *Centaurea calcitrapa*, is a different sort of plant, a much-branched biennial or perennial with many flower heads, each with a ruff of long, spine-tipped bracts beneath. Its grooved stems grow up to 60cm (2ft) tall and have a characteristic way of branching, each stiffly wavy branch arising from just beneath a flower head, so that younger flower heads overtop the older ones, and the older ones look as if they are growing on short side stems. The leaves are rough and deeply pinnately lobed, with bristle-pointed teeth on the margins, becoming simpler higher up the stems. The flower heads are formed of tubular red-purple florets, their involucral bracts ending in spreading, yellowish spines with smaller spines at the base. Star-thistles are found in cultivated land and waste places across much of Europe, except the north; they are sometimes found as casuals in southern England.

Yellow Star-thistle or St Barnaby's Thistle, *Centaurea solstitialis*, is an annual plant, its stiff, white-cottony stems much branched, with wavy wings running along their length and their leaves with bases merging into the wings. The lower leaves are pinnately lobed, the upper ones lance-shaped; all are white-cottony in appearance. The solitary flower heads are yellow, with an involucre formed of spine-tipped bracts, the terminal spines long and spreading, yellow in colour. This star-thistle comes originally from the Mediterranean region and southeastern Europe; it has become naturalized in cultivated land and waste places in central Europe, and may be found occasionally in southern and eastern England.

Members of the **Chicory tribe**, the Cichorieae, have basal or alternate leaves and flower heads formed entirely of herma-

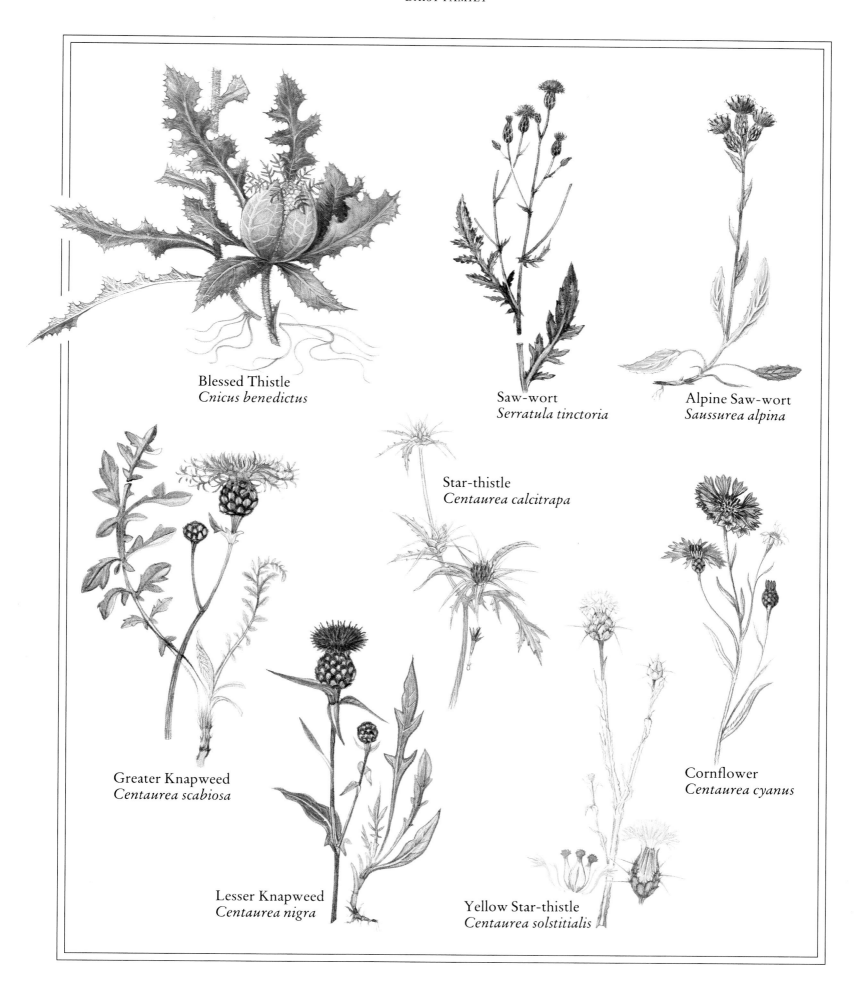

Blessed Thistle
Cnicus benedictus

Saw-wort
Serratula tinctoria

Alpine Saw-wort
Saussurea alpina

Star-thistle
Centaurea calcitrapa

Greater Knapweed
Centaurea scabiosa

Cornflower
Centaurea cyanus

Lesser Knapweed
Centaurea nigra

Yellow Star-thistle
Centaurea solstitialis

phrodite florets. The fruits often have a pappus of many hairs. Many plants in this tribe are common weeds.

Chicory, *Cichorium intybus*, grows wild in rough pastures and on roadsides, in fields and waste places throughout Europe and the British Isles, most commonly in lowland areas and on calcareous soils, becoming less common in Scotland and Ireland. It is also cultivated for its young shoots, which are blanched and eaten as a vegetable and in salads. The long tap roots are ground, roasted and added to coffee. Chicory is a striking plant, with its bright blue flowers catching the eye even from a moving car. It is a perennial, with an erect, branched stem up to 120cm (4ft) tall, alternate, wavy-toothed leaves forming a basal rosette, and similar clasping ones arranged alternately on the stem, and with many blue flower heads composed entirely of strap-shaped florets. They grow in clusters in the axils of the upper leaves.

Nipplewort, *Lapsana communis*, is an annual plant with erect, leafy stems growing up to 120cm (4ft) tall, the upper half branching into a complex inflorescence. The lower leaves are thin, each with a large terminal lobe and several small lobes or a wing near the base; the upper leaves are lance-shaped. The flower heads are small and numerous, formed of ray florets, lemon yellow in colour and borne in many clusters for much of the summer. Nipplewort grows as a weed in waste places and on roadsides, in woodland margins and hedgerows, on walls, in gardens and cultivated land throughout Europe and the British Isles. At one time it was used in herbal medicine, the name 'nipplewort' coming from the belief that it was effective in treating sore nipples. Its young leaves are edible; they can be eaten raw in salads or cooked like spinach.

Cat's-ear, *Hypochoeris radicata*, may be mistaken for a dandelion, but is a hairy plant; it flowers in early summer like a dandelion but later than that plant, and its tough, solid flower stems fork to bear several flower heads. There are small, dark bracts on the stems. The flower heads are formed of many bright yellow ray florets, the outer rays greenish-grey beneath; the heads are cupped in involucres formed of small, bristly, overlapping bracts. This is another common roadside plant found on grassy verges, also in meadows and pastures, on commons and stabilized sand-dunes, sometimes in gardens, throughout Europe and the British Isles. Smooth Cat's-ear, *H. glabra*, is a similar but annual plant, with more or less hairless leaves and smaller bright yellow flowers, opening wide only in sunlight. It grows in similar places across much of Europe, England and Wales but is far less common.

Autumnal Hawkbit, *Leontodon autumnalis*, resembles Cat's-ear. It is a perennial, has rosettes of more or less hairless, pinnately lobed leaves, the lobes deep and narrow, several solid stems forking near the top to bear yellow flower heads, small bracts on the flower stems and an involucre of overlapping bracts beneath each flower head. Cat's-ears and Autumnal Hawkbits are distinguished by botanical details, the receptacles of Cat's-ear flower heads being scaly, while those of Hawkbits are pitted and lack scales. One of the most obvious differences between these two species is that Autumnal Hawkbit flower heads are often streaked with red beneath instead of Cat's-ear green. Autumnal Hawkbits are common weeds of meadows and pastures, roadsides and other grassy places, found throughout Europe and the British Isles.

Rough Hawkbit, *Leontodon hispidus*, is another perennial, often forming several rosettes of wavy-toothed or pinnately lobed leaves, rough in texture from their many forked hairs. The flower stalks are unbranched, each bearing a solitary flower head opening from a drooping bud; the flowers are bright yellow in colour, the outermost ray florets often orange or reddish beneath. The involucre is formed of dark green, often blackish bracts. As in all Cat's-ears and Hawkbits, the flowers are followed by fruits with hairy parachutes, borne away by the wind to invade new areas. Rough Hawkbit grows in grassy places, in meadows and pastures, on rocky slopes and on roadsides, often on calcareous soils. It is found throughout Europe, in England, Wales and southern Scotland, in southern and central Ireland.

Bristly Ox-tongue, *Picris echioides*, has two distinctive features: the large, bristly, heart-shaped bracts which cup each flower head, and the large, bristly hairs with swollen, whitish bases dotted over the leaves. This is an annual or biennial plant found on roadsides and hedgebanks, in fields and waste places, particularly on stiff, calcareous clay soils; it is probably native to the Mediterranean region, but has become naturalized in central Europe, in lowland areas of England and Wales, and in southern and central Ireland. It has stout, much-branched stems up to 90cm (3ft) tall, covered with rigid, bristly hairs, and has many lance-shaped leaves, those higher up the stems with clasping bases, all with coarsely toothed or wavy margins and rough with their characteristic hairs. The flower heads appear in summer and into autumn, formed solely of yellow ray florets and borne in dense clusters on short side stems. They are followed by fruits with white, feathery hairs which fall off when the fruits come to earth.

Hawkweed Ox-tongue, *Picris hieracioides*, is also rough with bristly hairs, but the hairs lack swollen bases. This is a biennial or perennial plant, with much-branched, spreading stems growing up to 90cm (3ft) tall; its rough, lance-shaped leaves have wavy margins, the lowest ones up to 20cm (8in) long, those higher up the stems smaller with clasping bases. The flowers have yellow ray florets but their involucres have normal-size bracts, the inner bracts bristly and the outer ones short and narrow, spreading or even reflexed, with dark hairs. The fruits have feathery, cream-coloured hairs. This plant grows in grassy places, on roadsides and walls, on rocky slopes and in vineyards, especially on calcareous soils, throughout Europe, in lowland areas of England and Wales, in parts of Ireland and as a casual in southeast Scotland.

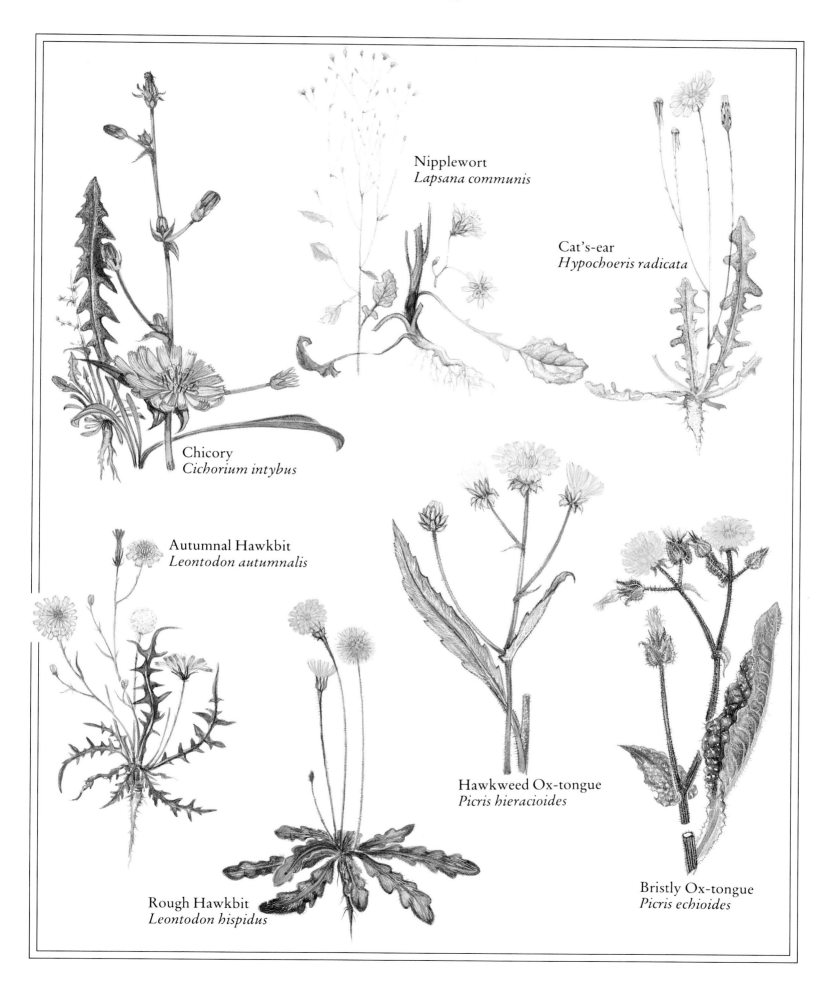

Nipplewort
Lapsana communis

Cat's-ear
Hypochoeris radicata

Chicory
Cichorium intybus

Autumnal Hawkbit
Leontodon autumnalis

Hawkweed Ox-tongue
Picris hieracioides

Bristly Ox-tongue
Picris echioides

Rough Hawkbit
Leontodon hispidus

Goatsbeard or Jack-go-to-bed-at-noon, *Tragopogon pratensis*, gets one common name from the long, silky hairs on the fruits, and the other from its flower heads which close up at lunch-time. It may grow as an annual or perennial, has a brown, cylindrical tap root and a rosette of long, linear leaves, white-veined, long-pointed at the tips and with somewhat sheathing bases. The flowering stem is little branched, about 60cm (2ft) tall, with many leaves like those of the basal rosette but even longer. The flower heads are borne at the tops of the stems; they are large and showy, formed of bright yellow, strap-shaped ray florets, with a series of slender bracts beneath the head, longer than the florets and projecting beyond them. The fruiting heads are spectacular—large balls of achenes, each with a feathery parachute, the hairs from one achene interwoven with those adjacent. Goatsbeard grows in grassy places, in meadows and pastures, on roadsides and in waste places, sometimes on stabilized sand-dunes, throughout much of Europe, in lowland areas of Great Britain and in central Ireland. Salsify, *T. porrifolius*, is a related plant grown for its tap roots (known as White Salsify) across much of Europe; it comes originally from the Mediterranean region. It is similar to Goatsbeard but has purple flower heads.

Viper's Grass, *Scorzonera humilis*, is widespread in Europe but is nevertheless a rare plant, found in only two localities in Britain: Dorset and Warwick. On the Continent it grows in acid soils, in marshes and wet moorlands, in pine woods and heaths. This small perennial plant has a clump of upright, linear leaves, woolly when young but losing most of their hairs as they age, growing from a shortened cylindrical stem at the base, which is black and scaly in appearance. Its flowering stems grow up to 50cm (20in) tall; they are unbranched with few leaves and bear solitary flower heads at the top. The heads are formed of yellow ray florets cupped in an involucre with many rows of blunt, overlapping bracts. The fruits which follow have several rows of dirty white, feathery hairs. Viper's Grass is one of about 25 *Scorzonera* species found in Europe. Black Salsify, *S. hispanica*, is a similar plant found in grassy places and scrub in central and southeastern Europe, but also cultivated in many areas for its fleshy tap root.

Lettuces are *Lactuca* species. Garden Lettuces are varieties of *L. sativa*, a plant which probably originated in Asia, but which has been cultivated for so long in so many different countries that its origins are obscure. There are about 16 species in Europe; they have alternate leaves and usually many flower heads in large compound inflorescences, some with yellow flowers, others with blue ones. **Prickly Lettuce**, *L. serriola*, grows in waste places and on walls, sometimes on stabilized sand-dunes, across much of Europe, in southern England and Wales. It is an annual, often overwintering plant, the leaves of its rosette more or less oblong in shape, often with wavy margins. Like those on the stems, these leaves are prickly on the margins and on the veins beneath. The stems grow up to

2m (6ft) tall and are very leafy, the upper leaves with clasping bases; when the plants grow in full sunlight, the leaves are all held vertically in the north/south plane (so that this species is sometimes called Compass Plant). The stems end in large, branched inflorescences of small, pale yellow flower heads, appearing in the latter half of summer and followed by clusters of parachuted seeds.

Wall Lettuce, *Mycelis muralis*, is a related perennial plant, with an erect stem up to 1m (3ft) tall, pinnately lobed leaves, the lower ones with winged stalks, the upper ones simpler, often reddish with clasping bases, and large, spreading inflorescences of small yellow flowers cupped in cylindrical involucres. Each head contains only five ray florets. Plants grow in walls and rocks, in hedgebanks and waste places, cultivated land and open woods, often on calcareous or base-rich soils, throughout Europe, England and Wales, more rarely in Scotland and Ireland.

Many **Sow-thistles**, also known as Milk-thistles, look like a cross between a thistle and a dandelion, but belong to the genus *Sonchus*. **Prickly Sow-thistle**, *S. asper*, and **Smooth Sow-thistle**, *S. oleraceus*, are common annual weeds of cultivated land, roadsides and waste places, found throughout the British Isles and much of Europe. They form branched, hollow stems up to 1.5m (5ft) tall. Prickly Sow-thistle has very prickly leaves, the lower ones with bases which curl around the stems, and few to several flower heads terminating the stems. Smooth Sow-thistle has weakly spiny leaves, the lower ones with bases which clasp but do not curl around the stem, and many flower heads. At the beginning of the flowering season its flower clusters are a tight mass of buds, but they gradually open out to form a large, branching inflorescence.

Field Milk-thistle, *Sonchus arvensis*, is a similar but perennial plant, forming spreading colonies of erect stems up to 1.5m (5ft) tall, with spiny-margined leaves, the lowermost lobed but the upper ones simple. It has open clusters of yellow flower heads, the stalks and involucres all covered with black, glandular hairs. This plant grows in a variety of places, in arable land and waste ground, beside streams, on the drift lines of brackish marshes, in sand-dunes and on shingle banks on the coast throughout Europe and the British Isles. Its young leaves are edible in salads or cooked as a potherb, provided the spines are removed.

Blue Sow-thistle, *Cicerbita alpina*, is a rare plant in Britain, found only in a few places in the Scottish mountains; however, it also grows in moist places in the mountains of France, Germany and Scandinavia. This is a perennial plant, with a stout, furrowed, often branched stem growing up to 2m (6ft) tall, bristly near the base and with red glandular hairs towards the top. The lowest leaves are pinnately lobed, each with a large, terminal lobe and smaller lobes near the base, and with winged stalks; the leaves become successively simpler higher up the stem and develop clasping bases, until the topmost leaves are

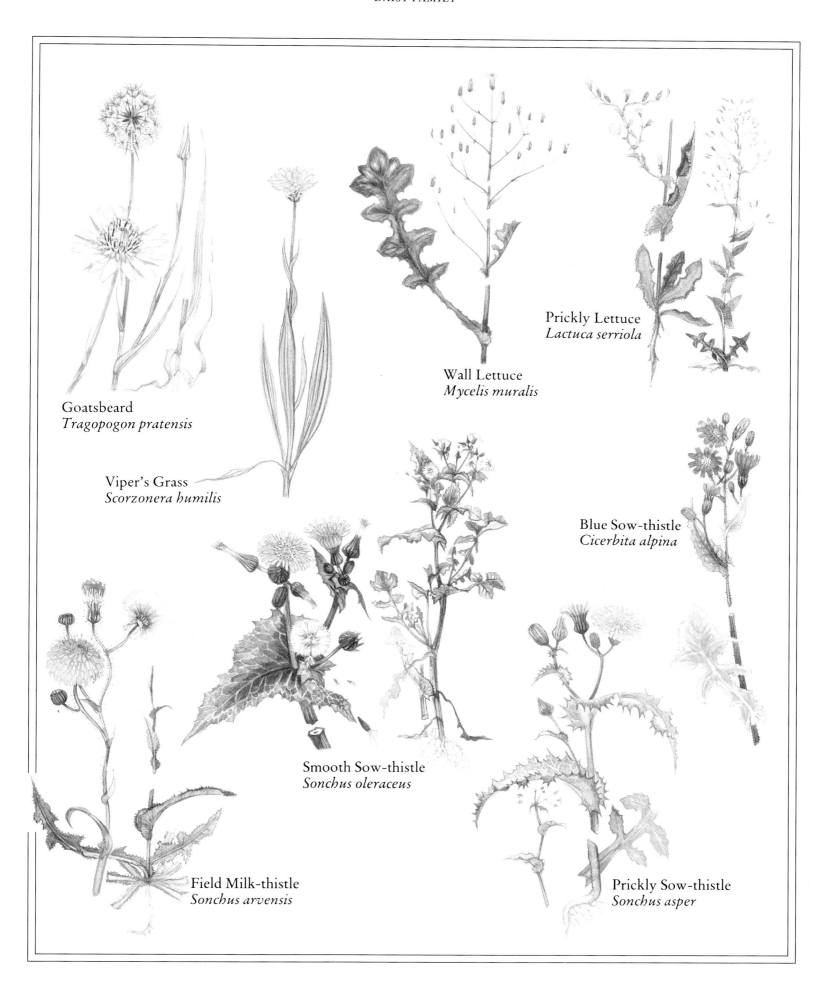

Goatsbeard
Tragopogon pratensis

Viper's Grass
Scorzonera humilis

Wall Lettuce
Mycelis muralis

Prickly Lettuce
Lactuca serriola

Blue Sow-thistle
Cicerbita alpina

Smooth Sow-thistle
Sonchus oleraceus

Field Milk-thistle
Sonchus arvensis

Prickly Sow-thistle
Sonchus asper

lance-shaped. The stems end in racemes of pale blue flower heads, each one formed of ray florets with purplish-green, glandular-hairy involucres.

Hawkweeds, *Hieracium* species, are a huge group, with somewhere between 10,000 and 20,000 species, mainly found in the temperate and Arctic regions of the northern hemisphere. It is impossible to be precise about the number of species in this group because many of them produce seeds apomictically, that is without pollination. This results in the formation of closed populations of plants, all descended from one individual. Since such a group is separated from all others by this process, it could be said to be a species. Hawkweeds are perennial plants, either with most of their leaves in a basal rosette or with leafy, erect stems. Their flowers are borne in flower heads composed of ray florets, like those of dandelions, but each erect stem is branched and carries several to many heads; most species have yellow flowers. Beneath each head the involucre is formed of bracts in overlapping rows.

Leafy Hawkweed, *Hieracium umbellatum*, grows in open woods, in grassland and heaths throughout lowland areas of Europe and the British Isles. It has a slender, leafy stem up to 80cm (30in) tall, with many narrow, linear, slightly toothed leaves and a branched cluster of yellow flower heads at the top. This is one of many species with this form. **Common Hawkweed**, *H. vulgatum*, by contrast, has a rosette of basal leaves and only 2–4 leaves on the stem. The basal leaves are softly hairy, oblong to lance-shaped, often with toothed margins and purplish beneath; the stem leaves are similar but smaller. The 1–20 small heads grow at the top of the stem. This is the commonest Hawkweed in Scotland and northern England, growing in grassy and rocky places, woods and heaths; it is also found in Ireland and northern and central Europe.

Mouse-ear Hawkweed, *Hieracium pilosella*, is rather different from most Hawkweeds and is separated from them into another subgenus. It forms spreading tufts of leaves, each rosette producing creeping stems which radiate out to form new plants at their tips. The leaves are usually lance-shaped and densely hairy beneath, with whitish, star-shaped hairs. The solitary flower heads are borne on leafless, stiffly hairy, erect stems, often only 15cm (6in) tall; each is lemon yellow in colour, quite different from the brassy yellow of most hawkweeds. The bracts which form the involucre are covered in black-tipped hairs. This plant grows in dry, grassy places, pastures and commons, on banks and walls, among rocks and in sand-dunes throughout Europe and much of the British Isles.

In the same group with Mouse-ear Hawkweed is a plant with some fascinating names. **Orange Hawkweed**, *Hieracium aurantiacum*, is also called Grim the Collier and Fox-and-cubs, the latter name describing its habit of spreading into mats, the mother plant putting out short runners from which young plants develop all around the original. This plant grows in meadows and among rocks in mountain ranges across Europe. It is grown in gardens in Great Britain, behaving as an aggressive weed in many places, becoming naturalized in waste places and roadsides, on walls and railway embankments. It forms rosettes of elliptical, hairy leaves and produces glowing brick-red flower heads on leafless stalks in summer.

Hawk's-beards, *Crepis* species, are similar to the hawkweeds, but there are only about 200 of them, mainly from Europe and Asia. **Smooth Hawk's-beard**, *C. capillaris*, grows in grassland, in waste places, on roadsides, walls and heaths throughout Europe and the British Isles. It is typical of many *Crepis* species, with sinuately lobed leaves, the largest in a basal rosette, the stem leaves smaller and simpler. From each rosette grows one or more stems up to 90cm (3ft) tall, leafy near the base, branching near the top to form erect inflorescences of many yellow flower heads. This species is an annual, almost hairless plant. The achenes which follow the flowers bear parachutes formed of many rows of soft, white hairs. This last feature serves to distinguish the *Crepis* from the *Hieracium* species, for the achenes of the latter have only one or two rows of brittle, pale brownish hairs.

Marsh Hawk's-beard, *Crepis paludosa*, is a perennial plant found in wet meadows and woods, beside streams and in fens in central and southern Europe, in Scotland and northern England, north Wales and Ireland. It has a rosette of toothed, ovate or lance-shaped leaves with winged stalks, and erect, leafy flowering stems growing up to 90cm (3ft) tall. The stem leaves become smaller higher up and they are stalkless with clasping bases. Plants flower in late summer, forming a branched cluster of yellow flower heads on straight, slender stalks at the tops of the flowering stems; each head is cupped in an involucre of dark bracts, sticky with black, glandular hairs. The heads are followed by clumps of achenes with brittle, brownish hairs.

Dandelions, *Taraxacum officinale*, are common weeds found throughout the temperate regions of the world, including Europe and the British Isles, growing in gardens and waste places, in cultivated ground and on roadsides, in moist or dry grassland, walls and sand-dunes, in acid and calcareous soils. Dandelions have persistent tap roots from which grow rosettes of wavy-lobed leaves; in early summer they bear several yellow flower heads, each one at the top of a hollow, slightly succulent stalk. Both stalk and leaves exude milky juice if broken. The flower heads are followed by 'clocks' of parachuted seeds which drift in thousands with a slight wind, enabling the plants to spread rapidly. This is another apomictic species, so closed colonies develop from a single individual; such colonies vary from one area to another in the shape of the leaves, in the colour of the stems (from green to red) and in the colour of the fruits. Dandelions are edible; their leaves, although bitter, make a useful addition to salads; their roots can be roasted and ground to make a caffeine-free substitute for coffee; and their flowers can be made into wine.

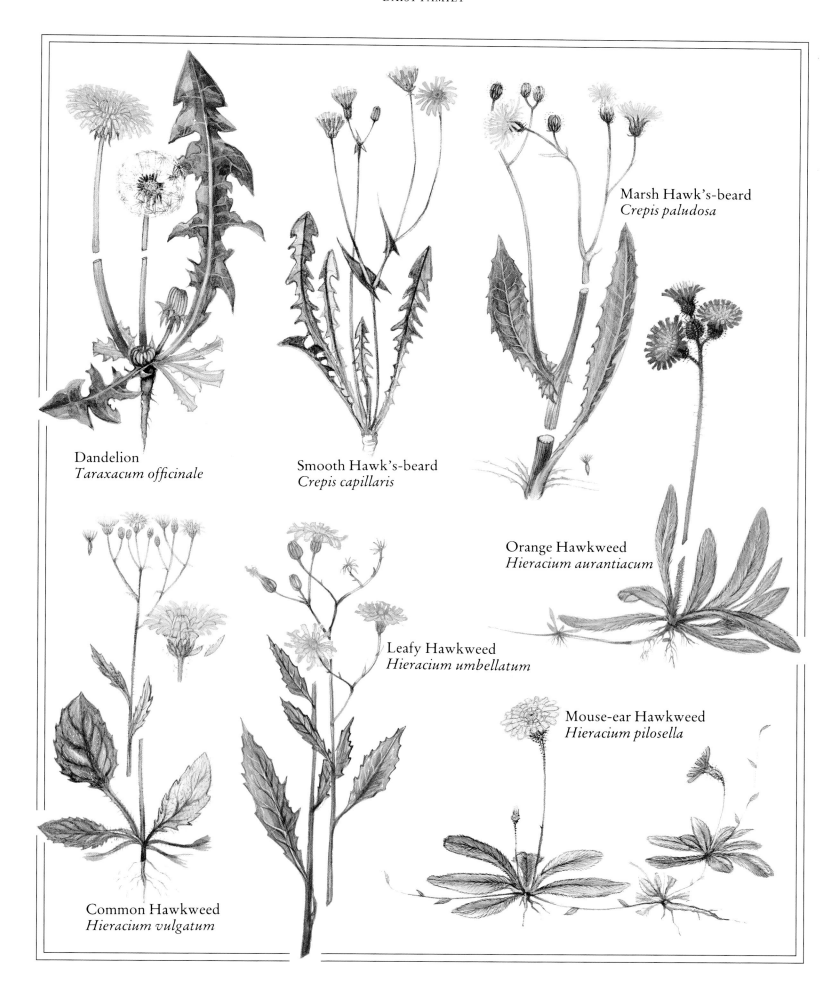

Dandelion
Taraxacum officinale

Smooth Hawk's-beard
Crepis capillaris

Marsh Hawk's-beard
Crepis paludosa

Orange Hawkweed
Hieracium aurantiacum

Leafy Hawkweed
Hieracium umbellatum

Mouse-ear Hawkweed
Hieracium pilosella

Common Hawkweed
Hieracium vulgatum

Water-plantain family
Alismataceae

A small family with 13 genera and about 90 species, mainly from temperate and tropical regions of the northern hemisphere. They are herbaceous, aquatic or wetland plants that bear an extraordinary resemblance to the buttercups; some experts consider the two families to be related, even though buttercups are dicotyledons and water-plantains monocotyledons. Other experts consider their resemblance to be because both families are primitive within their respective groups, and the features they have in common are primitive features.

Family features The flowers are usually hermaphrodite and are regular, often borne in whorls or racemes or in compound inflorescences. Each flower has six free perianth segments arranged in two whorls: the outer three are green and sepal-like, overlapping and persistent; the inner three are petal-like and overlapping, and soon fall. There are usually 3–6 stamens and many free carpels forming a superior ovary. The fruit is a cluster of achenes. The leaves are long-stalked, often basal with open, sheathing bases and linear to ovate, often arrow-shaped blades. The leaves have prominent veins.

There are three Water-plantains, *Alisma* species, in Europe. **Common Water-plantain**, *A. plantago-aquatica*, is found throughout Europe and much of the British Isles, becoming rare in the north; it grows in muddy places or in shallow water, beside ponds, slow-moving streams and ditches, its roots spreading into the mud at the bottom and its leaves and flowering stems emerging into the air to reach 1m (3ft) tall at most. It forms a clump of long-stalked leaves with elliptical or ovate blades; and in the early part of summer its branched flowering stalk bears numerous small, white or pale pink flowers in many umbel-like clusters. The flowers are followed by flattened, disk-like fruits borne in rings.

Lance-leaved Water-plantain, *Alisma lanceolatum*, is also found in ditches and ponds, scattered throughout much of Europe and the British Isles, becoming rare in the north; it is almost absent from Scotland. It has narrow, lance-shaped leaves but is otherwise similar to Common Water-plantain.

Lesser Water-plantain, *Baldellia ranunculoides*, is a much smaller plant, with a tuft of long-stalked, almost linear leaves, their stalks merging into the blades, and leafless flowering stems 20cm (8in) tall at most. The plants flower in summer, each stem forming an umbel (occasionally two whorls) of white flowers followed by rounded heads of achenes. Lesser Water-plantain grows beside streams, ponds and in ditches scattered throughout much of the British Isles, becoming rare in Scotland, in western Europe as far north as Norway.

Floating Water-plantain, *Luronium natans*, by contrast, has floating stems, the lower parts of the stems sinking and forming tufts of linear leaves, the higher parts forming floating leaves, their blades ovate or elliptical in shape. The plants flower in the latter half of summer, the white flowers borne in umbels on long stalks growing from the leaf axils and projecting above the surface of the water. The flowers are followed by hemispherical heads of achenes. This plant is not common, growing only in lakes and tarns with acid water, but is increasing in numbers; it is found in north Wales and central England, western and central Europe.

Starfruit, *Damasonium alisma*, is found in ponds and ditches in western Europe; this is not a common plant and it is rare in Britain, found only in a few localities in southeastern England. It forms tufts of long-stalked leaves, rooted in the substrate at the bottom of the water, their ovate or heart-shaped blades submerged or floating on the surface. The flowers are white with a yellow spot at the base of each petal, borne in whorls on leafless flowering stalks above the water surface. The name of Starfruit comes from the appearance of the fruits, for the carpels are arranged in six-pointed stars.

Arrowhead, *Sagittaria sagittifolia*, grows in shallow water at the edges of ponds and slow-moving rivers, in canals and ditches, scattered throughout much of Europe and England, more rarely in Wales and Ireland. This is a perennial plant, overwintering by means of tubers formed at the ends of long, undermud stems. It has long-stalked leaves, those beneath the water linear and translucent, those emerging from the water with dark green, arrow-shaped blades. In summer its flowering stalks grow up to 90cm (3ft) tall and bear whorls of white flowers, male flowers near the top and smaller female flowers lower down, followed by heads of dark achenes. The flowers have purple blotches at the base of each petal.

Flowering Rush family
Butomaceae

There is only one species in this family, the **Flowering Rush**, *Butomus umbellatus*. This is a very beautiful and uncommon plant, decreasing in numbers as its wetland habitats disappear or are degraded. It grows in ditches and ponds, or on the edges of canals and slow-moving rivers, throughout Europe, in England and Ireland, rarely in Wales. It is a perennial with short, creeping rhizomes, linear, twisted, three-angled leaves and separate flowering stems in the latter half of summer, both stems and leaves emerging above the water surface. The flowers are borne in a terminal umbel subtended by several bracts. Each has six perianth segments, pink in colour with darker veins, the three outer segments smaller than the inner ones and stained with green on the outside; there are nine red stamens and six carpels in the centre of each bloom. They are followed by reddish-purple follicles that are partly fused together at the base.

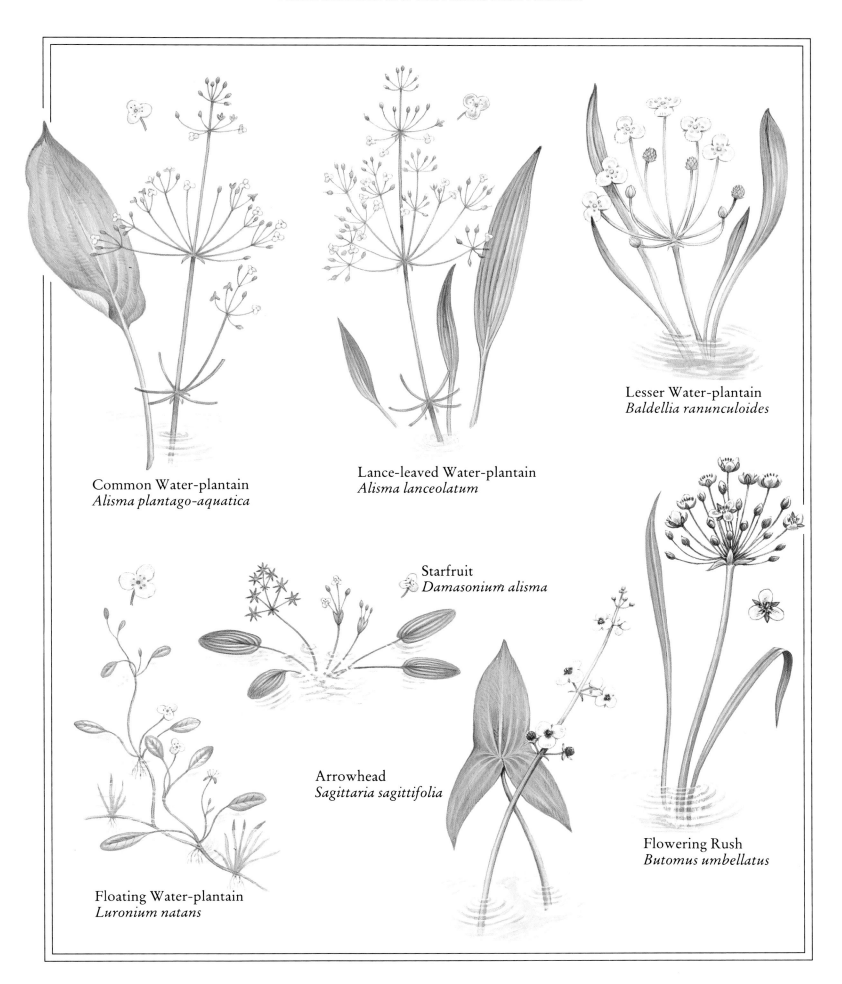

Common Water-plantain
Alisma plantago-aquatica

Lance-leaved Water-plantain
Alisma lanceolatum

Lesser Water-plantain
Baldellia ranunculoides

Starfruit
Damasonium alisma

Arrowhead
Sagittaria sagittifolia

Flowering Rush
Butomus umbellatus

Floating Water-plantain
Luronium natans

Frogbit family
Hydrocharitaceae

A small family of partly or wholly submerged aquatic plants, with about 16 genera and 80 species, found mainly in warmer parts of the world with few in temperate regions. Most grow in fresh water but some grow in the sea, a rare thing among flowering plants.

Family features The flowers are borne in a spathe formed of one or two bracts; where there are two bracts they are opposite and may or may not be joined. The flowers are regular and may be hermaphrodite but are more often unisexual. Male flowers are usually numerous while females are solitary. Each flower has three outer, sepal-like perianth segments and usually three inner, petal-like perianth segments but these may be missing. There are one to many stamens in male flowers and an inferior ovary with one cell in female flowers. The fruits may be dry or fleshy. The leaves may be borne in crowded rosettes or grow on the stems.

Frogbit, *Hydrocharis morsus-ranae*, is a small floating plant, at first glance like a miniature water-lily. However, the whole plant floats, its round-bladed leaves floating on the surface of the water, its leaf-stalks growing from the crown of the plant just beneath the surface and its long roots drifting downwards. From each of these leaf rosettes grow long stems, rooting at the nodes and forming fresh rosettes, until a tangled mass of plants develops by the end of the summer. The plants overwinter by means of turions (winter buds) which develop on the ends of the stems in autumn, so that when the plant dies back, the turions sink to the bottom of the water, rising and forming new plants in spring. Frogbit flowers in the latter half of summer, the small white blooms appearing above the surface, either male or female on any one plant. It grows in ponds, ditches and in sheltered places in lakes, scattered across Europe and in England, mainly in the north in Wales and in central Ireland; it is not found in Scotland.

Water-soldier, *Stratiotes aloides*, is another aquatic, rosette-forming plant, but a much larger one with unexpected rosettes of stiff, upright leaves like those of an aloe, growing up to 20cm (8in) tall. Each leaf is three-angled with prickles on the margins. For much of the year the rosettes are submerged but they rise to the surface around midsummer to flower, projecting above the surface and producing white flowers in their centres, male flowers in umbels and females solitary. However, fruits do not always form (never in British plants), and the plants reproduce by short stems which grow laterally and then form new rosettes. Water Soldier grows in still or slow-moving waters, in ponds and ditches, reservoirs and broads, scattered throughout much of Europe and locally common in some places, mainly in eastern and southeastern England in the British Isles.

Canadian Pondweed, *Elodea canadensis*, was introduced to Europe as an oxygenating plant for garden ponds; it escaped into the wild and has become widely naturalized in still and slow-moving waters throughout most of the British Isles, in western and central Europe. This submerged plant has long stems and whorls of dark green, translucent leaves, usually borne in threes. The flowers are small and floating, with white or purple petals, the females on long stalks, the males usually breaking free; most British plants are female.

Pondweed family
Potamogetonaceae

A small family of aquatic plants, with 2 genera and about 100 species, found throughout the world in fresh water.

All but one of the species in this family belong to the genus *Potamogeton*, the **Pondweeds**. These water plants have creeping rhizomes and alternate leaves; some species have only thin, submerged leaves, others have leathery, floating ones as well. The leaves have long stalks sheathed at the base with a membranous scale. The flowers are borne in spikes emerging from the water; they grow on bractless stalks in the leaf axils. They are small and inconspicuous, regular and hermaphrodite; each flower has four clawed perianth segments, four stamens inserted on the claws of the perianth segments and four free, one-celled carpels. The fruits are small drupes.

Pondweeds are a complex group, prone to hybridization and difficult to identify without flowers. The hybrids tend to be sterile and spread only by creeping stems and rhizomes and the production of turions (winter buds). These fall to the bottom of the water in autumn when the rest of the plant dies back and each one forms a new plant in spring. About 30 Pondweed species grow in Europe. **Broad-leaved Pondweed**, *Potamogeton natans*, is one of the most widespread, common throughout the British Isles and Europe in ponds, slow-moving rivers and ditches, usually where the water is less than 1m (3ft) deep and rich in organic matter. It has creeping rhizomes and linear, submerged leaves; its floating leaves have pointed-elliptical blades with heart-shaped bases and they appear to be jointed just where the blades meet the stalks. New leaves have inrolled bases for a time after they have emerged. The dense, cylindrical flowering spikes appear above water in summer and are followed by spikes of olive green fruits.

Perfoliate Pondweed, *Potamogeton perfoliatus*, is a submerged species, only its small flowering and fruiting spikes emerging above the surface of the water. It has creeping rhizomes and erect stems with thin, rounded leaves, their bases clasping the stems. This pondweed is common throughout the British Isles and Europe, growing in relatively deep water in lakes and ponds, canals and slow-moving rivers.

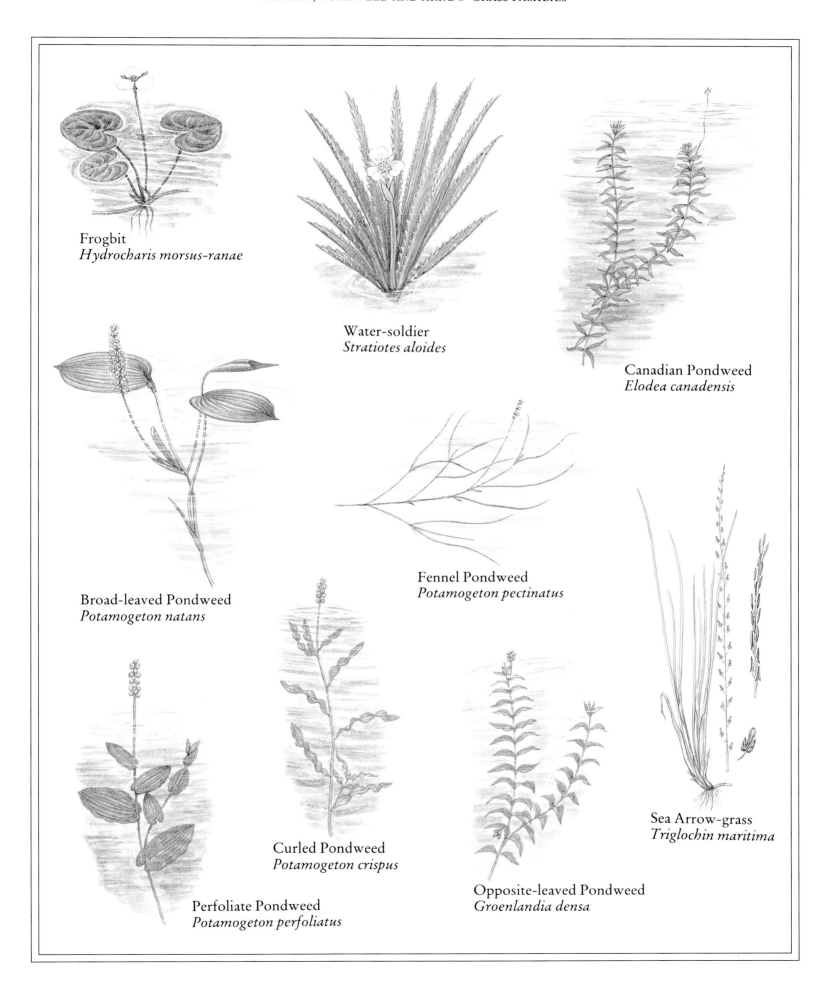

Frogbit
Hydrocharis morsus-ranae

Water-soldier
Stratiotes aloides

Canadian Pondweed
Elodea canadensis

Broad-leaved Pondweed
Potamogeton natans

Fennel Pondweed
Potamogeton pectinatus

Curled Pondweed
Potamogeton crispus

Perfoliate Pondweed
Potamogeton perfoliatus

Opposite-leaved Pondweed
Groenlandia densa

Sea Arrow-grass
Triglochin maritima

Curled Pondweed, *Potamogeton crispus* (p. 205), is another perennial, submerged species with creeping rhizomes. This one has four-angled, branched stems with wavy leaves; these are thin and translucent, often reddish, bluntly lance-shaped with serrated edges. The egg-shaped flowering spikes emerge above water in summer and are followed by beaked, dark olive fruits. This pondweed grows in lowland lakes and ponds, in slow-moving streams and canals throughout Europe north to southern Scandinavia, in much of the British Isles but rarely in western Wales and northern Scotland.

Fennel Pondweed, *Potamogeton pectinatus* (p. 205), has branched, slender, cylindrical stems growing from creeping rhizomes and dark green, translucent leaves, like pointed boot-laces. The membranous sheaths are conspicuous with white-edged margins. The flowers are borne in two-flowered whorls forming long, interrupted spikes, elongating even further in fruit. This plant grows across much of Europe and the British Isles (most commonly in England), in base-rich waters of canals and ditches, ponds and slow-moving rivers.

Opposite-leaved Pondweed, *Groenlandia densa* (p. 205), is similar to many of the *Potamogeton* species, with submerged stems and leaves and flowering spikes emerging above the water. However, its dark green, translucent, ovate or lance-shaped leaves are borne in opposite pairs or occasionally in whorls of three. The flowering spikes are small and dense, usually with only four flowers, and are followed by flattened, ovoid fruits borne on recurved stems. This plant grows in clear streams and ditches, in canals and ponds, usually in waters flowing over calcareous, stony substrates, across much of Europe, mainly in England in the British Isles.

Arrow-grass family
Juncaginaceae

A small family of 3 genera and about 25 species found in the temperate and Arctic regions of the world. They are aquatic and marshland plants.

Arrow-grasses, *Triglochin* species, are grass-like plants, with creeping rhizomes and fibrous roots. **Sea Arrow-grass**, *T. maritima* (p. 205), grows in salt marshes and in short turf near the sea around the coasts of Europe and the British Isles. It forms tufts of fleshy, very slender, linear or half-cylindrical leaves with sheathing bases, growing up to 45cm (18in) tall from stout rhizomes. The green flowers are borne in slender spikes on separate stems, appearing in the latter half of summer; each has three sepals, three stamens and a protruding ovary. They are followed by many green, egg-shaped fruits, each with six sections. Marsh Arrow-grass, *T. palustris*, is an inland species, growing in marshes, wet meadows and on stream banks throughout Europe and the British Isles.

Lily family
Liliaceae

A large and varied family of about 240 genera and 3000 species found throughout the world. Most are herbs, but a few are climbers. There are many beautiful garden plants in the family, including lilies, day lilies, tulips, hyacinths, red hot pokers and hostas. Many of these plants have showy flowers, others have attractive leaves. It would be difficult to imagine cooking without onions and garlic, two species from the large genus *Allium*; it also provides leeks and chives, as well as many attractive garden plants. Some members of the family, like Lily-of-the-valley and Autumn Crocus, contain chemicals which are active medicinally, either of beneficial use in medicine, or poisonous. Several species of *Aloe* are a source of the drug aloes, used as a laxative and in skin creams.

Family features The flowers are usually regular and hermaphrodite. There are usually six petal-like perianth segments in each flower; these may be free or partly fused into a tube and are mostly in two distinct but similar whorls. Each flower has six stamens opposite the perianth segments and a superior ovary; this usually has three cells and many seeds. The fruit is a capsule or fleshy berry. The leaves are either all basal, or alternate or whorled on erect stems. The plants have rhizomes, corms or bulbs.

Scottish Asphodel, *Tofieldia pusilla*, is a small, hairless plant, with a short rhizome and mostly basal tufts of sword-like leaves borne in two opposite rows so that they resemble a fan. In summer the flowering stems grow erect, reaching 20cm (8in) in height at most and each bearing a short terminal spike of greenish-white flowers; the flowers are followed by globular capsules. This plant grows beside streams and springs in mountain meadows and among rocks in northern Europe and Scotland, in high mountains in France and Germany.

Bog Asphodel, *Narthecium ossifragum*, is a more widespread and, to some extent, a more accessible plant. It grows in wet acid heaths and moors, especially on *Sphagnum* bogs, in western Europe north to Denmark and southern Scandinavia, mainly in northern and western areas of the British Isles. This little, hairless plant has fans of curved, sword-like leaves growing from creeping rhizomes; it blooms in the latter half of summer, producing erect flowering stems up to 45cm (18in) tall, with terminal racemes of conspicuous yellow flowers. They have distinctive stamens, their filaments covered with dense yellow hairs and orange anthers. The plant is most obvious as the fruiting capsules ripen, for both capsules and stems become deep orange. This species has the reputation of being poisonous to the sheep that graze on the moors.

White False Helleborine, *Veratrum album*, is a very poisonous plant that can easily be mistaken for Yellow Gentian, a plant much used in herb medicine. It causes symptoms

Bog Asphodel
Narthecium ossifragum

Streptopus
Streptopus amplexifolius

Scottish Asphodel
Tofieldia pusilla

Lily-of-the-valley
Convallaria majalis

May Lily
Maianthemum bifolium

White False Helleborine
Veratrum album

Common Solomon's Seal
Polygonatum multiflorum

similar to a heart attack. The helleborine is a stout, erect perennial plant, with clumps of leafy stems up to 1.5m (5ft) in height and alternate, broad, strongly veined leaves. Terminating the stems in the latter half of summer are impressive inflorescences formed of branched clusters of star-shaped flowers, hairy and greenish on the outside, white on the inside. Plants may be found in damp meadows and pastures in hills and mountains throughout much of Europe, but the species is absent from the British Isles.

Lily-of-the-valley, *Convallaria majalis* (p. 207), is most familiar as an old-fashioned garden plant, but is also a native British and European species. It grows in dry woodland and thickets, usually on calcareous soils, throughout much of Europe, mainly in England in the British Isles. It has far-creeping, branched rhizomes from which grow clusters of 2–4 leaves, carpeting the ground when they are growing thickly. The sheathing stalks of the leaves are wrapped around each other and resemble a single stem. From the axils of some of these leaves the flowering stems grow in late spring; each one bears a drooping, one-sided spray of fragrant white bells followed by red berries. Lily-of-the-valley contains convallaramin, a drug that can be used as a less powerful heart tonic than digitalin, the active ingredient in Foxglove.

May Lily, *Maianthemum bifolium* (p. 207), is another woodland carpeting plant growing in acid, humus-rich soils in woods across much of Europe; however, it is not a common species and is very rare in Britain, found only in a few localities in northern England. It has slender, creeping rhizomes from which grow erect stems up to 20cm (8in) tall; each has two scale leaves near the base, withering before flowering time, and two shiny, pointed heart-shaped leaves near the top of the stem. The starry, white, fragrant flowers appear in early summer in terminal racemes; each has four white petals and four protruding stamens and they are followed by red berries.

There are several species of Solomon's Seal in the genus *Polygonatum*. **Common Solomon's Seal**, *P. multiflorum* (p. 207), grows in woods, usually on calcareous soils, locally throughout much of Europe, mainly in southern England, south Wales and Cumbria in Great Britain. It has also escaped from gardens to grow wild in other areas. This is a perennial plant, with a thick, creeping rhizome and arching stems in summer, growing to 80cm (30in) tall, and with many alternate, broadly elliptical, parallel-veined leaves. In the axil of each leaf there hang small clusters of white, green-tipped, narrowly bell-shaped flowers followed by blue-black berries.

Streptopus, *Streptopus amplexifolius* (p. 207), has creeping rhizomes and erect, zigzag stems 30–80cm (12–30in) tall, with broadly ovate, clasping leaves. Solitary greenish-white, bell-like flowers on abruptly twisted stalks hang in the axils of the leaves. This plant grows in woods and among damp rocks in the hills and mountains of western and central Europe, south from France and Germany; it is not found in Britain.

Herb Paris, *Paris quadrifolia*, is a distinctive plant, forming patches of erect stems about 30cm (1ft) tall growing from creeping rhizomes. Each stem has a whorl of four glossy leaves halfway up and a single starry flower at the top, appearing in summer. This flower has four (sometimes five or six) broad green sepals, four thread-like, green petals and six prominent, erect stamens. At the centre of the flower the fruit develops, a fleshy, globular capsule turning black when ripe. Herb Paris grows scattered in damp woods on calcareous soils across most of Europe, mainly in England in Great Britain, but absent from many western areas and Ireland. This is a poisonous plant, at one time much used in herb medicine, but it is narcotic and dangerous.

Wild Asparagus, *Asparagus officinalis*, is similar to the cultivated variety, which is derived from it. In the wild it grows in woods and hedgerows, in waste places, in sand-dunes and on cliffs near the sea (where it is often found as a prostrate form) throughout Europe; it has been introduced into Britain, becoming naturalized in many places, mainly in England. This perennial plant has smooth, erect stems up to 1.5m (5ft) tall, much branched in the upper half. The stems appear to bear numerous clusters of needle-like leaves, giving the plant a feathery appearance and making it useful in flower arrangements; however, these 'leaves' are actually tiny, reduced stems and the true leaves are reduced to papery scales at the base of the 'leaf' clusters. Asparagus plants may be male or female, the flowers borne in the axils of the true scale-like leaves; the flowers are bell-like, the males yellow and the females yellow-green, followed by red berries. Young shoots of wild plants can be eaten like those of cultivated forms.

Butcher's Broom, *Ruscus aculeatus*, is unusual among members of this family for it is a small, dense shrub. It has much-branched, green stems up to 80cm (30in) tall, apparently with thick, dark green, spine-tipped leaves, each one twisted at the base. But as in Asparagus, these 'leaves' are reduced stems and the true leaves are the small papery scales, one at the base of each false leaf. The plants are either male or female, the small, greenish flowers borne on the surface of each false leaf cupped in a membranous bract. Female flowers are followed by red berries. Butcher's Broom grows in woods and dry, rocky places in western Europe, mainly in southern England and southwest Wales in Britain. It is also grown in gardens and has escaped to grow wild in other areas.

The true **Lilies**, *Lilium* species, are a large group of about 90 species, around nine found in Europe. Lilies are plants of temperate regions, many of them prized ornamentals for gardens, often not all that easy to grow and associated most successfully with woodland gardens. They form bulbs, underground overwintering organs that store food. Each year the plant grows from this bulb, forming a stem, leaves and flowers; towards the end of the growing season it forms a new bulb, overwintering again and persisting for many years in the same spot with this

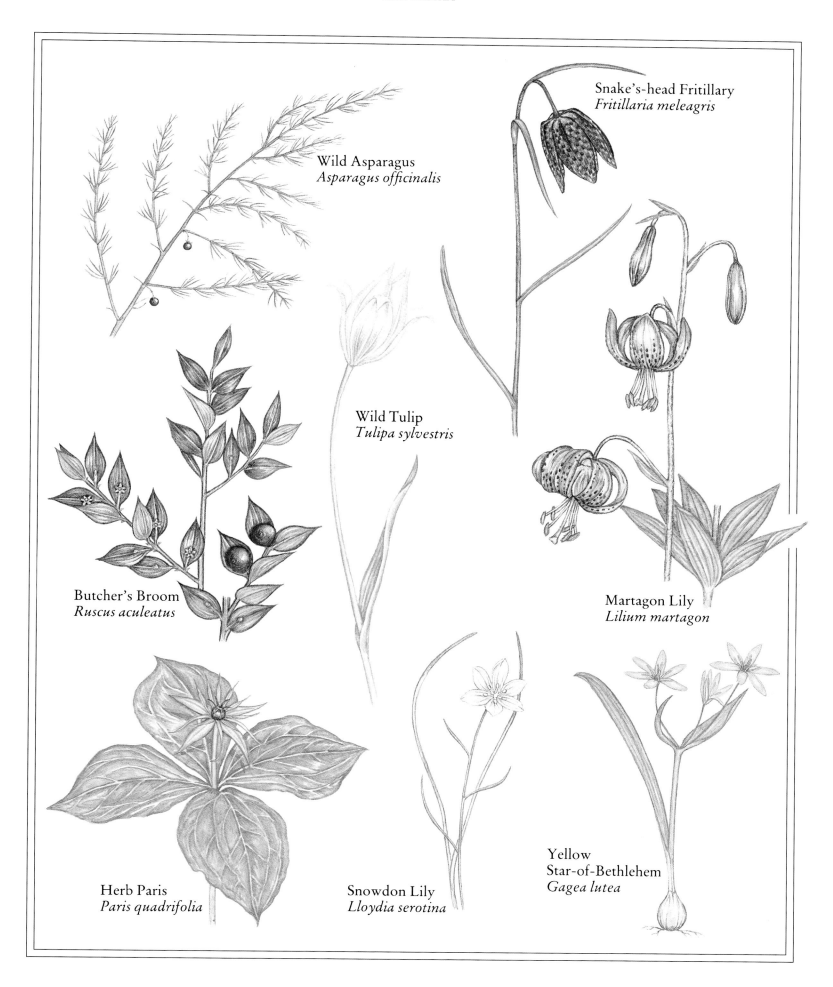

Wild Asparagus
Asparagus officinalis

Snake's-head Fritillary
Fritillaria meleagris

Wild Tulip
Tulipa sylvestris

Butcher's Broom
Ruscus aculeatus

Martagon Lily
Lilium martagon

Herb Paris
Paris quadrifolia

Snowdon Lily
Lloydia serotina

Yellow
Star-of-Bethlehem
Gagea lutea

cycle of growth and renewal. The bulb is actually an extremely shortened stem, with fleshy, food-storing leaves folded around it and a growing tip from which the new plant forms.

The **Martagon Lily**, *Lilium martagon* (p. 209), grows in woods and mountain pastures across much of Europe, except in the north, and has probably been introduced into Great Britain where it is often grown in gardens; in the wild it is found in a number of woodland localities in England. It forms an erect stem up to 1m (3ft) tall, with whorls of ovate or lance-shaped leaves and has a raceme of nodding flowers at the top of the stem in late summer. These are pink or pale purple with darker raised spots on the inside, the petals strongly recurved so that they form incomplete circles. The protruding stamens have versatile, reddish-brown anthers.

Fritillaries belong to the genus *Fritillaria*. They have bulbs formed of a single fleshy scale-leaf. Some are large and striking plants, like the Imperial Fritillaries grown in gardens, but others are small, delicate plants, like the native **Snake's-head Fritillary**, *F. meleagris* (p. 209). This beautiful species grows in damp meadows and pastures across most of Europe, mainly in southern England in Britain and not in Ireland. It has decreased to the point of extinction in many areas with the disappearance of the water meadows and is threatened everywhere by improved drainage techniques. In spring a single stem grows from each bulb, reaching about 30cm (1ft) tall and bearing several linear leaves and a single nodding flower at the top. The flower is like a lantern, with six petals chequered in light and dark purple. The plant is often planted in gardens but needs damp conditions to do well.

Wild Tulip, *Tulipa sylvestris* (p. 209), has a bulb formed of many fleshy scale leaves protected by dry brown scales (the tunic). Each spring it produces a single erect stem from each bulb, growing 30–60cm (1–2ft) tall, with three rather fleshy, linear leaves, their bases clasping the stems, and a single terminal flower. The flowers are like those of cultivated tulips, deeply bell-shaped and held upright, opening from drooping buds. In this species the flowers are yellow and the petal-like perianth segments are pointed; the outer 'petals' are tinged with red or green and turn back on themselves, while the inner ones are held erect at first, spreading as the flowers age. Fruits are oblong capsules but are rarely formed. Wild Tulips grow in fields and cultivated ground, in grassy places and woods across much of Europe, as native plants in the south, introduced further north. In Britain they have become naturalized in meadows and orchards in many parts of England.

Snowdon Lily, *Lloydia serotina* (p. 209), is an alpine species, growing on mountain ledges, among rocks and in pastures, in the mountains of central Europe and across Asia; it is rare in Britain, found only in the mountains of Snowdonia. It is a small plant, with a bulb from which grow two or more thread-like basal leaves and an erect flowering stem 15cm (6in) tall at most; this bears several linear leaves and a single flower

around midsummer. The flower is bell-shaped, upright or half-nodding, with six white, red-veined petals persisting beneath the globular capsule as it enlarges.

Yellow Star-of-Bethlehem, *Gagea lutea* (p. 209), is a spring-flowering plant, with a single bulb, one broad, linear to lance-shaped basal leaf and a flowering stem which grows in its axil, reaching 25cm (10in) in height at most. The starry, yellow flowers are borne in a terminal umbel on this stem, the umbel subtended by a pair of opposite leaves. Each petal has a streak of green on its outside. Plants grow in damp woods, hedgerows and meadows across most of Europe, scattered very locally in England north to central Scotland. There are about 20 *Gagea* species in Europe, all with similar starry, yellow flowers distinguished by differences in their leaves and in their distributions.

Star-of-Bethlehem, *Ornithogalum umbellatum*, at first glance may appear to resemble the previous species, but in fact is rather different in form. It has many white bulbs, new ones formed each year, so the plants spread into large patches. All the leaves are basal, linear and grooved, grass-like, each with a white stripe down the midrib. As well as leaves, larger bulbs produce leafless flowering stems growing up to 30cm (1ft) tall, the starry, white flowers borne in flat-topped terminal racemes. The backs of their petals are green-striped. The plants have bloomed, formed seed capsules and disappeared by late summer. The species is often grown in gardens, but is rather invasive and the bulbs are impossible to eradicate. In the wild it grows in grassy places and cultivated land across much of Europe, except the north; it has probably been introduced into Britain, but is now widespread in the wild in England and southern Scotland, more local in Wales and northern Scotland.

Drooping Star-of-Bethlehem, *Ornithogalum nutans*, comes originally from the Mediterranean region but has become widely naturalized in grassy places elsewhere in Europe, including eastern and central England. It has white-striped, grass-like leaves growing from an egg-shaped bulb, and an erect flowering stem up to 60cm (2ft) tall with a terminal, one-sided raceme of flowers in late spring. The flowers are white with a wide green band down the outside of each petal, nodding as they open from erect buds. The stamens are distinctive, with broad filaments deeply cleft at the tip, the anthers in the clefts. There are over 20 *Ornithogalum* species in Europe, all with basal leaves and racemes of white starry flowers marked with green.

Spring Squill, *Scilla verna*, is one of about 80 *Scilla* species, over 20 of which occur in Europe. Several are grown in rock gardens, notably *Scilla siberica*. Spring Squill is a small, delicate, bulbous plant, with a tuft of grass-like basal leaves appearing in spring before the flowers. Larger bulbs also produce leafless flowering stems, each bearing a dense, flat-topped cluster of starry, blue-violet flowers in late spring; the flowers are held more or less erect. This plant grows in dry, grassy

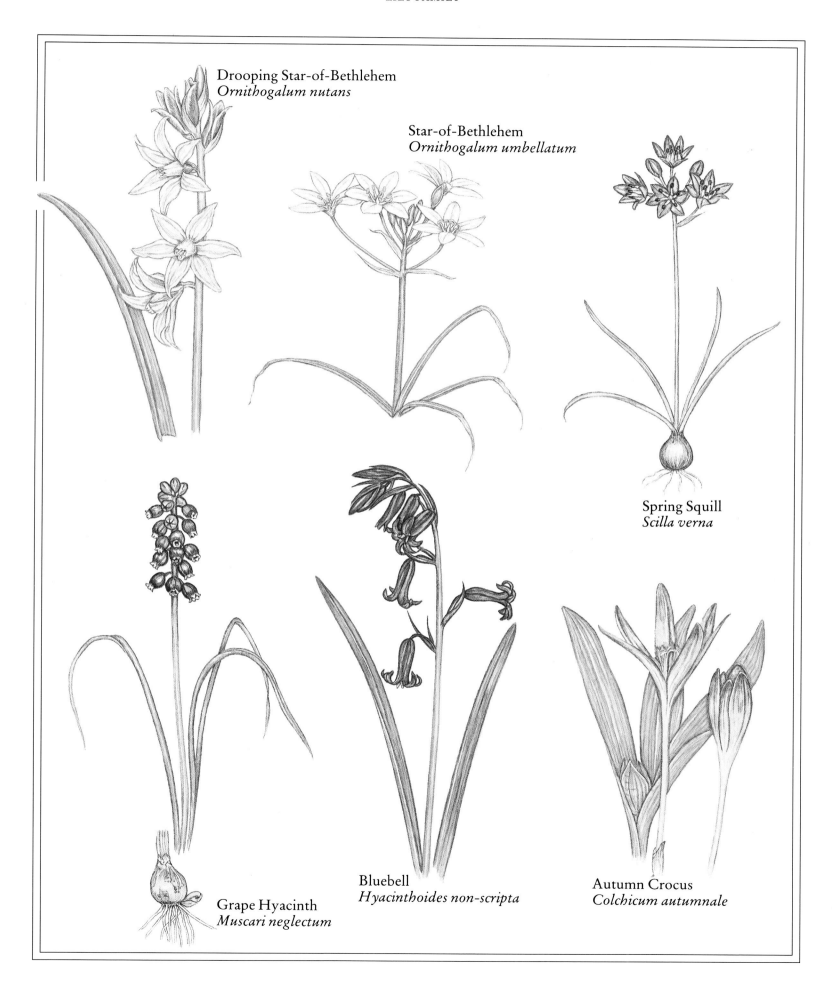

Drooping Star-of-Bethlehem
Ornithogalum nutans

Star-of-Bethlehem
Ornithogalum umbellatum

Spring Squill
Scilla verna

Grape Hyacinth
Muscari neglectum

Bluebell
Hyacinthoides non-scripta

Autumn Crocus
Colchicum autumnale

places and heaths in western Europe, very locally in the British Isles, mainly along the west coast of Great Britain, in the Hebrides, and on the east coast of Ireland. Autumn Squill, *S. autumnalis*, is a similar but somewhat larger plant, with a raceme of purple flowers borne in late summer and autumn; the leaves appear after the plants have flowered. This squill is found in dry grassland in the Mediterranean region, in France and England, mainly on the southwest coast, but also in a few places on the Isle of Wight and in the southeast.

The oak woods of western Europe and the British Isles provide homes for one of the most beautiful spring flowers, the **Bluebell**, *Hyacinthoides non-scripta* (p. 211). When growing in profusion they carpet the woodland floor with blue flowers in April and May. Bluebells have white bulbs and linear, grass-like leaves. Mature bulbs also produce flowers borne in drooping, one-sided racemes on leafless stalks up to 50cm (20in) tall. The flowers are narrowly bell-shaped with recurved tips, violet-blue in colour, nodding when fully open but with erect buds. They are followed by three-lobed capsules. Bluebells grow not only in oak woods, but also in hedges and sometimes in heathland, throughout western Europe and the British Isles but their numbers are declining from overpicking and with the disappearance of the woods and heaths.

Grape Hyacinths, *Muscari neglectum* (p. 211), are found in olive groves and vineyards, in cultivated ground and dry grassland in continental Europe, except for the north. They are not native to the British Isles but have been grown in gardens for many years, escaping into the wild in some places, particularly in East Anglia. Grape Hyacinths are bulbous plants with tufts of linear, almost cylindrical leaves appearing in winter long before the flowers. The flowering stems grow in spring, producing a dense, terminal spike of dark blue, flask-shaped flowers, each one with a small mouth surrounded by white recurved teeth. A few of the uppermost flowers of each spike are often smaller than the lower ones and sterile. Fertile flowers produce seed capsules.

Autumn Crocus, *Colchicum autumnale* (p. 211), is also known as Meadow Saffron and Naked Ladies. This last name comes from the appearance of the flowers, which seem to grow directly from the ground, without leaves or stems, in autumn. The flowers are like crocuses—shaped like goblets, pale purple in colour with orange anthers. In fact the flowers grow from corms buried in the soil. When the flowers die back they leave the developing fruiting capsule at soil level; this enlarges and emerges with the leaves in the following spring. The leaves are large, bright green, glossy and lance-shaped, growing directly from the corm like the flowers. This strange plant grows in damp meadows and woods across most of Europe, except the north, in England and eastern Wales in Great Britain, in a few places in southeastern Ireland. It is very poisonous, containing colchicine which disrupts cell division; this makes it a very useful substance for use in experimental genetics.

The **Onions** are a very large group, with about 700 species in the genus *Allium*, distributed throughout the northern hemisphere and Africa. About 90 are found in Europe. All the *Allium* species are more or less scented and many are eaten as vegetables or used for flavouring, including onions, chives, shallots, leeks and garlic. A variety of ornamental alliums are grown in gardens. Alliums are bulbous plants, with a bulb formed of fleshy scale leaves surrounded and protected by a tunic formed of one or two membranous leaves. Bulbs may be solitary or develop in clusters. From the bulb grows a clump of leaves, varying in shape from linear to ovate, from flattened to three-angled; mature bulbs also produce flowering stems with terminal umbels of flowers, the umbel at first enclosed in a leaf-like structure called a spathe. Some *Allium* species produce bulbils as well as flowers in their flower clusters, sometimes so many of them that they almost replace the flowers.

Cultivated Onions belong to the species *Allium cepa*, a plant native to southeastern Asia and grown throughout Europe and the British Isles. Its bulbs and cylindrical, hollow leaves are familiar to everyone, but its flowers less so. They are greenish-white and borne in dense, many-flowered, round umbels which may measure up to 10cm (4in) across.

Chives, *Allium schoenoprasum*, is another cultivated species, but this one is native to Europe. It grows in clumps, its soft, cylindrical leaves growing from clusters of narrow, elongated bulbs, its leafless flower stems with rounded umbels of pale purple flowers appearing around midsummer. It grows in damp meadows and among rocks, often beside streams, throughout much of Europe, in mountains in the south of its range, in a few scattered localities in England and Wales.

Ramsons, *Allium ursinum*, has a strong, distinctive scent like slightly rancid garlic, and the scent of the plants permeates the woods where they grow. Sometimes they grow in profusion, forming carpets of bright green, elliptical leaves on the woodland floor, especially in damp woods, but they also grow in smaller numbers in hedgerows and other shady places throughout Europe and the British Isles. The leaves grow from narrow, solitary bulbs, appearing in spring and early summer, two leaves and one flowering stem from each bulb. The white, starry flowers are borne in flat-topped umbels cupped in a membranous spathe, growing on two-angled or three-angled stems about 30cm (1ft) tall.

The three-angled leaves and stems of **Triquetrous Garlic**, *Allium triquetrum*, make it a distinctive species. It has a small, whitish bulb, its leaves are mostly basal and its flowers hang in a one-sided umbel from the top of the flowering stem, 20–50cm (8–20in) tall. The flowers are bell-shaped, white with green lines on the midrib of each petal. This allium grows in damp, shady places, in woods and hedgerows, beside streams in Spain and France, and has been introduced into the Channel Islands and southwestern England. It is also found in a few places in south Wales and southern Ireland.

212

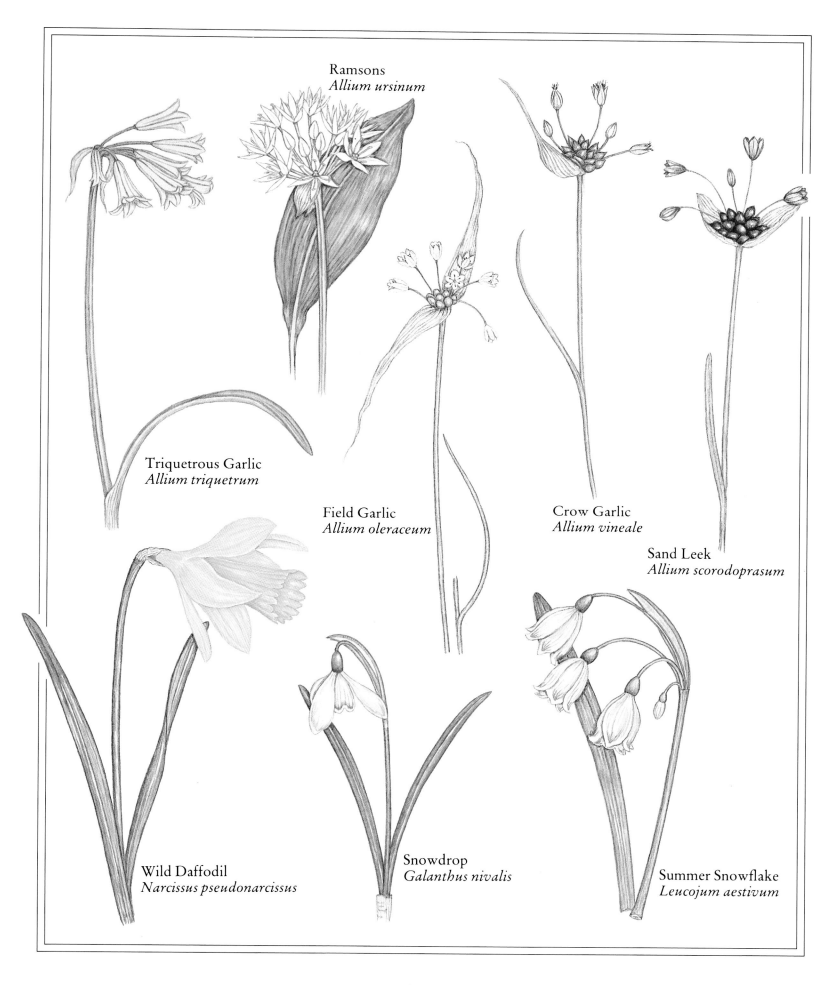

Ramsons
Allium ursinum

Triquetrous Garlic
Allium triquetrum

Field Garlic
Allium oleraceum

Crow Garlic
Allium vineale

Sand Leek
Allium scorodoprasum

Wild Daffodil
Narcissus pseudonarcissus

Snowdrop
Galanthus nivalis

Summer Snowflake
Leucojum aestivum

Field Garlic, *Allium oleraceum* (p. 213), forms clusters of bulbs and grass-like leaves, cylindrical at the base and sheathing the flowering stems, but merely channelled at the tops. This is one of those *Allium* species in which the flowers of the umbels may be replaced by bulbils; each umbel is subtended by a spathe formed of two pointed, membranous bracts, the bulbils are dark green and the flowers vary in colour from dull pink to greenish-white. Plants grow in cultivated ground, in orchards and vineyards, on roadsides and in rocky places across much of Europe. They have been introduced into Great Britain where they grow mainly in eastern areas of England.

Crow Garlic, *Allium vineale* (p. 213), also produces bulbils in its umbels, often to the complete exclusion of flowers; the bulbils are purple and the flowers are pink or greenish-white when they are present. The umbels appear at the tops of erect stems up to 60cm (2ft) tall, these stems sheathed by the linear leaves. Crow Garlic grows in dry, grassy places, in fields and vineyards, and on roadsides throughout Europe; it has been introduced into the British Isles, becoming a serious weed in some parts of eastern England and the Midlands.

Garlic, *Allium sativum*, is another cultivated allium that comes originally from Asia, now grown in many parts of Europe. Its bulbs are distinctive, formed of many bulblets covered with white scale leaves; its leaves are flat and broad. Its umbels often produce more bulbils than flowers, but the flowers are bell-shaped, white or greenish when present.

Sand Leek, *Allium scorodoprasum* (p. 213), has bulbs with many reddish-black bulblets and leaves that sheath the lower part of the flowering stem, like those seen in cultivated leeks. The leaves are wide and flat, keeled on the midrib so that they overlap each other, and very strongly scented. The red-purple flowers grow in loose umbels, but there are few of them and they are mixed with purple bulbils. This allium grows in dry, sandy and grassy places, in vineyards and fields across much of Europe, locally in northern England and Scotland.

Daffodil family
Amaryllidaceae

There are about 85 genera and 1100 species in this family, all bulbous herbaceous plants, the majority from warm temperate regions of the world. Many beautiful, ornamental bulbous plants come from the family, including daffodils, narcissi and snowdrops, popular spring-flowering species for flower borders, and hippeastrums, crinums and nerines, frost-sensitive species that are grown as house and greenhouse plants.

The family is very closely related to the Lily family, and the onions, *Allium* species, are included in the Daffodil family rather than the Lily family by some botanists because onions have their flowers in umbels, like many members of the Daffodil family. Other botanists believe that 'Daffodil family members have an inferior ovary, while Lily family members have a superior ovary'; on this basis the onions would remain in the Lily family. There may be no way of resolving this controversy once and for all!

Family features The flowers are solitary or borne in umbels enclosed in a membranous spathe in bud; they are hermaphrodite and usually regular. Each flower has six perianth segments in two separate whorls, sometimes with a corona. There are six stamens in two whorls opposite the perianth segments. The ovary is inferior with three cells and many seeds. The fruits are usually capsules, rarely berries. These are bulbous plants, with a clump of basal leaves.

Summer Snowflake or Loddon Lily, *Leucojum aestivum* (p. 213), forms clumps of bright green, strap-shaped leaves growing 30–50cm (12–20in) tall in late spring from clusters of large bulbs. The slightly taller flowering stems bear one-sided umbels of 3–7 nodding, bell-shaped flowers, white with green tips to the petals. They are followed by green capsules, formed from the ovaries already apparent beneath the flowers. Summer Snowflakes grow in wet meadows and marshes and beside streams across much of Europe, except the north; they are found only very locally in the British Isles, mainly in southern England, but also in Wales and Ireland. Spring Snowflake, *L. vernum*, is similar but smaller and has solitary or paired flowers appearing in late winter or early spring. It grows in damp woods and meadows in central and western Europe but is very rare in the wild in Britain. Both are grown in gardens.

Snowdrops, *Galanthus nivalis* (p. 213), are familar garden plants also found in the wild across much of Europe, except the north, and throughout Great Britain, becoming rare in Scotland. They are probably naturalized rather than native in many areas. Snowdrops grow in damp woods and hedgerows, in damp meadows and beside streams. They form small clumps of linear, grey-green leaves in late winter, joined before they are fully developed by flowering stems with solitary, nodding flowers. Each flower has three spreading, pure white, outer perianth segments and three smaller inner perianth segments which are green-spotted and notched at their tips.

Wild Daffodils, *Narcissus pseudonarcissus* (p. 213), are also wild versions of a flower more familiar in gardens than in their natural homes—damp woods and meadows, orchards and roadsides. Some are naturalized plants that have escaped from gardens, but others are truly native. They are found across much of Europe and locally throughout England and Wales. Like the garden forms, Wild Daffodils form springtime clumps of broad, linear leaves growing from bulbs, with leafless flowering stems and solitary, drooping flowers. Each flower has a spreading, pale yellow perianth and a deep yellow corona (the trumpet). This is one of about 40 *Narcissus* species found in Europe, several of them wild progenitors of garden forms, including Pheasant's Eyes, Hoop Petticoats and Jonquils.

An oak wood in spring, with Sessile Oaks on the left and coppiced Hazel on the right. In the foreground (from left to right) are Male Fern, Common Dog-violets, Primroses and Wood Anemones, with Bluebells beyond them and covering the woodland floor.

Iris family
Iridaceae

A large family with about 60 genera and 800 species of herbaceous plants distributed throughout the world. The family contains many ornamental garden plants. These include the many species and varieties of irises, as well as crocuses and montbretias. Freesias and gladioli make superb cut flowers.

Family features The flowers are hermaphrodite, usually regular, with one or two bracts forming a spathe around their base. Each flower has six perianth segments joined at their base into a tube and arranged in two whorls of three (the perianth segments may be alike in both whorls or very dissimilar). There are three stamens opposite the outer perianth segments. The ovary is inferior, with three cells. The fruits are three-celled capsules. These plants have rhizomes, bulbs or corms and form basal clumps of flattened, linear leaves, folded and overlapping at the base and sheathing the bases of the separate flowering stems.

Irises form one of the largest groups in the family, with about 300 species in the genus *Iris*, found throughout the temperate regions of the northern hemisphere. About 50 species grow wild in Europe and others grow in gardens. They are perennial plants with sword-shaped leaves growing in basal clumps and with a characteristic form—their bases fold over each other so that they form two opposite, overlapping rows. The flowers grow in terminal, often spike-like clusters on stems which originate between the overlapping leaves. Iris flowers are showy, with three clawed outer perianth segments (known as 'falls'), usually flexed downwards and larger than the inner segments, three clawed inner segments (the 'standards'), which are usually erect, and may be bearded in some species, and a three-cleft style (the 'crest'), with three petal-like sections, each one arching over a stamen.

Several of the garden species come originally from Europe, including the typical Garden Iris (the one with yellow-bearded, purple flowers), *Iris germanica*, which grows wild in rocky places in central and Mediterranean Europe. Siberian Iris, *I. sibirica*, is another garden species, this one with narrow, grass-like leaves and blue-purple flowers; it grows in damp, grassy places in central Europe.

Yellow Flag, *Iris pseudacorus*, is the most widespread wild iris, found in marshes and wet meadows, in ditches, beside rivers and ponds throughout Europe and the British Isles. It forms clumps of stiff, erect leaves about 1m (3ft) tall growing from dense, tangled rhizomes. Among the leaves grow the flowering stalks—about the same height as the leaves—each one with a terminal cluster of yellow flowers opening a few at a time around midsummer. Each flower has three broad, hanging falls, three smaller, upright standards and three arching styles, ragged at their tips. They are followed by green capsules containing brown seeds. The rhizomes of this iris are poisonous (like those of many others), causing inflammation of the stomach and intestines, and dangerous to livestock.

Stinking Iris or Gladdon, *Iris foetidissima*, gets its name from the unpleasant odour of its crushed leaves. It has evergreen, sword-shaped leaves and flowering stems about the same height, angled on one side. The flowers are purple, tinged or veined with yellow, the standards shorter than the falls and more yellow. They are followed by brownish capsules which split open to reveal bright orange seeds.

Blue-eyed Grasses, *Sisyrinchium* species, come entirely from the New World, except for one species found in western Ireland, where it grows in marshy meadows and on the shores of lakes. This **Blue-eyed Grass**, *S. bermudiana*, is a small, perennial, grass-like plant, which forms tufts of the distinctive, iris-family, overlapping leaves 50cm (20in) tall at most, growing from fibrous roots or short rhizomes. On separate stems it has umbels of delicate blue flowers with yellow centres, each one with six identical perianth segments. The plant is often grown in gardens.

Crocuses, *Crocus* species, are popular garden plants, their goblet-like flowers most familiar in spring; however, some species flower in autumn, like the **Autumn Crocus**, *C. nudiflorus*, which has purple flowers in early autumn, quite separately from the white-striped leaves which do not appear until spring. The plants have underground corms that produce creeping stems and new corms in spring so that a spreading colony of crocuses gradually forms. Autumn Crocus grows in grassy meadows and heaths in France and Spain; it has become naturalized in a few places in England.

Montbretia, *Tritonia crocosmiflora*, is a fertile hybrid plant, originating in France in the late nineteenth century from a cross between two species of South African origin. It is a popular garden plant in both France and the British Isles, spreading into large patches and seeding profusely so that it has become widely naturalized in hedgebanks and on roadsides, beside rivers and ponds, in woods and waste places. Beneath the ground are the corms, often several in a vertical row, together with creeping stems and the new corms that they form; above ground are the leaves, narrowly sword-shaped and overlapping, each shoot growing about 90cm (3ft) tall. The flowering stems appear from between the leaves in late summer; they have branching inflorescences which bear many funnel-shaped, deep orange flowers on zigzag stems.

Gladioli are more familiar as garden plants and cut flowers than as wild plants. Nevertheless, several are native to Europe, like the **Wild Gladiolus**, *Gladiolus illyricus*, which grows in bushy places, in heaths and marshes in southern and western Europe. It is also found very locally in the New Forest and the Isle of Wight in England. It grows from corms, producing erect tufts of sword-like, overlapping leaves and one-sided spikes of crimson-purple flowers.

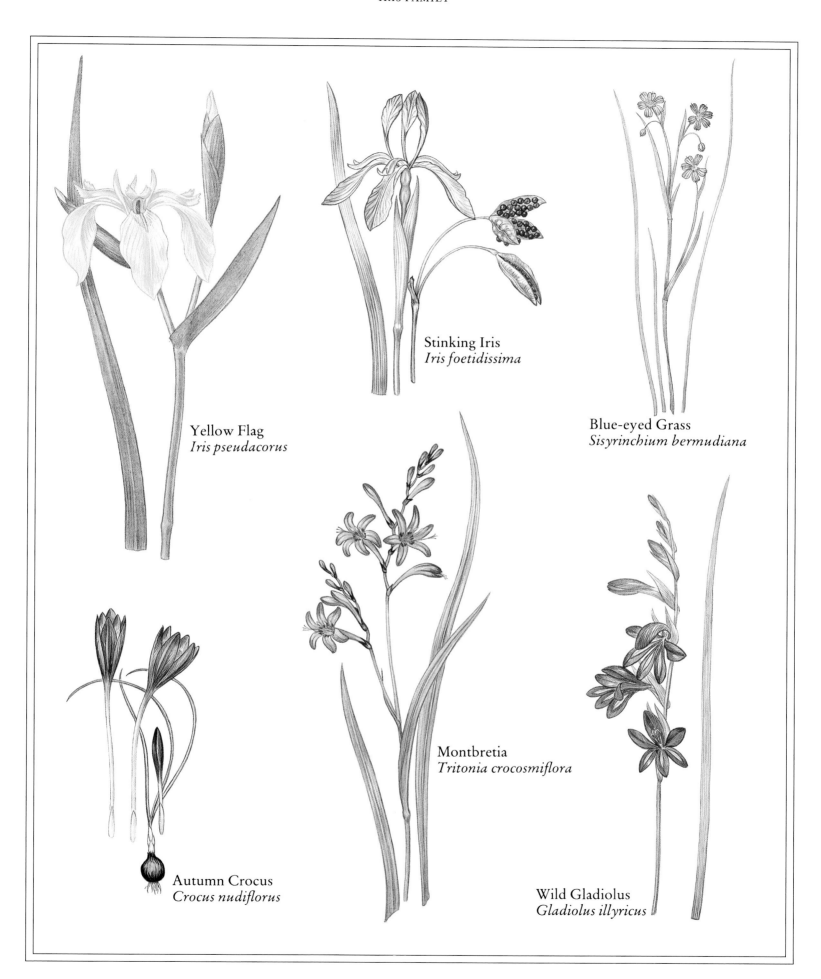

Yellow Flag
Iris pseudacorus

Stinking Iris
Iris foetidissima

Blue-eyed Grass
Sisyrinchium bermudiana

Montbretia
Tritonia crocosmiflora

Autumn Crocus
Crocus nudiflorus

Wild Gladiolus
Gladiolus illyricus

Yam family
Dioscoreaceae

A family of twining vines, with 8–9 genera and about 750 species, found in the tropical and warm temperate regions of the world. The tubers of Yams, *Dioscorea* species, are an important source of food in many tropical countries.

Only one species from the family is widespread in Europe, **Black Bryony**, *Tamus communis*, found across much of the Continent, except the north, in England and Wales. It grows in scrub and woodland margins, in hedgerows and on fences, twining around and through other shrubs and trees. It is a perennial plant, with a large tuber from which fresh stems grow each year, twining to the left, reaching a length of 2–4m (6–12ft); the stems are smooth and angular, unbranched and leafy, with pointed heart-shaped, shiny, dark green leaves. The flowers are yellowish-green with six perianth segments joined at the base. They are borne in the leaf axils but plants may be either male or female, the male flowers on long stalks and in elongated clusters, the females in smaller, shorter clusters on short recurved stalks. Female flowers are followed by berries, green at first and ripening bright red. This plant is dangerously poisonous; the berries in particular can be lethal.

Rush family
Juncaceae

A relatively small family of 9 genera and 400 species of herbaceous plants, found throughout the world. They are related to the Lily family, the difference in the appearance of the flowers in the two families coming from the method of pollination. Lilies are insect-pollinated plants whereas rushes are wind-pollinated.

Family features The flowers are usually borne in crowded cymes or heads; they are regular and hermaphrodite, with six perianth segments in two whorls, usually green or brown in colour. The stamens are free, either in two whorls of three or with the inner whorl missing; the ovary is superior with one or three cells. The fruit is a capsule. The leaves are linear, often grass-like, cylindrical or flat, with sheathing bases.

The **Rushes**, *Juncus* species, are tufted plants, often with creeping rhizomes. Their stem leaves have split, sheathing bases. This is a large group; out of a world total of 300 species, about 50 grow in Europe. **Soft Rush**, *J. effusus*, is one of the most common species, a perennial plant abundant in wet grassland, damp woods, marshes and bogs, beside streams and in flushes throughout Europe and the British Isles. It forms dense tufts of bright green, glossy, rather soft stems 30–150cm (1–5ft) tall, each with a single leaf and a loose cluster of dark brown flowers about halfway up. The similar Hard Rush, *J. inflexus*, has dull, grey-green stems, stiffly erect and strongly ridged. It grows in damp grassland on heavy soils throughout Europe and much of the British Isles, but is absent from northern Scotland.

Toad Rush, *Juncus bufonius*, is a much more delicate annual plant, with erect or prostrate stems branched from the base, channelled, thread-like leaves and solitary, pale green flowers borne at intervals along the stems. It grows in muddy places, along roads and paths, beside ponds and on cultivated land, abundantly throughout Europe and the British Isles.

Bulbous Rush, *Juncus bulbosus*, is an amphibious, perennial species, growing in damp places on land or floating in water. It is found in wet heathland and bogs, in damp woods, often in the ruts in rides and tracks, in muddy ponds and along riverbanks, usually on acid soils, throughout much of Europe, abundantly in the British Isles. It is a variable, grass-like plant, 20cm (8in) tall at most. Land forms are often mat-forming, either tufted with their leaves in basal clumps, or with prostrate stems rooting at the nodes. The stems are swollen at the base and may bear clusters of flowers near the top, often with leafy shoots growing from the clusters. Aquatic forms are submerged, with floating, thread-like, much-branched stems.

Sharp-flowered Rush, *Juncus acutiflorus*, has stout, far-creeping rhizomes and clumps of stiff, erect stems up to 1m (3ft) tall. Each stem has several straight leaves, rounded in cross-section, with 18–25 conspicuous transverse partitions inside. The terminal inflorescence has many branches, with numerous heads of chestnut brown flowers. This plant is common in wet meadows and woods, in bogs, moors and ditches across much of Europe and throughout the British Isles.

The **Woodrushes**, *Luzula* species, are also tufted, grass-like perennial plants, but their leaves tend to grow in basal clumps rather than on the stems, they are fringed with long colourless hairs and their sheathing bases are closed rather than split. This is another large group, with about 80 species worldwide, 25 in Europe. **Field Woodrush**, *L. campestris*, is a common plant of meadows and other grassy places throughout Europe and the British Isles. It forms small, loose tufts of bright-green, grass-like leaves growing from short creeping stems. The flowering stem grows 15cm (6in) tall at most and bears an umbel-like inflorescence at the top; this has curved branches, each with a cluster of chestnut brown flowers. There is also a stalkless flower cluster at the centre.

Great Woodrush, *Luzula sylvatica*, grows in acid soils, in woodland (particularly oak woods) and moorland across most of Europe and throughout the British Isles. It is by far the largest of the woodrushes, with tussocky clumps of glossy, broadly linear leaves and flowering stems growing up to 80cm (30in) tall in early summer. They bear numerous clusters of chestnut brown flowers in a loose, spreading, much-branched cyme at the top of the stem.

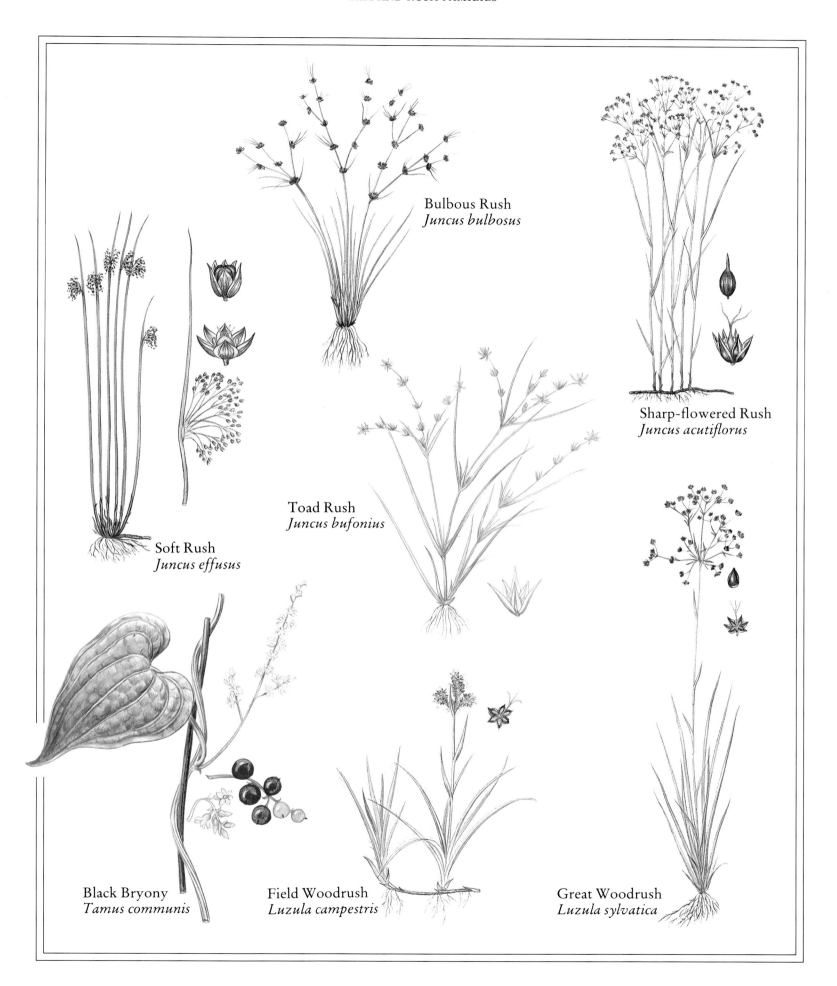

Bulbous Rush
Juncus bulbosus

Sharp-flowered Rush
Juncus acutiflorus

Soft Rush
Juncus effusus

Toad Rush
Juncus bufonius

Black Bryony
Tamus communis

Field Woodrush
Luzula campestris

Great Woodrush
Luzula sylvatica

Orchid family
Orchidaceae

This is one of the largest plant families, with about 735 genera and 17,000 species known to date; the figures increase every year as more are discovered and named. Many are found in temperate regions of the world, but far more grow in tropical jungles, and it is these jungle species which contribute most new species each year.

Family features Orchid flowers may be solitary, or borne in a spike, raceme or compound raceme. They are hermaphrodite and bilaterally symmetrical. Each flower has six perianth segments in two whorls; sometimes the two whorls are similar, but often they are unlike, the outer ones resembling sepals and the inner ones petals. Often there is one central sepal, which becomes the uppermost part of the flower, and two lateral sepals; and often there are two lateral petals, and a central one which becomes twisted to hang downwards, forming the lip or labellum. This latter structure is often complex and may be spurred, with nectar in the spur. The lateral sepals and petals often resemble each other. There are one or two stamens, their anthers borne together with the stigmas on a special structure known as the column. The pollen grains often adhere together to form small packets known as 'pollinia'. The ovary is inferior, usually with one cell. The fruit is usually a capsule containing numerous minute seeds (millions in some species). Orchids' leaves are entire and usually either arranged in two overlapping rows at the base of the stem or alternately on the stems; they are often fleshy with a sheathing base that encircles the stem, but they may be reduced to scales.

For many years horticulturalists failed to get orchid seeds to germinate. Finally it was realized that most orchids grow in a mycorrhizal association with a fungus. The fungus grows through and around the roots, and the orchid gets much of its water and nutrients from the fungus, not directly from the soil. Germinating orchid seeds have no food reserves and will die unless they connect with the right fungus very quickly.

There are about 50 **Lady's-slipper Orchids**, *Cypripedium* species, in the world but only three in Europe. Their name comes from the pouched lip of the flower, which is said to resemble a slipper; many of these beautiful orchids are now rare in the wild, their numbers reduced from overcollecting. **Yellow Lady's-slipper**, *C. calceolus*, has a creeping rhizome and an erect stem up to 45cm (18in) tall in early summer; this stem bears 3–4 large, elliptical leaves and one (sometimes two) flowers at the tip in the axil of a leafy bract. The flower is yellow and purple. It has wavy purple sepals, one erect at the top and the two lateral ones joined and pointing downwards, two purple, spirally twisted, linear lateral petals and a pale yellow pouched lip spotted with red on the inside. At one time this plant grew in woods and thickets, usually on calcareous

soils in hills and mountains, in many localities in Europe and in several places in northern England. It is now rare, eradicated in many of its former sites, with one small colony left in England.

Several Helleborines, *Epipactis* species, grow in Europe and the British Isles, some of them common (for orchids), others rare. **Marsh Helleborine**, *E. palustris*, is one of the more common ones, but its numbers are decreasing with the disappearance of its wetland habitats. It grows in fens and marshes, wet meadows and dune slacks locally across most of Europe, in England, Wales and Ireland. This is a perennial plant with a long-creeping rhizome, a slender, erect stem up to 45cm (18in) tall and several oblong to lance-shaped leaves, their bases clasping the stem; the lower part of the stem and the undersides of the lower leaves are often purplish. The flowers are borne in a terminal, more or less one-sided raceme, each one in the axil of a narrow, pointed bract. They have purplish-green sepals, hairy on the outside and paler on the inside, smaller whitish lateral petals veined with purple at their bases and a white lip veined with pink, spotted with yellow and frilly on the margin.

Broad-leaved Helleborine, *Epipactis helleborine*, has short rhizomes and one or more erect stems growing up to 80cm (30in) tall, with broadly ovate leaves, the largest in the middle of the stem and becoming smaller and narrower above and beneath. The flowers grow in one-sided, terminal racemes and vary in colour from dull purple to greenish; usually the sepals are greenish, the petals are purple and the heart-shaped lip may be purple or greenish-white, darker green or brown inside. This helleborine grows in woods and rocky places throughout Europe and the British Isles, but is rare in northern Scotland.

Dark Red Helleborine, *Epipactis atrorubens*, has a single erect stem about 30cm (1ft) tall, leafy with two rows of pointed-elliptical leaves. The flowers in the terminal raceme are red-purple and faintly scented. This plant grows among limestone rocks, in woods on calcareous soils, in grassy places and in dunes, locally across Europe, in north Wales and northern England, northern Scotland and western Ireland. Violet Helleborine, *E. purpurata*, has violet-tinged leaves and pale greenish-white flowers. This relatively rare plant grows in woods on calcareous soils in northern and central Europe, mainly in southern and central England in Britain.

The *Cephalanthera* species are also known as Helleborines. **White Helleborine**, *C. damasonium*, has a short, creeping rhizome and an erect, leafy stem up to 50cm (20in) tall. The leaves are ovate to lance-shaped, merging into leafy bracts near the top of the stem where the few flowers appear. These bracts are much larger than the flowers; the latter are creamy white, closed except for a brief time when they open into an up-facing bell, petals and sepals curved around the yellow-blotched lip. This plant grows in calcareous soils, in woods and shady places, scattered across Europe, mainly in southern England and the Midlands in Britain.

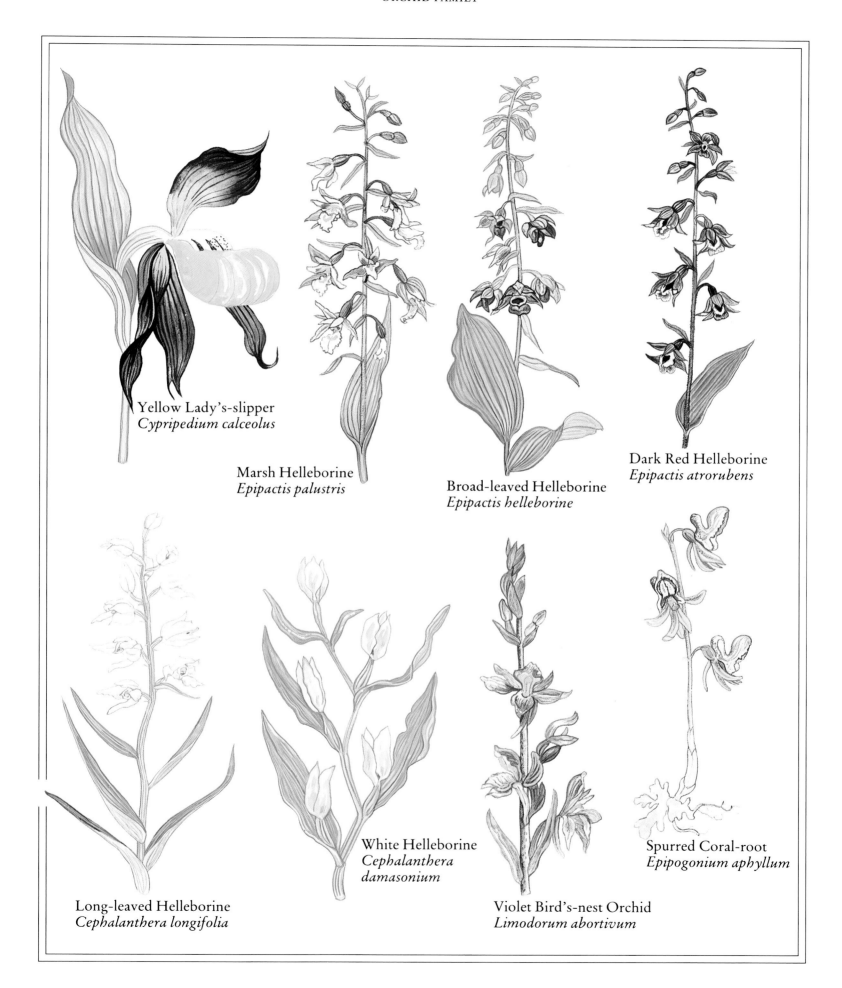

Yellow Lady's-slipper
Cypripedium calceolus

Marsh Helleborine
Epipactis palustris

Broad-leaved Helleborine
Epipactis helleborine

Dark Red Helleborine
Epipactis atrorubens

White Helleborine
Cephalanthera damasonium

Spurred Coral-root
Epipogonium aphyllum

Long-leaved Helleborine
Cephalanthera longifolia

Violet Bird's-nest Orchid
Limodorum abortivum

Long-leaved Helleborine, *Cephalanthera longifolia* (p. 221), is similar but its leaves are lance-shaped, becoming linear higher up the stem, and its bracts are smaller than the flowers. This is a relatively rare and declining plant of woodland and scrub, especially fond of calcareous soils, scattered across southern and central Europe; it is found in only a few places in England, Scotland and Ireland.

Violet Bird's-nest Orchid, *Limodorum abortivum* (p. 221), is one of several unrelated orchids which have lost all or most of their chlorophyll, becoming saprophytic in their lifestyles. They usually grow in shady woods where there is a deep layer of leaf litter on the ground, and they depend on the mycorrhiza in their roots to absorb water and nutrients from this leafy humus. This species grows in woods across much of Europe, except the north, but is not found in the British Isles. Most of its life is spent underground, only the flowering stems appearing at unpredictable intervals. The upright stems grow up to 80cm (30in) tall, have several scale leaves and a terminal raceme of flowers, all violet in colour. The flowers have spreading lateral sepals and petals, a helmet-shaped upper sepal, a yellow-tinged lip and a downward-pointing spur.

Spurred Coral-root or Ghost Orchid, *Epipogonium aphyllum* (p. 221), is another saprophyte, a rare plant found in the deep shade of oak or beech woods, scattered across Europe, in a few places in England and Wales, sporadic and unpredictable in its appearance. It has no roots but its rhizome has many short, flattened branches, like a piece of whitish coral. Its flowering stem grows only 20cm (8in) tall and is translucent white tinged with pink and streaked with red, its leaves reduced to a few brownish sheaths around the swollen base. It has few flowers (sometimes only one) and they are unusual in that the lip is at the top with the petals and sepals hanging downwards below. The lip is large, spurred and three-lobed, white with violet spots; the petals and sepals are yellow.

Creeping Lady's Tresses, *Goodyera repens*, has creeping rhizomes beneath the surface of the ground and creeping stems above ending in rosettes of ovate leaves. These are mottled dark green with a network of conspicuous veins. The flowering stem grows from this rosette, reaching 25cm (10in) in height, bearing a spirally twisted raceme of creamy white, fragrant flowers in the latter half of summer. Each flower grows in the axil of a large linear bract which is green on the outside, white on the inside; the upper sepal and the two petals of each flower form a hood, the lateral sepals are spreading and the lip is flat and triangular. This rather rare orchid grows in mossy coniferous woodland in the hills and mountains across much of Europe; it is found locally in East Anglia and the north of England, more frequently in northern Scotland.

The Lady's Tresses, *Spiranthes* species, are small orchids with leafy, erect stems and characteristic, spirally twisted racemes of flowers. **Autumn Lady's Tresses**, *S. spiralis*, grows in damp, grassy places, in meadows and pastures, on sand-dunes and hills, usually in calcareous soils, throughout much of Europe, except the north, in England, Wales and Ireland, more commonly in the south. It has a rosette of ovate or elliptical leaves appearing in late summer and developing an erect flowering stem in late summer and autumn of the following year. By this time the leaves have withered but a new rosette has formed to one side. The flowering stem grows about 30cm (1ft tall), has overlapping scale leaves near the base and a single twisted row of scented, white flowers at the top.

Twayblade, *Listera ovata*, is a small orchid flowering in the early part of summer. It has a slender, erect flowering stem growing up to 60cm (2ft) tall, with a pair of rounded, opposite leaves towards the base. The flowers are small and spurless, yellow-green in colour and numerous, borne in a slender, spike-like raceme terminating the stem. The petals and sepals are joined at the base to form an open hood over the long, dangling lip; this has a deep notch at the tip. **Lesser Twayblade**, *L. cordata*, is a smaller, even more slender plant, with a flowering stem growing up to 20cm (8in) tall and fewer flowers in a shorter raceme. The two leaves are rounded with heart-shaped bases and the flowers are reddish, with an open hood and a forked, dangling lip.

Bird's-nest Orchid, *Neottia nidus-avis*, is another saprophytic species, growing only in shady woodland, particularly beneath beech, throughout much of Europe, Great Britain and Ireland, most commonly in the south. The name of this plant refers to the ball of thick, fleshy roots which conceal the rhizome (the 'bird's nest'); this is buried in leaf litter on the woodland floor and the plant only appears above ground when it flowers. It has a stiff, erect flowering stem reaching 45cm (18in) tall, brownish in colour with many membranous, brown scale leaves and ending in a dense spike of many brown flowers. Each one has its sepals and petals joined into an open hood, and a long, dangling, lobed lip, pouched at the base and often darker than the rest of the flower.

Coral-root, *Corallorhiza trifida* is partly saprophytic in its lifestyle, with a much-branched, fleshy, rounded rhizome resembling a piece of coral. It grows in damp, mossy woods, often beneath pine or alder, also in dune slacks, scattered across much of Europe, in northern England and Scotland, but is nevertheless a rare plant and its presence can only be detected when it flowers. Often several stems are produced, but this is a small orchid and they grow only 25cm (10in) tall at most. They are yellow-green in colour, with brown-veined, sheathing scale leaves near the base and a few inconspicuous flowers at the top. The sepals and lateral petals are similar in colour to the stems, but the lip is whitish and spotted with crimson.

Fen Orchid, *Liparis loeselii*, is more nearly related to the tropical orchids than most British species, the relationship demonstrated by the way the base of the stem is swollen to form a structure known as a pseudo-bulb, a feature seen in many tropical species. Fen Orchid is a small plant with an erect

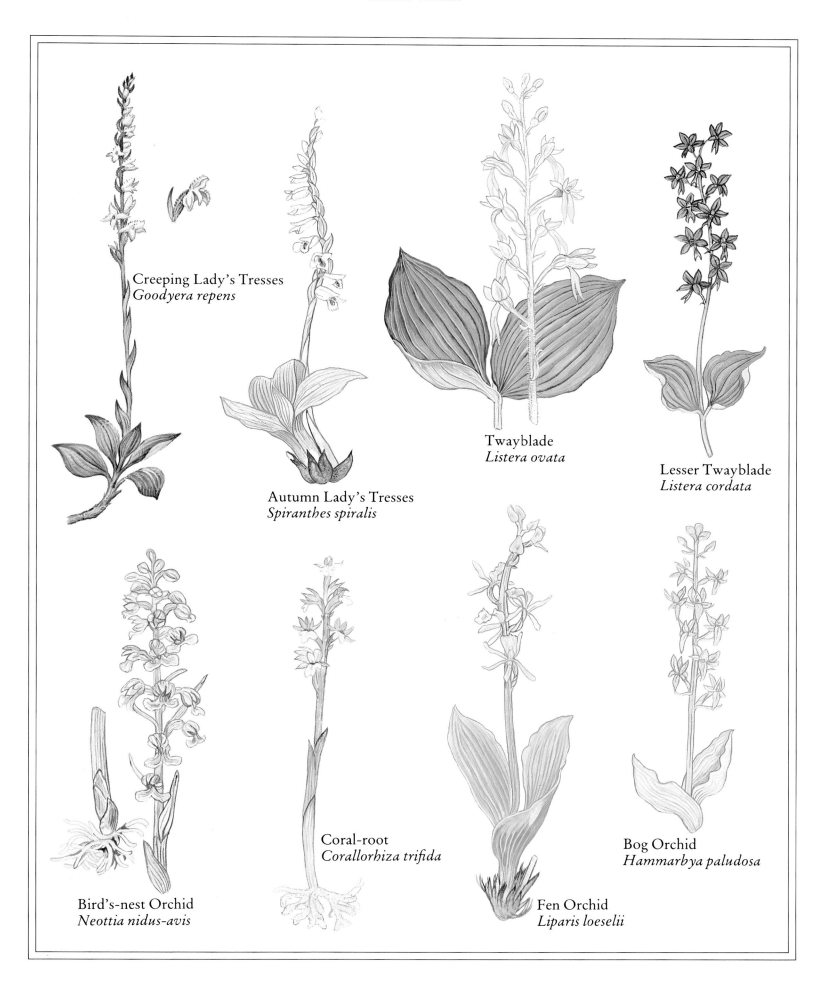

Creeping Lady's Tresses
Goodyera repens

Autumn Lady's Tresses
Spiranthes spiralis

Twayblade
Listera ovata

Lesser Twayblade
Listera cordata

Bird's-nest Orchid
Neottia nidus-avis

Coral-root
Corallorhiza trifida

Fen Orchid
Liparis loeselii

Bog Orchid
Hammarbya paludosa

stem 20cm (8in) tall at most, two shiny basal leaves and a loose, terminal raceme of yellow-green flowers. The flowers have spreading petals and sepals, and a broad, upward-pointing lip. Next to the pseudo-bulb at the base of the stem are the remains of the one from last year, covered by the withered remnants of last year's leaves. This rare plant grows in fens and bogs, in dune slacks and wet moorland, scattered across central Europe to southern Scandinavia; in Britain it is found in East Anglian fens and in the dune slacks of south Wales.

Bog Orchid, *Hammarbya paludosa* (p. 223), is a related plant that also forms pseudo-bulbs. It is a tiny species, its stem growing up to 12cm (5in) tall at most. It has a rosette of shiny, rounded leaves, their margins often fringed with tiny bulbils, and a spike of minute, yellow-green flowers. Each flower has spreading petals and sepals and a lip that points upwards. This tiny plant grows in wet *Sphagnum* bogs in northern and central Europe, mainly in Scotland in the British Isles. At one time it was much more widespread but it has disappeared with the elimination of its wetland habitats.

Musk Orchid, *Herminium monorchis*, has tuberous roots and slender, creeping stems which develop new tubers at their tips. At the time of flowering the plant has two elliptical-oblong leaves and a flowering stem growing betweem them. The stem grows about 15cm (6in) tall, has a small scale leaf halfway up and ends in a cylindrical spike of small, greenish, fragrant flowers formed of spreading petals and sepals and a three-lobed lip. This rare plant grows in short grassland, on chalk or limestone, scattered across Europe, mainly in southern and central England in Britain. Its numbers have decreased rapidly in recent years with the conversion of the downs and limestone hills from sheep grazing to arable farming.

The **Frog Orchid**, *Coeloglossum viride*, has an erect flowering stem about 25cm (10in) tall, with several brownish sheaths at its base and several leaves, the lowermost large and rounded, the upper ones smaller and narrower. Stem and leaves develop from two palmately lobed tubers beneath the ground. The small, slightly scented flowers are borne in a cylindrical spike; each has a hood formed from greenish or brownish sepals, green lateral petals often hidden by the hood, and a straight, green, dangling lip, three-lobed near the tip and tinged with reddish-brown. This plant grows in calcareous grassland, usually in hills and mountains, sometimes in dunes or on rock ledges; it is scattered across most of Europe and throughout the British Isles, more commonly in the north.

Fragrant Orchid, *Gymnadenia conopsea*, has a similar form to the Frog Orchid, with palmately lobed root tubers and a leafy flowering stem. But the stem grows up to 40cm (15in) tall and its leaves are narrow, the lower ones lance-shaped, slightly folded and hooded, the upper ones pressed close to the stem. The flowers are very fragrant, smelling of vanilla, often reddish-lilac but sometimes white or purple; they are borne in a dense, cylindrical spike. Each flower has a hood, two spread-ing lateral petals, a rounded, three-lobed lip and a long, slender, often curved spur. Fragrant Orchids grow in a variety of habitats, usually in grassland on calcareous soils, but also in heaths and woods; one variety grows in marshes. They are found throughout Europe and much of the British Isles.

Small White Orchid, *Pseudorchis albida*, is closely related to the Fragrant Orchid. It too has palmately lobed root tubers but these may be so deeply lobed as to appear separate. The erect, leafy flowering stem grows up to 30cm (1ft) tall and has glossy leaves, the lowermost keeled and lance-shaped, the upper ones narrow and bract-like. The flowers are very small, greenish-white with a faint scent of vanilla; they are half drooping and turned to one side, borne in a dense, cylindrical spike. Each has a broad hood formed from all the lateral petals and sepals, and a three-lobed lip with a triangular central lobe. This rather rare little orchid grows in dry grassland and heaths, on both calcareous and acid soils, in hills and mountains scattered across much of Europe, mainly in Scotland in the British Isles; its numbers are decreasing.

The **Butterfly Orchids** are a large group of about 200 species in the genus *Platanthera*, but few are found in Europe. They have tuberous roots and an erect flowering stem with few leaves, large ones near the base and the upper ones much smaller and bract-like. The flowers may be white or green and are borne in a broad spike; each has spreading lateral sepals, upper sepal and lateral petals joined to form a hood, and a narrow, strap-shaped lip with a long, slender spur. **Greater Butterfly Orchid**, *P. chlorantha*, has an erect stem up to 40cm (15in) tall, two bluntly elliptical basal leaves and a rather pyramidal spike of greenish flowers, sweetly scented at night. It grows in woods and in grassland, often on calcareous soils, scattered throughout much of Europe and the British Isles. **Lesser Butterfly Orchid**, *P. bifolia*, is a similar but smaller plant with a more cylindrical spike of whitish, less strongly scented flowers. It grows in wet places on moors and heaths, often in calcareous flushes, less frequently in open grassland and woods, scattered throughout Europe and much of the British Isles, more commonly in the north.

Lizard Orchid, *Himantoglossum hircinum*, is distinctive for the long, trailing lips of its flowers, said to resemble lizards. This species has a stout stem about 40cm (15in) tall, sometimes much taller, and a clump of elliptical-oblong leaves, the bases of the lowermost sheathing the stem, the upper ones smaller and bract-like. The conspicuous, untidy-looking flowers are borne in a loose spike; they smell of stale perspiration. Each has a pale grey-green hood formed of all the sepals and lateral petals joined together, often streaked with purple, and a distinctive lip, three-lobed, with curly lateral lobes and the long, strap-shaped, undulating central lobe, furry and whitish at the base with purple spots, and brownish-green towards the end, notched at the tip. This lobe is coiled like a watch spring in the buds and uncoils rapidly as the flowers open. Lizard Orchids

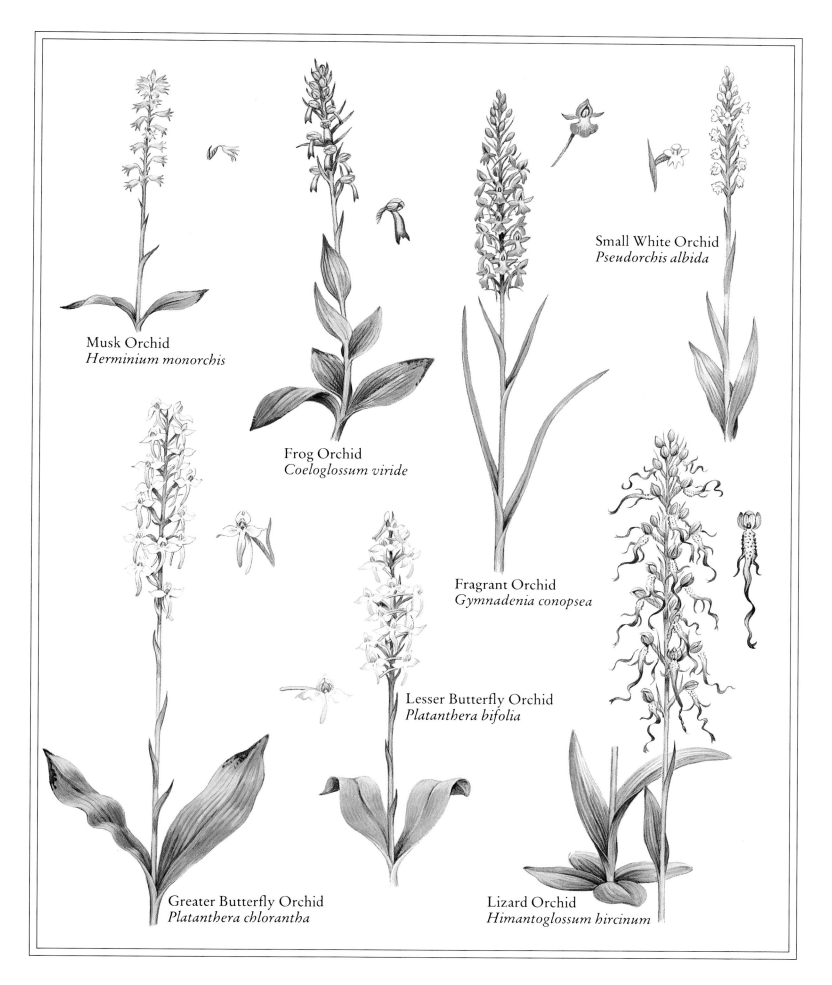

Musk Orchid
Herminium monorchis

Frog Orchid
Coeloglossum viride

Small White Orchid
Pseudorchis albida

Fragrant Orchid
Gymnadenia conopsea

Lesser Butterfly Orchid
Platanthera bifolia

Greater Butterfly Orchid
Platanthera chlorantha

Lizard Orchid
Himantoglossum hircinum

are rare; they grow in woodland margins and clearings, on roadside verges and in grassland, usually on chalk and limestone, scattered across Europe, except in the north, mainly in southeastern England in Great Britain.

The *Ophrys* species are a group of about 30 very distinctive orchids, many with flowers resembling insects or spiders; the majority come from the Mediterranean region. The **Bee Orchid**, *O. apifera*, has elliptical leaves, a stem 45cm (18in) tall at most and a spike of 2–5 flowers around midsummer. Each flower has three broad sepals, pink or white on the inside, green on the back, two small, lance-shaped, pinkish-green lateral petals and a lip that looks like a bumblebee. The lip is three-lobed; the two lateral lobes are small and hairy and the central lobe is globular, dark brown and velvety, with two yellow spots near the base, and a pointed tip that curves backwards. Bee Orchids grow in grassland, on the edges of fields, on roadsides and in quarries, often on chalk and limestone, also in fixed sand-dunes and on clay soils. They are scattered across much of Europe, except the north, mainly in England in the British Isles, more rarely in Wales and Ireland; their numbers are decreasing.

Early Spider Orchid, *Ophrys sphegodes*, is similar but its flowers resemble spiders rather than bees. They are borne 2–8 together in a spike in spring and early summer; their sepals are green, their smaller petals yellow-green and the rounded lip dark velvety brown with a bluish H- or X-shaped cross. This orchid grows in short grassland on chalk or limestone scattered across much of Europe, except the north, and in southern England; its numbers have decreased rapidly in recent years.

Fly Orchid, *Ophrys insectifera*, is a taller, more slender plant, growing up to 60cm (2ft) in height, with an elongated spike of 4–12 flowers. Each bloom has oblong, yellow-green sepals, purple-brown, velvety, thread-like petals and a narrow, three-lobed lip like a fly. The lip is velvety brown with a broad, bluish band across the middle, two small lateral lobes and a notched tip. Fly Orchids are not as rare as Spider Orchids but are not common; they grow in woods and coppices, on grassy banks and slopes, in fields and on roadsides, sometimes in fens, usually on calcareous soils, across much of Europe, mainly in southern England in Britain, more rarely in northern England, in parts of Wales and central Ireland.

The Spotted Orchids and the Marsh Orchids are a group of about 30 species belonging to the genus *Dactylorhiza*. They all have characteristic root tubers, deeply and palmately lobed into several almost separate finger-like lobes; their leaves may be plain or spotted and in their flowers the lateral sepals are always spreading, never contributing to the helmet often formed by the upper sepal and petals.

Early Marsh Orchid, *Dactylorhiza incarnata*, has several keeled, lance-shaped, erect leaves, usually unspotted, hooded at their tips, held erect and with their bases sheathing the flowering stem, becoming smaller higher up the stem. The stem grows about 60cm (2ft) tall and bears a dense, cylindrical spike of many flowers in summer; these are often flesh-coloured marked with spots and lines of darker colour, but they vary from pale yellow to magenta-purple. The upper sepal and the petals fall forwards over the flower, the lip has a short spur and the margin of the lip is reflexed backwards so that it appears very narrow. This orchid grows in marshes and wet meadows, in peaty fens and bogs, sometimes in dune slacks, scattered across most of Europe and the British Isles.

The **Spotted Orchids** are a variable complex of subspecies placed in the species *Dactylorhiza fuchsii* and *D. maculata*, recognizable from the dark spots on their leaves. They are among the most common European orchids. **Common Spotted Orchid**, *D. fuchsii*, often forms large colonies in open woods and scrub, in short grassland, often in calcareous soils, also in marshes and stabilized sand-dunes throughout much of Europe and the British Isles, becoming much less common in northern Scotland. Its leaves are keeled, marked with elongated, often confluent dark spots, the largest, broadest leaves at the base of the stem, smaller, narrower ones higher up. The flowers are borne in spikes which are conical when young, becoming cylindrical as they age; they vary from white to bright reddish-purple but are always marked with a symmetrical pattern of lines and blotches. Each flower has spreading lateral sepals, a helmet formed of the upper sepal and the petals, and a three-lobed lip with a slender spur. The central lobe of the lip is narrow and longer than the rounder lateral lobes.

The **Heath Spotted Orchid**, *Dactylorhiza maculata*, has leaves with much smaller, lighter, rounded spots; it is not uncommon for spots to be faint or absent. The leaves are much more uniform in shape than those of Common Spotted Orchids, narrowly lance-shaped or even linear, and the stem grows 15–50cm (6–20in) tall. Its pyramidal spikes have a few large flowers varying from pale to deep lilac-pink, but usually pale and marked with darker loops and dots. The flowers are similar in shape to those of Common Spotted Orchid, but the lip is broader than long and its central lobe is much smaller than its lateral lobes. This orchid grows in acid, peaty soils, in damp moors and dry heaths, in oak and beech woods, and in grassland across Europe and much of the British Isles, most commonly in the north and west.

The **Marsh Orchids**, the subspecies of *Dactylorhiza majalis*, are an even more complex group, very variable, difficult to distinguish from each other and freely hybridizing. Marsh Orchids have palmately lobed root tubers, a flowering stem up to 60cm (2ft) tall or more, and leaves which vary from unspotted to heavily spotted, the lowermost leaves sheathing the base of the stem. The flowers vary in colour from very pale to deep reddish-purple; they have upward-spreading lateral sepals (that look like wings), a helmet formed from the upper sepal and the lateral petals, and a lip which is broader than long. All Marsh Orchids grow in wet places.

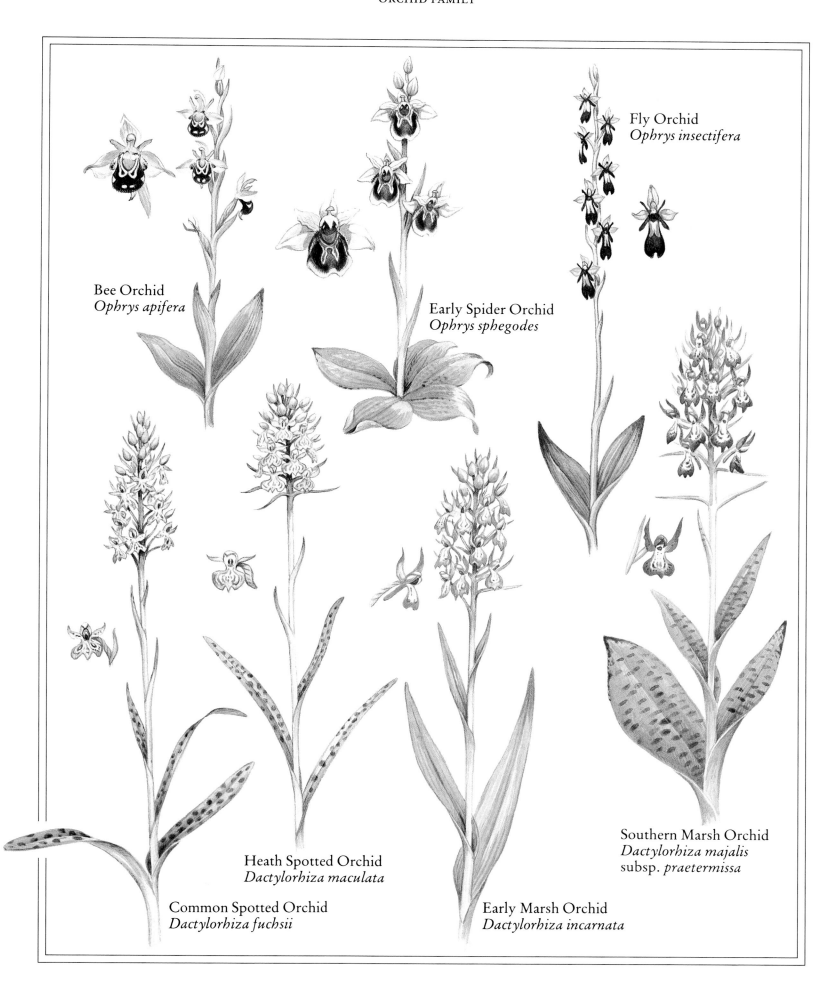

Bee Orchid
Ophrys apifera

Early Spider Orchid
Ophrys sphegodes

Fly Orchid
Ophrys insectifera

Heath Spotted Orchid
Dactylorhiza maculata

Common Spotted Orchid
Dactylorhiza fuchsii

Early Marsh Orchid
Dactylorhiza incarnata

Southern Marsh Orchid
Dactylorhiza majalis
subsp. *praetermissa*

227

Southern Marsh Orchid, *Dactylorhiza majalis* subsp.

The **Burnt-tip Orchid**, *Orchis ustulata*, gets its name from

Arum family
Araceae

A family of herbaceous plants, with about 115 genera and 2000 species mainly from the tropics. Tropical species often come from damp and steamy jungles, while more temperate species are frequently found in wet places. Several popular house plants come from this family, mostly grown for their large and impressive leaves rather than for their curious flowers. They include philodendrons, dieffenbachias and monsteras. Garden species include arums and calla lilies. Many of the plants in this family contain poisonous juice; however, they rarely cause serious poisoning because the juice is so acrid that it burns the lips and mouth, and is therefore not swallowed.

Family features The flowers are very small, often with an offensive scent, and borne in a dense spike (a spadix), usually subtended by a leafy bract (a spathe). The flowers may be hermaphrodite or unisexual; if unisexual, then the male flowers are borne on the upper part of the spadix, the females below. Hermaphrodite flowers usually have a perianth, with 4–6 lobes, free or forming a cup, but this is absent in unisexual flowers. There are 2–8 stamens opposite the perianth segments. The ovary is superior or embedded in the spadix and has 1–3 cells. The fruit is usually a berry, but may be leathery and split open. The leaves often have sheathing bases; they usually form a basal clump growing directly from the rhizome. The plants have watery or milky, acrid juice.

Sweetflag, *Acorus calamus*, is found in shallow water on the margins of slow-moving rivers and canals, ponds and lakes across much of Europe, except the north, mainly in England in the British Isles; it has been introduced from Asia. It spreads by stout rhizomes that creep in the mud, forming colonies of sword-like, wavy-edged leaves up to 1m (3ft) tall. The leaves have a scent of tangerines and cinnamon when bruised. Stems that look like three-angled leaves also grow from the rhizomes to bear flower spikes about halfway up, growing at an angle of about 45 degrees to the stems. The spikes bear densely packed, yellowish, hermaphrodite flowers with an unpleasant scent. Sweetflag rhizomes yield a volatile oil known as Calamus Oil, used in perfumery; the rhizomes are also used in herb medicine and in the production of Stockton Bitters. In medieval times the leaves were strewn as rushes on the floors of churches, castles and manor houses for their sweet scent.

Cuckoo-pint or Lords-and-ladies, *Arum maculatum*, is one of those plants with a multitude of names and much folklore, a lot of it sexual in nature (perhaps inevitably, given the appearance of its flowers). It grows in hedgerows and woods across much of Europe, except the north, and throughout England, Wales and Ireland, less frequently in Scotland. The large leaves unfurl in spring; they are shiny green, often black-spotted, arrow-shaped with long stalks. They are followed by the spathe, pale yellow-green and edged or streaked with purple, containing the dull purple spadix. Once the flowers are pollinated the spathe and leaves gradually wither, leaving the cluster of green berries at the top of a bare stalk; these gradually turn red as they ripen in late summer. They are very poisonous and the whole plant contains acrid, irritant sap.

Duckweed family
Lemnaceae

A small family of floating aquatic plants, with 3 genera and about 40 species, found in fresh water throughout the world.

The **Duckweeds**, the *Lemna* species, are found in the still waters of ponds and ditches. They have floating, leaf-like fronds (known as the 'thallus') and minute flowers which lack petals or sepals. **Common Duckweed**, *L. minor*, has opaque, rounded thalli which constantly divide into new ones; these may remain attached to the original thallus, or split off and float away. Each thallus has a single root beneath and may form flowers, which are developed in a cavity on the upper surface; flowers usually appear only in plants growing in shallow water in full sunlight. This is easily the most common species, growing in ponds and ditches (often covering the whole surface by late summer) throughout Europe, much of Great Britain and Ireland, becoming rare in northern Scotland.

Ivy-leaved Duckweed, *Lemna trisulca*, is a submerged species floating just beneath the surface of the water in ponds and ditches throughout Europe and much of the British Isles, but rare in Scotland and in the west. Its thalli are translucent and pointed-oval in shape; they float in clumps, several thalli joined together by their stalks, new ones arising in opposite pairs and at right angles to the parent.

Bulrush family
Typhaceae

A very small family, with only one genus, *Typha*, and 10 species, found throughout the world. All are aquatic plants, growing in shallow water, in marshes and reed-beds, along the edges of ponds and slow-moving rivers, and in ditches.

They are tall, perennial plants with creeping rhizomes, forming wide colonies in the right conditions—in marshes, for instance, where shallow water covers mud. Such places form excellent hiding and nesting places for aquatic birds. The erect stems grow up to 2.5m (9ft) tall in the largest species, with thick, sword-like leaves growing from the bases of the stems in overlapping rows. The stems are stiff and unbranched and bear the flowers in distinctive, terminal, cylindrical heads, the

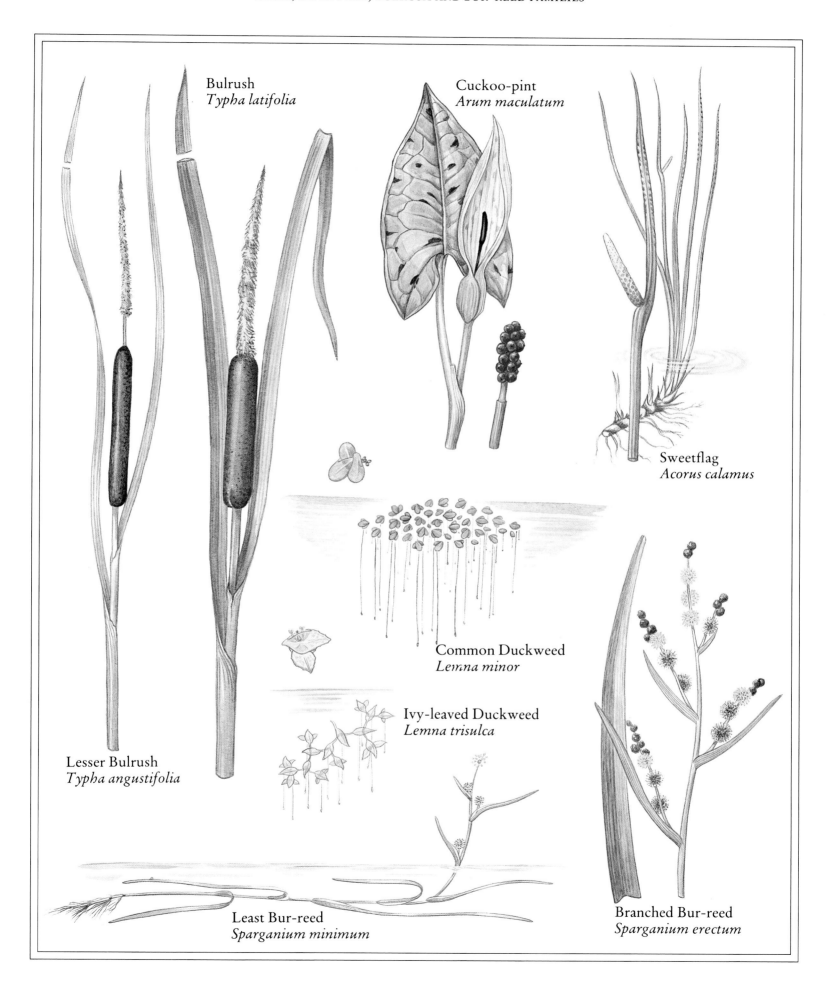

Bulrush
Typha latifolia

Cuckoo-pint
Arum maculatum

Sweetflag
Acorus calamus

Lesser Bulrush
Typha angustifolia

Common Duckweed
Lemna minor

Ivy-leaved Duckweed
Lemna trisulca

Least Bur-reed
Sparganium minimum

Branched Bur-reed
Sparganium erectum

greenish female flowers below and the male flowers above, yellow with pollen when in full bloom. The male flowers are shed after the pollen has blown away to pollinate the females, leaving a bare stalk, but the female flowers go on to form the brown fruiting heads. These are more familiar, as they last for months, persisting into autumn and winter.

Bulrush, *Typha latifolia* (p. 231), is the largest, growing up to 2.4m (9ft) tall, with leaves up to 20mm ($^3/_4$in) across. Its male and female flowers form one continuous cylindrical flower spike. It is also known as Cat's-tail and Greater Reedmace. The **Lesser Bulrush** or Lesser Reedmace, *T. angustifolia* (p. 231), is smaller, usually not more than 2m (6ft) tall, with narrow leaves only 6mm ($^1/_4$in) wide. Its male and female flowers are separated by a section of stem up to 8cm (3in) long. Both species are widespread in Europe north to southern Scandinavia, but the Bulrush is common while the Lesser Bulrush is much rarer. In the British Isles Bulrushes are common in England, Wales and Ireland, rare in Scotland; Lesser Bulrushes are scattered in England, rare in other areas.

Bur-reed family
Sparganiaceae

A small family of aquatic plants, with only one genus and about 20 species, but found in many parts of the world.

The **Bur-reeds**, *Sparganium* species, are perennial plants which spread by creeping rhizomes in marshes, or in shallow water on the edges of ponds and slow-moving rivers; they may form extensive stands. They have erect or floating stems and narrow, grass-like leaves, the bases of the leaves sheathing the stems. Their flowers are borne in small green balls, male flowers near the tip of the stem, female ones below.

Branched Bur-reed, *Sparganium erectum* (p. 231), varies in height, often 30–60cm (1–2ft) but sometimes up to 2m (6ft) tall. It has clumps of erect, three-angled leaves and branched flowering stems in the latter half of summer, the balls of male flowers borne above the females on the branches. Unbranched Bur-reed, *S. emersum*, has unbranched flowering stems and some of its leaves are floating. Both bur-reeds grow in shallow water throughout much of Europe and the British Isles, becoming much less common in the north. Branched Bur-reed is common in ponds, slow-moving rivers and ditches and in marshes; Unbranched Bur-reed is less common, growing on the margins of ponds and lakes.

Least Bur-reed, *Sparganium minimum* (p. 231), is a floating species, its stems and translucent, ribbon-like leaves floating on the surface of lakes, ponds and ditches in many areas of Europe and much of the British Isles; it is rare in the south. It is a small plant, its stems growing 30cm (1ft) long at most; its flowers are borne on stems emerging from the water, the females in balls on the stem, the males on stalks.

Sedge family
Cyperaceae

A large family of herbaceous plants, with about 100 genera and 4000 species, found throughout the world. Many are inconspicuous plants which go unnoticed among the grasses and they are of little economic importance. Papyrus, used as paper in ancient Egypt, came from a member of this family.

Family features The flowers are very small and inconspicuous; they may be hermaphrodite or unisexual and are arranged in small spikes (known as spikelets), each one solitary in the axil of a special bract called a glume. The spikelets are gathered into flower spikes and within these the glumes may be spirally arranged or borne in two opposite rows. In each flower there may be a perianth formed of scales or hairs, or the perianth may be absent; there are usually 2–3 stamens and a superior, single-celled ovary with two or three styles. The fruits are indehiscent nutlets. These plants often have rhizomes. Their leaves are basal or crowded at the bottom of the stem, linear in shape with a sheathing base and a narrow blade, or the blade may be absent.

The **Cotton-grasses**, *Eriophorum* species, are often the most conspicuous plants in their landscape (unlike most members of this family). About 20 species grow in fens and bogs, or on wet moors, in northern temperate and Arctic regions of the world. **Common Cotton-grass**, *E. angustifolium*, has creeping rhizomes and forms extensive colonies, with broadly linear, channelled leaves. The plants flower in early summer, the flower spikes borne in umbels at the tops of slender stems; the white cottony tufts of hairs that are such a conspicuous feature of this plant appear with the fruits and remain through the summer. It grows in wet bogs and fens across most of Europe and throughout the British Isles, much more commonly in the north, disappearing with improved drainage in many southern areas. Cotton-grass or Hare's-tail, *E. vaginatum*, is also common in the north; this species forms leafy tussocks and has a single tuft of white perched at the top of each stem.

Deer-grass, *Trichophorum cespitosum* (for many years *Scirpus caespitosus*), grows in damp upland heaths and moors, especially in blanket bogs, forming tussocks of slender stems. It is found throughout most of Europe and much of the British Isles, much more widespread and common in the north than in the south, and absent from parts of central England. It is a small plant, only 25cm (10in) tall at most, and its smooth stems are almost leafless, the leaves replaced by brownish sheaths at the base of the stem; only the uppermost sheath has a tiny blade. At the tip of each stem is a solitary, pale brown spikelet.

The **Spike-rushes**, *Eleocharis* species, are similar in form to Deer-grass, but in these species the uppermost sheath on the stem lacks a blade. **Common Spike-rush**, *E. palustris*, has far-creeping rhizomes and single stems or small tufts of stems

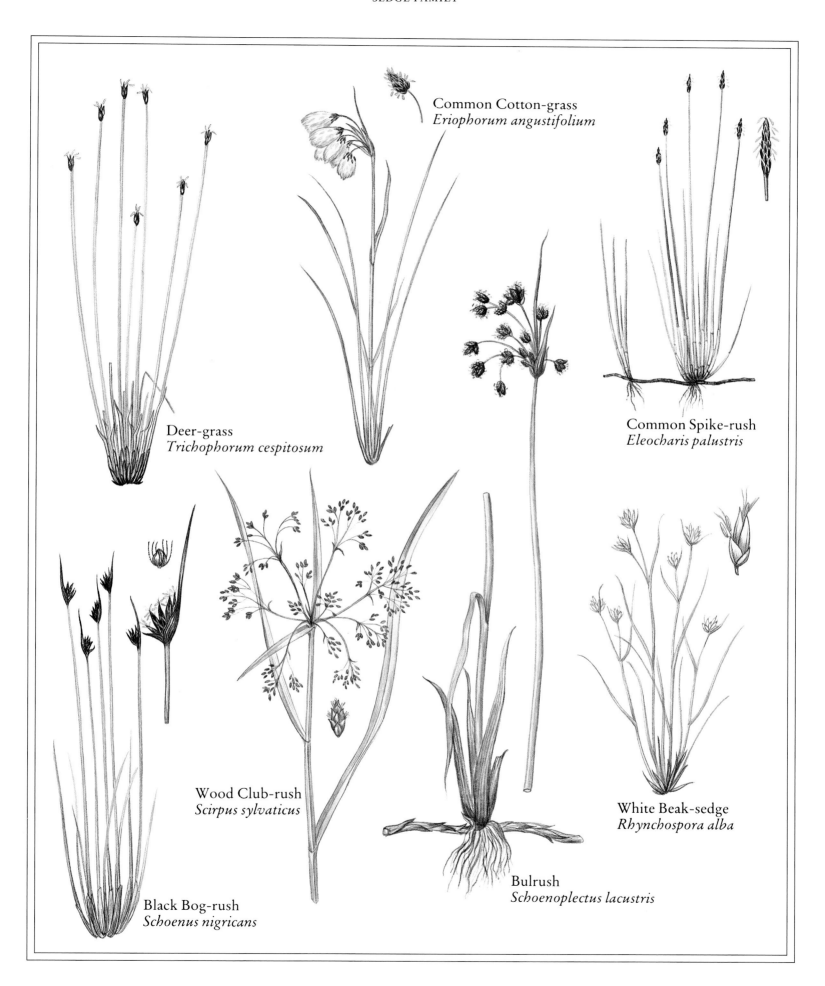

Common Cotton-grass
Eriophorum angustifolium

Deer-grass
Trichophorum cespitosum

Common Spike-rush
Eleocharis palustris

Wood Club-rush
Scirpus sylvaticus

White Beak-sedge
Rhynchospora alba

Black Bog-rush
Schoenus nigricans

Bulrush
Schoenoplectus lacustris

which may grow 60cm (2ft) tall, reddish at the base and with no blades on any of its yellow-brown sheaths. Solitary spikes of brown flowers tip the stems, the two lowest glumes sterile and much shorter than the spikelet. Plants grow in marshes and wet meadows, at the margins of lakes and ponds, and in ditches throughout Europe and the British Isles.

The **Club-rushes**, *Scirpus* species, are perennial plants with leafy stems and much-branched, terminal inflorescences. About 15 are found in Europe. **Wood Club-rush**, *S. sylvaticus* (p. 233), grows in wet places in woods and in marshes throughout most of Europe; it is scattered across the British Isles, but absent from northern Scotland and much of Ireland. This is a tall plant, with stout, erect, three-angled stems up to 120cm (4ft) in height, many broad, flat leaves with rough margins, and branched clusters of numerous greenish-brown spikelets in summer. Sea Club-rush, *S. maritimus*, is similar but smaller, with narrower leaves and red-brown spikelets. It grows in ditches and ponds near the sea and in tidal estuaries around the coast of Europe and the British Isles.

Black Bog-rush, *Schoenus nigricans* (p. 233), forms dense perennial tufts of wiry stems and leaves up to 75cm (30in) tall in marshes and other damp, peaty places, particularly near the sea, in most of Europe and the British Isles; it is much more common in Scotland and Ireland than in England or Wales. The leaves are cylindrical with inrolled margins, growing as tall as the stems, and the tips of the stems bear dense tufts of blackish flowers in early summer.

White Beak-sedge, *Rhynchospora alba* (p. 233), grows in bogs and marshes, in peaty, acid soils, scattered across Europe and the British Isles, mainly in the north and west. It is a tufted perennial, its stems slender and growing up to 50cm (20in) tall, its shorter, channelled leaves growing from the bases of the stems. The lowermost sheaths produce no leaves, but often have bulbils in their axils. In summer the distinctive whitish spikelets are borne in dense clusters at the tips of the stems, often with one or two lateral clusters as well, all of them on long stalks in the axils of leaf-like bracts.

Bulrushes, *Schoenoplectus lacustris* (p. 233), are familiar to many people, not as living plants but as the rushes with which mats, baskets and chair-seats are made; they are also used for thatching. The plant is ideal for this kind of use, since the stems grow straight and up to 3m (9ft) long, they are flexible and they have a natural waterproofing (from growing in wet places). Bulrushes grow in ponds and lakes, usually when they are silting up, across Europe and scattered throughout the British Isles. They have creeping rhizomes, round stems with the lowermost leaves linear and submerged, upper ones reduced to sheaths. The plants flower in summer, producing dense clusters of reddish-brown spikelets at the tops of the stems.

The true **Sedges** are a huge group, with about 2000 species in the genus *Carex*, found throughout the world; about 160 grow wild in Europe. They have solid, three-angled stems and linear, often keeled leaves. The flowers are unisexual, borne in one-flowered spikelets, each with a glume; the spikelets are gathered into several spikes, often male flowers in the terminal spike(s) and females in the lower one(s).

Sand Sedge, *Carex arenaria*, spreads rapidly with its far-creeping rhizomes, helping to stabilize sand-dunes around the coasts of the British Isles and Europe. It often grows in straight lines, marked by tufts of rigid leaves with inrolled margins. The erect flowering stems appear in summer, growing up to 40cm (15in) tall, with several dense, terminal flower spikes, male flowers in the upper spikes, mixed flowers in the middle and female flowers in the lower ones.

The **Flea Sedge**, *Carex pulicaris*, is unusual among sedges in having a solitary, terminal flower spike, with a cluster of male flowers above and females below. The female flowers are erect at first, spreading and drooping as the spindle-shaped fruits ripen and soon losing their reddish-brown glumes. This is a small but creeping plant, forming dense patches of narrow channelled leaves and slender stems only 30cm (1ft) tall at most. It grows in damp, calcareous grassland, base-rich fens and moors across most of Europe and the British Isles, but is uncommon in the south and east.

The **Hairy Sedge**, *Carex hirta*, grows in woods and rough grassland, in damp meadows, on roadsides and in hedgerows throughout Europe and much of the British Isles, becoming rare in Scotland. It is typical of many sedges in that the male and female flower spikes are quite separate, the female spikes lower down the stem and the males at the top. In this species there are 2–3 widely spaced, green, female spikes, the lowest often near the base of the stem, and 2–3 erect, reddish-brown male spikes at the top. This sedge is readily recognizable from its hairy leaves and shaggy leaf sheaths, and from its hairy fruits. It is a perennial, with tufts of leafy stems about 15–60cm (6–24in) tall.

Carnation Sedge, *Carex panicea*, grows in wet places like many other sedges, this species in fens and marshes, in wet, grassy places and mountain moors across much of Europe and throughout the British Isles, becoming less common in the south. It is a tufted perennial plant, with bluish or greyish leaves (like those of carnations) and erect stems up to 60cm (2ft) tall, flowering in summer. The female spikes are erect, solitary or widely spaced with few flowers, the single male spike brown. The fruits are distinctive—inflated and egg-shaped, smooth and grey-green, often purple-tinged.

Spring Sedge, *Carex caryophyllea*, is one of the smallest sedges, a perennial with tufts of leaves and slender stems often only 5–15cm (2–6in) tall, growing from short, creeping rhizomes. It has a single brown, club-shaped male spike at the top of each stem and 1–3 touching female spikes below, followed by olive-green, three-angled fruits. The tufts of leaves remain green in winter and the plants flower in spring; they grow in dry grassland, usually on calcareous or base-rich soils,

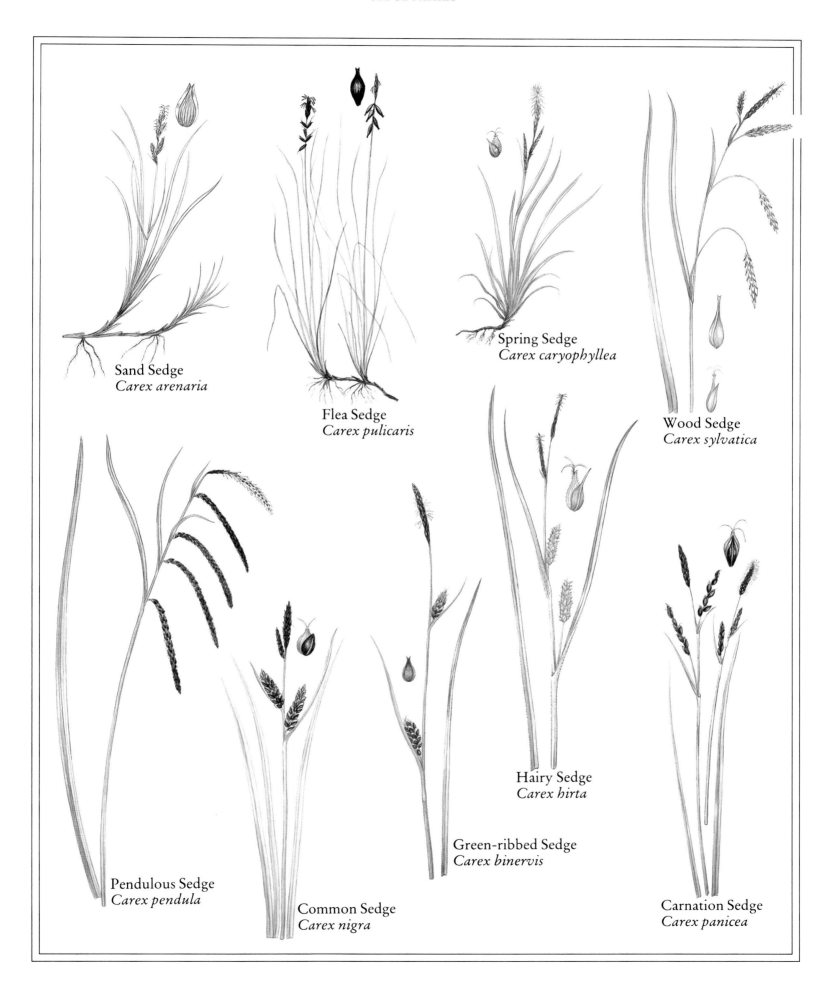

Sand Sedge
Carex arenaria

Flea Sedge
Carex pulicaris

Spring Sedge
Carex caryophyllea

Wood Sedge
Carex sylvatica

Pendulous Sedge
Carex pendula

Common Sedge
Carex nigra

Green-ribbed Sedge
Carex binervis

Hairy Sedge
Carex hirta

Carnation Sedge
Carex panicea

often on chalk and limestone, throughout the British Isles and much of Europe north to southern Scandinavia.

Green-ribbed Sedge, *Carex binervis* (p. 235), grows in acid soils, on heaths and moors, and in rough grassland, in western Europe and throughout the British Isles, more commonly in the north and west than in the south and east. It is a tufted perennial, with keeled leaves and stems up to 150cm (5ft) tall; the flowering spikes appear around midsummer, the single purplish male at the top and the 2–3 widely separated, erect, cylindrical female spikes lower down. The fruits are distinctive, three-angled, pale green or purplish, each with two prominent dark green stripes.

Common Sedge, *Carex nigra* (p. 235), is a variable plant, often with tufts of leaves and stems up to 60cm (2ft) tall, the leaves rough and more or less as long as the stems, the stems slender with a mass of blackish fibres at the base (the remains of dead leaves). In summer the plant produces one or two purplish male spikes at the top of the stem, the lower one smaller than the upper, and two or more female spikes below; the female flowers have black glumes which persist beneath the greenish or purplish fruits. This plant grows beside water, in marshes and other wet, grassy places, often on acid soils, throughout Europe and the British Isles.

Wood Sedge, *Carex sylvatica* (p. 235), grows in wet places, on clay soils in woods and in damp grassland across most of Europe and throughout the British Isles, becoming less common in Scotland and Ireland. It forms dense tufts of soft, shiny green leaves and leafy stems growing up to 60cm (2ft) tall, bearing distinctive flowering spikes. The single male spike grows erect above several nodding, few-flowered females.

Pendulous Sedge, *Carex pendula* (p. 235), is another woodland species, growing in damp woods and on the banks of shaded streams, scattered across most of Europe and the British Isles, becoming much rarer in the north. This is one of the tallest sedges, with clumps of broad, yellow-green leaves and graceful, leafy flowering stems up to 180cm (6ft) in height. The plants flower in summer; each stem has 1–2 narrow male spikes at the top and 4–5 elongated, hanging, dense-flowered female spikes lower down, widely separated from each other.

Grass family
Gramineae

A very large family, mostly of herbaceous plants, found throughout the world, with about 620 genera and 10,000 species. Many of these are found in grasslands, a habitat the grasses have made their own and which only came into being with the origin of the grasses some 15 million years ago (a very short time in the history of the Earth, which is 4.6 billion years old, and not very long before the origin of man).

Economically, as well as ecologically, the grasses are arguably the most influential plant family on Earth; they provide the cereals which are the staple foods for most people—wheat, rice, millet, maize, oats, barley and rye—and also sugar cane; they are the main source of fodder for grazing animals raised for meat and dairy products—cattle, sheep and goats; and the bamboos are used as building materials. Other grasses are used in paper-making and grown as ornamentals.

Family features The flowers are hermaphrodite, consisting usually of three stamens and a single-celled ovary with two feathery stigmas. Each flower is enclosed in two bracts, the lower one (the lemma) leathery or membranous, the upper one (the palea) usually thin, and the whole of this structure forms one floret. One to many florets are arranged on a short axis with two bracts (the glumes) at the base, the whole forming a spikelet; where there are many florets, they are often overlapping and arranged in two rows in the spikelet. The spikelets may be borne on stalks and arranged in loose racemes or compound inflorescences, or they may be stalkless and borne in dense spikes. The fruits are specialized achenes. Grasses grow from the base (this is why they can withstand mowing or grazing). Their leaves are linear, with a sheathing base encircling the stem and a narrow blade; there is a flap-like structure at the junction of the blade and the sheath which is known as the ligule—this may be membranous or hair-like.

The **Fescues**, *Festuca* species, are a large group of about 300 grasses, all from temperate regions of the world or tropical mountain ranges, with about 60 in Europe. Some of them are among the best fodder plants for domestic grazing animals, others among the most important grass species for lawns.

Red Fescue, *Festuca rubra*, is an important component of hay meadows and pastures throughout Europe and the British Isles, a valuable fodder plant spreading into large patches with its creeping rhizomes. It is also found on roadsides and other open, grassy places. It has many non-flowering shoots with thread-like leaves, and erect, leafy flowering stems up to 60cm (2ft) tall with flat leaves; their sheathing bases are pinkish and soon decay into threads. The plants flower in early summer, with attractive, branched inflorescences of greenish or purplish spikelets. Red Fescue has several subspecies: subsp. *rubra* is the one found in meadows and pastures; others grow in coastal habitats like dunes and salt marshes.

Sheep's Fescue, *Festuca ovina*, is another important pasture grass, this one growing in well-drained, shallow soils on uplands and moors, where it provides valuable grazing for sheep. It is found throughout Europe and the British Isles. It forms dense tufts of stiff, bristle-like, grey-green leaves, their sheaths split often to the base. The plants flower in summer, the flowering stems growing about 50cm (20in) tall and producing quite dense, erect inflorescences with green, often violet-tinged spikelets. Several very similar species also grow in dry grassland and heathland.

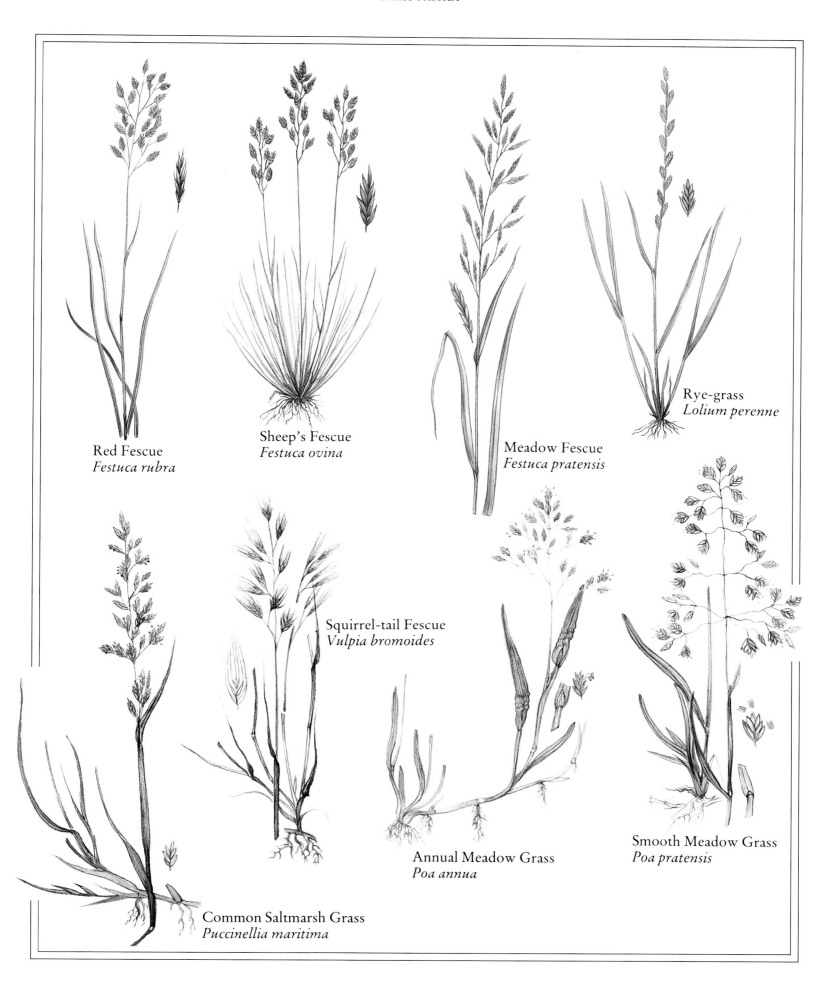

Red Fescue
Festuca rubra

Sheep's Fescue
Festuca ovina

Meadow Fescue
Festuca pratensis

Rye-grass
Lolium perenne

Squirrel-tail Fescue
Vulpia bromoides

Annual Meadow Grass
Poa annua

Smooth Meadow Grass
Poa pratensis

Common Saltmarsh Grass
Puccinellia maritima

Meadow Fescue, *Festuca pratensis* (p. 237), also grows in meadows, pastures and other grassy places throughout Europe and the British Isles, but rarely in northern Scotland. It is a perennial plant with tufts of dark green leaves, the base of the plant clothed with the dark brown remains of old leaf sheaths. It flowers around midsummer, with slender, nodding, one-sided inflorescences of greenish or purplish spikelets.

Rye-grass, *Lolium perenne* (p. 237), is another valuable grass, an important component of rich hay meadows and pastures, also sown in leys (often with clover) for hay, silage and grazing. It is found throughout Europe and the British Isles, not only in meadows, but also on roadsides and in waste places. Rye-grass is a tufted perennial plant, its leaves folded when young, becoming flat with maturity. It has distinctive green flowering spikes in summer, long and narrow, up to 90cm (3ft) tall, their stems flexed in a zigzag pattern, their spikelets borne edge on and alternately on each side.

Squirrel-tail Fescue, *Vulpia bromoides* (p. 237), is an annual grass which has short, narrow leaves with inrolled margins and slender flowering stems growing up to 60cm (2ft) tall, well above the leaves. The flowers are green, borne in little-branched, one-sided inflorescences around midsummer; the spikelets have long awns. This grass grows in dry places on hills and heaths, on roadsides and waste places across most of Europe and the British Isles, becoming rare in Scotland and absent from northern Europe. It is one of about 15 *Vulpia* species in Europe, all with slender, one-sided inflorescences and awned spikelets with unequal glumes.

The **Meadow Grasses** are a large group of about 300 species in the genus *Poa*, found in cold and temperate regions of the world; about 35 grow in Europe. They are annual or perennial grasses, with spreading, branched inflorescences of soft, flattened spikelets. They characteristically have a tuft of cottony hairs on the lemma of each floret.

Smooth Meadow Grass, *Poa pratensis* (p. 237), is another component grass of good pastures and hay meadows, growing wild in these and other grassy places throughout Europe and the British Isles. Several varieties have been developed, some to increase fertility in meadows, others as fine grasses for lawns. This is a small perennial plant, with creeping rhizomes and tufts of flat or pleated leaves. It flowers in summer, with branched, pyramidal inflorescences on stems 50cm (20in) tall at most, 3–5 branches arising at each of the lower nodes.

Annual Meadow Grass, *Poa annua* (p. 237), is often found on bare ground and in waste places, growing as a weed in gardens and on cultivated land, also in grassy places and tracks, throughout Europe and the British Isles. It is a little, annual grass, with tufts of pale green, often transversely wrinkled leaves and sprawling stems only 30cm (1ft) tall at most (often much shorter). It flowers throughout the year, with branched, more or less pyramidal inflorescences, the lowermost branches spreading or turned backwards in fruit.

Common Saltmarsh Grass, *Puccinellia maritima* (p. 237), is one of several species in this genus found near the sea, in damp, muddy ground and salt marshes. This one is a creeping perennial which can form a grassy sward if conditions suit it, where the mud is mixed with sand; it forms thick tufts of leaves and creeping stems, its leaves narrow, flat or folded and somewhat fleshy. It flowers in summer, the inflorescences one-sided and rather narrow, but much branched with 2–3 more or less erect branches arising at each node; they are borne on erect stems growing up to 80cm (30in) tall. This grass grows in salt marshes around the coast of Europe and the British Isles.

Cock's-foot, *Dactylis glomerata*, is a coarse grass, its large clumps of leaves and harsh greenish flowers common and easily recognized in meadows and waste places, beside roads and in other rough, grassy places. It is found throughout Europe and the British Isles and, surprisingly, is a valuable hay and pasture grass. Cock's-foot is a perennial, with rough, more or less keeled, grey-green leaves and flowering stems growing up to 2m (6ft) tall, but often much less. The inflorescences are erect and dense, the lower spikelets in dense clusters on long, somewhat spreading stems but the uppermost ones clustered together on very short stems.

Crested Dog's-tail, *Cynosurus cristatus*, is a perennial species found in hay meadows and pastures on a wide range of soils throughout Europe and the British Isles. It has rough, more or less keeled leaves and characteristic flowering spikes about 60cm (2ft) tall, long and narrow with clusters of awned spikelets borne alternately on each side of the stem, creating a zigzag effect. There are two kinds of spikelet in each cluster, the upper ones fertile with brown stamens, the lower ones sterile, with rigid comb-like lemmas.

The **Sweet-grasses** are a group of about 40 aquatic grass species in the genus *Glyceria*, found in temperate regions of the world, with about 13 in Europe. They have submerged stems creeping over the mud at the bottom of lakes and rivers, with more erect stems growing towards the surface. **Floating Sweet-grass**, *G. fluitans*, is one of the most common, found throughout Europe and the British Isles in shallow, slow-moving or still water, at the sides of lakes and rivers or in ditches. It is a succulent perennial plant, forming a dense mass of vegetation, its upward-growing stems floating beneath the surface and then growing erect above it, reaching a height of 90cm (3ft). The leaves are flat, bright green and often rough. In summer the green flowers appear, borne in branched inflorescences, wide-spreading while the flowers are open, but then contracting into a narrow, often nodding spike in fruit.

Quaking Grass, *Briza media*, is one of the most attractive grasses, with a delicate inflorescence trembling in every breeze. It is a tufted perennial plant, with flat leaves and erect flowering stems in summer growing up to 60cm (2ft) tall. The purplish spikelets are borne in distinctive, broadly egg-shaped or triangular clusters, nodding on fine, wavy stalks in a spread-

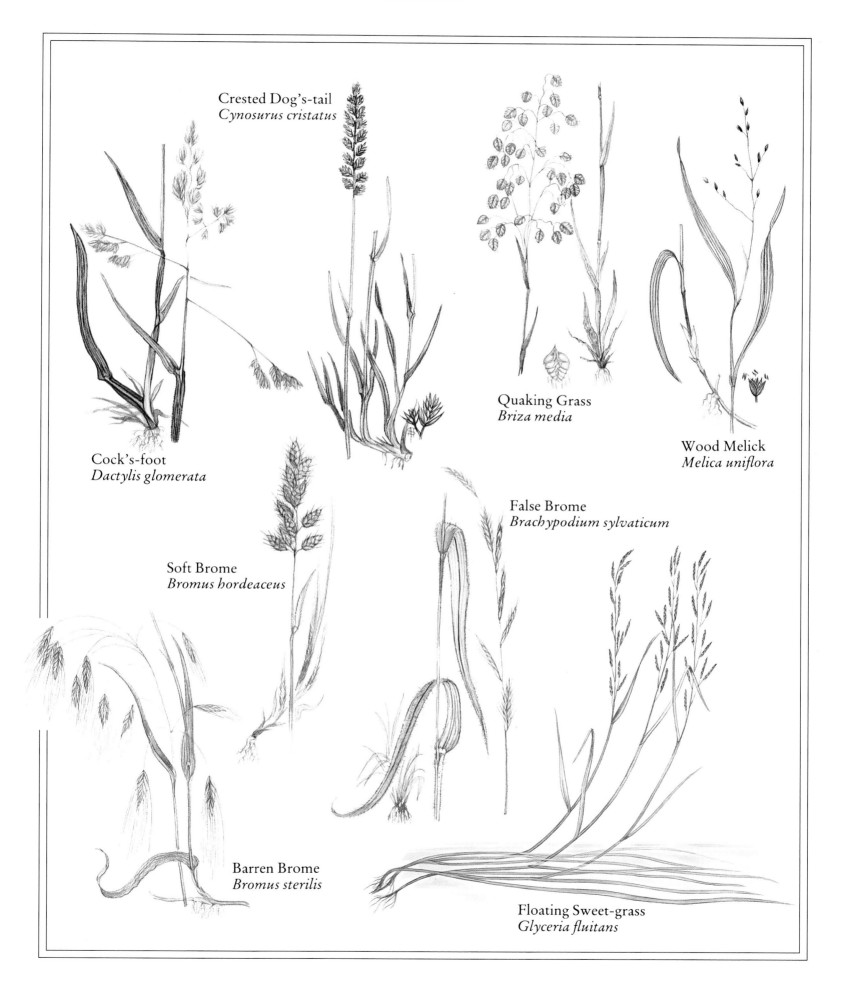

Crested Dog's-tail
Cynosurus cristatus

Quaking Grass
Briza media

Wood Melick
Melica uniflora

Cock's-foot
Dactylis glomerata

False Brome
Brachypodium sylvaticum

Soft Brome
Bromus hordeaceus

Barren Brome
Bromus sterilis

Floating Sweet-grass
Glyceria fluitans

ing inflorescence. Quaking Grass grows in a variety of grassy places, often in calcareous soils. It is found across much of Europe and the British Isles, becoming rare or absent in northern and western Scotland.

Wood Melick, *Melica uniflora* (p. 239), is one of the few plants to grow in beech woods, in clearings and rides, also more generally in woodland margins and shady hedgerows. It is found throughout most of Europe and the British Isles, less commonly in Ireland and Scotland. This is another attractive grass with a delicate inflorescence. It is a perennial, with creeping rhizomes and bright green, flat leaves, rough on their undersides and with long hairs on their upper surfaces. In early summer the flowering stems grow about 60cm (2ft) tall, ending in branched, arching inflorescences with erect spikelets; each spikelet contains only two florets, one fertile and the other sterile, cupped in two purplish-brown glumes.

The **Brome Grasses** are a group of about 50 species in the genus *Bromus*, found mostly in northern temperate areas; about 35 grow in Europe. They may be annuals, biennials or perennials; they have flat leaves and flattened spikelets formed of numerous overlapping florets. The glumes are unequal —usually the upper one is the larger of the two. In many species the florets have long awns.

Barren Brome, *Bromus sterilis* (p. 239), is an untidy annual plant with soft, downy leaves and sprawling, hairless stems growing up to 1m (3ft) tall. In summer the inflorescence droops with the weight of its flattened, long-awned spikelets, one spikelet to each branch. This is a common grass, growing in waste places and beside roads, on the margins of fields and as a garden weed throughout Europe and much of Great Britain, but absent from much of Scotland and scattered in Ireland.

Soft Brome or Lop-grass, *Bromus hordeaceus* (p. 239), also has awned spikelets but in this species the awns are much shorter. This plant may be annual or biennial; it has soft, often hairy leaves, and flowers in summer, with a flowering stem up to 80cm (30in) tall and an erect, dense inflorescence of hairy, short-awned spikelets. It grows in grassy places, meadows, on roadsides and waste ground, often in sand-dunes and on cliffs beside the sea, throughout Europe and the British Isles; however, it is much more common in the south than the north.

False Brome, *Brachypodium sylvaticum* (p. 239), is a woodland grass found in woods and hedgerows, sometimes in grassland where a wood once existed, throughout Europe and the British Isles. It is a perennial, with broad, yellow-green, drooping leaves, rough to the touch, erect flowering stems up to 90cm (3ft) tall and slender, nodding inflorescences formed of alternate spikelets. These are so narrow as to be almost linear in shape, finely awned and borne on short stalks.

The **Couch Grasses** are a large group of about 100 species, many of them until recently placed in the genus *Agropyron*, but now moved to *Elymus*. They are tough perennial plants, usually with creeping rhizomes and narrow, zigzag flowering spikes, the spikelets arranged broadside on to the stem. **Couch Grass** or Twitch, *E. repens*, is a notorious garden weed, extremely difficult to eradicate, invading and taking over lawns, vegetable gardens and flower beds if left unchecked. It also grows on roadsides and in waste places, in arable land and rough grassland throughout Europe and the British Isles. It has many prostrate non-flowering shoots and erect flowering stems up to 120cm (4ft) tall, with dull green leaves and zigzag spikes of overlapping spikelets. The similar Sea Couch Grass, *E. pycnanthus*, is a coastal species found in sand-dunes and on sandy shores; its stems and leaves are stiff and rigid, and its leaves often have inrolled margins and pointed tips.

Lyme Grass, *Leymus arenarius* (formerly called *Elymus arenarius*), is a coastal plant found with Marram Grass on the shifting sands of sand-dunes (on the fore dunes, not in the relative safety of the fixed dunes), its creeping stems and ability to form new shoots when buried helping it to survive in this unstable environment and ultimately helping to bring stability. It is a stout perennial plant, forming large tufts of stems growing up to 2m (6ft) tall, with rigid, sharp-pointed, blue-grey leaves, their margins inrolled to cut down water loss. The plants flower in the latter half of summer, producing long, dense inflorescences with two spikelets at each node arranged in two rows alternating all along the stem. Each spikelet has two large glumes, often placed at the front of it.

Wild Oats, *Avena fatua*, are widespread in Europe, only common in southern and eastern England in Britain, scattered elsewhere, growing in arable land and waste places and flowering in late summer. This is an annual plant, growing up to 1m (3ft) tall, with a spreading inflorescence of dangling spikelets, silky-hairy in texture with tawny hairs and tipped with bent awns. The spikelets readily fall apart when the seeds are ripe. Cultivated Oats belong to a similar species.

Meadow Oat-grass, *Avenula pratensis* (formerly *Helictotrichon pratense*), grows in short grassland on chalk and limestone throughout western and central Europe and in Great Britain. It is a perennial plant with erect stems up to 80cm (30in) tall, stiff, grey-green, often channelled leaves, and a narrow inflorescence of large spikelets held erect on short branches. It flowers around midsummer. Downy Oat-grass, *A. pubescens*, has soft, downy leaves and a spreading inflorescence, with erect spikelets. It grows in rough grassland, on basic soils throughout the British Isles and Europe. In both these species the spikelets have long, abruptly bent awns.

False Oat-grass, *Arrhenatherum elatius*, is a robust, tufted perennial grass, with erect stems up to 50cm (20in) tall, sometimes swollen at the base. The leaves are flat and weak, often rough but with smooth sheaths. Plants flower in summer; the inflorescence is rather narrow but loose and often nodding, with several branches arising at every node and shiny, often purplish spikelets. Each spikelet has two florets, the upper one essentially awnless and the lemma of the lower one with a long,

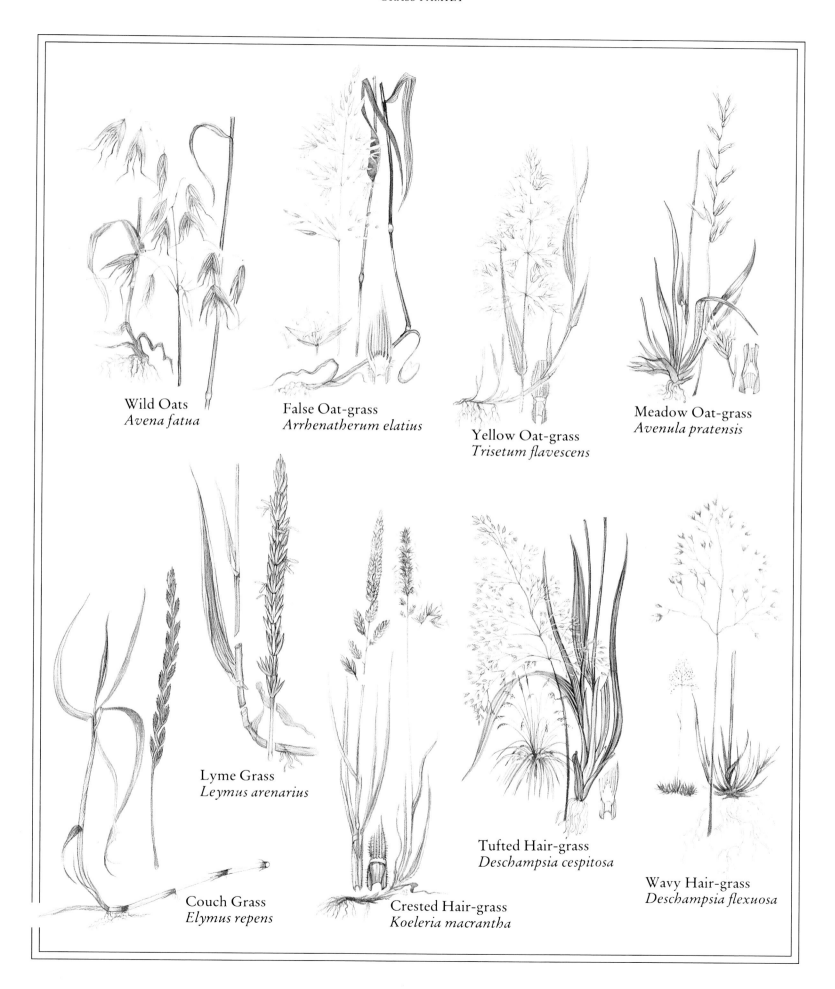

Wild Oats
Avena fatua

False Oat-grass
Arrhenatherum elatius

Yellow Oat-grass
Trisetum flavescens

Meadow Oat-grass
Avenula pratensis

Lyme Grass
Leymus arenarius

Couch Grass
Elymus repens

Crested Hair-grass
Koeleria macrantha

Tufted Hair-grass
Deschampsia cespitosa

Wavy Hair-grass
Deschampsia flexuosa

bent awn. This common grass grows in meadows, on rough, grassy roadsides, on waste ground, in scree and shingle throughout Europe and the British Isles.

Crested Hair-grass, *Koeleria macrantha* (p. 241), is another tufted perennial grass, this one found in short grassland on chalk and limestone scattered across much of Europe, except the north, and in many areas of the British Isles. It has tufts of narrow, flat or folded leaves with the old sheaths from last year persisting at the base, and erect stems up to 40cm (15in) tall, flowering in summer. The inflorescence is narrow and often lobed, formed of flattened, glistening spikelets, varying in colour from green to purplish.

Yellow Oat-grass, *Trisetum flavescens* (p. 241), gets its name from its numerous glistening, yellowish spikelets. It resembles Wild Oat in its appearance and in the bent awns on the spikelets, but the spikelets are much smaller and may be erect or nodding. Yellow Oat-grass is a loosely tufted perennial, with leaves softly hairy on their upper surface and erect flowering stems up to 80cm (30in) tall, flowering in early summer. It grows in meadows, pastures and other grassy places, especially in dry, calcareous soils, throughout Europe and much of the British Isles, but is absent from the north.

Tufted Hair-grass, *Deschampsia cespitosa* (p. 241), is one of about 10 species in this genus found in Europe, all stout, tufted perennial plants. It grows in damp meadows and woods, usually on heavy, poorly drained soils, also in marshes and wet moors, throughout Europe and the British Isles. This may be a large plant, with dense tussocks of coarse leaves and stiff stems up to 2m (6ft) in height. It flowers in the latter half of summer, with lax, nodding inflorescences of numerous spikelets on slender stems; these spikelets are shiny, often silvery or purplish in colour, with straight awns.

Wavy Hair-grass, *Deschampsia flexuosa* (p. 241), is a smaller, more slender but also densely tufted plant, which has bristle-like, rough-edged leaves and stems up to 1m (3ft) tall. It flowers around midsummer, forming a delicate inflorescence with long, wavy branches and shiny spikelets, often silvery or purplish with bent awns. This grass grows in acid soils, in poor grassland, on dry moors, heaths and in open woods throughout Europe and the British Isles. It is often the only plant that can grow in the acid 'soil' of colliery spoil tips.

Sweet Vernal Grass, *Anthoxanthum odoratum*, gets its name from its scent of coumarin, more familiar to most people as the smell of new-mown hay (which actually gets its scent from Sweet Vernal Grass). It grows in meadows and pastures, heaths and moors, and in open woodland throughout Europe and the British Isles. This is a tufted perennial grass, with short flat, somewhat hairy leaves, and flowering stems up to 50cm (20in) tall. It flowers in spring and early summer, producing spike-like inflorescences of green spikelets with bent awns.

Yorkshire Fog, *Holcus lanatus*, is an apt name for this plant, with its soft leaves and grey-purple flowers. It is a tufted, short-lived perennial grass found on roadsides and waste places, in woods, fields and meadows throughout Europe and the British Isles. It has flat, softly downy leaves, flowering stems up to 1m (3ft) tall in summer and bushy inflorescences, starting out dense and then opening up, varying in colour from whitish to pinkish-green or purple, attractive to the sight and touch. The spikelets have hooked awns.

Creeping Soft-grass, *Holcus mollis*, is a true perennial plant, with creeping rhizomes and tufts or mats of rough leaves. It flowers around midsummer, with stiff, erect flowering stems up to 1m (3ft) tall, their joints conspicuously hairy, and branched inflorescences of brownish or purplish spikelets with bent awns. This grass grows in acid soils, usually in woodland but also on heaths and in pastures, throughout Europe and the British Isles.

The **Bent-grasses** are a large group of about 200 species in the genus *Agrostis*, found in temperate regions of the world. They are tufted or creeping perennial plants with small spikelets, each spikelet containing only one floret. **Brown Bent-grass**, *A. canina*, grows in damp, grassy places in acid soils, one of several common *Agrostis* species found throughout Europe and the British Isles. It forms loose tufts of stems with flat leaves, up to 60cm (2ft) tall, some of the stems sprawling and rooting at the nodes, others erect. It flowers around midsummer, producing purplish-brown inflorescences that are compact before and after flowering, loosely branched while the flowers are open.

Marram Grass, *Ammophila arenaria*, is the most obvious of the sand-dune grasses, forming large, untidy clumps on the fore dunes all around the coasts of western Europe and the British Isles. It spreads by means of far-creeping rhizomes, rooting at the nodes and producing new plants, penetrating through the sand and gradually stabilizing it until other plants can also begin to colonize the dunes. Its leaves are distinctive, long and narrow with sharp points, rolled almost into a cylinder, smooth and polished on the outside, ribbed on the inside, superbly adapted for conserving water. Marram Grass flowers in the latter half of summer, producing erect stems up to 120cm (4ft) tall and dense, cylindrical inflorescences of whitish, one-flowered spikelets.

The **Small-reeds**, *Calamagrostis* species, are a large group of about 280 tall, perennial grasses found in damp places in the temperate regions of the world; about 20 grow in Europe, together with their hybrids. **Wood Small-reed** or Bushgrass, *C. epigejos*, forms dense patches of stout, erect stems up to 2m (6ft) tall in damp woods and fens, in ditches and beside streams across most of Europe and in England; it is found more rarely in Wales and Scotland. It has flat, long-pointed, rough leaves and branched, spreading inflorescences of purple-brown spikelets in the latter half of summer. Each spikelet contains only one floret with numerous silky hairs at its base (this is true for all small-reeds).

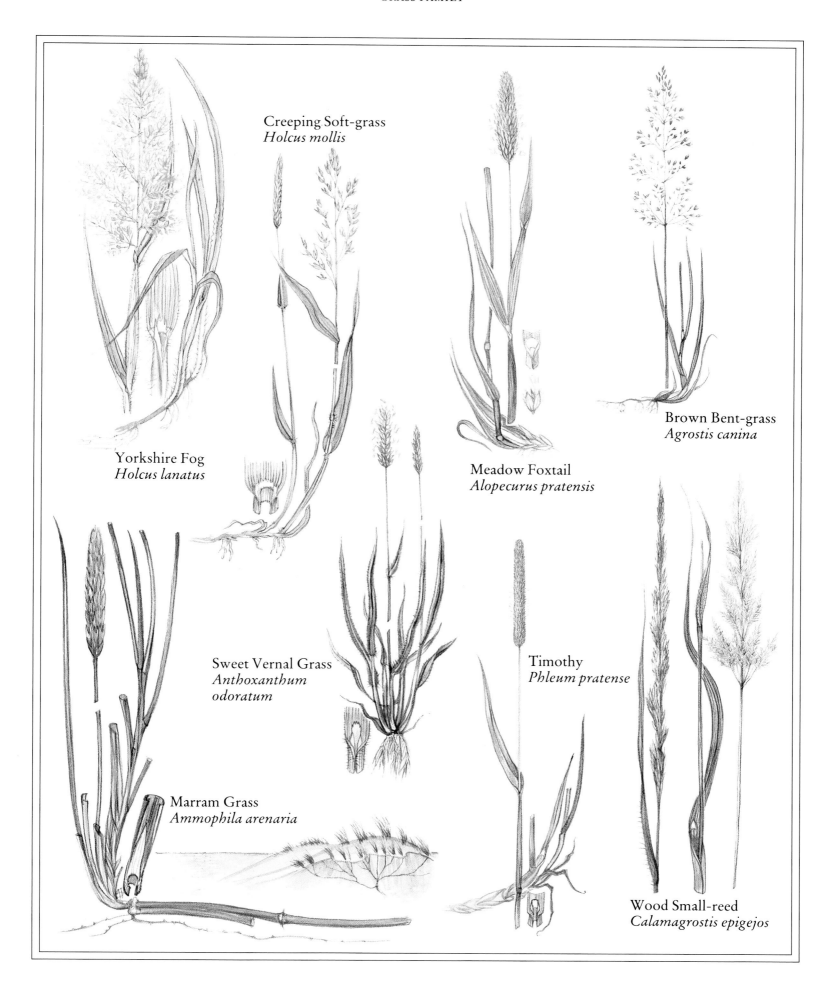

Creeping Soft-grass
Holcus mollis

Brown Bent-grass
Agrostis canina

Yorkshire Fog
Holcus lanatus

Meadow Foxtail
Alopecurus pratensis

Sweet Vernal Grass
*Anthoxanthum
odoratum*

Timothy
Phleum pratense

Marram Grass
Ammophila arenaria

Wood Small-reed
Calamagrostis epigejos

Timothy, *Phleum pratense* (p. 243), is cultivated for fodder and in hay meadows, but also grows wild in many grassy places, on roadsides and waste ground throughout Europe and the British Isles. It is a tufted perennial, with stems up to 1.5m (5ft) tall, the lower nodes sometimes swollen and with firm, rough leaves. It flowers in summer, with a dense, cylindrical inflorescence, greenish or purplish in colour, packed with flattened, stalkless, one-flowered spikelets.

Meadow Foxtail, *Alopecurus pratensis* (p. 243), is one of about 50 species in this genus, all found in temperate regions of the world, with about 12 in Europe; they have inflorescences like those of the *Phleum* species, cylindrical and densely packed with flattened, one-flowered spikelets, but those of foxtails readily fall apart when the fruits are ripe. Meadow Foxtail is a loosely tufted perennial plant, with flat, rough leaves and stems up to 1m (3ft) tall; it flowers in spring and early summer, with soft spikes of green, bent-awned spikelets. It grows in damp, grassy places, meadows and pastures throughout Europe and much of the British Isles; this is an important forage grass, providing grazing early in the season.

Hard-grass, *Parapholis strigosa*, is a coastal plant, growing in salt marshes and in waste places beside the sea around the coasts of western and southern Europe and the British Isles, north to southern Scotland. It is a little annual plant, with sprawling, whip-like stems up to 40cm (20in) tall at most, much branched, jointed in appearance, with short, narrow leaves. It flowers in summer, but the flowering spikes are barely noticeable, the one-flowered spikelets embedded singly in the hollow curves of the stems.

Wood Millet, *Milium effusum*, grows in damp, shady woods throughout Europe and the British Isles. It is a loosely tufted, tall perennial grass, with stems growing up to 180cm (6ft) in height, flat, pale green leaves and delicate, airy inflorescences around midsummer. Each inflorescence has several branches at each node, spreading at first but drooping later, and many green, flattened, one-flowered, unawned spikelets.

Reed Canary-grass, *Phalaris arundinacea*, grows in reed beds, in shallow water in marshes and fens, in wet woods and meadows and beside riverbanks throughout Europe and the British Isles. This tall, reed-like grass has far-creeping rhizomes and forms stands of stout stems up to 2m (6ft) in height which retain their leaves in winter. The plants flower around midsummer, with dense, lobed inflorescences of purplish, unawned spikelets.

Common Reed, *Phragmites australis*, forms extensive reed beds in shallow water at the edges of ponds and lakes, on the sides of rivers and estuaries, in fens and marshes, colonizing wide areas with its stout, creeping rhizomes; it is found throughout Europe and the British Isles. It is one of the tallest grasses, with erect, leafy stems growing up to 3.5m (12ft) in height and bearing plumes of soft, purple flowers in late summer and early autumn. The leaves are smooth, wide and flat, tapering to a point and falling off in winter, leaving the dead stems with their flower plumes still standing. The flowers are erect at first, later opening out and nodding, with long, silky hairs on the spikelets. The stems are smooth and tough, somewhat like bamboo; dried stems are the most common material used for thatching.

Heath Grass, *Danthonia decumbens*, is a moorland plant found in damp, acid grassland, scattered throughout Europe and the British Isles on moors and heaths. It is a perennial tufted species, growing up to 45cm (15in) tall, some shoots half lying on the ground. The leaves are flat and greyish, the ligules consisting of a ring of hairs; the flowers appear in summer and consist of a few large, green spikelets borne in an erect or spreading inflorescence.

Unlike Heath Grass, which grows scattered among other species, some moorland grasses become dominant over large areas. **Purple Moor-grass**, *Molinia caerulea*, forms a grassland habitat of its own on wide areas of moorland, especially in the west and north of the British Isles; it also grows throughout Europe. It grows in acid, peaty soils, in damp fens and bogs, on moors and mountains, forming large tussocks with stems up to 1.5m (5ft) tall when conditions really suit it, smaller tufts in other areas. It is a wiry, perennial plant, with rough, blue-green leaves and a ring of hairs for a ligule. The flowering stems are swollen at the base and in summer they bear narrowly erect, slate-blue or purplish inflorescences. Sheep like to graze on its tussocks in early summer.

Mat-grass, *Nardus stricta*, is another moorland grass but one that sheep dislike and therefore common on over-grazed areas. It tends to grow on the poorest acid, peaty and siliceous soils throughout Europe and the British Isles, often dominating wide areas on mountains and moorlands. It forms dense tufts of stems, growing up to 40cm (15in) tall with hard, rough, wiry leaves which persist and become bleached after they have died so that mat-grass moorland looks white from a distance. The flowers appear in summer in narrow inflorescences, with two rows of awned spikelets on one side of the stem; each spikelet contains only one flower.

Rice-grass, *Spartina* x *townsendii*, first appeared on the south coast of Britain in the middle of the nineteenth century, a fertile hybrid resulting from the cross between the native Cord-grass, *S. maritima*, and a recently introduced alien, *S. alterniflora*, from South America. The hybrid turned out to be far more vigorous than either parent and set about colonizing the tidal mud flats of the south coast; nowadays it is often planted in soft mud flats in Britain and western Europe, in estuaries and salt marshes to stabilize the mud. Rice-grass has short, creeping rhizomes, tough networks of interlaced roots and large, circular tufts of stems and leaves, usually about 60cm (2ft) tall. Its flat, yellow-green leaves end in stout points; the plants flower in summer, with several erect, slender spikes of golden-yellow spikelets borne in clusters.

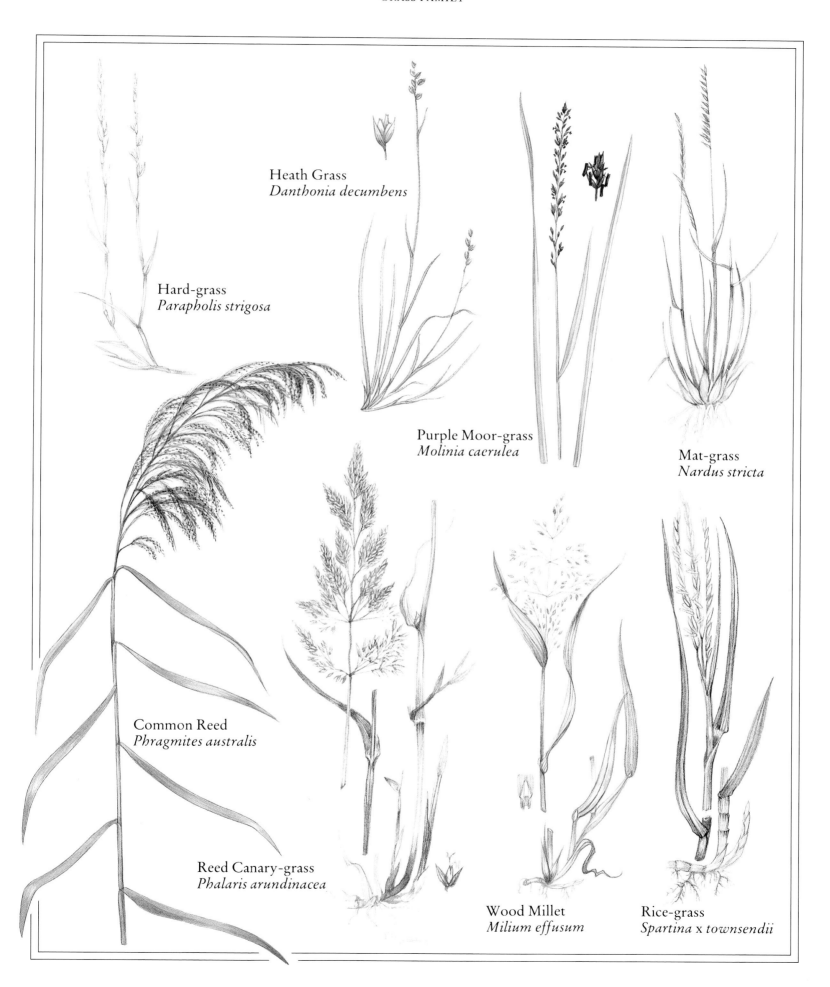

Heath Grass
Danthonia decumbens

Hard-grass
Parapholis strigosa

Purple Moor-grass
Molinia caerulea

Mat-grass
Nardus stricta

Common Reed
Phragmites australis

Reed Canary-grass
Phalaris arundinacea

Wood Millet
Milium effusum

Rice-grass
Spartina x *townsendii*

GLOSSARY

Note: Where botanical terms are specific to a family, they have been defined within the **Family features** of that family in the main text.

Achene A small, dry, indehiscent fruit with a single seed. Its thin wall distinguishes it from a nutlet.

Alien An introduced plant which has become naturalized.

Alternate An arrangement of leaves on a stem, such that each node bears one leaf on alternate sides of the stem (see Fig. 2).

Annual A plant completing its life cycle within a single year: germinating from seed, flowering and setting seed itself, then dying.

Anther The portion of a stamen in which the pollen is formed (see Fig. 5).

Awn A stiff terminal bristle, on a fruit for example, or on the lemma in grasses.

Axil The place between a lateral branch of a stem, twig or leaf and the main stem.

Bearded With bristly hairs.

Berry A fleshy fruit, usually containing several seeds. Often used as a more general term for any fleshy fruit.

Fig. 1 Parts of a Plant

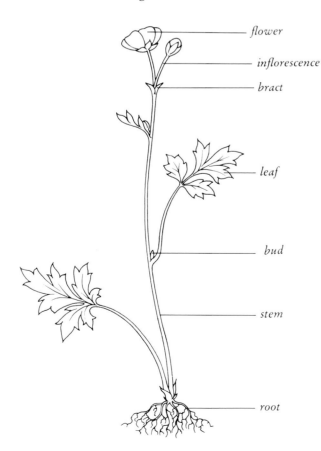

flower
inflorescence
bract
leaf
bud
stem
root

Fig. 2 Leaf Arrangements

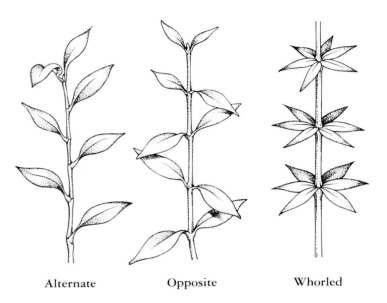

Alternate   Opposite   Whorled

Biennial A plant which completes its life cycle in two years: developing a root and leaves in its first year, overwintering by means of food stored in the root, then flowering and setting seed in the second year, and dying.

Blade The expanded flat portion of a leaf, in contrast to the stalk.

Bract A specialized leaf with a flower growing in its axil. Bracts may closely resemble leaves, or may differ in size, colour or texture, cf Spathe (see Fig. 1).

Bud An undeveloped flower or shoot protected by sepals (flower bud) or bud scales (shoot).

Bulb An extremely shortened underground stem with many swollen fleshy leaves or leaf bases in which food is stored. Bulbs may or may not be enclosed in a protective tunic. They are common overwintering and food storage organs in some monocotyledonous plants.

Bulbil A small bulb produced by some plants in the axils of leaves or in the inflorescence.

Calyx The sepals of a flower form the calyx. They are usually green and leaf-like, and enclose and protect the flower in bud. They may be joined or free, coloured or absent. In many families the calyx persists to enclose the fruit. In a calyx where the sepals are joined the basal tubular portion is the calyx-tube, and the upper free parts are the calyx-lobes (see Fig. 5).

Capsule A dry fruit formed of several cells, which splits open to release the seeds.

Carpel One of the segments or cells which make up the ovary.

Claw The narrow basal section of some petals and sepals.

Fig. 3 Leaf Types

Simple Leaves

entire *serrated* *sinuate* *linear*

elliptical *lance-shaped* *ovate* *spoon-shaped*

heart-shaped *pinnately lobed* *palmately lobed*

Compound Leaves

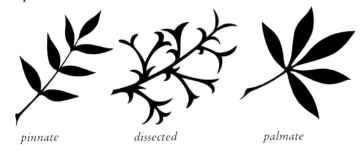

pinnate *dissected* *palmate*

Compound inflorescence A branched inflorescence composed of several racemes or cymes.

Compound leaf A leaf composed of several leaflets (see Fig. 3).

Corm A short, erect underground stem, swollen with food and often acting as an overwintering organ. It is usually protected by a scaly tunic. The following year's corm develops on top of the spent one of the previous year.

Corolla The petals of a flower form the corolla. They are often coloured and conspicuous, and may bear nectaries, all features designed to attract insects. In some plants they are small, insignificant or absent (see Fig. 5).

Corona In some plants the flowers have an additional structure between the petals and the stamens (as in the milk-

weeds). This is called the corona.

Creeping With stems growing along the ground, rooting at the nodes.

Cyme A flat-topped or conical inflorescence in which the branches develop equally from the centre, the central flower opening first in each branch. Each flower is the terminal one when it is formed (see Fig. 4).

Dehiscent Splitting open to release the seeds.

Disk The central portion of the flower head in a member of the Daisy family. It contains only tubular florets.

Dissected Of a leaf, one cut deeply into segments, and where the segments are themselves deeply cut (see Fig. 3).

Divided Of a leaf, cut into segments, the divisions extending as far as the midrib or the base, cf Lobed (see Fig. 3).

Drupe A fleshy fruit, usually with a single seed surrounded by a hard or stony layer.

Elliptical Of a leaf (see Fig. 3).

Entire Of a leaf, with an unbroken margin, not toothed (see Fig. 3).

Evergreen A plant that does not lose its leaves in winter.

Family A unit of biological classification consisting of a collection of genera sharing particular features, cf Genus.

Fertile Capable of reproduction; of a stamen, one which produces pollen; of a flower, one which produces viable seed.

Filament The stalk of a stamen (see Fig. 5).

Floret A single flower in the flower head of a member of the Daisy family. Disk florets are tubular, ray florets are strap-shaped. Flower heads may be composed wholly of disk florets or of ray florets, or may have disk florets in the centre (forming the central disk) and ray florets around the margin.

Follicle A dry, dehiscent fruit, opening along one side only.

Free Not joined to other organs.

Fruit A ripened ovary which contains matured seeds, ready for dispersal.

Fused At least partially joined together, united.

Genus (plural Genera) A unit of biological classification consisting of a group of species considered to be related through common descent, and indicated by sharing the same first name, cf Species.

Gland An area on a plant which secretes a liquid, usually an oil or resin. When a plant has many glands, it is described as glandular; when the glands are situated on hairs, it is described as glandular-hairy.

Hair A small, usually slender outgrowth from a plant.

Head A dense flower cluster consisting of many stalkless flowers (see Fig. 5).

Herb A non-woody annual, biennial or perennial plant. If perennial, then dying back to ground level at the end of the season.

Herbaceous Having the texture of a herb; dying back to the ground each year.

Hermaphrodite Containing both male and female organs (stamens and carpels).

Hybrid A plant originating from the cross between two species.

Indehiscent Not opening at maturity to release the seed(s).

Inferior Of an ovary, located beneath the other flower parts (see Fig. 5).

Inflorescence The flower cluster of a plant, including the branches, bracts and flowers (see Fig. 4).

Inserted The point of attachment, e.g. of stamens to the corolla.

Introduced Not native; having been brought to the country by man within historic times.

Involucre A set of bracts forming a structure like a calyx, beneath an inflorescence. Often used specifically for the structure beneath the condensed, head-like inflorescence of the members of the Daisy family.

Irregular Bilaterally symmetrical.

Lance-shaped Of a leaf (see Fig. 3).

Latex Milky juice or sap.

Legume A dry, dehiscent fruit characteristic of the Pea family. It opens along both sides to release the seeds.

Linear Of a leaf (see Fig. 3).

Lobed Of leaves, divided but with the divisions cutting less than halfway to the midrib. The leaves are therefore not divided into leaflets (see Fig. 3).

Membranous Thin and flexible, but usually not green.

Midrib The central vein of a leaf.

Mycorrhiza An association between the roots of certain plants and soil fungi. Orchids cannot survive without their mycorrhizal partners.

Native Endemic; not introduced by man.

Fig. 4 Inflorescence Types

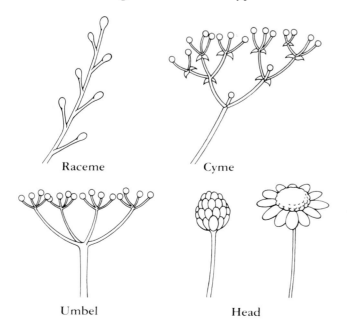

Raceme   Cyme

Umbel   Head

Fig. 5 Parts of a Flower

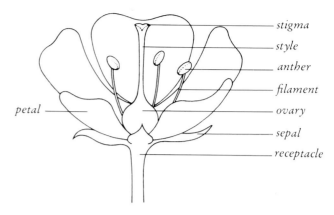

stigma
style
anther
filament
petal — *ovary*
sepal
receptacle

Naturalized Well established and growing wild in an area, but coming from another region or part of the world.

Nectary A gland which secretes nectar, usually found on the receptacle or the petals of the corolla.

Node A point on a stem where leaves or roots, or both, arise.

Nodule A small swelling.

Nutlet A small, dry, indehiscent fruit with a relatively thick wall and only one seed.

Opposite Two organs, such as leaves, growing opposite each other at a node (see Fig. 2).

Ovary The part of a flower which contains the ovules (see Fig. 5).

Ovate Of a leaf (see Fig. 3).

Ovule The structure which contains the egg. It develops into a seed after fertilization.

Palmate Of leaves, divided into three or more lobes or leaflets, all arising from the same point on the leaf stalk (see Fig. 3).

Pappus The crown of hairs, bristles or scales on the achene of a member of the Daisy family.

Parasite A plant which obtains its water and nutrients from another plant, to which it becomes attached.

Perennial A plant which lives for several years, usually flowering each year, and (of herbaceous perennials) dying back at the end of the growing season.

Perianth The petals and sepals together.

Perianth segments The separate 'segments' which make up the perianth—they may be like petals or like sepals. This term is often used when all the parts of the perianth are similar and there is no clear division into sepals and petals.

Persistent Remaining attached to the fruit, especially of sepals or petals.

Petal One segment of the corolla. The petals are often brightly coloured and may have nectaries at the base (see Fig. 5).

Pinnate A compound leaf composed of more than three leaflets, arranged in two rows on either side of the central axis or midrib (see Fig. 3).

Pod A dry, dehiscent fruit which opens along both sides. Usually used specifically to describe the fruits of the Pea family.

Pollen grains The structures which develop inside the anthers and which contain the male cells. They are carried to the stigma and there develop a pollen tube which grows down the style, carrying the male nucleus with it. When the pollen tube reaches the ovary, the male nucleus fuses with the ovule and the fertilized ovules develop into seeds.

Pollination The carrying of pollen from the anthers to the stigma. It is usually transferred by wind or by insects.

Prickle A sharp outgrowth from a stem or leaf, but irregularly arranged, cf Spine.

Prostrate Lying flat on the ground.

Raceme An inflorescence with an elongated, unbranched central axis and flowers growing on stalks on each side. The lowermost flowers open first. In theory a raceme can go on elongating indefinitely as the youngest flowers are at the growing tip (see Fig. 4).

Receptacle The flat end of a flower stalk on which the flower parts arise (see Fig. 5).

Regular Radially symmetrical.

Rhizome A perennial, underground stem growing horizontally. Rhizomes may act as an overwintering device, as a food storage organ, or as a method of spreading the plant.

Rosette A basal clump of leaves appearing to radiate outwards from a single spot.

Saprophyte A plant which lacks green colouring and which feeds on dead organic material, often with the help of mycorrhizal fungi.

Scale A thin, membranous bract or leaf.

Seed A ripened ovule.

Sepal One segment of the calyx. The sepals are usually green and leaf-like, and together they enclose and protect the flower bud (see Fig. 5).

Serrated Of a leaf, with a toothed margin where the teeth are pointed.

Siliqua A specialized capsule produced by members of the Mustard family; it has a central axis on which the seeds develop and two valves, one on each side of the axis. The valves open from the bottom upwards to release the seeds.

Simple With a single, undivided blade.

Sinuate Of a leaf, with a wavy margin (see Fig. 3).

Species A group of similar-looking individual plants which can interbreed and produce similar-looking offspring true to type.

Spike Strictly, a raceme in which the flowers lack stalks. In more general use, any spike-like inflorescence.

Spikelet The flower of a sedge or grass, together with its bract(s).

Spine A stiff, sharp-pointed projection from a plant, often a modified leaf or stipule, cf Prickle.

Fig. 6 Flower Types

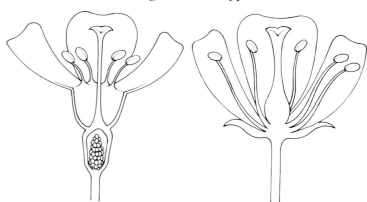

Flower with an inferior ovary   Flower with a superior ovary

Spur A hollow, often slender projection from the base of a sepal or petal, usually containing nectar.

Stamen One of the male reproductive organs of a flower (see Fig. 5).

Sterile Incapable of producing viable pollen (of stamens) or seeds (of plants).

Stigma The receptive tip of the style on which pollen grains must land and adhere for pollination to occur (see Fig. 5).

Stipule An often leaf-like appendage found at the base of the leaf stalk where the stalk is attached to the stem. They often occur in pairs, one on each side of the stalk (see Fig. 1).

Style The structure at the top of the ovary connecting it to the stigma where the pollen grains land (see Fig. 5).

Superior Of an ovary, located above the other floral parts and free from them (see Fig. 5).

Tendril A climbing organ formed from part of a stem or leaf. In the Pea family, where tendrils are common, they are formed from the terminal leaflet of a compound leaf.

Ternate Of a leaf, divided into three equal leaflets, which may be in turn be divided.

Thallus The name given to the body of a plant when it is not clearly differentiated into stems and leaves, and often lacking roots.

Tuber A thickened portion of a root or rhizome acting as a food storage organ.

Tubercle A rounded swelling.

Tunic The dry, often brown and papery covering around a bulb or corm.

Turion A special winter bud produced by aquatic plants and by which they overwinter.

Umbel An umbrella-like inflorescence in which all the flower stalks arise from the same point on the stem (see Fig. 4).

Versatile A term used to describe an anther which is attached to the filament only at its middle, so that it is free to swing.

Weed A plant growing where it is not wanted.

Whorl A circle of three or more leaves or flowers growing from a node (see Fig. 2).

Xerophyte A plant adapted to life in a dry environment.

INDEX

(Figures in **bold** type indicate illustrations.)

Aaron's Rod 150
Abraham, Isaac and Joseph
  (*Trachystemon orientalis*) **133**, 134
Acanthus family (Acanthaceae) 160
Aconite, Winter (*Eranthis hyemalis*) 32, **33**
Agrimony (*Agrimonia eupatoria*) 64, **65**
Alexanders (*Smyrnium olusatrum*) 104, **105**
Alfalfa (*Medicago sativa*) 76, **77**
Alisons (*Alyssum* spp.) 50
  Mountain (*A. montanum*) 50, **53**
Alkanet (*Anchusa officinalis*) 134, **135**
  Green (*Pentaglottis sempervirens*) 134, **135**
Alliums (*Allium* spp.) 212
Allseed (*Radiola linoides*) 82, **83**
Amaranth family (Amaranthaceae) 16
Amaranth, Common (*Amaranthus retroflexus*) 16, **17**
Anemones (*Anemone* spp.) 34
  Wood (*A. nemorosa*) 34, **35**
  Yellow Wood (*A. ranunculoides*) 34, **35**
Angelica, Garden (*Angelica archangelica*) 112
  Wild (*A. sylvestris*) **111**, 112
Archangel, Yellow (*Lamiastrum galeobdolon*) 144, **145**
Arnica (*Arnica montana*) 182, **183**
Arrow-grass family (Juncaginaceae) 206
Arrow-grass, Marsh (*Triglochin palustris*) 206
  Sea (*T. maritima*) **205**, 206
Arrowhead (*Sagittaria sagittifolia*) 202, **203**
Artichoke, Jerusalem (*Helianthus tuberosus*) 173
Arum family (Araceae) 230
Asparagus, Wild (*Asparagus officinalis*) 208, **209**
Asphodel, Bog (*Narthecium ossifragum*) 206, **207**
  Scottish (*Tofieldia pusilla*) 206, **207**
Aster, Sea (*Aster tripolium*) 176, **177**
Aster tribe (Astereae) 174
Asarabacca (*Asarum europaeum*) **39**, 40
Avens (*Geum* spp.) 64
  Water (*G. rivale*) 64, **65**
  Wood (*G. urbanum*) 64, **65**
Avens, White Mountain (*Dryas octopetala*) 64, **65**
Azalea, Trailing (*Loiseleuria procumbens*) 114, **115**

Baldmoney 108
Balm (*Melissa officinalis*) 140, **141**
  Bastard (*Melittis melissophyllum*) 142, **143**
Balsam, Small (*Impatiens parviflora*) 86, **87**
Baneberry 34
Bartsia, Alpine (*Bartsia alpina*) 156, **157**
  Red (*Odontites verna*) 156, **157**
  Yellow (*Parentucellia viscosa*) 156, **157**
Basil (*Ocimum basilicum*) 140
  Wild (*Clinopodium vulgare*) 140, **141**
Basil Thyme (*Acinos arvensis*) 140, **141**
Bastard Toadflax (*Thesium humifusum*) 16, **17**
Bats-in-the-belfry (*Campanula trachelium*) 168, **169**
Beak-sedge, White (*Rhynchospora alba*) 233, **234**
Bearberry (*Arctostaphylos uva-ursi*) 114, **115**
Bear's Breeches (*Acanthus mollis*) 160, **161**
Bedstraw family (Rubiaceae) 128
Bedstraws (*Galium* spp.) 128

Heath (*G. saxitile*) 128, **129**
Hedge (*G. mollugo*) 128, **129**
Lady's (*G. verum*) 128, **129**
Marsh (*G. palustre*) 128, **129**
Beet, Sea (*Beta vulgaris* subsp. *maritima*) 22, **23**
Belladonna (*Atropa belladonna*) 148, **149**
Bellbine 130
Bellflower family (Campanulaceae) 168–70
Bellflower, Ivy-leaved (*Wahlenbergia hederacea*) 168, **169**
Bellflowers (*Campanula* spp.) 168
  Clustered (*C. glomerata*) 168, **169**
  Creeping (*C. rapunculoides*) 168, **169**
  Giant (*C. latifolia*) 168, **169**
  Peach-leaved (*C. persicifolia*) 168, **169**
Bell-heather (*Erica cinerea*) 116, **117**
Bent-grasses (*Agrostis* spp.) 242
  Brown (*A. canina*) 242, **243**
Betony (*Stachys betonica*) 142, **143**
Bilberry (*Vaccinium myrtillus*) 114, **115**
  Bog (*V. uliginosum*) 114, **115**
Bindweed, Black (*Fallopia convolvulus*) **19**, 20
  Field (*Convolvulus arvensis*) 130, **131**
  Hedge (*Calystegia sepium*) 130, **131**
  Sea (*Calystegia soldanella*) 130, **131**
Bindweed family (Convolvulaceae) 130–2
Bird's-foot (*Ornithopus perpusillus*) 80, **81**
Bird's-foot Trefoil (*Lotus corniculatus*) 78, **81**
  Greater (*L. uliginosus*) 78
Bird's-nest family (Monotropaceae) 118
Bird's-nest, Yellow (*Monotropa hypopitys*) 118, **119**
Birthwort (*Aristolochia clematitis*) **39**, 40
Birthwort family (Aristolochiaceae) 40
Bistorts (*Polygonum* spp.) 18
  Amphibious (*P. amphibium*) 18
  Common (*P. bistorta*) 18, **19**
Bittercresses (*Cardamine* spp.) 52
  Hairy (*C. hirsuta*) 52, **53**
Bittersweet 148
Blackberry (*Rubus fruticosus*) 68, **69**
Black-eyed Susan (*Rudbeckia hirta*) 173
Bladderworts (*Utricularia* spp.) 162
  Greater (*U. vulgaris*) 162, **163**
  Lesser (*U. minor*) 162, **163**
Blinks (*Montia fontana*) 17, 18
Blood-spot-emlets (*Mimulus luteus*) 152
Bluebell (*Hyacinthoides non-scripta*) **211**, 212
Bluebottle 194
Blue-eyed Grass (*Sisyrinchium bermudiana*) 216, **217**
Blue-eyed Mary (*Omphalodes verna*) **133**, 134
Bogbean family (Menyanthaceae) 124
Bogbean (*Menyanthes trifoliata*) 124, **125**
Bog Myrtle family (Myricaceae) 90
Bog Myrtle (*Myrica gale*) **89**, 90
Bog-rush, Black (*Schoenus nigricans*) 233, **234**
Borage (*Borago officinalis*) **133**, 134
Borage family (Boraginaceae) 132
Bouncing Bett 24
Brandy-bottle 38
Brome, False (*Brachypodium sylvaticum*) **239**, 240
Brome Grasses (*Bromus* spp.) 240
  Barren (*B. sterilis*) **239**, 240
  Soft (*B. hordeaceus*) **239**, 240
Brooklime (*Veronica beccabunga*) 154, **155**
Brookweed (*Samolus valerandi*) 122, **123**
Broom (*Cytisus scoparius*) 70, **71**
  Spanish (*Spartium junceum*) 70, **71**
Broomrape family (Orobanchaceae) 160
Broomrapes (*Orobanche* spp.) 160
  Common (*O. minor*) 160, **161**
  Greater (*O. rapum-genistae*) 160, **161**
  Hemp (*O. ramosa*) 160

Ivy (*O. hederae*) 160
Yarrow (*O. purpurea*) 160, **161**
Bryony, Black (*Tamus communis*) 218, **219**
  White or Red (*Bryonia cretica*) 96, **97**
Buckbean 124
Buckwheat (*Fagopyrum esculentum*) 20, **21**
Bugle (*Ajuga reptans*) 146, **147**
  Pyramidal (*A. pyramidalis*) 146, **149**
Bugloss (*Anchusa arvensis*) 134, **135**
  Purple Viper's (*Echium plantagineum*) 136, **137**
  Viper's (*Echium vulgare*) 136, **137**
Bulrush family (Typhaceae) 230
Bulrush (*Schoenoplectus lacustris*) **233**, 234
Bulrush (*Typha latifolia*) **231**, 232
  Lesser (*T. angustifolia*) **231**, 232
Burdock, Greater (*Arctium lappa*) 188, **191**
  Lesser (*A. minor*) 188, **191**
  Woolly (*A. tomentosum*) 190, **191**
Bur-marigolds (*Bidens* spp.) 173
  Nodding (*B. cernua*) 174, **175**
  Tripartite (*B. tripartita*) 174, **175**
Burnet, Great (*Sanguisorba officinalis*) 64, **65**
  Salad (*S. minor*) 64, **65**
Burnet Saxifrage (*Pimpinella saxifraga*) **105**, 106
  Greater (*P. major*) 106
Burning Bush (*Dictamnus albus*) 87, **88**
Bur-reed family (Sparganiaceae) 232
Bur-reeds (*Sparganium* spp.) 232
  Branched (*S. erectum*) **231**, 232
  Least (*S. minimum*) **231**, 232
  Unbranched (*S. emersum*) 232
Bushgrass 242
Butcher's Broom (*Ruscus aculeatus*) 208, **209**
Butterbur (*Petasites hybridus*) 182, **183**
  White (*P. albus*) 182, **183**
Buttercup family (Ranunculaceae) 32–8
Buttercups (*Ranunculus* spp.) 36
  Bulbous (*R. bulbosus*) 36, **37**
  Creeping (*R. repens*) 36, **37**
  Meadow (*R. acris*) 36, **37**
Butterfly Orchids (*Platanthera* spp.) 224
  Greater (*P. chlorantha*) 224, **225**
  Lesser (*P. bifolia*) 224, **225**
Butterwort, Alpine (*Pinguicula alpina*) 162, **163**
  Common (*P. vulgaris*) 162, **163**
  Pale (*P. lusitanica*) 162, **163**
Butterwort family (Lentibulariaceae) 162

Cabbage, Hare's-ear (*Conringia orientalis*) 48, **49**
  Wild (*Brassica oleracea*) 46, **47**
Calamint, Common (*Calamintha sylvatica* subsp. *adscendens*) 140, **141**
  Lesser (*C. nepeta*) 140
  Wood (*C. sylvatica* subsp. *sylvatica*) 140
Campions (*Silene* spp.) 30
  Bladder (*S. vulgaris*) 30, **31**
  Moss (*S. acaulis*) 30, **31**
  Red (*S. dioica*) 30, **31**
  Sea (*S. vulgaris* subsp. *maritima*) 30
  White (*S. alba*) 30, **31**
Canary-grass, Reed (*Phalaris arundinacea*) 244, **245**
Caraway (*Carum carvi*) **109**, 110
Carrot family (Umbelliferae or Apiaceae) 102–12
Carrot, Wild (*Daucus carota*) **111**, 112
Catchflies (*Silene* spp.) 30
  Nightflowering (*S. noctiflora*) 30, **31**
  Sand (*S. conica*) 30
  Small-flowered (*S. gallica*) 30
Catchfly, Red German (*Lychnis viscaria*) 30, **31**
Catmint (*Nepeta cataria*) 146, **147**

Cat's-ear (*Hypochoeris radicata*) 196, **197**
  Smooth (*H. glabra*) 196
Cat's-foot 186
Cat's-peas 74
Cat's-tail 232
Celandine, Greater (*Chelidonium majus*) **43**, 44
  Lesser (*Ranunculus ficaria*) 37, **38**
Celery, Wild (*Apium graveolens*) **109**, 110
Centauries (*Centaurium* spp.) 126
  Common (*C. erythraea*) 126, **127**
Chaffweed (*Anagallis minima*) 120, **121**
Chamomile (*Chamaemelum nobile*) 176, **179**
  Corn (*Anthemis arvensis*) 178, **179**
  Stinking (*Anthemis cotula*) 178, **179**
  Wild (*Matricaria recutita*) 178, **179**
  Yellow (*Anthemis tinctoria*) 178, **179**
Chamomiles 176
Charlock (*Sinapis arvensis*) 46, **47**
  White (*Raphanus raphanistrum*) 46
Chervil, Bur (*Anthriscus caucalis*) 104
  Rough (*Chaerophyllum temulentum*) **103**, 104
Chickweed, Common (*Stellaria media*) **26**, 27
  Jagged (*Holosteum umbellatum*) **27**, 28
  Water (*Myosoton aquaticum*) 26, **27**
Chickweeds, Mouse-ear (*Cerastium* spp.) 26
  Common (*C. fontanum*) 26, **27**
  Field (*C. arvense*) 26, **27**
  Sticky (*C. glomeratum*) 26, **27**
Chicory (*Cichorium intybus*) 196, **197**
Chicory tribe (Chicorieae) 194
Chives (*Allium schoenoprasum*) 212
Cinquefoils (*Potentilla* spp.) 64
  Creeping (*P. reptans*) 64, **67**
  Hoary (*P. argentea*) 66, **67**
  Marsh (*P. palustris*) 66, **67**
  Shrubby (*P. fruticosa*) 66, **67**
Clary, Meadow (*Salvia pratensis*) **141**, 142
  Whorled (*S. verticillata*) **141**, 142
  Wild (*S. verbenaca*) **141**, 142
Cleavers (*Galium aparine*) 128, **129**
Clematises (*Clematis* spp.) 34
Cloudberry (*Rubus chamaemorus*) 68, **69**
Clovers (*Trifolium* spp.) 76
  Alsike (*T. hybridum*) 78, **79**
  Crimson (*T. incarnatum*) 78, **79**
  Hare's-foot (*T. arvense*) 78, **79**
  Red (*T. pratense*) 78, **79**
  Strawberry (*T. fragiferum*) 78, **79**
  White (*T. repens*) 76, **79**
  Zigzag (*T. medium*) 78, **79**
Club-rushes (*Scirpus* spp.) 234
  Sea (*S. maritimus*) 234
  Wood (*S. sylvaticus*) **233**, 234
Cocklebur, Common (*Xanthium strumarium*) 174, **175**
  Spiny (*X. spinosum*) 174, **175**
Cock's-foot (*Dactylis glomerata*) 238, **239**
Codlins-and-cream 98
Coltsfoot (*Tussilago farfara*) 180, **183**
  Alpine (*Homogyne alpina*) 182, **183**
Columbine (*Aquilegia vulgaris*) **35**, 36
Comfrey, Common (*Symphytum officinale*) 132, **133**
  Tuberous (*S. tuberosum*) 132, **133**
Compass Plant 198
Coneflowers (*Rudbeckia* spp.) 173
  Green-headed (*R. laciniata*) 173, **175**
Coral-root (*Cardamine bulbifera*) 52, **53**
Coral-root (*Corallorhiza trifida*) 222, **223**
  Spurred (*Epipogium aphyllum*) **221**, 222
Cord-grass (*Spartina maritima*) 244
Corncockle (*Agrostemma githago*) 30, **31**
Cornel, Dwarf (*Cornus suecica*) **97**, 98
Cornflower (*Centaurea cyanus*) 194, **195**
Corn Salad 166
Corydalis, Bulbous (*Corydalis solida*) **41**, 42
  Climbing (*C. claviculata*) **41**, 44
  Yellow (*C. lutea*) **41**, 42

Cotton-grass (*Eriophorum vaginatum*) 232
  Common (*E. angustifolium*) 232, **233**
Cotton-grasses (*Eriophorum* spp.) 232
Cowbane (*Cicuta virosa*) 109, 110
Cowberry (*Vaccinium vitis-idaea*) 114, **115**
Cowslip (*Primula veris*) 120, **121**
Cow-wheats (*Melampyrum* spp.) 158
  Common (*M. pratense*) 158, **159**
  Crested (*M. cristatum*) 158, **159**
  Field (*M. arvense*) 158, **159**
  Small *M. sylvaticum* 158
Cranberry (*Vaccinium oxycoccus*) 114, **115**
Crane's-bills, Wild (*Geranium* spp.) 82
  Bloody (*G. sanguineum*) 84, **85**
  Cut-leaved (*G. dissectum*) 84, **85**
  Dove's-foot (*G. molle*) 84, **85**
  Dusky (*G. phaeum*) 84
  Hedgerow (*G. pyrenaicum*) 84, **85**
  Meadow (*G. pratense*) 82, **85**
  Small-flowered (*G. pusillum*) 84, **85**
  Wood (*G. sylvaticum*) 84, **85**
Creeping Jenny (*Lysimachia nummularia*) 122, **123**
Cress, Hoary (*Cardaria draba*) 48, **49**
  Shepherd's (*Teesdalia nudicaulis*) 50, **51**
  Smith's (*Lepidium heterophyllum*) 48, **49**
  Thale (*Arabidopsis thaliana*) 56, **57**
Crested Dog's-tail (*Cynosurus cristatus*) 238, **239**
Crocus, Autumn (*Colchicum autumnale*) **11**, 212
Crocuses (*Crocus* spp.) 216
  Autumn (*C. nudiflorus*) 216, **217**
Crosswort (*Cruciata laevipes*) 128, **129**
Crowberry (*Empetrum nigrum*) 116, **119**
Crowberry family (Empetraceae) 116
Crowfoots (*Ranunculus* spp.) 36
  Celery-leaved (*R. sceleratus*) 36, **37**
Cuckoo-flower (*Cardamine pratensis*) 52, **53**
Cuckoo-pint (*Arum maculatum*) 230, **231**
Cucumber family (Cucurbitaceae) 96
Cudweeds (*Filago* spp.) 188
  Common (*F. vulgaris*) 188, **189**
  Small (*F. minima*) 188, **189**
Cudweeds (*Gnaphalium* spp.) 186
  Dwarf (*G. supinum*) 188, **189**
  Heath (*G. sylvaticum*) 186, **189**
  Marsh (*G. uliginosum*) 188, **189**
Cudweed tribe (Inuleae) 184

Daffodil family (Amaryllidaceae) 214
Daffodil, Wild (*Narcissus pseudonarcissus*) **213**, 214
Daisies, Michaelmas (*Aster* spp.) 176
Daisy (*Bellis perennis*) 176, **177**
  Ox-eye (*Leucanthemum vulgare*) 178, **181**
Daisy family (Asteraceae or Compositae) 173–200
Dame's Violet (*Hesperis matronalis*) 54, **55**
Dandelion (*Taraxacum officinale*) 200, **201**
Danewort (*Sambucus ebulus*) 164, **167**
Daphne family (Thymelaeaceae) 94
Deadnettles (*Lamium* spp.) 144
  Red (*L. purpureum*) 144, **145**
  Spotted (*L. maculatum*) 144, **145**
  White (*L. album*) 144, **145**
Deer-grass (*Trichophorum cespitosum*) 232, **233**
Dewberry (*Rubus caesius*) 68, **69**
Diapensia (*Diapensia lapponica*) 116, **119**
Diapensia family (Diapensiaceae) 116
Dill (*Anethum graveolens*) **107**, 108
Dock family (Polygonaceae) 18
Docks (*Rumex* spp.) 20
  Broad-leaved (*R. obtusifolius*) 20, **21**
  Curled (*R. crispus*) 20, **21**
  Fiddle (*R. pulcher*) 20
  Golden (*R. maritimus*) 20, **21**
  Sharp (*R. conglomeratus*) 20, **21**

Dodders (*Cuscuta* spp.) 132
  Common (*C. epithymum*) **131**, 132
  Great (*C. europaea*) **131**, 132
Dogbane family (Apocynaceae) 124
Dog-violet, Common (*Viola riviniana*) 92, **93**
  Heath (*V. canina*) 92, **93**
Dogwood family (Cornaceae) 98
Dovedale Moss (*Saxifraga hypnoides*) 60, **61**
Dragon's Teeth (*Tetragonolobus maritimus*) 78, **81**
Dropwort (*Filipendula vulgaris*) 62, **63**
Duckweed family (Lemnaceae) 230
Duckweeds (*Lemna* spp.) 230
  Common (*L. minor*) 230, **231**
  Ivy-leaved (*L. trisulca*) 230, **231**

Earthnut 106
Edelweiss (*Leontopodium alpinum*) 186, **189**
Eglantine 68
Elder (*Sambucus nigra*) 164
  Dwarf (*Sambucus ebulis*) 164
  Ground (*Aegopodium podagraria*) **105**, 106
Elecampane (*Inula helenium*) 184, **187**
Eryngo, Field (*Eryngium campestre*) **103**, 104
Evening Primroses (*Oenothera* spp.) 100
  Common (*O. biennis*) **99**, 100
Everlasting Flowers 186
Everlasting, Mountain (*Antennaria dioica*) 186, **189**
  Pearly (*Anaphalis margaritacea*) 186, **187**
  Sand (*Helichrysum arenarium*) 186, **187**
Eyebrights (*Euphrasia* spp.) 156
  Common (*E. rostkoviana*) 158, **159**

Fat Hen (*Chenopodium album*) 22, **23**
Felwort (*Gentianella amarella*) 126, **127**
  Marsh (*Swertia perennis*) 126, **127**
Fennel (*Foeniculum vulgare*) **107**, 108
Fenugreek, Bird's-foot (*Trifolium ornithopodioides*) 76, **79**
  Classical (*Trigonella foenum-graecum*) 76, **77**
  Star-fruited (*Trigonella monspeliaca*) 76
Fescues (*Festuca* spp.) 236
  Meadow (*F. pratensis*) **237**, 238
  Red (*F. rubra*) 236, **237**
  Sheep's (*F. ovina*) 236, **237**
Fescue, Squirrel-tail (*Vulpia bromoides*) **237**, 238
Feverfew (*Tanacetum parthenium*) 180, **181**
Figwort family (Scrophulariaceae) 150–60
Figworts (*Scrophularia* spp.) 152
  Common (*S. nodosa*) 152, **153**
  Water (*S. auriculata*) 152, **153**
  Yellow (*S. vernalis*) 152, **153**
Flag, Yellow (*Iris pseudacorus*) 216, **217**
Flax, Common (*Linum usitatissimum*) 82, **83**
  Fairy (*L. catharticum*) 82, **83**
  Pale (*L. bienne*) 82, **83**
  Perennial (*L. perenne*) 82, **83**
Flax family (Linaceae) 82
Fleabane (*Pulicaria dysenterica*) 186, **187**
  Canadian (*Conyza canadensis*) 176, **177**
  Small (*Pulicaria vulgaris*) 186, **187**
  Irish (*Inula salicina*) 184, **187**
Fleabanes (*Erigeron* spp.) 176
  Alpine (*E. borealis*) 176, **177**
  Blue (*E. acer*) 176, **177**
Flixweed (*Descurainia sophia*) 56, **57**
Flowering Rush (*Butomus umbellatus*) 202, **203**
Flowering Rush family (Butomaceae) 202
Flower-of-an-hour (*Hibiscus trionum*) **91**, 92
Fluellen, Round-leaved (*Kicksia spuria*) 152, **153**

Sharp-leaved (*Kicksia elatine*) 152, **153**
Forget-me-not, Bur (*Lappula myosotis*) 132, **133**
Forget-me-not family (Boraginaceae) 132
Forget-me-nots (*Myosotis* spp.) 134
  Changing (*M. discolor*) **135**, 136
  Field (*M. arvensis*) 134, **135**
  Water (*M. scorpioides*) 134, **135**
  Wood (*M. sylvatica*) 134, **135**
Foxglove (*Digitalis purpurea*) 156, **157**
  Large Yellow (*D. grandiflora*) 156, **157**
  Small Yellow (*D. lutea*) 156
Foxglove, Fairy (*Erinus alpinus*) 156, **157**
Foxtail, Meadow (*Alopecurus pratensis*) **243**, 244
Fritillaries (*Fritillaria* spp.) 210
  Snake's-head (*F. meleagris*) **209**, 210
Frogbit family (Hydrocharitaceae) 204
Frogbit (*Hydrocharis morsus-ranae*) 204, **205**
Fuchsia, Hedge (*Fuchsia magellanica*) **99**, 100
Fumana (*Fumana procumbens*) **95**, 96
Fumitory, Common (*Fumaria officinalis*) **41**, 42
Fumitory family (Fumariaceae) 42, 44

Gallant Soldier (*Galinsoga parviflora*) 174, **175**
Garlic (*Allium sativum*) 214
  Crow (*A. vineale*) **213**, 214
  Field (*A. oleraceum*) **213**, 214
  Triquetrous (*A. triquetrum*) 212, **213**
Gentian family (Gentianaceae) 124, 126
Gentian, Field (*Gentianella campestris*) 126, **127**
Gentians (*Gentiana* spp.) 126
  Great Yellow (*G. lutea*) 126, **127**
  Marsh (*G. pneumonanthe*) 126, **127**
  Spring (*G. verna*) 126, **127**
Geranium family (Geraniaceae) 82, 84
Germanders (*Teucrium* spp.) 146
  Wall (*T. chamaedrys*) 146, **147**
Gilliflower 54
Gipsywort (*Lycopus europaeus*) 138, **139**
Gladdon 216
Gladiolus, Wild (*Gladiolus illyricus*) 216, **217**
Glasswort (*Salicornia europaea*) 22, **23**
Globe Flower (*Trollius europaeus*) **33**, 34
Goatsbeard (*Aruncus dioicus*) 62, **63**
Goatsbeard (*Tragopogon pratensis*) 198, **199**
Goat's-rue (*Galega officinalis*) 72, **73**
Golden Drop (*Onosma echioides*) 136, **137**
Goldenrods (*Solidago* spp.) 174
  Canadian (*S. canadensis*) 174
  European (*S. virgaurea*) 174, **177**
Golden Saxifrages (*Chrysosplenium* spp.) 60
  Alternate-leaved (*C. alternifolium*) 60, **61**
  Opposite-leaved (*C. oppositifolium*) 60, **61**
Goldilocks (*Aster linosyris*) 176, **177**
Goldilocks (*Ranunculus auricomus*) 36, **37**
Gold-of-pleasure (*Camelina sativa*) 56, **57**
Good King Henry (*Chenopodium bonus-henricus*) 22, **23**
Goosefoot family (Chenopodiaceae) 22–4
Goosefoots (*Chenopodium* spp.) 22
Goosegrass 128
Gorse (*Ulex europaeus*) 70, **71**
  Hedgehog (*Erinacea anthyllis*) **71**, 72
  Spanish (*Genista hispanica*) 70, **71**
  Western (*Ulex galli*) 70
Gourd family (Cucurbitaceae) 96
Goutweed 106
Grass, Common Saltmarsh (*Puccinellia maritima*) **237**, 238
  Couch (*Elymus repens*) 240, **241**
  Heath (*Danthonia decumbens*) 244, **245**
  Lyme (*Leymus arenarius*) 240, **241**
  Marram (*Ammophila arenaria*) 242, **243**

Quaking (*Briza media*) 238, **239**
  Sea Couch (*Elymus pycnanthus*) 240
  Sweet Vernal (*Anthoxanthum odoratum*) 242, **243**
Grasses, Brome (*Bromus* spp.) 240
  Couch (*Elymus* spp.) 240
  Meadow (*Poa* spp.) 238
Grass family (Gramineae) 236–45
Grass of Parnassus (*Parnassia palustris*) 61, 62
Grass Poly (*Lythrum hyssopifolia*) 96, 97
Gratiole (*Gratiola officinalis*) 152, **153**
Greenweed, Dyer's (*Genista tinctoria*) 70, **71**
  Hairy (*G. pilosa*) 70
Gromwells (*Lithospermum* spp.) 136
  Blue (*L. purpurocaeruleum*) 136, **137**
  Common (*L. officinale*) 136, **137**
  Corn (*L. arvense*) 136, **137**
Ground Elder (*Aegopodium podagraria*) 105, 106
Ground Ivy (*Glechoma hederacea*) 146, **147**
Ground Pine (*Ajuga chamaepitys*) 148
Groundsel (*Senecio vulgaris*) 184, **185**
  Sticky (*S. viscosus*) 184, **185**
Groundsels (*Senecio* spp.) 182
Gypsophila, Annual (*Gypsophila muralis*) **25**, 26
  Cultivated (*G. paniculata*) 26

Hair-grass, Crested (*Koeleria macrantha*) **241**, 242
  Tufted (*Deschampsia cespitosa*) **241**, 242
  Wavy (*Deschampsia flexuosa*) **241**, 242
Hard-grass (*Parapholis strigosa*) 244, **245**
Hardheads 194
Harebell (*Campanula rotundifolia*) 168, **169**
Hare's-ear (*Bupleurum rotundifolium*) 107, 108
  Sickle-leaved (*B. falcatum*) **107**, 108
  Slender (*B. tenuissimum*) 108
Hare's-tail 232
Hawkbit, Autumnal (*L. autumnalis*) 196, **197**
  Rough (*L. hispidus*) 196, **197**
Hawk's-beards (*Crepis* spp.) 200
  Marsh (*C. paludosa*) 200, **201**
  Smooth (*C. capillaris*) 200, **201**
Hawkweeds (*Hieracium* spp.) 200
  Common (*H. vulgatum*) 200, **201**
  Leafy (*H. umbellatum*) 200, **201**
  Mouse-ear (*H. pilosella*) 200, **201**
  Orange (*H. aurantiacum*) 200, **201**
Heartsease 92
Heath, Cornish (*Erica vagans*) 116, **117**
  Cross-leaved (*E. tetralix*) 116, **117**
  Dorset (*E. ciliaris*) 116, **117**
  Irish (*E. erigena*) 116, **117**
Heather (*Calluna vulgaris*) 114, **117**
  Bell- (*Erica cinerea*) 116, **117**
Heath family (Ericaceae) 114–16
Heath, St Dabeoc's (*Daboecia cantabrica*) 114, **115**
  Sea (*Frankenia laevis*) **95**, 96
Hedge-parsley, Spreading (*Torilis arvensis*) 112
  Upright (*T. japonica*) **111**, 112
Heliotrope, Winter (*Petasites fragrans*) 182, **183**
Hellebore, Stinking (*Helleborus foetidus*) 32, **33**
Helleborines (*Cephalanthera* spp.) 220
  Long-leaved (*C. longifolia*) **221**, 222
  White (*C. damasonium*) 220, **221**
Helleborines (*Epipactis* spp.) 220
  Broad-leaved (*E. helleborine*) 220, **221**
  Dark Red (*E. atrorubens*) 220, **221**
  Marsh (*E. palustris*) 220, **221**
  Violet (*E. purpurata*) 220
Helleborine, White False (*Veratrum album*) 206, **207**
Hemlock (*Conium maculatum*) **107**, 108
Hemp Agrimony (*Eupatorium cannabinum*) 184, **185**
Hemp Agrimony tribe (Eupatorieae) 184
Hemp family (Cannabaceae) 14

Hempnettles (*Galeopsis* spp.) 144
  Common (*G. tetrahit*) 144, **145**
  Large-flowered (*G. speciosa*) 144, **145**
  Red (*G. angustifolia*) 144, **145**
Henbane (*Hyoscyamus niger*) 148, **149**
Henbit (*Lamium amplexicaule*) 144, **145**
Hepatica (*Hepatica nobilis*) 34, **35**
Herb Bennet 64
Herb Christopher (*Actaea spicata*) **33**, 34
Herb Paris (*Paris quadrifolia*) 208, **209**
Herb Robert (*G. robertianum*) 84, **85**
Hogweed (*Heracleum sphondylium*) 112
  Giant (*H. mantegazzianum*) **111**, 112
Hollyhock (*Alcea rosea*) 90, **91**
Honesty (*Lunaria annua*) 50
  Perennial (*L. rediviva*) 50, **51**
Honeysuckle family (Caprifoliaceae) 164, 166
Honeysuckle (*Lonicera periclymenum*) 166, **167**
  Perfoliate (*L. caprifolium*) 166
Hop (*Humulus lupulus*) 14, **15**
Hop-trefoil (*Trifolium campestre*) 78, **79**
Horehound, Black (*Ballota nigra*) 146, **147**
  White (*Marrubium vulgare*) 146, **147**
Horned-poppy, Yellow (*Glaucium flavum*) **43**, 44
Horsemint (*Mentha longifolia*) 138, **139**
Houndstongue (*Cynoglossum officinale*) 132, **133**
Houseleek (*Sempervivum tectorum*) 58, **59**
Hutchinsia, Rock (*Hornungia petraea*) 50, **51**
Hyacinth, Grape (*Muscari neglectum*) **211**, 212

Irises (*Iris* spp.) 216
  Garden (*I. germanica*) 216
  Siberian (*I. sibirica*) 216
  Stinking (*I. foetidissima*) 216, **217**
Iris family (Iridaceae) 216
Ivy family (Araliaceae) 98
Ivy (*Hedera helix*) **97**, 98
  Ground (*Glechoma hederacea*) 146, **147**

Jack-by-the-hedge 54
Jack-go-to-bed-at-noon 198
Jacob's Ladder (*Polemonium caeruleum*) 130, **131**

Kingcup 32
Knapweeds (*Centaurea* spp.) 194
  Brown (*C. jacea*) 194
  Greater (*C. scabiosa*) 194, **195**
  Lesser (*C. nigra*) 194, **195**
Knawel, Annual (*Scleranthus annuus*) 28, **29**
Knotgrass (*Polygonum aviculare*) 18, **19**
Knotweed, Japanese (*Reynoutria cuspidatum*) **19**, 20

Ladies' Fingers 80
Lady's Mantles (*Alchemilla* spp.) 62
  Alpine (*A. alpina*) 62, **63**
  Common (*A. vulgaris*) 62, **63**
Lady's-slipper Orchids (*Cypripedium* spp.) 220
  Yellow (*C. calceolus*) 220, **221**
Lady's Smock 52
Lady's Tresses, Creeping (*Goodyera repens*) 222, **223**
Lady's Tresses (*Spiranthes* spp.) 222
  Autumn (*S. spiralis*) 222, **223**
Lamb's Lettuce (*Valerianella locusta*) 166, **167**
Larkspurs (*Consolida* spp.) 32
  Forking (*C. regalis*) 32, **33**
  Garden (*C. ambigua*) 32
Leek, Sand (*Allium scorodoprasum*) **213**, 214
Leopard's-banes (*Doronicum* spp.) 182
  Great (*D. pardalianches*) 182, **183**
Lettuces (*Lactuca* spp.) 198

Garden (*L. sativa*) 198
Prickly (*L. serriola*) 198, **199**
Lettuce, Wall (*Mycelis muralis*) 198, **199**
Liquorice (*Glycyrrhiza glabra*) 72, **73**
Wild (*Astragalus glycyphyllos*) 72, **73**
Lilac, French 72
Lilies (*Lilium* spp.) 208
Martagon (*L. martagon*) **209**, 210
Lily family (Liliaceae) 206
Lily, Loddon 214
May (*Maianthemum bifolium*) **207**, 208
Snowdon (*Lloydia serotina*) **209**, 210
Lily-of-the-valley (*Convallaria majalis*) **207**, 208
Ling 114
Lobelias (*Lobelia* spp.) 170
Heath (*L. urens*) 170
Water (*L. dortmanna*) 170, **171**
London Pride (*Saxifraga x urbium*) 60
Longleaf (*Falcaria vulgaris*) **109**, 110
Loosestrife family (Lythraceae) 96
Loosestrife, Purple (*Lythrum salicaria*) 96, **97**
Loosestrifes (*Lysimachia* spp.) 120
Tufted (*L. thyrsiflora*) 122, **123**
Yellow (*L. vulgaris*) 122, **123**
Lop-grass 240
Lords-and-ladies 230
Lousewort (*Pedicularis sylvatica*) 158, **159**
Marsh (*P. palustris*) 158, **159**
Louseworts (*Pedicularis* spp.) 158
Lovage (*Levisticum officinale*) **111**, 112
Scots (*Ligusticum scoticum*) 110, **111**
Lucerne 76
Lungwort (*Pulmonaria officinalis*) 134, **135**
Narrow-leaved (*P. longifolia*) 134
Lupins (*Lupinus* spp.) 72
Common (*L. polyphyllus*) **71**, 72
Tree (*L. arboreus*) **71**, 72
White (*L. albus*) 72

Madder family (Rubiaceae) 128
Madder (*Rubia tinctorum*) 130
Field (*Sherardia arvensis*) **129**, 130
Wild (*Rubia peregrina*) **129**, 130
Madwort (*Asperugo procumbens*) 132, **133**
Mallow family (Malvaceae) 90–2
Mallow, Marsh (*Althaea officinalis*) 90, **91**
Small Tree (*Lavatera cretica*) **91**, 92
Tree (*Lavatera arborea*) 90, **91**
Mallows (*Malva* spp.) 90
Common (*M. sylvestris*) 90, **91**
Dwarf (*M. neglecta*) 90, **91**
Musk (*M. moschata*) 90, **91**
Mare's-tail family (Hippuridaceae) 100
Mare's-tail (*Hippuris vulgaris*) 100, **101**
Marigold, Corn (*Chrysanthemum segetum*) 178, **179**
Marsh (*Caltha palustris*) 32, **33**
Marjoram, Sweet (*Origanum majorana*) 140
Wild (*O. vulgare*) **139**, 140
Marsh Orchid, Early (*Dactylorhiza incarnata*) 226, **227**
Northern (*D. majalis* subsp. *purpurella*) 228
Southern (*D. majalis* subsp. *praetermissa*) **227**, 228
Masterwort (*Peucedanum ostruthium*) **111**, 112
Great (*Astrantia major*) 102, **103**
Mat-grass (*Nardus stricta*) 244, **245**
Mayweeds 176
Rayless 178
Scented 176
Scentless (*Tripleurospermum inodorum*) 178, **179**
Sea (*Tripleurospermum maritimum*) 178
Mayweed tribe (Anthemideae) 176
Meadow Grasses (*Poa* spp.) 238
Annual (*P. annua*) **237**, 238
Smooth (*P. pratensis*) **237**, 238
Meadow Rue, Common (*Thalictrum flavum*) **35**, 36

Great (*T. aquilegifolium*) 36
Meadowsweet (*Filipendula ulmaria*) 62, **63**
Medick, Black (*Medicago lupulina*) 76, 77
Spotted (*M. arabica*) 76
Melick, Wood (*Melica uniflora*) **239**, 240
Melilot, Ribbed (*Melilotus officinalis*) 76, 77
Tall (*M. altissima*) 76, 77
White (*M. alba*) 76, 77
Mercury, Annual (*Mercurialis annua*) 88
Dog's (*M. perennis*) 88, **89**
Mezereon (*Daphne mezereum*) 94, **95**
Michaelmas Daisies (*Aster* spp.) 176
European (*A. amellus*) 176
Mignonette family (Resedaceae) 56
Mignonette, White (*Reseda alba*) 56, **57**
Wild (*R. lutea*) 56
Milfoil 178
Milk-parsley, Cambridge (*Selinum carvifolia*) **109**, 110
Milk-thistles (*Sonchus* spp.) 198
Field (*S. arvensis*) 198, **199**
Milk-vetches (*Astragalus* spp.) 72
Purple (*A. danica*) 72
Milkweed family (Asclepiadaceae) 124
Milkwort family (Polygalaceae) 86
Milkwort, Sea (*Glaux maritima*) 122, **123**
Milkworts (*Polygala* spp.) 86
Common (*P. vulgaris*) 86, **87**
Heath (*P. serpyllifolia*) 86, **87**
Tufted (*P. comosa*) 86, **87**
Millet, Wood (*Milium effusum*) 244, **245**
Mimosa subfamily (Mimosoideae) 70
Mind-your-own-business (*Helxine soleirolii*) 14, **15**
Mint family (Labiatae or Lamiaceae) 138
Mints (*Mentha* spp.) 138
Corn (*M. arvensis*) 138, **139**
Corsican (*M. requienii*) 138
Water (*M. aquatica*) 138, **139**
Mistletoe family (Loranthaceae) 14
Mistletoe (*Viscum album*) 14, **15**
Moneywort, Cornish (*Sibthorpia europaea*) 156, **157**
Monkeyflower (*Mimulus guttatus*) 152, **153**
Monkshood (*Aconitum napellus*) 32, **33**
Monkshoods (*Aconitum* spp.) 32
Montbretia (*Tritonia crocosmiflora*) 216, **217**
Moor-grass, Purple (*Molinia caerulea*) 244, **245**
Moschatel (*Adoxa moschatellina*) 162, **163**
Moschatel family (Adoxaceae) 162
Mossy Cyphel (*Minuartia sedoides*) 28
Mother-of-thousands 14
Motherwort (*Leonurus cardiaca*) 144, **147**
Mouse-tail (*Myosurus minimus*) **35**, 36
Mudwort (*Limosella aquatica*) 152, **153**
Mugwort (*Artemisia vulgaris*) 180, **181**
Mugwort (*Cruciata laevipes*) 128
Mulleins (*Verbascum* spp.) 150
Dark (*V. nigrum*) 150, **151**
Great (*V. thapsus*) 150, **151**
Moth (*V. blattaria*) 150, **151**
White (*V. lychnitis*) 150, **151**
Mustard, Black (*Brassica nigra*) 46, **47**
Field (*Brassica rapa*) 46, **47**
Garlic (*Alliaria petiolata*) 54, **57**
Hedge (*Sisymbrium officinale*) 54, **57**
Tower (*Arabis glabra*) 52, **55**
Treacle (*Erysimum cheiranthoides*) 54, **55**
White (*Sinapis alba*) 46, **47**
Wild (*Sinapis arvensis*) 46
Yellow Ball (*Neslia paniculata*) 50, **51**
Mustard family (Cruciferae or Brassicaceae) 46–56

Navelwort (*Umbilicus rupestris*) **59**, 60
Needle Furze 70
Nettle family (Urticaceae) 14
Nettle, Small (*Urtica urens*) 14, **15**
Stinging (*U. dioica*) 14, **15**
Nightshade, Enchanter's (*Circaea lutetiana*) **99**, 100

Alpine Enchanter's (*C. alpina*) 100
Nightshade family (Solanaceae) 148
Nightshades (*Solanum* spp.) 148
Black (*S. nigrum*) 148, **149**
Woody (*S. dulcamara*) 148, **149**
Nipplewort (*Lapsana communis*) 196, **197**

Oat-grass, Downy (*Avenula pubescens*) 240
False (*Arrhenatherum elatius*) 240, **241**
Meadow (*Avenula pratensis*) 240, **241**
Yellow (*Trisetum flavescens*) **241**, 242
Oats, Wild (*Avena fatua*) 240, **241**
Old Man's Beard 34
Oleaster family (Elaeagnaceae) 94
Onions (*Allium* spp.) 212
Cultivated (*A. cepa*) 212
Oraches (*Atriplex* spp.) 22
Common (*A. patula*) 22, **23**
Hastate (*A. hastata*) 22
Orchid, Bee (*Ophrys apifera*) 226, **227**
Bird's-nest (*Neottia nidus-avis*) 222, **223**
Bog (*Hammarbya paludosa*) **223**, 224
Early Spider (*Ophrys sphegodes*) 226, **227**
Fen (*Liparis loeselii*) 222, **223**
Fly (*Ophrys insectifera*) 226, **227**
Fragrant (*Gymadenia conopsea*) 224, **225**
Frog (*Coeloglossum viride*) 224, **225**
Lizard (*Himantoglossum hircinum*) 224, **225**
Man (*Aceras anthropophorum*) 228, **229**
Musk (*Herminium monorchis*) 224, **225**
Pyramidal (*Anacamptis pyramidalis*) 228, **229**
Small White (*Pseudorchis albida*) 224, **225**
Spurred Coral-root or Ghost (*Epipogonium aphyllum*) **221**, 222
Violet Bird's-nest (*Limodorum abortivum*) **221**, 222
Orchid family (Orchidaceae) 220
Orchids, Butterfly (*Platanthera* spp.) 224
Lady's-slipper (*Cypripedium* spp.) 220
Marsh and Spotted (*Dactylorhiza* spp.) 226
Orchids (*Orchis* spp.) 228
Burnt-tip (*O. ustulata*) 228, **229**
Early Purple (*O. mascula*) 228, **229**
Green-winged (*O. morio*) 228, **229**
Lady (*O. purpurea*) 228, **229**
Monkey (*O. simia*) 228, **229**
Soldier (*O. militaris*) 228, **229**
Oregano 140
Orpine (*Sedum telephium*) 58, **59**
Oxlip (*Primula elatior*) 120, **121**
Ox-tongue, Bristly (*Picris echioides*) 196, **197**
Hawkweed (*P. hieracioides*) 196, **197**
Oyster Plant (*Mertensia maritima*) 136, **137**

Pansies (*Viola* spp.) 92
Field (*V. arvensis*) **93**, 94
Mountain (*V. lutea*) **93**, 94
Wild (*V. tricolor*) 92, **93**
Parsley, Corn (*Petroselinum segetum*) **109**, 110
Cow (*Anthriscus sylvestris*) **103**, 104
Fool's (*Aethusa cynapium*) 106, **107**
Garden (*Petroselinum crispum*) **109**, 110
Parsley family (Umbelliferae or Apiaceae) 102
Parsley Piert (*Aphanes arvensis*) 62, **63**
Parsnip, Cow (*Heracleum sphondylium*) **111**, 112
Lesser Water (*Berula erecta*) **105**, 106
Water (*Sium latifolium*) **105**, 106
Wild (*Pastinaca sativa*) **111**, 112
Pasque Flower (*Pulsatilla vulgaris*) 34, **35**
Pea family (Leguminosae) 70–80

Pearlworts (*Sagina* spp.) 28
  Knotted (*S. nodosa*) 28
  Procumbent (*S. procumbens*) 28, **29**
Pea subfamily (Papilionoideae) 70
Peas, Wild (*Lathyrus* spp.) 72
  Narrow-leaved Everlasting (*L. sylvestris*) 73, 74
  Sea (*L. japonicus*) 74, **75**
  Tuberous (*L. tuberosus*) 72, **73**
Pellitory-of-the-wall (*Parietaria judaica*) 14, **15**
Pennycress, Field (*Thlaspi arvense*) 50, **51**
Pennyroyal (*Mentha pulegium*) 138, **139**
Pennywort, Marsh (*Hydrocotyle vulgaris*) 102, **103**
  Wall (*Umbilicus rupestris*) 60
Peppermint (*Mentha* x *piperita*) 138, **139**
Pepper Saxifrage (*Silaum silaus*) 107, 108
Pepperworts (*Lepidium* spp.) 48
  Field (*L. campestre*) 48, **49**
Periwinkles (*Vinca* spp.) 124
  Greater (*V. major*) 124, **125**
  Lesser (*V. minor*) 124, **125**
Persicaria (*Polygonum persicaria*) 18
  Pale (*P. lapathifolium*) 18, **19**
Pheasant's Eye (*Adonis annua*) 34, **35**
Phlox family (Polemoniaceae) 130
Pignut (*Conopodium majus*) 105, **106**
Pilewort 38
Pimpernel, Bog (*Anagallis tenella*) 120, **121**
  Scarlet (*Anagallis arvensis*) 120, **121**
  Yellow (*Lysimachia nemorum*) 122, **123**
Pineapple Weed (*Matricaria matricarioides*) 178, **179**
Pink family (Caryophyllaceae) 24–30
Pinks (*Dianthus* spp.) 24
  Cheddar (*D. gratianopolitanus*) 24, **25**
  Common (*D. plumarius*) 24
  Deptford (*D. armeria*) 24, **25**
  Large (*D. superbus*) 24, **25**
  Maiden (*D. deltoides*) 24, **25**
Pitcher-plant family (Sarraceniaceae) 40
Pitcher-plant (*Sarracenia purpurea*) 39, 40
Plantain family (Plantaginaceae) 162, 164
Plantains (*Plantago* spp.) 162
  Branched (*P. arenaria*) 164, **165**
  Buck's-horn (*P. coronopus*) 164, **165**
  Greater (*P. major*) 162, **165**
  Hoary (*P. media*) 164, **165**
  Sea (*P. maritima*) 164, **165**
Pokeweed family (Phytolaccaceae) 16
Pokeweed (*Phytolacca americana*) 16, **17**
Policeman's Helmet (*Impatiens glandulifera*) 86, **87**
Pondweed, Canadian (*Elodea canadensis*) 204, **205**
  Opposite-leaved (*Groenlandia densa*) 205, 206
Pondweed family (Potamogetonaceae) 204–6
Pondweeds (*Potamogeton* spp.) 204
  Broad-leaved (*P. natans*) 204, **205**
  Curled (*P. crispus*) 205, 206
  Fennel (*P. pectinatus*) 205, 206
  Perfoliate (*P. perfoliatus*) 204, **205**
Poppy family (Papaveraceae) 44
Poppy, Field or Common (*Papaver rhoeas*) 43, 44
  Long-headed (*P. dubium*) 43, 44
  Opium (*P. somniferum*) 43, 44
  Prickly Long-headed (*P. argemone*) 43, 44
  Welsh (*Meconopsis cambrica*) 43, 44
  Yellow Horned- (*Glaucium flavum*) 43, 44
Primrose family (Primulaceae) 118–22
Primrose (*Primula vulgaris*) 118, **121**
  Bird's-eye (*P. farinosa*) 120, **121**
Primulas (*Primula* spp.) 118
Purslane family (Portulacaceae) 16–18
Purslane (*Portulaca oleracea*) 17, 18
  Sea (*Halimione portulacoides*) 22, **23**
  Water (*Ludwigia palustris*) 99, 100
  Water (*Lythrum portula*) 96, 97

Radish, Horse (*Armoracia rusticana*) 52, **53**

  Wild (*Raphanus raphanistrum*) 46, **47**
Ragged Robin (*Lychnis flos-cuculi*) 30, **31**
Ragweed, Common (*Ambrosia artemisiifolia*) 174, **175**
  Great (*A. trifida*) 174
Ragworts (*Senecio* spp.) 182
  Common (*S. jacobaea*) 182, **185**
  Hoary (*S. erucifolius*) 184, **185**
  Marsh (*S. aquaticus*) 184, **185**
  Oxford (*S. squalidus*) 184, **185**
Ragwort tribe (Senecioneae) 180
Ramping-fumitory, Common (*Fumaria muralis*) 42
  White (*F. capreolata*) 41, 42
Rampions (*Phyteuma* spp.) 168
  Round-headed (*P. orbiculare*) 170, **171**
  Spiked (*P. spicatum*) 168, **171**
Ramsons (*Allium ursinum*) 212, **213**
Raspberry (*Rubus idaeus*) 68, 69
Rattle, Greater Yellow (*Rhinanthus angustifolius*) 158
  Red 158
  Yellow (*Rhinanthus minor*) 158, **159**
Redshank (*Polygonum persicaria*) 18, **19**
Reed, Common (*Phragmites communis*) 244, **245**
Reedmace, Greater 232
  Lesser 232
Restharrows (*Ononis* spp.) 74
  Common (*O. repens*) 74, **77**
  Spiny (*O. spinosa*) 76, **77**
Ribwort (*Plantago lanceolata*) 164, **165**
Rice-grass (*Spartina* x *townsendii*) 244, **245**
Rock-cresses (*Arabis* spp.) 52
  Hairy (*A. hirsuta*) 52, **55**
Rock-cress, Northern (*Cardaminopsis petraea*) 52
  Tall (*C. arenosa*) 52, **53**
Rocket, Dyer's (*Reseda luteola*) 56, **57**
  Eastern (*Sisymbrium orientale*) 56
  London (*Sisymbrium irio*) 56
  Perennial Wall (*Diplotaxis tenuifolia*) 48, **49**
  Sea (*Cakile maritima*) 48, **49**
  Tall (*Sisymbrium altissimum*) 56, **57**
  Wall (*Diplotaxis muralis*) 48
  Yellow 52
Rockrose, Common (*Helianthemum nummularium*) 94, **95**
  White (*H. apenninum*) 94, **95**
Rockrose family (Cistaceae) 94
Rose family (Rosaceae) 62–8
Rosemary, Bog (*Andromeda polifolia*) 114, **115**
Roseroot (*Sedum rosea*) 58, **59**
Roses (*Rosa* spp.) 66
  Burnet (*R. pimpinellifolia*) 68, **69**
  Dog (*R. canina*) 68, **69**
  Field (*R. arvensis*) 68, **69**
  French (*R. gallica*) 66, **69**
Rue family (Rutaceae) 86, 88
Rue (*Ruta graveolens*) 87, 88
Rupturewort (*Herniaria glabra*) 28, **29**
Rushes (*Juncus* spp.) 218
  Bulbous (*J. bulbosus*) 218, **219**
  Hard (*J. inflexus*) 218
  Sharp-flowered (*J. acutiflorus*) 218, **219**
  Soft (*J. effusus*) 218, **219**
  Toad (*J. bufonius*) 218, **219**
Rush family (Juncaceae) 218
Rye-grass (*Lolium perenne*) 237, 238

Sage (*Salvia officinalis*) 140
  Wood (*Teucrium scorodonia*) 146, **147**
Sages (*Salvia* spp.) 140
Sainfoin (*Onobrychis viciifolia*) 80, **81**
St Barnaby's Thistle 194
St John's-wort, Common (*Hypericum perforatum*) 41, 42
  Slender (*H. pulchrum*) 41, 42
  Square-stalked (*H. tetrapterum*) 41, 42
  Trailing (*H. humifusum*) 41, 42
St John's-wort family (Hypericaceae) 40
Salsify (*Tragopogon porrifolius*) 198
  Black (*Scorzonera hispanica*) 198
Saltmarsh Grass, Common (*Puccinellia maritima*) 237, 238
Saltwort, Prickly (*Salsola kali*) **23**, 24

Samphire, Golden (*Inula crithmoides*) 186, **187**
  Marsh (*Salicornia europaea*) 22
  Rock (*Crithmum maritimum*) **105**, 106
Sandalwood family (Santalaceae) 16
Sandwort, Sea (*Honkenya peploides*) 28, **29**
  Thyme-leaved (*Arenaria serpyllifolia*) 28, **29**
Sandworts (*Minuartia* spp.) 28
  Spring (*M. verna*) 28
Sanicle (*Sanicula europaea*) 102, **103**
Satin Flower 26
Saw-wort (*Serratula tinctoria*) 194, **195**
  Alpine (*Saussurea alpina*) 192, **195**
Saxifrage, Burnet (*Pimpinella saxifraga*) **105**, 106
  Greater Burnet (*Pimpinella major*) 106
  Pepper (*Silaum silaus*) **107**, 108
Saxifrage family (Saxifragaceae) 60–2
Saxifrages, Golden (*Chrysosplenium* spp.) 60
Saxifrages (*Saxifraga* spp.) 60
  Meadow (*S. granulata*) 60, **61**
  Mossy (*S. hypnoides*) 60
  Purple (*S. oppositifolia*) 60, **61**
  Rue-leaved (*S. tridactylites*) 60, **61**
  Starry (*S. stellaris*) 60, **61**
Scabious, Devil's-bit (*Succisa pratensis*) 170, **171**
  Field (*Knautia arvensis*) 170, **171**
  Small (*Scabiosa columbaria*) 170, **171**
Scurvy-grass, Common (*Cochlearia officinalis*) 50, **51**
Sea-blite, Annual (*Suaeda maritima*) **23**, 24
Sea-buckthorn (*Hippophaë rhamnoides*) 94, **95**
Sea Heath family (Frankeniaceae) 96
Sea Heath (*Frankenia laevis*) **95**, 96
Sea-holly (*Eryngium maritimum*) **103**, 104
Seakale (*Crambe maritima*) 48, **49**
Sea Lavender family (Plumbaginaceae) 122, 124
Sea Lavender (*Limonium vulgare*) 122, **125**
Sea Pink 122
Sea-spurrey, Greater (*Spergularia marginata*) 28
  Lesser (*S. marina*) 28, **29**
Sedge family (Cyperaceae) 232
Sedges (*Carex* spp.) 234
  Carnation (*C. panicea*) 234, **235**
  Common (*C. nigra*) **235**, 236
  Flea (*C. pulicaris*) 234, **235**
  Green-ribbed (*C. binervis*) **235**, 236
  Hairy (*C. hirta*) 234, **235**
  Pendulous (*C. pendula*) **235**, 236
  Sand (*C. arenaria*) 234, **235**
  Spring (*C. caryophyllea*) 234, **235**
  Wood (*C. sylvatica*) **235**, 236
Self-heal (*Prunella vulgaris*) 142, **143**
  Cut-leaved (*P. laciniata*) 142, **143**
Senna subfamily (Caesalpinioideae) 70
Sheep's-bit (*Jasione montana*) 168, **171**
Shepherd's Needle (*Scandix pecten-veneris*) **103**, 104
Shepherd's Purse (*Capsella bursa-pastoris*) 50, **51**
Shore-weed (*Littorella uniflora*) 164, **165**
Sibbaldia (*Sibbaldia procumbens*) 64, **65**
Silverweed (*Potentilla anserina*) 66, **67**
Skullcap (*Scutellaria galericulata*) 146, **147**
  Lesser (*S. minor*) 146
Small-reeds (*Calamagrostis* spp.) 242
  Wood (*C. epigejos*) 242, **243**
Snake-root 18
Snapdragon (*Antirrhinum majus*) 150, **151**
Sneezeweed tribe (Helenieae) 174
Sneezewort (*Achillea ptarmica*) 180, **181**
Snowdrop (*Galanthus nivalis*) 213, 214
Snowflake, Spring (*Leucojum vernum*) 214
  Summer (*L. aestivum*) **213**, 214
Snow-in-summer (*Cerastium tomentosum*) 26
Soapwort (*Saponaria officinalis*) 24, **25**

Soft-grass, Creeping (*Holcus lanatus*) 242, **243**
Solomon's Seal, Common (*Polygonatum multiflorum*) 207, 208
Sorrel, Mountain (*Oxyria digyna*) 20, **21**
Sorrel, Procumbent Yellow (*Oxalis corniculata*) 82, **83**
  Wood (*O. acetosella*) 80, **83**
  Upright Yellow (*O. europaea*) 80, **83**
Sorrels (*Rumex* spp.) 20
  Common (*R. acetosa*) 20, **21**
  Sheep (*R. acetosella*) 20, **21**
Southernwood, Field (*Artemisia campestris* 180
Sowbread (*Cyclamen hederifolium*) 120, **121**
Sow-thistle, Blue (*Cicerbita alpina*) 198, **199**
Sow-thistles (*Sonchus* spp.) 198
  Prickly (*S. asper*) 198, **199**
  Smooth (*S. oleraceus*) 198, **199**
Spearmint (*Mentha spicata*) 138, **139**
Spearworts (*Ranunculus* spp.) 36
  Great (*R. lingua*) 36
  Lesser (*R. flammula*) 36, **37**
Speedwells (*Veronica* spp.) 154
  Buxbaum's (*V. persica*) 154, **155**
  Germander (*V. chamaedrys*) 154, **155**
  Heath (*V. officinalis*) 154, **155**
  Ivy-leaved (*V. hederifolia*) 154, **155**
  Pink Water (*V. catenata*) 154
  Slender (*V. filiformis*) 154
  Spiked (*V. spicata*) 154, **155**
  Thyme-leaved (*V. serpyllifolia*) 154, **155**
  Wall (*V. arvensis*) 154, **155**
  Water (*V. anagallis-aquatica*) 154, **155**
Spignel (*Meum athamanticum*) 107, **108**
Spikenard, Ploughman's (*Inula conyza*) 186, **187**
Spike-rushes (*Eleocharis* spp.) 232
  Common (*E. palustris*) 232, **233**
Spotted Orchids (*Dactylorhiza* spp.) 226
  Common (*D. fuchsii*) 226, **227**
  Heath (*D. maculata*) 226, **227**
Spring Beauty (*Montia perfoliata*) 16, **17**
Spurge family (Euphorbiaceae) 88
Spurge-laurel (*Daphne laureola*) 94, **95**
Spurges (*Euphorbia* spp.) 88
  Cypress (*E. cyparissias*) 88, **89**
  Leafy (*E. esula*) 88, **89**
  Petty (*E. peplus*) 88, **89**
  Sun (*E. helioscopia*) 88, **89**
  Wood (*E. amygdaloides*) 88, **89**
Spurrey, Corn (*Spergula arvensis*) 28, **29**
  Sand (*Spergularia rubra*) 28, **29**
Squill, Autumn (*Scilla autumnalis*) 212
  Spring (*S. verna*) 210, **211**
Squinancy-wort (*Asperula cynanchica*) 128, **129**
Starfruit (*Damasonium alisma*) 202, **203**
Star-of-Bethlehem (*Ornithogalum umbellatum*) 210, **211**
  Drooping (*Ornithogalum nutans*) 210, **211**
  Yellow (*Gagea lutea*) 209, 210
Star-thistle (*Centaurea calcitrapa*) 194, **195**
  Yellow (*C. solstitialis*) 194, **195**
Star-thistles (*Centaurea* spp.) 194
Starwort family (Callitrichaceae) 102
Starworts (*Callitriche* spp.) 102
  Common (*C. stagnalis*) **101**, 102
  Intermediate (*C. hamulata*) **101**, 102
Stinkweed 48
Stitchworts (*Stellaria* spp.) 26
  Bog (*S. alsine*) 26
  Greater (*S. holostea*) 26, **27**
  Lesser (*S. graminea*) 26, **27**
  Marsh (*S. palustris*) 26
  Wood (*S. nemorum*) 26
Stitchwort, Water (*Myosoton aquaticum*) 26, **27**
Stock, Hoary (*Matthiola incana*) 54, **55**
Stonecrop family (Crassulaceae) 58, 60
Stonecrops (*Sedum* spp.) 58
  Biting (*S. acre*) 58, **59**
  English (*S. anglicum*) 58, **59**
  Reflexed (*S. reflexum*) 58, **59**
  White (*S. album*) 58, **59**

Stork's-bills (*Erodium* spp.) 84
  Common (*E. cicutarium*) 84, **85**
Strawberry, Barren (*Potentilla sterilis*) 66, **67**
  Wild (*Fragaria vesca*) 66, **67**
Streptopus (*Streptopus amplexifolius*) 207, 208
Sundew family (Droseraceae) 38–40
Sundew, Great (*Drosera anglica*) **39**, 40
  Long-leaved (*D. intermedia*) **39**, 40
  Round-leaved (*D. rotundifolia*) 38, **39**
Sunflower family (Compositae or Asteraceae) 173
Sunflower (*Helianthus annuus*) 173, **175**
Sunflower tribe (Heliantheae) 173
Swallow-wort (*Vincetoxicum hirundinaria*) 124, **125**
Sweetbriar (*Rosa rubiginosa*) 68, **69**
Sweet Cicely (*Myrrhis odorata*) 103, **104**
Sweetflag (*Acorus calamus*) 230, **231**
Sweet Gale 90
Sweet-grasses (*Glyceria* spp.) 238
  Floating (*G. fluitans*) 238, **239**
Sweet William (*Dianthus barbatus*) 24, **25**
Swine-cress (*Coronopus squamatus*) 48, **49**
  Lesser (*C. didymus*) 48

Tansy (*Tanacetum vulgare*) 180, **181**
Tares (*Vicia* spp.) 72, 74
  Hairy (*V. hirsuta*) 74, **75**
  Smooth (*V. tetrasperma*) 74
Teasel family (Dipsacaceae) 170
Teasel, Wild (*Dipsacus fullonum*) 170, **171**
Thistle, Blessed (*Cnicus benedictus*) 192, **195**
  Carline (*Carlina vulgaris*) 188, **191**
  Milk (*Silybum marianum* 192, **193**
  Scotch or Cotton (*Onopordon acanthium*) 192, **193**
  Stemless Carline (*Carlina acaulis*) 188, **191**
Thistles (*Carduus* spp.) 190
  Musk (*C. nutans*) 190, **191**
  Slender (*C. tenuiflorus*) 190, **191**
  Welted (*C. acanthoides*) 190, **191**
Thistles (*Cirsium* spp.) 190
  Cabbage (*C. oleraceum*) 192, **193**
  Creeping (*C. arvense*) 190, **193**
  Marsh (*C. palustre*) 192, **193**
  Melancholy (*C. helenoides*) 192, **193**
  Spear (*C. vulgare*) 190, **193**
  Stemless (*C. acaule*) 192, **193**
Thistle tribe (Cynareae) 188
Thorn-apple (*Datura stramonium*) 148, **149**
Thorow-waxes (*Bupleurum* spp.) 108
  False (*B. subovatum*) 108
Thrift (*Armeria maritima*) 122, **125**
Thyme, Basil (*Acinos arvensis*) 140, **141**
Thyme, Garden (*Thymus vulgaris*) 140
  Large (*T. pulegioides*) 140
  Wild (*T. praecox*) 140, **141**
Thymelaea, Annual (*Thymelaea passerina*) 94, **95**
Timothy (*Phleum pratense*) 243, **244**
Tinegrass 74
Toadflax, Bastard (*Thesium humifusum*) 16, **17**
  Ivy-leaved (*Cymbalaria muralis*) 152, **153**
  Small (*Chaenorhinum minus*) 151, **152**
Toadflaxes (*Linaria* spp.) 150
  Common (*L. vulgaris*) 150, **151**
  Pale (*L. repens*) 150, **151**
Toothwort (*Lathraea squamaria*) 158, **161**
Tormentil (*Potentilla erecta*) 66, **67**
Touch-me-not family (Balsaminaceae) 86
Touch-me-not (*Impatiens noli-tangere*) 86, **87**
Traveller's Joy (*Clematis vitalba*) 34, **35**
Trefoil, Bird's-foot (*Lotus corniculatus*) 78, **81**
  Greater Bird's-foot (*Lotus uliginosus*) 78
  Hop- (*Trifolium campestre*) 78, **79**

Lesser Yellow (*Trifolium dubium*) 78
Tulip, Wild (*Tulipa sylvestris*) **209**, 210
Tutsan (*Hypericum androsaemum*) 41, 42
Twayblade (*Listera ovata*) 222, **223**
  Lesser (*L. cordata*) 222, **223**
Twinflower (*Linnaea borealis*) 166, **167**
Twitch 240

Valerian family (Valerianaceae) 166
Valerian, Red (*Centranthus ruber*) 166, **167**
Valerians (*Valeriana* spp.) 166
  Common (*V. officinalis*) 166, **167**
  Marsh (*V. dioica*) 166, **167**
Venus' Looking Glass (*Legousia hybrida*) 168, **169**
Vervain family (Verbenaceae) 136
Vervain (*Verbena officinalis*) 136, **137**
Vetch, Bitter (*Lathyrus montanus*) 74, **75**
  Crown (*Coronilla varia*) 80, **81**
  Horseshoe (*Hippocrepis comosa*) 80, **81**
  Kidney (*Anthyllis vulneraria*) 80, **81**
Vetches (*Vicia* spp.) 72, 74
  Bush (*V. sepium*) 74, **75**
  Common (*V. sativa*) 74, **75**
  Tufted (*V. cracca*) 74, **75**
  Wood (*V. sylvatica*) 74, **75**
  Yellow (*V. lutea*) 74, **75**
Vetchlings (*Lathyrus* spp.) 72
  Meadow (*L. pratensis*) 72, **73**
  Yellow (*L. aphaca*) 72, **73**
Violet family (Violaceae) 92–4
Violets (*Viola* spp.) 92
  Common Dog (*V. riviniana*) 92, **93**
  Hairy (*V. hirta*) 92
  Heath Dog (*V. canina*) 92, **93**
  Marsh (*V. palustris*) 92, **93**
  Sweet (*V. odorata*) 92, **93**
  Yellow Wood (*V. biflora*) 92, **93**
Violet, Water (*Hottonia palustris*) 120, **123**
Viper's Bugloss (*Echium vulgare*) 136, **137**
  Purple (*E. plantagineum*) 136, **137**
Viper's Grass (*Scorzonera humilis*) 198, **199**

Wallflower (*Cheiranthus cheiri*) 54, **55**
Wall-pepper 58
Wart-cress 48
Watercress (*Nasturtium officinale*) 54, **55**
  Fool's (*Apium nodiflorum*) **109**, 110
Water-crowfoots (*Ranunculus* spp.) 38
  Common (*R. aquatilis*) **37**, 38
  Ivy-leaved (*R. hederaceus*) **37**, 38
Water-dropworts (*Oenanthe* spp.) 106
  Fine-leaved (*O. aquatica*) 106
  Hemlock (*O. crocata*) **105**, 106
  Tubular (*O. fistulosa*) **105**, 106
Water-lily family (Nymphaeaceae) 38
Water-lily, Fringed (*Nymphoides peltata*) 124, **125**
  White (*Nymphaea alba*) 38, **39**
  Yellow (*Nuphar lutea*) 38, **39**
Water-milfoil family (Haloragidaceae) 100
Water-milfoils (*Myriophyllum*) 100
  Spiked (*M. spicatum*) 100, **101**
  Whorled (*M. verticillatum*) 100, **101**
Water Parsnip (*Sium latifolium*) **105**, 106
  Lesser (*Berula erecta*) **105**, 106
Water-pepper (*Polygonum hydropiper*) 18, **19**
Water-peppers (*Polygonum* spp.) 18
Water-plantain family (Alismataceae) 202
Water-plantain, Common (*Alisma plantago-aquatica*) 202, **203**
  Floating (*Luronium natans*) 202, **203**
  Lance-leaved (*Alisma lanceolatum*) 202, **203**
  Lesser (*Baldellia ranunculoides*) 202, **203**
Water-soldier (*Stratiotes aloides*) 204, **205**
Water Violet (*Hottonia palustris*) 120, **123**
Weld 56

Whin (*Ulex europaeus*) 70
 Petty (*Genista anglica*) 70
Whitlow Grasses (*Draba* spp.) 50
 Common (*Erophila verna*) 50, **53**
Whortleberry 114
Willowherb family (Onagraceae) 98–100
Willowherb, Rosebay (*Chamaenerion angustifolium*) 98, **99**
Willowherbs (*Epilobium* spp.) 98
 Broad-leaved (*E. montanum*) **99**, 100
 Great Hairy (*E. hirsutum*) 98, **99**
 Small-flowered (*E. parviflorum*) 98, **99**
Windflower 34
Wintercress (*Barbarea vulgaris*) 52, **53**
Wintergreen, Chickweed (*Trientalis europaea*) 122, **123**
 Nodding (*Orthilia secunda*) 118, **119**

One-flowered (*Moneses uniflora*) 118, **119**
Wintergreen family (Pyrolaceae) 118
Wintergreens (*Pyrola* spp.) 118
 Small (*P. minor*) 118, **119**
Woad (*Isatis tinctoria*) 50, **51**
Wolfsbane (*Aconitum vulparia*) 32, **33**
Woodbine 166
Woodruff, Sweet (*Galium odoratum*) 128, **129**
Woodrushes (*Luzula* spp.) 218
 Field (*L. campestris*) 218, **219**
 Great (*L. sylvatica*) 218, **219**
Wood Sorrel family (Oxalidaceae) 80, 82
Wood Sorrel (*Oxalis acetosella*) 80, **83**
Wormwood (*Artemisia absinthium*) 180, **181**

Sea (*A. maritima*) 180, **181**
Wormwoods (*Artemisia* spp.) 180
Woundworts (*Stachys* spp.) 142
 Annual (*S. annua*) **143**, 144
 Field (*S. arvensis*) 142, **143**
 Hedge (*S. sylvatica*) 142, **143**
 Marsh (*S. palustris*) 142, **143**

Yam family (Dioscoreaceae) 218
Yarrow (*Achillea millefolium*) 178, **181**
Yellowcresses (*Rorippa* spp.) 54
 Marsh (*R. palustris*) 54, **55**
Yellow Odontites (*Odontites lutea*) 156
Yellow-wort (*Blackstonia perfoliata*) 126, **127**
Yorkshire Fog (*Holcus lanatus*) 242, **243**

Bibliography

The following books are floras—books with technical details of the plants.

Blamey, Marjorie and Grey-Wilson, Christopher, *The Illustrated Flora of Britain and Northern Europe* (Hodder & Stoughton, London, 1989)

Clapham, A.R., Tutin, T.G. and Moore, D.M., *Flora of the British Isles* (Cambridge University Press, Cambridge, third edn. 1987)

Polunin, Oleg, *Flowers of Europe* (Oxford University Press, London, 1969)

The following are field guides or books which contain more general information.

Phillips, Roger, *Wild Flowers of Britain* (Pan Books, London, 1977)

Reader's Digest, *Field Guide to the Wild Flowers of Britain* (Reader's Digest, London, 1981)

Schauer, Thomas, *Field Guide to the Wild Flowers of Britain and Europe* (William Collins Sons & Co Ltd, London, 1982)

The following are books with information on particular groups or special aspects of wild flowers.

Fitter, Richard and Fitter, Alastair, *Guide to the Grasses, Sedges, Rushes and Ferns of Britain and Northern Europe* (William Collins Sons & Co Ltd, London, 1984)

Grieve, M., *A Modern Herbal* (Penguin Books, Harmondsworth, 1976)

Grigson, Geoffrey, *The Englishman's Flora* (Paladin, London, 1975)

Halliday, Geoffrey and Malloch, Andrew (eds), *Wild Flowers, Their Habitats in Britain and Northern Europe* (Peter Lowe, Glasgow, 1981)

Hepburn, Ian, *Flowers of the Coast* (Collins New Naturalist Series, London, 1952)

Hutchinson, J., *The Families of Flowering Plants, Vols I & II* (Oxford University Press, London, 1959)

Launert, Edmund, *Edible and Medicinal Plants of Britain and Northern Europe* (Hamlyn, London, 1981)

Salisbury, Sir Edward, *Weeds and Aliens* (Collins New Naturalist Series, London, 1961)

Summerhayes, V.S., *Wild Orchids of Britain* (Collins New Naturalist Series, London, 1951)